The Builder's Guide to SOLAR CONSTRUCTION

Rick Schwolsky
James I. Williams

An Energy Learning Systems Book

McGRAW-HILL BOOK COMPANY

New York, St. Louis, San Francisco, Auckland, Bogotá, Hamburg, Johannesburg, London, Madrid, Mexico, Montreal, New Delhi, Panama, Paris, São Paulo, Singapore, Sydney, Tokyo, and Toronto

Illustrated by Alan S. Ross

CREDITS:
Graph 2.1, reprinted by permission from *ASHRAE Handbook, 1977 Fundamentals,* American Society of Heating, Cooling and Air conditioning Engineers, N.Y. N.Y.; Table 2.1, Table 2.2, Table 2.5, Table 10.1 reprinted by permission from *Insulation Manual,* National Association of Home Builders Research Foundation, Rockville, Maryland; Table 2.1, Graph 5.1, Table 5.1, Table 5.2, Table 9.4, reprinted by permission from *The Passive Solar Energy Book,* © 1979, Edward Mazria, Rodale Press, Emmaus, Pennsylvania; Figure 3.6, Graph 3.1, Table 3.1, Table 3.2, Table 9.3, reprinted by permission from *Construction Principles, Materials, and Methods,* by H. B. Olin, Chicago, 1980; Figure 4.1, reprinted by permission from *Design With Climate,* page 4, © 1963, Victor Olgay, Princeton University Press, Princeton, N.J.; Figure 5.11, reprinted by permission from *Designing, Building and Selling Energy Conserving Homes,* National Association of Home Builders, Washington, D.C.; Chart 8.1, Table 8.1, reprinted by permission from *Thermal Transmission Measurements of Insulation,* R. P. Tye, Editor, copyright American Society for Testing and Materials, 1916 Race Street, Philadelphia, Pennsylvania, 19103; Chart 9.1, Chart 9.2, reprinted by permission from *Fundamentals of Residential Attic Ventilation,* H. C. Products Co., Princeville, Illinois; Figure 9.47, reprinted by permission from New England Solar Energy Association slide sets, Brattleboro, Vermont; Table 10.3, reprinted by permission from *Modern Carpentry,* Willis H. Wagner, The Goodheart Willcox Co., Inc., South Holland, Illinois.

Library of Congress Cataloging in Publication Data
Schwolsky, Rick.
    The builder's guide to solar construction.

    (An Energy learning systems book)
    Includes index.
      1. Solar houses—Design and construction.
I. Williams, James I.   II. Title.   III. Series.
TH7414.S38   1982   690'.869   82–8947
                            AACR2

ISBN 0-07-055786-1

Copyright © 1982 by McGraw-Hill, Inc. All rights reserved. Printed in the United States of America. No part of this publication may be reproduced, stored in a retrieval system, or transmitted, in any form or by any means, electronic, mechanical, photocopying, recording, or otherwise, without the prior written permission of the publisher.

CONTENTS

PART I
BASIC PRINCIPLES OF SOLAR CONSTRUCTION   1

CHAPTER 1
WHAT'S DIFFERENT ABOUT SOLAR CONSTRUCTION   3
What Is Solar Construction? 3 • What's Different About Solar Construction? 3 • Introduction to Part I 4

CHAPTER 2
HEAT IN BUILDINGS   7
Introduction 7 • Basic Principles of Heat Energy 7 Sources of Heat in Buildings 14 • Heat Loss in Buildings 16 • Heat Gain in Buildings 31

CHAPTER 3
MOISTURE AND AIR QUALITY IN TIGHT CONSTRUCTION   32
Introduction 32 • Water Vapor 32 • Effects of Water Vapor on Materials 34 • Controlling Water Vapor 37 Indoor Air Quality 43

CHAPTER 4
CLIMATE AND SITE   45
Introduction 45 • Macroclimate—the Climate of a Region 45 • Microclimate—the Climate at the Building Site 47 • Air Temperature 51 • Humidity and Precipitation 52 • Air Movement 53 • Topography 54 Vegetation 58 • Siting the Building 58

CHAPTER 5
PASSIVE SOLAR HEATING AND COOLING   60
Introduction 60 • Building Shape and Orientation 60 Suntempering 65 • Thermal Mass 73 • Earth Sheltered Construction 82 • Sunspaces and Greenhouses 83 • Double Shell and Superinsulated Houses 86

CHAPTER 6
SOLAR WATER HEATING   91
Introduction 91 • Energy Conservation First 91 Solar Water Heating 93 • Sizing and Selecting Water Heaters 97 • Siting Solar Collectors 97 • System Layout 99 • Solar Contractors 100

PART II
MATERIALS, DETAILS, AND TECHNIQUES OF SOLAR CONSTRUCTION   101

CHAPTER 7
THE PHASES OF SOLAR CONSTRUCTION   103
Introduction to Part II 103 • Materials, Details, and Techniques 103 • Building Codes 104 Regulations 106 • The Phases of Construction 128

CHAPTER 8
SITEWORK AND FOUNDATIONS   113
Introduction 113 • Sitework 113 • Foundation 124 Moistureproofing Foundations 127 • Insulating Foundations 128

CHAPTER 9
THE INSULATED BUILDING SHELL   139
Introduction 139 • Floors 140 • Walls 149 • Roofs and Ceilings 163 • Additional Details: Roof and Ceiling Systems 175

CHAPTER 10
DOORS, WINDOWS AND GLAZINGS   177
Introduction 177 • Notes About Materials 177 Doors 185 • Operable Windows 190 • Fixed Glazings 195

CHAPTER 11
HVAC, PLUMBING, ELECTRICAL, AND SOLAR DHW   201
Introduction 201 • HVAC 201 • Plumbing 206 Electrical 207 • Roughed-in Ductwork, Piping and Wiring 208 • Solar DHW 211

CHAPTER 12
INTERIOR FINISHES AND SPECIAL CONSTRUCTION 227

Introduction 227 • Interior Finishes 227 • Special Construction 233

CHAPTER 13
CASE STUDIES 237

Introduction 237 • Peterson Construction Company, Lincoln, Nebraska 238 • Mayhill Homes Corporation, Gainesville, Georgia 243 • Green Horizon, Santa Fe, New Mexico 249 • Sunrise Solar Services, Suffield, Connecticut 252 • Dennis Davey, Inc., Tolland, Connecticut 256

GLOSSARY 259

INDEX 263

PREFACE

(I)

"You don't have to preach honesty to a man with creative purpose. Let a human being throw the energies of his soul into the making of something and the instinct of workmanship will take care of this honesty. . . . A genuine craftsman will not adulterate his product. The reason is not that duty says he shouldn't, but because passion says he couldn't."

Walter Lippman

This book about homebuilding is written for all the people it takes to put a home together. It is culled from my own experiences as an architect, builder, teacher, student, and personal observations and conversations with every building trade. Rick and I started writing this book over three years ago, after spending several years on drawing boards and building sites working with the principles and materials of solar construction. We wanted to write the book we thought we would need if we were starting off in solar construction: a book to help us avoid all the mistakes we've made and heard about.

This book is written for all those builders who are still looking for that better mousetrap . . . and wall section, stair detail, or floor plan. It's written in the spirit of creative dialogue. It discusses basic principles and then applies them to the job of putting a home together. It raises a lot of questions and asserts many new priorities for home construction.

One of the most critical factors in successful solar construction is quality workmanship which necessitates an innate understanding of the priorities, the links between the phases of construction, an understanding of where corners can be cut, and where they cannot. It is knowing where to slow down and pay close attention to detail; and where cutting corners is not cutting quality.

There are many ways a book like this could be organized. This one is organized in two parts, with the first part emphasizing an understanding of the basic principles of solar construction. It is organized by topic—Heat, Moisture and Air Quality, Climate, Passive Solar, and Solar Hot Water. This understanding of principles allows builders to look closely at their particular construction situation and see what works. Part II is focused on the job site and organized by construction sequence, emphasizing the changes required at all stages to meet the rigorous demands of solar construction.

* * *

There have been many sources of help, insight, clarification, and review, both in defining our content and helping to produce this work. I do want to express my deepest gratitude to each one of the following people: Susan Luster, for her editing, criticism and understanding and support during this long and often painful process; Larry Purcell, for covering me at Brattleboro Design Group in my hibernation periods of writing; Alan Ross, for his architectural sense, his technical review, those long nights writing the book in pictures, and for his pen; Mollie Beattie for her comments and review, and all that she's missed because of this; Janet Ross, for her mylar pencil, her eye for detail, and her cooking; Jim McCall, for his need to know the right answer; Nancy Shaw, for typing under pressure and her help in the quest for the right word; our technical reviewers, Charles Michal, Steve Brown, John Crowley, Mike Bell and Don Carr, for their comments on our early drafts; EHW, Gary Williams and Michael Jhin for early financial faith; my family in so many ways; and many other friends and colleagues who have shaped this effort.

And thanks to Rick Schwolsky, my comrade in this endeavor, for trying to reach past the present.

J.W.

(II)

The Builder's Guide to Solar Construction is about change. All who work in the building industry approach change differently. In many ways builders are adverse to changing anything about the way they design or build because it is so hard to achieve efficient production levels when materials, details, and techniques are not standardized. Change in this case is equated with risk and creating resistance to new concepts. On the other hand, builders are forever changing; using new components, designs, and tools in order to improve their products and profits. The problem that faces them is one of balancing these two. If they focus too closely on one, they are in danger of either changing too slowly and being left behind by their competition, or changing too rapidly and practicing risky pioneering at potentially great expense. Most builders fall somewhere between. They are strongly influenced by local markets, the availability of materials and components, and the other builders in their areas. They want to be different enough for buyers to distinguish their buildings, but not too different.

We have written this book to help builders, tradespeople, architects, engineers, and lumber dealers to understand and adapt to the many changes occurring in our industry due to changes in world energy supplies and economic conditions. Some of what we present may be new to you. Our goal is to guide you through an organized discussion and visual presentation of in-use features that minimize energy consumption in new and existing buildings. The materials, details, and techniques included in our book are not experimental. The concepts upon which these features are based are not new; they are only now being combined into practical building systems.

We have tried to present a wide range of options for different climatic conditions, architectural types, and market groups. We have attempted to assign priorities to practical options in terms of simplicity, cost, and risk—even though simplicity and risk are subjective judgments, and costs vary from builder to builder. We ask that you take the information offered and interpret it for yourself based on your own experiences and perspectives. We have not attempted to teach building construction to builders; rather, we identify what's different about solar construction at each phase. We assume that you have a professional familiarity with the construction process, materials used, and roles and responsibilities of the people involved during each step.

We are home builders. We build solar homes. This book is our attempt to present practical information for your use. It represents our direct experience as designers and builders, as well as our honest interpretations of information gathered from other builders and authors.

Builders will either see the current turmoil in the building industry as the collapse of the good old days ... or they will be challenged by the opportunity to respond and grow and adapt and survive and succeed.

* * *

First, I want to dedicate my share of this project to my friend, Doug Taff, a pioneer in solar energy who gave me my first opportunity to learn and work in this great field. The flame you lit will never die. This is also dedicated to Mollie Beattie, my beautiful wife, for her support and commitment during a truly hard period. Her acceptance of total disruption made me believe in "life after the book." And, as is true with everything I do, this small piece of me is dedicated to my loving parents, Arnold and Ruby Schwolsky.

There are many people to thank for making various types of contributions to me and to this project. Charles Michal, John Crowley, and Steve Brown offered valuable technical review. Mike Bell and Don Carr gave of their NAHB office, staff, home, and friendship. My partner Jim McCall firmly held our business together during my absence and reviewed portions of the manuscript. Jay and Laurie Tucker were always there when I needed to talk. Lew Boyd was always there with guidance.

Thanks go to Richard Blazej for taking the point on a booby-trapped trail; Ed Jones for sincere interest and helpful dialogue; Peter Tobey for faith and understanding; Marilyn Jackson for speedy hands and eagle eyes; and to the case study builders for their openness and for answering their telephones.

Thanks also go to the people at *Solar Age Magazine*, Total Environmental Action, Inc., Parallax and Sunplace Corporations, Brattleboro Design Group, National Association of Home Builders, National Association of Solar Contractors, the New England Solar Energy Association, and the Brattleboro Public Library.

My special gratitude goes to Bob Entwistle, Dixie Clark, and Jeremy Robinson for their patience and to everyone to whom I said "yes," when I should have said "no."

Finally I must thank Jim Williams for the deep friendship that we will always share. We pulled through this together, a rare experience with a truly rare person.

R.S.

PART I BASIC PRINCIPLES OF SOLAR CONSTRUCTION

(Downing and Leach)

(Communico, Inc.)

(Mayhill Homes)

CHAPTER 1: WHAT'S DIFFERENT ABOUT SOLAR CONSTRUCTION

WHAT IS SOLAR CONSTRUCTION?

Solar construction is a practical way to design and build homes both comfortable to live in and economical to operate, using techniques which reduce energy requirements for space heating and cooling, domestic water heating, lighting, and operating appliances. Solar homes are oriented carefully on their sites to receive the sun for winter heating, and use vegetation to help divert winter winds, direct summer breezes, and shade roof and glazed areas during the summer. The materials used to construct solar homes form energy conserving shells, overhangs that block summer sun, and glazed areas that allow winter sun to enter the building directly. Building materials also are used to intercept incoming solar radiation and store its heat for later delivery to the living space. In solar construction, special components may also collect, absorb, and transport solar energy for heating domestic water.

The tremendous amount of flexibility in the definition of solar construction allows these principles to be applied to all types of buildings, constructed for all markets, in all climates. A variety of approaches enables builders to plan for different levels of energy efficiency in their buildings, and to apply a technique that is suitable for their own climates, markets, and styles. Our definition is broad because: (1) the appropriate use of solar energy covers a wide range of options; (2) the business of building varies everywhere; and (3) until recently builders tended to take a narrow view of solar construction. Simply stated, our definition of solar construction is "a well built house."

Fig. 1.1 A wide variety of solar homes is being built and sold in all geographic regions and economic markets throughout the country.

WHAT'S DIFFERENT ABOUT SOLAR CONSTRUCTION?

All buildings are designed to provide shelter for their occupants, but their success at doing so often depends on the materials and techniques used in construction. Buildings also are designed to provide comfortable conditions for their occupants. While standard building techniques assure shelter from the environment, standard approaches to providing comfort do not always succeed, and in many homes they actually cause discomfort. **Solar construction, however, offers a more even distribution of comfortable conditions within homes.**

The measures taken to improve comfort in solar homes also improve the economy of living in them. Reduced heat loss and gain, controlled moisture and drafts, and natural ventilation and daylighting are features of solar construction that affect both comfort and economy. Reduced operating costs are considered a priority by new home buyers and a means for lenders to evaluate a buyer's ability to meet mortgage payments. These factors create a different market for builders, encouraged both by the banks and by increased public demand for affordable housing.

Solar construction requires changes in a builder's approach to siting. Along with site concerns for access, views, drainage, septic, and presentation to the road, builders should consider slope and orientation, wind direction and velocities, vegetation, and the availability of solar radiation. Careful placement of all buildings on their sites results in reduced energy consumption and increased comfort. Solar homes in the Northern Hemisphere are oriented towards the south in order to take advantage of solar radiation coming from that direction.

Site considerations for solar construction also affect the layout of subdivisions to allow access to solar radia-

(Steven Lazar)

Fig. 1.2 Both traditional and new forms of buildings can include solar features.

tion for as many lots as possible. Road layout, lot size and shape, and setback guidelines can be adjusted during the design of a subdivision or planned community to accomplish this. In some parts of the country, incentives—and regulations—have been developed to initiate these changes.

No one approach to solar heating and cooling is generally applicable to any building located in any climate. Rather, the best approach to solar construction depends on specific local conditions of site, climate, style, selling price, and builder's approach to construction. The first priority always is energy conservation. Features that increase the amount of solar radiation that enters and warms the building interior also are important. As the amount of sunlight allowed to enter increases, further measures are taken to store the heat for use later, which helps to even the daily temperature swings. In some cases new features are integrated into standard building forms; in others totally new forms of housing are developed (Fig. 1.2). Although there are basic differences attributed to solar construction, one thing remains the same: building materials are delivered to a site and, according to specific plans, are assembled in a predetermined sequence.

The materials, details, and techniques used in solar construction also may differ from past standard practices (Fig. 1.3). Changes occur at each phase of construction, ranging from insulating foundations and slabs at the foundation phase to the selection and application of interior finishes. The use of new materials, details, and techniques requires adjustments in estimating, purchasing, scheduling, and supervision, and also must be approved by local building codes and lender's regulations.

Another major difference is the importance of the quality of workmanship to energy efficiency in solar construction. Solar homes often cost more initially due to increased levels of insulation, double or triple glazed windows, vestibules, solar water heaters, and other practical features. However, if any of these features are improperly installed, their potential energy savings will be negated by their inefficient operation. Workmanship, even in areas that are eventually "buried," must be of good quality.

The business of solar construction can also be different from other types of construction businesses. We have already mentioned the effects on business management and job planning. Changing markets too quickly can be risky for builders; they should enter new markets gradually, gaining experience with new products and the best ways to sell them. The approach used to market solar homes depends on their location and type. In some areas builders have found it most effective to promote heavily the energy features of their buildings, while in other areas builders sell solar homes with the same approach used throughout the years for their other houses. Throughout the country builders are selling solar homes quickly, often well before completion. This reduces the amount of interest paid on financing, which improves cash flow and increases profits (Fig. 1.4). See the case studies for a more in-depth look at the business considerations in solar construction.

INTRODUCTION TO PART I

The rest of the chapters in Part I present the basic principles of solar construction, including heat in buildings, moisture and air quality in tight construction, climate and siting, and passive solar heating and cooling.

Chapter 2, **Heat in Buildings,** discusses the conditions within buildings that, when combined, create a comfortable environment. The chapter provides an explanation of the basic principles of heat energy and describes the different sources of heat in buildings, and continues by presenting the ways in which heat is lost

WHAT'S DIFFERENT ABOUT SOLAR CONSTRUCTION

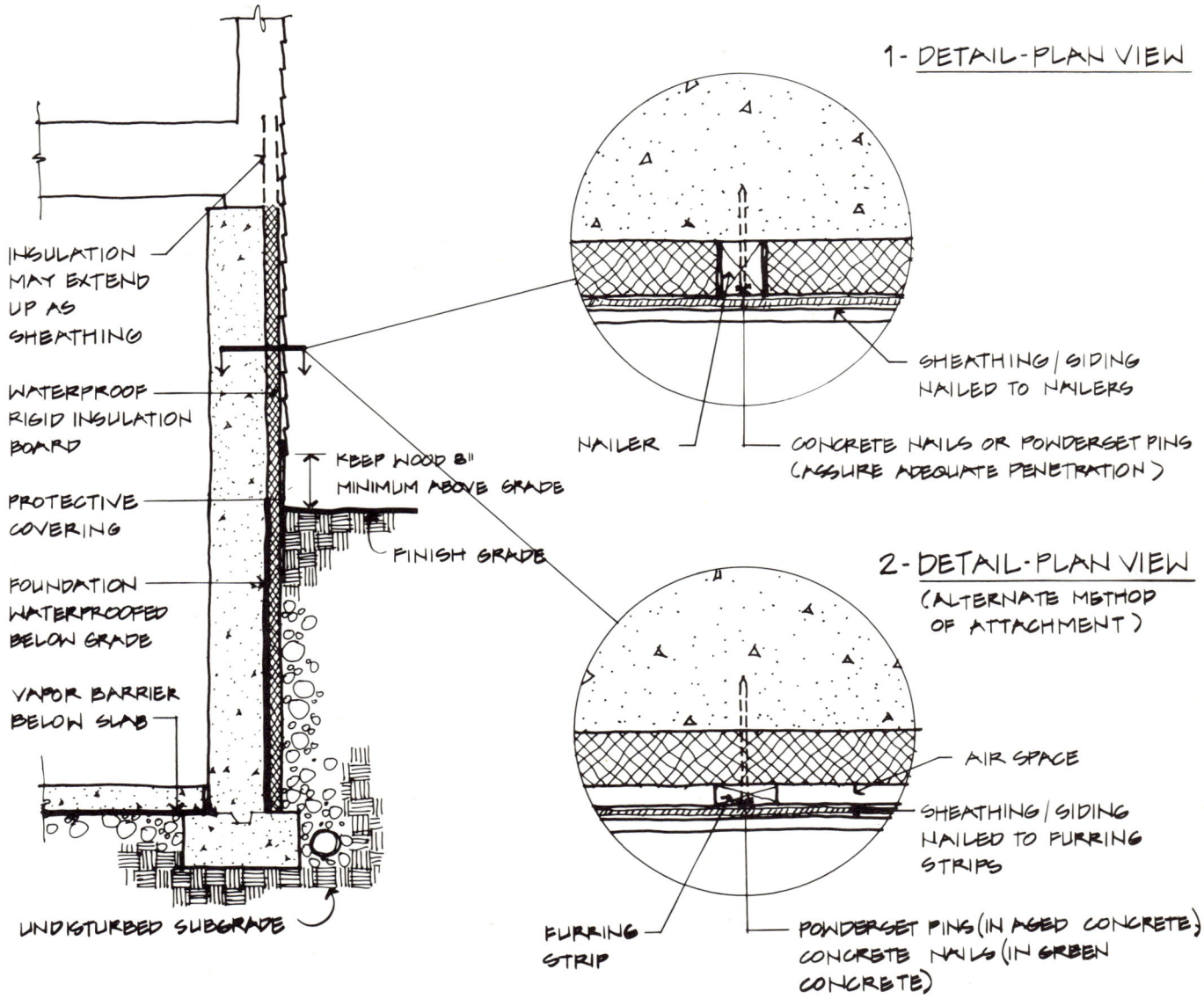

Fig. 1.3 Insulating foundations may be new to many builders, but it is common practice in solar construction.

and gained by buildings, with recommendations for controls.

Chapter 3, **Moisture and Air Quality in Tight Construction,** presents the sources, effects, and recommended controls of water vapor and indoor air pollutants generated within buildings. This chapter also discusses the way water vapor and pollutants move, the causes for their accumulation, their effect on building materials, and effects on human health and comfort.

Chapter 4, **Climate and Siting,** introduces the elements of regional and local climatic conditions and their effects on buildings. Topics include the availability of solar radiation at a site, and the effects of air temperature, precipitation, wind, topography, and vegetation on a specific site's climate. Then these site features are assessed in order to properly fix the location of a building.

Chapter 5, **Passive Solar Heating and Cooling,** begins with an examination of building shape and orientation, and recommendations for actual placement of the building on its site. A discussion of practical approaches to passive solar heating and cooling covers various building materials and configurations available to builders, and gives recommendations for their use.

Chapter 6, **Solar Water Heating**, offers recommendations for reducing energy requirements for domestic hot water. The chapter first discusses energy/water conserving measures and then continues with a discussion of solar domestic hot water (DHW) systems. Various types of systems commonly in use, as well as considerations for siting collectors, laying-out pipes and components, and selecting solar contractors, are considered.

CHAPTER 2
HEAT IN BUILDINGS

INTRODUCTION

One of the most important functions of any home is to provide a comfortable interior environment. However, achieving this simple goal is by no means a simple task. A number of factors determine whether comfortable conditions are present in a particular home. The climate at a building site defines the seasonal needs for heating or cooling. Climatic conditions of air temperature, wind movement, and precipitation determine the priorities for heating or cooling in different parts of the country. However, in every building, heat control is central to providing human comfort. Sometimes we need heat, and sometimes we want relief from it; in all cases we want to control it. This chapter discusses the many aspects of heat in buildings and is organized into four parts:

1. **the basics of heat energy**
2. **sources of heat in buildings**
3. **heat loss in buildings**
4. **heat gain in buildings**

The first part discusses basic principles of heat energy. These properties of heat in buildings—how heat moves, how heat is measured, thermal properties of building materials, human thermal comfort—are all important for builders to understand, since they will be applied repeatedly in selecting the materials and details of solar construction.

The second part discusses sources of heat in buildings, including the sun's radiation, mechanical heating systems, lights, equipment, and human activity. The concept of an insulated building shell the primary function of which is to control the loss or gain of heat is introduced.

The third part discusses heat loss in buildings: how it is lost, where it is lost, and how to reduce these losses. The use of insulating materials, caulking, weatherstripping, and multiple glazing are all introduced as ways to reduce heat loss through the building shell.

This chapter concludes with a discussion of heat gain in residences: how and where heat is gained, and how to control unwanted heat gain to provide more comfortable homes. This fourth part is primarily concerned with controlling excessive solar heat gain by using shading and ventilation.

BASIC PRINCIPLES OF HEAT ENERGY

Several basic principles of heat energy must be introduced, since we refer to them throughout this book. Many of these concepts have strict definitions from the laws of science; in common usage, they often are misunderstood and misused.

Heat is a form of energy associated with the motion of molecules. All materials contain heat so *cold* can be defined as the absence of heat. When you feel a cold wind penetrating your clothing, it is heat being lost from the body too quickly that makes you feel cold.

Heat is always moving from higher to lower temperatures, trying to equalize the temperatures. This heat movement is referred to by many terms which can be used interchangeably: heat flow, heat transfer, heat exchange (Fig. 2.1).

The difference between temperatures powers the heat exchange. The rate of heat transfer is proportional to the difference in temperature (ΔT): the greater the difference, the faster the heat moves. For example, the heat transfer through a wall from 68°F indoor temperature to -10°F outdoor temperature would be much greater than if the outdoor temperature were 50°F. This heat movement will not stop until the inside and outside temperatures are equal, but it can be slowed down. Insulations are building materials whose sole function in walls

8 BASIC PRINCIPLES OF SOLAR CONSTRUCTION

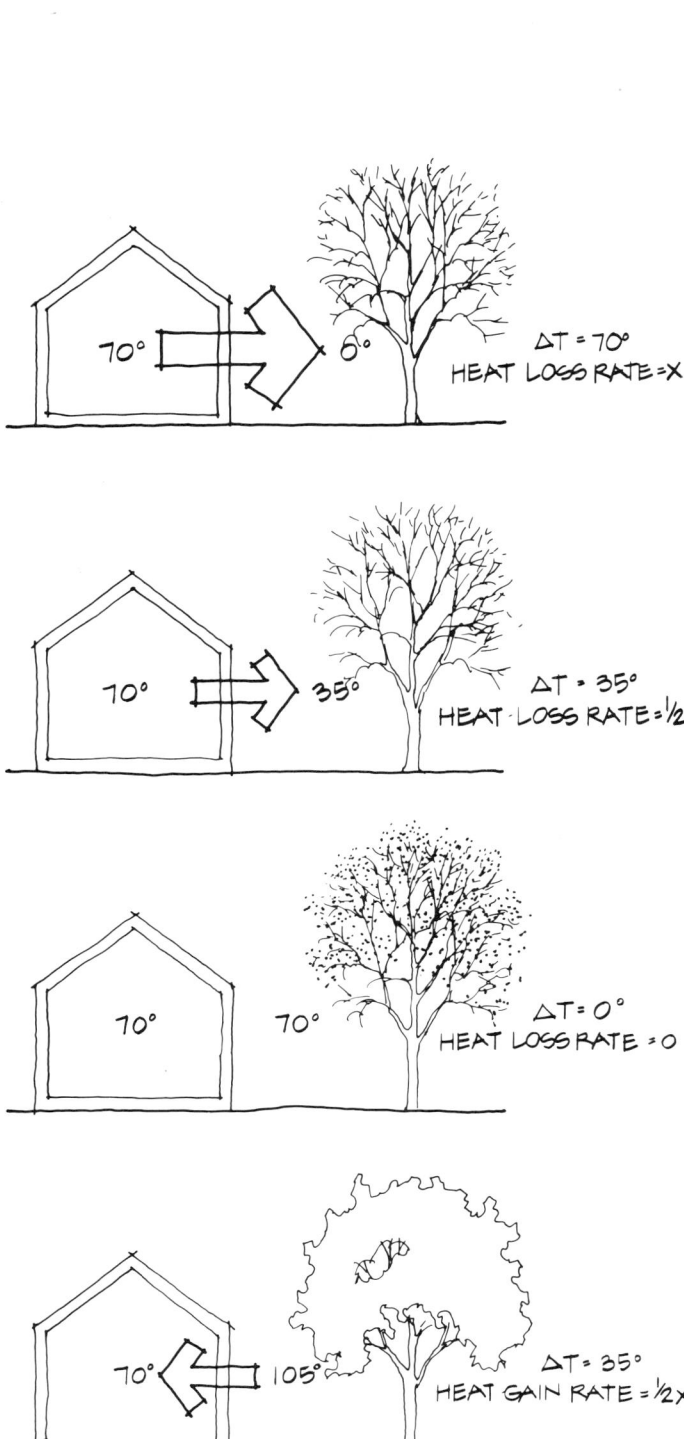

Fig. 2.1 Heat is always moving from higher to lower temperatures at a rate governed by the difference in temperature (ΔT) and the resistance to heat flow (R) of the material separating the two temperatures.

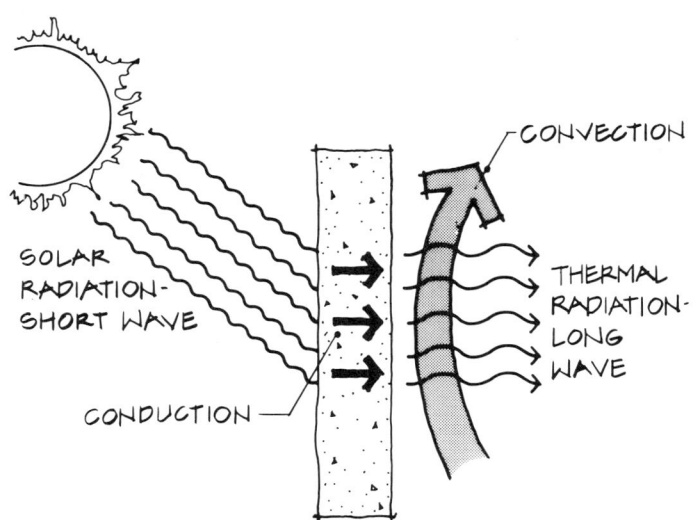

Fig. 2.2 Heat moves by conduction, convection, and radiation. *Note:* The symbols in this drawing are used throughout this book to signify heat movement by conduction, convection, or radiation.

or roofs is to slow the passage of heat through the building section.

How Heat Moves

Heat always moves by three means: conduction, convection, or radiation. These natural forces work separately and together in transferring heat between objects, but in different situations one force often provides the dominant method of heat exhange. These methods of heat transfer and the thermal properties of building materials are closely related. For example, the different materials that make up a wall (or roof or floor) determine how easily heat can move through that wall. The priority in solar construction is to keep the heat in the building during winter and out of the building during summer, by making it more difficult for heat to move through the wall section.

A building is constantly exchanging heat between the indoor environment and the outdoor climate. Heat moves through all materials that make up a building's floors, walls, ceilings, and roofs. A building's occupants also are continuously exchanging heat with the building materials and objects which affect their thermal comfort. Heat is constantly being reflected, transmitted, absorbed, and distributed by the materials and mechanisms that make up the building. The following discussion explains how heat conduction, convection, and radiation work in buildings to move heat around (Fig. 2.2).

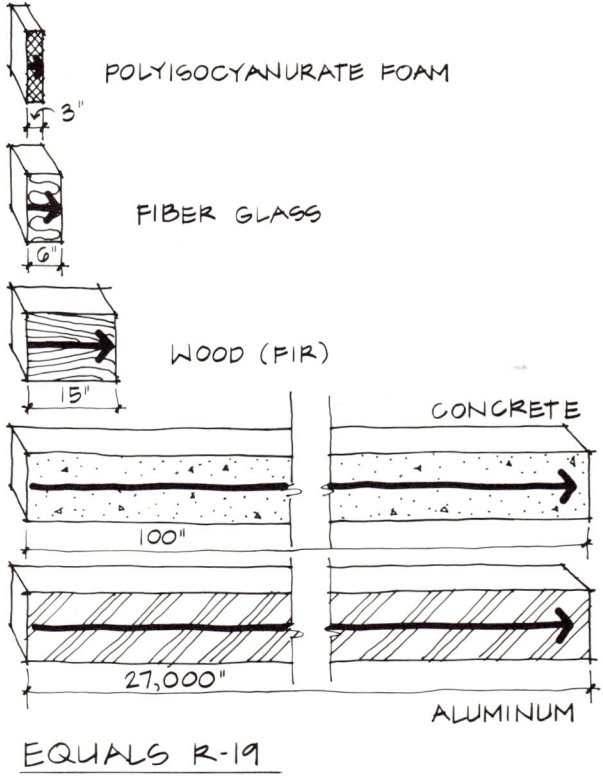

Fig. 2.3 Some materials conduct heat more readily than others. For example, these different thicknesses of certain materials are required to achieve an R-value of 19.

Conduction

Conduction is the transfer of heat through a solid material, or from one material to another where their surfaces are touching. Heat is conducted more easily through a solid material than through layers, even if the surfaces are held tightly together. The rate of heat flow through a building material is crucial to the selection of materials for solar construction.

Every material has a different ability to either resist or transmit heat flow through it. The *thermal conductivity* (k) of a material is defined as the amount of heat that passes through one square foot of a solid material with a 1°F temperature difference on either side, so the lower the k-value, the higher the insulating value. The *conductance* (C) of a material is similar to conductivity, but it measures the heat flow through a given thickness. Mathematically expressed, C = k/thickness. *Resistance* (R) is the measure of a material's ability to resist the flow of heat through it, so the higher the R-value of a material, the greater its resistance to heat flow. Insulating materials have high R-values. R-values of different materials are rated per inch or per given thickness (Fig. 2.3). In determining the resistance to heat flow of a built-up section using different materials, the individual R-values for each material (for the thickness installed) are added to give the total resistance of that section. Mathematically expressed,

$$R_{total} = R_1 + R_2 + R_3 + \ldots$$

Throughout this book we refer to the R-values of materials primarily for two reasons: first, resisting heat flow is an important function of the exterior shell in solar construction; second, most builders are more familiar with R-values, from purchasing insulation for their buildings, than with rates of conduction.

Another measure of conductive heat flow through materials is known as U, the overall coefficient of heat transmission of a building section. U refers to the ability of an entire built-up section, such as the wall or window section, to permit the flow of heat; in other words, it is the combined thermal value of all materials that make up that building section, plus air spaces and air films. The U-value is important in calculating heat loss and when comparing window units. U is the inverse of the total R, so, the lower the U-value, the higher the insulating value.

$$U = \frac{1}{R_1 + R_2 + R_3 + \ldots}$$

The conduction of heat through building materials is a major source of heat loss. For this reason, you should compare the different heat flow resistances when specifying materials or components. For instance, most residential windows are built with either metal or wood frames. A metal frame will conduct much more heat through it; however, metal windows usually are less expensive than wood windows. The low resistance of metals to heat movement has led to the development of *thermal breaks* in metal building components, which block the passage of heat from inside to out with an insulating material between the metal. Chapter 10 examines the use of thermal breaks in doors and windows. An in-depth discussion of conductive heat loss in buildings follows later in this chapter.

Convection

Convection is the transport of heat by a moving fluid, typically air or water. For example, convective heat transfer occurs as cool air moves along a warm surface, absorbing heat as it moves. Convective heat transfer is an important factor in the thermal behavior of buildings and operates in conjunction with conductive heat transfer. Heat initially is transferred to the air by conduction

10 BASIC PRINCIPLES OF SOLAR CONSTRUCTION

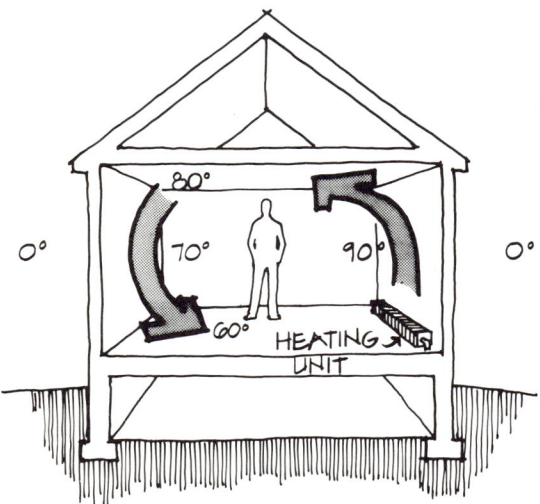

Fig. 2.4 Convective air movements are an important means of distributing heat within rooms.

between the surface and the adjacent air molecules, and the moving air carries the heat away. This convective transfer in turn accelerates the rate of conduction through a material by reducing its surface temperature.

Natural convection is caused by the heating and cooling of air as it contacts objects. As the air changes temperature it also changes density, causing the cooler air to fall and warmer air to rise. As warm air rises, cool air is drawn in to replace it, establishing a convective cycle of air movement (Fig. 2.4). This convective pattern is an important means of distributing heat in rooms. Natural convection also transfers substantial amounts of heat across an uninsulated wall cavity, as the air flow carries heat from the warm inside wall surfaces to the cool face of the exterior sheathing. Remember that it is hot air, not heat, that rises.

Wind is another form of convective air movement that significantly affects the energy performance of buildings. A building fully exposed to cold winter wind requires more energy for heating than one sheltered from it. Wind sweeps heat away from the exterior surfaces, accelerating the rate of conduction through the materials. Wind also contributes to heat loss and gain by increasing air leakage (infiltration) through the shell, as discussed later in this chapter. Wind convection is an important means of providing cooling in summer. The speed of the moving air determines the rate of convective heat transfer; the faster the air is moving, the more heat it will carry away. Chapter 4 examines the importance of siting to take advantage of wind for cooling benefits in summer and provide protection in winter.

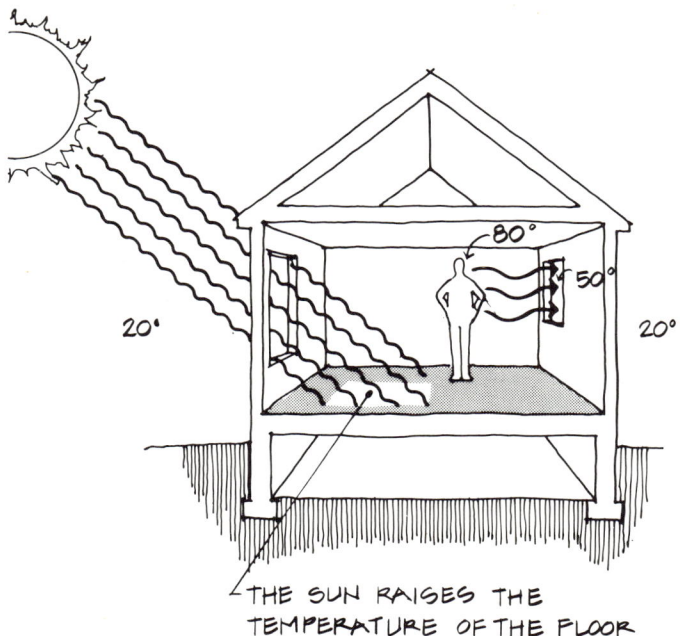

Fig. 2.5 Sunlight entering the building through windows raises the surface temperature of the floor and the air temperature of the room. The body radiates heat in all directions to surfaces at lower temperature.

Fig. 2.6 On hot sunny days we commonly seek the shelter of a shade tree. Trees can shade buildings too, helping to keep them cool by blocking the sun's radiant energy.

Radiation

Radiation is the direct transfer of heat through space by electromagnetic waves from a warm object to a cooler one. Heat radiates in all directions from a warm material; it warms all surfaces, including body surfaces in direct line of sight with that material (Fig. 2.5). Most objects that stop the flow of visible light will also stop the flow of radiant heat. The sun delivers its heat to earth as radiation. If you stand in the direct sun and then move to a shaded area, the temperature drop you feel is due to the blockage of radiant heat (Fig. 2.6). Radiant heat can be transmitted directly or indirectly through the building shell. Building materials emit radiant heat *in all directions*, to any surfaces that are at a lower temperature. If the surface is opaque, such as wood, gypsum, or concrete, some of the heat will be absorbed by the surface and either conducted through the materials or immediately picked up by convection.

The rate of radiant heat exchange between two objects depends on the temperature differential and the distance between the objects. There is little net heat transfer between objects at nearly the same temperature or at a great distance apart.

Measurement of Heat

The quantity of heat energy in a material is measured in British Thermal Units, or BTUs. A BTU is defined as the quantity of heat required to raise the temperature of one pound of water 1°F. The following examples give an idea of the heat contained in one BTU. One BTU is approximately the energy that would be released by completely burning a single wooden kitchen match. A gallon of water weighs 8.33 pounds; therefore, it will take 333 BTUs to raise the temperature in a 40-gallon water heater by 1°F. The rate of heat flow is expressed in BTUs per hour (BTU/hr or BTUH). When comparing building materials, it is often useful to consider the rate of heat transfer per square foot of area of a given thickness. This unit becomes BTUs per hour per square foot or BTU/hr/ft^2.

Human Thermal Comfort

The human body produces its own heat, and constantly exchanges heat with its surrounding environment. Generally, a comfortable thermal environment is one where the body achieves a thermal equilibrium with its surroundings (heat gains to the body balance heat losses from the body). Since the temperature of the body is almost always higher than the temperature of its surroundings, providing thermal comfort consists of con-

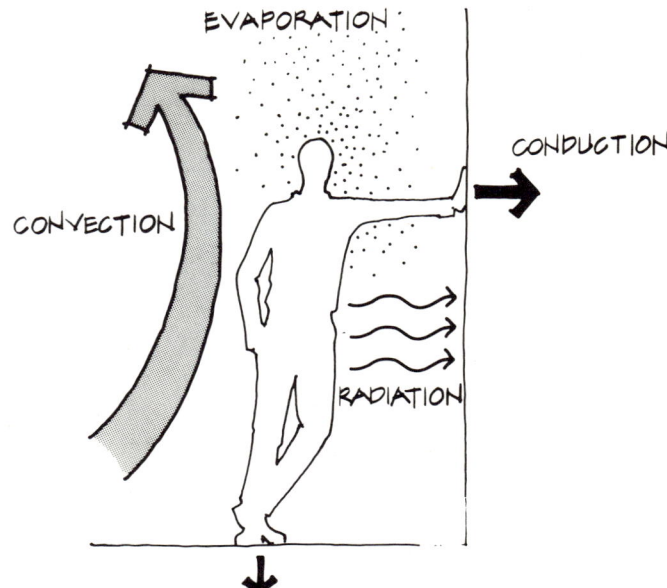

Fig. 2.7 The body loses heat by conduction, convection, radiation and evaporation.

trolling the rate of body heat loss. Inside a building, the body exchanges heat with the surrounding surfaces, and the building itself constantly exchanges heat with the outdoor climate.

Heat transfer between the body and its surroundings occurs in several ways. The body gains heat by conduction, convection, and radiation and loses heat by conduction, convection, radiation, and evaporation (Fig. 2.7). Heat transfer by conduction, convection, and radiation was covered earlier in this chapter. Evaporative heat loss from the body occurs through respiration and perspiration. Evaporation causes heat loss because it requires heat energy to turn liquid water into water vapor. The rate of evaporative cooling depends on the quantity of moisture in the air and the speed of moving air. If the air is very dry, perspiration will readily evaporate, substantially cooling the body even at high air temperatures. The total heat exchange between the body and surroundings is a function of all these mechanisms operating simultaneously, but their relative importance varies with climatic differences. For instance, at higher air temperatures evaporative losses tend to dominate, but at lower temperatures convective and radiative losses are most significant.

Criteria of Thermal Comfort

Four characteristics of the indoor environment combine to shape the comfort requirements within a building: (1) air temperature; (2) relative humidity; (3) mean radiant temperature of surrounding surfaces; and (4) velocity of

12 BASIC PRINCIPLES OF SOLAR CONSTRUCTION

air movement. The prevailing outdoor climate at a building site, which varies greatly for different regions of the country at different times of the year, determines the indoor requirements that a building must provide for human comfort. Additionally, a number of occupant-related factors, such as clothing, age, metabolism, health, and level of activity, all determine individual thermal preferences. Nonetheless, through many studies of optimum comfort levels, certain criteria have been established defining the range of thermal conditions within which most adults feel comfortable. Graph 2.1 summarizes the current ASHRAE recommendations. These guidelines provide an estimate for human comfort levels from which the designer can evaluate outdoor climatic conditions and achieve a comfortable interior environment. The influence of outdoor climate on defining building shape, orientation, and placement on the site is discussed in Chapter 4.

Air temperature is a common environmental factor that directly affects thermal comfort, and is used as the point of reference to which other criteria are compared. Air temperature affects heat exchange by convection, conduction, and evaporation, all of which are critical to

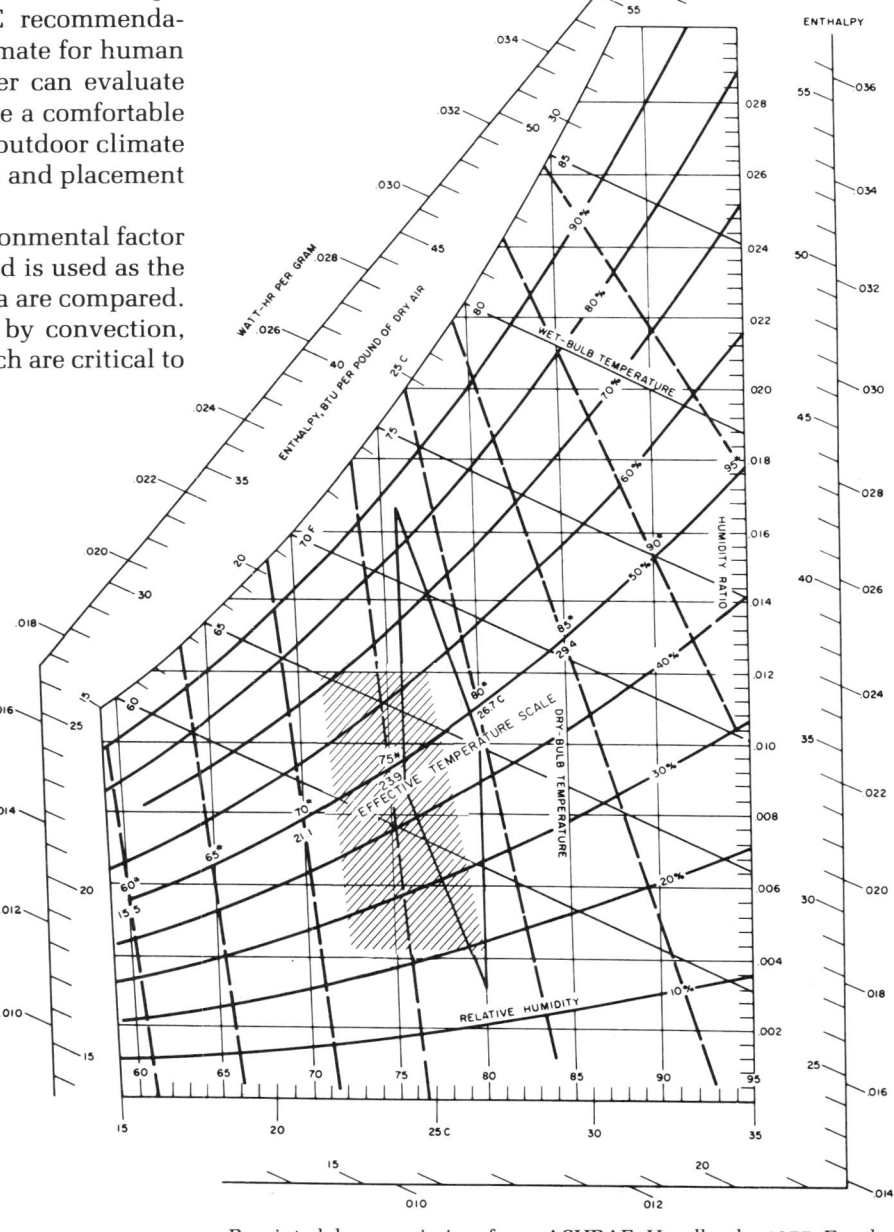

Graph 2.1 Effective temperature scale

Reprinted by permission from ASHRAE *Handbook*, 1977 Fundamentals.

the energy balance of the body. When the other conditions are close to optimum comfort levels, air temperature is the single most important variable. Many heating systems are designed exclusively to control air temperature.

Relative humidity (RH), an important element of comfort, is defined as the quantity of water vapor present in the air. Expressed as a percentage, relative humidity refers to the actual amount of moisture contained in air at a given temperature as a fraction of the total amount that the air could potentially hold. For example, air at 50 percent relative humidity contains half the moisture it could hold at that temperature. Relative humidity is closely linked with air temperature, since warmer air will hold more moisture. As air cools, its capacity to retain moisture decreases to the point where relative humidity reaches 100 percent. Air at 100 percent RH can hold no more moisture and is said to be *saturated*. If the air is heated and water vapor quantity is fixed, the relative humidity decreases since the warmer air can hold more moisture. If the air drops below the temperature of saturation (100 percent RH), the water vapor will condense out of the air. The temperature at which condensation occurs is known as the *dew point*.

Excessive humidity creates a moist atmosphere that hinders evaporative body cooling, and also may cause condensation on cool surfaces such as window glass and metal door and window frames. Conversely, low humidity levels can cause dryness of skin, respiratory passages, and eyes. Long periods of low humidity also can cause furniture and building materials to shrink. Chapter 3 presents a more detailed discussion of problems and solutions associated with water vapor, condensation, and humidity levels.

Winter air has a low moisture content due to its cool temperatures. When cool air leaks into a building and becomes heated, it lowers the relative humidity of the inside air, requiring more heat to maintain comfort. "Tight" buildings require less energy because the occupants simply use less heat as a result of higher relative humidities. Relative humidities in the range of 25 to 40 percent strike an acceptable balance between the need for comfort and dangers of condensation.

Mean radiant temperature refers to the surface temperature of walls, floors, and ceilings that surround the body. It is a very significant factor in establishing the rate of radiant heat transfer between surfaces and the body. Radiant surface temperature has approximately 40 percent more direct effect on comfort than air temperature. Well insulated homes will maintain higher interior surface temperatures in winter and cooler surface temperatures in summer; this leads to greater comfort in both seasons. People are more comfortable at lower air temperatures, which means a lower thermostat setting and lower heat losses through the shell.

Air velocity is the speed of air movement within a space. The cooler the temperature of the air, the less velocity is desirable for comfort. The speed of air movement affects both convective and evaporative heat losses from the body. In winter, at lower air temperatures, excessive air movements can cause uncomfortable "cold drafts." In summer, however, air movement at higher speeds can increase comfort by cooling the body at a faster rate. This moving air can be provided by natural and/or mechanical ventilation. Wind speed and direction at different sites greatly affects the patterns and speeds of indoor air movement.

Air speed is also directly related to fresh air supply. Low velocities may cause moisture or odor build-up. The recommended minimum air speed that will avoid stagnation is 10 feet per minute (FPM) although 20-50 FPM is preferred. These higher flow rates translate to an air exchange rate of 25 cubic feet per minute per person, or one complete air change per room per hour. Maintaining air quality in tight construction is also discussed in greater detail in Chapter 3.

Providing Thermal Comfort
It must be emphasized that the four criteria we have discussed are heavily interdependent in a building. Sunlight entering through a window warms the surfaces of the floors and walls that it strikes, heats the air, and radiates back from the surfaces to the body. As the air is warmed, the relative humidity drops and convective currents of air motion are established. The driving force of all these heat exchanges is the natural tendency of heat to equalize its distribution. Controlling these variables is the basis of providing human comfort (Fig. 2.8).

The relationship of the building to its site is the first consideration in establishing a controlled indoor environment. The prevailing climate at the site defines outdoor air temperature, wind speeds, and relative humidity. Proper orientation and placement of the building on the site can utilize these site conditions to provide thermal comfort. The building shell controls the passage of sun, air, heat, moisture, light, and sound; the shape, materials, and construction details all determine how heat moves through it. Mechanical systems have been developed to control interior environments. They may manipulate any or all of these four criteria depending on their type and sophistication. For instance, a forced hot air heating system heats the air, reduces humidity, blows air through a room, and warms the surfaces as the air sweeps past. The trend in designing heating systems has been towards greater control, but these sophisticated systems can be complex, expensive, and dependent on external supplies of fuel and electricity.

The primary goal of solar construction is to utilize the capabilities of siting, orientation, building shape, materials, and construction assemblies to provide human comfort without dependence on mechanical systems. This is not to say that mechanical systems have no place in solar construction. However, their role is restricted to fine tuning the interior environment, resulting in smaller, less expensive, less imposing systems.

Remember that while controlling the inside environment often is accomplished by heating or cooling systems, there is seldom a net flow of heat to the body. All mechanical systems and natural techniques that provide for comfort do so by adjusting the indoor thermal conditions to allow a comfortable rate of heat loss from the body. Heating systems allow the body to cool less rapidly during heating seasons while cooling systems accelerate body heat loss during periods when cooling is desired.

SOURCES OF HEAT IN BUILDINGS

There are many sources of heat in buildings. The sun's energy, mechanical heating systems, lights, appliances and human activity all contribute heat energy to the interior environment, which is either an asset to comfort during the heating season or a liability when cooling is desired. The resistance of the exterior building shell to the passage of heat between indoors and outdoors is a very strong determinant of the building's requirements for heating or cooling.

The effect of the sun's energy on heat movement through the building shell is very important. Solar energy travels through space as electromagnetic radiation, passes though the atmosphere, and strikes the earth. The intensity of solar energy at the surface varies at different times of day and different times of year. Chapter 4 discusses in more detail these principles of solar radiation that affect solar construction. As the solar radiation strikes the earth's surface or the surface of the building shell, it is either reflected, transmitted or absorbed, depending on the nature of the material it strikes. As the solar radiation is absorbed by the material, it is transformed to thermal radiation or heat. A black asphalt roof will absorb much more solar energy than a lightly colored roof, which reflects a significantly higher percentage. This absorbed heat is then conducted through the building shell to the interior. Window glass and other glazing materials transmit most of the solar radiation that strikes them directly through to the building interior; a small percentage is reflected and

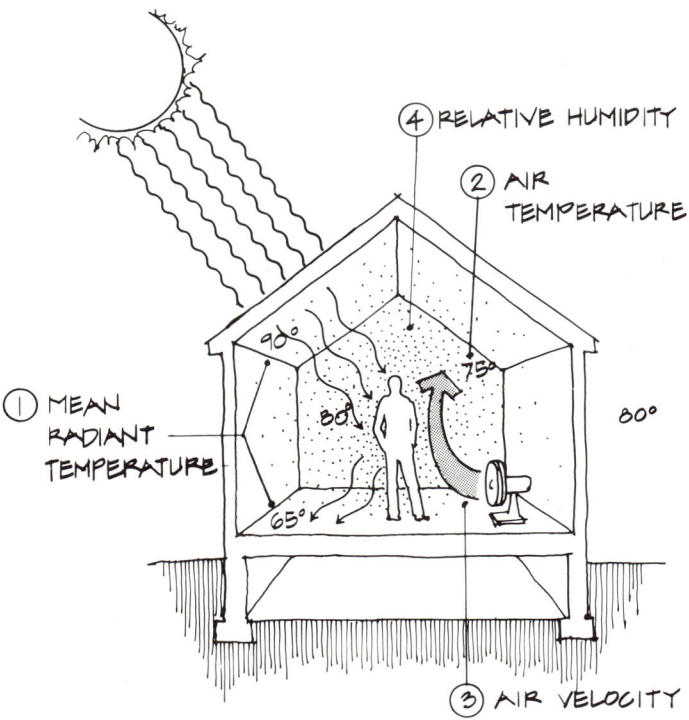

Fig. 2.8 Providing thermal comfort in a building consists of regulating four factors: (1) mean radiant temperature, (2) air temperature, (3) air velocity, (4) relative humidity.

absorbed, but most of the energy turns to heat as it is absorbed by the materials inside. This trapping of the sun's energy by glazed areas is known as the greenhouse effect (Fig. 2.9). This is true of windows, actual greenhouses, and glazings used for solar collectors. Certain building materials are used in solar construction because of their capability to absorb the sun's energy. These materials, such as concrete, stone, or brick, when properly used, can prevent the room from overheating by absorbing the solar heat (Fig. 2.10). Chapter 5 discusses several alternative approaches for the use of glazed areas for collection of solar energy and the use of materials to store heat.

Mechanical heating systems, fueled by external energy sources of wood, coal, gas, oil, or electricity control the interior environment of living spaces to ensure thermal comfort for inhabitants. Solar construction techniques lower the requirements for nonrenewable energy sources by reducing a building's dependence on mechanical systems to provide these human needs. Mechanical systems control four main factors in maintaining thermal comfort in buildings: 1) air temperature, 2) relative humidity of the air, 3) air motion and supply, 4) mean radiant temperature of floor, wall and ceiling surfaces. The objective of mechanical systems is to adjust these four factors to maintain "comfort zone" conditions within a space. There are many ways that mechanical systems accomplish this and these form an important basis for selecting a particular mechanical system. Air temperature may be controlled by a supply of warm or cool air delivered to a space through air, water, or electricity. Mean radiant temperature of surfaces may be controlled by radiant panels heated by water, electric resistance heating, or warm air, or by convective warm air distribution warming the surface. Homes using solar construction techniques maintain more desirable surface temperatures (warmer in winter, cooler in summer) due to the increased levels of thermal protection from outside temperature fluctuations. Solar radiation that penetrates the building skin also contributes to higher radiant temperatures and higher air temperatures. Relative humidity is controlled by the introduction or elimination of water vapor concentrations in the air. Energy conserving residences maintain more comfortable humidity levels in winter without humidification.

Mechanical systems must be accurately sized to provide the proper quantity of heating or cooling to maintain comfortable conditions. The size of unit required and the amount of fuel consumed depends on climate factors, the resistance of the building shell to the movement of heat through it, and the lifestyle of the occupants. The sun's energy also plays a dominant role in mechanical requirements for comfort. In the winter, the sun can reduce the quantity of fuel required by directly warming the living spaces and in the summer, if the living spaces are not adequately protected from the sun's heat, mechanical cooling requirements will be greatly increased. Simple strategies to protect from the sun's heat are discussed at the end of the chapter and in Chapters 4 and 5.

The particular approach to delivery of heat to the living space is another important means of comparing mechanical heating systems. Convection, conduction, and radiation are all utilized by different systems. Conduction of heat is utilized in hydronic central heating systems to transfer heat energy from the hot water inside baseboard pipes to the attached metal fins. Electric baseboards also rely on conduction to transfer heat. Common heat delivery systems that rely heavily on radiation include radiative ceiling and wall panels and slab floors, steam radiators, wood stoves, and fireplaces. Hydronic and electric baseboards rely on convective heat transfer for delivery of heat to the living space. Heat that has been conducted to the metal fins is picked up by the natural convective air movement that sweeps heat from the baseboards, and rises into the room. As heated air comes in contact with cooler surfaces, it loses its heat

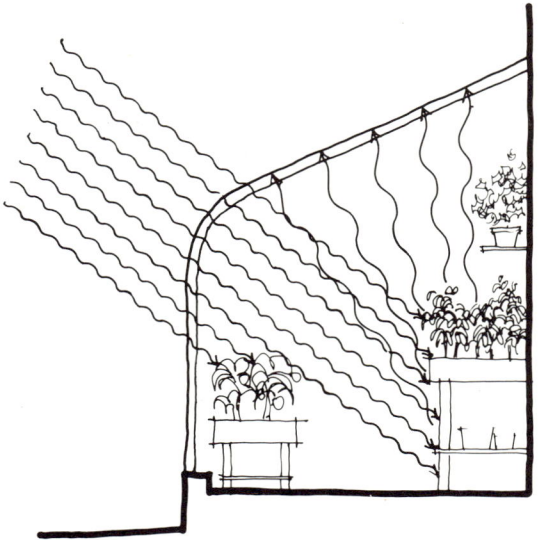

Fig. 2.9 The Greenhouse Effect Most sunlight (short wave radiation) passes directly through glazing materials. A small percentage is reflected or absorbed, depending on the sunlight angle and the type of glazing. Objects within the building (or solar collector absorber plates) absorb the sun's energy and heat up. This heat is then re-radiated as long wave radiation. Since glass blocks the passage of long wave radiation, a large percentage of the original solar energy is effectively trapped as heat.

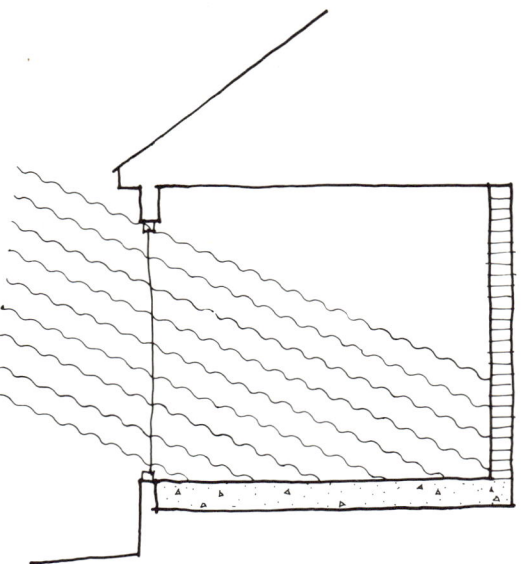

Fig. 2.10 The Use of Thermal Mass Thick, heavy materials such as concrete, stone, and brick absorb more direct solar energy than thin, lightweight materials like wood, carpet, or fabric. A room designed to admit solar energy and employing adequate thermal mass will not overheat during sunny periods because more energy is stored in the mass and less is available to heat the air. At night this stored heat is re-radiated into the room to help keep it warm.

and sinks to floor level to replace air that has just been heated. Convective heat transfer can be assisted mechanically by the use of fans and blowers. Forced warm air heating systems utilize this approach. The building's air supply is blown past a central point where it sweeps heat away from the furnace and moves it through ducts and registers into the living space. As the air cools, and loses its heat to the living space, it sinks to the floor, and is circulated to the furnace to be heated once again.

In addition to solar radiation and mechanical systems, electric lighting, appliances, and human activity also contribute heat to a building. In superinsulated construction, these internal heat gains may even provide the primary source of heating. In these homes, the insulation levels and resistance to air infiltration are so high that the need for mechanical heating systems is often eliminated. However, mechanical ventilation to assure adequate fresh air may be required; this can be accomplished with an air to air heat exchanger to prevent excessive heat loss. Maintaining air quality in tight construction is discussed in Chapter 3.

HEAT LOSS IN BUILDINGS

A building's heat loss occurs through its exterior shell, as heat moves from warm interior spaces toward the colder outdoors. As previously stated, the heat moves by conduction, convection or radiation. The rate of heat flow depends on the difference in temperature between inside and outside, and on the resistance of the building shell to the passage of heat. A large temperature differential (65°F indoor to 10°F outdoor) causes a greater flow of heat than a smaller differential (65°F indoor to 50°F outdoor). The resistance of the shell is determined by the sum of the individual resistances of each material that make up a particular floor, wall, or roof section. All three mechanisms of heat transfer operate to transmit heat through the building section. For example, consider the path of heat movement through an uninsulated wall. Heat is delivered to the inside wall surfaces by radiation and convection, absorbed by the interior finish, and conducted through it. Where the finish is nailed to the studs, heat conduction continues through the studs to the cooler sheathing. Across the cavity between the studs, the heat is both convected and radiated to the inside face of the sheathing; then it is conducted through the sheathing and siding to the outside surface of the building, where it is both radiated and carried away by convection.

Though heat moves from indoors to outdoors by all three methods of heat transfer, in different places in the building one method often predominates. It is important to understand where the different types of heat loss occur, and to what degrees, in order to determine how heat loss can be reduced.

Conductive Heat Loss

The conduction of heat through materials is the primary means of heat loss in buildings (Fig. 2.11). Conductive losses are most prevalent where the same material is exposed to both inside and outside temperatures. This "thermal bridging" is present in many locations in residential construction. Areas of particular concern include bandjoists, plates, built-up headers, studs, corners, rafters, window sash and glazings, doors, basement walls, and concrete slab floors. New building materials and techniques reduce the effects of "thermal bridging" by interrupting the conduction of heat directly through these components. In some cases this requires covering one surface with a continuous layer of insulation, while in others it may mean that an insulating material is laminated between their inside and outside surfaces. Every material in a building section has a different rate of conduction. Compared to metal, wood is a poor conductor of heat, but it is a good conductor compared to insulation materials (Table 2.1). Insulations are used in construction specifically to reduce the conductive flow of heat; generally, the more wood there is in a building frame, the less area available for insulation, and the more paths for conductive heat loss.

Convective Heat Loss

Convection contributes to heat loss in a number of ways, both inside and outside the building, and it usually works in conjunction with conductive heat transfer. Within living spaces, natural convection patterns are important means of distributing heat. Outside walls are typically the coldest surfaces within a room; warm air that has risen to the ceiling moves toward the cooler walls, gives up its heat to the cold wall and sinks to the floor, drawing more warm air off the ceiling. This pattern serves to cool living spaces, as it delivers heat to the exterior walls where it is absorbed and conducted to the outside. A well insulated exterior wall lowers the effect of this pattern since the inside surface temperatures are higher; however, the problem still occurs near windows. Heating units often are placed in front of glazed areas to eliminate this cold draft falling down along the glass. This practice increases comfort in front of windows but actually accelerates heat loss through them by increasing the temperature difference across the glass.

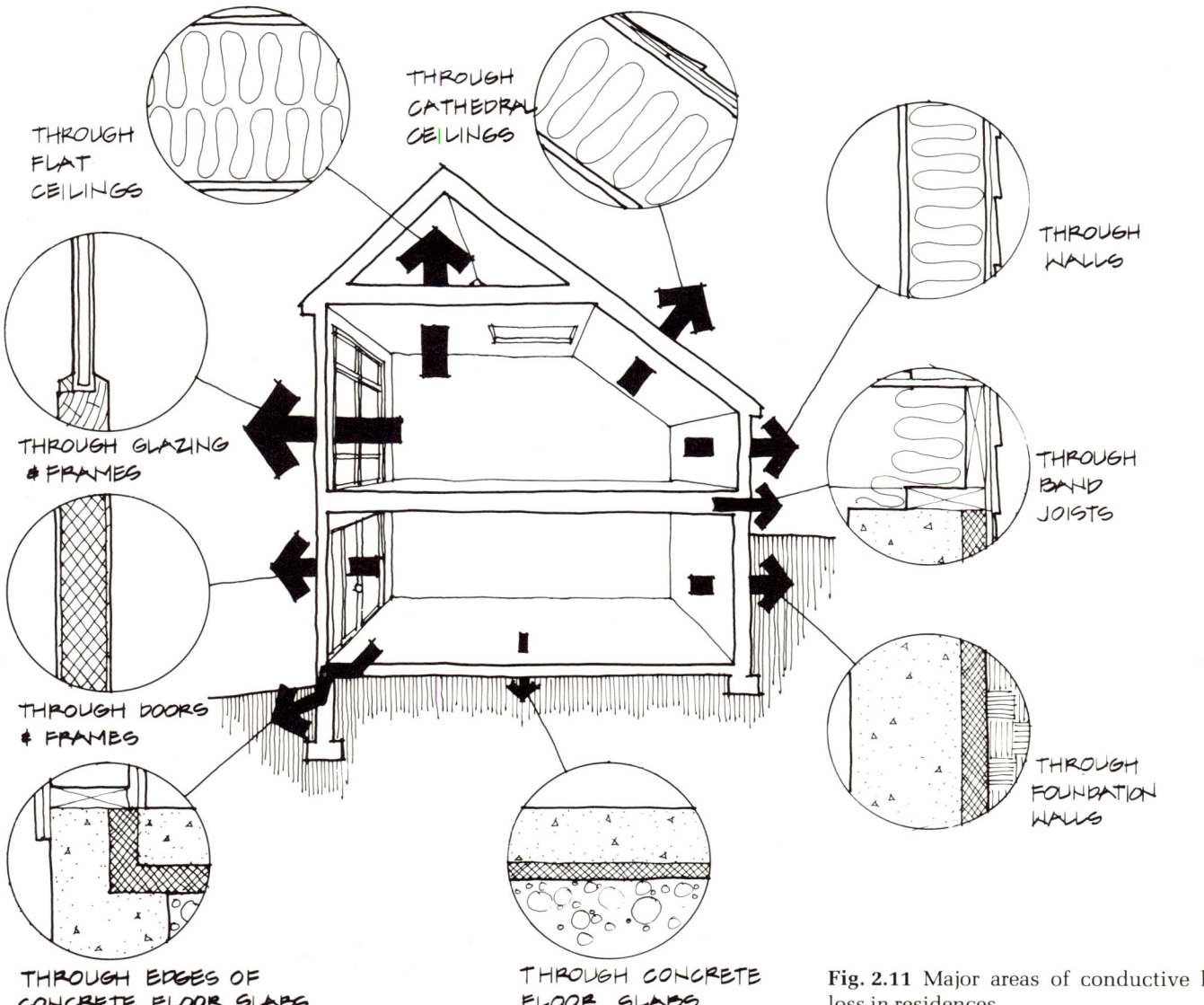

Fig. 2.11 Major areas of conductive heat loss in residences.

Another place where convective loss occurs is within a wall section, including uninsulated stud cavities, or between multiple layers of glass. Inside the wall cavity, air contacts warm interior surfaces and rises, drawing heat as it moves; then it sinks as it loses heat to the exterior sheathing. Convective cycles form in each empty stud cavity, resulting in increased transfer of heat from the warm inside to the cooler outside. Convective flows also can be established between layers of glazing in windows and doors. This is only likely to occur on site fabricated windows with air spaces of ¾ inch or more. The air space on most commercial window units usually is too small for this to occur. Air spaces between glazings and the effects of air films are discussed in more detail later in this section.

Wind movement at a site greatly affects convective heat loss. Cold winter winds convect heat away from building surfaces. This rapid cooling of the exterior accelerates the conductive loss through the shell. Sheltering a building from predominant winter winds at a site is a very simple and effective way to reduce heat loss. Techniques for siting the building to reduce heat loss are discussed in Chapter 4.

The most significant area of convective heat loss is *infiltration*—the leakage of cold air into a building and warm air out through the exterior shell (Fig. 2.12). This

Table 2.1
Resistance values of structural and finish materials, insulation air spaces and air films[a]

Material	R-value	Material	R-value
Wood bevel siding, ½" × 8", lapped	0.81	Approximately 12" thick	38.00
Wood siding shingles, 16", 7½" exposure	0.87	*Insulation board*	
Asbestos-cement shingles	0.03	Glass fiber, organic bonded, 1"	4.00
Stucco, per inch	0.20	Extruded polystyrene, cut cell, 1"	4.00
Building paper, permeable felt	0.06	Extruded polystyrene, smooth, 1"	5.00
½" Nail-base insulation board sheathing	1.14	Expanded polystyrene, molded beads, 1"	3.57
½" Insulation board sheathing, regular intermediate density	1.22	Expanded polyurethane, 1" or more	6.25
		Polyisocyanurate, 1"	7.20
½" Insulation board sheathing, regular density	1.32	Mineral fiber with resin binder	3.45
		Insulation blown loose fill	
25/32" Insulation board sheathing, regular density	2.06	Cellulosic, per inch	3.13–3.70
		Perlite expanded, per inch	2.70
¼" Plywood	0.31	Mineral fiber (rock, slag, glass)	
⅜" Plywood	0.47	3¾" to 5"	11.00
½" Plywood	0.62	6½" to 8¾"	19.00
⅝" Plywood	0.77	7½" to 10"	22.00
¼" Hardboard, high-density, standard tempered	0.25	10¼" to 13¾"	30.00
		13" to 17¼"	38.00
¼" Hardboard, underlayment	0.31	Vermiculite exfoliated, per inch	2.13–2.27
⅝" Particleboard, underlayment	0.82	*Air spaces (¾")*[b]	
Softwood, per inch	1.25	Heat flow up	
Softwood board, ¾" thick	0.94	Nonreflective	0.75 (summer)
			0.87 (winter)
Concrete blocks, three oval cores		Reflective, one surface	2.22 (summer)
Cinder aggregate, 4" thick	1.11		2.21 (winter)
Cinder aggregate, 12" thick	1.89	Heat flow down	
Cinder aggregate, 8" thick	1.72	Nonreflective	0.85 (summer)
Sand and gravel aggregate, 8" thick	1.11		1.02 (winter)
Lightweight aggregate (expanded clay, shale, slag, pumice, etc.), 8" thick	2.00	Reflective, one surface	3.29 (summer)
			3.59 (winter)
Concrete blocks, two rectangular cores		Heat flow horizontal	
Sand and gravel aggregate, 8" thick	1.04	Nonreflective	0.84 (summer)
Lightweight aggregate, 8" thick	2.18		1.01 (winter)
Common brick, per inch	0.20	Reflective, one surface	3.24 (summer)
Face brick, per inch	0.11		3.46 (winter)
Sand and gravel concrete, per inch	0.08	*Surface air films, inside (still air)*	
Sand and gravel concrete, 8" thick	0.64	Heat flow up (through a horizontal surface)	
½" Gypsumboard	0.45		
⅝" Gypsumboard	0.56	Nonreflective	0.61
½" Lightweight aggregate gypsum plaster	0.32	Reflective	1.32
¾" Hardwood finish flooring	0.68	Heat flow down (through a horizontal surface)	
Asphalt, linoleum, vinyl, or rubber floor tile	0.05		
Carpet and fibrous pad	2.08	Nonreflective	0.92
Carpet and foam rubber pad	1.23	Reflective	4.55
Asphalt roof shingles	0.44	Heat flow horizontal (through a vertical surface)	
Wood roof shingles	0.94		
⅜" Builtup roof	0.33	Nonreflective	0.68
Insulation, mineral wool blanket and batt		Heat flow in any direction, surface in position	
Approximately 3" to 3½" thick	11.00		
Approximately 5¼" to 6½" thick	19.00	15-mph wind (winter)	0.17
Approximately 6" to 7" thick	22.00	7.5-mph wind (summer)	0.25
Approximately 8½" to 9" thick	30.00		

[a] Additional resistance values can be obtained from the 1977 ASHRAE *Handbook of Fundamentals* published by the American Society of Heating, Refrigerating and Air-Conditioning Engineers.
[b] The addition of a second reflective surface facing the first reflective surface increases the thermal resistance value of an air space only 4 to 8 percent.

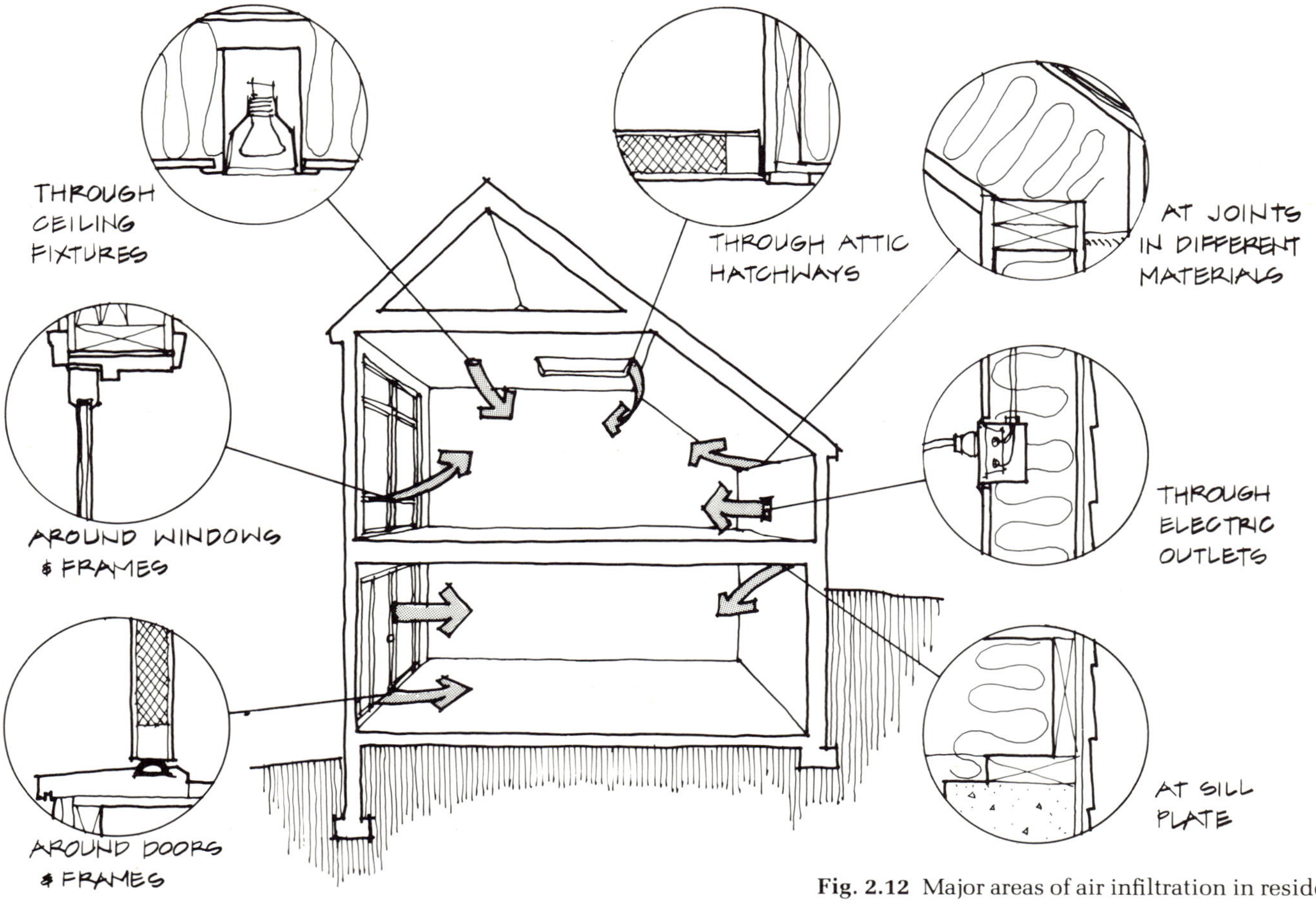

HEAT IN BUILDINGS 19

Fig. 2.12 Major areas of air infiltration in residences.

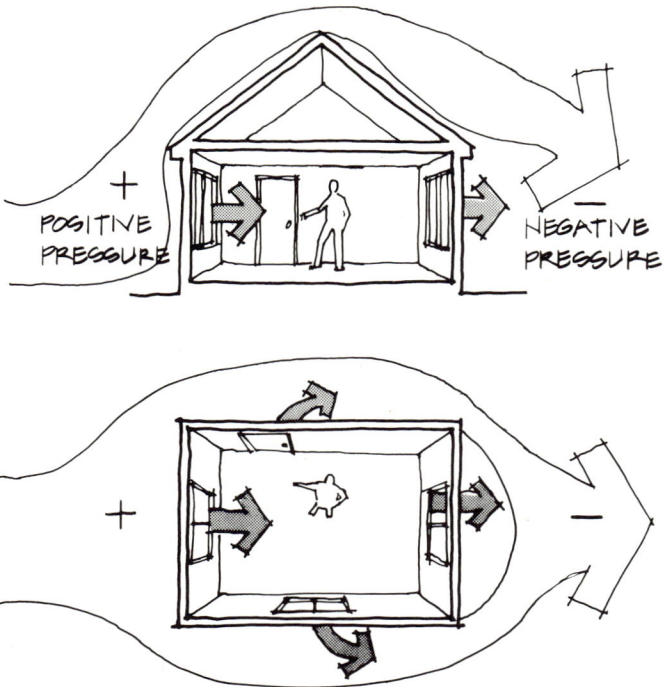

air leakage occurs through cracks around windows and doors, exhaust fan openings, utility penetrations, intersection of sill and foundation—any place that materials intersect can leak air through the building shell. As other sources of heat loss are reduced, infiltration becomes more significant, and it can account for up to 40 percent of the total heat loss in a well insulated building. The amount of infiltration depends on construction details, quality of building components, and the level of workmanship; however, workmanship is the most important factor in achieving a tight building.

When wind strikes the walls and roof of a building, it changes the air pressure on all sides. On the windward side (toward the wind) the pressure is positive, causing air to flow into the building at each point of leakage. Pressure on the leeward side (away from the wind) is negative, causing air to flow from inside the building, through leaks in the building shell to the outside (Fig. 2.13).

Fig. 2.13 Wind creates areas of positive and negative pressure around buildings which cause air leakage into and out of the building.

Another cause of air leakage is the combustion of fuel for space and domestic water heating that requires fresh makeup air as oxygen is burned. The venting of warm exhaust gases through the chimney draws air up and out of the building. This air is replaced by air within the building (already heated), which causes negative inside pressure resulting in increased infiltration of cold air. This effect also occurs with fireplaces.

Radiative Heat Loss

Radiative heat loss occurs when exterior surfaces of the building are warmer than the outdoor environment. As with other types of heat loss, radiation works in conjunction with conduction and convection. It is much more significant in distributing heat inside rooms and dissipating conducted heat to the outdoors than it is in transmitting heat through the shell. Windows and glazings contribute significantly to radiative heat loss. Heat from warm interior surfaces and objects (including the occupants) is radiated to the glass (which is opaque to radiation) and then is conducted through the glass and lost to the outdoors by radiation and convection. Techniques for reducing this form of heat loss are discussed later in this chapter.

Controlling Heat Losses

A variety of materials and techniques may be used to reduce heat loss from buildings. Since heat loss occurs through the building shell, our discussion concentrates on that phase of construction. Other techniques for reducing heat loss, such as siting, landscaping, and building shape, are discussed in Chapter 4. Construction measures to reduce heat loss through the shell are specifically aimed at slowing the rate of conduction, convection, and infiltration. These controls include: increasing insulation levels; insulating areas usually left uninsulated; choosing good quality windows with multiple layers of glass; and proper selection and construction of other details to reduce infiltration. This section introduces insulating materials and concepts, and presents the relative priorities for reducing heat loss through the various components of the building shell—foundations, floors, walls, doors, windows, roofs. Table 2.2 presents a summary of heat losses at different places in a building for typical uninsulated and insulated residences.

It is important to remember that energy performance depends on the combined effects of conduction, radiation, convection, and infiltration, as well as the climate that surrounds the building. The relationship between these elements is a very direct one; change one element, and they are all affected. For example, reducing the velocity of wind striking a wall by planting shrubs reduces convective cooling of the wall. This in turn slows conduction through the wall section, keeping the interior wall surface warmer, which reduces interior convection. The slower wind speed does not exert as much pressure on the windward surfaces, so infiltration is also reduced.

The Use of Insulation

The first priority in reducing heat loss is increasing insulation levels. As discussed earlier, insulating materials are those with high resistance to heat flow (high R-values). All materials with the same R-value, regardless of thickness, have the same insulating value. Products developed specifically for this purpose include fiberglass (batts and loose), foam boards, cellulose (loose), liquid foams that solidify after installation, reflective aluminum, and vermiculite. All of these products (except aluminum foil, which reduces radiative losses) reduce conductive heat loss by creating "dead air spaces" within or next to wall, roof, and floor cavities (Fig. 2.14). This concept of "dead air spaces" is the basis for the use of multiple glazings.

It is important to select the proper insulation material for use in different areas of the building. Insulations should be compared on the basis of insulating value, ease of installation, life expectancy, cost, availability, and fire and toxicity dangers. Different insulations often are used in different places in the building; for example, insulation suitable for use in sidewall cavities may not be appropriate for use below grade (Table 2.3).

Fiberglass insulation is the most commonly applied of these materials. Fiberglass batts can be installed in stud walls, roof/ceiling, and floor cavities. They are available with kraft paper or foil facing, and with stapling tabs or unfaced for a pressure fit. Typical thicknesses and R-values include 3½-inch (R-11), 6-inch (R-19), and 9½-inch (R-30). Fiberglass insulation is also available as semi-rigid sheets, of 1-inch (R-4), 1½-inch (R-6), or 2-inch (R-8) thickness. These sheets are also available faced or unfaced. Another form of fiberglass insulation is a loose fill that is poured or blown into framing cavities.

Fiberglass insulation must be used in conjunction with an effective, continuous interior vapor barrier. As the facings on these products do not provide the necessary moisture protection in most climates, installation of a separate barrier of 6-mil polyethylene or aluminum foil is required. Also, these facings (and adhesives) may be combustible and should be covered with a fire resistant finish.

Table 2.2
Summary of heat losses of uninsulated residence (Btuh)

Room or space	Walls	Ceiling and roof	Floor	Glass and door	Infiltration	Totals
Bedroom A	5870	8350	—	1530	3080	18,830
Bedroom B	3840	5630	—	1530	2080	18,830
Bedroom C	2810	4280	—	1030	1580	9,700
Bedroom D	2910	3640	1140	770	1350	9,810
Bathroom 1	740	1820	—	540	670	3,770
Bathroom 2	1750	1190	360	340	430	4,070
Living Room	8050	—	—	1910	5730	15,690
Dining Room	4090	—	—	3300	3270	10,660
Kitchen	3170	—	—	1040	2440	6,650
Lavette	3350	—	—	1160	590	5,100
Entrance Hall	960	2990	—	680	1700	6,330
Garage	−1180[a]	−1500[b]	1180	4120	2120	4,740
Recreation	950	—	720	770	3080	5,520
Design totals	37,310	26,400	3,400	18,720	28,120	113,950
Operating totals[c]	37,310	26,400	3,400	18,720	14,060	99,890
Percentages[d]	37	27	3	19	14	100

[a] Wall heat loss of 2420 Btuh minus wall heat gains of 1470, 800, and 1330 Btuh.
[b] Heat gains of 1140 and 360 Btuh.
[c] Based on 0.5 computed infiltration.
[d] Based on operating totals.

Summary of heat losses of insulated residence (Btuh)

Room or space	Walls	Ceiling and roof	Floor	Glass and door	Infiltration	Totals
Bedroom A	2620	2770	—	1530	3080	10,000
Bedroom B	1720	1870	—	1530	2080	7,200
Bedroom C	1260	1470	—	1030	1580	5,340
Bedroom D	1300	1220	790	770	1350	5,430
Bathroom 1	330	610	—	540	670	2,150
Bathroom 2	870	280	250	340	430	2,170
Living room	3630	—	—	1910	5730	11,270
Dining room	1830	—	—	3300	3270	8,400
Kitchen	1430	—	—	1040	2440	4,910
Lavette	1520	—	—	1160	590	3,270
Entrance hall	430	960	—	680	1700	3,770
Garage	−580[a]	−1040[b]	1180	4120	2120	5,800
Recreation	950	—	720	770	3080	5,520
Design totals	17,310	8,140	2,940	18,720	28,120	75,230
Operating totals[c]	17,310	8,140	2,940	18,720	14,060	61,170
Percentages[d]	28	13	5	31	23	100

[a] Wall heat loss of 1080 Btuh minus wall heat gains of 680, 370, and 610 Btuh.
[b] Heat gains of 790 and 250 Btuh.
[c] Based on 0.5 computed infiltration.
[d] Based on operating totals.

Note the reduction in percent of heat loss in walls and ceiling/roofs due to increased insulation in these areas. These reductions result in increased importance to control heat loss through floors, windows/doors and air leakage throughout the building as indicated by their increased percentage of total heat loss in the insulated residence. These tables are taken from an example in the NAHB/RF *Insulation Manual*.

22 BASIC PRINCIPLES OF SOLAR CONSTRUCTION

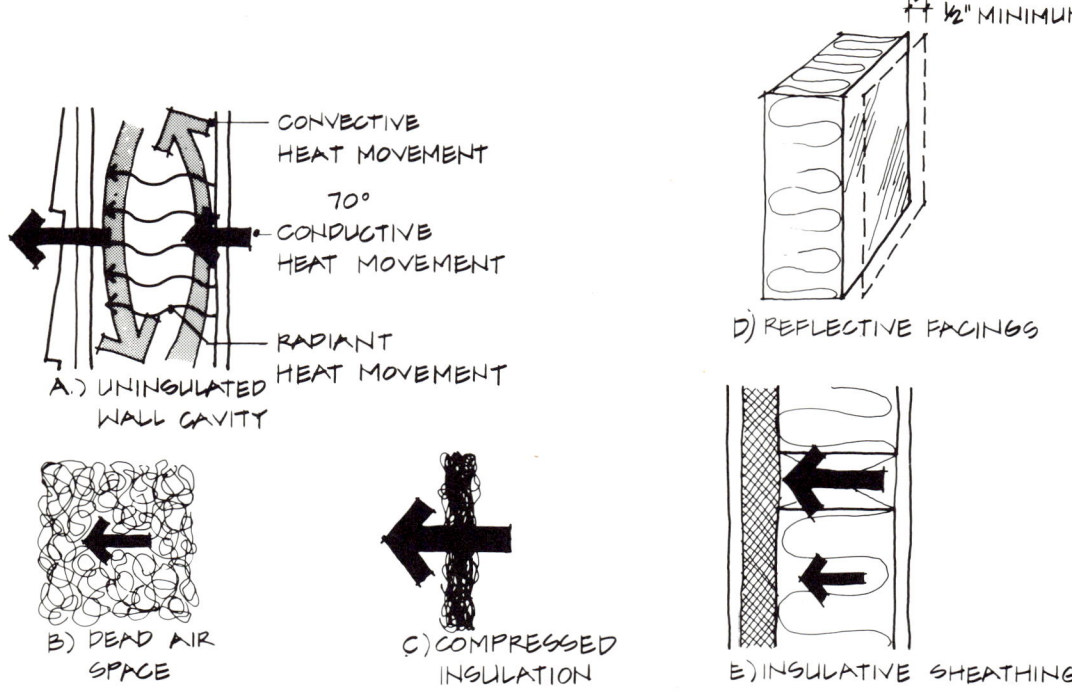

Fig. 2.14 Principles of Insulation A) Heat moves through an uninsulated wall by conduction, convection and radiation. B) Insulation materials create dead air spaces which block the flow of heat. C) Compressing insulation lowers its R-value. Six inches of fiberglass that is crammed into a 3½″ wall cavity will perform the same as only 3½″ of insulation. D) Some insulations have reflective facings which can increase their R-value. These facings require ½″ *minimum air space* between foil and adjacent wall surface. E) Rigid foam insulation used as sheathing will block conductive heat flow through wood frame structure.

Table 2.3
Comparison of insulations used in residential construction

	Material	R-value/inch	Available as	Appropriate applications	Specification
Blown Loose Fill	Cellulose	3.5	20–30 lb bags	• Wood framed • Ceilings, floors, walls	• Expect 10% settling • Good for retrofits • Specify by R-value rather than thickness
	Fiberglass	3.14	20 lb bags	• Wood framed ceilings, floors • Walls	• Expect settling • Good for retrofits • Specify by R-value rather than thickness
	Rockwool	2.9	20–30 lb bags	• Wood framed ceilings, floors • Walls	• Expect 10% settling • Good for retrofits • Specify by R-value rather than thickness
	Perlite	2.7	20–30 lb bags	• Wood framed ceilings, floors	• Expect settling • Specify by R-value rather than thickness

(Continued)

Table 2.3 *(Continued)*
Comparison of insulations used in residential construction

	Material	R-valve/inch	Available as	Appropriate applications	Specification
Blanket or Batt	Fiberglass or Mineral Wool	3.14	*Thicknesses:* 3½, 6, 9, 12 inch *Widths:* 16, 24 inch • Paper or foil faced	• Wood framed ceilings, floors, walls	• Specify by thickness and width • Order by square footage • Install at full thickness • Requires fire protection
Rigid Board Insulation	Expanded Polystyrene (beadboard)	3.6	*Thicknesses:* 1, 2, 4 inch *Surface Dimensions:* 2 × 8 4 × 8 • Squared edges	• Interior insulative sheathing • Exterior insulative sheathing (above grade)	• Requires protection from fire, UV degradation, and moisture • Use only compatible panel adhesives
	Extruded Polystyrene (Blueboard or Pinkboard) smooth cell cut cell	 5.4 4	*Thicknesses:* ¾, 1, 1½, 2 inch *Surface Dimensions:* 2 × 8 • T&G or squared edges	• Interior insulative sheathing • Exterior insulative sheathing (above grade) • Interior foundation • Exterior foundation (below grade) • Beneath concrete slabs • Along slab edges	• Requires protection from fire, UV degradation • Use only compatible panel adhesives and foundation sealants
	Expanded Polyurethane	6.25	*Thicknesses:* ¾, 1, 2, 4 inch *Surface Dimensions:* 4 × 8 • Squared edges • Foil or wax paper facing	• Interior insulative sheathing • Exterior insulative sheathing	• Requires protection from fire
	Polyisocyanurate	7.2	*Thicknesses:* 1, 1¼, 1½, 1¾, 2, 2¼, 3 inch *Surface Dimensions:* 4 × 8 • Squared edges • Foil or wax paper facing	• Interior insulative sheathing • Exterior insulative sheathing	• Requires protection from fire
	Rigid Glass Fiberboard	4.4	*Thicknesses:* 1 inch *Surface Dimensions:* 4 × 8 4 × 9 • Squared edges • Foil facing	• Interior insulative sheathing	• Requires protection from fire

Cellulose, a commonly used insulation, consists of shredded newspaper which has been treated for fire resistance. This material is applied as a loose fill and is poured or blown into framing cavities, achieving R-3.5 per inch. Cellulose insulation will tend to settle 10 percent after its initial installation, which reduces its R-value. It is important to use a continuous vapor barrier on the warm side (interior) of this material.

Rigid foam board insulations increasingly are used in many areas of energy conserving buildings—as exterior insulation on foundations, under slabs and along their perimeters, as exterior sheathing on wood frames, and as interior sheathing. Foams may be polyurethane, polyisocyanurate, extruded polystyrene, or expanded polystyrene. The various types of foam boards available differ as to R-value, available thickness, resistance to moisture, flame spread and toxicity, cost, and dimensions. Special attention should be paid to selection of foams for use below grade (exterior foundation, under slab) and to fire safety.

Foam insulations also can be installed in framing cavities as liquids which then solidify. These foams include urethane (R-8 per inch), urea formaldehyde (R-4.8 per inch), and tripolymer (R-4.5 per inch). The actual R-value, amount of shrinkage, and lingering odor levels depend largely on the installer who prepares and installs the foam. Most often this is done by specialized subcontractors. Most foam-in-place installations are on existing buildings with uninsulated walls. Foams rarely are used in ceilings. Liquid foams also perform differently from one another in terms of toxicity, flame spread, cost per square foot installed, moisture resistance, odor problems, and shrinkage. There have been problems with lingering vapors (such as formaldehyde) after installation of some foams, and a few states have banned their use. Builders should be alert to regulations concerning the use of these foams.

Aluminum foil sometimes is used alone, or as a facing on one of the insulations already mentioned to reduce heat loss. Its reflective nature is very useful in reflecting radiant heat. To be effective, reflective surfaces must be separated from the adjacent warm side surface by at least ½ inch; without this air space, reflected heat is lost immediately by conduction through the foil.

Masonry and concrete walls. Depending on construction, these walls can suffer from high conductive losses due to large areas of thermal bridging, where the materials make a direct connection between interior and exterior temperatures, either above or below grade. Basement walls conduct substantial amounts of heat, especially if a heating system is located in the basement. Walls below grade are subject to conductive heat loss only. Because the temperature of the ground below frost remains fairly constant throughout the year, many energy efficient homes (especially in cold climates) place living space below grade to shelter the living space from convective losses and permit a moderate temperature differential. The moisture content of the surrounding soil has a dramatic effect on the rate of conduction. Wet soil has a much higher conductance than well drained material like gravel, so it draws more heat from the building. Techniques to ensure adequate site and foundation drainage are discussed in Chapter 8.

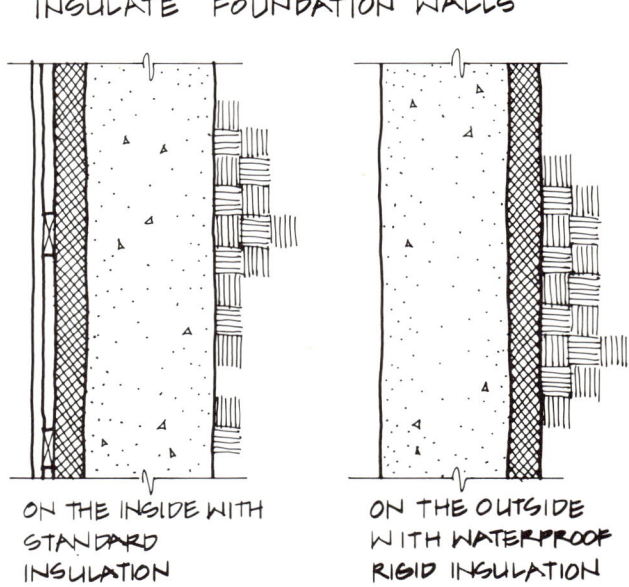

Fig. 2.15 Reducing heat loss through foundation walls.

Rigid board insulation can be used on the exterior of foundations to reduce heat loss through these walls (Fig. 2.15). The insulation must be able to withstand the presence of moisture, multiple freeze/thaw cycles, and frost pressure without losing its insulating qualities or deteriorating. A more detailed discussion of the selection and performance of materials suitable for this use follows in Chapter 8.

Foundation walls typically have been insulated on the interior surfaces by furring out from the wall and insulating the resulting cavity. This approach may create problems with moisture moving from inside towards the outside. Insulation on the interior reduces the surface temperature of the masonry, which encourages condensation as moisture-laden air contacts it. This condensation may damage both the insulating value of the insulation and the structure of the furring strips. Interior insulation also isolates the thermal storage capacity of the masonry walls from interior spaces. Application of appropriate insulation on the exterior of foundation walls increases their interior surface temperature, thus reducing condensation. This approach also leaves the masonry more exposed to air movement and heat radiation, allowing it to store and reradiate heat. Masonry walls can play an important role in solar construction; their capability to provide thermal storage is discussed in Chapter 5.

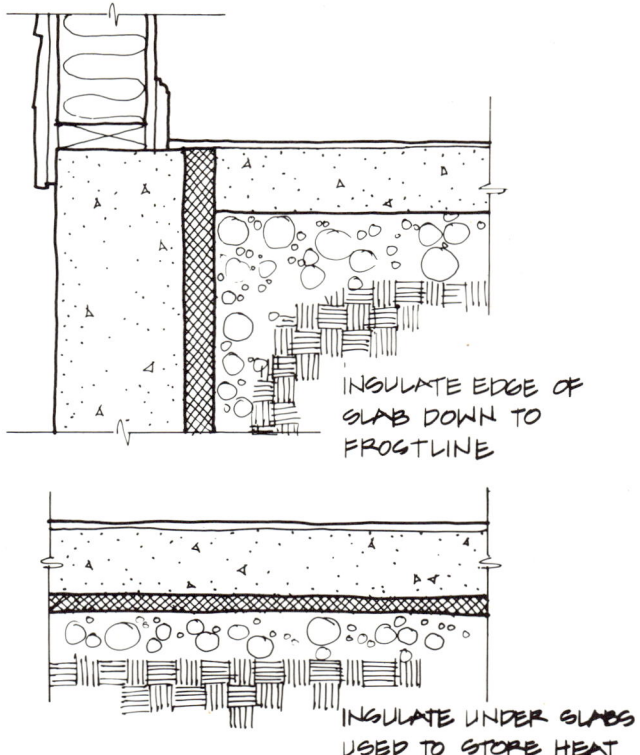

Fig. 2.16 Reducing heat loss through concrete slab on grade floors.

Table 2.4
Minimum recommended levels of insulation along the perimeter of concrete slab floors

Degree days/years	Heated (R)	Unheated (R)
8,000 and higher	9.4	7.6
6,000	7.1	4.9
4,000	5.5	3.5
2,500	4.6	2.7

Note: In cold regions it is recommended that insulation also be placed beneath slab floors in heated areas or in unheated areas that may be heated in the future.

Concrete slab floors. Depending on their location within the building, concrete slab floors may lose considerable heat by conduction. Heat moves into the slab; while some heat is conducted through the slab to the ground below, most heat moves toward the cold edges. Concrete slab floors used in living spaces will conduct more heat than those used in basements, because these slabs are exposed to higher temperatures within the heated living space. Also, the exposure of the edges to outside temperatures increases the rate of heat transfer to the edges. Slab on grade floors should be well insulated with a material suited for below grade application. Insulation placed beneath the slab reduces conduction to the soil, and insulation around the perimeter reduces heat movement to the cool edges and blocks thermal bridging to footings and frost walls (Fig. 2.16). Perimeter insulation also serves as a good expansion joint for slab floors. Techniques used to insulate concrete slab floors are presented in Chapter 8.

Table 2.4 presents recommended levels of insulation for slab floors. By insulating beneath the slab and around its perimeter, the thermal storage capacity of the concrete is contained within the insulated envelope where it can benefit the building's energy performance. This is very important if heating equipment is located on slab floors, or if the slab is used for radiant heat delivery to the room from heating ducts or pipes cast into it or from heat gained by solar radiation.

Wood frame floors. Heat loss through wood frame floors depends on the conditions above and below it and around its perimeter. Wood framed floors divide the living spaces within a building as well as separate them from crawl spaces (vented or unvented) and basements (heated or unheated). Three areas in floors require attention: the sill, where floor deck meets foundation; the band joists; and the space between floor joists. These first two should be addressed in every situation, while the third depends on the particular situation.

The intersection between the sill and foundation can be a source of significant air leakage. The use of fiberglass sill seal between the top of the foundation wall and sill reduces this infiltration. The sill seal fills the gaps between the wood and irregular masonry surfaces; however, fiberglass may retain moisture from water leaks or condensation, jeopardizing the wood frame. Extra supervision to ensure that the foundation is both level and square minimizes air leakage at this intersection. Rigid board insulation used to insulate the foundation on the outside can be installed to extend past the sill connection and continue as exterior sheathing of wood frame walls. This detail laps the sill area with sheathing, which reduces air leakage (Fig. 2.17).

Band joists typically are left uninsulated, which creates a band of heat loss around the building. The band joist at all floors should be insulated to the same level as walls. This may be done on the inside between floor joists or outside over the band joist.

Wood frame floors over vented crawl spaces conduct heat to the crawl space and allow cold air leakage. These floors should be well insulated to reduce heat conduction. A 6-mil polyethylene vapor barrier should be placed on the floor (ground) of the crawl space to resist the movement of moisture into the building. If

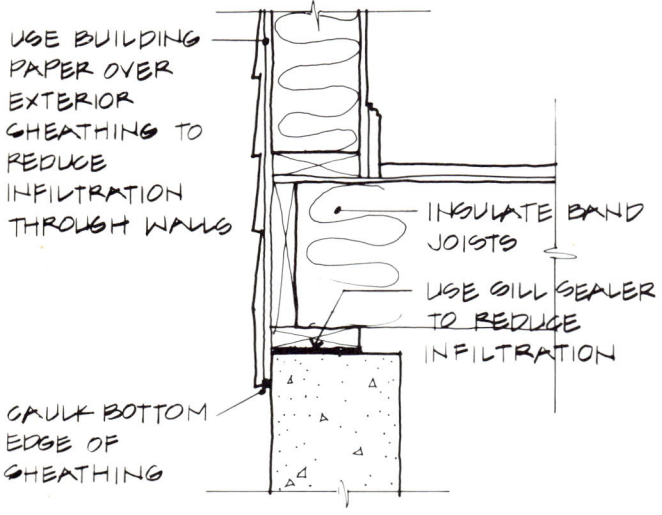

Fig. 2.17 Reducing heat loss through wood frame floors.

moisture collects in floor insulation it saturates the material, which reduces its effective R-value while holding moisture against the framing and flooring. Wood frame floors over unvented crawl spaces used as warm air plenums do not need to be insulated. Heat generated in the crawl space rises into the living space, adding to comfort by warming the first floor deck. The best location for insulation in this situation is along the perimeter of frostwall, inside or outside, extending down to the footing. Band joists should be insulated as described above.

Wood floors over heated basements should be left uninsulated to encourage the natural movement of heat through them. Band joists also should be insulated in this case. Unheated basements should be isolated from the rest of the building by an insulated first floor. This reduces heat loss to the basement, but in summer it may cause increased condensation on foundation walls due to reduced temperature.

Wood frame walls. Generally wood is thought to be a good insulator but, compared to insulation products, it is not. In typical residential construction, solid and built-up framing members create many areas that rely solely on the insulating properties of wood to prevent heat loss. These thermal bridges, such as headers over windows and doors, plates, corners, and jack and stud assemblies, should be avoided when possible.

Changes in building techniques to improve energy performance must not compromise structural integrity. There are many areas where improvement can take place without risking strength. New framing details at headers and corners that incorporate insulation to increase the R-value of these components are presented in Chapter 9. Insulative exterior sheathing wraps the frame in insulation, which reduces the impact of thermal bridging through it (Fig. 2.18). When using these rigid board insulations for sheathing, diagonal bracing

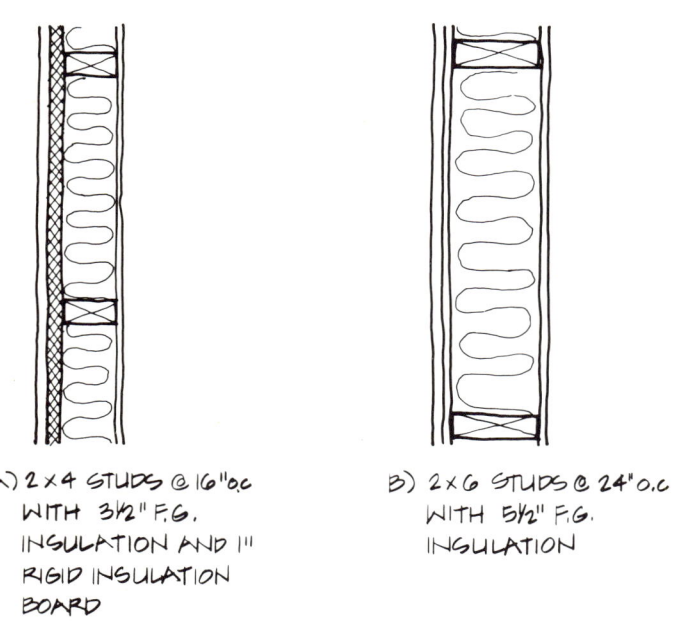
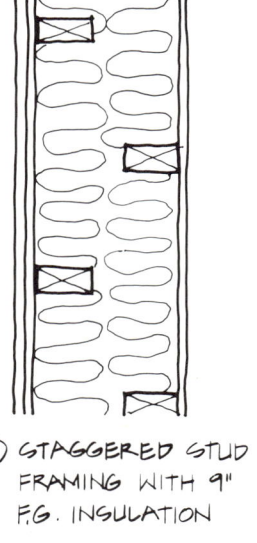

Fig. 2.18 Reducing heat loss through wood frame walls. A) Use of rigid board insulation as exterior sheathing. B) Increasing stud size to 2 × 6 creates larger wall cavity for insulation. C) Staggered stud framing permits more insulation.

to resist horizontal and racking forces is required. The R-value in wood framed walls can be increased in new construction with any one or a combination of practical techniques. The use of insulative exterior sheathings allows builders to increase R-value without changing from standard framing (except to require more nailers and bracing). A typical 2x4 wall provides an approximate R-13. By substituting foam board sheathing for plywood, the new wall section becomes R-19.

Framing methods can be changed to create a larger cavity permitting thicker insulation. Builders are adopting 2x6 studs framed 24 inches on center in an effort to achieve higher R-values. Combining a thicker insulation blanket with insulative sheathing creates an even better insulated wall section, reaching R-25–28. Some builders are stressing increased insulation levels to the point where their houses are considered "super insulated." These buildings often have R-36 walls and R-48 ceiling/roofs. Superinsulated buildings generally involve modifications to framing methods, such as double wall stud construction; these approaches are discussed in more detail in Chapter 9.

Reducing infiltration losses through walls requires attention at several locations in the wall section, because any place different materials meet can be a source of air leakage. The more joints in the shell, the greater potential exists for air leakage. Exterior sheathing materials in sheet form, including plywood, fiberboards, and rigid foams, all offer good resistance to air leakage if installed tightly. Sheets should be cut accurately and tightly fitted around openings to minimize air leakage. Exterior siding materials vary in their ability to reduce infiltration. Adequate lapping and securing of sidings is important. Exterior trim at corners, around windows and doors, and at the bottom of the siding covers areas that are susceptible to leakage. Trim must be accurately cut and installed to provide protection.

With increased levels of insulation, it is especially important to install a vapor barrier on the warm side of the insulation. While insulation materials are often faced with a vapor barrier material (such as asphalt-impregnated kraft paper), the use of a separate, continuous barrier such as 6-mil polyethylene is recommended. Vapor barriers are discussed in detail in Chapter 3. Installation of a separate vapor barrier also provides excellent protection against air infiltration. It is crucial that any holes in the barrier be patched.

Mechanical and electrical lines have conventionally been run in wall, floor, and roof sections. This practice seriously compromises the overall R-value of a building section by making it difficult to insulate, and requiring many holes in vapor barriers for outlets. There are a number of alternatives to this practice. The preferred approach is for the layout of floor plan to provide for all utility chases to occur in interior walls. Electric lines can run in raceway conduits that mount on walls rather than between studs. Double wall framing uses the inner wall to provide an easy path for all utility lines and may place the vapor barrier between the two walls so it can be installed with no penetrations.

The controlled introduction of outside air for combustion, through 4-inch solid drain pipe, will help reduce infiltration through all areas of the exterior shell. By piping outside air directly to the combustion unit, much less air is pulled into the living areas by the combustion and chimney updraft. Exterior air feeds are practical for combustion heating systems fired by any fuel source.

Ceiling, roofs, and attic spaces. The best approach to insulating ceilings and roofs depends on the building configuration, framing plan, and use of attic space. Heat generated inside the building tends to collect at upper levels. This causes upper levels to have a higher inside-to-outside temperature differential than other sections of the building, so it loses more heat through its exterior surface (the roof). Thus, roof and ceiling spaces should be insulated more heavily than walls and floors. Attics are considered unheated if the insulation is located in attic floor joists (ceiling joists for rooms below it), and heated if insulation is applied to the rafters or on roof deck. The use of vapor barriers on the warm side of insulation and proper venting are both extremely important with ceiling and roof insulation. These are discussed in detail in Chapter 3.

Unheated attics not used for storage permit easy installation of increased amounts of insulation (Fig. 2.19). Fiberglass fill or batts and/or cellulose fill can be installed between joists or the bottom chords of trusses to the desired level, without being restricted to the depth of the framing members. In cold attics where storage space is desired, the amount of insulation that can be placed between the joists is limited by their depth. Floor boards placed on the joists over the insulation should be spaced apart slightly to allow venting. Increasing the level of insulation here requires the use of materials with higher R-value in attic floor, or installation of insulative sheathing on ceilings of rooms directly below.

Heated attics or rooms with finished vaulted ceilings are generally insulated with fiberglass batts placed between the rafters. However, insulation must not fill the entire cavity; it should allow at least a 1-inch air space for venting between the fiberglass and roof sheathing.

Air moving from soffit vents to ridge vents helps keep the insulation, framing, and roof sheathing dry. Increasing R-value in this section of the building

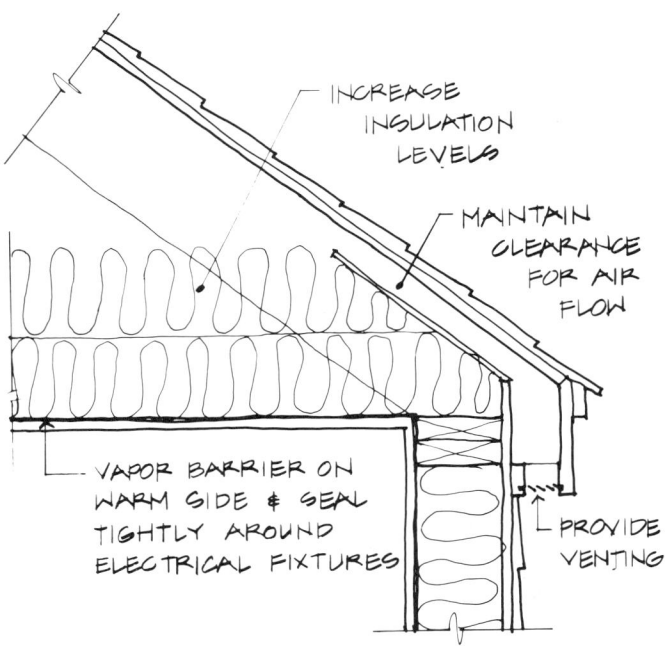

Fig. 2.19 Reducing heat loss through ceilings.

requires larger rafters (for thicker fiberglass) and/or insulative sheathing applied to the interior of the rafter prior to installation of the interior finish. Vaulted ceilings with exposed roof frame and deck require increased deck insulation, and provisions for adequate ventilation of roof deck and insulation are also important.

Insulation can be run between rafters along sloped roofs, until it reaches and follows horizontal collar ties. Ventilation is still important with this approach, but gable end vents can be used in place of ridge vents. Soffit vents always are required. Another insulation plan for attics/upper floors utilizes knee walls and collar ties as insulated cavities. Collar ties can be oversized to house a thicker blanket of insulation. If the space will be unused, insulation levels can exceed the depth of the framing, and larger framing depths are unnecessary.

Any penetrations of utility chases, chimneys, or plumbing stacks through the attic space must be treated carefully. Again, as the insulative levels of the shell are tightened up, seemingly insignificant areas take on greater importance. All these areas of penetration through the insulative envelope should be stuffed with insulation, or caulked if there is inadequate room for insulation. Attic hatchways should be insulated and weatherstripped, as if an exterior door.

Doors and windows. Doors and windows are two of the most important components in a residence. They provide light, ventilation, views, and physical access

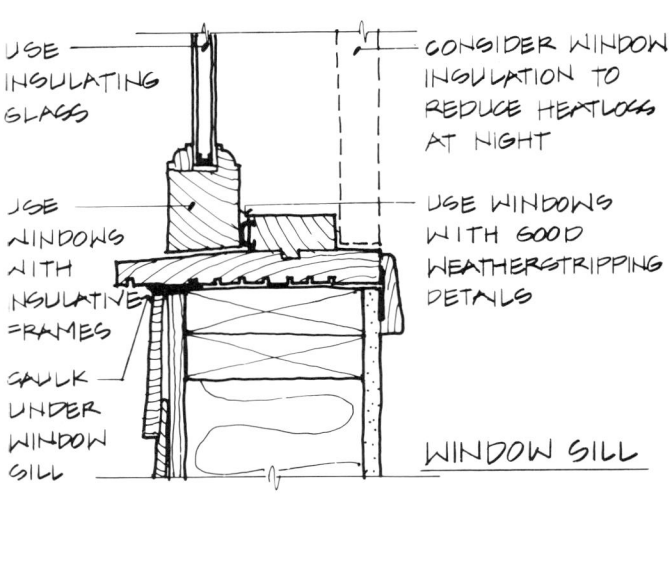

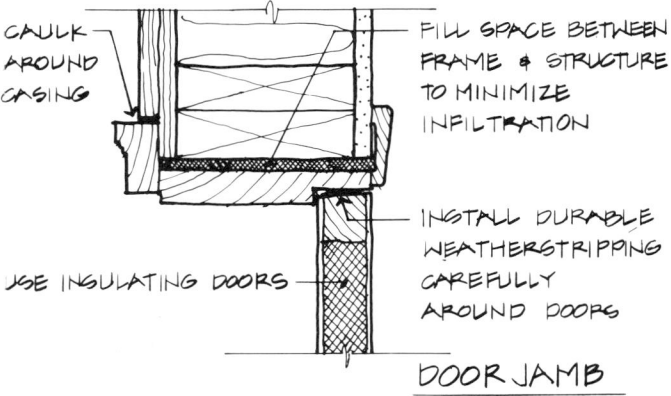

Fig. 2.20 Reducing heat loss through doors and windows.

through the building shell. When closed they must provide a weathertight seal and maintain the insulative value of the wall section. Additionally, windows are a primary means for collection and utilization of solar energy. In the past, heat loss through the uninsulated shell has been the primary path of total building heat loss; as the shell is tightened up, doors and windows account for a much greater percentage of the total (Fig. 2.20).

Many types of doors are used in residential construction. Components of the door assembly include the frame, threshold, casings, and the door and its hardware. Heat loss at exterior doors consists of conductive loss through the door and frame and infiltration loss through the assembly. A thermal door should be used to reduce conductive loss. Metal doors should be the insulated type with thermal breaks. Wooden doors should also be insulated, and sliding glass doors should be equipped with double or triple glazed panels and thermal breaks on all metal components.

If a door is weatherstripped properly, infiltration losses can be further controlled by careful installation of components. There are many places for air to leak through a door assembly, and measures to seal them should be taken. The shim space between jambs and framing should be filled with insulation (stuffed with fiberglass or sprayed with urethane), and caulking should be applied around sills and behind casings. Chapter 10 discusses the selection and installation of exterior doors in more detail.

A swinging door properly installed and weatherstripped provides the best thermal performance. Installation of a storm door or utilization of an air lock entry will increase thermal performance. Storm doors cut heat loss by both infiltration and conduction. Sliding glass doors are often used in solar construction for collection of solar heat; however, these doors are not as airtight as hinged doors, so they can lose considerable heat by infiltration. They should not be used as primary doors, and they should have double glazed panels and thermal break frames.

The use of windows in solar construction is one of the most important issues to be considered, because windows admit light and heat, control ventilation and views, and shelter from the outside elements. They may be operable or fixed, and they are available in a wide variety of sizes, shapes, and configurations. In solar construction, windows must balance the potential for solar heat gain in some orientations with the potential for heat loss in others, while still achieving comfortable levels of daylighting without glare.

All windows consist of the same basic components: the window frame including jambs and sills; the window sash including rails, stiles and glazing; and interior and exterior casings. Storm windows and screens are often used and mounted inside or out, depending on the unit chosen. The energy performance of operable windows is similar to that of exterior doors. Conductive losses occur through the sash, frame, and glazing; infiltration losses occur between the rough opening and the window frame, past casings and operable sash.

Reducing the energy losses through windows is accomplished as we discussed for doors. Air leakage around casings is sealed by caulking behind casings as the window is installed or selecting windows with compressible foam on the back of the casing. Also, the shim space between window and framing should be filled with insulation as discussed for doors. The second major path of window infiltration—the cracks around operable window sash—can be reduced effectively by proper weatherstripping. Inspection and comparison of

Table 2.5
U-values for single, double and triple glazings

Configuration	U-value
Glass	
Single glass, winter	1.10
Single glass, summer	1.04
Insulating glass, double	
3/16" Air space, winter	0.62
3/16" Air space, summer	0.65
1/4" Air space, winter	0.58
1/4" Air space, summer	0.61
1/2" Air space, winter	0.49
1/2" Air space, summer	0.56
Storm windows	
1" to 4" Air space, winter	0.50
1" to 4" Air space, summer	0.50
Triple glass	
Winter	0.31–0.39
Summer	0.39–0.44

weatherstripping details is an important part of choosing quality windows for solar construction.

Reducing conductive losses through windows requires the use of frame materials with low rates of conductance and the use of multiple glazing. The two most popular materials that are used for window frames and sash are wood and aluminum. Aluminum windows are generally less expensive than wood but are less energy efficient due to the metal's conductance. However, manufacturers have added thermal breaks to extruded aluminum channels to cut off this flow of heat. Wood used for frame material has better insulating value than metal, but aluminum window frames with thermal breaks can approach the insulating value of wood frames.

The use of multiple glazing layers is an important way to reduce heat loss through glass. All heat passing through glass is conducted, though it may reach the glass and be released to the outside by other means. Glass is a good conductor of heat; the thin films of stagnant air that cling to both sides of the glass are poor conductors. These air films to a large degree determine the resistance of the glass to heat loss. The film's resistance varies with its thickness and stability. Wind currents disturb the air films and increase conduction and infiltration losses. Additional layers of glazing trap the air films and greatly reduce losses by conduction. The R-value of a 1/8-inch sheet of glass is only .01, so the influence of air films is critical to reducing heat loss. Table 2.5 lists the U-values for single, double, and triple glazings. There are many possible ways to obtain multiple glazing: a storm window over single glazed win-

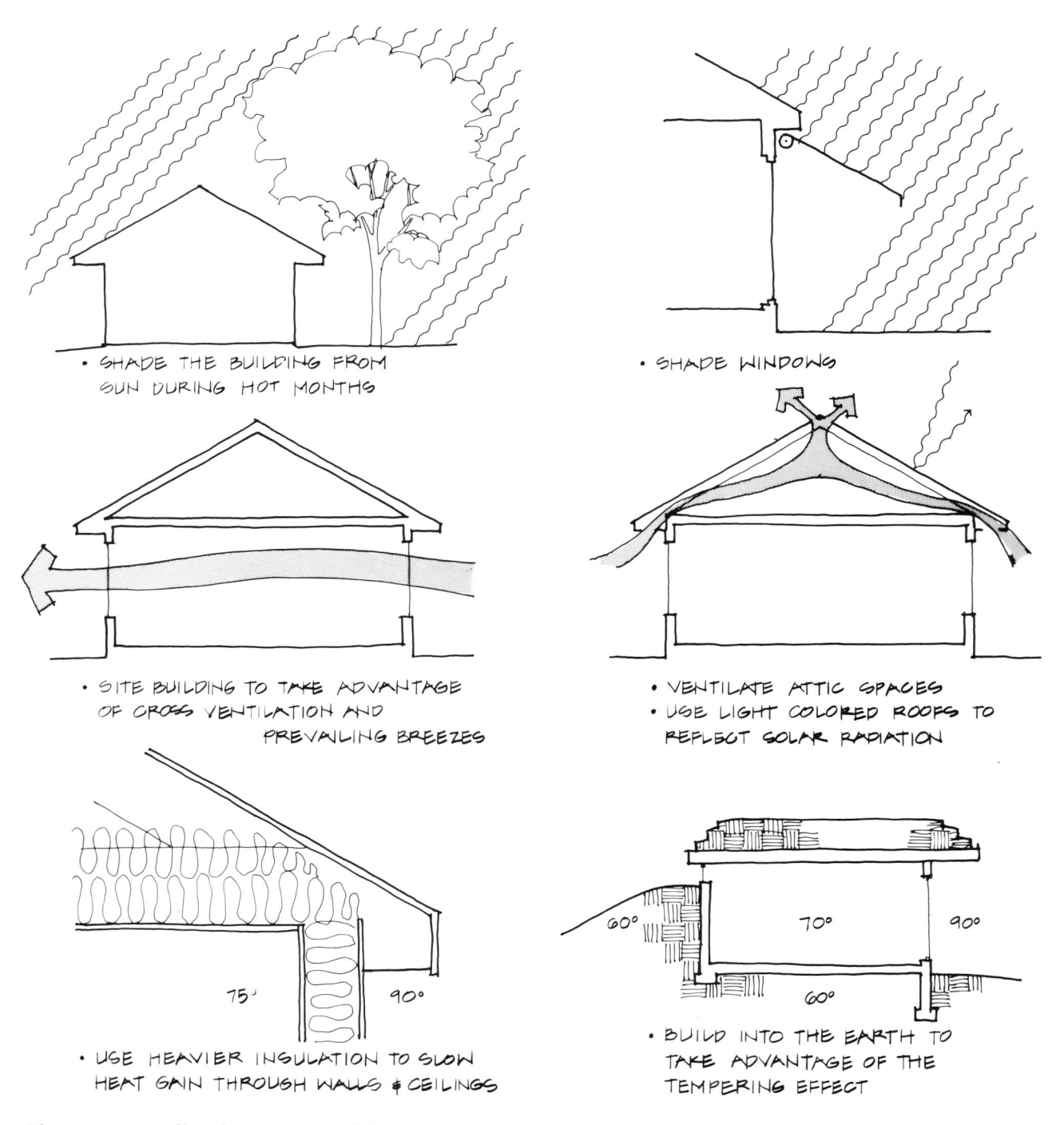

Fig. 2.21 Controlling heat gain in buildings.

dows, double glazed window units, or triple glazing in severe climates.

The choice of which approach to use must take many factors into account. Additional layers of glazing cut the transmittance of light and heat from the sun. Storm windows must be removed each spring; however, many windows now have better integration of storm sash details that make this operation less tedious than it used to be. The best choice for builders in most situations is to go with double glazing; most window units currently are available with insulating glass. By using windows with double glazed sash, the homeowner has the option to add a third layer in the future.

The use of movable insulation over windows can reduce both conduction and infiltration losses by placing a material of low conductance in front of the glass with tight edge seals. These products often require some custom finish work to complete their installation.

As mentioned earlier, different types of windows will perform differently regarding energy. Fixed glazings offer the best seal against air infiltration, though the airtightness of these units depends on the quality of installation. Fixed windows often are used when view is a prime consideration, or to increase glazed areas for solar access. Depending on the quality of their thermal details, hinged windows including casement, awning, and hopper offer greater potential for energy efficiency than sliding windows. This is due primarily to the tighter closure against air infiltration. Hinged windows open more fully for ventilation and they can divert air moving along the exterior wall surfaces into the building.

HEAT GAIN IN BUILDINGS

Controlling heat gain in buildings is just as important to providing a comfortable residence as controlling heat loss. However, in most climate zones within the United States, the need for heating is more prevalent than the need for cooling. Solar construction techniques aimed primarily at reducing heat loss will also reduce heat gain. Thus, the preceding discussion concerning increasing insulation levels throughout the building shell and reducing air infiltration also applies to controlling unwanted heat gain. Just as the strategies for reducing heat loss all essentially boil down to "keep the heat in," the simple strategies for reducing heat gain boil down to "keep the heat out" and "ventilate" (Fig. 2.21). These simple strategies are introduced here and also discussed in more detail in Chapters 4 and 5.

External heat gain occurs through the building's walls and roofs, and the heat of the sun is the principal source. The shape, orientation, and materials of the building shell in relation to the position of the sun in the sky all influence the amount of heat that will be gained. In cool climates during winter, it is desirable to let the heat of the sun penetrate through glazed areas to warm the interior spaces and lower the requirements for mechanical heating. In the northern hemisphere, the winter sun is low in the sky and less intense than the summer sun, which is much higher in the sky. Thus, a majority of the beneficial warming rays of the sun strike the vertical walls of the building, even when the sun reaches its highest point at noon. However, the summer sun strikes east and west walls with intense solar radiation in the morning and afternoon and the roof of the building with the most intense midday sun. The south wall does not receive as much sunlight in the summer due to the high solar angle. The principles of seasonal and daily sun angles are discussed in Chapter 4. These sun angles for a particular site determine the most effective configurations for shading glazed areas. South facing vertical glass can be easily shaded by simple overhangs or deep eaves. East and west facing glass are more difficult to shade since the sun is at a lower angle. Plantings, vertical louvers, deep awnings, or reflective glass may be required on east and west to prevent overheating.

As mentioned earlier, the increased levels of insulation in walls and roofs helps to prevent the passage of the sun's heat through these building sections to the interior. In addition, for warm climates, light colored materials for finish roofing and siding increase the reflection of solar energy and thus reduce absorption of heat through wall sections.

Natural ventilation is a very simple and effective cooling strategy. Attic spaces that are well ventilated reduce heat buildup in addition to preventing moisture buildup and condensation problems. Operable windows should be laid out for cross ventilation of all interior spaces and oriented to prevailing summer winds.

The use of earth berming and below grade living spaces can be an effective way to escape temperature extremes of hot and cold. The relatively stable temperatures of the earth eliminate the temperature fluctuations of the air.

CHAPTER 3: MOISTURE AND AIR QUALITY IN TIGHT CONSTRUCTION

INTRODUCTION

As a building becomes "tighter" through reduced air infiltration, the presence and movement of moisture within it becomes more important. This is due not to an increase in the amount of moisture generated within buildings, but to the reduced ability of moisture to diffuse into the air, and be carried through the shell and released into the atmosphere. Therefore, reduced air leakage can cause an accumulation of moisture within the building. Builders are well versed in the construction requirements for controlling moisture in its liquid state (water). All the exterior components and finishes of the building shell are designed to shed water or resist its entry into the building. (See Chapters 8 and 10.) Moisture is also present in colder climates as a solid (ice). Builders commonly deal with ice, as frost, in determining the depth of excavation for footings and soil drainage surrounding the foundation. Seasonal freezing and thawing cycles contribute to the deterioration of materials that have absorbed moisture.

Moisture also exists as an invisible gas (water vapor), and its behavior is not fully understood by builders. Water vapor, always present in the air, is found also in a building's walls, floors, ceilings, and roof cavities, as well as in wood, concrete, and masonry materials. Its effect on the comfort and performance of a building can be significant. Builders must understand the sources of moisture, the way it moves, and its effects on building materials and human comfort, so it can be controlled effectively. This chapter discusses the generation and movement of water vapor within a building; problems caused as it condenses into water; and controls that can be used to avoid these problems.

Reducing air leakage limits not only the diffusion of water vapor, but also the diffusion of odors and dust particles generated and contained within a building. Whereas uncontrolled infiltration brings fresh air into the building and allows odors to escape, controls used to tighten the shell will result in their accumulation. Builders should be aware of the effects of tight construction on indoor air quality, and steps that can be taken to provide a comfortable and safe environment. A discussion of the sources of indoor pollutants and options for controlling their accumulation follows the sections on moisture.

WATER VAPOR

Water vapor is introduced into the air inside a building by its occupants and their activities. Respiration, bathing, cooking, dishwashing, and laundering contribute as much as one gallon of vapor per person per day. Other sources of water vapor include dirt floors in crawl space or basement, wet basements, newly installed building materials such as poured concrete, masonry or plaster, lumber, and unseasoned firewood.

Water vapor is actually a mixture of moisture and air; although vapor movement is influenced by air movement, vapor also moves independently of the air. As with any gas, the driving force of water vapor movement is the diffusion from an area of high concentration to an area of low concentration. Just as heat seeks to equalize temperature differentials, water vapor moves to equalize its pressure. Water vapor creates a pressure that is proportional to the quantity of water vapor in the air.

Relative Humidity

Relative humidity is a measurement of the actual moisture content of air at a given temperature compared to the

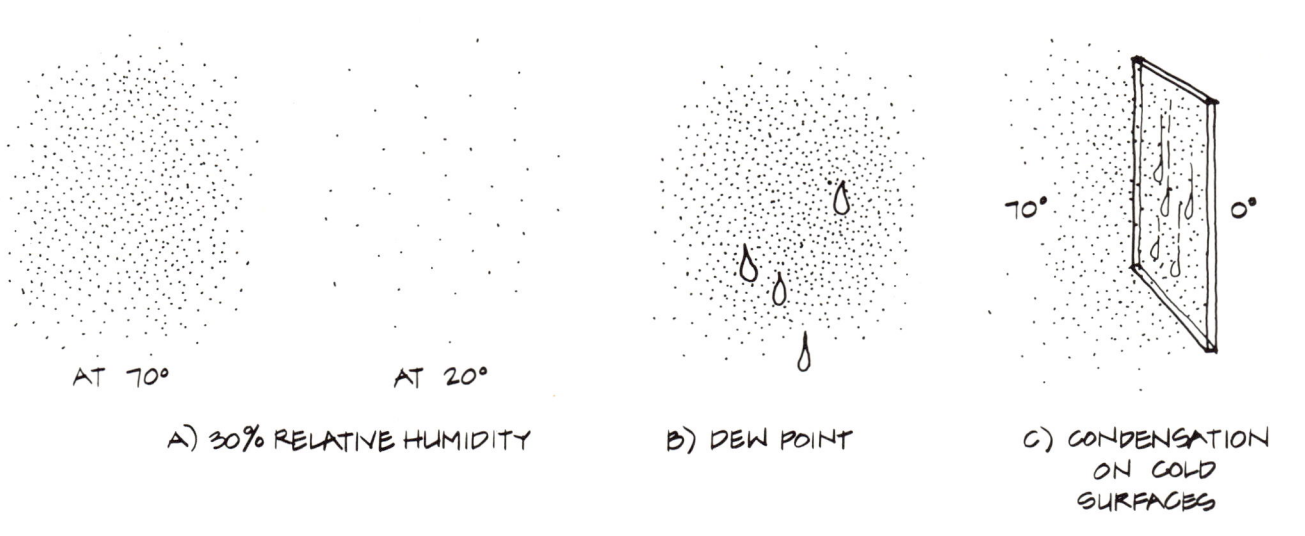

Fig. 3.1 The Relationship Between Relative Humidity, Air Temperature and Condensation A) Relative humidity is a measure of how much water vapor air can hold at various temperatures. Warm air can hold more water vapor than cold air. B) When air becomes saturated, it can no longer hold any more water vapor at that temperature. The air temperature at the saturation point is known as the dew point; condensation will occur if humidity increases or temperature decreases. C) Condensation occurs on cold, impermeable surfaces (like window glass), when the surface temperature is below the dew point of the air.

potential amount it could hold (Fig. 3.1). Vapor pressure is directly affected by relative humidity; that is, when the relative humidity is high, the vapor pressure also is high. Another important concept to understand is the effect of air temperature on its capacity to retain or release moisture; the warmer the air temperature, the more moisture it can hold. As the air cools, its capacity to hold moisture decreases to the point where it reaches 100 percent RH. Further cooling will cause the air to release moisture as condensation. The temperature at which condensation occurs is known as the *dew point*. Moisture affects the thermal and structural performance of a building, and it is an important factor in determining the comfort of its occupants. The influence of relative humidity on human comfort was discussed in more detail in Chapter 2.

Vapor Movement

Differences in water vapor pressure cause vapor to move from an area of high pressure to one of lower pressure. In the winter, vapor generated by the occupants and their activities creates higher vapor pressure inside than outside, causing vapor to move through the exterior shell to equalize with the lower outside pressure. Water vapor moves directly through the materials that make up the building shell as well as through gaps between materials (Fig. 3.2).

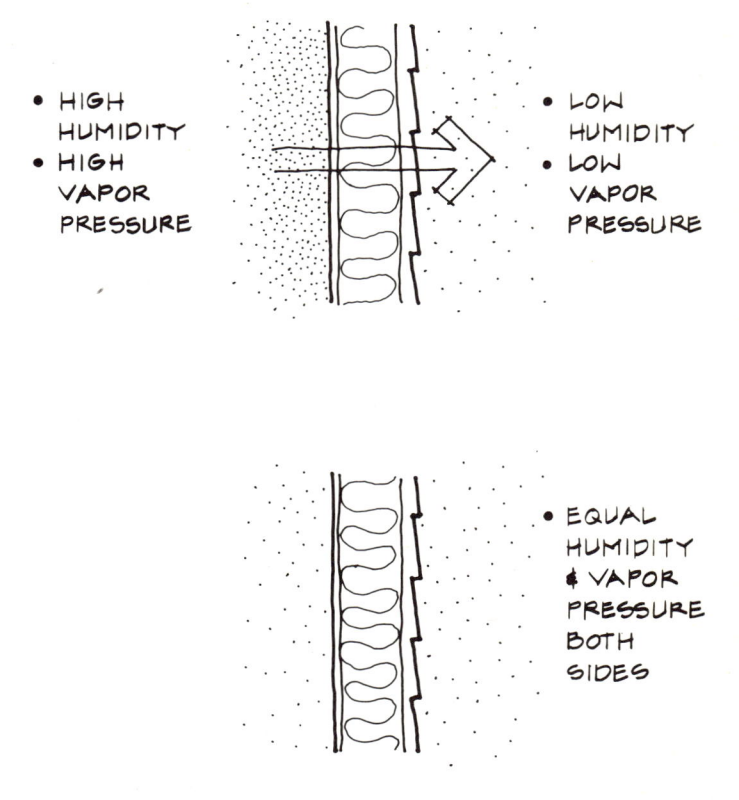

Fig. 3.2 Moisture as vapor will move through a permeable material from an area of high vapor pressure to an area of low vapor pressure until the pressure is equalized.

BASIC PRINCIPLES OF SOLAR CONSTRUCTION

Table 3.1
Water vapor permeance of building materials

Materials used in construction	
1″ Concrete (1:2:4 mix)	3.2
Brick masonry (4″ thick)	0.8
Concrete block (8″ cored, limestone aggregate)	2.4
Asbestos-cement board (0.2″ thick)	0.54
Plaster on metal lath (¾″)	15.0
Plaster on plain gypsum lath (with studs)	20.0
Gypsum wallboard (⅜″ plain)	50.0
Gypsum sheathing (½″ asphalt impregnated)	10.0
1″ Structural insulating board (sheathing)	20–50
Structural insulating board (interior, uncoated, ½″)	50–90
Hardboard (⅛″ standard)	11.0
Hardboard (⅛″ tempered)	5.0
Built-up roofing (hot-mopped)	0.0
1″ Wood, sugar pine	0.4–5.4
Plywood (douglas fir, interior, glue, ¼″ thick)	1.9

Thermal insulations, 1″ thick	
Air (still)	120.0
Cellular glass	0.0
Corkboard	2.1–9.5
Mineral wool (unprotected)	116.0
Expanded polyurethane (R-11 blown)	0.4–1.6
Expanded polystyrene—extruded	1.2
Expanded polystyrene—bead	2.0–5.8
Unicellular synthetic flexible rubber foam	0.02–0.15

Plastic and metal foils and films	
Aluminum foil (1 mil)	0.0
Aluminum foil (0.35 mil)	0.05
Polyethylene (2 mil)	0.16
Polyethylene (4 mil)	0.08
Polyethylene (6 mil)	0.06

Building papers, felts, roofing papers*	
Duplex sheet, asphalt laminated, aluminum foil one side (43)	0.002
Saturated and coated roll roofing (326)	0.05
Kraft paper and asphalt laminated, Reinforced 30-120-30 (34)	0.3
Blanket thermal insulation back-up paper, asphalt coated (31)	0.4
Asphalt-saturated and coated vapor-barrier paper (43)	0.2–0.3
Asphalt-saturated but not coated sheathing paper (22)	3.3
15 lb asphalt felt (70)	1.0
15 lb tar felt (70)	4.0
Single-kraft, double infused (16)	31.0

Protective coatings	
Paint—2 coats	
Aluminum varnish on wood	0.3–0.5
Enamel on smooth plaster	0.5–1.5
Various primers plus 1 coat flat oil paint on plaster	1.6–3.0
Water emulsion on interior insulating board	30.0–85.0
Paint—3 coats	
Exterior paint, white lead and oil on wood siding	0.3–1.0
Exterior paint, white lead-zinc oxide and oil on wood	0.9
Styrene-butadiene latex coating, 2 oz/sq ft	11.0
Polyvinyl acetate latex coating, 4 oz/sq ft	5.5
Asphalt cut-back mastic, 1/16″ dry	0.14
Hot melt asphalt, 2 oz/sq ft	0.5

*Numbers in parentheses are weights in lbs per 500 sq ft.

Permeance to moisture is an important physical property of building materials. Just as R-value defines resistance to heat movement, *permeance* measures a material's resistance to the movement of moisture through it. Table 3.1 lists the permeances of many common building materials. The lower the perm-rating, the lower the amount of moisture movement through. Materials with a perm-rating of less than 1 can be considered for use as a barrier to vapor movement; however, lower ratings can be achieved with proper installation.

EFFECTS OF WATER VAPOR ON MATERIALS

The movement of water vapor through materials will not damage them, but condensation of vapor resulting from its contact with cooler surfaces or the freezing of moisture contained in a material can cause significant damage. Older buildings permit large amounts of air leakage, allowing moisture to diffuse freely in the cooler, drier outside air; they also offer less resistance to the outward flow of moisture through gaps. This built-in diffusion does dissipate moisture, but also drastically increases the total heat loss. If you reduce infiltration, you increase the indoor relative humidity; and if the relative humidity becomes too high, moisture may condense as it strikes cooler surfaces. The resulting accumulation of water could be a serious problem.

Exposure to water over a period of time (from condensation or other sources) degrades building materials. Metal rusts, wood rots, and if the temperature drops

MOISTURE AND AIR QUALITY IN TIGHT CONSTRUCTION

Graph 3.1
Recommended maximum interior RH to prevent condensation damage*

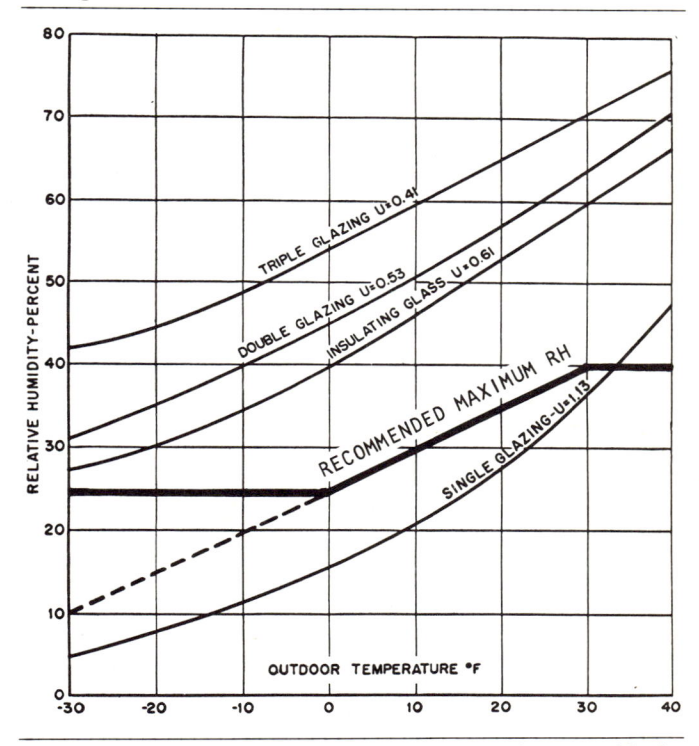

*Below 0°F, RH values maintained at 25% to provide acceptable degree of occupant comfort (solid line); however, to minimize condensation on single glazing, use RH values represented by dashed line.

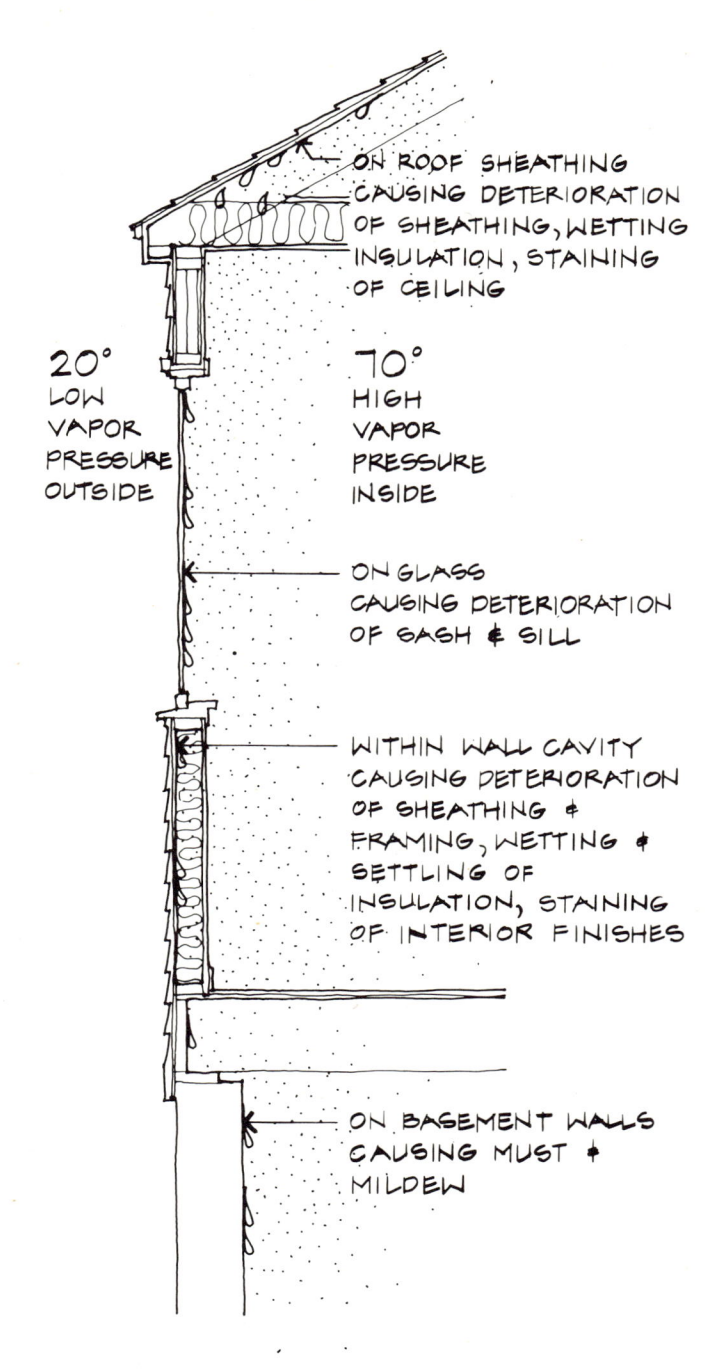

Fig. 3.2 Moisture as vapor will move through a permeable material from an area of high vapor pressure to an area of low vapor pressure until the pressure is equalized.

below freezing, frost action causes the spalling of masonry and other materials. Many building materials change dimension when their moisture content changes. Wood is well known for this; high moisture content causes it to swell, and lowering the moisture content makes it shrink.

The heat conduction properties of building materials also are affected by the presence of condensed moisture. Water is an excellent heat conductor; when present in a material, it reduces that material's resistance to heat flow. Insulation materials, too, react this way when saturated.

Condensation

In winter the movement of water vapor from inside a building through the exterior shell to the outside brings moisture into contact with all of the materials that make up the foundation; floors, walls, ceilings, and roof sections. If the surfaces of these materials are cooler than the dew point of the moisture-laden air, the vapor condenses into a film of water. Depending on the permeance of the material, some of this moisture will be absorbed by it, while the rest remains as water on the surface (Fig. 3.3)

Surface Condensation

Condensation occurs on cool interior surfaces including walls, window glazings, metal window frames, doors,

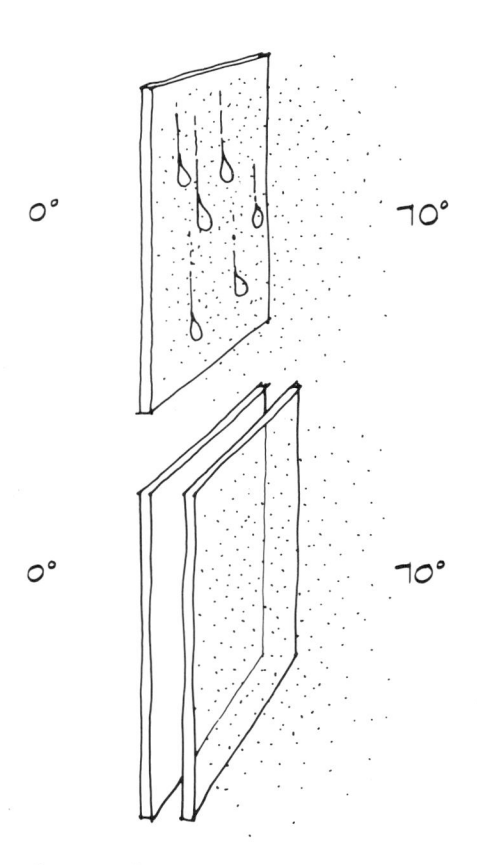

Fig. 3.4 The use of multiple layers of glazing can prevent condensation on windows. Since single glass has little resistance to heat loss, its surface temperature is often below the dew point of interior air. A double layer of glass resists condensation on the interior surface because the R-value is twice that of single glazing and thus the interior surface temperature is usually above the dew point of the air.

sliding glass doors, and metal electrical boxes when the temperature of these surfaces is below the dew point of the indoor air. Graph 3.1 shows the interior relative humidities at which surface condensation occurs for different exterior temperatures.

Windows and sliding glass doors most frequently experience condensation. They are usually the coolest areas of a wall, and because of their impermeance to water vapor, they collect surface condensation sooner than other materials. Surface condensation in winter is best controlled by warming the interior surfaces to temperatures above the dew point. This higher surface temperature can be achieved by properly insulating floors, walls, and ceiling/roof sections, and by using multiple glazings on windows and doors (Fig. 3.4).

Multi-layered glazings reduce the amount of condensation on the innermost layer of glass; however, if improperly designed and built, they can cause condensation problems between the layers. Factory sealed, airtight units should not suffer from condensation between layers of glass unless the seal has been damaged during shipment or installation. These seals may deteriorate over the life of the unit, requiring either replacement or venting the air space to the outside through small holes drilled in the sides. Fixed glass, assembled at the job site, should have a tight, caulked seal at the layer closest to the building interior; exterior layers should be uncaulked. Moisture within the building cannot leak into the air space and condense against the cool outside glazing due to tight seal inside. Any moisture introduced into the air space by the atmosphere will be vented to the outside due to the relatively loose fit of the exterior glazings. Chapter 10 talks in more detail about windows.

Surface condensation can form also in summer on the interior surface of concrete foundation walls and floors. These materials are cooled by their contact with the soil; because of their thermal mass, they remain at fairly stable temperatures throughout the year. This is usually above the dew point of dry winter air and does not cause surface condensation in winter; however, the higher relative humidity during summer may cause moisture to condense on these surfaces, resulting in damage to interior finishes. The use of below grade construction for primary living space offers many advantages in energy performance over construction above grade, including elimination of convective heat loss by wind movement and heat storage in foundation material. Surface condensation in this situation must be controlled, and measures that help control this problem include:

- limiting the introduction of warm, humid air from outside during the day
- creating warmer interior surface temperatures through the use of rigid insulation on exterior surfaces
- mechanical dehumidification

Hidden Condensation

The movement of water vapor from inside to outside in winter introduces moisture into the walls, floors, and ceiling/roofs of a building. If the temperature within a section of the building is low enough, the moisture will cool until it reaches its dew point and then condense on materials within the section. This hidden condensation damages the structural and thermal performance of these materials, and it is not apparent until interior or exterior finishes show signs of peeling paint or moldy interior gypsum.

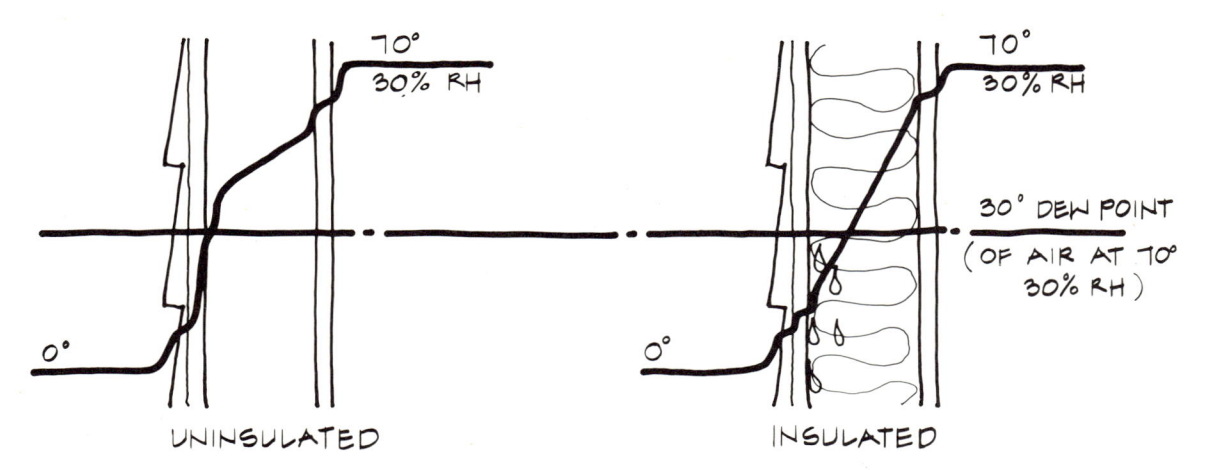

Fig. 3.5 The Location of Dew Point Within a Wall Section
In an uninsulated wall section, indoor vapor pressure forces moisture to move from inside toward the outside. It moves through the stud cavity and condenses on the sheathing. If temperatures are low enough, it may freeze on sheathing. As this ice melts with warm weather, it is carried away by air currents moving through gaps in sheathing and siding. In an insulated wall section, the dew point moves into the insulation cavity itself. The moisture moves through the insulation and condenses on the sheathing. However, since the stud cavities are filled with insulation, air movements are blocked from dissipating the moisture from the stud cavity where it is trapped. This trapped moisture can cause rotting of sheathing, studs, plates and deterioration of insulation. The use of a continuous vapor barrier on the warm side of insulations is important to prevent moisture from penetrating the stud cavities.

Older buildings that are leaky and uninsulated suffer less from hidden condensation than newer buildings. Heat moving on its way out of the building usually keeps wall and roof cavities above dew point temperature. Air leakage at joints in the siding and sheathing boards ventilates the cavities, which greatly reduces moisture accumulation. Figure 3.5 shows that when insulation is added to a wood frame wall, the dew point occurs nearer the middle of the cavity than in an uninsulated wall. This is due to cooler temperatures inside the wall resulting from reduced heat movement through the insulated wall. Because fiberglass insulation is permeable, the water vapor will not condense at this point, and it moves to the cool surface of the exterior sheathing where it does condense. Older buildings sheathed with boards have numerous gaps through which air can enter the cavity and carry moisture away from the materials.

The most common sheathing materials presently in use are large sheets. Rigid insulation, plywood, and composition sheathings offer greater coverage with fewer joints than sheathing boards, thus reducing the venting of moisture from the cavity by air movement. Insulative sheathing and plywood also are relatively impermeable to moisture, which accelerates the formation of condensation on their surfaces. The trapping of moisture within a building cavity can be avoided by using a combination of the approaches discussed below.

CONTROLLING WATER VAPOR

Moisture control in floor, wall, and ceiling/roof cavities can be accomplished with three primary strategies:

1. using a continuous vapor barrier on the interior surfaces;
2. ventilation of the building (or dehumidification) to reduce the level of vapor pressure within; and/or
3. the deliberate venting of the cavities to allow air movement to carry moisture away from structural and insulative materials.

The particular configuration of moisture protection depends on a number of factors: interior and exterior relative humidity, length and intensity of winter, and local materials and construction methods. The continental United States can be divided into three condensation hazard zones (Fig. 3.6). *The use of vapor barriers with proper ventilation details* is recommended in all areas where severe or moderate hazard exists; in wall sections the use of the vapor barrier is important, since air movement within the wall cavity will increase heat loss. Table 3.2 recommends vapor barrier and ventilation requirements for different condensation zones and different locations in the building. In the warm southern portions of the United States, large temperature and vapor differentials are not present and vapor barriers

38 BASIC PRINCIPLES OF SOLAR CONSTRUCTION

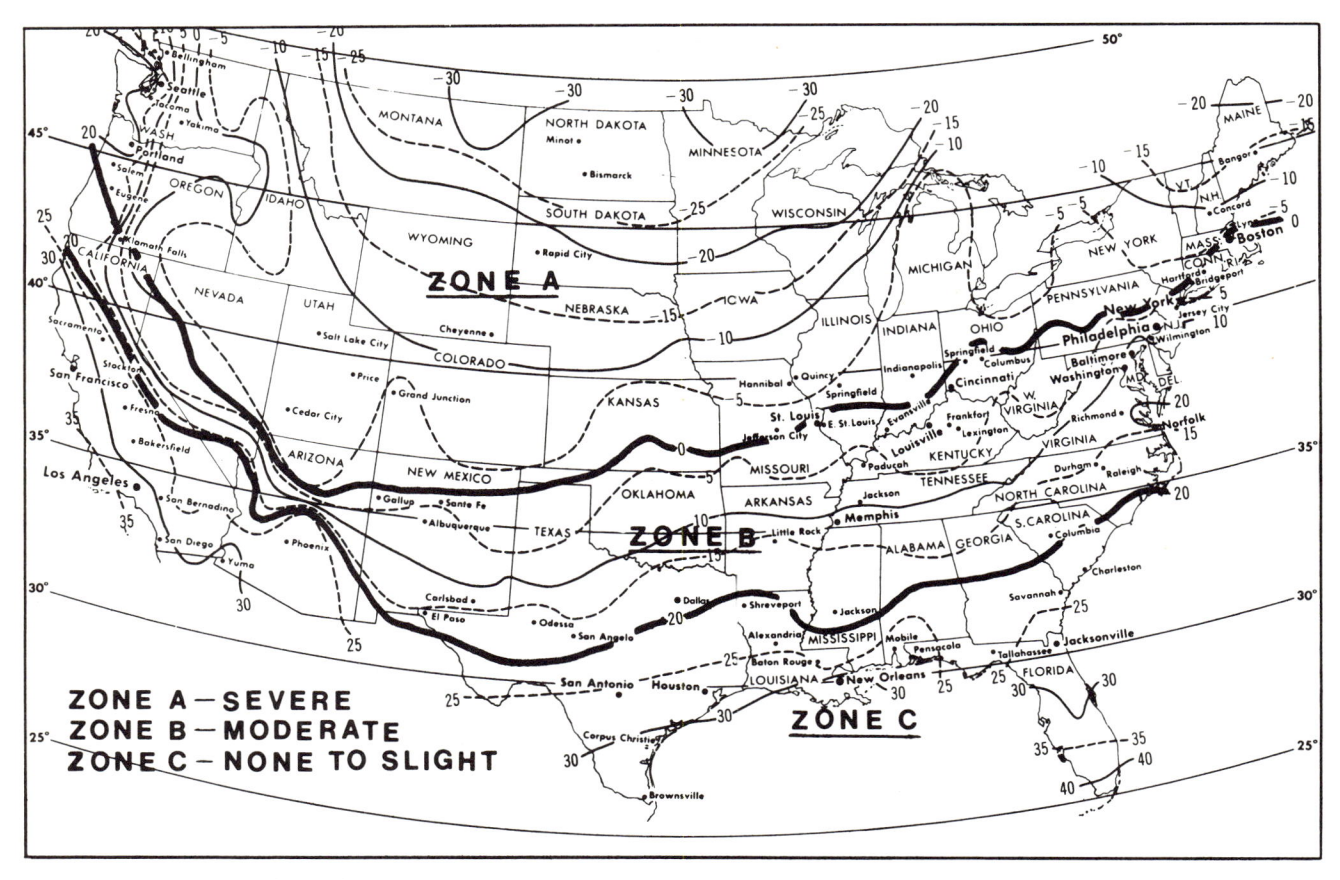

Fig. 3.6 Condensation hazard zones.

Table 3.2
Recommended vapor barriers and structural ventilation in different condensation zones

Condens. zone	Attic-less joist roof/ceiling Ceiling V.B., perms	Struc. ventil.[c]	Attic-type joist roof/ceiling Ceiling V.B., perms	Struc. ventil.[c]	Crawl space Ground V.B., perms	Struc. ventil.[a,c]	Floor over open unheated area— V.B., perms	Exterior walls V.B., perms	Slab-on-ground V.B., perms	Insulated wood plank roof V.B., ventil.	Struc.
Zone A	0.1	1/300	0.5	1/300	1.0	1/1500	1.0	1.0[d]	3.0	None[e]	Edge venting and/or stack venting when V.B. is provided.
Zone B	0.5	1/300[b]	1.0	1/300[b]	1.0	1/1500	1.0	1.0[d]	3.0	None	
Zone C	1.0	1/300[b]	None	1/300[b]	1.0[f]	1/1500[f]	None	None	3.0	None	

[a] Ventilation to atmosphere not required when crawl space is heated or cooled and foundation wall is insulated.
[b] Ratio of 1/150 preferred to relieve high summer solar heat gain.
[c] Ratio of net free ventilating area (NFA) to total floor or ceiling area.
[d] Venting of walls may be desirable where highly impermeable exterior finish is used.
[e] V.b. recommended in areas with winter design temperature of −10°F or lower, or occupancies with average winter interior humidites in excess of 40% RH.
[f] When crawl space is not heated or cooled, v.b., may be omitted provided vent area is increased to 1/150.

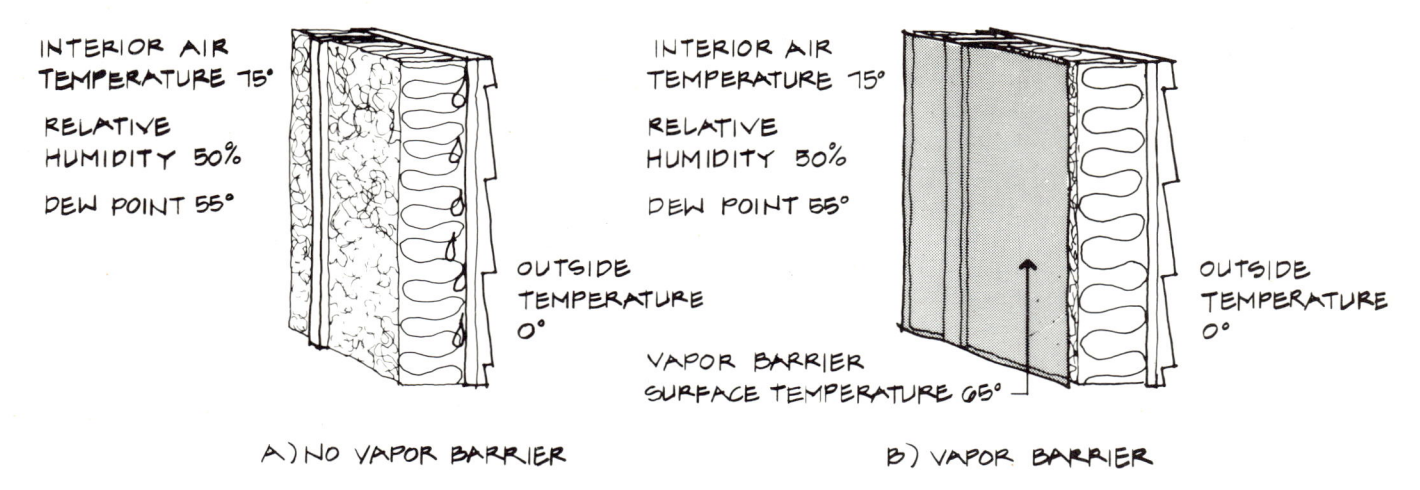

Fig. 3.7 How a Vapor Barrier Works A) With no vapor barrier in an insulated wall section, moisture will move through the insulation and condense as it reaches the cold surface of sheathing. B) A vapor barrier prevents moisture from entering the wall cavity. Condensation does not occur on the vapor barrier since its surface temperature is above the dew point of the interior air.

generally are not required. However, ventilation requirements may be increased to dissipate summer heat gains in attics.

Vapor Barriers

A continuous interior vapor barrier is the most effective means of retarding the movement of moisture into building cavities. The use of a vapor barrier should be combined with ventilation, especially in crawl spaces and ceiling/roof sections. Vapor barriers can be very effective in reducing the amount of moisture that enters the area they protect (Fig. 3.7).

By definition, a vapor barrier is any material that has a rating of 1 perm or less. Many materials are available for use as vapor barriers; their effectiveness depends on proper selection for the appropriate situation and on careful installation. Common vapor barriers include polyethylene sheets of various thicknesses, foil and paper facings on fiberglass batts, aluminum foils, closed cell rigid board insulation, foil backed wallboards, and moisture resistant paints. Generally, the separate sheet vapor barriers such as plastic films or aluminum papers are the most effective; the actual performance of any vapor barrier depends on the quality of installation.

A few essential principles apply to all vapor barrier installations. The barrier should be located as close as possible to the warm (heated in winter) side of the section. The barrier should be installed with as few joints, breaks, or openings as possible. Any joints in the vapor barrier should be backed up by a structural member to prevent any leakage. Barriers should form an unbroken surface over all insulation enclosing a heated area (Fig. 3.8). Any openings for fixtures, pipe penetrations, or around windows and doors should be sealed carefully with vapor resistant patch or tape.

Vapor barriers are recommended as the primary means of moisture control. They should be used as ground cover in crawl spaces, below concrete slab on grade floors, and on the warm side of floors, walls, and ceiling/roof sections. A detailed discussion of selection and installation of different vapor barriers follows in Chapter 9.

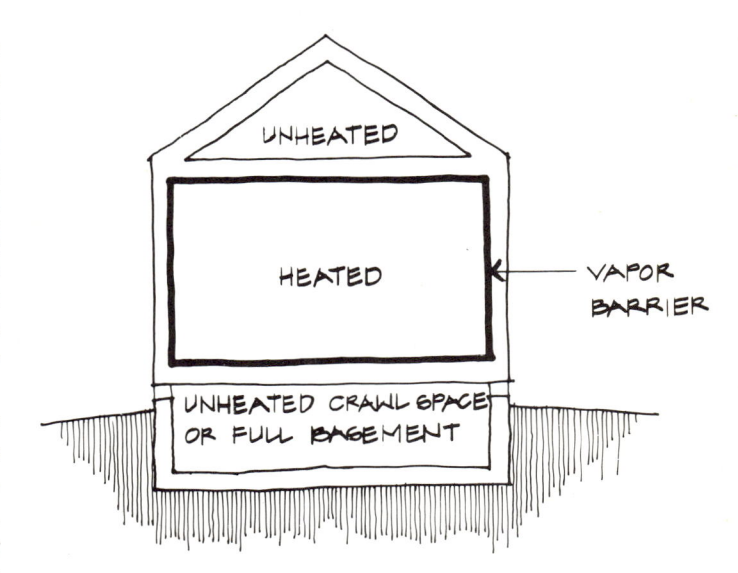

Fig. 3.8 The vapor barrier should enclose the entire heated area.

Venting the Living Space

The installation of a continuous and effective vapor barrier which retards the movement of water vapor to the outside results in both the accumulation of water vapor inside and an increase in vapor pressure. To relieve this pressure, it is very important to eject moisture close to where it is generated. Bathroom fans, range hoods, and dryer vents can be used to remove moisture from the living space. Reduced air infiltration in a building requires not only more planning for moisture ventilation, but also controlling odors generated in kitchen, bathroom, and laundry. If moisture from these sources is not vented to the outside, the relative humidity will rise, and with it the likelihood of surface and hidden condensation.

Venting the Structure

Ventilation of building structure is an important adjunct to the use of vapor barriers in controlling potential condensation problems (Fig. 3.9). Ventilation of attic and roof/ceiling spaces aids the escape of water vapor and lowers the chance of condensation in winter. It also lowers the temperature of these areas in summer. Ventilation of a crawl space will dissipate moisture from that location. Ventilation of wall sections is used only when finish sidings are impermeable to moisture; normally, the primary control of moisture in walls is accomplished with the use of inside vapor barriers.

Ventilation requirements are given in terms of the net free vent area, which is the space actually available to the moving air. Most ventilating openings have louvers to keep out wind and rain, and screening to keep out insects and animals. The area of the obstructions to the movement of air must be taken into account in determining the area requirements for ventilation.

All houses with crawl spaces should have a vapor barrier laid directly over the soil as ground cover to prevent movement of moisture up into the building. This barrier may be 4- or 6-mil polyethylene or 15-pound roll roofing. When the crawl space is below a heated area, it usually is economical to insulate the foundation and heat the crawl space. Ventilation to the outside is required in all zones when the foundation is not insulated. The requirements depend on whether or not the ground is covered with a vapor barrier. When the barrier is included, a minimum of two vents are needed, with a total net free area at least 1/1500 of the crawl space area. Vents should be placed as high as possible in

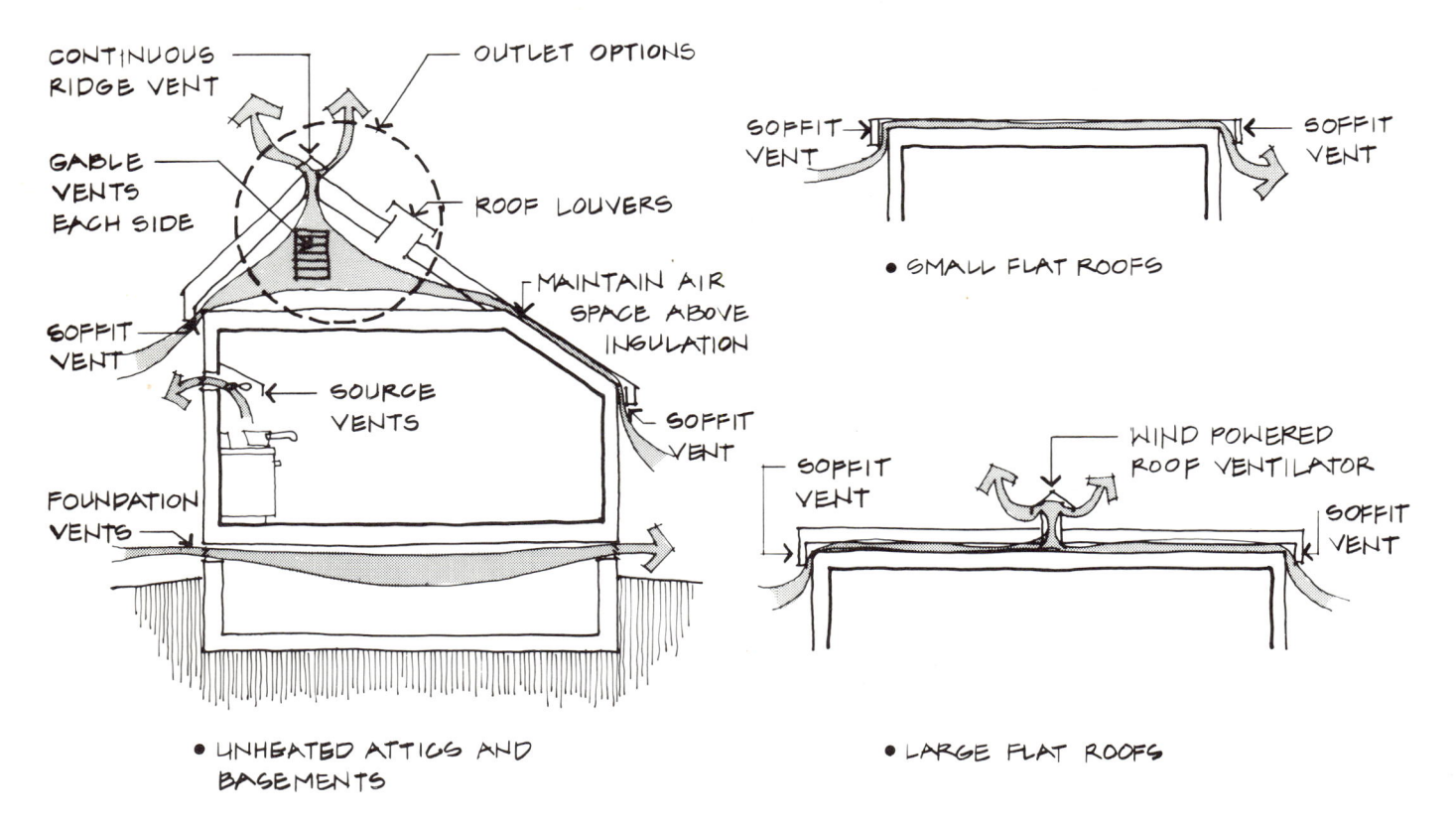

Fig. 3.9 Principles of structural venting.

opposite walls. When the ground cover is not provided, more ventilation is required; the vent area should increase at least ten times to 1/150 of crawl space area, with at least four vents, or one in each wall.

Installation of special vents in wood frame walls generally is not recommended (especially in homes built in colder climates) due to the increased heat loss by convection. In homes without interior vapor barriers, exterior painted finishes may impede the outward flow of moisture, and the resulting vapor pressure may cause blistering and peeling. In these situations, the stud cavity may need to be vented with individual vents to allow it to breathe. It is usually necessary to introduce some type of interior vapor barrier to halt this vapor movement.

To insure the safe outward diffusion of moisture that may penetrate the wall cavity, it is important to consider the combined permeance of the built-up wall section. A safe rule of thumb is that the combined permeance of exterior materials should be at least five times the permeance of interior vapor barrier plus interior finishes. When you know that the exterior finish materials will be impermeable to moisture, the importance of the interior vapor barrier is amplified and quality of installation is even more critical.

Ventilation in roof areas is extremely critical. When used with a suitable vapor barrier, a minimum net free area of 1/300 of ceiling area is required. When no vapor barrier is used, the vent area should be doubled. The effectiveness of roof venting depends on the volume of air moved and the extent to which the air is moved through all areas of the attic or joist space. The roof spaces are natural places for moisture within a building to accumulate. Moisture will make its way up through wall cavities past chimneys, through holes left in plates, and through light fixtures and other equipment installed in ceilings. In certain roof constructions (unheated attics), moisture may be dissipated by ventilation alone. A vapor barrier then should be used to maintain the internal levels of relative humidity. However, in joist roofs where there is no attic, the air flow is not as great and the quality and continuity of the vapor barrier is much more important.

Ventilation tests have determined that wind direction and velocity as well as vent type greatly affect the distribution and volume of air movement within attic spaces. Vents must be selected carefully and located for maximum air flow and uniform distribution. It is recommended that one-half of the vent requirement be provided at the ridge and the balance at the eaves.

The following vent types are typically used in residential solar construction: roof louvers, continuous soffit vents, gable end louvers, and continuous ridge

Fig. 3.10 The best type of venting system to use depends upon specific site conditions and construction details. Shown are soffit *(upper photo)* and gable *(lower photo)* vents.

vents (Fig. 3.10). Roof louvers when used alone contribute little to air flow through the attic; however, when used in the upper portions of the attic as outlets and combined with soffit vents as inlets, the distribution and air flow are greatly improved. Continuous soffit vents provide substantial flow regardless of wind direction. They do require outlets in the upper roof or ridge for good circulation. Gable louvers are most effective for winds perpendicular or diagonal to the louver face. Air flow is cut by one-half to one-third when wind is parallel to louvers or perpendicular to the ridge; the addition of soffit vents will increase the effectiveness of louvers under poor wind conditions by 50 percent. Continuous

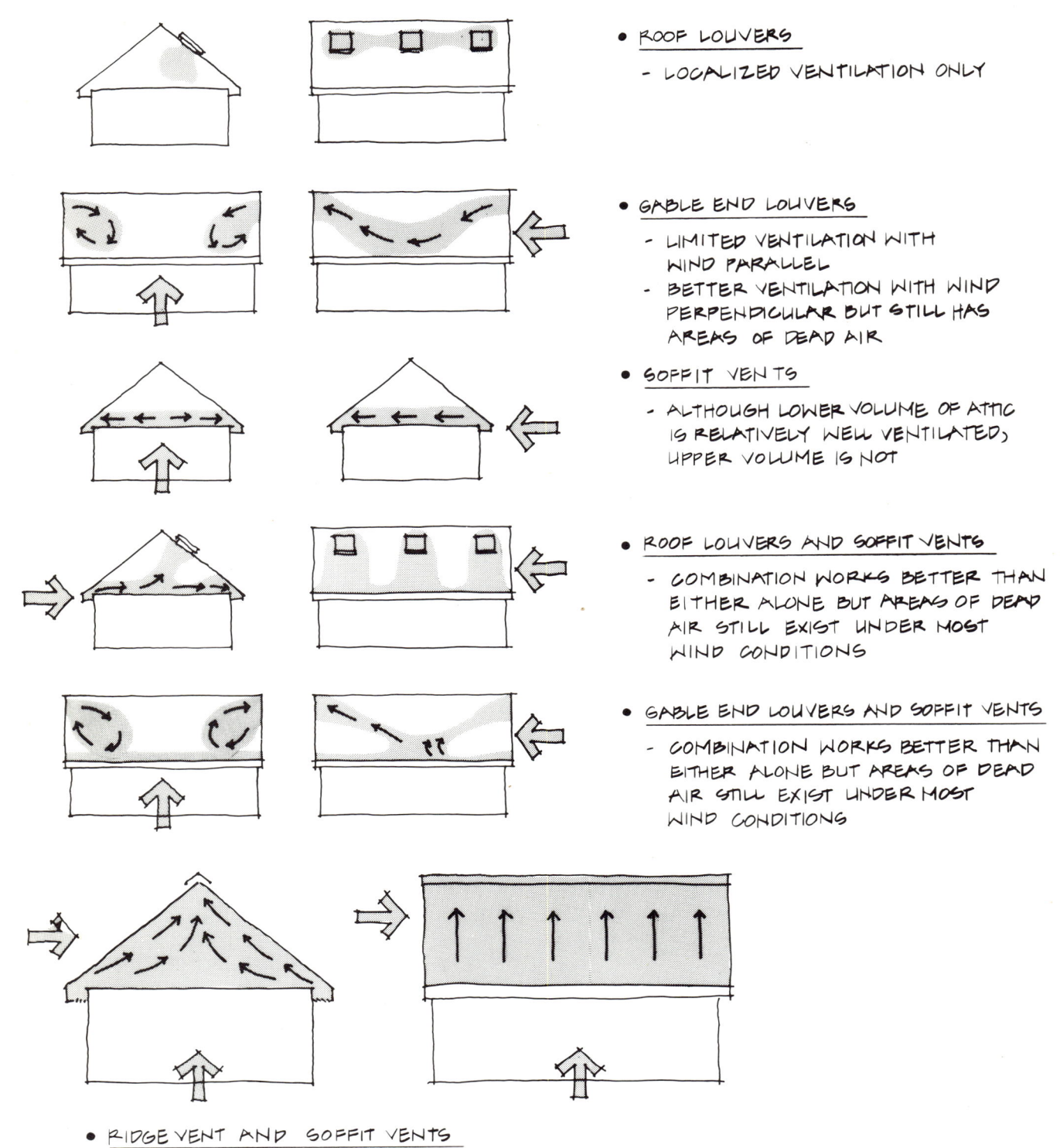

42 BASIC PRINCIPLES OF SOLAR CONSTRUCTION

- ROOF LOUVERS
  - LOCALIZED VENTILATION ONLY

- GABLE END LOUVERS
  - LIMITED VENTILATION WITH WIND PARALLEL
  - BETTER VENTILATION WITH WIND PERPENDICULAR BUT STILL HAS AREAS OF DEAD AIR

- SOFFIT VENTS
  - ALTHOUGH LOWER VOLUME OF ATTIC IS RELATIVELY WELL VENTILATED, UPPER VOLUME IS NOT

- ROOF LOUVERS AND SOFFIT VENTS
  - COMBINATION WORKS BETTER THAN EITHER ALONE BUT AREAS OF DEAD AIR STILL EXIST UNDER MOST WIND CONDITIONS

- GABLE END LOUVERS AND SOFFIT VENTS
  - COMBINATION WORKS BETTER THAN EITHER ALONE BUT AREAS OF DEAD AIR STILL EXIST UNDER MOST WIND CONDITIONS

- RIDGE VENT AND SOFFIT VENTS
  - MOST COMPLETE VENTING UNDER VARYING WIND CONDITIONS

Fig. 3.11 The comparative effectiveness of roof venting combinations.

ridge vents provide air flow due to temperature differential as well as wind velocity; air flow will be most effective with wind parallel to the ridge. Continuous ridge vents coupled with continuous soffit vents generally provide the most consistent air flow (Fig. 3.11).

Joist roofs (where there is no attic) should have adequate ventilation and an effective vapor barrier. Each joist space must be provided with an inlet, through continuous soffit venting or single plug vents for each joist space.

INDOOR AIR QUALITY

The quality of indoor air can be affected in a number of ways by the techniques of solar construction designed to reduce air infiltration. In the past, air infiltration through opening and closing of doors and windows and leakage through the building shell has been the primary source of fresh air for indoor spaces. A typical new house has an air infiltration rate of approximately one complete air change per hour (ACH); an older, leaky house may approach 3 to 4 ACH, which assures plenty of fresh air but also a high rate of heat loss. Energy conserving homes greatly reduce air infiltration, in some cases to as low as 0.3 ACH. As discussed in Chapter 2, other factors such as temperature differential and wind speed affect infiltration rates; in most cases, though, the tighter the construction, the lower the infiltration. These low infiltration rates can lead to a build-up of indoor air pollutants in tight homes. Many of these pollutants always have been present inside homes, but it is only with the greatly reduced air changes of tight construction that they build up to levels that may be uncomfortable or even harmful. There is a great deal of uncertainty regarding what concentrations of various pollutants constitute a health hazard, and currently a good deal of research is taking place to determine guidelines for construction. In any event, builders must be aware of indoor air quality, and they should take several steps presented below to minimize adverse health impacts while still constructing a tight building.

Sources of Indoor Pollution

There are three primary sources of indoor air pollution: (1) outdoor generated pollutants entering the building through infiltration; (2) indoor pollutants generated by combustion, and (3) indoor pollutants generated by occupants or building materials.

Reduced air infiltration actually lowers the presence of outdoor generated pollutants in tight homes. The accumulation of combustion by-products includes carbon monoxide, nitrogen dioxide, particulates, and hydrocarbons. These can build up from a number of sources, including wood combustion, fossil fuel combustion (especially gas) for heating and cooking, and tobacco smoke. A lack of makeup air for combustion can result in incomplete combustion of the fuel. Building materials themselves can give off formaldehyde, radon, and asbestos. Formaldehyde resins are used in manufacture of particle board and foam insulations. Radon is a radioactive gas present in most homes in insignificant amounts. Stone, concrete, brick, and earth berming can cause higher concentrations of the gas to be found in tight homes.

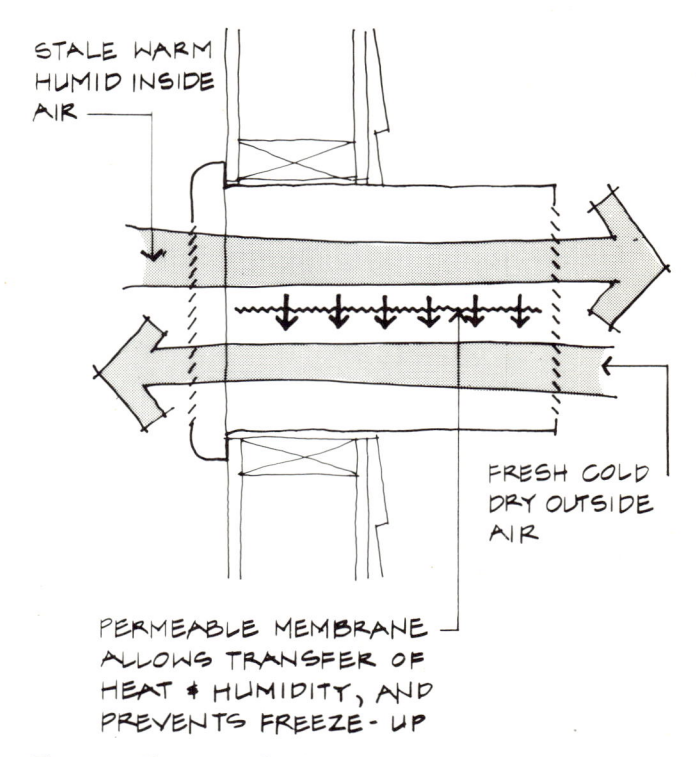

Fig. 3.12 The principle of an air to air heat exchanger.

Reducing Indoor Pollution

A number of strategies can control indoor pollution. Ventilation is the key component, and the challenge is to provide indoor air quality without compromising the thermal efficiency of the building. A minimum ventilation standard of 0.5 ACH has been proposed in European countries and is being considered by ASHRAE for adoption as an American standard. With this level of infiltration, it is important to provide outdoor air feed for combustion air. Substituting different materials for those that emit excessive quantities of formaldehyde, radon, or asbestos can eliminate those sources of pollutants.

Electric cooking appliances can substitute for gas. Exhaust ventilation at the source also lowers the concentration of potential pollutants.

The use of air-to-air heat exchangers permits continued ventilation while minimizing heat loss. These heat exchangers are simply boxes with air channels and blowers inside (Fig. 3.12). The incoming fresh air and stale exhaust air pass through adjacent channels while never coming in direct contact. Because heat moves from a warmer to cooler surface, the warm outgoing air gives up its heat to the cooler incoming air. Efficiency varies with the design of the unit and the rate of air flow, but heat transfer rate of up to 70 percent is possible. Two fans are required to power the unit, one for intake and one for exhaust.

CHAPTER 4 CLIMATE AND SITE

INTRODUCTION

A building's ability to provide shelter and comfort economically depends on how it is placed on the site, and on the climate at the site. Adapting the design of the building to take advantage of these factors is a fundamental principle of solar construction. Because climate varies from one region of the country to another and from one site to another within the same region, builders need to know both the effects of climate on energy performance and how to apply this knowledge when siting a building. *Macroclimate* refers to the general climate of a large area or region of the country. *Microclimate* is the specific climate of a small area, in this case of a particular building site. The combined influence of different climatic factors greatly affects the ability of a building to shelter its inhabitants. This chapter discusses both regional and site specific elements of climate, and develops guidelines for placing a building on its site to take advantage of favorable elements and protect it from unfavorable ones.

MACROCLIMATE—THE CLIMATE OF A REGION

Macroclimate can be defined as the average prevailing weather condition of a region during various seasons over a period of years. The primary elements that characterize local and regional climates are air temperature, humidity, precipitation, wind speed and direction, and solar radiation. Numerous attempts have been made to classify climatic regions within the United States, but it is very difficult to generalize. This discussion utilizes a breakdown of four climatic regions: cool, temperate, hot-arid, and hot-humid. While we accept that this breakdown is greatly oversimplified, it has been used in numerous studies of the impact of climate on housing, and it does provide a basis for comparing alternative climatic priorities. Figure 4.1 shows the different areas of the United States that fall within these predominant climatic patterns. Remember that each zone blends gradually into the other and that one region will often exhibit weather patterns characteristic of another.

Climate Zones of the United States

The **cool** regions of the country are characterized by a wide range of temperatures, generally with hot summers and cold winters. Predominant winds are from the northwest in winter and southeast in summer. Sites in these northern regions typically receive less sun on an annual and daily basis than southern regions. Housing adaptations sensitive to climate try to maximize the warming effects of solar radiation, to shelter from the cold winter wind and to avoid localized cold spots on a site.

The **temperate** regions are characterized by a balance between heating and cooling seasons. As a general rule, winter winds are from the northwest and summer winds are from the south; high humidity levels and large amounts of precipitation are common. Periods of cloudy days often follow periods of clear sunny days. Housing types should maximize solar gain in winter and provide solar shading in summer. Although winter wind should be blocked, access to prevailing summer breezes should be encouraged.

The **hot-arid** regions of the southwestern United States typically experience clear sky, low humidity, long periods of overheating, and large day/night temperature extremes. Wind direction is predominantly from east or

46 BASIC PRINCIPLES OF SOLAR CONSTRUCTION

Fig. 4.1 Four basic climatic regions of the country.

west with day/night variations. Housing forms in this region typically should provide maximum shelter from the sun, especially in late morning and afternoon. Exposure to wind movement in the summer should also be maximized, and humidity is desirable.

Hot-humid regions of the southeastern United States are characterized by high temperatures and high humidities. Wind speeds and directions vary throughout both the day and the year. Hurricane force winds are common every year from the east-southeast direction. Housing forms should provide maximum shelter from the sun and maximum exposure to the cooling wind.

Elements of Regional Climate

As we learned earlier, the primary elements that differentiate regional climates are air temperature, precipitation, humidity, wind speed and direction, and availability of solar radiation. Builders are familiar with using maximum/minimum temperatures and degree-day figures to size (usually oversize) mechanical heating and cooling systems. However, the design and construction of energy conserving housing must consider other climatic elements as well (Fig. 4.2). For example, average air temperature and wind speed are very important in determining the level of insulation for walls and roofs and the number of layers of glass in windows. Site latitude plays an important role in determining the optimum angle for sloped glazings and solar heat collectors for domestic hot water. Latitude and precipitation affect the shape and dimensions of shading overhangs, while the combined effect of all of these elements should influence the shape and orientation of the whole building. The most important element of climate is the availability of solar radiation, which also varies greatly—for different regions, for different sites, for different seasons.

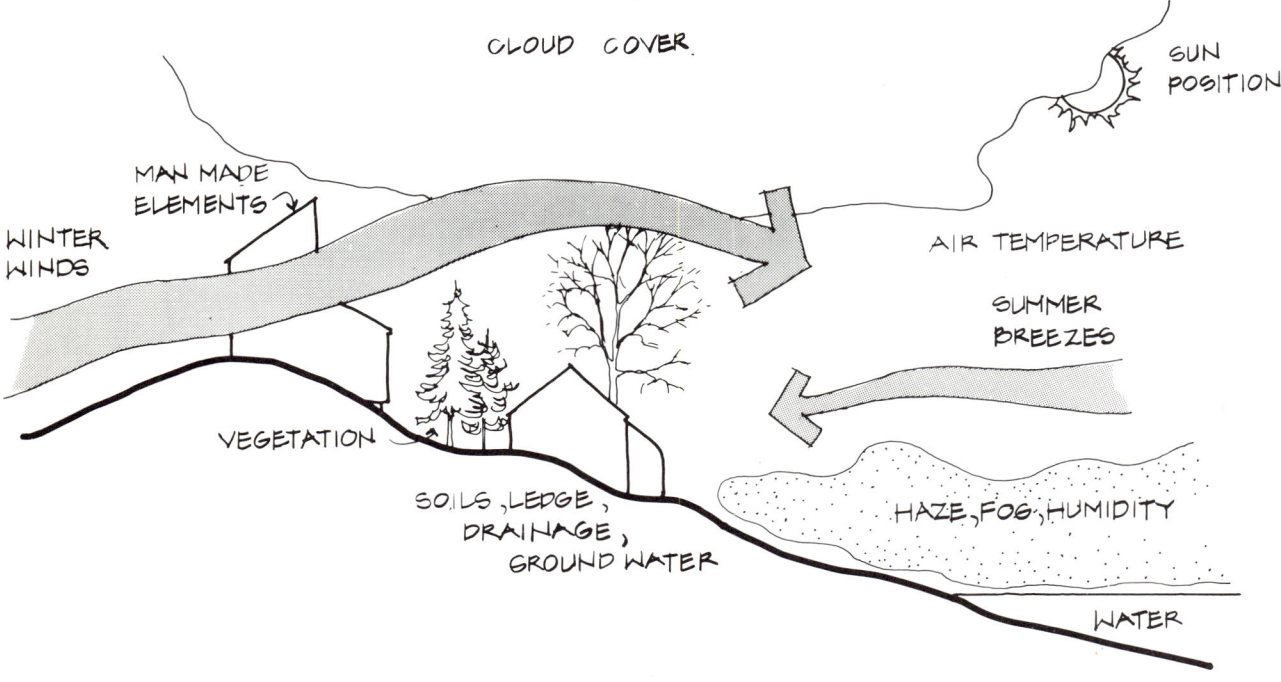

Fig. 4.2 Typical climatic elements at a building site.

MICROCLIMATE—THE CLIMATE AT THE BUILDING SITE

While macroclimate defines the general climate of a region, microclimate refers to the more specific climate of an individual building site. These site specific climatic factors play the most important role in the performance of any building. No two sites are exactly alike; the microclimate at a particular site may share most characteristics of the regional climate, but it also has specific characteristics. The elements that vary for different sites include topography (slope and orientation), vegetation, soil types, surface materials, and views. These combine to influence the regional elements of air temperature, wind speed and direction, humidity, solar radiation, and precipitation in defining a particular microclimate, the effects of which vary throughout the day and night and can change significantly within distances of only a few feet. Macroclimate analysis determines general thermal design priorities, and microclimate assessment determines exact details, especially placement of the building on the site. Although the combined effect of these elements defines the microclimate, it is simpler to consider them individually.

THE SUN

Of all the climatic elements to be considered in constructing a home, the sun is the most important. Solar radiation determines the air temperature, wind movement, precipitation patterns, and vegetation characteristics at a site. In addition, it is a primary source of heat gain (an asset or liability, depending on the climatic region and time of year). In either case, the control of solar radiation by the building is the critical factor. The sun's rays should penetrate the building when desirable (during heating season) and be blocked when undesirable (during cooling season). Builders must understand the characteristics of solar radiation in order to effectively control the impact of the sun on the building.

Solar Radiation

Solar energy is electromagnetic radiation, and the visible light perceived by the human eye is only part of the total radiation transmitted from the sun to the earth. A constant 429 BTU per square foot per hour of solar energy reaches the outer atmosphere, and this amount is known as the *solar constant*. However, the actual radiation that reaches the earth's surface, called *insolation*, is considerably less, due to losses that occur as the radiation passes through the atmosphere. Of all the solar radiation intercepted by the atmosphere, approximately

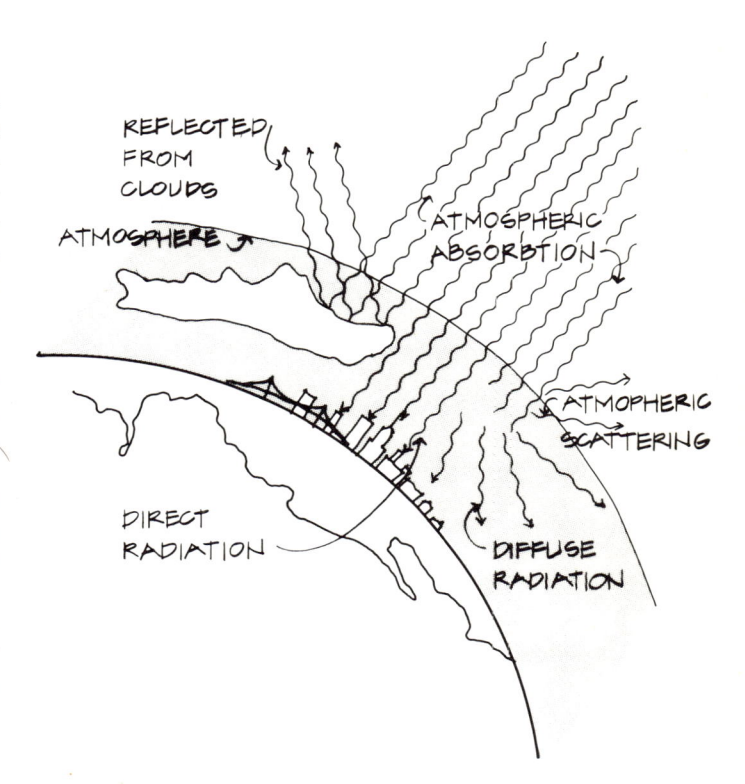

Fig. 4.3 Solar radiation is reflected, diffused, absorbed, and scattered as it passes through the atmosphere.

33 percent is reflected by cloud surfaces back into space. Approximately 42 percent of the energy is scattered or deflected by moisture and dust, and another 10 to 15 percent is absorbed by water vapor, carbon dioxide, and ozone (Fig. 4.3). *Direct radiation* strikes the earth's surfaces in parallel rays after passing directly through the atmosphere in cloudless conditions, and it is the most intense form of solar heat energy. *Diffuse radiation* reaches the ground after being scattered in all directions by reflection off particles in the atmosphere. Even in "clear sky conditions," up to 10 percent of total insolation may arrive at a site as diffuse radiation. Additionally, radiation reaching a building site may be reflected from the ground surface or adjacent structures.

The total amount of solar energy available at a site is the combined amount of direct, diffuse, and reflected radiation. Diffuse radiation can contribute as much as 50 percent of the total, when the sun is at low angles in winter, and 100 percent on cloudy days. On clear days, direct radiation contributes the greatest percentage of the total.

The distances of the atmosphere through which solar radiation must pass also affect its intensity when it finally reaches the site. Because of the earth's tilt and its

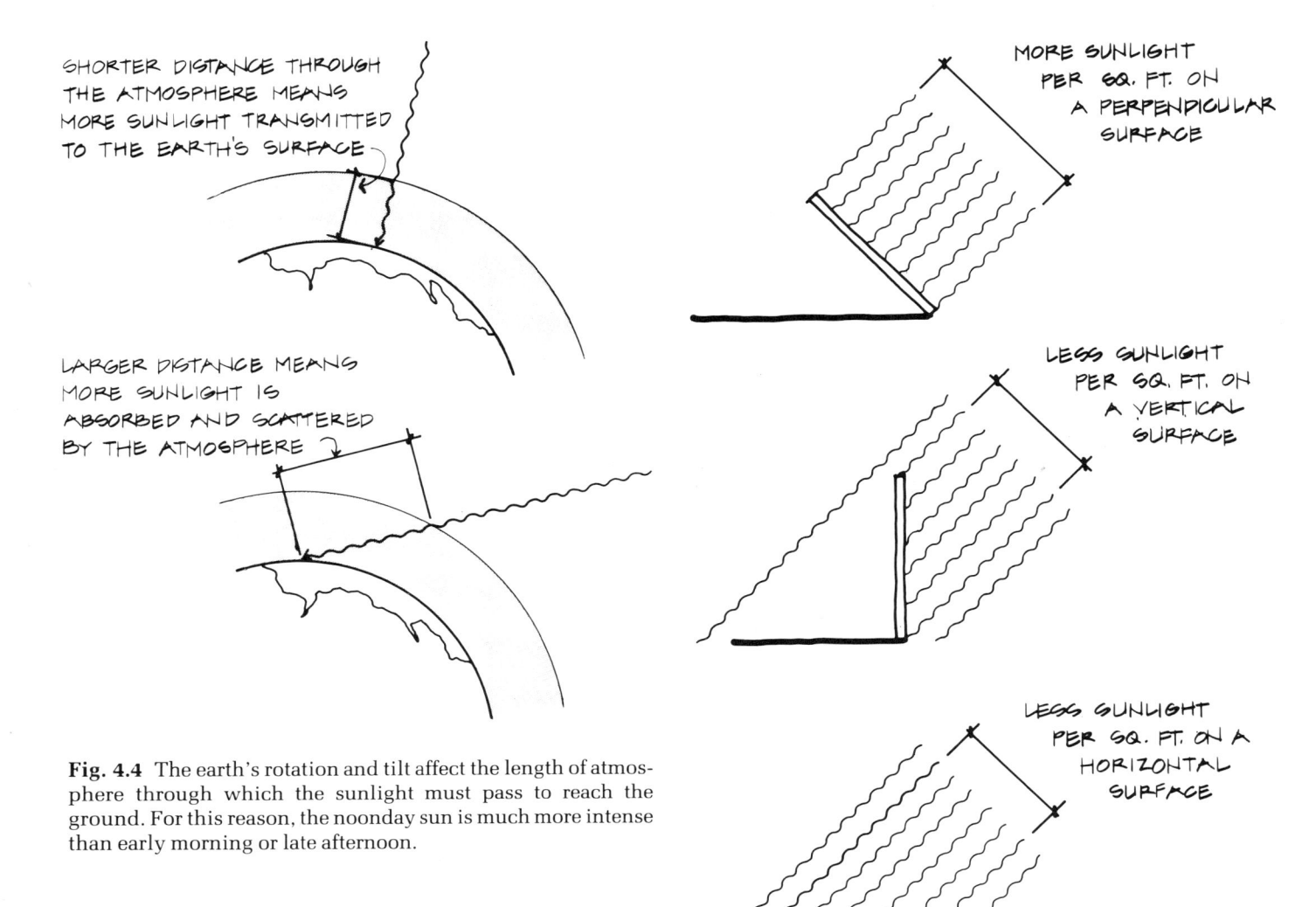

Fig. 4.4 The earth's rotation and tilt affect the length of atmosphere through which the sunlight must pass to reach the ground. For this reason, the noonday sun is much more intense than early morning or late afternoon.

Fig. 4.5 Surfaces that are perpendicular to the sun's rays receive maximum solar radiation per square foot.

rotation around the sun, the length of atmosphere that solar radiation must penetrate varies with time of day and month of year. As the earth goes through its rotation, it places different atmospheric conditions between the site and the sun at different times of day. In the morning and afternoon, low angle radiation must pass through more of the atmosphere to reach a site. Its intensity is greatly reduced along the way by energy loss through reflection and absorption. During midday, the sun is higher overhead and has less atmosphere to penetrate; thus, the energy received during this period is more intense (Fig. 4.4).

The amount of solar energy received by a surface is also affected by the angle at which the sunlight is received. A surface which is perpendicular to the sun's rays will receive the most energy per square foot while surfaces that are tilted away receive proportionally less (Fig. 4.5).

Solar Angles

As the earth revolves around the sun, its tilt remains constant, and this tilt creates the seasonal changes. In winter the Northern Hemisphere is tilted away from the sun. Solar radiation strikes the surfaces in the Northern Hemisphere at low angles. Sites that are farther north (Northern Hemisphere) receive solar radiation at lower angles, resulting in lower intensity of the radiation, fewer hours of daylight, and a colder climate. The sun rises to the south of east during winter, and sets south of west.

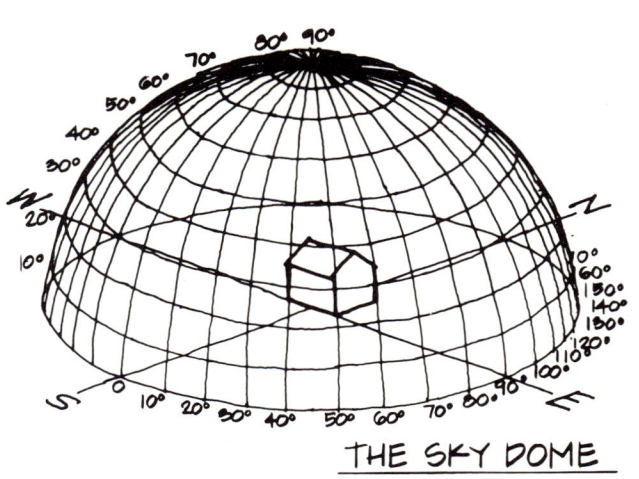

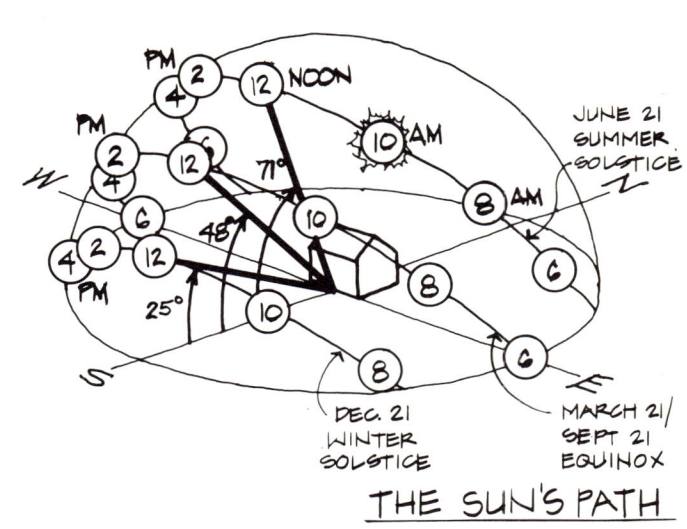

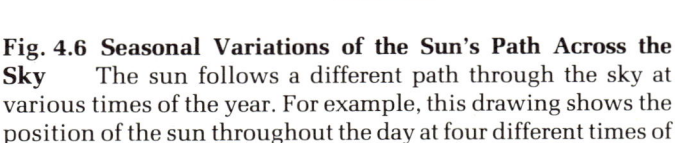

Fig. 4.6 Seasonal Variations of the Sun's Path Across the Sky The sun follows a different path through the sky at various times of the year. For example, this drawing shows the position of the sun throughout the day at four different times of the year for a site at 42°N latitude. The angles 25°, 48° and 71° are the height of the sun above the horizon at noon for the times of year shown.

In summer, the Northern Hemisphere is tilted toward the sun. More heat energy is absorbed by the earth due to the high sun angle and longer hours of daylight. The sun rises north of east in the summer, and sets north of west. Four dates mark the sun's position in the sky:

- December 21. Winter solstice, when the sun has reached its lowest point on the horizon, has the shortest hours of daylight of the year.
- June 21. Summer solstice, when the sun has reached its highest point in the sky, has the longest daylight hours of the year.
- March 21 and September 21. The equinox, when the sun is midway between high and low position, and days are equally divided between daylight hours and hours of darkness (Fig. 4.6).

The daily revolving of the earth around its own axis causes "sunrise" and "sunset." The orbit of the earth around the sun causes the sun to appear close to the horizon in winter and high overhead in summer. The angle of the sun above the horizon for a given site is called the *solar altitude*. This angle is different for different sites (dependent on latitude) and it changes throughout the day, reaching its highest point at noon. As the sun traverses the sky, it also makes an angle on the ground called *solar azimuth* which is measured with respect to the observer and the points of the compass.

The solar altitude angle and azimuth angle for latitude, date, and time of day are listed in tables which can be used to plot the sun's position as it moves across the sky at different times of year. This information is necessary when determining the degree to which trees, hills, buildings, or other features block the sun at a particular site at various times of year. Figure 4.7 illustrates a simple method for determining solar access at a site.

The availability of solar radiation at various times of the year, as well as day to day, also depends on climatic factors. The *percent of possible sunshine* refers to the percentage of the total daylight hours that are sunny. It refers strictly to direct radiation, and therefore is misleading due to the significant role that diffuse radiation can play. For this reason, it is important to combine both direct *and* diffuse radiation when determining available solar energy.

Microclimate Effect on Solar Radiation

Local climatic conditions can affect greatly the availability of solar radiation. Large bodies of water create early morning fog or localized cloud cover and storms. Urban industrial areas receive reduced amounts of solar radiation due to reflection by air pollutants. Site conditions that influence the availability of solar radiation include localized fogs, mountains, hills, buildings, and vegetation that may shade the site from solar radiation at various times of day or at different seasons.

50 BASIC PRINCIPLES OF SOLAR CONSTRUCTION

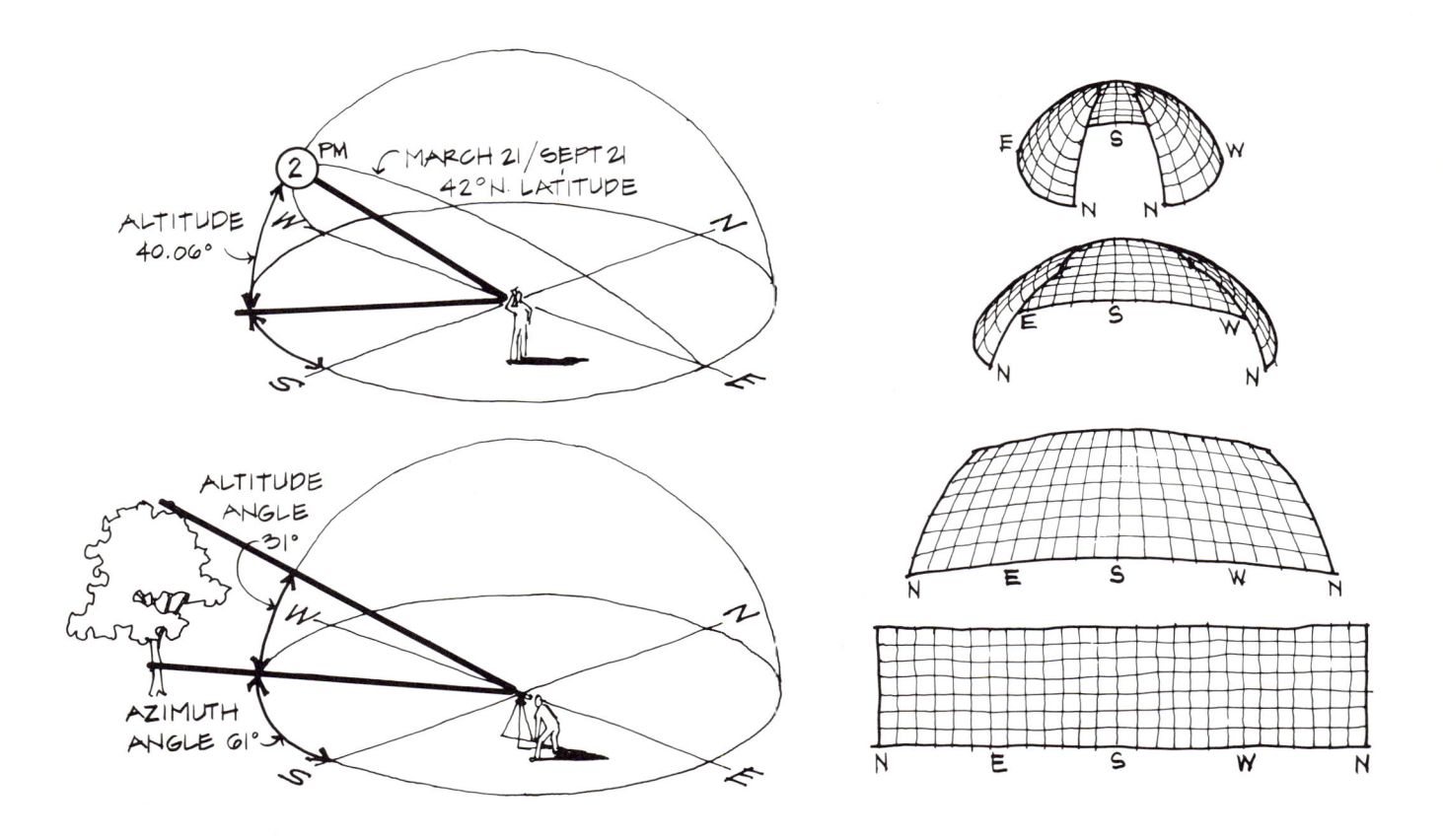

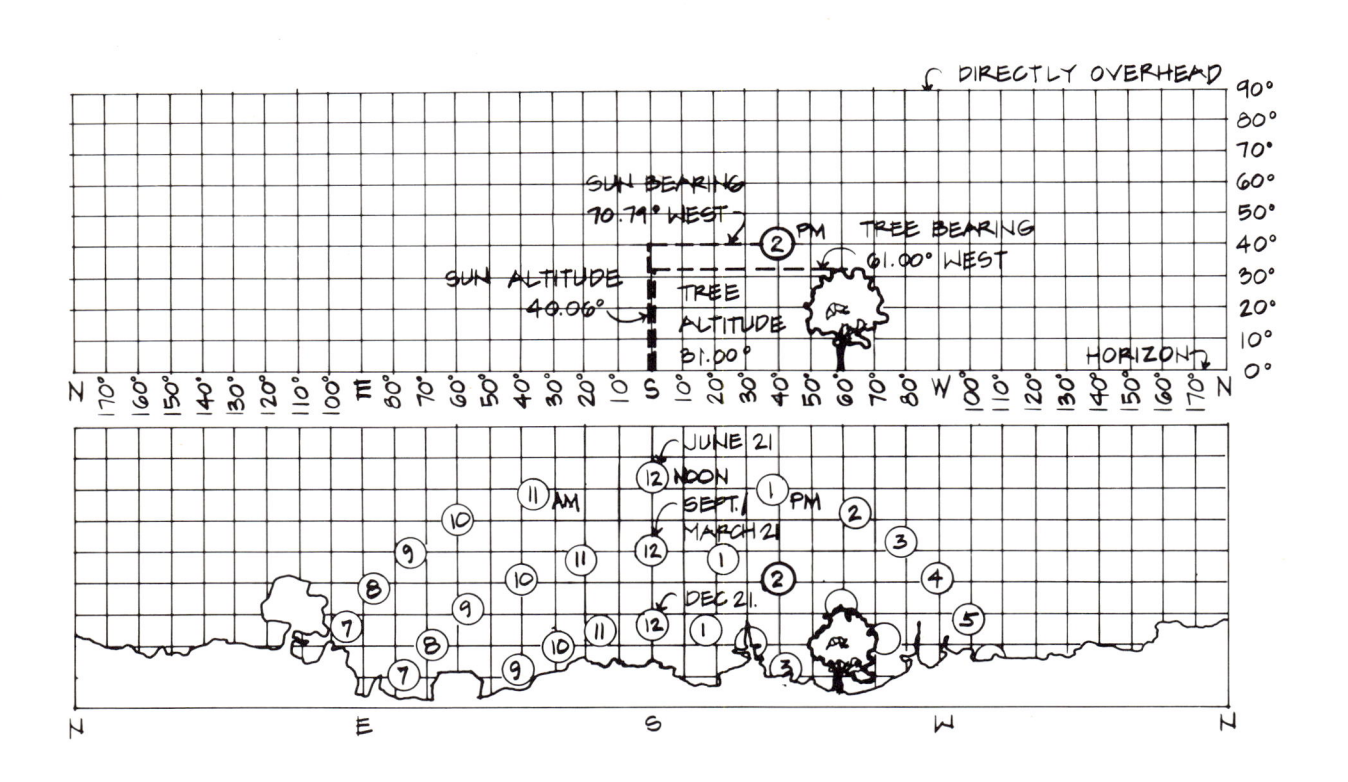

Fig. 4.7 Ending the Position of the Sun A) The sun's position in the sky can be found by obtaining the altitude and azimuth angle for the appropriate latitude, date and time of day from a table of sun angles. This example is for latitude 42°North, March or September 21 at 2:00 p.m. B) A transit can be used to determine if trees, hills or other buildings will block the sun's rays. The azimuth and altitude angles of possible obstructions can be plotted on a sky map. C) A sky chart is a *mercator projection* of the sky dome around the observer's point of view. D) The position of the sun and potential obstruction can be plotted to determine if a shading problem exists. E) It is useful to plot the sun's path for three times of the year—June 21 (summer solstice), March and September 21 (equinox), and December 21 (winter solstice). This plot indicates a good solar heating site as long as the trees to the south do not grow excessively.

The actual warmth of a site depends not only on the amount of solar radiation striking it, but also on the composition of its surface materials. Solar radiation striking the surface of a site is either absorbed or reflected; the properties of the surface materials determine how much is absorbed and how much is reflected. For example, fresh snow is highly reflective, as is any white or light colored material, while asphalt paving is highly absorptive, as is any black or dark colored material. The absorptive or reflective properties of the surface materials at a site, combined with their heat conduction properties (the rate at which heat moves through the material), help define the microclimate (Fig. 4.8). Site surface materials that absorb and conduct heat well create a mild and stable microclimate. Excess solar heat is absorbed quickly and conducted into the earth. When the air temperature drops at night or under cloud cover, the earth gradually releases this stored heat into the atmosphere, which slows the cooling process. Site surface materials which are highly reflective and poor heat conductors create a microclimate of temperature extremes, since the materials do not help balance the high daytime and low nighttime air temperatures. These same principles apply to the collection, storage, and release of solar heat by a building's interior surface materials, as discussed in the next chapter.

AIR TEMPERATURE

Outdoor air temperature is a basic criterion for determining heat loss or gain from a building. Analysis of the temperature difference between indoors and out defines the heating and cooling load for a building. The degree-day concept has been developed as a means of comparing the relationship between desired indoor temperatures with expected outdoor temperatures. *Heating degree-days* measure the difference between the outdoor temperature and an indoor standard of 65°F. For example, a day with an average outdoor temperature of 32°F has 33 degree-days (65 − 32 = 33). Monthly degree-day records for many cities are available from the National Weather Bureau. There is a direct correlation between quantity of degree-days for a site and the amount of fuel required to heat a building on that site. Degree-days for the total heating season in the United States can range from 600 (Tampa, Florida) to 10,800 (Anchorage, Alaska). The higher the number of degree-days, the more heat that is required in the building.

Patterns of air temperature fluctuation also are required to estimate the requirements that climate imposes on a building's heating system. The range of air temperatures experienced throughout the year, as well as day/night cycles, is important. The average low temperature expected during a winter is called the *design temperature*, because the heating system is sized to maintain comfort for the lowest temperature expected. Minimum outdoor design temperatures for various locations are tabulated by ASHRAE. The design temperature should be selected carefully; conventional practice has been to design for a very low, conservative temperature, which has resulted in many oversized heating systems. The reduced requirement for heating equipment is one of the many benefits of solar construction, and proper sizing to meet reduced loads is important in achieving that savings (Fig. 4.9).

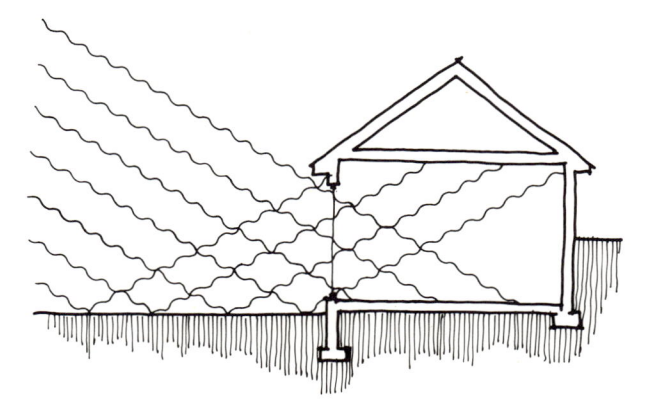

Fig. 4.8 Sunlight reflected off snow or other reflective ground cover increases the total solar radiation striking a vertical surface.

52 BASIC PRINCIPLES OF SOLAR CONSTRUCTION

A.) BUILDING SHAPE
B.) INSULATION LEVELS
C.) HEATING AND COOLING SYSTEMS
D.) EARTH SHELTERED

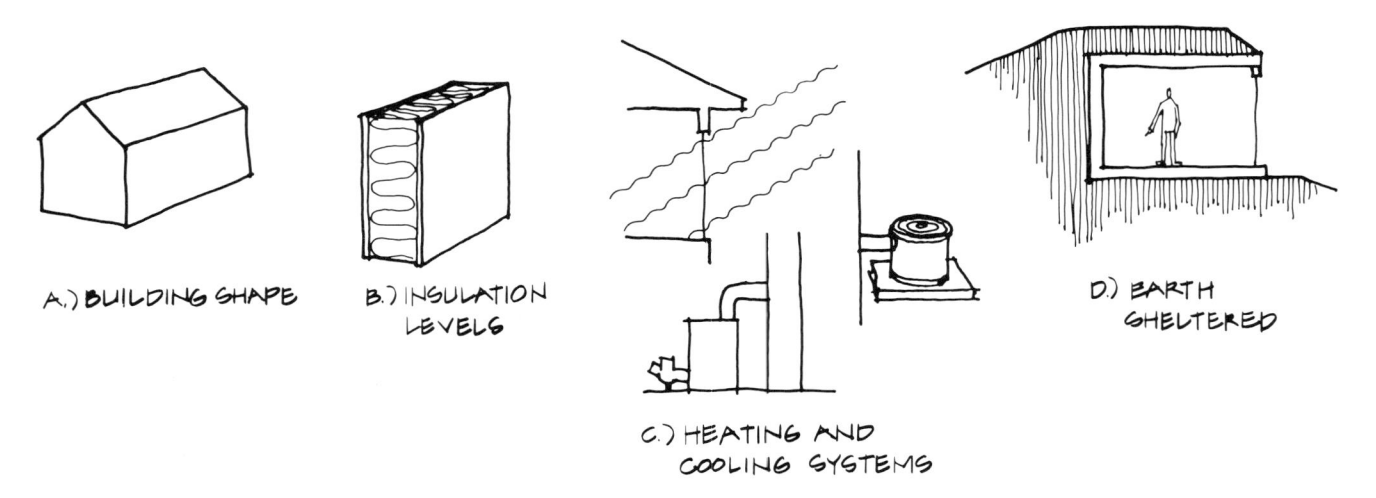

Fig. 4.9 Effect of Design Temperature (Average Minimum and Maximum on Building Forms) A) Surface area—less surface area means less heat loss and heat gain. B) Insulation levels—colder climates require more insulation. C) Heating and cooling systems—these systems are sized according to design temperatures and rates of building heat loss or gain. D) Earth sheltering—the tempering effect of the earth minimizes the impact of outside temperature extremes.

HUMIDITY AND PRECIPITATION

The importance of humidity in solar construction was discussed in Chapters 2 and 3. To review, relative humidity is the percentage of the actual amount of moisture in the air compared to the amount of moisture the air could hold at a given temperature. The amount of moisture the air can hold depends on temperature; the higher the air temperature, the more moisture the air can hold. Humidity may need to be added or reduced to provide comfort in buildings (Fig. 4.10).

Precipitation (rain and snow) affects building form and structure. Reflection from snow and frequency of rain storms affects the amount and intensity of insolation striking a building. The direction of the storm, and ice or snow build-up, also are important design considerations, as is the quantity of water movement on a site, which affects the requirements for site drainage.

A.) MEDIUM HIGH HUMIDITY
B.) HIGH HUMIDITY
C.) FOG

Fig. 4.10 Effect of Humidity on Building Forms A) Medium high humidity—natural ventilation or attic fans increases evaporative cooling. B) High humidity—mechanical cooling and dehumidification require a tight house. A hot climate may require a vapor barrier on the outside of the insulation. C) Fog—Weather patterns at a site influence building orientation. For example, recurring morning fog may dictate orientation to the west of south since the sun's rays will be blocked until the fog is burned off.

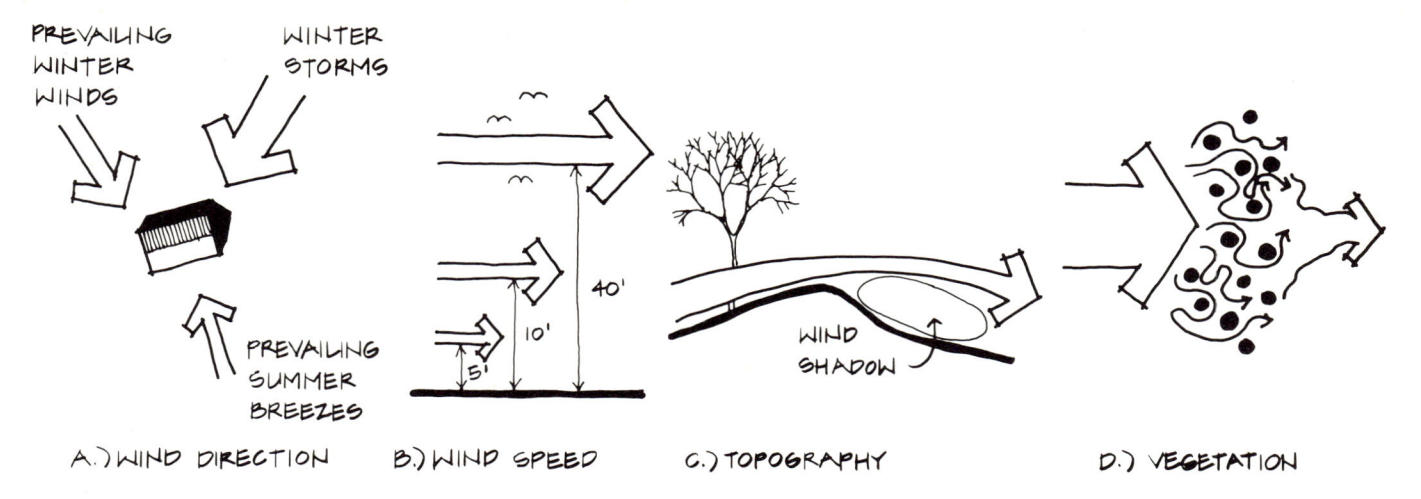

Fig. 4.11 Principles of Wind Analysis and Building Placement A) Wind direction—the direction of prevailing winds varies with location and season. B) Wind speed—wind speeds are lower close to the earth because of ground friction. C) Topography—slopes can create areas of wind shadows where calmer air exists. D) Vegetation—wooded areas lower wind speed by causing frictional eddies between the trees.

AIR MOVEMENT

Air movement is another important component of a site's climate. Regional information helps determine the prevailing wind directions and average velocities for different seasons. However, wind patterns at a site can be altered by topography, slope, orientation, vegetation, and other buildings. Wind movement has a major impact on the energy requirements for heating and cooling of any building on any site. Wind causes increased heat loss by convection, increased infiltration by wind pressure, and the cooling of living space through cross ventilation of summer breezes. So, warm weather winds should be utilized to cool the building, while cold winter winds should be blocked.

Wind Speed

Wind speed increases with distance from the ground, as surface friction is reduced. Wind speed at 3 inches off the ground may be 30 percent of the speed at 6 feet off the ground. Higher wind speeds accelerate the rate of heat loss from a building. Wind moving 30°F air at 30 miles per hour has six times the cooling effect of still air at 10°F. It pays to control air movement at a site. For example, by reducing the wind speed of 32°F air from 12 miles per hour to 3 miles per hour before it hits the building, the energy requirements for heating can be cut in half. This reduction in wind speed can be achieved through the use of shrubs, trees, topography, and other buildings (Fig. 4.11).

Wind Control

Methods of controlling wind movement attempt to reduce its velocity and divert its direction. The shape, orientation, and placement of a building on the site should utilize natural and created site features to protect it from the effects of wind. The rate of air infiltration into a building is affected by its orientation to the prevailing winds. A building with a corner pointing into the winter wind loses much more heat than one with a wall square to the wind. The design and location of garage space, outbuildings, and vestibules can effectively protect the heated spaces in a building. Earth berming, either on a natural slope or with a created berm, also reduces the amount of heat lost due to wind movement (Fig. 4.12).

Wind velocity can be reduced by using windbreaks consisting of various trees and shrubs. Wind striking a windbreak placed square to prevailing winds either moves through the dense branches and dissipates, or is diverted over and around the windbreak. Windbreaks should contain different heights, species, and ages of trees and shrubs. The various heights create a jagged crown which helps reduce wind velocity, and the variety in species helps protect the windbreak from disease. Year-round wind protection is improved by including coniferous species (evergreen). A variety of ages provides for a new generation to replace the mature trees and shrubs; this assures long term protection and forms a "stable" windbreak.

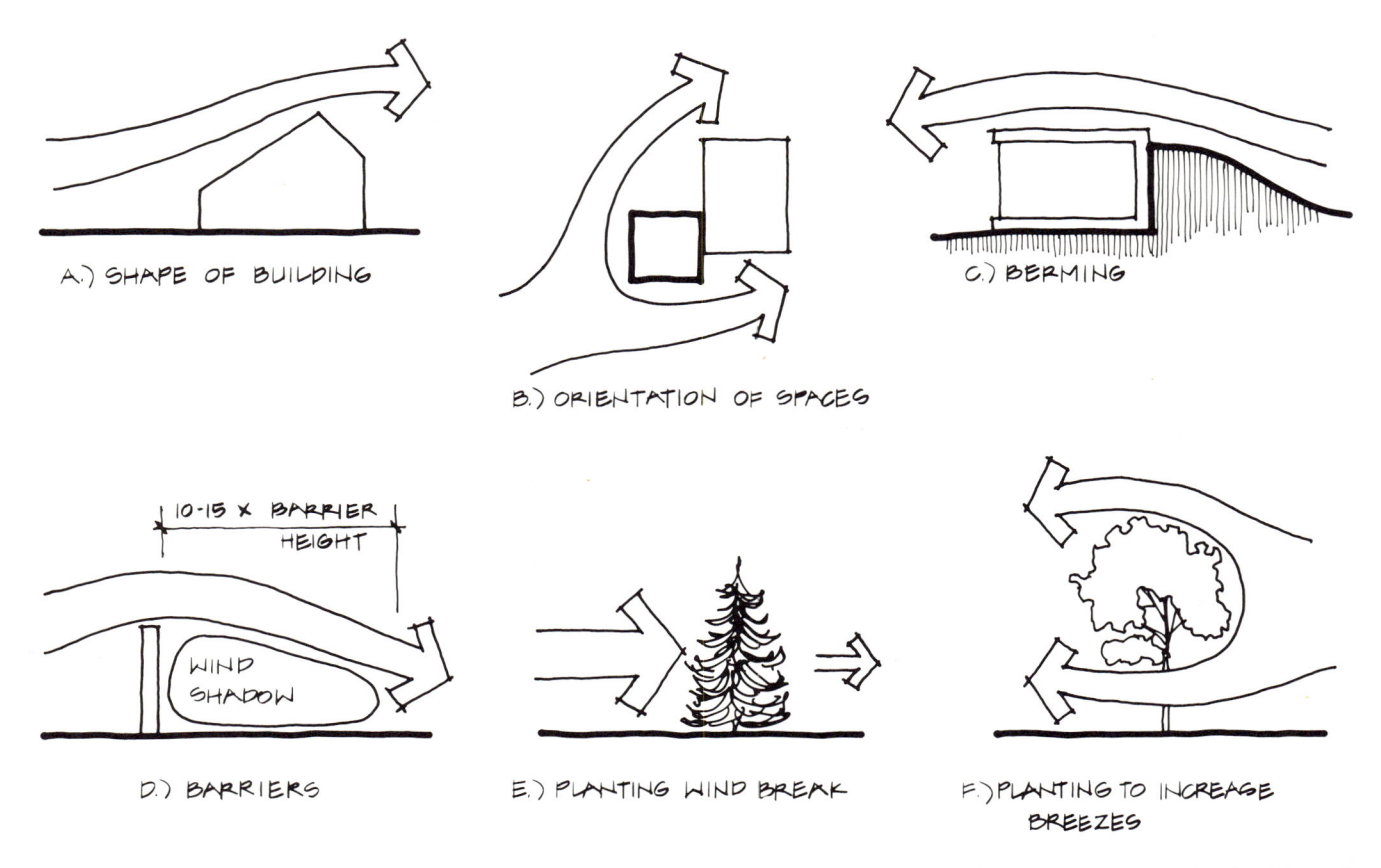

Fig. 4.12 Techniques for Wind Control A) Building shape can reduce wall surface and windows toward prevailing winds. B) Orientation of spaces—unheated elements of the building can be used to deflect prevailing winds. C) Earth berms can also be used to deflect prevailing winds. D) Barriers create a wind shadow 10–15 times the building height. E) Wind breaks—the best planting of winter wind barriers is dense grouping of evergreens which branch close to the ground. F) Trees which do not branch to the ground can be used to increase wind speeds for cooling.

Wind deflection over and around the windbreak depends on its density, height, and shape. Height is the most important factor in determining the area of protection on the leeward side of a windbreak. Wind diverted over the windbreak flows over the top and begins to drop back to the ground. A building on the leeward side of the windbreak close to the buffer would not be affected much by the diverted winds. Placement of the building further downwind, however, exposes it to air currents returning to ground level after being diverted over the windbreak, so the higher the windbreak, the more area downwind that is protected from wind. Chapter 8 discusses windbreaks as part of the site work and foundation phase of construction.

Summer winds prevail from a different direction than winter winds, and they are usually welcome. Because they come to a site from different seasonal directions, wind controls for winter will not block the cooling summer breezes. The need for cooling varies with the region. Heavy insulation, the use of thermal mass, and inclusion of shading devices all help keep houses cool in summer. One of the most important architectural measures that can be taken is careful placement of operable windows for cross ventilation. Trees and shrubs can also assist in summer cooling by shading south and west glazings, and also by diverting cool summer breezes towards the house, where open windows can allow it to enter and exit the building.

TOPOGRAPHY

Topography of a site includes the slope, shape, and orientation of the land. These are important microclimatic factors to consider when determining the exact siting of the building. The steepness of a site influences accessibility, equipment operation, soil stability, waste

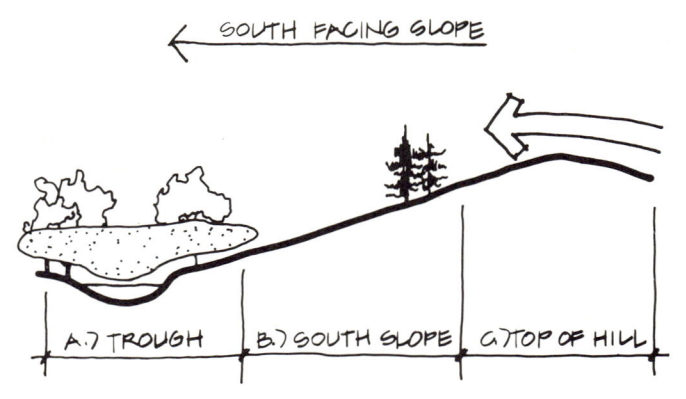

Fig. 4.13 Topography Can Create Colder or Warmer Building Sites A) Trough—colder air collects in lower areas and can create morning ground fog. B) Cold air does not collect on sloped areas and wind speeds are lower than at top of hill. C) Wind speeds from any direction are higher at the crest of the hill.

disposal, footing, and foundation plans, and costs related to all phases of construction. Sites that exceed 10 percent pitch are generally regarded as too steep for building. Varying temperature conditions at different locations on a slope form three basic areas: the cold ridge, moderate mid-slope, and cold basin at the bottom (Fig. 4.13).

Site Slope

Wind speed at the top of a slope may be 20 percent greater than the wind speed on a flat site, given the same conditions. This acceleration is due to the shape of the land and makes this area along the ridge a "cold site." Increased wind velocities accelerate convective heat loss and infiltration from the building shell, as described in Chapter 2. A building sited at the top of a slope probably has a colder climate affecting it than regional factors may indicate. Consequently, this location should be avoided in climates where the heating load dominates, but it would be desirable in locations where the cooling load dominates.

Another "cold site" forms at the foot of long open slopes and in hollows. At night, the earth through radiation loses heat absorbed during the day. This creates a thin layer of cool air near the surface, which behaves somewhat like water and flows downhill towards the low points in the topography. The cold air flood gathers into a stream in open valleys, or in pools where its flow has been blocked by a topographic dam or ground cover and trees. If large enough, a cold air pool may persist through the following day, especially if a fog or haze remains to prevent the sun from warming the ground.

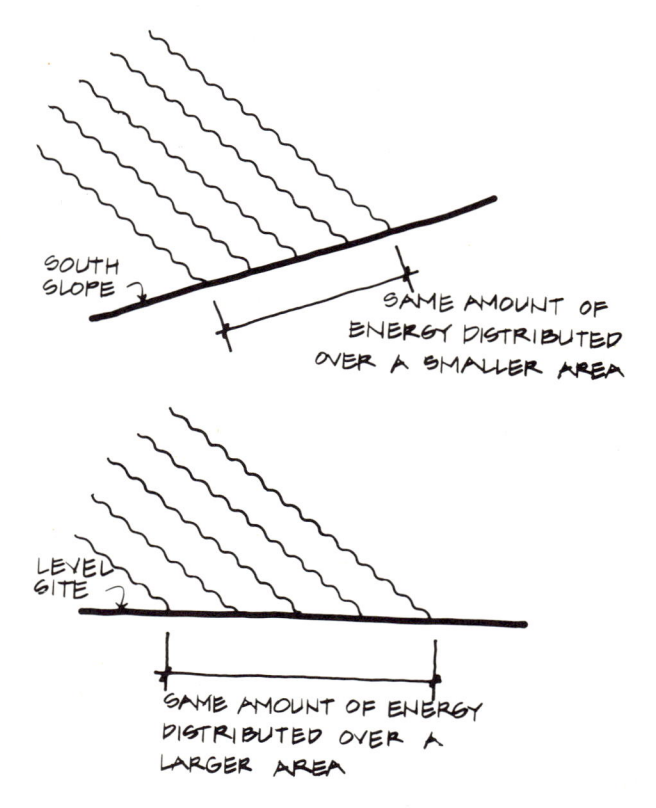

Fig. 4.14 A south facing slope receives more solar radiation than a level site.

The presence of a layer of cold air near the ground during the day is the opposite of normal daytime conditions, and is called an *inversion*. Cold air is heavier and stays near the ground, reducing the usual upward movement of warm, light surface air. Inversions are fairly stable conditions that may remain until wind movement breaks up the temperature stratification. These cold air pockets should be avoided in cold climates.

From an energy standpoint, the best location for any building placed on a sloping site is at the upper or middle portions, rather than at the crest or at the bottom. Mid-slope areas generally are protected from extreme winds and are not subject to cold air pools, unless a local topographic feature causes a damming effect.

Site Orientation

Another important aspect of site slope is its orientation with respect to the sun. The amount of solar radiation received by a sloping site is determined by its pitch and orientation. A south facing slope receives more solar radiation than a level site (Fig. 4.14). In winter, when the sun is low in the southern sky (Northern Hemisphere), solar radiation strikes the earth at a low angle. Sites

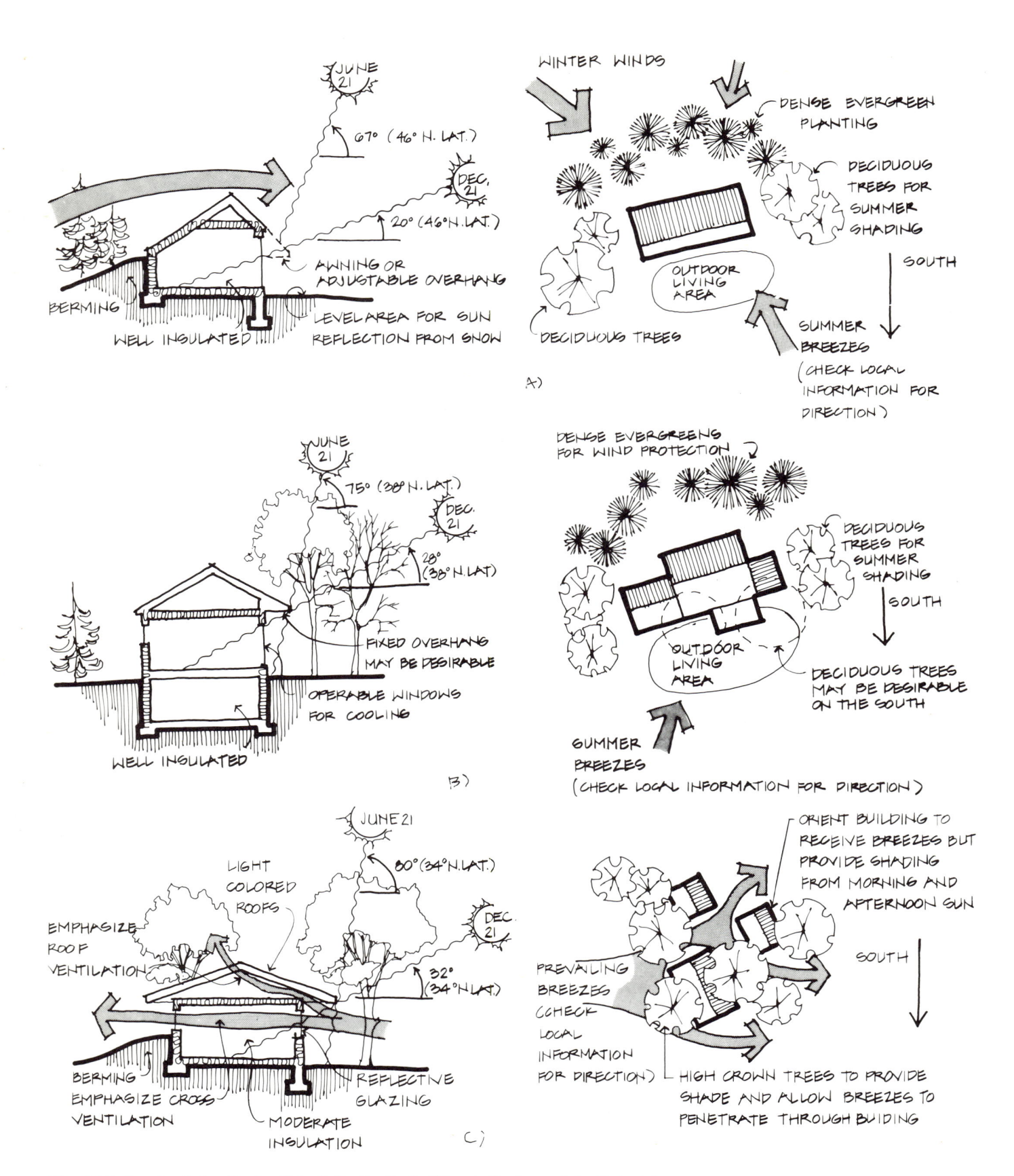

Fig. 4.15 Passive Solar Design Principles for Basic Climate Regions of the United States

56

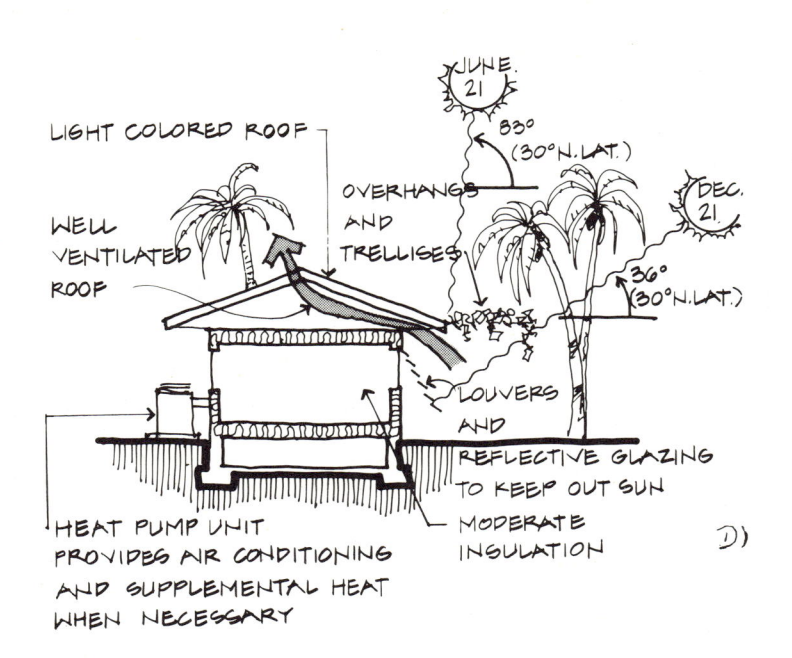

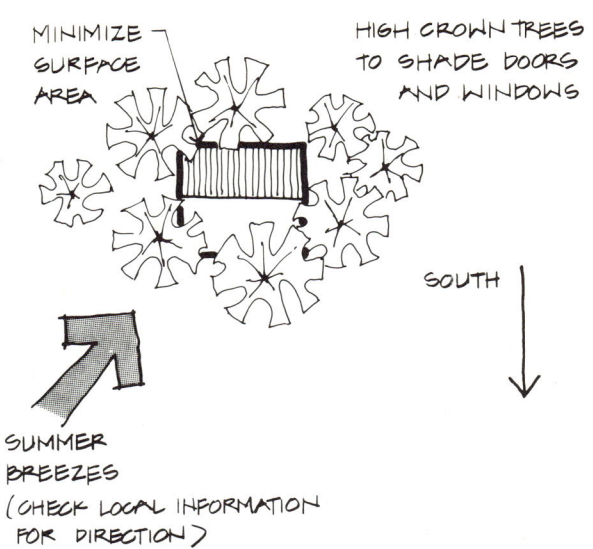

A) Cool Regions   Site and organize building to:
- Minimize windows and exposure on the north.
- Elongate building east to west to maximize solar gain in winter and minimize in summer.
- Maximize insulation levels.
- Minimize surface area of building to reduce heat loss.
- Provide evergreen wind screens to block prevailing winter winds & storms.
- Provide deciduous trees to east & west to block morning and afternoon summer sun.
- Consider movable awnings or other adjustable overhangs to reduce summer sun penetration on the south.
- Face south facade east of south to encourage faster warm up in the winter and discourage afternoon heat up in summer.
- Consider earth berming to temper air temperature extremes.
- Use steep roofs and snow slides to shed snow.
- Provide level area in front of south windows to hold snow and reflect sun into buildings.

B) Temperate regions   Site and organize building to:
- Minimize windows on the north.
- Elongate building east to west to maximize solar gain in winter and minimize solar gain in summer.
- Optimize insulation levels.
- Provide evergreen wind screens to block prevailing winter winds and storms.
- Provide deciduous trees to east and west to block morning and afternoon sun in summer.
- Consider deciduous trees to the south if summer shading is a high priority (since some winter sun will be blocked by branches).
- Consider fixed overhangs instead of adjustable (for cost savings) if cooling is a higher priority (since some late winter sun will be blocked by a large fixed overhang).
- Face south facade east of south to encourage faster warm up in winter and discourage afternoon heat up in summer.
- Consider using a heat pump for summer cooling and winter back up heat.

C) Hot Arid Regions   Site and organize building to:
- Take advantage of breezes.
- Provide large overhangs to shade south windows and walls.
- Provide light colored and well-ventilated roof.
- Provide moderate insulation.
- Consider earth berming to help cool and humidify.
- Take advantage of natural water features like lakes to help cool and humidify.
- Provide high crown trees to help shade building and direct breezes.
- Break up forms and provide operable windows to encourage cross ventilation
- Provide reflective glazing on windows that receive sun.

D) Hot Humid Regions   Site and organize building to:
- Take advantage of breezes for exterior spaces and venting.
- Provide large overhangs, trellises, exterior louvers, and reflective glazings to minimize solar gain.
- Provide light colored and well-ventilated roof.
- Provide moderate insulation.
- Provide high crown trees to help shade building and direct breezes.
- Provide operable windows to take advantage of cooler breezes and temperatures.
- Minimize surface area to minimize conductive heat gain.
- Provide air conditioning to cool, dehumidify, and heat when necessary.

sloped to the south are actually pitched towards the winter sun and receive more of its energy, making these sites the warmest of all in winter. A 10 percent slope to the south will receive as much radiation as a level site 6 degrees in latitude to the south. A south facing sloped site that receives 20 percent more winter radiation than a level site at the same latitude will be approximately two weeks ahead in the arrival of spring. Sites that slope to the north receive much less direct solar radiation in winter than south facing or level building sites, and for this reason they are also considered "cold sites."

In many cases selecting a well drained site is more important for solar construction than for typical buildings. If the site slopes toward the south, the building can be set into the slope, and the foundation used as primary living space with the south facing elevation open to the sun. The use of foundation areas as heat storage and living space requires that backfill materials provide good drainage, and that perimeter drains are installed properly. Drainage is even more important when earth sheltering surrounds all of the building except its south elevation. In both instances the waterproofing of the foundation is critical, as discussed in Chapter 8. The insulating value of the surrounding soil depends on its consistency and moisture content. Moisture increases the rate at which heat is conducted through the soil. Well drained, coarse materials make the best backfill for foundations. If existing materials removed for excavation offer poor drainage (such as clay), then proper material should be brought in, though this will increase site costs.

Site Excavation

Ease of excavation has a great effect on construction costs, especially if ledge or bedrock is encountered, requiring blasting or a change in foundation plans. These problems are the same for any type of construction; however, an energy conserving building built on ledge has other problems. The mass of the foundation, though insulated on the outside, will be tied directly to a virtually infinite heat sink, the earth. This connection, another form of thermal bridge between material within the heated envelope and the material outside, will be a path of heat loss from the building. These subsurface foundation conditions dictate the most sensible way to insulate the foundation. In this case, foundation insulation would be better placed on the inside.

VEGETATION

All microclimatic conditions are influenced by plant cover. Plants increase the surface area for radiation and transpiration, shade the ground, and slow air movement, resulting in a cooler, more humid and stable microclimate. Thick belts of shrubs or trees can be used effectively as windbreaks that will reduce velocities by more than 50 percent, for a distance downwind of ten times their height. Shrubs located close to the building will reduce wind speed further. Grass or wet ground tends to stabilize temperature extremes at a site. Moisture increases the conductivity of the soil, which increases the amount of heat it will absorb, thus reducing daytime temperatures. Grass cover and ground moisture also help cool the site through evaporation.

SITING THE BUILDING

The siting of a sun-tempered building must respond to as many climatic factors as possible. Proper siting with respect to climate is the most cost effective step a builder can take to improve energy performance. Any additional costs incurred for careful siting will be very low, yet the effects on energy performance will be significant. The placement of the building on its site must always achieve a balance between the requirements for proper drainage, ease and depth of excavation, waste disposal, orientation towards roads, and views. Builders must recognize energy performance as a priority in siting (Fig. 4.15).

The positioning of a building on its site must also be sensitive to aesthetics. The site planning of subdivisions has traditionally been focused on laying out building lines with relation to roads. This concern can easily be incorporated in solar construction by modification of building plans. There is also some leeway in optimum orientation for solar energy gain, as we will discuss later.

Other important aesthetic considerations for siting include noise, privacy, and access to views. Besides its usefulness as shade and wind control, vegetation can also serve as a buffer against noise from roads, neighbors, or industrial processes. Landscape planning also can provide for privacy. Both of these features will add value to the property by increasing the comfort of its inhabitants. Visual access to pleasant views and protection from unpleasant ones are important elements of siting. Although solar heated buildings usually are designed to minimize glazed areas on the north exposure, a builder should not ignore special features that may give that exposure the preferred view. If this is the case, then it is important for the builder to provide that view in the most energy efficient manner—by careful sizing and selection of glazings (multiple layers, mostly fixed), proper installation to minimize infiltration, and possible inclusion of movable insulation or heavy drapes.

Solar heated buildings incorporate more glazed area on the south than on other elevations, offering inhabitants wide views to the south. The value of this depends on what can be seen now, as well as what might be built later. This can affect the approach to material selection or choice of solar system. For instance, glazings can be perfectly clear (transparent) or somewhat clouded (translucent); direct gain systems create large glazed areas with increased visual access and thermal storage walls lessen visual access to the outside. The site criteria determine the appropriate response.

CHAPTER 5 PASSIVE SOLAR HEATING AND COOLING

INTRODUCTION

In the preceding chapters we emphasized the conservation of heat energy within the building and the placement of the building on the site to take advantage of the microclimate in providing thermal comfort. We discussed the importance of site climate in defining a building's requirements for heating and cooling. The strongest influence on a building's climate, both at the site and in the region, is the sun. Now we will examine the use of a building's shape, orientation, and configuration to control the impact of solar radiation on indoor comfort requirements; this involves selectively opening and closing the building shell to admit the sun's warmth to living spaces when heating is required, and to protect them from the sun's rays when cooling is required. Our discussion focuses on collection of solar radiation, heat storage and delivery of heat to building spaces. We again emphasize that sun tempered buildings must be energy conserving.

All buildings utilize solar radiation to some extent. The sun illuminates building interiors and heats the walls and roofs. Wherever solar radiation passes directly though a glazed area, it strikes the interior surfaces and warms the space. This is true for all buildings. Solar heated buildings are designed and built to take greater advantage of radiation available at the site (Fig. 5.1).

Simple, practical approaches to solar heat collection, storage, and distribution can be applied to all residential building designs. Buildings can be built to use the sun in many different ways; solar radiation can pass directly into living space or accumulate in another location for later use. In all approaches the building materials transmit and absorb solar radiation, and retain its heat to temper the space. These applications, where the collection and storage of the heat energy operate by the natural natural energy flows of radiation, conduction, and convection, are known as *passive solar heating* approaches.

Since the need for heating dominates the comfort requirements of most housing built in the United States, passive solar heating techniques dominate our discussion. Simple *passive cooling* techniques also can significantly reduce the demand for mechanical cooling in most climate zones. In contrast to approaches using the sun for heating, passive cooling requires shading the building from overheating by excess sun, and opening the building for ventilation by wind flows. The higher levels of insulation to keep heat in also serve to keep the building cooler in summer (Fig. 5.2).

Throughout this book, our emphasis is on simplicity. In this chapter we develop a simple, one-step-at-a-time approach for builders to begin applying solar concepts in their work. This does not imply that the final steps represent an ultimate evolution for housing types or that these steps are mutually exclusive. Rather, builders should understand the principles and alternatives, and selectively begin to test them on their building types and specific marketplaces.

BUILDING SHAPE AND ORIENTATION

A building's shape and orientation determine the amount of solar radiation, both direct and diffuse, that will strike it. Buildings positioned to increase solar energy gain in winter, and reduce solar gain in summer, will perform best if rectangular in shape, with the length running east to west. This exposes long vertical walls to south, where low winter sun can penetrate the glazed areas and warm the interior while high summer sun will be either shaded by overhang, trellis, or tree crown, or reflected due to oblique angle of incidence. This shape and orientation

PASSIVE SOLAR HEATING AND COOLING 61

Fig. 5.1 Solar construction is based on designing buildings to suit their climates. Each climatic region has its own special concerns that influence building design.

(Communico, Inc.)
(Downing and Leach)
(Peterson Construction Co.)

62   BASIC PRINCIPLES OF SOLAR CONSTRUCTION

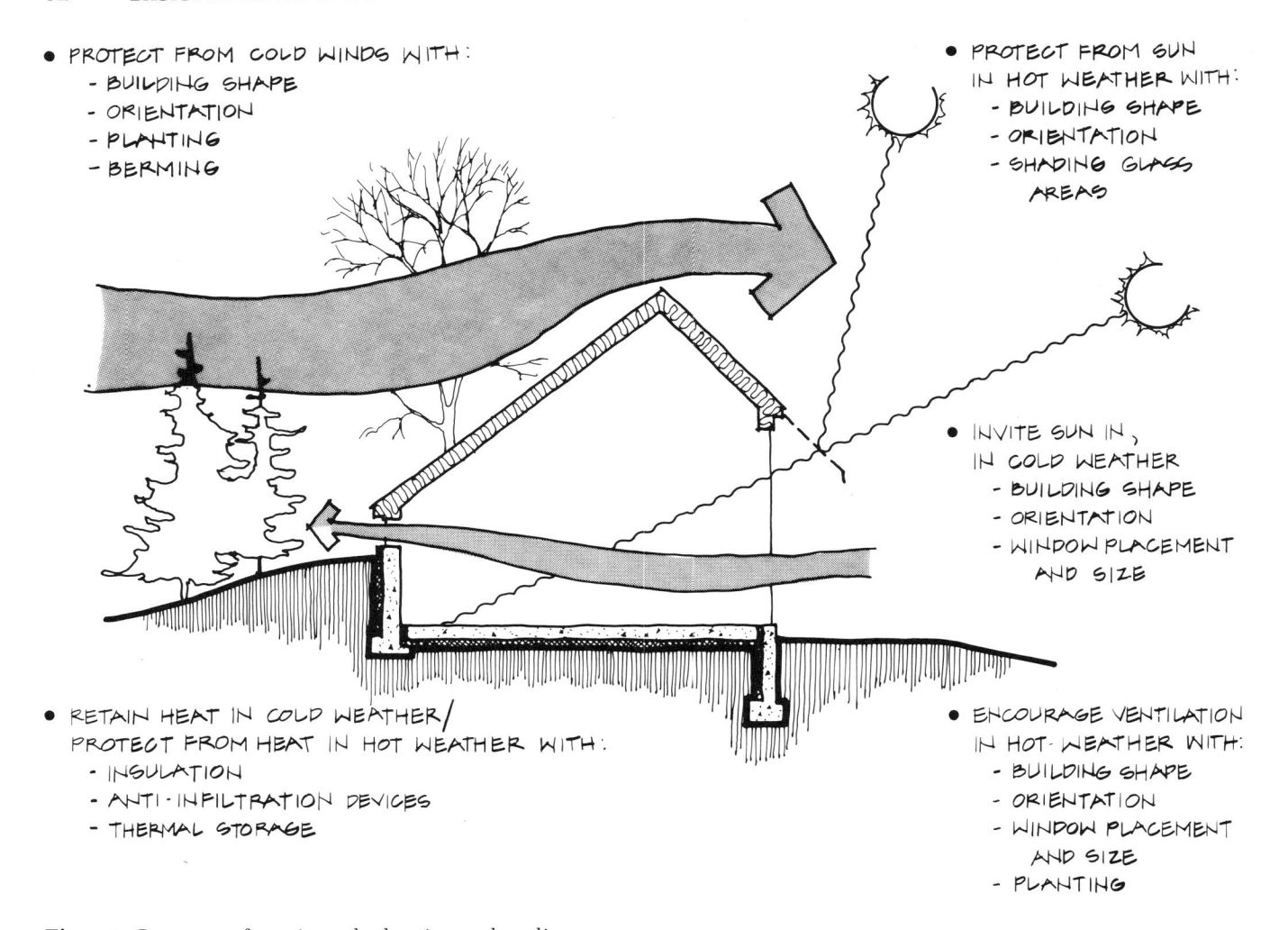

- PROTECT FROM COLD WINDS WITH:
  - BUILDING SHAPE
  - ORIENTATION
  - PLANTING
  - BERMING

- PROTECT FROM SUN IN HOT WEATHER WITH:
  - BUILDING SHAPE
  - ORIENTATION
  - SHADING GLASS AREAS

- INVITE SUN IN, IN COLD WEATHER
  - BUILDING SHAPE
  - ORIENTATION
  - WINDOW PLACEMENT AND SIZE

- RETAIN HEAT IN COLD WEATHER / PROTECT FROM HEAT IN HOT WEATHER WITH:
  - INSULATION
  - ANTI-INFILTRATION DEVICES
  - THERMAL STORAGE

- ENCOURAGE VENTILATION IN HOT WEATHER WITH:
  - BUILDING SHAPE
  - ORIENTATION
  - WINDOW PLACEMENT AND SIZE
  - PLANTING

Fig. 5.2 Concepts of passive solar heating and cooling

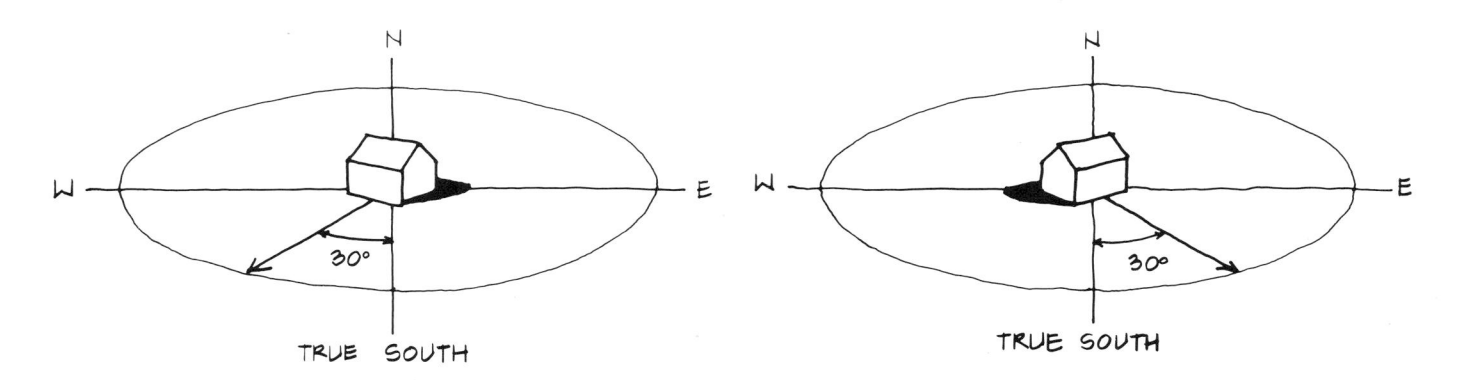

Fig. 5.3 **Acceptable Building Orientation for Passive Solar Heating**   A variation of 30° east or 30° west of true south reduces solar gain on a vertical wall by only 10%.

PASSIVE SOLAR HEATING AND COOLING 63

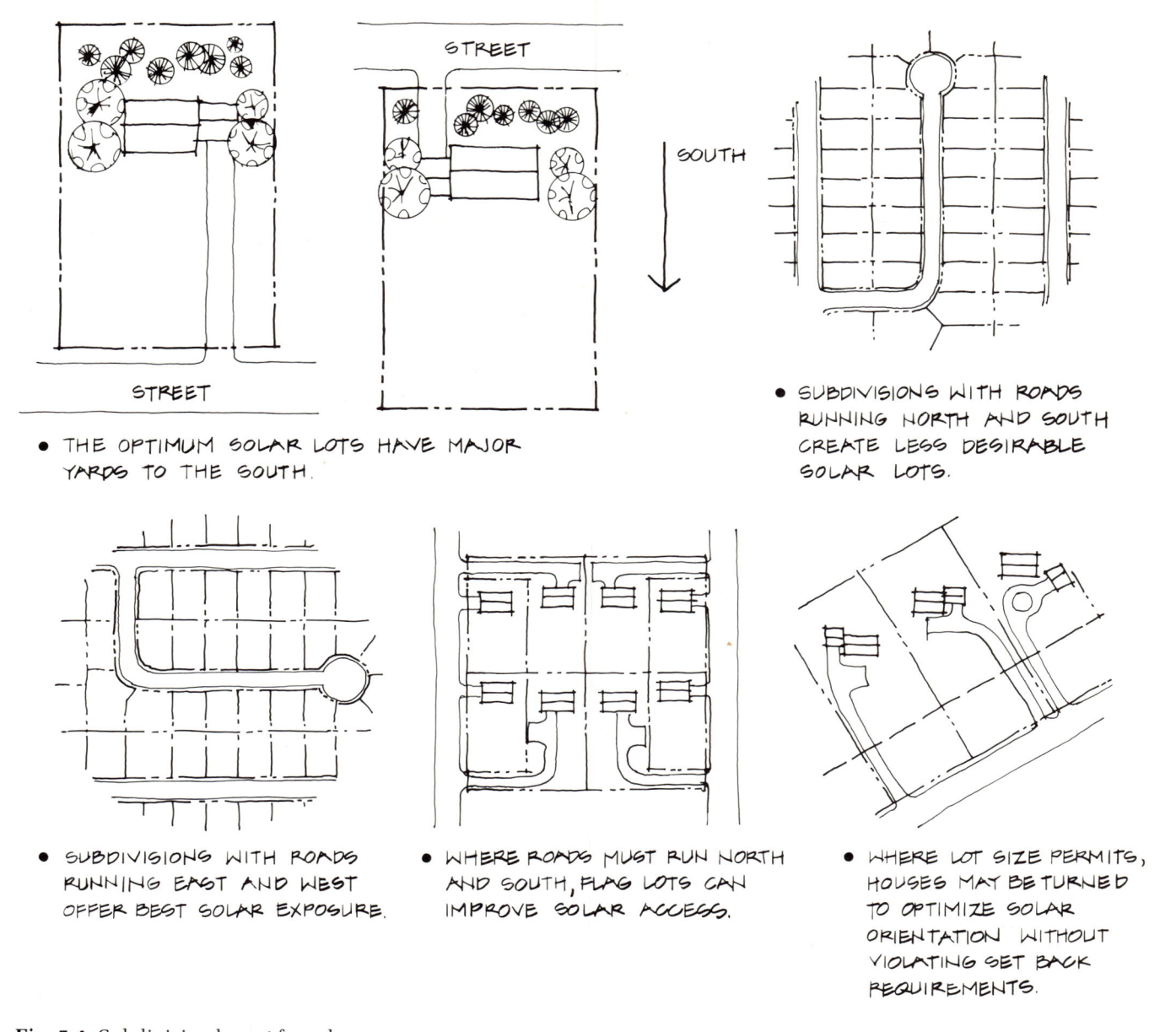

- THE OPTIMUM SOLAR LOTS HAVE MAJOR YARDS TO THE SOUTH.

- SUBDIVISIONS WITH ROADS RUNNING NORTH AND SOUTH CREATE LESS DESIRABLE SOLAR LOTS.

- SUBDIVISIONS WITH ROADS RUNNING EAST AND WEST OFFER BEST SOLAR EXPOSURE.

- WHERE ROADS MUST RUN NORTH AND SOUTH, FLAG LOTS CAN IMPROVE SOLAR ACCESS.

- WHERE LOT SIZE PERMITS, HOUSES MAY BE TURNED TO OPTIMIZE SOLAR ORIENTATION WITHOUT VIOLATING SET BACK REQUIREMENTS.

Fig. 5.4 Subdivision layout for solar access

reduces the wall area exposed to direct solar radiation in summer by exposing only the narrow end walls to the low angles of morning and afternoon sun. The solar altitude at these times is too low for fixed overhangs to be effective as shading devices; therefore, vegetation, awnings, and other shading devices should be used to reduce heat gain through these areas in summer. This affects the sizing and selection of windows for end walls.

Most solar radiation in summer strikes the roof. If the attic space or rafter cavities are properly insulated and vented, heat build-up will not be a problem. Failure to take either into account will cause heat transmission from the roof area into the building, which decreases comfort while increasing air conditioning (energy) loads.

Buildings oriented with length running north to south expose smaller end walls to the sun (reducing the potential winter solar collection area) while exposing major wall surfaces to the east and west summer sun

64 BASIC PRINCIPLES OF SOLAR CONSTRUCTION

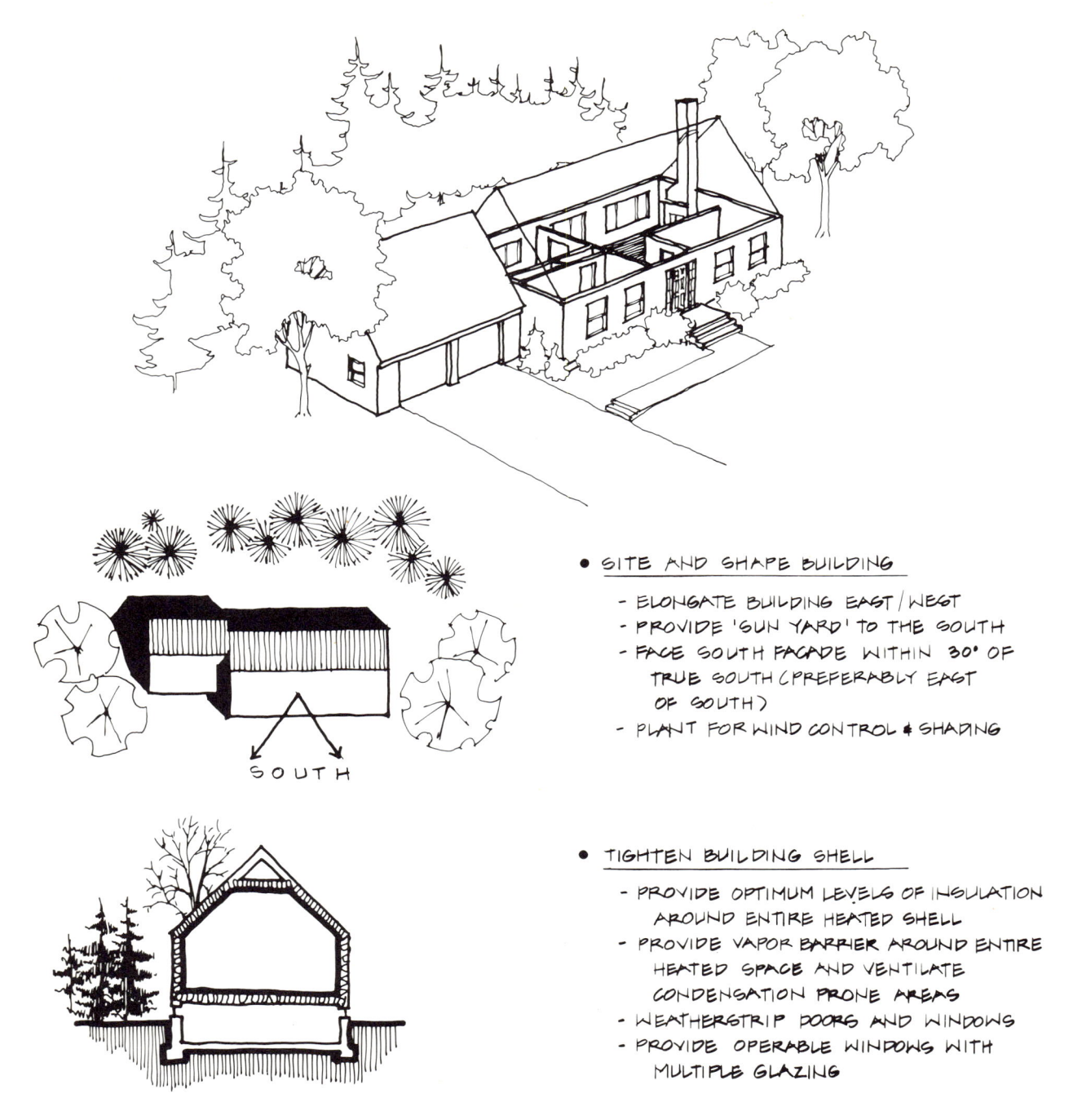

- SITE AND SHAPE BUILDING
    - ELONGATE BUILDING EAST/WEST
    - PROVIDE 'SUN YARD' TO THE SOUTH
    - FACE SOUTH FACADE WITHIN 30° OF TRUE SOUTH (PREFERABLY EAST OF SOUTH)
    - PLANT FOR WIND CONTROL & SHADING

- TIGHTEN BUILDING SHELL
    - PROVIDE OPTIMUM LEVELS OF INSULATION AROUND ENTIRE HEATED SHELL
    - PROVIDE VAPOR BARRIER AROUND ENTIRE HEATED SPACE AND VENTILATE CONDENSATION PRONE AREAS
    - WEATHERSTRIP DOORS AND WINDOWS
    - PROVIDE OPERABLE WINDOWS WITH MULTIPLE GLAZING

Fig. 5.5 The First Step A tight building shell sited to minimize heat loss in cold weather and maximize cooling in hot weather.

(raising chances for overheating). In northern latitudes (40°N+) with a harsh winter climate, a south facing vertical wall receives twice as much radiation in winter as in summer, while the east and west receive two and one-half times more radiation in summer than in winter. In more southerly latitudes (35°N) a south facing vertical wall will receive an even higher ratio of radiation between winter and summer than in the north and the east and west walls of a building receive two to three times more solar radiation than the south wall in summer.

This is the advantage of the rectangular shape. The exposure of the long wall to the winter sun is accomplished by running the length of the building east to west. This may be difficult due to lot dimensions, zoning restrictions, and orientation to roads. However, there is usually adequate leeway to allow builders to site the home to optimize all these criteria.

Although it is usually best to orient solar buildings towards true south, a 30° variance east or west will reduce solar gain by only 10 percent on a vertical wall (Fig. 5.3). Microclimate factors must be considered in determining building orientation (see Chapter 4). Shading and sky conditions influence orientation: For example, a building on a site that often experiences early morning fog which clears by late morning would perform better (from a solar gain standpoint) if oriented a bit west of true south, thus taking advantage of solar radiation available later in the day. The building on a site that experiences late afternoon shading in winter from other buildings, trees, or hilltops may perform better if oriented somewhat east of true south, to take advantage of the sun earlier in the morning.

The 60 degree leeway in acceptable orientation becomes very important when determining site feasibility for solar options on existing buildings. The leeway is less than 30° for solar water heaters, as discussed in Chapter 6. Builders and planners usually orient buildings for access to view, privacy, and roads. Many alternatives are available to developers; subdivisions can be laid out to offer each building access to the sun and other elements of site microclimate without risking market value. To the contrary, as discussed in Chapter 4, these features enhance property value in the increasingly energy conscious housing market. Subdivision layouts can plan roads to run east/west, allowing builders to orient towards the road and gain optimum solar exposure (Fig. 5.4). Building lots easily can be arranged on east/west roads to eliminate shade cast from one lot to the next.

If roads must run predominantly north/south, siting for proper solar orientation is more difficult. Two simple ways to optimize building orientation in these situations are to combine lots and to use "flag lots." These involve redesigning the shape of the lot to simplify access to the road and guarantee enough space to the south of the building to prevent shading. Both options must be considered in relation to local zoning restrictions (some towns encourage solar siting) and market response.

The easiest option of all, however, is to orient the *building* for solar gain regardless of lot orientation. Modest changes in building design can maintain an attractive, easy orientation to the road while presenting the most effective building shape towards the sun. Theoretically, the best orientation for a rectangular building is with its long sides perpendicular to the true south axis, which is not the same as compass south. The compass defines magnetic readings, which in most locations vary substantially from true orientations. Determining the magnetic deviation for a site is discussed in more detail in Chapter 8.

The site planning phase of construction, from large tract developments to custom homes, is critical to the energy efficiency of each building. Careful siting, for energy conservation and solar heat collection, can be the most cost effective measure taken on any project (Fig. 5.5).

SUNTEMPERING

After a building has been positioned on the site to receive solar radiation in winter, there are many ways to capture and utilize that radiation. In properly oriented buildings solar energy contributes to the annual heating load by entering the building directly through windows and warming the interior surfaces. This approach to solar heating, often called suntempering, is the simplest form of solar application for space heating (Fig. 5.6). However, to ensure occupant comfort, suntempering also requires careful planning for:

- building shape and orientation
- adjustment of floor plans
- careful sizing and placement of glazings with consideration for shading and reducing heat loss.

Room Layout

An important change in solar construction, especially suntempering applications, is the redesign of floor plans. Room layout should consider daily usage patterns; for example, rooms used during the day should be located on the south side to benefit from the direct heat. These include living room, family room, and dining room. Kitchens usually are best placed on the north and east sides for two reasons: (1) the kitchen appliances will contribute to heating the space; and (2) eastern morning sun is very pleasant to kitchen and breakfast areas. Because bedrooms are primarily used at night, they can benefit from natural circulation of heat into them during the day so that they are comfortable when required. Bedrooms located on the south can also be allowed to overheat somewhat during the day, when not in use, so that warmth remains into the night. Entryways should be sheltered from the winter winds, as discussed in Chapter 2, while room and window placement should provide for cross ventilation whenever possible.

66 BASIC PRINCIPLES OF SOLAR CONSTRUCTION

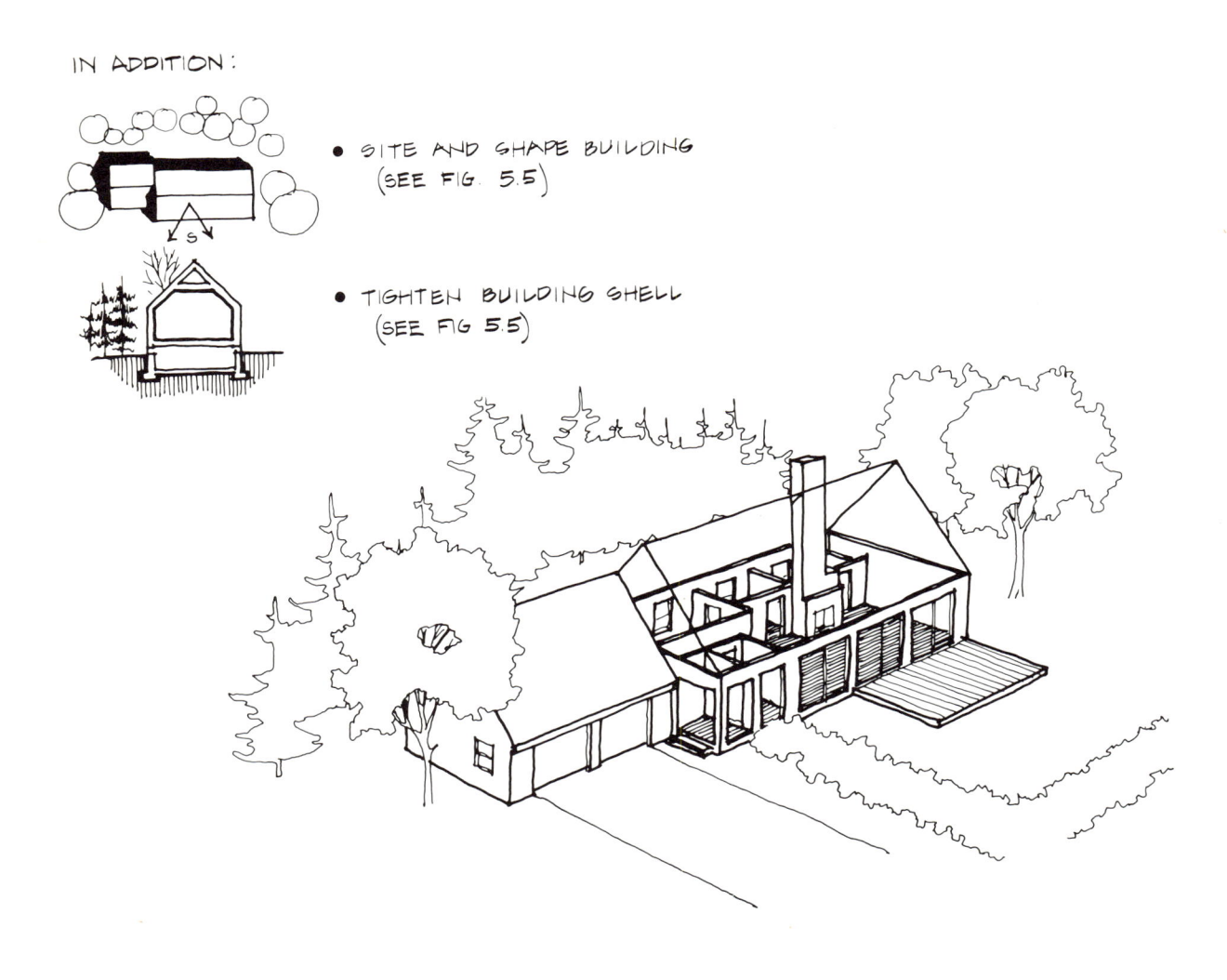

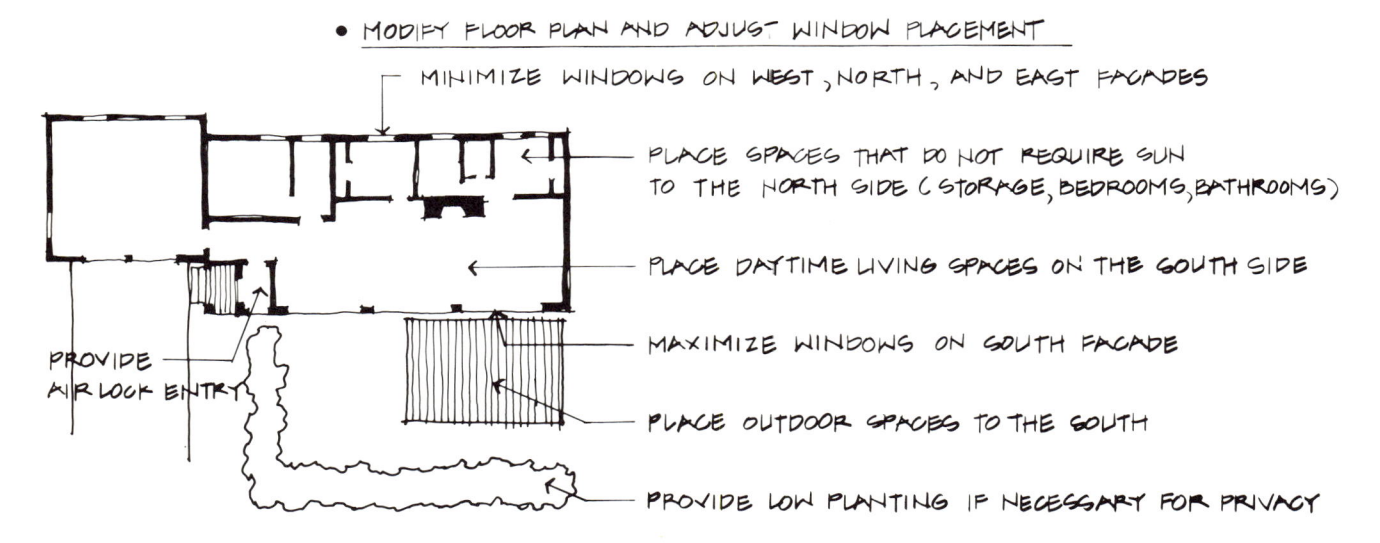

IN ADDITION:

- SITE AND SHAPE BUILDING (SEE FIG. 5.5)

- TIGHTEN BUILDING SHELL (SEE FIG 5.5)

- <u>MODIFY FLOOR PLAN AND ADJUST WINDOW PLACEMENT</u>
  - MINIMIZE WINDOWS ON WEST, NORTH, AND EAST FACADES
  - PLACE SPACES THAT DO NOT REQUIRE SUN TO THE NORTH SIDE (STORAGE, BEDROOMS, BATHROOMS)
  - PLACE DAYTIME LIVING SPACES ON THE SOUTH SIDE
  - MAXIMIZE WINDOWS ON SOUTH FACADE
  - PLACE OUTDOOR SPACES TO THE SOUTH
  - PROVIDE LOW PLANTING IF NECESSARY FOR PRIVACY
  - PROVIDE AIRLOCK ENTRY

Fig. 5.6 Basic suntempering and floor plan modifications

Window Placement

Another important change involves the placement and sizing of glazed areas, which will affect both solar heat gained and total heat lost. This requires relocation of windows to maximize exposures that contribute to winter heating (south, southeast, southwest), and to minimize window area on walls that contribute most to winter heat loss (north) or summer overheating (east, west). Graph 5.1 illustrates window performance in relation to solar gain for different orientations.

Window distribution for a typical house plan shows 50 percent located on the front, 10 percent on end walls, and 30 percent on the back (Fig. 5.7). If this house were oriented with the front elevation facing within 30 degrees east or west of true south, there would be significant solar heat gained through southerly exposed windows, but there would also be a large amount of heat lost through the northern windows. Changing the distribution of the same windows increases the amount of solar heat gained through the larger southern glazed area and reduces heat loss through the smaller northern windows. East and west end windows are increased enough to allow for daylight and good cross ventilation, but not enough to cause summer overheating.

Windows, fixed glazed units, and sliding patio doors are three common building components used to admit solar energy directly into the building (Fig. 5.8). Selection and placement of glazed areas must consider view to the outside, ventilation, and possible egress from the building. If window orientation on an otherwise conventional building is to be changed, the glazed portion of the southern wall should be limited to a maximum of 25 percent of floor area. It is quite possible for rooms on the southern side of the house to gain more solar heat than they need or can store, causing temperatures to rise beyond the comfort range. Overheating can occur even on very cold days with bright sunshine, especially if snow is in a position to reflect more radiation into the building. At night, the temperature drops quickly due to heat loss through the larger southern glazings. This drop begins as soon as the sun is shaded from the windows. This can create an uncomfortable

Graph 5.1
Comparison of window orientations

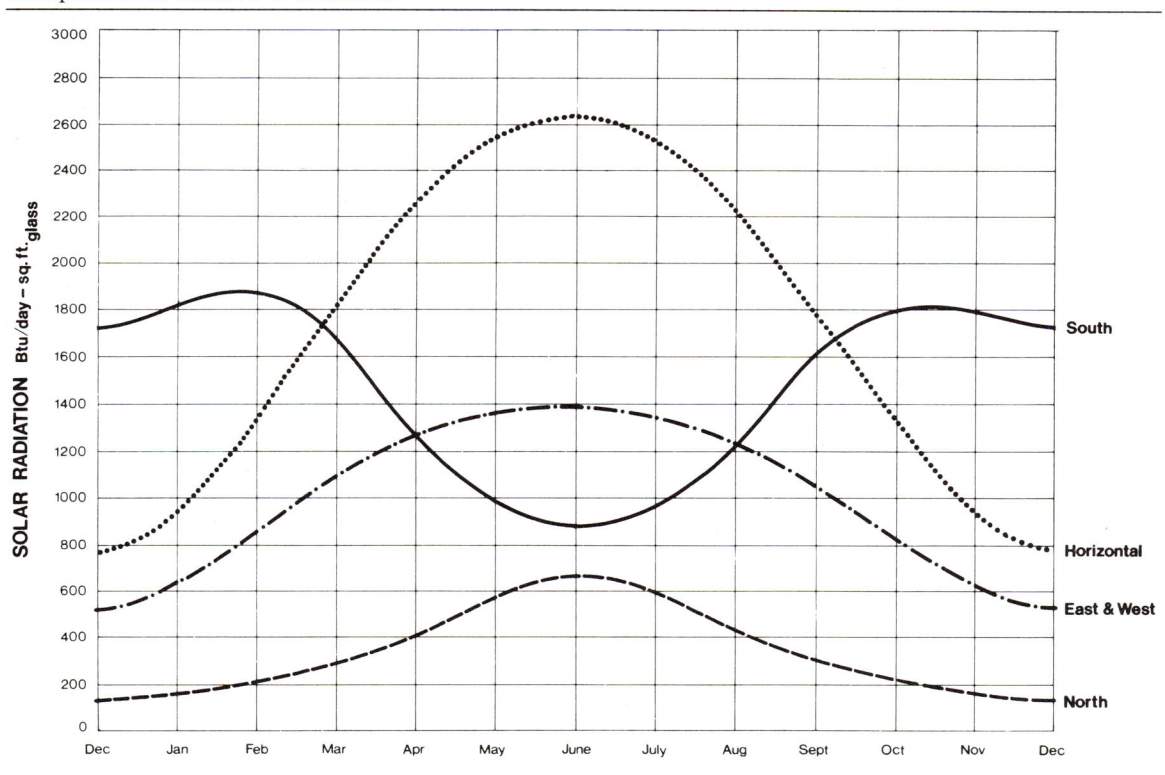

Note: This graph represents clear-day solar radiation values, on the surfaces indicated, for 40°NL.

68   BASIC PRINCIPLES OF SOLAR CONSTRUCTION

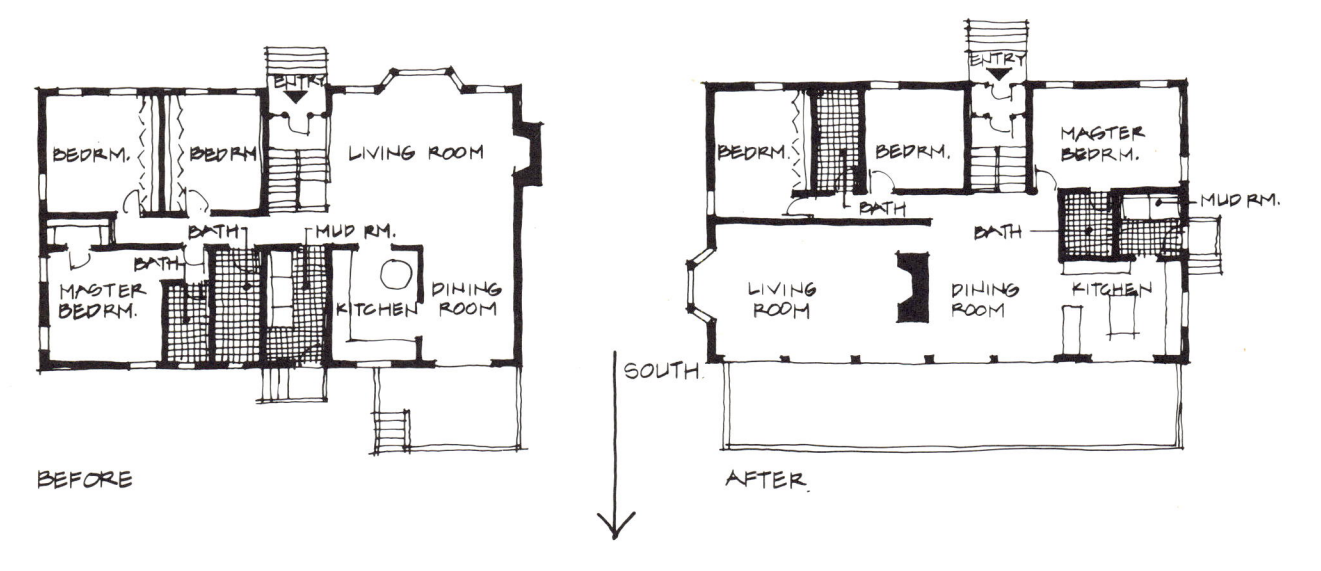

Fig. 5.7 Relocation of windows for suntempering

Fig. 5.8 A suntempered house is often characterized by a moderate amount of south glass, simple overhangs and proper orientation.

situation where the temperature rapidly declines as much as 30°F (80 to 50°F) from daily high to low, and back the next day. Builders should use restraint in sizing glazed areas for solar collection. Approaches that utilize large glazed areas are discussed later in this chapter.

Increasing the glazed area in the south wall allows additional solar gain; it also increases the total heat load of the building, due to considerable nighttime loss through windows. There are many solutions to this problem. As discussed in Chapter 2, multiple glazing is the first step to reducing heat loss. Multiple glazing can take many forms: single glazed window with storm sash or insert panels, hermetically sealed insulating glass units (fixed or sliding), or site assembled glazing components. Chapter 10 details materials and techniques used for installing glazings properly. A poorly installed window will lose as much heat from infiltration as it allows into the building from the sun. Builders should study the thermal details of different windows when selecting units for use in solar construction.

Use of heavy drapes over enlarged glazed areas also reduces nighttime heat loss. If drapes are drawn as soon as the sun sets, heat loss from a window can be reduced. A more effective and more costly approach is the use of insulating drapes, curtains and/or shutters. These products are designed specifically to reduce heat loss through glazed areas (Fig. 5.9). (The use of window insulation is discussed in Chapter 12.) Many new products for controlling the transmission of solar and thermal radiation through glass are under development. However, their questionable availability at present limits their application for residential construction.

PASSIVE SOLAR HEATING AND COOLING

TRIPLE OR QUADRUPLE GLAZING

INSULATING DRAPES – INTERIOR

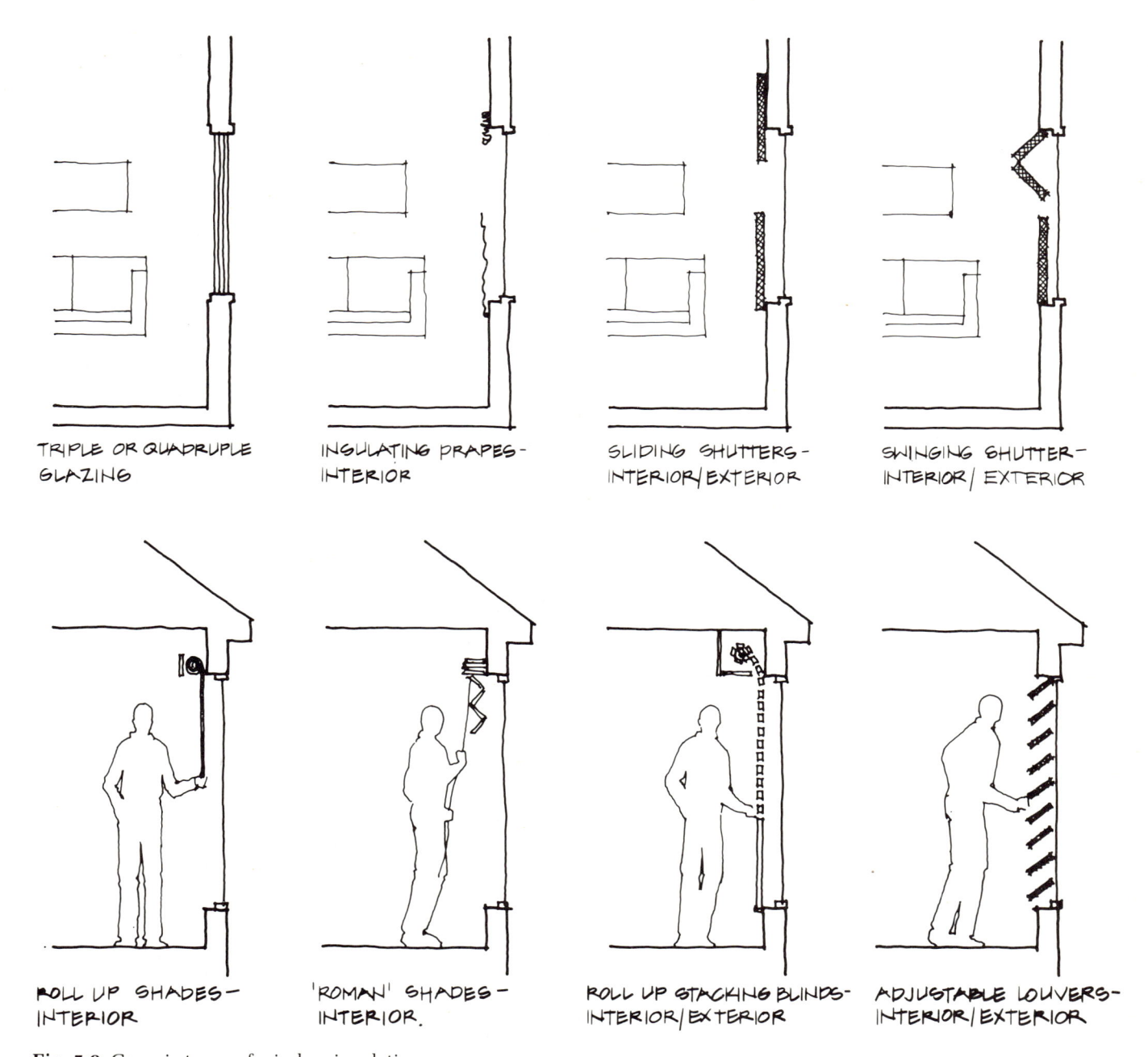

SLIDING SHUTTERS – INTERIOR/EXTERIOR

SWINGING SHUTTER – INTERIOR/EXTERIOR

ROLL UP SHADES – INTERIOR

'ROMAN' SHADES – INTERIOR.

ROLL UP STACKING BLINDS – INTERIOR/EXTERIOR

ADJUSTABLE LOUVERS – INTERIOR/EXTERIOR

Fig. 5.9 Generic types of window insulation

Two other considerations for increased south glazing are the increased potential for glare and for ultraviolet degradation of materials and finishes. Careful spacing of glass units with the use of light colored surfaces to reflect light can avoid glare problems. Increased direct gain also can accelerate aging of materials and finishes. Solar radiation may fade natural upholstery, cause discoloring and cracking of plastics, and cloud wood finishes. Building design for increased direct gain must consider the increased levels of ultraviolet admitted and protect any vulnerable materials and finishes from degradation (see Chapter 12).

Window Shading

One of the most important components of the suntempering approach is the integration of shading features (Fig. 5.10). Increased glazing areas also mean increased

70 BASIC PRINCIPLES OF SOLAR CONSTRUCTION

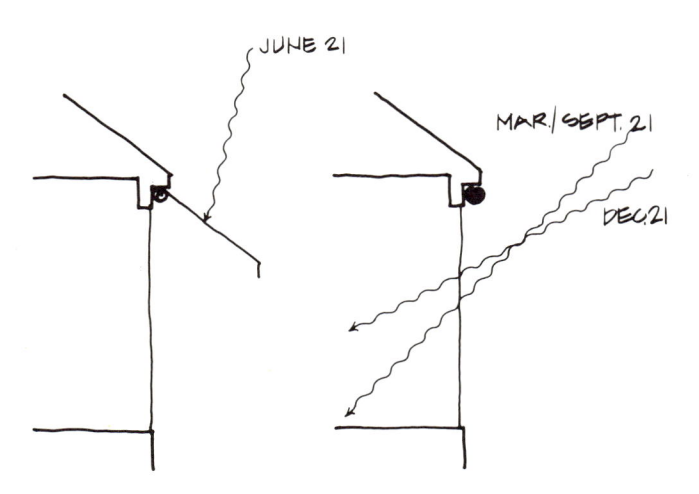

AWNINGS OR EXTERIOR SHADES
ON EAST, WEST & SOUTH WINDOWS

- REMOVE FOR BEST WINTER SOLAR GAIN
- REQUIRES SEASONAL MAINTENANCE

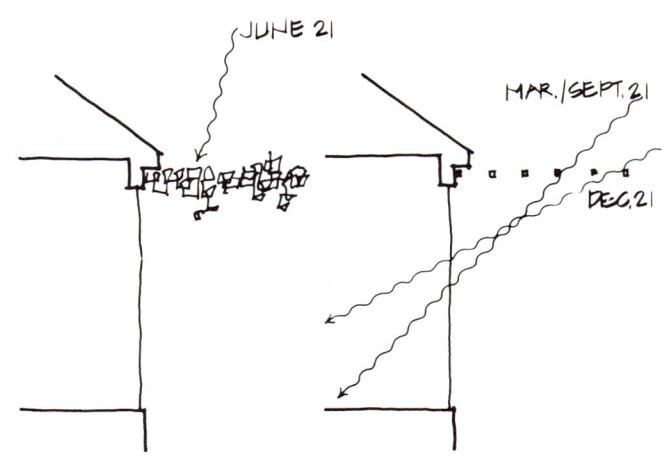

TRELLISES
ON EAST, WEST & SOUTH WINDOWS

- REQUIRE PRUNING
- ALTHOUGH LEAVES FALL IN WINTER, FRAME & BRANCHES CAST SOME SHADOW

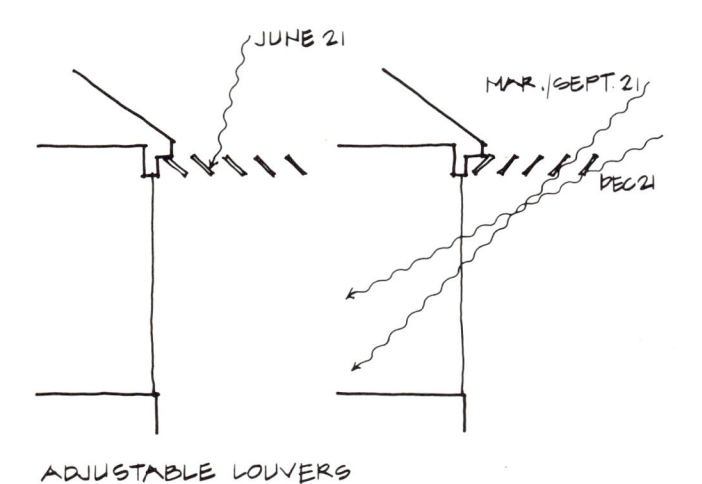

ADJUSTABLE LOUVERS
ON SOUTH

- REQUIRE SEASONAL ADJUSTMENT
- CAST SOME SHADOW IN WINTER

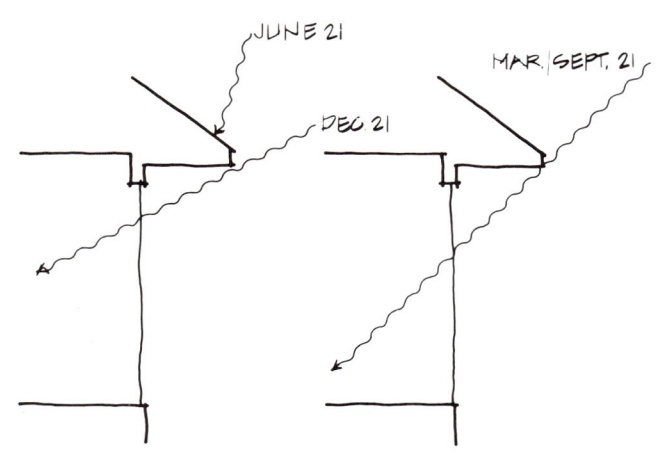

FIXED OVERHANGS
ON SOUTH

- REQUIRE NO MAINTENANCE OR ADJUSTMENT
- WORK WELL IN EARLY WINTER AND EARLY SUMMER BUT COMPROMISE OTHER SEASONS TO VARYING DEGREES

Fig. 5.10 Options for window shading

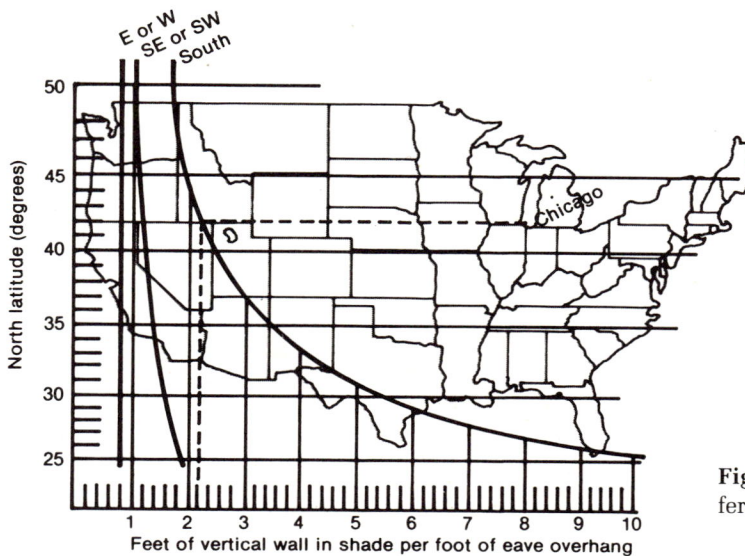

Example: Chicago is very near the 42 degree latitude line. Coming straight across the graph to the heavy curved lines, it may be seen that for each foot of overhang on the south side, about 2.2 feet of vertical wall will be in shade. Similarly for walls facing southeast or southwest, about 1.2 feet of vertical shade corresponds to a one foot overhang. Note that east and west walls have a constant 0.8 feet of shade per foot of overhang regardless of latitude.

Fig. 5.11 Recommendations for sizing fixed overhangs for different latitudes

heat gain in summer, when it is not desirable. The simplest means of rejecting this unwanted heat combines siting with shading devices which block solar radiation and keep it from penetrating through windows. Built-in shading often takes the form of fixed overhangs. While they usually are architecturally integrated, which may be desirable, their limitation lies in the fact that a fixed overhang allows the same amount of solar transmission in September as in March, because the sun angle is the same for spring and fall. This is a problem because a building has different heating requirements in September, when solar gain is undesirable, than in March, when the solar energy is welcome. Figure 5.11 demonstrates shading with various overhang dimensions for different latitudes at different times of the year.

Awnings also can be used to reduce summer heat gain effectively. Awnings are especially useful on east and west end walls, which are areas of high heat gain in summer. Because the solar gain through east and west windows occurs in the morning and afternoon when the sun angle is low, it is difficult to create an overhang that works properly. An adjustable awning enables the occupants to admit sun to the building in March when it is needed, yet block it from entry in September when it is not, though the incident sun angle is the same.

Other options for shading include tinted glass, interior blinds, shutters, and curtains; however, shading outside the building is most effective. With interior shades, solar energy is transmitted through the glass and strikes the reflective surface. Much of the energy is reflected through the glass, but a significant amount is converted to heat and conducted through the material to add unwanted heat to the space. When the shading is accomplished outside the building, the heat never penetrates the space.

Sloped Versus Vertical Glazing

Windows, sliding glass doors, and fixed glazed areas must satisfy requirements of daylighting, ventilation, egress, view, and solar energy transmission. Properly designed glazed areas for direct solar gain require much more than simply increasing the square footage of glazing on the south elevation. If the glazed area is too large for the room, winter overheating occurs; if shading is insufficient for the area of glazing on east, south, and west elevations, summer and fall overheating occurs.

The types and configurations of southern glazings determine the effect of overheating and glare. Sloped glazed areas over living spaces encourage overheating problems. Because of the slope, it is difficult to incorporate overhang-type shading devices that would not also cause shade in winter, so an adjustable awning or interior shading device is required. This glazing configuration also accelerates winter heat loss, since the glazed area presents low resistance where highest resistance is required. Glare also can be a problem. Sloped glazings are best applied in situations where solar heat gain will be isolated from living space (such as an attached greenhouse) and delivered as needed, and where they will not contribute to the nighttime heat loss of the building.

The most practical configuration from the standpoint of shading, heat loss, weather resistance, and solar transmission in winter is the installation of glazings in a vertical position. Windows and sliding glass doors mounted vertically allow the builder to increase glazed area on the south and properly shade it without drastically changing the overall architectural appearance of a building. Additionally, vertical glazing will receive solar gain reflected off the snow during winter months (Fig. 5.12).

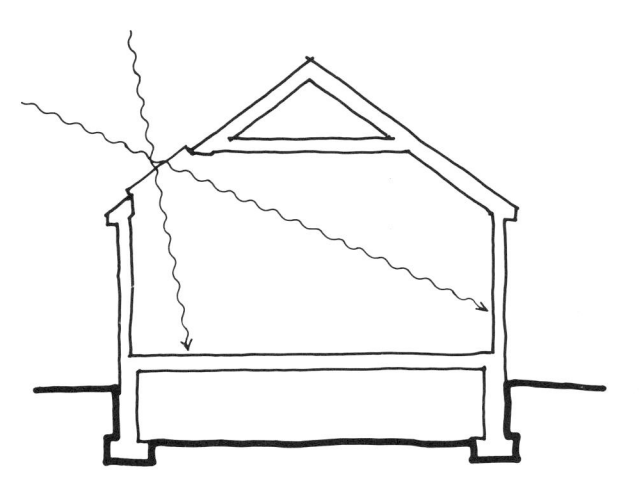

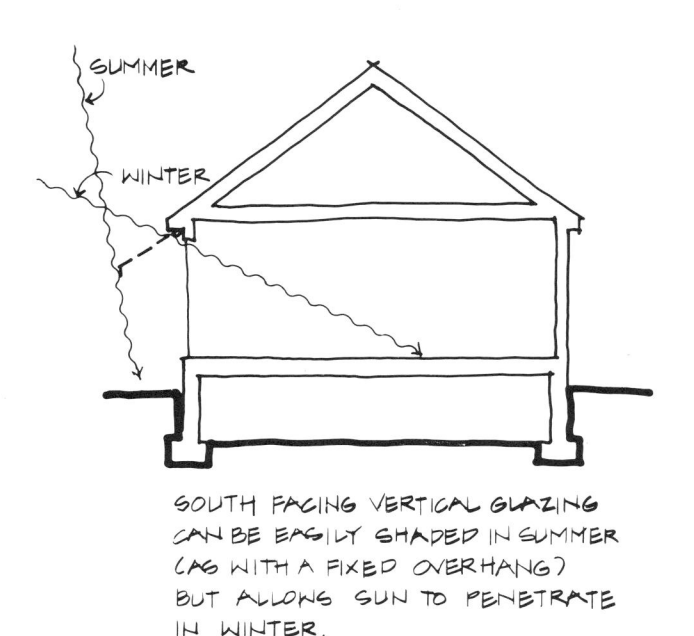

Temperature Swings

One problem with early solar buildings has been overheating due to an overglazed south wall. The large expanse of transmitting glass allows more solar radiation to enter the building than is required. Surfaces of floors, walls, ceilings, and furnishings (in typical light construction) absorb as much heat as they can and then heat the air at a rate that quickly brings its temperature past the comfort range. The solution usually has been the natural or forced ventilation of excess heat from a room, which results in a very inefficient use of solar heat gain.

This same area of glass allows for accelerated heat loss, resulting in wide temperature swings within the building. Often the nighttime low may be 30°F lower than the daytime high, and this temperature swing is unacceptable to most homeowners. A more acceptable range of temperatures would be 60 to 75 °F depending on the relative humidity inside the building (see Chapter 2).

There are two solutions to the problem of wide temperature swings. One is to reduce the size of glazed areas, which reduces the amount of solar radiation admitted into the building as well as the amount of heat loss. This tends to stabilize the temperature swing in a well insulated house, keeping it more within the comfort range. The solar gain is moderate to avoid overheat-

Fig. 5.12 Considerations for using sloped or vertical glazing over living spaces

Fig. 5.13 The heat retaining capabilities of masonry and stone have been known and used by people throughout history.

Table 5.1
Thermal storage material properties

Material	Conductivity (k) Btu hr/ft²-°F/ft	Specific heat (Cp) Btu/lb-°F	Density (^{4}) lb/ft
Concrete (dense)	1.00	0.20	140.0
Brick (common)	0.42	0.20	120.0
Brick (magnesium) additive)	2.20	0.20	120.0
Adobe	0.30	0.24	106.0

ing, and the annual solar contribution to space heating may be 15 to 20 percent.

The other solution involves the storage of excess heat generated during the day, and its reradiation at night. Storage of excess heat lowers the daytime high, and reradiation at night slows cooling. As introduced in Chapter 2, some materials can absorb and retain more heat than others; these materials are said to have more thermal mass (storage capacity). Table 5.1 compares common building materials and their ability to store heat (thermal mass). It is important to understand that the use of thermal mass is not a new concept developed recently in solar heated buildings. The tempering effects of massive materials have been put to use in shelters throughout history (Fig. 5.13).

THERMAL MASS

By including materials with high heat storage capacity, such as concrete slab and tile floors, gypsum walls, and stone or brick chimneys built within the insulated shell, the heat storage capacity of the entire building increases. With this increased mass, heat energy from any source will be absorbed, stored, and reradiated to the building, smoothing temperature swings and utilizing the energy more efficiently by retaining it inside the building longer. The thermal storage characteristics of building materials can be used to store and reradiate heat generated by solar gain. While thermal mass functions in many locations in the building, it functions best as solar storage when the radiation strikes its surfaces directly or reflects off light colored surfaces (Fig. 5.14).

Increased amounts of mass are more costly than lighter construction due to added materials and labor costs; therefore, the most practical materials to use are those that serve structural *and* thermal functions. (Where another approach is required, mass materials used strictly for their storage/radiation qualities may be employed. In these instances, the cost of including storage materials should be closely related to the actual benefit they offer.) Mass configurations that serve dual purposes include concrete slab floor with masonry finish, chimney mass, foundation, and masonry bearing walls. Those that serve strictly a thermal function include water walls and masonry partitions (Fig. 5.15).

Concrete Slab Storage

One of the most common forms of thermal mass is a concrete slab floor with a masonry finish. This approach is often used in direct gain buildings with southerly glazed areas over 25 percent of the floor area. Solar energy enters the building through the large glazed area and strikes the floor. Heat is stored in the finish surface and insulated slab until the slab becomes warmer than the adjacent air, when heat begins to radiate to the space. There is usually a time lag between the initial absorption of solar radiation and its reradiation. The period of lag depends upon the type of material, its thickness and density, its temperature, the air temperature, the amount of solar radiation striking it, and its surface color.

Concrete slabs used for heat storage must be well insulated underneath and along their perimeters, with an insulating material suitable for below grade application (see Chapters 2 and 8). Concrete slabs used for thermal storage are often thicker than typical slab floors, ranging from 4 to 8 inches. Storage of absorbed solar heat is accomplished through conduction of energy from the hot collecting surface to cooler depths of the material, so it is important for a slab floor to be in excellent thermal contact with the finish surface above it. Masonry tiles, floor slates, and paving bricks are common finishes on slab floors. The connection between the two surfaces must conduct heat from the top layer into the concrete. Masonry mortar will conduct heat at this point, and is better than most materials used for this purpose. For example, mastic adhesive applications actually insulate the hot finish surface from the cooler slab. This reduces the actual amount of mass (storage) available to solar gain and contributes to overheating problems. Floor tiles or brick alone do not add significant mass for large solar gain.

The portion of a masonry floor that receives winter radiation should be free of furnishings and rugs to present a large area of storage material for solar gain. Because the transfer of heat from storage to the space is radiative, furnishings and rugs will block its movement and create problems with heat distribution. Slab storage is especially suited for slab-on-grade construction (Fig. 5.16).

74 BASIC PRINCIPLES OF SOLAR CONSTRUCTION

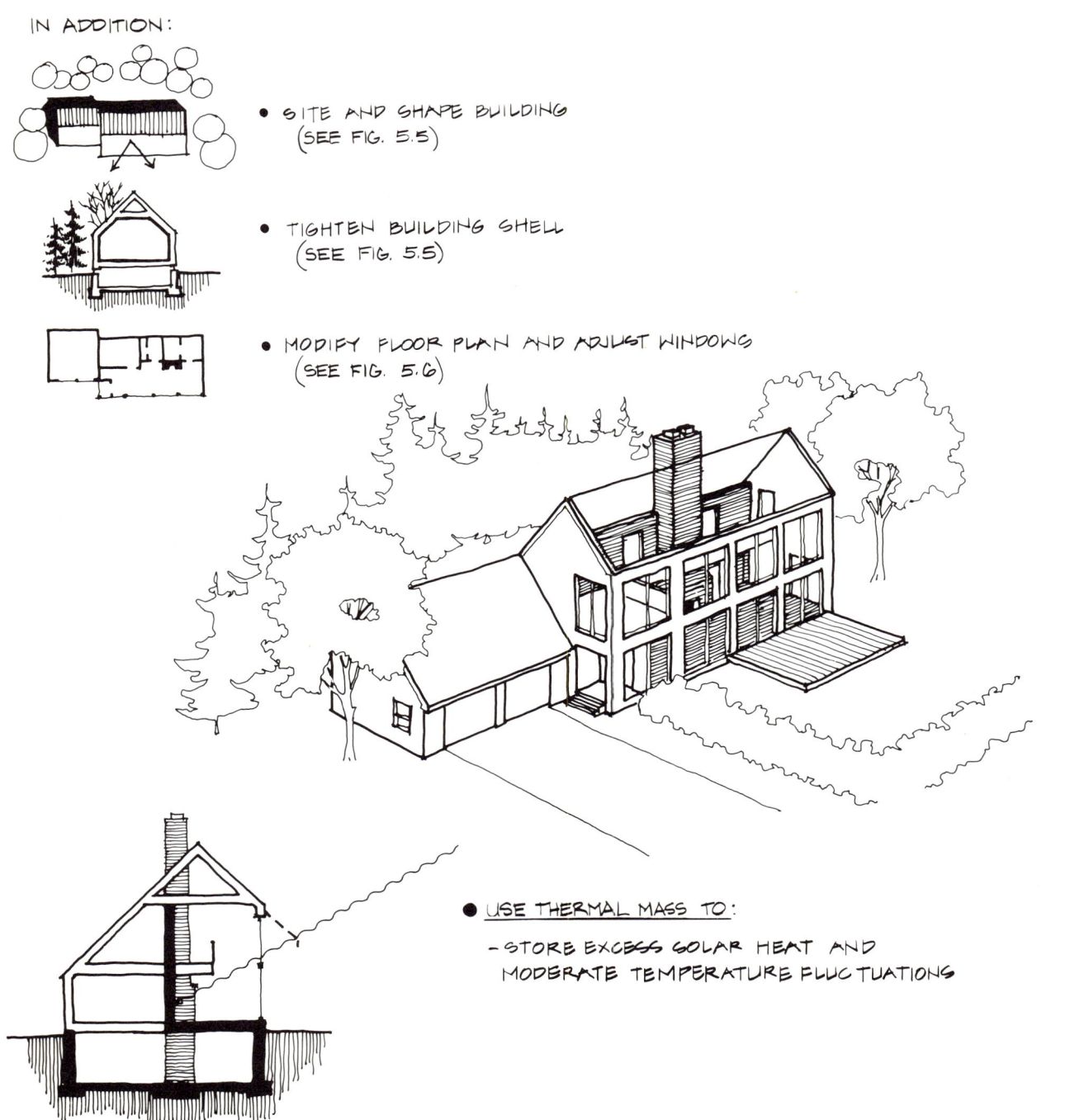

IN ADDITION:

- SITE AND SHAPE BUILDING (SEE FIG. 5.5)

- TIGHTEN BUILDING SHELL (SEE FIG. 5.5)

- MODIFY FLOOR PLAN AND ADJUST WINDOWS (SEE FIG. 5.6)

- USE THERMAL MASS TO:
  - STORE EXCESS SOLAR HEAT AND MODERATE TEMPERATURE FLUCTUATIONS

Fig. 5.14 The use of thermal mass

Internal Mass

Another way to introduce thermal mass for solar heat storage is by locating a masonry fireplace and chimney where it will receive direct or reflected radiation.

Most brick, stone, or block chimneys have considerable heat storage and delivery capacities, especially if exposed to sufficient solar radiation and air circulation, but may permit more storage by enlarging the overall dimensions beyond the minimum required for the num-

PASSIVE SOLAR HEATING AND COOLING 75

- FOUNDATION WALLS AND SLAB ON GRADE

- INTERIOR CHIMNEYS

- INTERIOR MASONRY WALLS, BEARING OR VENEER

- ELEVATED SLABS

- THERMAL STORAGE WALLS

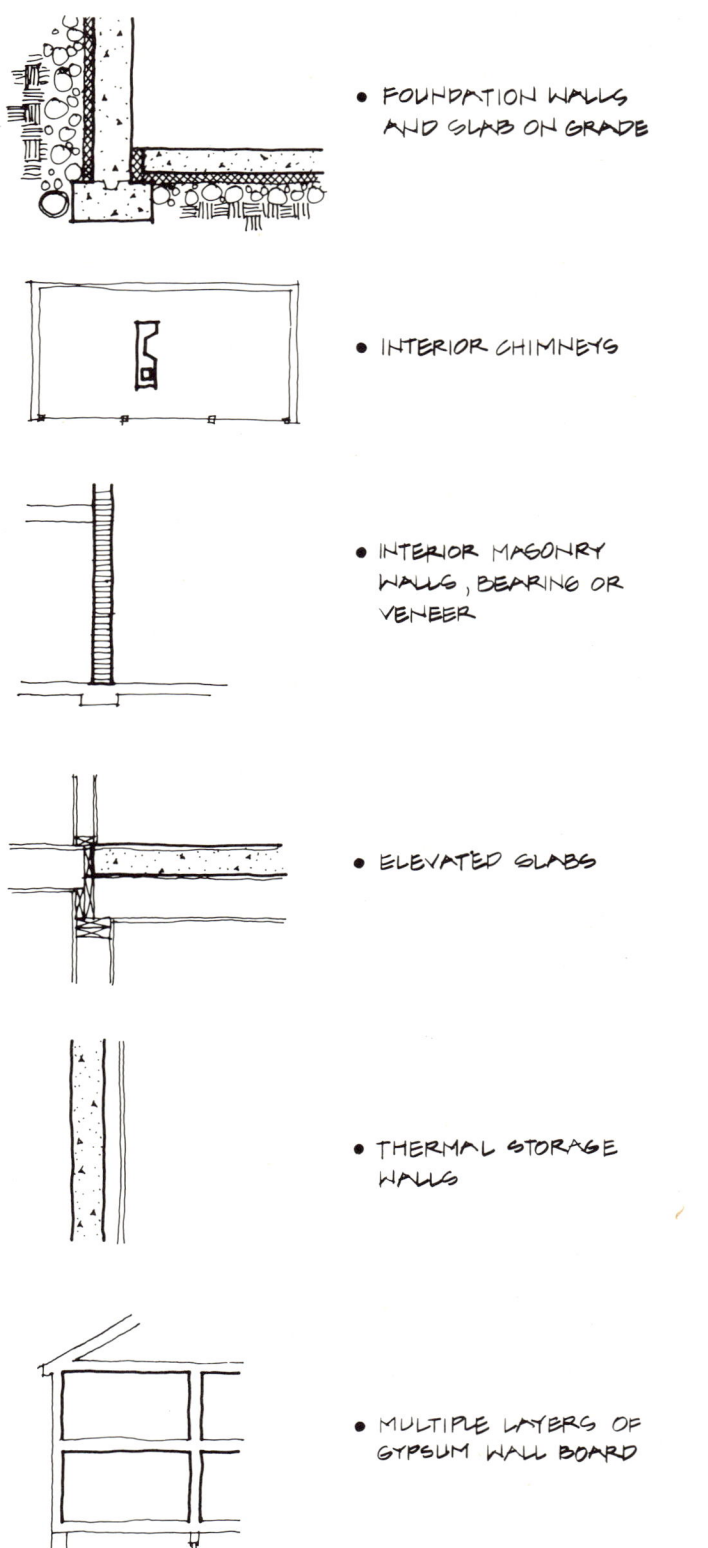

- MULTIPLE LAYERS OF GYPSUM WALL BOARD

Fig. 5.15 Common thermal mass configurations

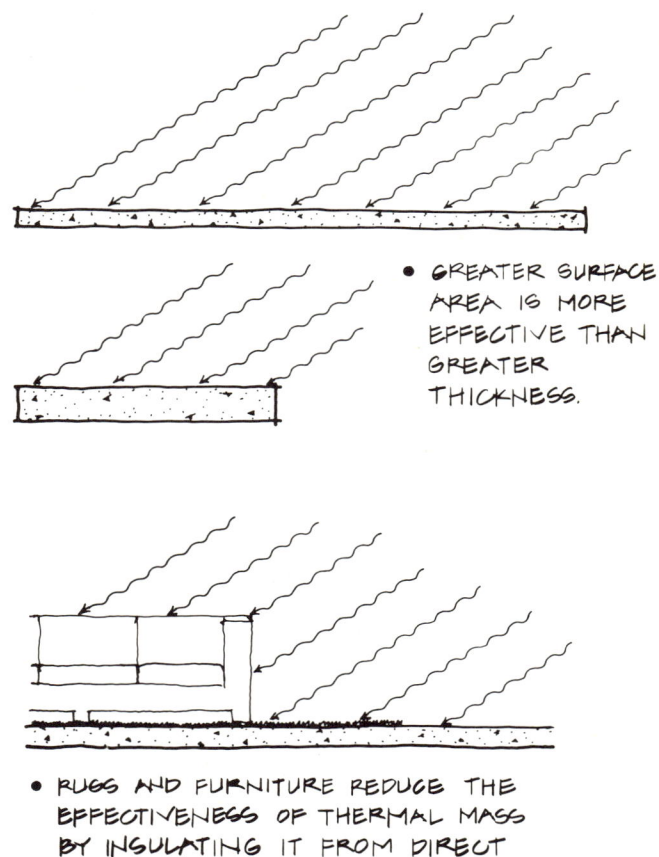

- GREATER SURFACE AREA IS MORE EFFECTIVE THAN GREATER THICKNESS.

- RUGS AND FURNITURE REDUCE THE EFFECTIVENESS OF THERMAL MASS BY INSULATING IT FROM DIRECT SUNLIGHT.

Fig. 5.16 Considerations when using concrete slab floors for thermal storage

ber of flues within the chimney. A portion of the chimney mass can act as an interior partition exposed to solar radiation, or may be an enlargement of a central core that absorbs heat by indirect radiation and convection.

Masonry (closed) wood stoves, such as the Russian fireplace, rely on a greatly increased amount of masonry material. Increasing the area and volume of mass enlarges the surface area that absorbs excess heat, conducts it to deeper storage, and then radiates it to the room as it is needed.

The use of chimney mass as storage and radiant heat delivery requires that the mass is exposed directly to the heated space, rather than running it through an enclosed chase or closet. If the material used in a masonry chimney or wall is undesirable as an interior finish, it can be treated directly with a masonry stucco or trowelled surface, and then dyed or painted, without interrupting its thermal functions (Fig. 5.17).

76   BASIC PRINCIPLES OF SOLAR CONSTRUCTION

- LOCATING CHIMNEYS ON EXTERIOR WALLS HAS DISADVANTAGES:
  - MASONRY NOT AVAILABLE AS THERMAL MASS FOR THE SPACE
  - MASONRY FORMS A THERMAL 'SHORT CIRCUIT' THROUGH THE WALL

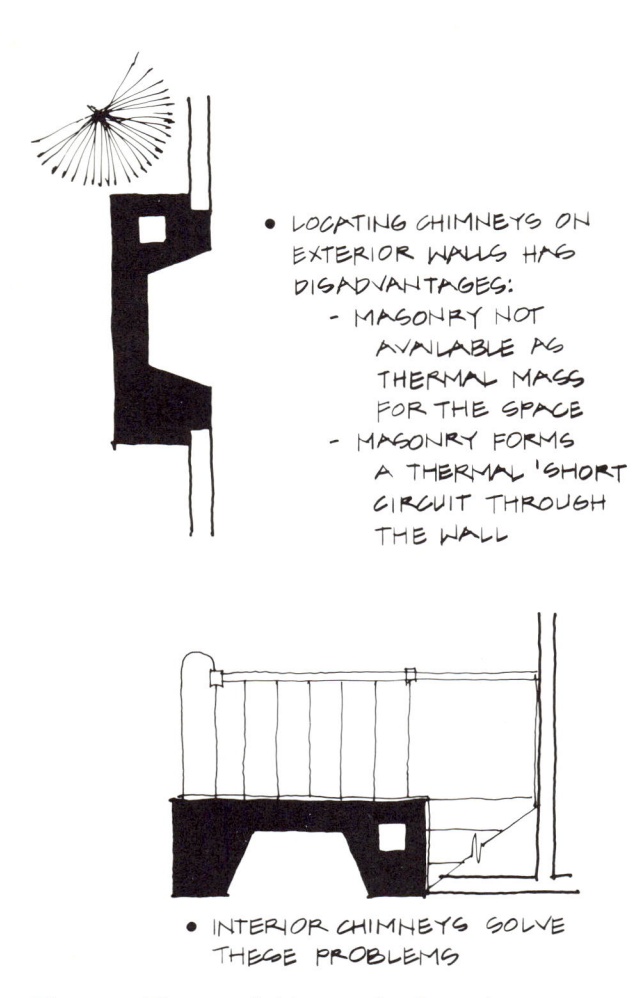

- INTERIOR CHIMNEYS SOLVE THESE PROBLEMS

Fig. 5.17 The use of chimneys for thermal mass

Fig. 5.18 Foundation walls and masonry partitions are commonly used as thermal mass in solar homes. They can be attractively finished with plaster as shown in this photo.

Foundation walls also serve as practical thermal storage components. They should be treated with a good sealant, well insulated outside with a material suitable for use below grade, and backfilled with coarse, well drained material (see Chapter 8).

Many passive solar homes utilize the basement as finished and conditioned living space, thus combining direct solar gain with storage in the slab floor and concrete bearing walls (Fig. 5.18). While poured concrete offers structural, water resisting, and thermal advantages, designers and builders also use concrete block walls in which the blocks are "cored" with cement.

In order to use this large area of storage more effectively, the surfaces close to glazings should be light in color. This will bounce the radiation deeper into the building, giving it a chance to be absorbed by the walls in a more even pattern. Heat also will be transferred into storage by natural convective air movement, but this is less efficient and will not protect areas from overheating. The mechanical movement of air is more effective for removing excess heat, but it is expensive to install and operate.

Adobe walls function similarly to concrete, and in the Southwest, where they are commonly used, they help protect buildings from the summer heat. The mass both absorbs excess heat and presents a cool surface that encourages radiative heat loss from the occupants' bodies. Poured concrete, cement block, and adobe walls also can be finished with a masonry parge, either stucco or smooth. The thermal use of foundation walls requires as direct contact between the wall material and room air as possible. This calls for the use of exterior insulation and interior finishes applied directly to the masonry. Typical foundation finishes of interior insulation, fur-

PASSIVE SOLAR HEATING AND COOLING 77

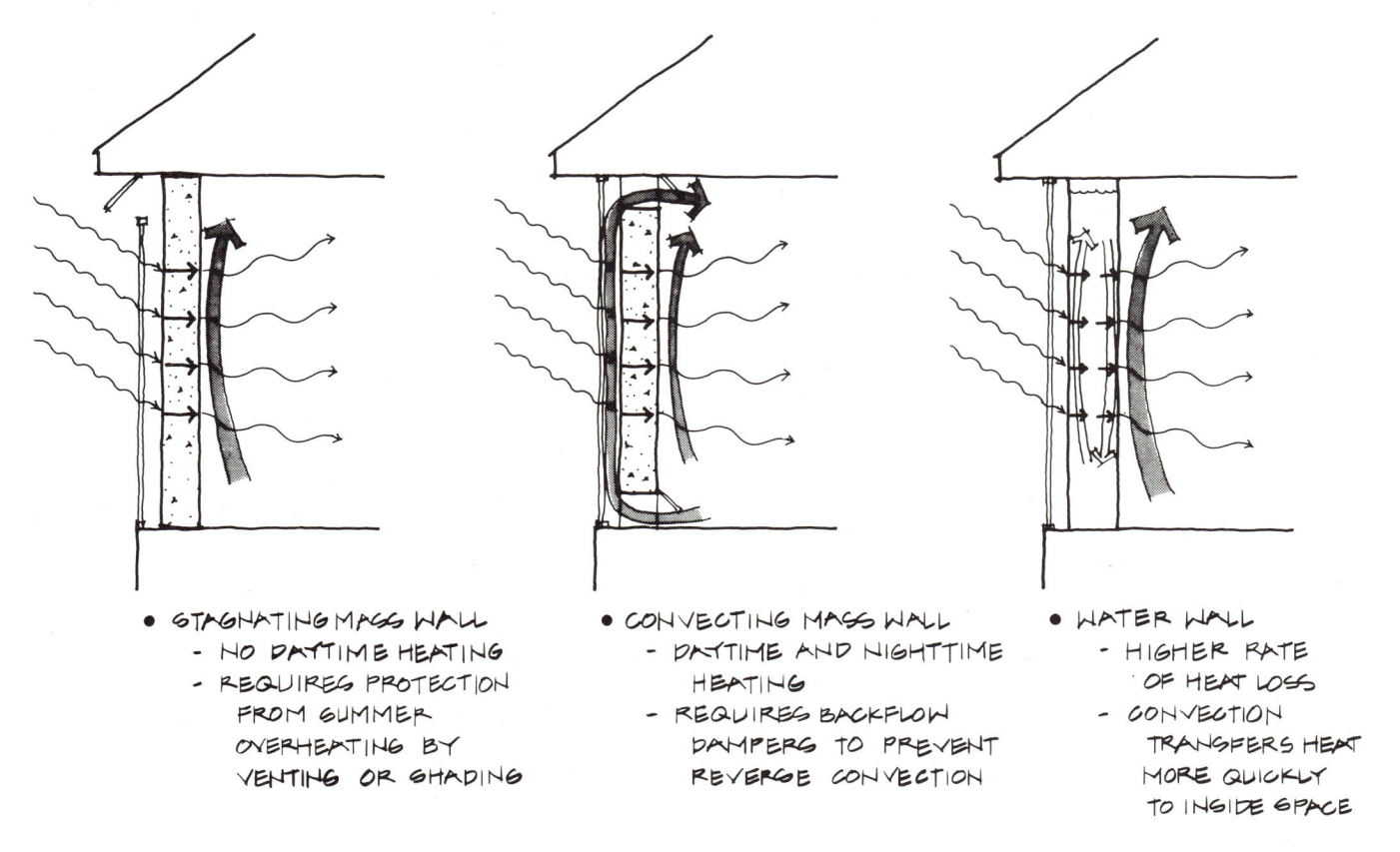

- **STAGNATING MASS WALL**
  - NO DAYTIME HEATING
  - REQUIRES PROTECTION FROM SUMMER OVERHEATING BY VENTING OR SHADING

- **CONVECTING MASS WALL**
  - DAYTIME AND NIGHTTIME HEATING
  - REQUIRES BACKFLOW DAMPERS TO PREVENT REVERSE CONVECTION

- **WATER WALL**
  - HIGHER RATE OF HEAT LOSS
  - CONVECTION TRANSFERS HEAT MORE QUICKLY TO INSIDE SPACE

Fig. 5.19 Thermal Storage Walls When the thermal mass is positioned directly behind the glass, the combination is called a thermal storage wall. Its heating effectiveness relies on the conductive rate and thickness of the wall to produce the correct "time lag" that will deliver heat to the space during the night when the heat is most needed.

ring strips and wood, sheetrock, or paneling will isolate (and insulate) the mass from the room.

Thermal Storage Walls—Concrete and Masonry

Where foundation walls are exposed above grade to the south, and therefore receive a large amount of direct radiation, they can be used as solar heat collectors. If a wall is finished with a dark colored surface outside (exposed to the sun), and covered with one or two layers of glazing, it will trap, absorb, and conduct solar heat through the wall and into the space directly behind it (Fig. 5.19). This configuration can include vents in the walls to promote convective heat transfer to the rooms.

Another similar use of southern foundation walls exposed above grade is the construction of an attached greenhouse or sunspace onto the wall. Solar radiation trapped in this area is conducted and/or vented into the building. Because the time lag between absorption and delivery to the space can be planned, the wall can store heat all day and radiate it into the space in the evening as the building starts to cool. The rate at which mass radiates heat into the night depends on its properties, the amount of solar radiation stored the previous day, and the rate of heat loss from the building at any given moment. This configuration is also used on other levels of the building's south elevation where the exterior wall is masonry.

Although mass walls work well when properly designed and constructed, they are best used in conjunction with south facing windows. Solar energy passing through the windows warms the building early in the day, and the mass wall will begin delivering its heat later. The next morning, the sunlight will warm the space directly as it also stores heat in the wall for later use.

Mass walls used as outside bearing walls on south elevations can be built with openings for windows and doors that admit light and heat energy through the wall. A glazing system, typically consisting of two layers, is

78 BASIC PRINCIPLES OF SOLAR CONSTRUCTION

(Dennis Davey, Inc.)

(Downing and Leach)

Fig. 5.20 Masonry veneers can be used to increase the thermal mass in light frame construction.

Fig. 5.21 Special building components, such as the water wall systems shown above, are available for heat storage.

fastened to the exterior of the solid wall. The glass traps the heat by creating a dead air space, thus reducing heat loss from the wall. Installation of heavy drapes or other nighttime insulation, which reduces heat loss through the glass, helps maximize the solar contribution of this approach. Outside masonry bearing walls not exposed to southern sun should be well insulated on the outside, and thermally exposed on the inside of the building.

Brick partitions and interior veneers also can increase mass in buildings. Solar heat storage occurs in the same manner as in slab floors and masonry exterior walls; however, these walls may not be serving as structural components. If the partitions or veneers are small, their heat storage capacity will be reduced. Do not rely on these forms for storage in areas with large solar gain; reduced mass and enlarged gain adds up to overheating.

Some interior mass walls are built just inside the glazed areas of framed exterior walls (Fig. 5.20). Heat is trapped, absorbed, conducted, and radiated or convected as has been described for exterior mass walls. Interior masonry walls and partitions require stable footings.

Thermal Storage Walls—Water

Another way to increase thermal mass inside a building is to install properly sized and placed water storage containers. These storage tanks or tubes can be either black or colored, so that the surface absorbs solar radiation and conducts it to the water, or clear, so that the water absorbs heat directly as light passes through it (Fig. 5.21). This system functions in the same manner as the other mass wall approaches; however, water has a higher capacity for absorbing, storing, and reradiating solar heat energy. A given volume of water will store more heat than the same volume of most materials. This means that a lesser volume of water is necessary to store a given amount of solar heat than for stone, brick, or concrete. Water storage systems are most often nonstructural and require proper framing or footing support for such a concentrated load. Provision for drainage, both planned and emergency, must also be incorporated.

A number of products are available for use as water/heat storage containers. The water usually requires

80 BASIC PRINCIPLES OF SOLAR CONSTRUCTION

IN ADDITION:

- SITE AND SHAPE BUILDING (SEE FIG. 5.5)
- TIGHTEN BUILDING SHELL (SEE FIG. 5.5)
- MODIFY FLOOR PLAN AND ADJUST WINDOWS (SEE FIG. 5.6)
- USE THERMAL MASS (SEE FIG. 5.14)

- IN HARSH CLIMATES
- ON SOUTH SLOPING SITES

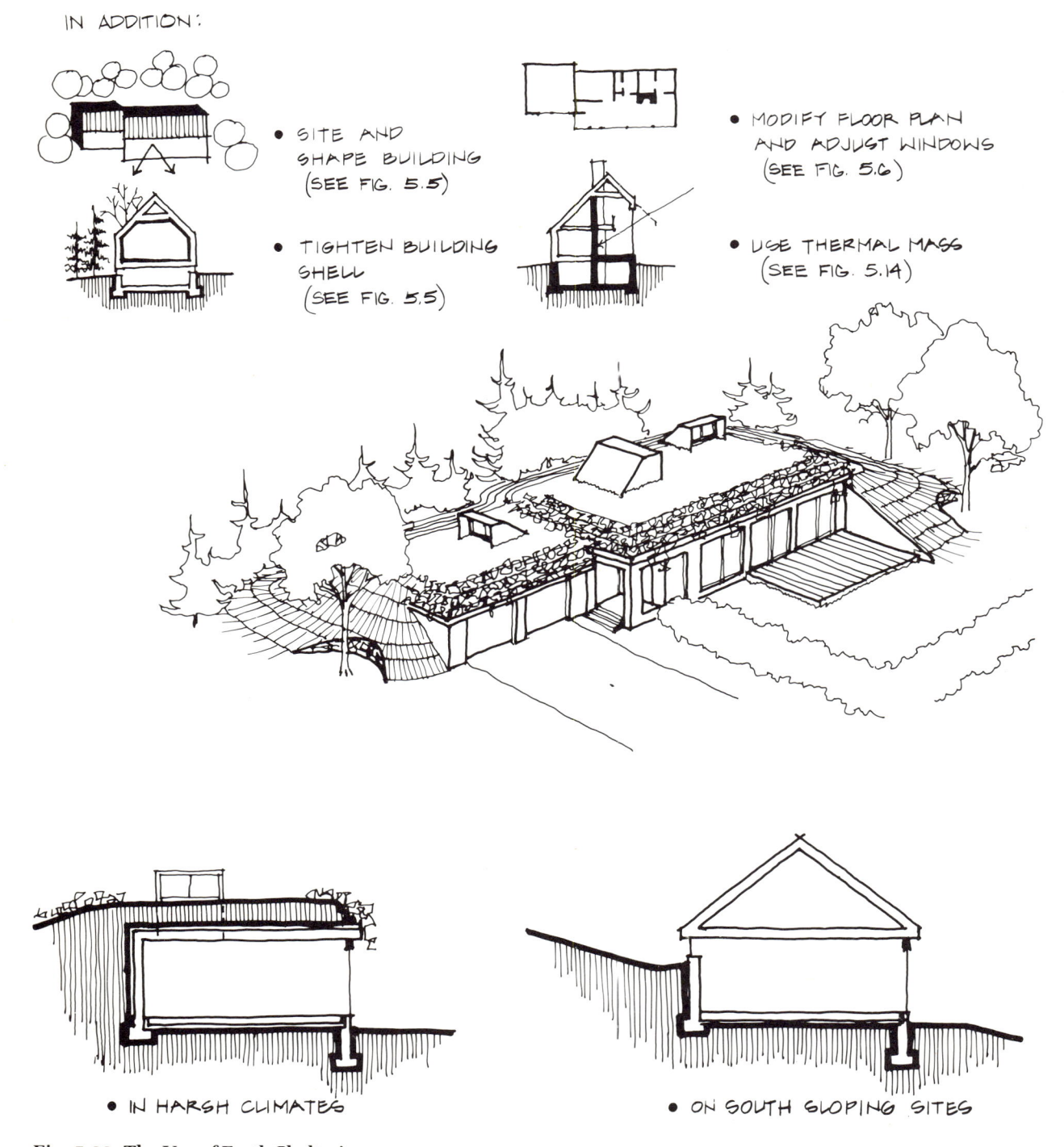

Fig. 5.22 The Use of Earth Sheltering

- Earth sheltering is effective in coping with extreme climatic conditions where very high or low temperatures and strong winds prevail. By shielding building surfaces with a mantle of earth at relatively stable temperatures, conductive, radiative, and convective heat loss and infiltration are dramatically reduced.

- On south sloping sites earth sheltering can be an economical means of achieving energy efficiency by providing living space, passive solar heat gain, and thermal mass through use of below grade areas as primary living space.

Fig. 5.23 The use of earth berms reduces the amount of wall areas, and in some cases roof areas, exposed to wind and cold temperatures.

treatment with copper sulfate to prevent algae growth. Covering the surface of the water with a mineral oil will reduce evaporative losses. Clear tubes of water located directly behind glazing also can serve to redirect light passing through, this helps diffuse radiation throughout the interior which aids both heat transfer and daylighting. The term "water walls" often is used to describe this system.

Remember, thermal mass (as masonry or water) must be properly sized to the conditions of the space it serves, and located carefully to assure that it does serve the space. The combined effects of direct, reflected, and convective heatgain are the determining factors to consider.

The color of the mass affects its rate of absorption, and its thickness and conductance determine the storage capacity and rate of reradiation of heat. Generally, interior materials of low mass should be light in color to avoid overheating themselves, and to aid in reflecting radiation towards high mass materials. High mass materials do not necessarily have to be dark in color, but they work best when they are. Dark colors of new red brick, grey slates, and a wide range of colored tiles are acceptable.

EARTH SHELTERED CONSTRUCTION

Earth sheltered construction can take many forms, two of which are shown in Fig. 5.22, where earth is placed in contact with the building to varying degrees depending on the climate, site, and preference of the designer or builder. Earth sheltered buildings are typically constructed using poured or pre-cast concrete walls, concrete slab floors, and ceiling/roof decks of either poured concrete, precast concrete plank or wood framing.

Of greatest importance with this form of solar construction are the site considerations of orientation, topography, soil type, and groundwater. Earth sheltered buildings make use of the tempering effect of the surrounding earth berm that protects the building from extreme climatic conditions. These buildings can be properly oriented on building lots to take advantage of passive solar heating in winter and can either be recessed deeply or partially bermed to moderate the effects of ambient temperatures and wind movement. Depending on the topography of the site, earth sheltering often can be accomplished rather easily, with minimal added costs for earthwork. On sites that do not naturally lend themselves to these configurations, this design may involve increased costs, depending on the degree of difficulty.

Because primary living space is placed below grade, builders should evaluate soil types and groundwater conditions in order to avoid moisture problems (Fig. 5.23). Careful selection and proper application of a reliable moistureproofing system are crucial to successful earth sheltered construction. Recommendations for these site considerations are made in Chapter 8.

Earth sheltered buildings need to be well-insulated with materials suitable for use below grade. This insulation is required because even though the temperatures of the soil will moderate the effect of air temperature extremes, and therefore slow the rate of heat loss from the inside, the earth will provide an infinite heat sink for heat being lost at the slower rate. The insulation is placed beneath concrete slab floors and to the exterior of walls and roofs. Because the materials typically used in the construction of these buildings are concrete or masonry, placement of the insulation on the exterior increases the heat storage capacity of the building. Insulating on the outside of concrete walls also creates higher surface temperatures for the concrete in warm weather which helps to control condensation.

82 BASIC PRINCIPLES OF SOLAR CONSTRUCTION

IN ADDITION:

- SITE AND SHAPE BUILDING (SEE FIG. 5.5)
- TIGHTEN BUILDING SHELL (SEE FIG. 5.5)
- MODIFY FLOOR PLAN AND ADJUST WINDOWS (SEE FIG. 5.6)
- USE THERMAL MASS (SEE FIG. 5.14)

- ATTACHED GREENHOUSE
- SUNSPACE

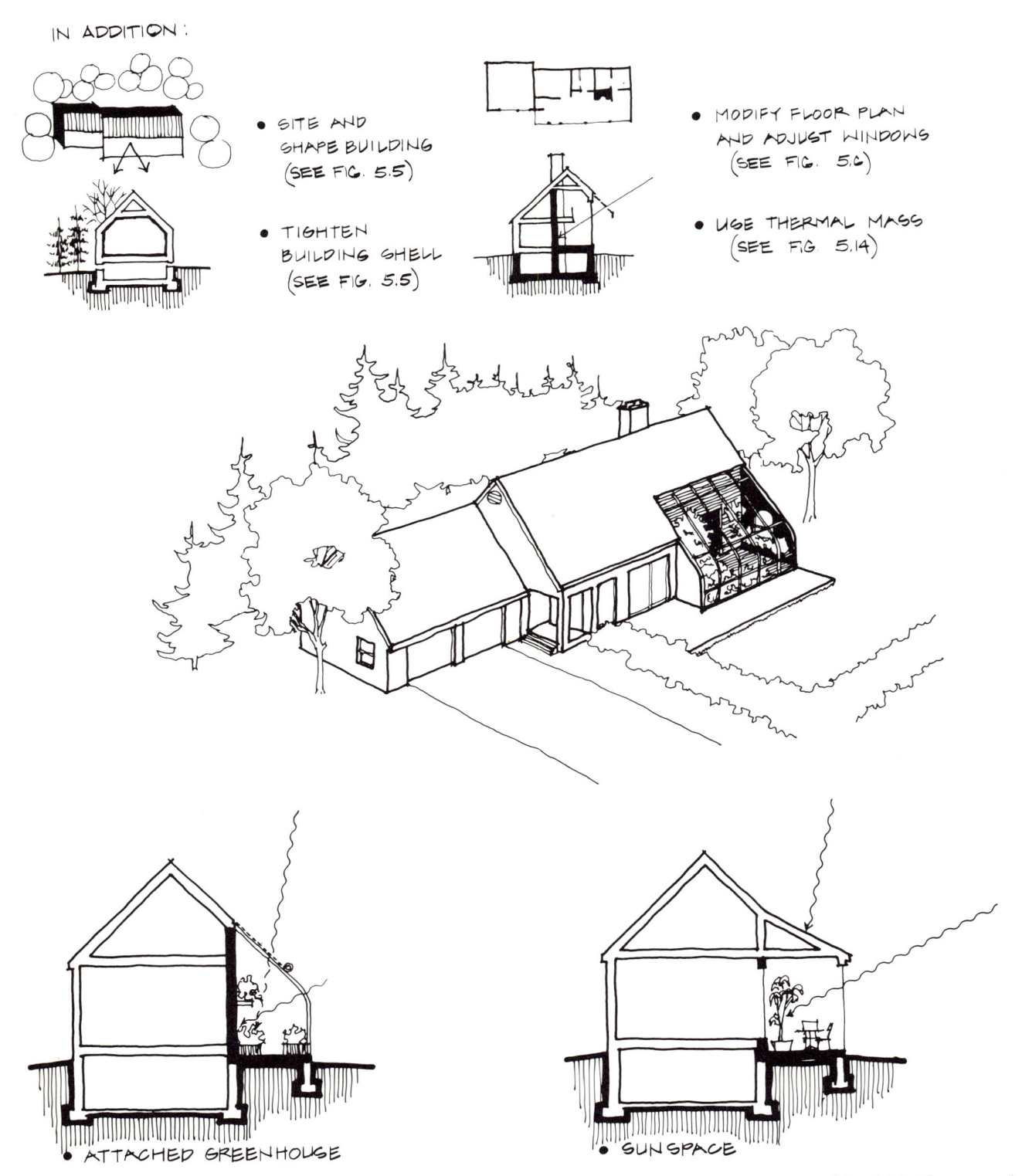

Fig. 5.24 The use of sunspace or greenhouse.

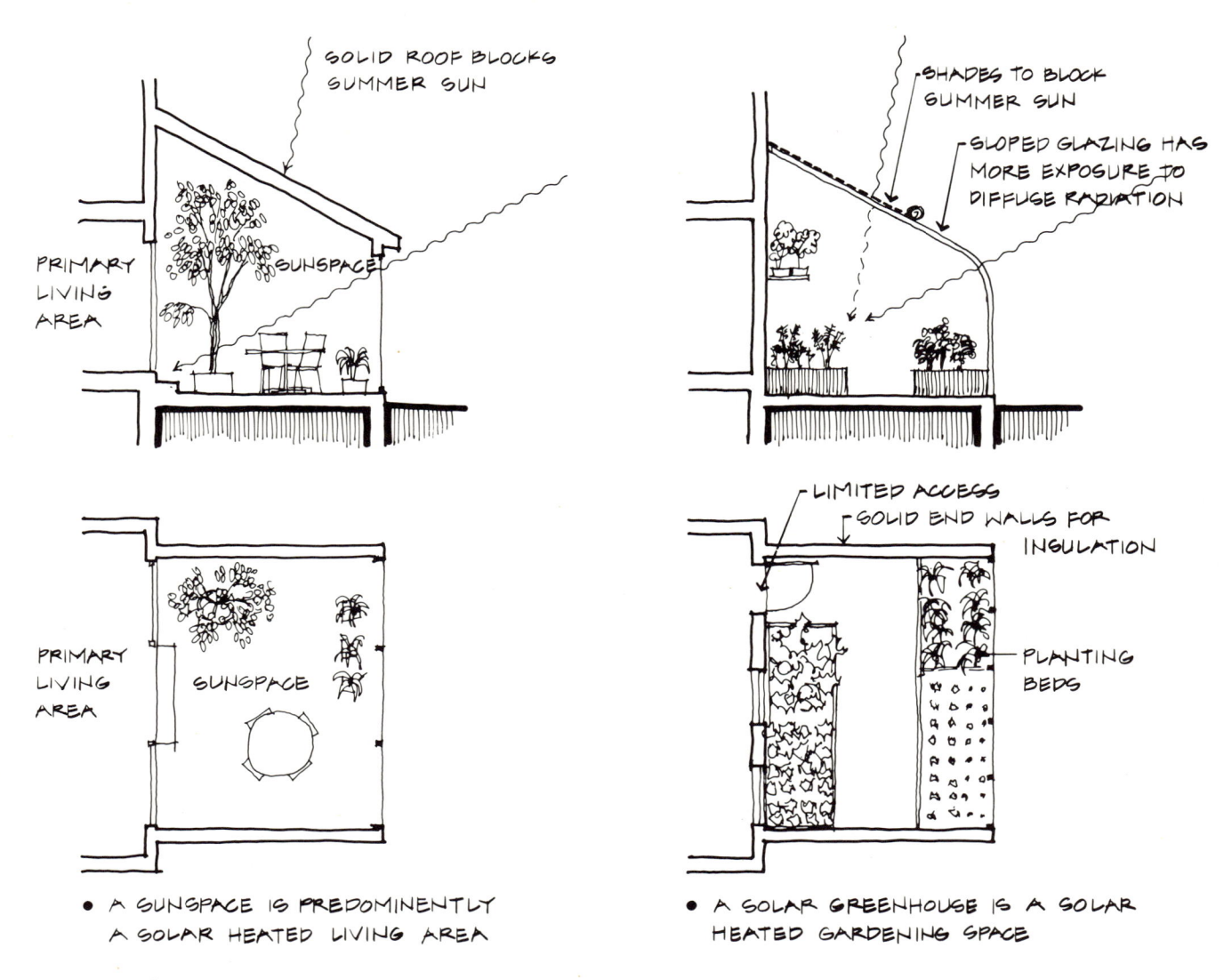

Fig. 5.25 The Difference Between a Sunspace and a Greenhouse Sunspace—The primary differences between a sunspace and a sun porch are the higher levels of insulation, weatherstripping, and thermal mass in a sunspace. Since plant growing is not the primary function of the sunspace, vertical glazing (which overheats less in the summer) is often preferred.

Greenhouse—In order to maintain high humidity levels and prevent insects from entering the house, it generally remains closed to the house except for access. Since it requires high light levels as well as solar heat, its glazed roof is usually sloped to "see" more diffuse radiation. Summer overheating, though more difficult to handle with sloped glazing, can be helped with exterior blinds or shades and positive venting techniques including fans.

SUNSPACES AND GREENHOUSES

One of the most popular approaches to solar heating is the use of built-in or attached sunspaces and greenhouses on the south side of a building (Fig. 5.24). These features can add significantly to the value of a building through their solar heat collection and storage, added living space, potential vegetable and flower production, and contribution to the warmth and brightness of the house. Many different configurations are currently in use (Fig. 5.25). The selection of a suitable approach depends on the primary purpose of the space (i.e., solar heated living space or plant growing), microclimatic

Fig. 5.26 Sunspaces and greenhouses often serve dual purposes as living space and plant space at different times of the year.

elements, budget limitations, and the architectural style of the building.

Sunspaces and greenhouses usually consist of large glazed areas used either as an integral part of the total heated space or as a separate space isolated by an exterior wall. A variety of glazing materials and components, installed in vertical or sloped positions, allow the solar radiation to enter the building. Because the glazing area is so large, the amount of solar heat collected, even on cold days, can create relatively high temperatures in the sunspace/greenhouse. These temperatures must be kept within an acceptable range for the space. For our discussions we define *sunspace* as solar heated living area, and *greenhouse* as solar heated indoor gardening area. In reality many homeowners combine uses of the space at various times of the year (Fig. 5.26).

In concept, all greenhouses are solar greenhouses, but in practice many features distinguish an energy conserving solar greenhouse from a conventional greenhouse. The primary distinction is the requirement for heating fuel; a conventional greenhouse requires much fuel to maintain suitable growing temperatures throughout the winter, while a solar greenhouse is designed to conserve energy and use little supplemental fuel beyond the solar energy it collects during the day. The solar greenhouse usually has thermal storage built into it, and it may produce a net heat gain to the building during daylight hours.

Integrated with Floor Plan

Sunspaces or greenhouses integrated directly into the floor plan of a house must be designed carefully using the guidelines for direct gain options. Because this configuration places a high heat gain area in continuous contact with the rest of the building, plans for heat storage, heat distribution, and summer shading must be considered. Also, the large glazed areas will lose a significant amount of heat, so provisions for multiple layers and nighttime insulation should be included. Many builders incorporate sloped skylights into their sunspace/greenhouse designs, while others use standard windows in a vertical position. Sloped glazings used as the roofs of integrated sunspaces/greenhouses can cause uncomfortable summer overheating and accelerate winter heat loss. Depending on the area of glazing, it can be very difficult to shade the sloped surface from the high summer sun.

The location of glazing material in the roof also creates an area of high heat loss in the winter. The roof requires higher levels of insulation than anywhere else in the building, due to the build-up of heat near the

PASSIVE SOLAR HEATING AND COOLING

Table 5.2
Recommended thickness of thermal storage walls for use with attached greenhouse.

Material	Recommended thickness (in)
Adobe	8–12
Brick (common)	10–14
Concrete (dense)	12–18
Water	8 or more (or 0.67 cu ft for each one sq ft of south-facing glass)

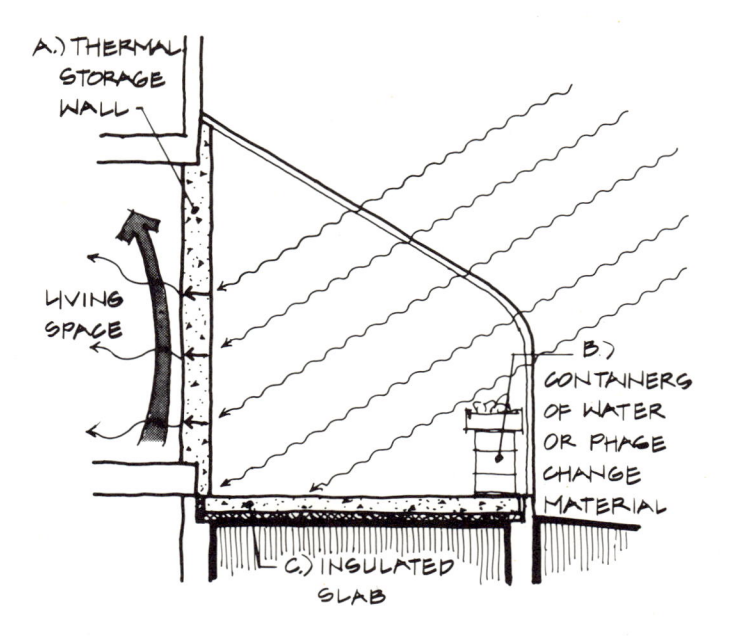

Fig. 5.27 The Use of Thermal Mass in Sunspaces and Solar Greenhouses A) Thermal Storage Walls—Heat may be transferred into the house by conduction through thermal storage walls. This is useful in greenhouses where it may be undesirable to transfer air between the greenhouse and the living space. B) Containers of water or phase change material are often used to provide effective thermal storage in greenhouses. C) Insulated Slabs—These are more effective in sunspaces than in greenhouses where plants often shade the floor.

ceiling. Replacing large areas of insulated roof with glazed areas greatly reduces the resistance of the roof to heat loss. The use of nighttime insulation will improve the performance of this area; however, the slope of the roof affects the efficiency of those products.

Greenhouses integrated into living space of houses can be very pleasant, but they can cause problems other than overheating and accelerated heat loss. Depending on the extent of plantings, greenhouses may contribute high levels of water vapor and increase surface and hidden condensation in the house. Another problem that often arises is the presence of insects in and around the greenhouse area.

Attached Sunspace/Greenhouse

The most versatile approach to the application of sunspaces and greenhouses is the attached structure. This configuration isolates the sunspace/greenhouse from the living space by building it onto the southern exterior wall. Access typically is provided through patio or french doors that allow the occupants to enter the room from the house and control the circulation of air between the attached sunspace/greenhouse and the rest of the living space. As this area is separate from the rest of the building, it can heat up during the day and cool down at night without adversely affecting the comfort of the house. Solar heat gain can be stored in a slab floor or mass wall and vented into the house through the doors and windows that open into the sunspace/greenhouse. Louvered vents and electric fans can be used to move heat from this high gain area into the building. Where the sunspace/greenhouse is built onto a masonry wall, heat will conduct through the wall where it radiates into the living space (Fig. 5.27, Table 5.2).

Heat storage is more important for areas used in plant production than as primarily living space. This means that less heat can be taken from the greenhouse to use in the house. Greenhouses must store heat during the day to keep plants from freezing at night. However, attached sunspaces usually are used during the day and left to cool at night. Solar heat can be vented into the house when the sunspace is warmer than the living space. When the sunspace is cooler than the house, it can be isolated by closing vents, doors, and windows, which reduces the flow of heat from the house (Fig. 5.28).

The control of air and heat flow between the attached sunspace/greenhouse and the living space is very important. If a greenhouse has not stored sufficient heat during the day to protect the plants at night, then vents, doors, and windows can be opened to allow heat to flow into it from the house. Depending on the configuration, summer overheating can be a problem in the sunspace/greenhouse, but the ability to isolate it from the house minimizes the effects on the comfort of the occupants. All openings between the house and greenhouse should be screened to prevent any insects from the greenhouse getting into the house.

Overheating in the attached sunspace/greenhouse may occur at any time of year. In the winter, excess heat

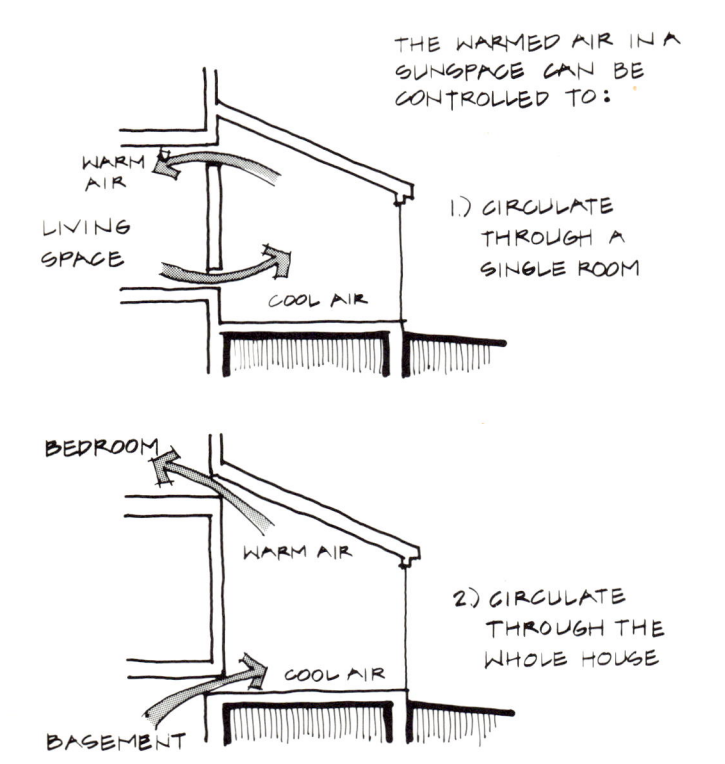

Fig. 5.28 Circulate heated air from a sunspace/greenhouse to the house.

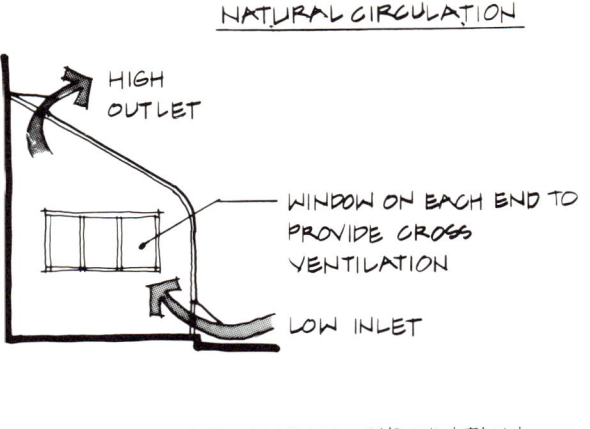

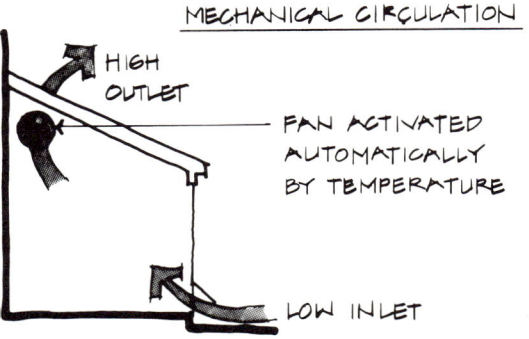

Fig. 5.29 Vent the sunspace/greenhouse to minimize overheating.

usually is vented into the house, while in the summer it should vent to the outside. Again, depending on the design, venting can be achieved by introducing air at a low point and allowing it to exit at the ridge or gables or by cross ventilation between opposite operable windows (Fig. 5.29). Attached sunspace/greenhouse areas also serve as a buffer between the south exterior wall and ambient conditions (temperature and wind), which helps reduce heat loss through the wall.

Builders use sunspaces and greenhouses in many different ways. Some use them to form sun tempered air-lock entries, while others incorporate them into kitchen, living, and dining areas. Many builders are offering them for their potential to produce a year round environment for plants. The demand for each of these applications, especially in remodeling existing buildings, is increasing. The components, materials, and techniques used in constructing these features are discussed in Chapter 10.

DOUBLE SHELL AND SUPERINSULATED HOUSES

One of the more recent approaches to solar construction incorporates double wall and ceiling framing, creating an air space surrounding the interior living space (or shell) with warm air. These buildings are known as *double shell houses*. A primary benefit of double framing is the increased level of insulation that can be achieved by insulating both "shells." Many builders also provide these high R-values using other construction methods, thus making their houses *superinsulated*.

Although both double shell and superinsulated houses take advantage of solar heat gain, their primary focus is on drastically reducing heating loads (Fig. 5.30). These approaches require careful control of solar heat collection, using solar energy for daylighting as much as heating. Builders are utilizing internal heat gains from refrigerator compressors, and heat contributed by water heater losses, light bulbs, and occupants, as supplemental sources. Both types of building design can result in lower initial costs for backup heating equipment efficiently designed for reduced loads (Fig. 5.31).

Double shell houses are typically built over crawl spaces, using the crawl space as an earth tempered air plenum. The double framed walls are built with a 4 to 8-inch space between them that is open to air flowing

PASSIVE SOLAR HEATING AND COOLING 87

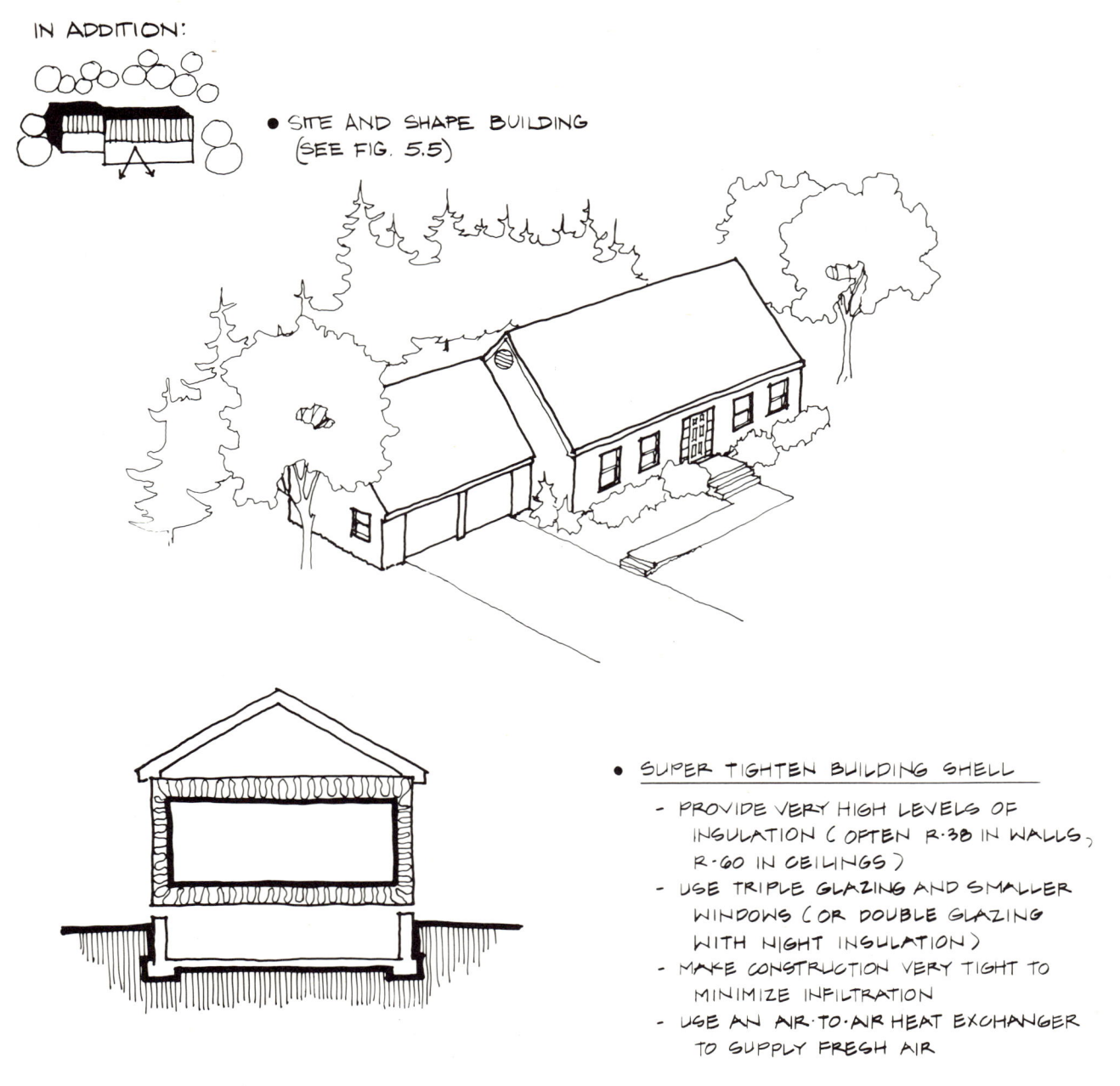

IN ADDITION:

- SITE AND SHAPE BUILDING (SEE FIG. 5.5)

- SUPER TIGHTEN BUILDING SHELL
    - PROVIDE VERY HIGH LEVELS OF INSULATION (OFTEN R-38 IN WALLS, R-60 IN CEILINGS)
    - USE TRIPLE GLAZING AND SMALLER WINDOWS (OR DOUBLE GLAZING WITH NIGHT INSULATION)
    - MAKE CONSTRUCTION VERY TIGHT TO MINIMIZE INFILTRATION
    - USE AN AIR-TO-AIR HEAT EXCHANGER TO SUPPLY FRESH AIR

Fig. 5.30 The use of superinsulated construction

out of the crawl space and from the wall back into the crawl space. The air space in the wall also opens to an air space between the top plates that allows air flow into an air space created by double framed ceiling. Figure 5.32 illustrates the air blanket that surrounds the building's interior shell. The presence in the wall of air that is at least as warm as the earth in the crawl space reduces the heat loss from the house by lowering the temperature differential between the building's interior and exterior wall surfaces. The warmer air in the wall, the less heat is lost from the living space.

The designs for double shell houses rely on an attached sunspace or greenhouse to collect solar heat. Air heated in the sunspace/greenhouse rises into the ceiling air space and is replaced at the floor of the sunspace/greenhouse with cool air from the crawl space. This convective air movement is driven by the solar heating of air in the sunspace/greenhouse. The warm air

Fig. 5.31 Double shell house (top) and superinsulated house (bottom). Note the differences in glazed areas.

that collects at the top of the sunspace/greenhouse enters the roof cavity through vents and moves along the roof to the north wall, where it drops through the double wall air space and reenters the crawl space. The convective flow draws the air through the crawl space on its way back to the sunspace/greenhouse on the south of the building. This air movement must sometimes be supplemented with mechanical blowers. At this point the air is supposed to transfer the heat gained in the sunspace/greenhouse to the soil in the crawl space. The soil is then responsible for storing and reradiating heat into the crawl space and subsequently the entire air space.

This approach uses the sunspace/greenhouse, ceiling cavity, double framed north wall, and crawl space as air passages and plenum. Its design relies on the theory that a high amount of solar heat gain will move the warm air to the crawl space where it will be stored in the earth for later use. Typical designs utilize large expanses of south facing glass on the exterior shell, which has led to

PASSIVE SOLAR HEATING AND COOLING

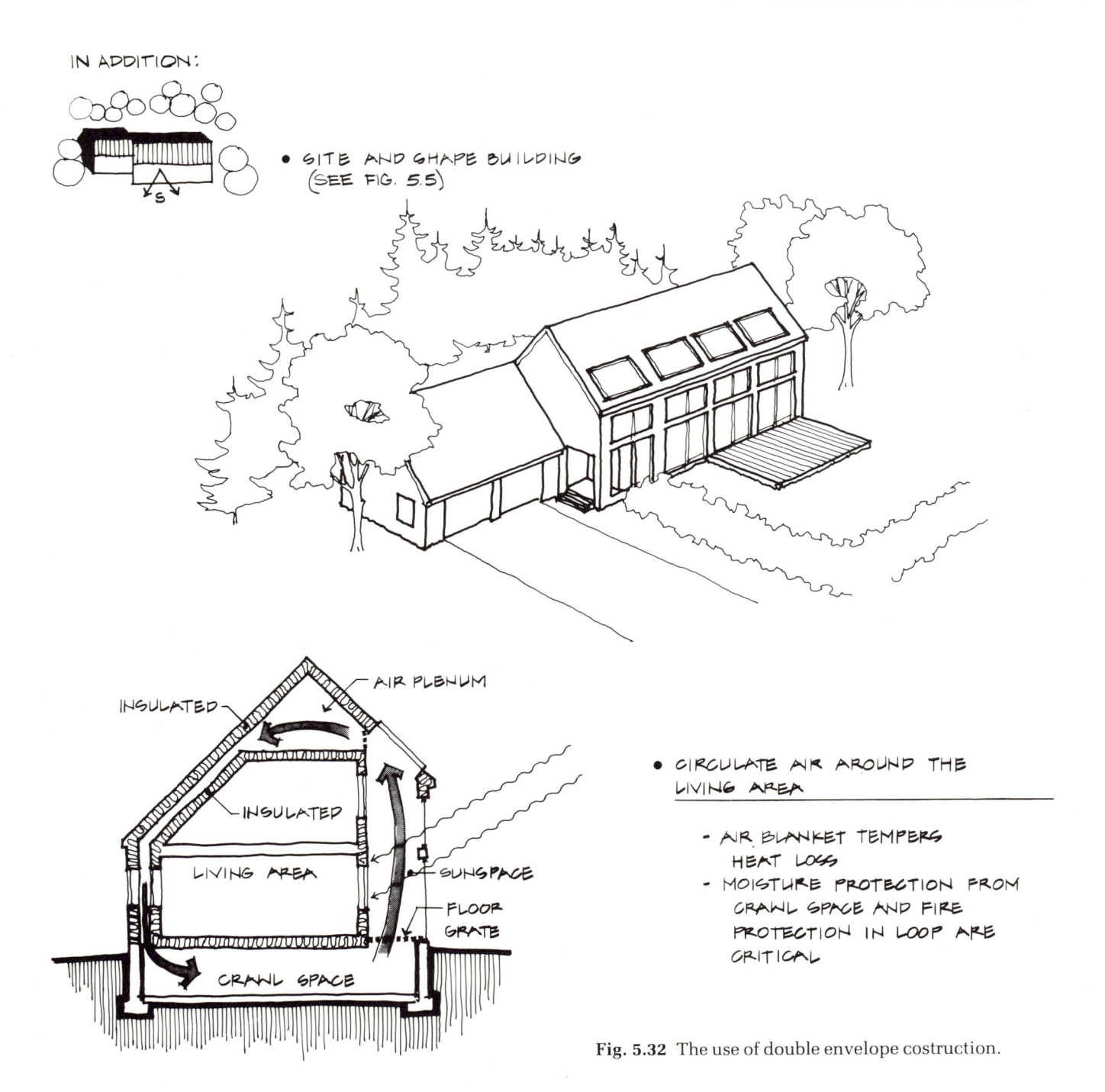

IN ADDITION:

- SITE AND SHAPE BUILDING (SEE FIG. 5.5)

- CIRCULATE AIR AROUND THE LIVING AREA
  - AIR BLANKET TEMPERS HEAT LOSS
  - MOISTURE PROTECTION FROM CRAWL SPACE AND FIRE PROTECTION IN LOOP ARE CRITICAL

Fig. 5.32 The use of double envelope costruction.

overheating problems in early houses of this type. Also, builders question the actual amount of heat delivered from the sunspace/greenhouse to storage in the soil.

Many builders of double shell houses are using restraint in sizing south facing windows. This is due in part to their feelings that the benefits of the double shell approach derive from the high levels of insulation and the air blanket warmed by the earth in the crawl space (or cooled in summer or hot climates). The difference with this approach is that the air in the crawl space is heated by the naturally occuring earth temperatures and not by stored solar heat. These ideas have led to a different style of double shell house that uses a reduced area of south facing windows, often opens up all of the walls to the crawl space, and relies on high levels of insulation.

Both approaches utilize the thermal mass of the earth in the crawl space rather than internal mass located within the living space. Therefore, window sizing and placement on the south wall must control the amount of solar heat gain to avoid overheating.

Double shell construction can take many forms. Chapter 9 presents construction details for double framing. Control of moisture rising out of the earth floor of the crawl space is especially important. Without a vapor barrier a significant amount of moisture will rise into the crawl space and be carried by air convection through the framing of the walls and ceiling. Water vapor also will rise through the first floor and enter the living space. The effect and control of this moisture movement is discussed in Chapter 3.

CHAPTER 6 SOLAR WATER HEATING

INTRODUCTION

The cost of energy for domestic hot water can contribute up to one-third of a building's total operating expenses. Builders, therefore, should offer energy conserving features that reduce consumption, encourage occupants to use hot water wisely, and include solar water heaters on appropriate sites.

The use of hot water for bathing, laundering, and dishwashing varies from family to family. For sizing purposes, hot water consumption of 20 gallons per person per day is assumed. This is based on a 15-gallon daily usage plus some water heater inefficiencies. Thus, a family of four would require either an 80-gallon hot water tank, an appropriately sized tankless coil, or an instantaneous heater to meet their demand. The proper sizing of a water heater is critical to its efficient operation.

ENERGY CONSERVATION FIRST

As in every aspect of solar construction, the first priority is energy conservation. Reduce the demand for fuel at every opportunity. With domestic water heating a number of simple steps can easily be taken, including:

- Insulate the water tank.
- Insulate the pipe runs.
- Install water saving fixtures.
- Consider off-peak electric storage water heating.
- Lower the thermostat setting.

Insulate the Tank

Most water heating tanks are not well insulated in their manufacture and should be wrapped with additional fiberglass insulation. Hot water tanks often are located in unheated areas; regardless of location, the temperature difference between the air outside and the water inside the tank accelerates heat loss through its shell. This occurs every hour of every day, and can increase the load by as much as 35 percent. By adding R-6 to tanks supplied with R-4, the heat loss from the tank can be reduced significantly (Fig. 6.1).

Fig. 6.1 Vinyl jacketed duct insulation can be used to insulate tank-type water heaters, a very important measure for energy conservation.

interior surface (gypsum) and on pipes in unheated or vented crawl spaces (Fig. 6.2).

Install Water Saving Fixtures

Insulating hot water lines improves the delivery of hot water to the fixtures. Another very effective way to reduce the cost of hot water is to install water conserving appliances and fixtures. Typical showerheads which operate at 5 gallons per minute can be replaced by fixtures that use 3 gallons per minute, and still provide a comfortable shower. Also available are toilets that require half the water normally used for operation, washers and dishwashers that use less water, and water conserving aerators for sink faucets.

All of these features should be part of the builder's complete energy efficient package. They are as basic to the builder's efforts to reduce the operating expenses of a building as the insulation in the walls, but should be accompanied by an effort to encourage the occupants to reduce their consumption and use hot water wisely. As is true with the energy performance of a building, the efficiency of a water heating system, whether conventional or solar fueled, largely depends on how it is used.

Off-Peak Electric Water Heating

Electric water heaters that are designed to use off-peak electric power can save considerable expense for the homeowner, because many electric companies offer lower rates for electricity consumed during off-peak demand periods. Water heaters of this type should be sized for the entire daily anticipated load, since they heat the whole tank overnight for use the following day. An additional meter for off-peak periods must be installed. The units often are combined with solar water heating components.

Lower Thermostat Setting

Typical thermostat settings for domestic water heaters range from 140° to 160°F. Tank type water heaters set for these high temperatures continuously cycle, as the water loses heat and the thermostat energizes the burner or resistance coil, in an effort to maintain the minimum setting. The higher the setting, the more energy consumed to maintain it, due to the higher rate of heat loss that accompanies the higher water temperatures.

By lowering the thermostat setting to 120°F, most domestic hot water demands, except dishwashing, can be met. In fact, bathing water at 120°F still needs to be

Fig. 6.2 All hot water distribution lines should be well insulated between the water heater and fixtures.

Insulate Pipe Runs

Pipe runs for domestic hot water systems should be located in interior walls and partitions with other plumbing lines rather than in exterior walls. Pipes run in exterior walls are subject to increased heat loss due to cold temperatures a few inches away, and they can freeze in extreme conditions. Avoid running water lines in unheated or vented crawl spaces. Even well insulated water lines in these areas will lose heat and may freeze if the temperature is low enough. All plumbing lines, especially hot water lines, should be laid out for short pipe runs. Many builders achieve lower costs and reduced heat loss with well designed plumbing cores.

Pipe runs for hot water should be well insulated between the water heater and the fixtures. Several types of pipe insulations are available (see Chapter 11). Selection of insulation type and R-value depend on where it is installed. For example, pipe insulation that is highly toxic and flammable should not be used within the building. These materials typically offer higher R-values and can be used in exterior walls behind a fire rated

Table 6.1
Comparative costs to maintain various water heater thermostat settings

Thermostat setting (°F)	Tank insulation level		
	R-3	R-6	R-10
120°	$11.40	$5.70	$3.90
140°	$15.30	$7.80	$5.10
160°	$19.50	$9.90	$6.60

Note: Based on a 100 gallon electric tank located in a room at 65°F. Costs based on electricity at $.07/kWh.

mixed with cold water. Laundering with lower temperatures is also common, with many appliances and laundry supplies now made especially for cooler water. A water heater set at 120°F will cost much less to operate than one set at 140° or 160°F (Table 6.1).

SOLAR WATER HEATING

Builders have available many approaches to solar water heating, including the use of systems that are commercially manufactured as well as job built, and systems that are installed by solar contractors or plumbing and heating contractors. Most systems utilize flat plate solar collectors exposed to the sun. A fluid that circulates through the collectors absorbs the heat and carries it to the domestic water heater, where it is then stored (Fig. 6.3).

Types of Solar Water Heaters

The materials used in flat plate solar collectors vary with different collectors, yet their basic operations are very similar. Differences between various generic systems can be found in the type of fluid that circulates through the collectors, the means of transferring heat to the domestic water, and the type of freeze protection incorporated in their design when used in freezing climates. Basic types of solar water heaters include:

- closed loop
- thermosiphoning
- recirculating
- drain back
- batch heaters

The names are derived from the systems operation or means of freeze protection.

A **closed loop** system is very similar to a typical hydronic heating system; in fact, most of the components used in the solar loop are the same (Fig. 6.4). The main difference is that the sun is now the "burner" and the collector is the "boiler." The term "closed loop" refers to the fact that a fluid other than domestic water is circulated through the system. This heat transfer fluid is introduced into the closed loop and pressurized, and it remains there until changed as part of periodic maintenance. Heat transfer fluids absorb solar heat as they pass through the collectors, carry the heat from the collectors to the heat exchanger, and release the heat to the domestic water by conduction through the wall of the heat exchange coil.

The heat transfer fluids used in closed loop systems include water, propylene glycol, glycerin, freon, and silicone oil. Criteria for comparing them include compatibility with system piping and components, relative heat transfer efficiency, durability, toxicity, flammability, and cost (Table 6.2). Most collector manufacturers recommend particular heat transfer fluids for use in their systems.

Mechanically circulated closed loop systems are used most often. Controlled by a differential thermostat, two sensors are placed in the system: one at the collectors, and one on the side of the water heater. As the morning sun warms the collector sensor mounted on the collector outlet to a temperature of 15°F warmer than the

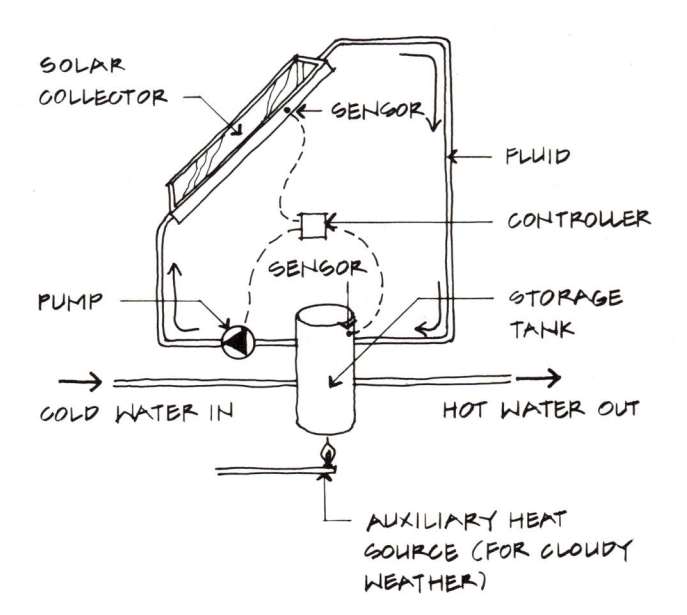

Fig. 6.3 Simplified operation of solar water heater

94 BASIC PRINCIPLES OF SOLAR CONSTRUCTION

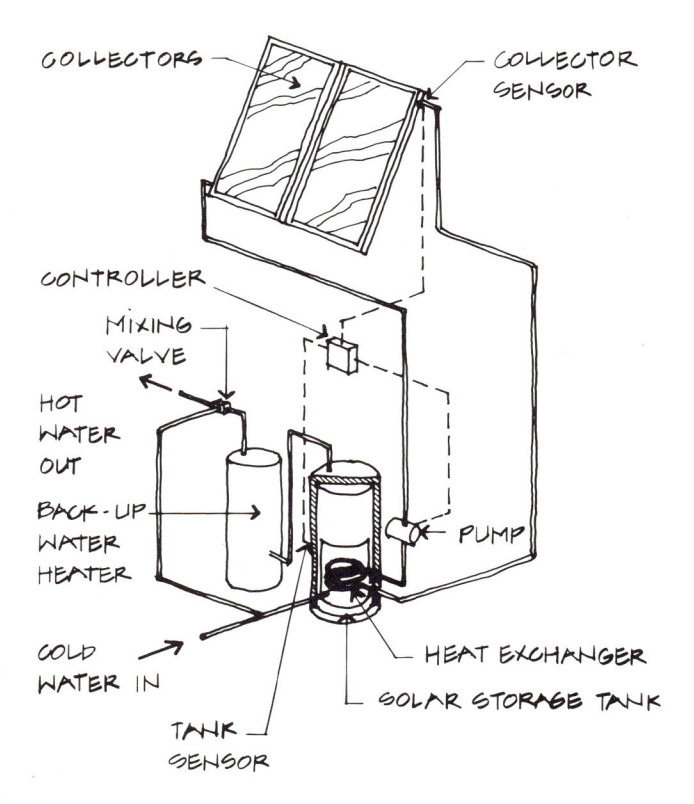

Fig. 6.4 Schematic layout of closed loop antifreeze system

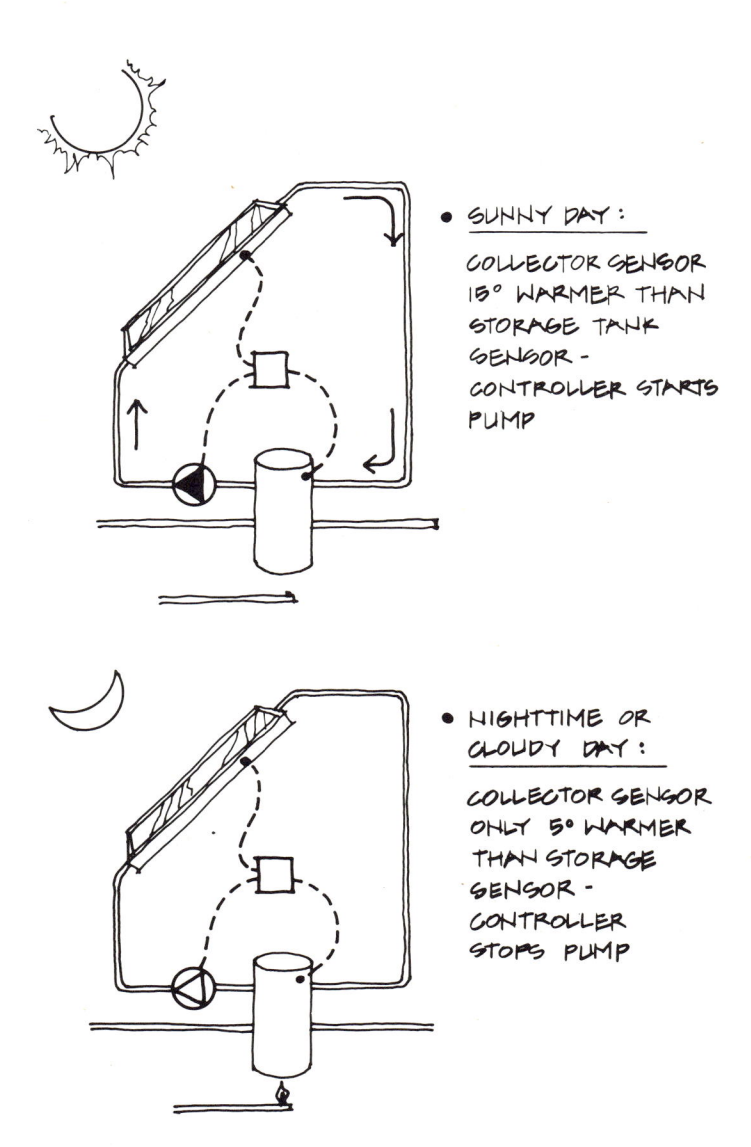

Fig. 6.5 Operation of differential thermostatic controller

tank sensor, the controller activates the circulator to start the day's collection. On cloudy days or when the sun goes down, the collector immediately begins to cool. When it reaches a temperature that is only 5°F warmer than the tank sensor, the controller cuts power to the circulator and ends the day's collection (Fig. 6.5). Many systems stop operation automatically when the domestic water reaches 180°F, to protect the tanks from overheating.

Closed loop systems also can operate on the convective flow of heat transfer fluid through the loop. This convective, or **thermosiphoning**, movement between the collectors and the tank begins as collectors heat up from solar radiation and the fluid in the absorber passages rises like warm air; the fluid is replaced by heavier, cooler fluid at the bottom of a sloped collector (Fig. 6.6). Thermosiphoning collectors must be located such that the top of the collector is lower than the bottom of the storage tank. A difference of 2 feet between top of collectors and bottom of tank prevents reverse cycling at night or on cloudy days. This configuration allows the rising fluid to move into the heat exchanger above and the sinking fluid to create head pressure, which helps the overall natural circulation. The sun is the "control"

of thermosiphoning systems. They start operating when solar energy is available and stop when it is not; the rate of flow depends on the intensity of solar radiation striking the collectors and the temperature of incoming fluid. Thermosiphoning closed loop systems utilize either water, freon, or antifreeze as heat transfer fluids.

Water has more capacity to pick up and store heat than all of the other fluids used for heat transfer. This physical property makes water very efficient as a heat transfer fluid and has led to the development of two generic types of solar water heaters: *recirculating* and *drain back*. These systems are also called **open loop.** This approach is very efficient, because it reduces the

SOLAR WATER HEATING

Table 6.2
Comparison of heat transfer fluids commonly used in solar water heaters

Material	Compatibility with fluid passages	Specific heat (relative efficiency)	Toxicity	Maintenance	Freezing point (°F)
Water	• Check pH and hardness • Drain-back—use demineralized water	1	• No special requirements	• If open system—replace evaporative losses	+32
50% Water/ ethylene glycol	• For use with copper or high temp. plastic tubing • Monitor pH especially after period of high temp. stagnation.	.83	• Requires use of dye tracers, backflow preventer and/or wall heat exchanger	• Replace when pH is less than 5	−33
50% Water/ propylene glycol	• For use with copper or high temp. plastic tubing • Monitor pH especially after period of high temp. stagnation	.85	• Requires use of dye trace • May also be required to use backflow preventive • Single-wall heat exchanger generally acceptable	• Replace when pH is less than 5	−28
Silicone oils	• For use with copper or high temp. plastics • Tends to leak more easily than other fluids —requires use of special pipe dope, seals on circulators, and packings on valve stems	.38	• Non-toxic • Single wall heat exchanger generally acceptable	• Relatively stable • Promoted as not requiring replacement	−120
Freon	• For use with copper fluid passages		• Presence in atmosphere damages ozone layer	• No fluid change required	None

number of heat exchanges that take place which increases the amount of energy that is actually delivered for use. The relatively high freezing temperature of water is a drawback, and systems that utilize water for heat transfer are designed to avoid this problem.

Recirculating systems pump the actual domestic water through the collectors. Their day-to-day operation is similar to the closed loop controls, except that an ambient sensor activates the circulator whenever there is a chance of water freezing in the collectors and exterior piping; warm water then is circulated from the water tank through the cold piping and collectors to keep the system from freezing (Fig. 6.7). This recirculation will result in tremendous heat loss; but a callback to repair frozen pipes and water damaged materials is far more costly. These systems should be used in mild climates where there are less than 20 days of freezing temperatures per year (Fig. 6.8).

Drain back systems prevent water from freezing by draining automatically when the pump stops for any reason. These systems are similar to closed loops, since they circulate the same water through a heat exchanger each day. When the collectors are sufficiently warmed by the sun, a differential thermostatic controller turns the pump on to begin collecting and transferring heat. When the sun sets, or when clouds cause cooling of the collectors, the controller cuts power to the pump and the water drains by gravity into a holding tank. The next sunny day will cause the system to begin operation automatically, filling the loop with the water (Fig. 6.8).

96 BASIC PRINCIPLES OF SOLAR CONSTRUCTION

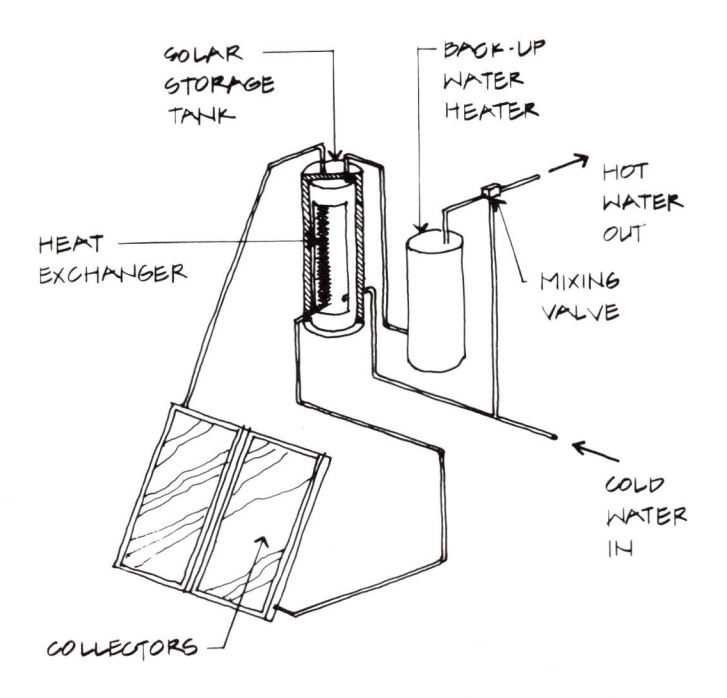

Fig. 6.6 Schematic layout of thermosiphon system

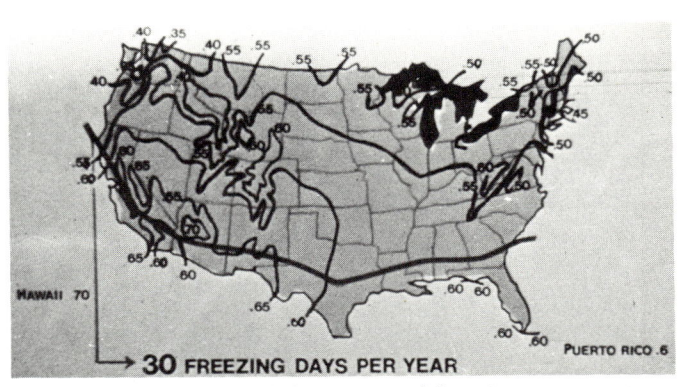

Fig. 6.8 Average annual frequency of freezing temperatures for different regions

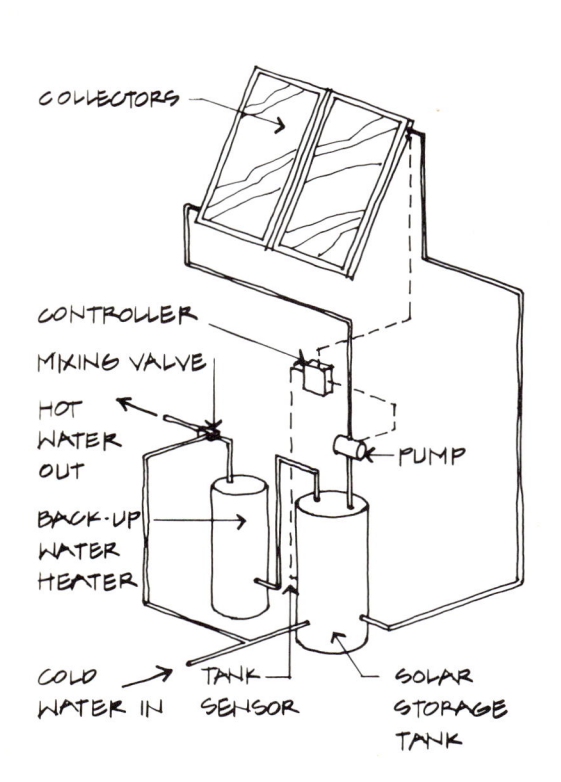

Fig. 6.7 Schematic layout of recirculating system

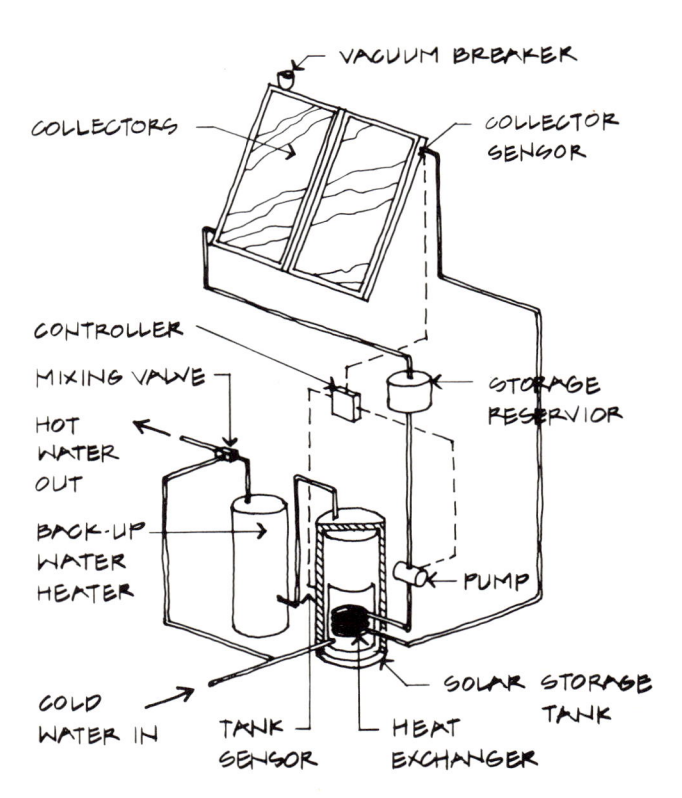

Fig. 6.9 Schematic layout of drainback system

Thermosiphoning systems also use the open loop approach, where domestic water is heated directly in the solar collector and rises from the collectors into the storage tank. These systems are used all year in warmer sections of North America or as seasonal heaters in cooler climates.

While other types of solar water heaters use flat plate collectors to heat a small amount of fluid many times, batch heaters use large volume collectors to heat a

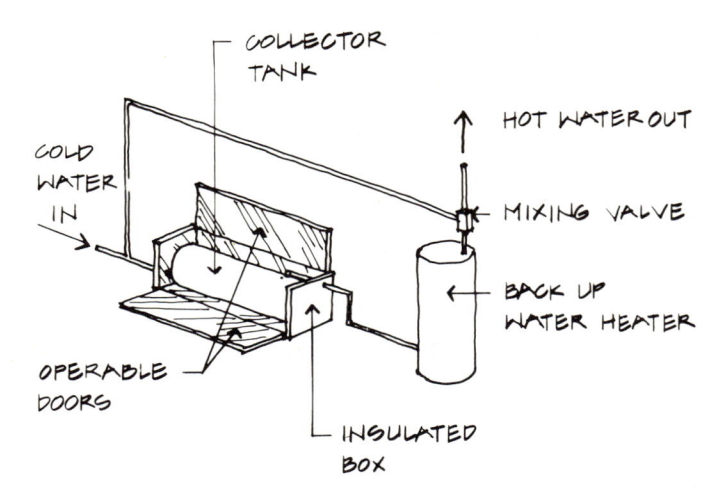

Fig. 6.10 Schematic layout of batch heater system.

Fig. 6.11 Batch-type solar water heaters are simple, inexpensive, and effective.

few "batches" of water during the day. These systems place special absorbers or small tanks in line between cold water supply and conventional water heater (Fig. 6.10). Water flows on demand into the solar heat collector, where it is preheated before moving to the water heater. When there is no demand, the water sits in the collectors, absorbing and storing solar heat (Fig. 6.11).

SIZING AND SELECTING WATER HEATERS

Solar water heaters are usually sized by the system supplier or installing subcontractor. Considerations for determining the size of collector arrays and storage tanks (sometimes with heat exchangers) include:

- Hot water demand (gallons per day) and percent of solar contribution desired
- Generic type of solar domestic hot water
- Type of supplemental water heating
- Availability of solar radiation
- Collector tilt and orientation
- Architectural limitations

A review of the solar equipment as to aesthetics, performance, durability, installation details, cost, and service warrantees is important. The quality and cost of available systems cover a wide range, and equipment selection must adhere to the budget planned for the system. However, choosing the lowest initial costs for lower quality equipment and installation may result in higher maintenance and earlier replacement costs. Builders often underestimate the installed cost of solar water heaters; then they are pressured by the budget to cut corners and buy for low price rather than long term quality. Chapter 11 presents construction and installation details for solar hot water equipment, both factory and job-built.

SITING SOLAR COLLECTORS

Solar heat collectors should be placed on the building's roof, side wall, or on a ground mounted rack to receive direct sunlight for at least 6 hours on clear days. Three factors that affect the amount and intensity of solar radiation striking a collector are the collector's orientation, collector tilt, and shading (Fig. 6.12).

Orientation

Solar heat collectors, like the buildings of which they are part, must be oriented to receive solar radiation. The optimum orientation depends very much on the microclimate of the site, and can be influenced by the local characteristics of early morning fog, late afternoon clouds, or shading elements. The acceptable range of orientation lies within 15 degrees east or west of true south. This wide range of orientation allows many existing homes sufficient exposure to make a solar domestic hot water retrofit practical. Builders who orient their houses properly in new construction for passive solar heat gain will be providing for solar domestic hot water at the same time.

Tilt

The most intense collection of heat by a flat plate collector occurs when the solar radiation strikes the outside

98 BASIC PRINCIPLES OF SOLAR CONSTRUCTION

- ORIENTATION:
  WITHIN 15° OF SOUTH

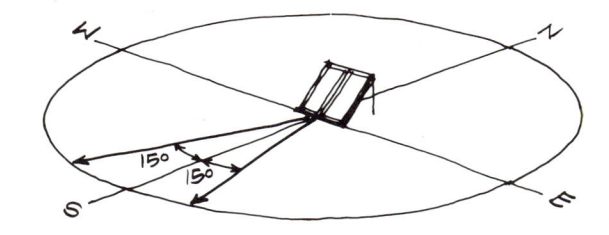

- OPTIMUM TILT FOR YEAR ROUND COLLECTION:
  EQUALS LATITUDE (± 5° ALLOWABLE)

- SHADING:
  COLLECTORS SHOULD BE IN FULL SUN FOR A MINIMUM 6 HOURS PER DAY (SEE CHAPTER 4 ON SITING BUILDING FOR SHADE ANALYSIS)

Fig. 6.12 Considerations in siting solar collectors

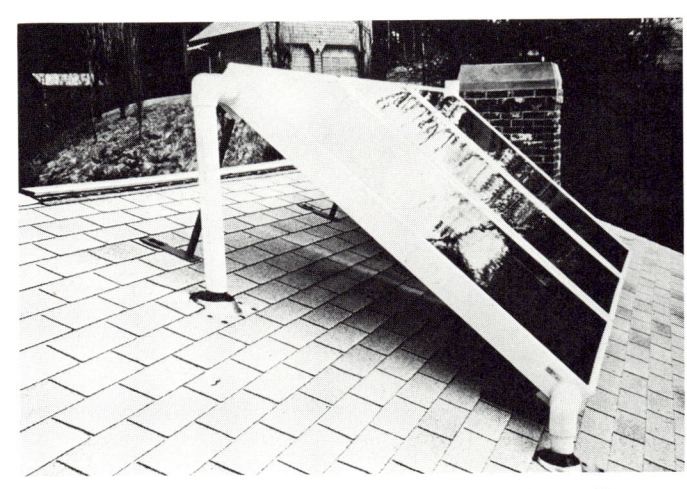

Fig. 6.13 On shallow roofs or ground mounted installations, solar heat collectors can be held at the proper tilt by a well-built rack.

cover at approximately a 90° angle. At this angle more radiation passes through the cover and strikes the absorber than at indirect angles, because less radiation is reflected.

As the sun's position on the horizon changes with the seasons, the angle at which solar radiation strikes a collector also varies, so that at different times of the year, collector glazings will transmit varying amounts of radiation through them. This is the most critical factor in determining a system's performance; therefore, collectors must be installed at a tilt that allows them the most opportunity to collect solar radiation. Since domestic water heating is a year round load (compared to space heating, which occurs only part of the year), collectors should be tiled towards the south at an optimum angle for year round collection. For domestic hot water, this optimum angle equals the site latitude. For example, at a site located at 45°N latitude, the collectors should be tilted towards the south at a 45° angle from the horizontal. This optimum angle is derived from the fact that on both September 21 and March 21, the sun is in the same position relative to the horizon, and solar radiation strikes the collectors at near the 90° angle desired. At other times of the year, when the sun is lower or higher in the sky, reflection of radiation by the glazing increases. However, the annual average collection is best for collectors installed at this tilt.

Very few roofs are built to offer the optimum tilt for solar heat collectors. Table 6.3 shows various roof pitches and their equivalent angles so builders can compare site latitude and roof frame design. Roofs that are within plus or minus 5 degrees of site latitude are within an acceptable range for solar heat collectors. The system performance will be affected significantly by this variation, and the collectors can be mounted parallel to the roof surface. The acceptable range for collectors at a site of 45°N latitude is between 40° and 50° from the horizontal.

Collectors placed at more shallow tilts absorb more heat from the high summer sun and reflect more of the low winter sun, while the opposite is true of collectors at a steeper pitch. Arrays installed at these angles perform in a very inconsistent manner. If the array has been sized for year round use, collectors at too shallow a pitch may

Table 6.3
Angle/roof pitch conversion table

Roof pitch	Angle (degrees)
1/12	5
2/12	10
3/12	14
4/12	18
5/12	23
6/12	27
7/12	30
8/12	34
9/12	37
10/12	40
11/12	43
12/12	45
13/12	47
14/12	49
15/12	51
16/12	53

absorb more heat in summer than is required, causing the system to overheat.

Collectors installed on roofs can be mounted parallel to the roof pitch if it is within the acceptable range. Collectors also can be mounted on racks or dormers built to the proper tilt if the roof pitch is not acceptable, which is common in existing buildings (Fig. 6.13). Wall mounted racks and ground mounted stands also are used to hold the collectors at the proper tilt when the roof is not suitable. Chapter 11 discusses construction details for roof, wall, and ground mounted collector arrays, installed parallel to the roof as well as on racks.

The use of collectors built at the job rather than bought as premanufactured units offers some constraints regarding tilt. Most often job-built collectors utilize a portion of rafter cavities as the enclosures and the rafters as glazing supports. This requires that the section of roof that houses the collector be built within 5 degrees of site latitude.

Shading

The third factor to consider when siting solar heat collectors is shading, for it is useless to tilt and orient collectors to receive solar radiation if they will then be shaded by trees, other buildings, chimneys, dormers, or hilltops. Collectors should not receive more than 5 percent shading between 9:00 A.M. and 3:00 P.M. for optimum performance.

Roof installations to avoid shade are especially practical in urban and suburban locations. Trees and shrubs located to the south of a potential site may require thinning or removal if they will cast shadows on the array. Deciduous trees and shrubs pose less of a problem in winter than conifers (softwoods); however, the use of the collectors throughout the year requires determining their shading effects in each season. Builders should determine the effects of shading from these elements by plotting the path of the sun across the sky for January 21, September/March 21, and June 21. Assessment of solar shading with a transit is discussed in Chapter 8.

SYSTEM LAYOUT

The exact location of solar collectors determines the layout of the rest of the system, so it must be carefully planned. The length and location of pipe runs connecting collectors with domestic water storage influence the efficiency and operation of the system. To reduce the length of runs outside the building, insulated pipes from collectors on roofs, walls, or ground mounted racks should enter the building as quickly as possible through properly sealed penetrations (Fig. 6.14). Even well insulated pipes lose considerable heat between the collectors and storage, especially when directly exposed to outdoor temperatures. Chapter 11 offers a detailed discussion of pipe insulation.

Pipe runs for solar water heaters should be located in interior partitions, closets, or chases in new construction and retrofits. Distance from the cooler temperatures of exterior walls helps reduce the rate of heat loss from these lines; it also leaves the wall cavities open for more complete insulation.

Fig. 6.14 All pipe penetrations must be properly sealed. Here a standard 3" roof flange is used to flash around an insulated pipe.

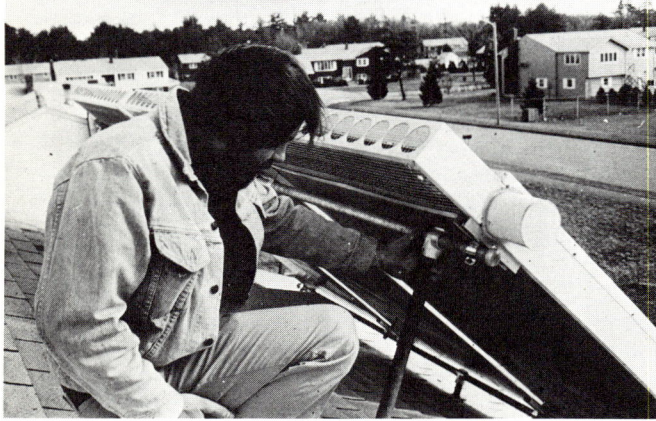

Fig. 6.15 Many different mounting details are used with solar collectors.

The exact layout of components in the mechanical area depends on the type of system. Although manufacturers and designers will specify the schematic plan, exact layout in the mechanical room is defined by the installing subcontractor and the space available for insulated pipes and components. Chapter 11 offers detailed suggestions for system layout regarding ease of installation, proper operation, aesthetics, and future maintenance. Builders should become familiar with these details so they can prepare for system installation, select and schedule the installing subcontractors, and knowledgeably supervise their work (Fig. 6.15).

SOLAR CONTRACTORS

Subcontractors who install solar water heaters may be specialized solar contractors or plumbing and heating contractors. Builders should select this contractor the same way others are chosen: by past experience working together, the contractor's previous work with solar water heaters, the quality and cost of equipment offered, and the contractor's service agreement.

The solar installation can be subcontracted as part of the total plumbing and heating job or separately, depending on the availability of qualified contractors. Even the best equipment will not work if it is installed improperly, and many problems can occur with contractors installing their first system. Builders should visit at least one system installed by a potential subcontractor and check references for other installations. Do not assume that a plumber can successfully install a solar water heater the first time.

PART II MATERIALS, DETAILS, AND TECHNIQUES OF SOLAR CONSTRUCTION

Fig. 7.1 Phases of solar construction.

(Boyd Associates)

102

CHAPTER 7
THE PHASES OF SOLAR CONSTRUCTION

INTRODUCTION TO PART II

Part I presented the principles of solar construction upon which builders should base their design and construction decisions; the application of these principles in specific building configurations is the focus of Part II (Fig. 7.1).

In many ways solar construction is identical to past standard practices; in many ways, of course, it differs. Builders must understand the differences in each phase of construction, because these differences affect the selection of materials, details, and construction techniques. Although each builder's business is different, common concerns in selection of materials, detail design, or definition of construction technique include:

- estimating and purchasing
- production scheduling
- supervision and workmanship
- codes and regulations

MATERIALS, DETAILS, AND TECHNIQUES

The selection of building materials and components for use in a particular application is influenced by special requirements of solar construction. These requirements may make certain standard materials unsuitable, and may necessitate selection of new materials or products more appropriate for that application. Generally, at every phase of construction the option to use new materials exists. Available options at each phase are discussed in the chapters in Part II, which follow a logical construction sequence. Builders are accustomed to change in building materials and their applications; however, change should be made only after evaluating the requirements of an application and the properties of those materials under consideration. Energy efficiency is not the only criterion to apply during this process.

The process of estimating and purchasing new materials used in solar construction may vary from a builder's standard method due to unfamiliar specifications and prices, or problems with availability from local suppliers. When obtaining pricing information, estimators should make sure they receive pricing from all suppliers on exactly the same material or component as specified for the job. Additionally, builders should not assume that substitutions readily can be made if the specified material is unavailable; they should hold orders until the proper material can be located or a suitable replacement is verified.

A builder's production schedule also can be affected by the use of new materials during any phase of construction; problems in the availability of new materials may cause delivery delays. Builders should plan for delays by placing orders for new materials far in advance of when they are needed. If subcontractors are to provide special materials and components, such as flat plate collectors, builders should be sure the materials will be available when the subcontracted work is scheduled to start. Subcontractor delays set back all subsequent phases of construction.

When using new materials in solar construction, builders should supervise layout and help work crews to set up and work efficiently with the materials. Workmanship is critical throughout all phases of solar construction; although many of the new products are applied easily, workers should be given direction to establish the proper pace and level of quality. At some points, as discussed later in Part II, work *should* slow down to allow adequate attention to detail; however, as the materials become more familiar, workmanship will remain at a high level, while productivity improves.

Construction details and techniques also may be affected at each phase by the need to incorporate new materials and new features into buildings. As always, details should be carefully planned and drawn, and then explained to the crew foremen so they can understand the materials used and the sequence of assembly.

The use of new details and techniques in solar construction may affect a builder's cost estimating procedures. Although the materials take-offs can be accomplished as usual, estimates of labor requirements for unfamiliar details will be more difficult to calculate accurately. When preparing job estimates, builders should plan on slower production whenever a new feature is encountered. New details must be designed both to serve their intended functions, and, even if new materials are used, to be assembled using practical construction techniques.

The production scheduling at each phase of construction is just as critical in solar construction as it has been in the past; however, changes in scheduling will result from additional steps taken during the construction sequence, or slower production at critical points where good quality must be assured. The schedule must account for these added delays in order for builders to plan the completion of each phase and the job as a whole. These concerns are especially important in planning for subcontracted work, to make sure the job is ready for the subcontractors in proper sequence.

Job supervision affects the cost of construction, quality of workmanship, and ultimately the energy efficiency of a building. The person responsible for supervision must be aware of any changes in materials, details, and techniques used during any phase to make sure they are properly included before progressing too far into the next phase. The supervisor or foreman should double-check layout of new features as well as inspect the final product. As stated throughout this book, good workmanship is a critical element of solar construction, and careful supervision is one means of assuring it.

BUILDING CODES

Building codes protect public health and safety, and they affect every aspect of the building industry from material production to building. Codes define the types of materials that can be used in various applications as well as the techniques used to assemble them. Codes therefore have a direct impact on the costs of construction (Fig. 7.2).

Builders and contractors must comply with local restrictions that cover carpentry, plumbing, heating, and electrical work, so they must learn whether any new practices under consideration are acceptable under the codes:

Structural stability is a primary concern in building codes. As discussed later in Part II, solar construction may require changes in foundations, framing, bracing, and sheathing used to support vertical loads and to resist horizontal forces. These changes can be made within the limits of local codes using standard construction practices.

Fire prevention and protection also are identified and enforced through local codes. Most materials used in residential construction are flammable, some more than others. Flame spread and smoke toxicity potential of some building materials used in solar construction affect their location in the building and the need for fire-resistant finishes between the material and the living space. For example, foam board insulation used on interior wall and ceiling surfaces typically must be finished with gypsum wallboard.

Solar construction also uses features that encourage natural heat and moisture distribution by convection within a building. Some builders enclose a convective air passage between double framed exterior walls, which allows free air movement but also allows the free spread of fire. Local codes define the appropriate means of controlling fire in these areas. Woodstoves, fireplaces, and plastic glazing materials also must be approved by local codes for fire safety.

Fire protection usually involves measures that slow a fire's progress in order to allow occupants to escape. Codes also define the requirements for location and size of windows and doors in order to provide emergency egress. As well as affecting the layout of exterior windows and doors, codes may dictate the location of interior rooms and hallways. Any floor plan adjustments made for fire safety should weigh energy considerations as well.

Natural light and ventilation levels in buildings often are set by local codes. Such regulations prescribe placement and size of windows throughout the building and a minimum percentage of operable window area for ventilation. Window area and natural ventilation are also important concerns in solar construction. In most cases, code requirements can be balanced with solar requirements.

Other areas of solar construction affected by codes include: solar domestic hot water (DHW) installation; sizing of supplemental heating and cooling systems; placement of electrical outlets along exterior walls; and rates of mechanical ventilation.

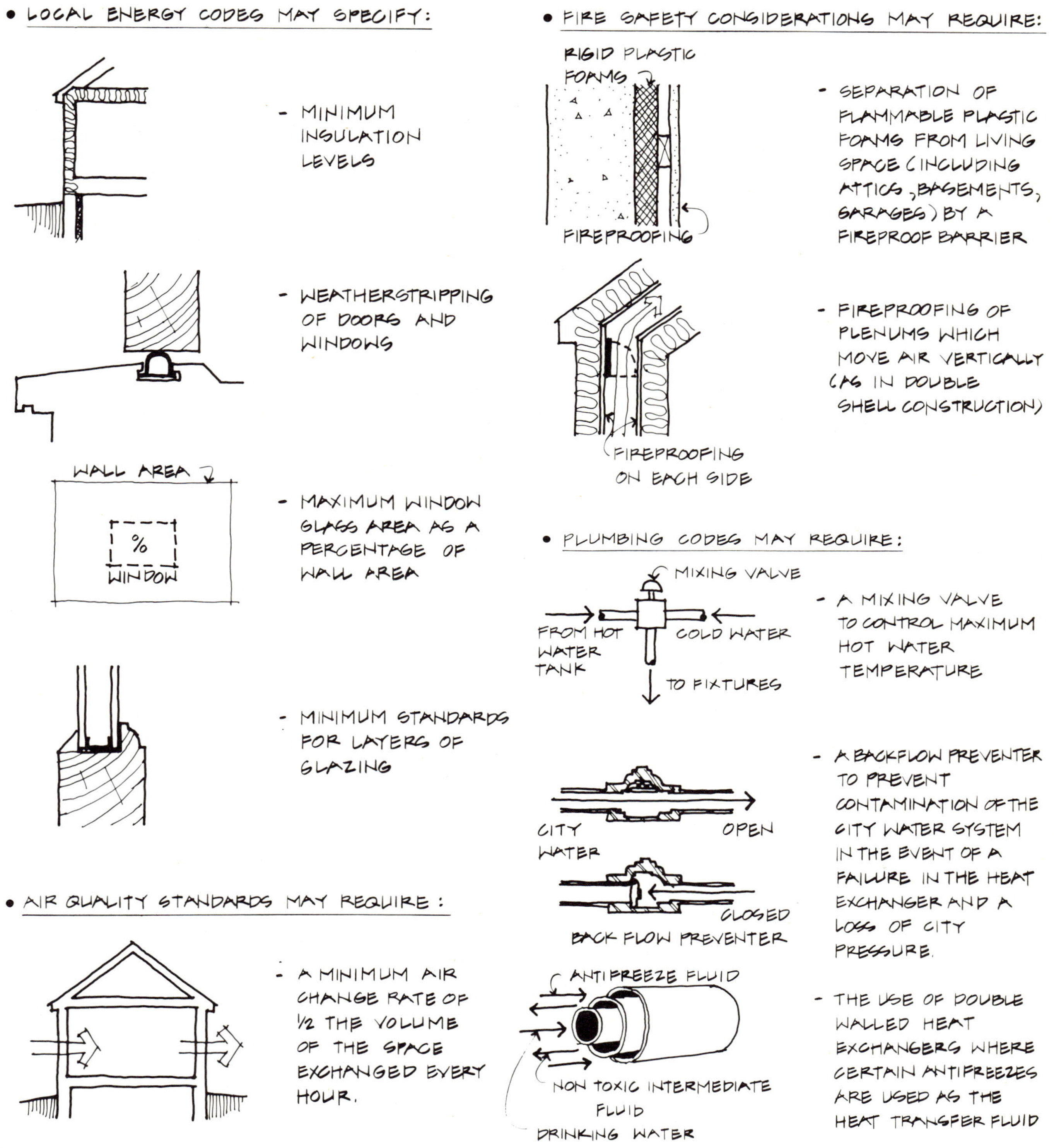

- LOCAL ENERGY CODES MAY SPECIFY:
  - MINIMUM INSULATION LEVELS
  - WEATHERSTRIPPING OF DOORS AND WINDOWS
  - MAXIMUM WINDOW GLASS AREA AS A PERCENTAGE OF WALL AREA
  - MINIMUM STANDARDS FOR LAYERS OF GLAZING

- AIR QUALITY STANDARDS MAY REQUIRE:
  - A MINIMUM AIR CHANGE RATE OF ½ THE VOLUME OF THE SPACE EXCHANGED EVERY HOUR.

- FIRE SAFETY CONSIDERATIONS MAY REQUIRE:
  - SEPARATION OF FLAMMABLE PLASTIC FOAMS FROM LIVING SPACE (INCLUDING ATTICS, BASEMENTS, GARAGES) BY A FIREPROOF BARRIER
  - FIREPROOFING OF PLENUMS WHICH MOVE AIR VERTICALLY (AS IN DOUBLE SHELL CONSTRUCTION)

- PLUMBING CODES MAY REQUIRE:
  - A MIXING VALVE TO CONTROL MAXIMUM HOT WATER TEMPERATURE
  - A BACKFLOW PREVENTER TO PREVENT CONTAMINATION OF THE CITY WATER SYSTEM IN THE EVENT OF A FAILURE IN THE HEAT EXCHANGER AND A LOSS OF CITY PRESSURE.
  - THE USE OF DOUBLE WALLED HEAT EXCHANGERS WHERE CERTAIN ANTIFREEZES ARE USED AS THE HEAT TRANSFER FLUID

Fig. 7.2 Building regulations that may apply to solar construction

REGULATIONS

Several government housing agencies have adopted energy regulations designed to improve the energy efficiency of homes built under their programs. Typically, these set minimum levels of insulation throughout the building according to different climates; they may even make recommendations for site plantings, orientation of entry doors, building shape, and glazing area. Some of these agencies have approved passive solar features and solar DHW systems.

New regulations developed by state and local authorities also will affect builders in the near future. They are likely to call for minimum levels of insulation, compliance with energy performance standards, and the installation of solar DHW. (Many states now require at least roughed-in pipe runs for DHW). Regulations mandating lot plans and zoning setbacks adjusted for solar access are also probable.

THE PHASES OF CONSTRUCTION

The remaining chapters of Part II are organized in the chronological progression of construction phases, with emphasis on those phases in which solar construction requires a departure from standard practice. The interrelation of phases is such that the early ones affect work done later, and the reverse is also true. Some work, such as plumbing, heating, and electrical installation, affects each phase and has a large impact on the control of heat conduction, air leakage, and moisture. Builders must be aware of these overlapping areas of work as they are critical in the scheduling, supervision, and energy performance of solar construction.

The following chapters introduce the energy related decisions that must be made throughout the construction process. Available options and critical areas which affect scheduling and workmanship are discussed. The work at each phase is discussed with an eye towards its effect on the overall energy efficiency of the building. New materials, details, and techniques used at each phase, and the priorities involved in their selection and use, are identified. The discussion is organized into the following five construction phases:

1. sitework and foundation
2. the insulated building shell
3. doors, windows, and glazings
4. HVAC, plumbing, electrical, and solar DHW
5. interior finishes and special construction

Chapter 8, **Sitework and Foundation**, presents the first phase of construction in which the specific location of a building is selected (Fig. 7.3). The elements of microclimate, as introduced in Chapter 4, are reviewed and recommendations for building orientation and layout are made within the context of other features important in this phase. The materials, details, and techniques used during excavation, construction, waterproofing, insulating and backfilling of several foundation configurations are discussed, and special areas of concern for solar construction identified. Additional details found at the end of the chapter include saving trees on building sites, construction of retaining walls, and features of earth-sheltered buildings.

Chapter 9, **The Insulated Building Shell**, presents that phase most critical in solar construction (Fig. 7.4). Structural and material changes made to aid in the control of heat loss and gain, air leakage, moisture, and ventilation are discussed. Options for new materials and details are presented and the importance of scheduling, supervision, and workmanship are reemphasized. The discussion follows the sequence of shell construction and offers additional details of special features in floors, walls, and roofs/ceilings.

Chapter 10, **Doors, Windows, and Glazings**, focuses on the important functions of these components in solar construction, including entry and exit, transmission of solar radiation, ventilation, daylighting, views, and weatherproofing (Figure 7.5). Materials and components are compared and recommended installation techniques presented with emphasis on reducing heat loss by conduction and infiltration in both operable and fixed units. Special applications of fixed glazings for thermal storage walls, sunspace/greenhouses, skylights, and site-built solar heat collectors are also included.

Chapter 11, **HVAC, Plumbing, Electrical and Solar DHW**, discusses the installation and operation of these mechanical components in residential solar construction (Fig. 7.6). These systems are the energy consumers in a building and their impact can be reduced through careful selection of energy efficient products sized to meet specific requirements and through new installation techniques. Because work done in this phase extends into all phases of construction, the impact of scheduling and workmanship on the successful completion and energy performance of buildings is emphasized. The section on solar DHW installation includes the selection of components, subcontractors, and installation techniques and scheduling for flat plate collectors used in mechanical systems. Additional details covered are options for thermosiphoning and batch solar water heaters.

Chapter 12, **Interior Finishes and Special Construction**, considers the selection of interior finish materials for floors, walls, and ceilings and of woodwork installed

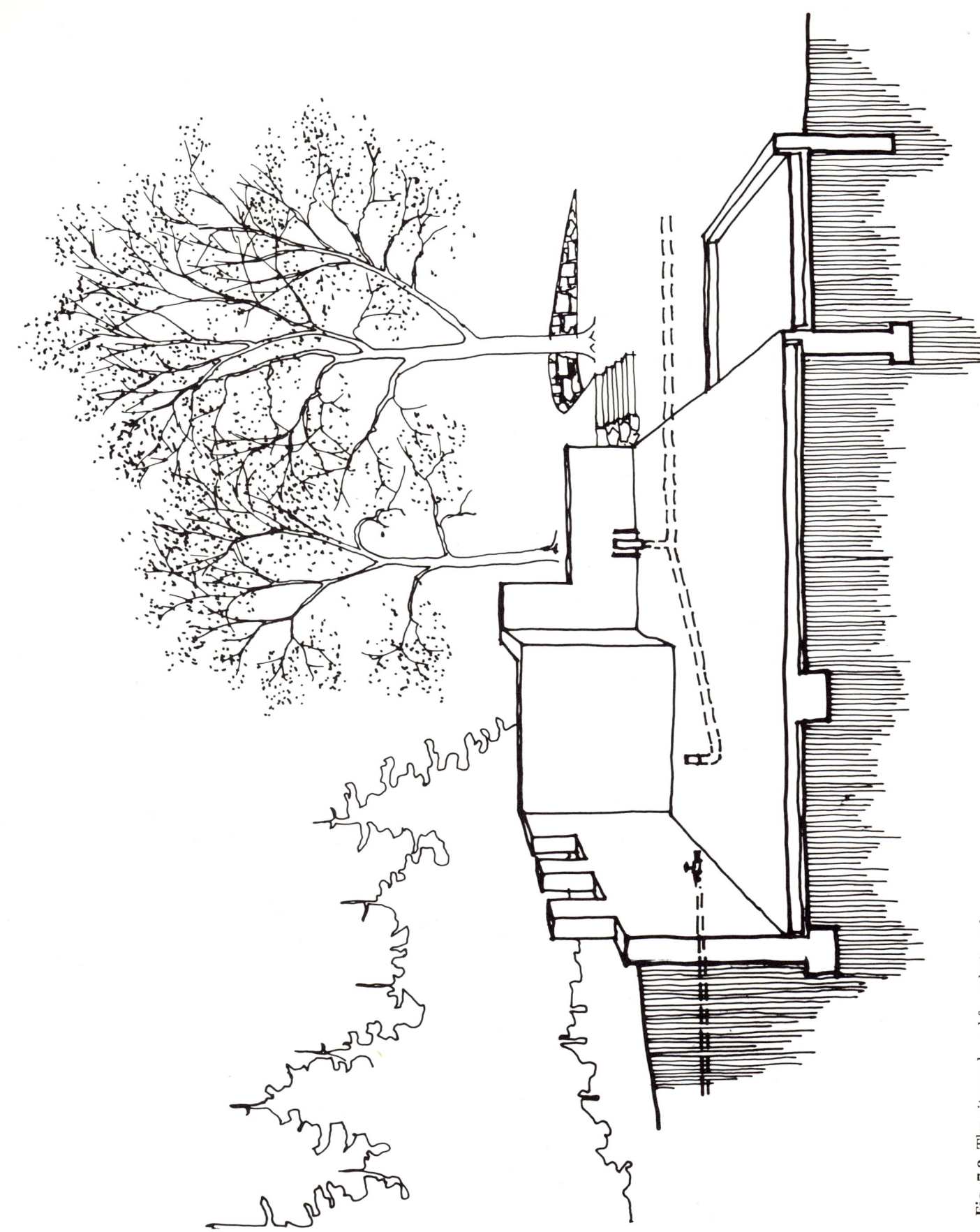

Fig. 7.3 The sitework and foundation phase.

Fig. 7.4 The insulated building shell phase.

Fig. 7.5 The doors, windows and glazings phase.

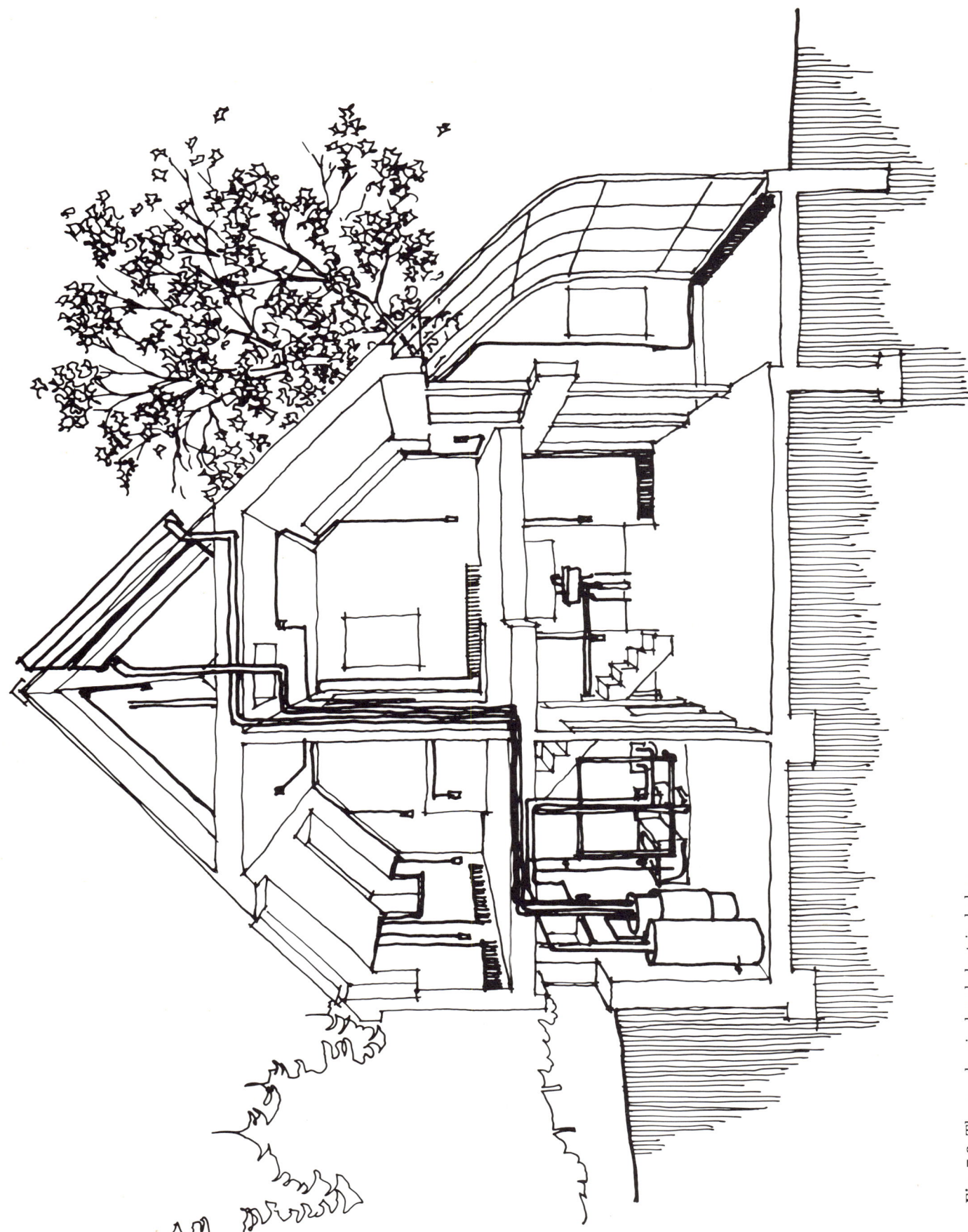

Fig. 7.6 The mechanical and electrical phase.

Fig. 7.7 The interior finishes and special construction phase.

112 MATERIALS, DETAILS, AND TECHNIQUES OF SOLAR CONSTRUCTION

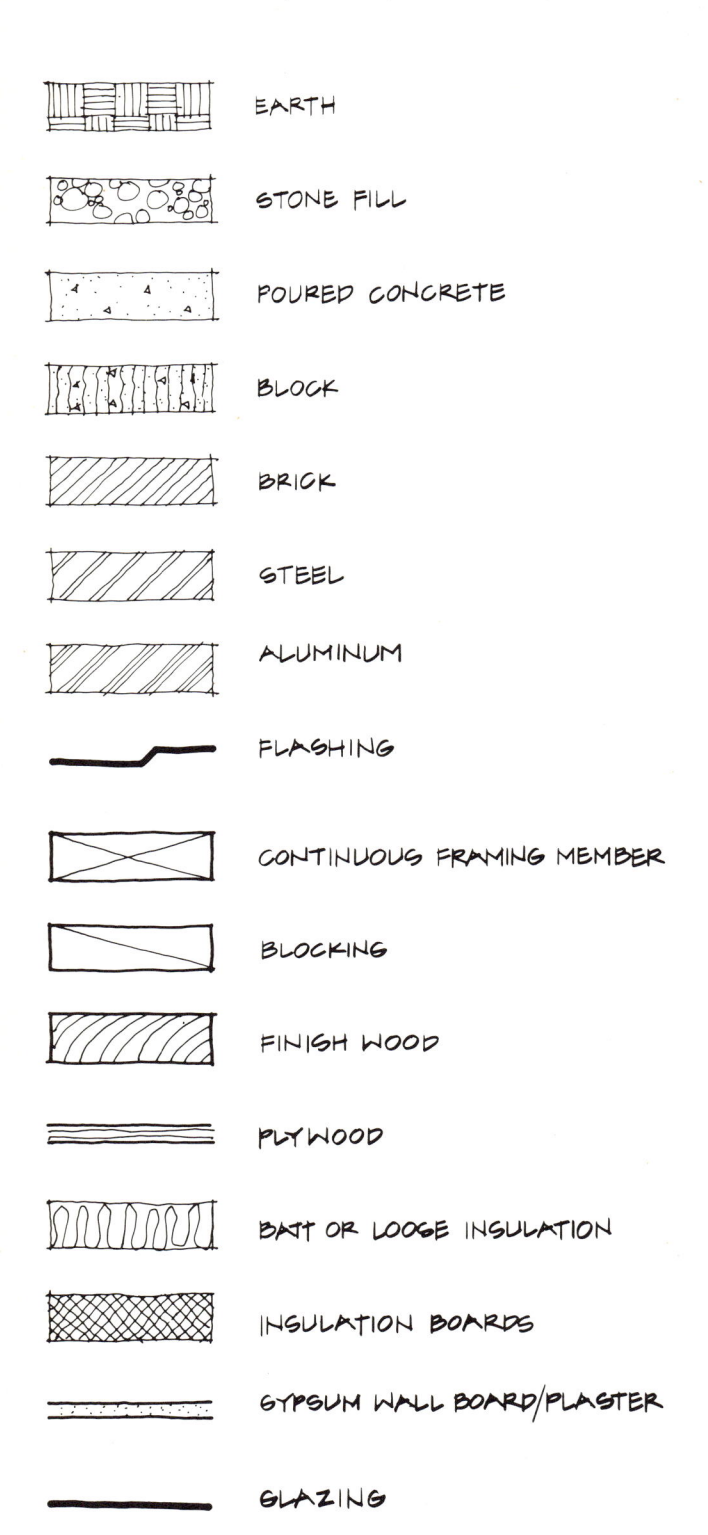

during this final phase of construction (Fig. 7.7). The use of color and materials to reflect or absorb solar radiation and special techniques required for their application are discussed. This chapter also presents special features installed in this phase, including options for movable insulation, and shading devices.

Throughout Part II, discussions are supplemented with comparative tables and charts, photographs, and drawings. The drawings of construction details utilize the symbols presented in Figure 7.8.

- EARTH
- STONE FILL
- POURED CONCRETE
- BLOCK
- BRICK
- STEEL
- ALUMINUM
- FLASHING
- CONTINUOUS FRAMING MEMBER
- BLOCKING
- FINISH WOOD
- PLYWOOD
- BATT OR LOOSE INSULATION
- INSULATION BOARDS
- GYPSUM WALL BOARD/PLASTER
- GLAZING

Fig. 7.8 List of building symbols.

CHAPTER 8 SITEWORK AND FOUNDATIONS

INTRODUCTION

The sitework and foundation phase of construction can be affected to a large extent by the details and techniques of solar construction. In Chapter 4 we examined the importance of placing a building on its site so that it is sheltered from the winds and open to the sun in winter, and sheltered from the sun and open to breezes in summer. Additionally, below grade areas increasingly are used as primary living spaces to take advantage of the sheltering effects of the earth. Proper site drainage and close attention to waterproofing details can ensure comfortable conditions. The ability of materials such as concrete and masonry to store heat for periods of time increases their application in solar construction. As such, basement walls and slab on grade floors should be insulated. The use of rigid foam insulations below a slab or outside a foundation requires careful selection and installation, due to the material's exposure to multiple freeze/thaw cycles below grade and to the effects of solar radiation above grade (Fig. 8.2).

The foundation connects a building to its site; it supports the building and transmits its loads directly to the soil. Reinforced concrete and masonry products have traditionally been used for foundations, and they still remain the primary materials used to satisfy the different structural requirements of various buildings and sites. Foundations serve two main structural functions: (1) distributing loads from the building to the ground, as footings distribute loads from walls, posts, or fireplaces; and (2) retaining the earth, as with basement walls and retaining walls in the side of a hill. Solar construction may affect structural requirements in several ways. The increased weight of thermal storage materials may require larger footings. The use of earth berming against walls or covering roofs with soil can increase structural importance in foundation selection (Fig. 8.3).

Other important considerations in the selection of foundation materials are differing capabilities to waterproof, insulate, store heat, and provide a durable finish. Reinforced concrete commonly is used in solar construction for its high strength and heat storage capacity. Poured concrete also is more resistant than cement block to the movement of ground moisture through it, and therefore has greater potential for use as walls and floors of dry, warm, below grade living spaces. Cement block foundations are often less expensive than poured concrete, and they have lower conductive heat loss due to the air spaces between the block webbing. Both materials should be insulated, as discussed later in this chapter. Brick, stone, slate, and other masonry products often are used in combination with concrete because of their more attractive finish, texture, and ease of handling.

SITEWORK

Site Analysis

The proper placement of a building on its site requires an accurate survey of site resources, including topographic features and orientation, location and types of trees and shrubs, shading obstructions, surface drainage patterns, and soil types (See Chapter 4). Builders should evaluate each site separately and work to find the best location for each house. No matter what approach to solar heating is included, all buildings benefit from careful siting (Fig. 8.4).

Topographic features including outcroppings of ledge, site slope, and earth mounds can help determine where a building should be placed on a site. If you encounter ledge, try to locate an alternate site. A foun-

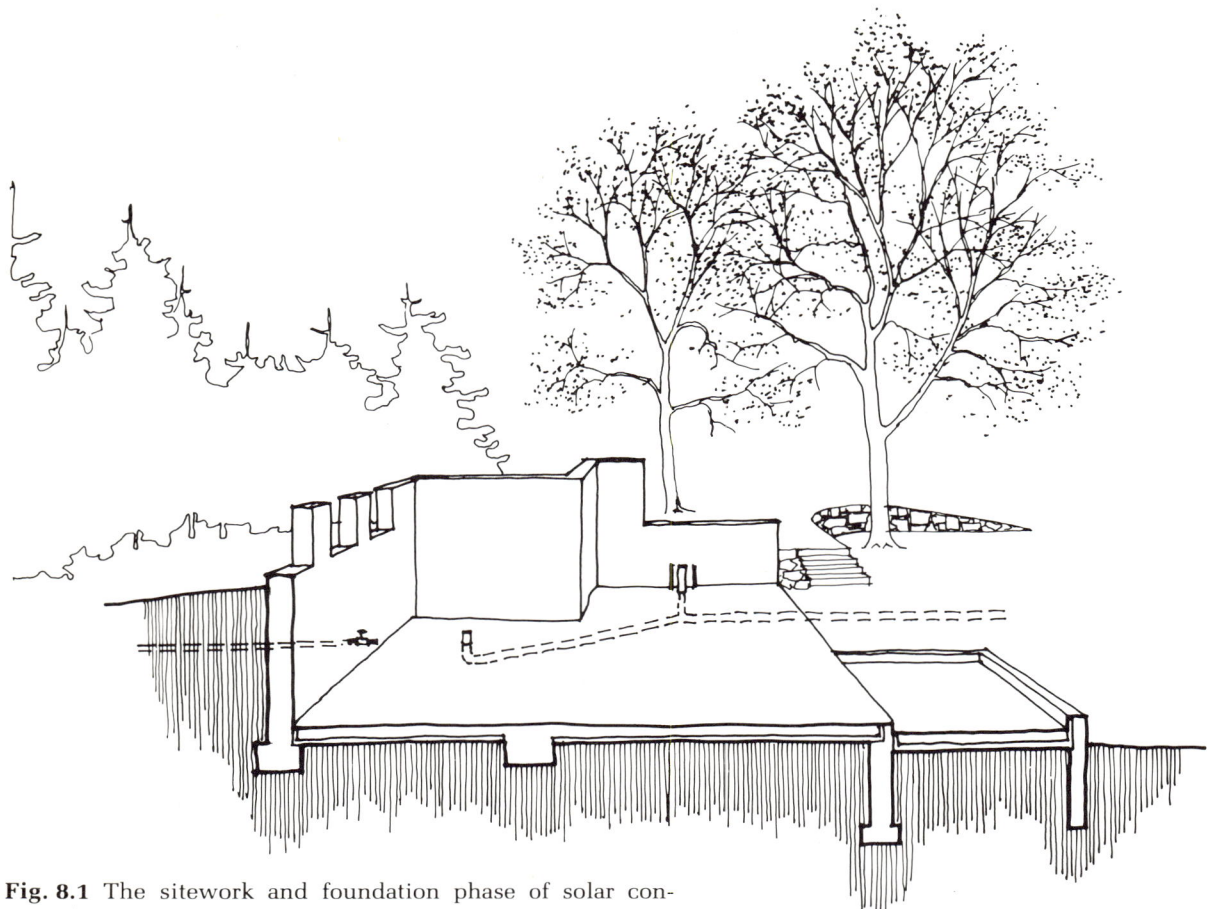

Fig. 8.1 The sitework and foundation phase of solar construction

dation connected to ledge will transmit heat away from the building into the almost limitless mass of the earth.

Site slope and orientation should be assessed for access to solar energy, elements of the microclimate, sewage and utilities, vehicle access, and ease of construction. Sites sloping to the south are most desirable in northern latitudes and offer the potential to earth berm the sides of the building. These sites are especially suitable for earth sheltered designs. Mounds of earth may be used beneficially to earth berm a building. If located on the side of a slope, however, they may serve as dams to cool air, causing cold pockets. In this case, the earth mounds should be broken down to allow cool air to drain past.

Location and types of trees are other important site considerations. Building placement should take advantage of wind protection offered by vegetation. By reducing wind velocity, trees and shrubs reduce the rate of heat loss from the building. A more detailed discussion of wind control is presented in Chapter 4.

Shading from trees and/or other buildings reduces the amount of solar energy striking a site. In the summer, shading helps keep a building cool; in the winter, however, shading should be avoided between the hours of 9:00 A.M. and 3:00 P.M. when the sun is most intense. Proper placement of the building and selective clearing of some trees can result in a building that receives shade in summer and full exposure to the sun in winter. It is important to assess the effects of shading from potential obstructions to the southeast, south, and southwest of the site. The longest shadows occur on December 21 when the sun is lowest in the sky. (The various sun angles during the year are discussed in Chapter 4.) A transit can be used to "shoot" the position of the sun at different times of day and different days of the year, thus allowing the builder to plan for solar access to the building (Fig. 8.5).

Water movement on the site is always a critical concern. Ground water affects the heat loss from the foundation by increasing the rate of heat conducted

Fig. 8.2 Builders and their subcontractors must become familiar with changes that occur at each phase of solar construction.

through the adjacent soil. It has long term effects on exterior foundation insulation, and water can damage interior finishes in below grade living spaces if it leaks through walls. (Foundation moistureproofing is discussed later in this chapter.) Surface drainage patterns and soil types also should be considered; natural drainage patterns should be left undisturbed whenever possible, and finish grading sloped to divert water away from the building and towards the natural drainage pattern. Soil types that hold water (clay types) should be avoided, or at least replaced with gravel as backfill for a building on a wet site (Fig. 8.6).

Building Orientation and Layout

Once an appropriate site has been selected, the building and excavation lines can be established. The orientation of a building on its site affects its comfort, economy, and marketability. When orienting the building, consider access to the road, view, privacy, and solar radiation—

116 MATERIALS, DETAILS, AND TECHNIQUES OF SOLAR CONSTRUCTION

- MORE GRADING IS OFTEN REQUIRED TO FIT THE BUILDING INTO THE SITE ESPECIALLY IF BERMING IS DONE

- BELOW GRADE AREAS ARE MORE OFTEN USED AS LIVING SPACE NECESSITATING DRIER WARMER CONDITIONS THAN NORMALLY ASSOCIATED WITH BASEMENTS

- INCREASED SITEWORK REQUIRES MORE ATTENTION TO CONSTRUCTION STAGING TO AVOID CONFLICTS OF PHASES

- ATTENTION TO DRAINAGE IS MORE CRITICAL TO ASSURE DRY INTERIOR SPACE

- FOUNDATION INSULATION IS OFTEN PLACED ON THE OUTSIDE OF FOUNDATION WALLS

- NEW AND EXISTING SITE PLANTING IS EXTREMELY IMPORTANT IN CONTROLLING SUN, WIND AND PRIVACY

- FOUNDATION SHOULD BE SQUARE AND LEVEL WITHIN CLOSE TOLERANCES (1/4") TO REDUCE INFILTRATION AT CONNECTIONS WITH OTHER CONSTRUCTION.

- INTERIOR CHIMNEYS AND OTHER THERMAL MASS PLACE INCREASED STRUCTURAL LOADS ON FOUNDATIONS

- STORING SOLAR HEAT IN SLABS REQUIRES INSULATION UNDER THE SLAB IN ADDITION TO INCREASED PERIMETER INSULATION

- UTILITY CONNECTIONS, EXTRA UNDER SLAB PIPING AND DUCTWORK (SUCH AS OUTSIDE AIR FEEDS FOR COMBUSTION APPLIANCES) REQUIRE CAREFUL PLANNING

Fig. 8.3 What's different for sitework and foundations in solar construction

all factors which should be weighed carefully before the first layout stake is in the ground.

In Chapter 5 we discussed the impact of shape and orientation on a building's thermal efficiency and solar heat collection. A wide range of orientations are acceptable for collecting solar heat. Generally, it is best to place the building with the long axis running east to west.

Many buildings are "sited" on maps in an office without a site visit. While this approach may be appropriate for properly designed subdivisions built on flat open sites, variations in topography or the presence of trees require a site inspection. Buildings should be integrated into the topography even at the expense of altering the solar orientation. In most locations in the United States, the acceptable range of orientation toward the south falls between 30 degrees east or west of true south. This range allows wide flexibility in responding to the other important considerations for building orientation.

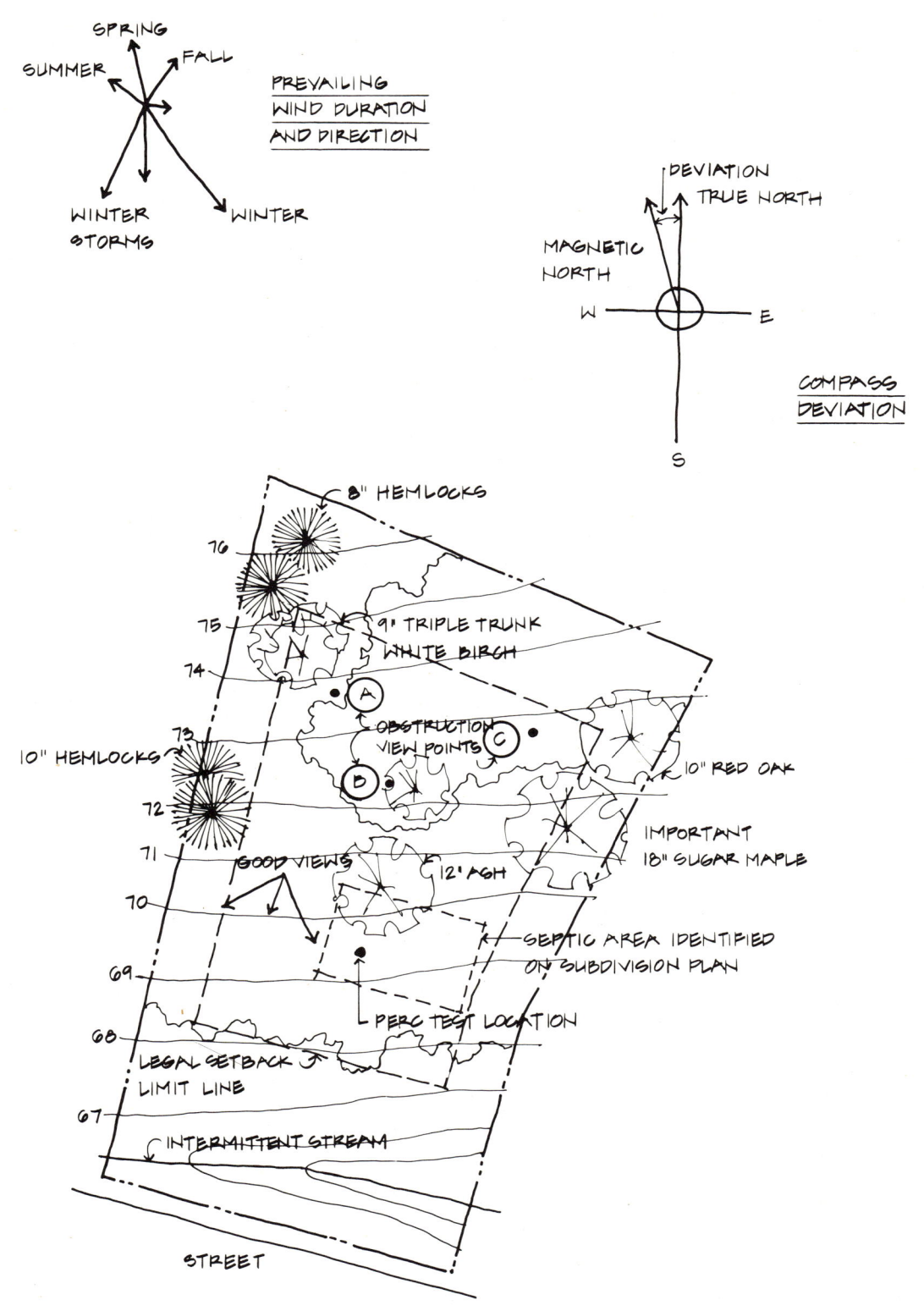

Fig. 8.4 An example of a comprehensive site analysis for a fictitious site. *Note:* Figures 8.5, 8.6, 8.8, 8.11 and 8.13 all present different elements of a comprehensive site plan for this site.

118 MATERIALS, DETAILS, AND TECHNIQUES OF SOLAR CONSTRUCTION

Fig. 8.5 (Top) Builders can use a transit to plot the path of the sun in the sky in order to avoid unwanted shading in winter. (Bottom) A plot of the sun's path across the sky at different times of the year as viewed from different places on the sample site to check for shading obstructions.

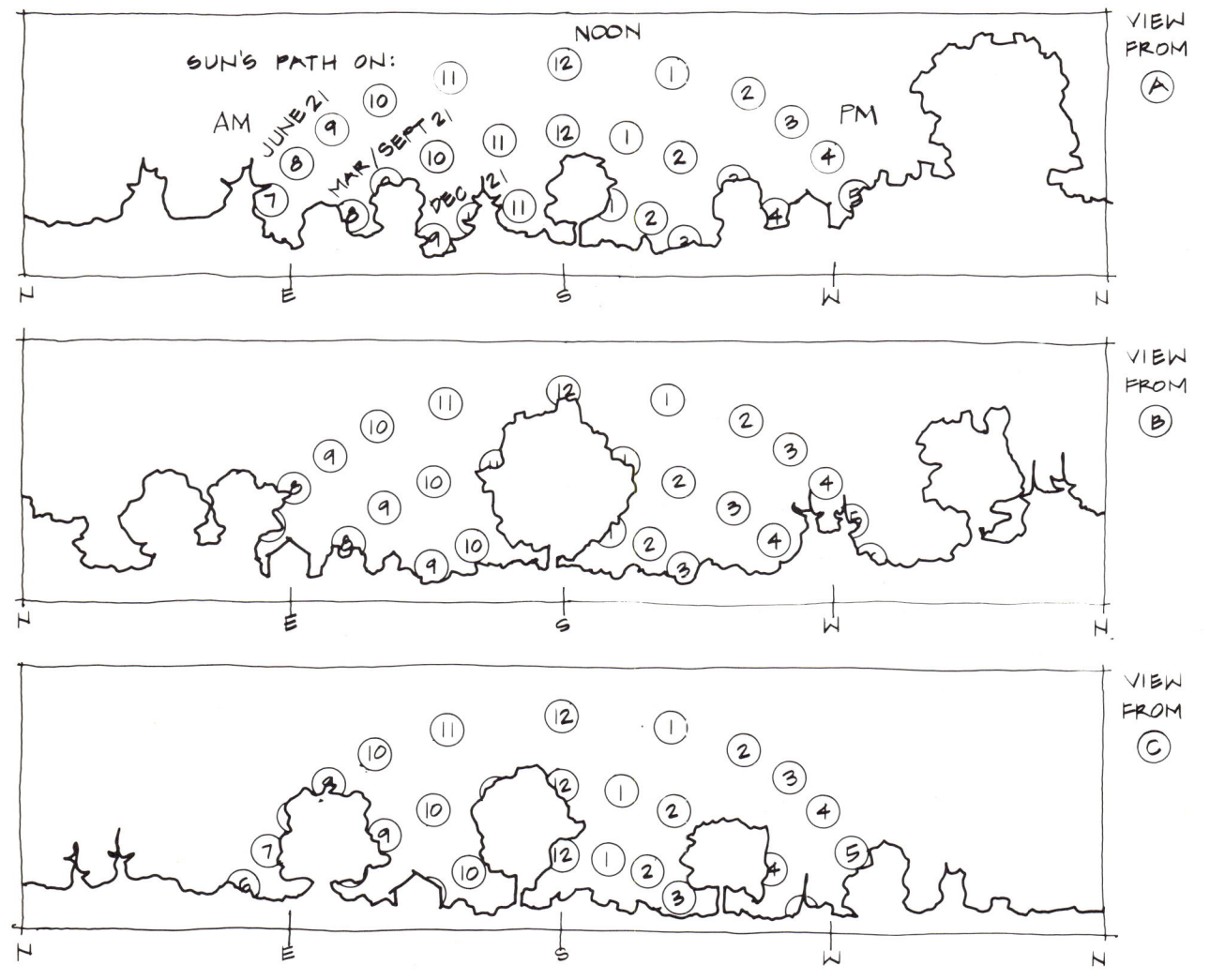

SITEWORK AND FOUNDATIONS 119

Fig. 8.6 (Left) Properly installed footing drains are essential for keeping below grade living areas dry. (Below) A grading and drainage plan for the sample site.

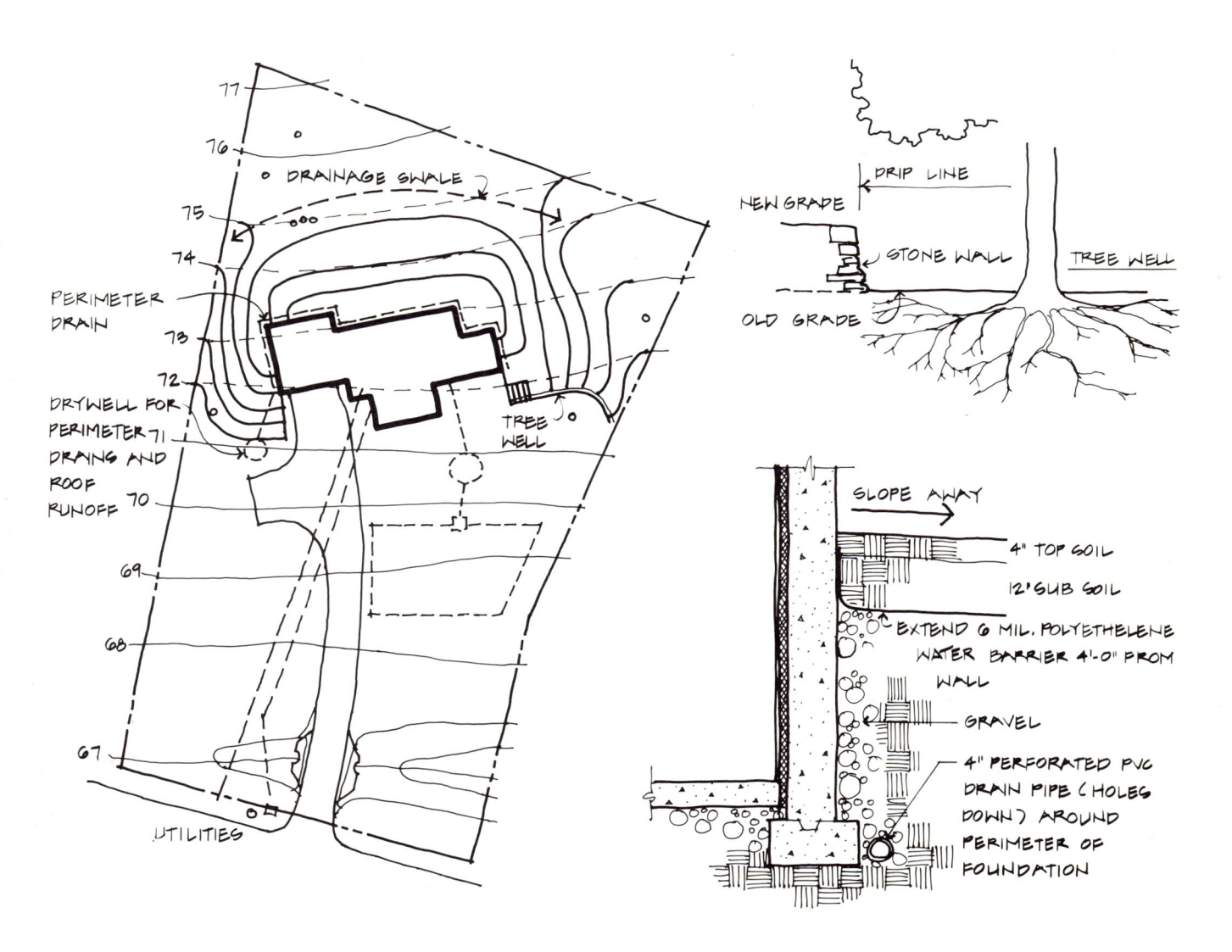

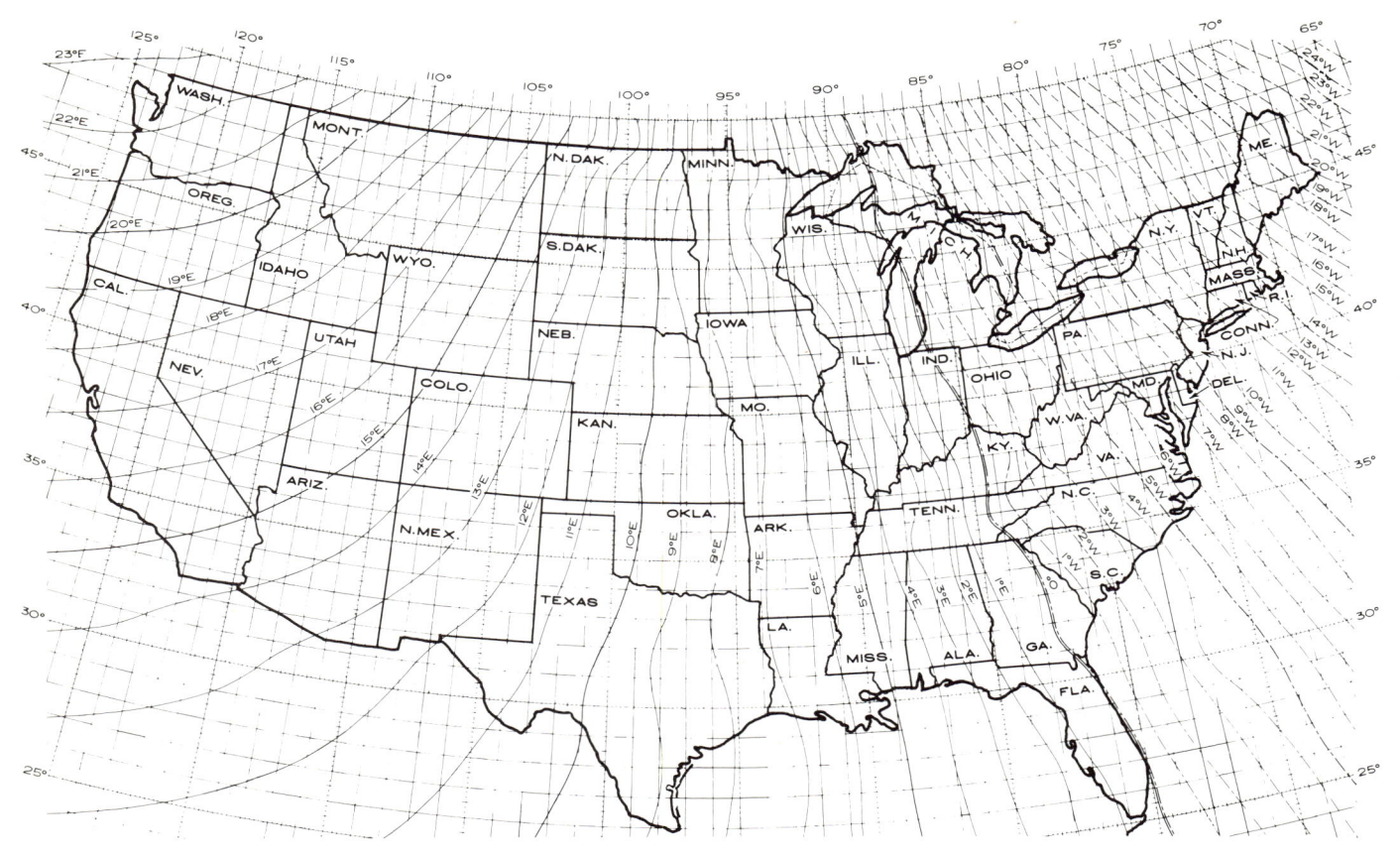

120 MATERIALS, DETAILS, AND TECHNIQUES OF SOLAR CONSTRUCTION

Fig. 8.7 An isogonic map of the United States showing magnetic deviation from true north south orientation. (From U.S. Department of Commerce, Coast & Geodetic Survey 1965)

True south differs from the magnetic south found with a compass; this difference is known as deviation, and it varies with the location. To find true south, first take an accurate compass reading and locate magnetic south; then either add or subtract the number of degrees of deviation from this reading. The deviation for sites in North America can be obtained from the map in Figure 8.7. For a more accurate determination of magnetic deviation, consult a local surveyor or U.S. Geodetic Survey.

Clearing and Planting

During an initial site evaluation to determine types and location of trees and shrubs, a preliminary plan for clearing wooded lots or planting open slopes should be developed (Fig. 8.8). Wooded lots may require clearing for road, septic, power, building site, and solar access. In selecting trees to be cut, consider species, age, health, and location with respect to the building. A consulting forester can assist in developing the clearing and planting plan (Fig. 8.9).

Deciduous trees, such as maple, birch, and oak, can form shade in summer while allowing sunlight to pass through bare winter branches. They should be cut selectively on the south of a building, but left to shade the east, west, and southwest and to help form a windbreak on the north and northwest.

Coniferous trees, such as pine, cedar, and spruce, will form shade in both summer and winter. They should

SITEWORK AND FOUNDATIONS 121

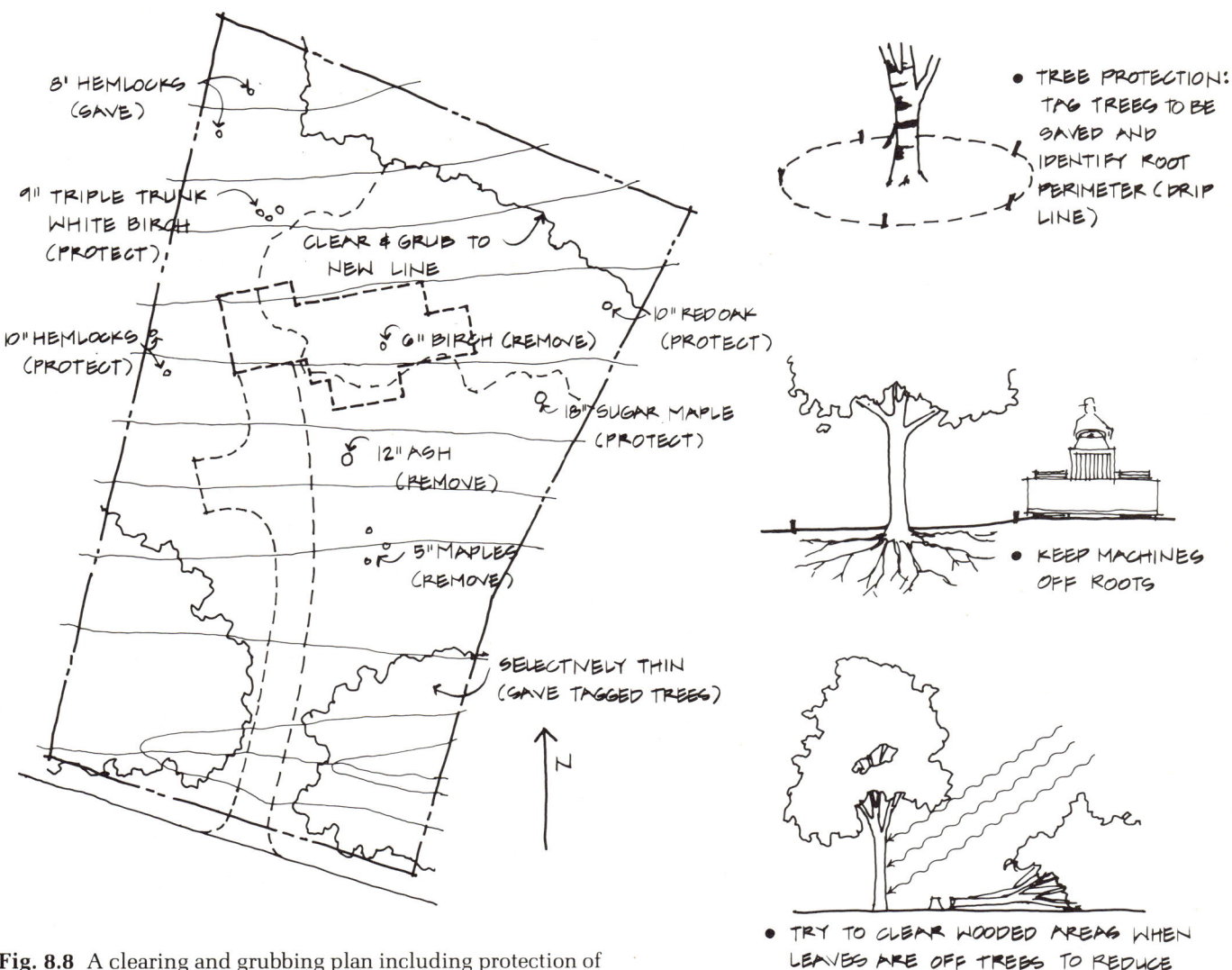

Fig. 8.8 A clearing and grubbing plan including protection of existing trees

- TREE PROTECTION: TAG TREES TO BE SAVED AND IDENTIFY ROOT PERIMETER (DRIP LINE)

- KEEP MACHINES OFF ROOTS

- TRY TO CLEAR WOODED AREAS WHEN LEAVES ARE OFF TREES TO REDUCE SUMMER SUN SHOCK ON SAVED TREES

Fig. 8.9 Consult a local forester to learn how best to save trees on wooded building sites, and how to plant them on open sites.

122 MATERIALS, DETAILS, AND TECHNIQUES OF SOLAR CONSTRUCTION

Fig. 8.10 Work closely with excavation contractors so that trees to be left on the site are not damaged by their equipment.

be cut to the south of the building, and left to form shade and windbreak on the north and northwest.

The trees left on a wooded site should range in age and be free from disease. A diversity of species and age forms a more effective windbreak and reduces the spread of disease, as well as providing for regenerative replacement of older trees that die.

The location of trees with respect to the building site should be considered. Distance from the building determines if trees to the south will shade the site and if trees to the north will be effective as wind deflectors. Distance also determines whether the building could be damaged by falling limbs or tops. The position of trees around the building determines whether certain species located to the south should be cut to prevent shading; whether trees to the east, southwest, and west should be left to promote shading; and whether trees to the north and northwest should be left to divert and slow the winter wind.

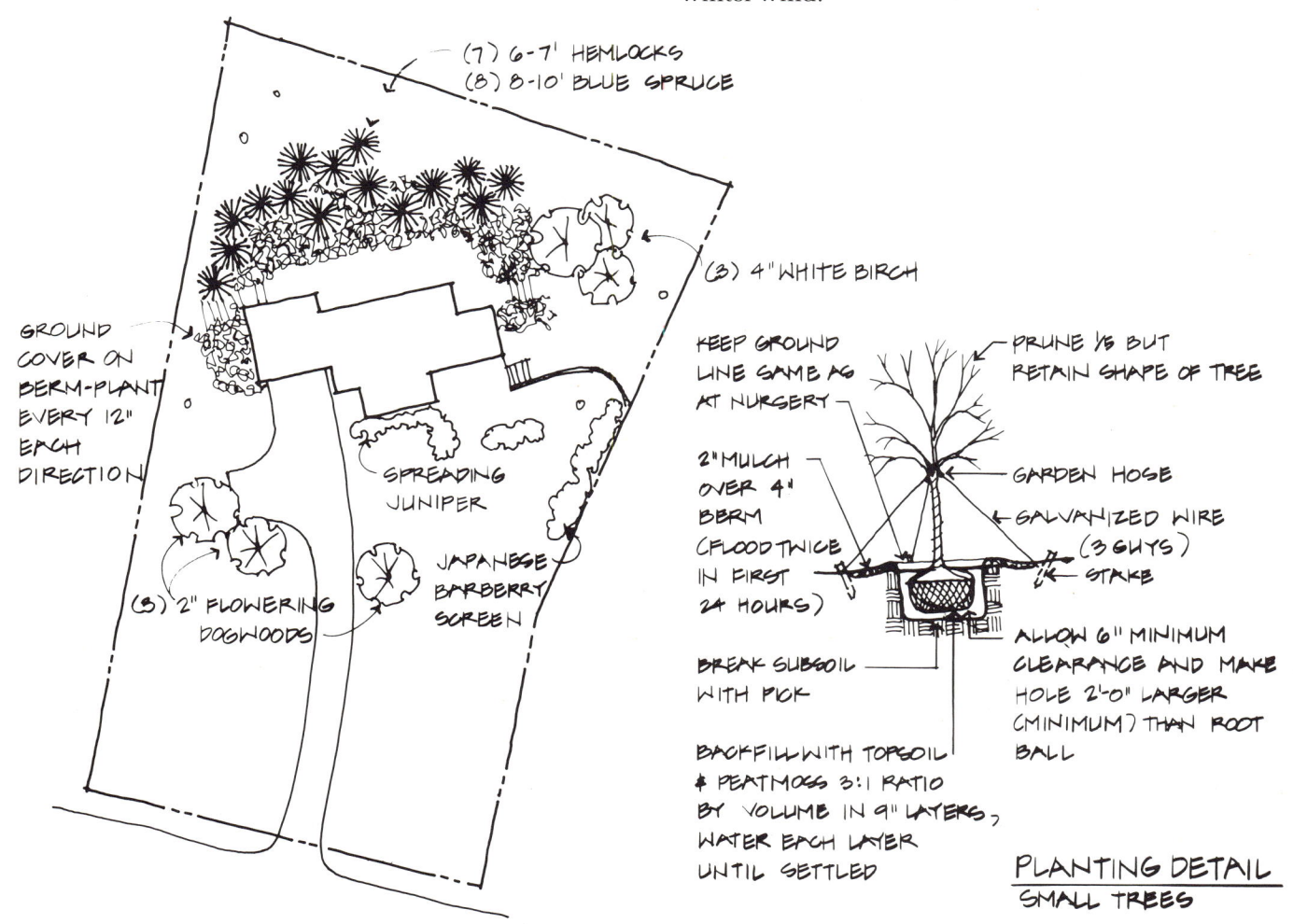

Fig. 8.11 A planting plan for the sample site

Fig. 8.12 Skinned bark, broken branches, root compaction and changes in grade can kill trees left on building sites. Effects of the damage may not be apparent for 2–5 years.

All trees to be left on a wooded site close to the building should be flagged to remind heavy equipment operators to avoid them. Broken branches, skinned bark, soil compaction, or dirt piled around the roots will weaken a tree and leave it susceptible to disease. Supervision and inspection by the builder are critical at this stage (Fig. 8.10).

Open lots require much less site work prior to construction than wooded lots. There are usually very few natural features to utilize for wind protection, so earth berming and the positioning of the garage or a fence to shed winter winds are important measures. Buildings properly oriented on open lots may have easier access to solar radiation than those on wooded lots, though the lack of trees on the site results in higher temperatures in summer, when shading is desired. Deciduous trees planted on the east, southwest, and west of the building help reduce these temperatures and keep the building cooler. One method of planting is to plant short- and long-lived species. Short-lived trees, such as aspen, grow rapidly and will offer shade sooner than the long-lived trees like maple or oak. It is important to allow for future tree growth when spacing plantings in relation to each other and to the building (Fig. 8.11).

Buildings placed on either wooded or open lots should be protected further from wind movement by thick shrubs planted close to the building. However, trees and shrubs located too close to a building can disrupt foundations, walls, and drainage or sewage lines, depending on their root structures.

Trees are valuable elements of microclimate; their use in diverting wind and creating shade are basic to the proper siting of a building. They add value to property, act as a buffer against noise, and offer privacy to homeowners. Saving trees on a building site requires extra planning and care during construction. Although we have touched upon these issues earlier in this chapter and in Chapter 4, they are important enough to add the following details.

Damage to the root system poses the largest threat to trees on a building site, although broken branches and skinned bark also cause serious problems (Fig. 8.12). Root systems are commonly damaged by: (1) compaction from heavy equipment operating or parked within the root zone; (2) chemicals, including petroleum products, lime, and mortar; and (3) excavation, including changes in finish grade, water table, or from trenching. Trees should no longer be considered obstacles to construction.

Excavation, Footings, Drainage, and Retaining Walls

Excavation is not significantly different for solar construction, though supervision of this phase is equally important. As always, the depth of excavation and levelness of the floor of the hole should be accurate (Fig. 8.13). Equipment operators should be instructed to leave a minimal impact on the site. Some changes that may be required include:

- Foundation holes may have to be larger, to allow easier access to work on footings, foundation, and drainage.
- Earth sheltering and berming may require more machine time for site work and backfilling.
- The use of below grade living space may require more gravel to improve drainage around and under the building.
- Schedule of backfill may be delayed due to installation of exterior foundation insulation.

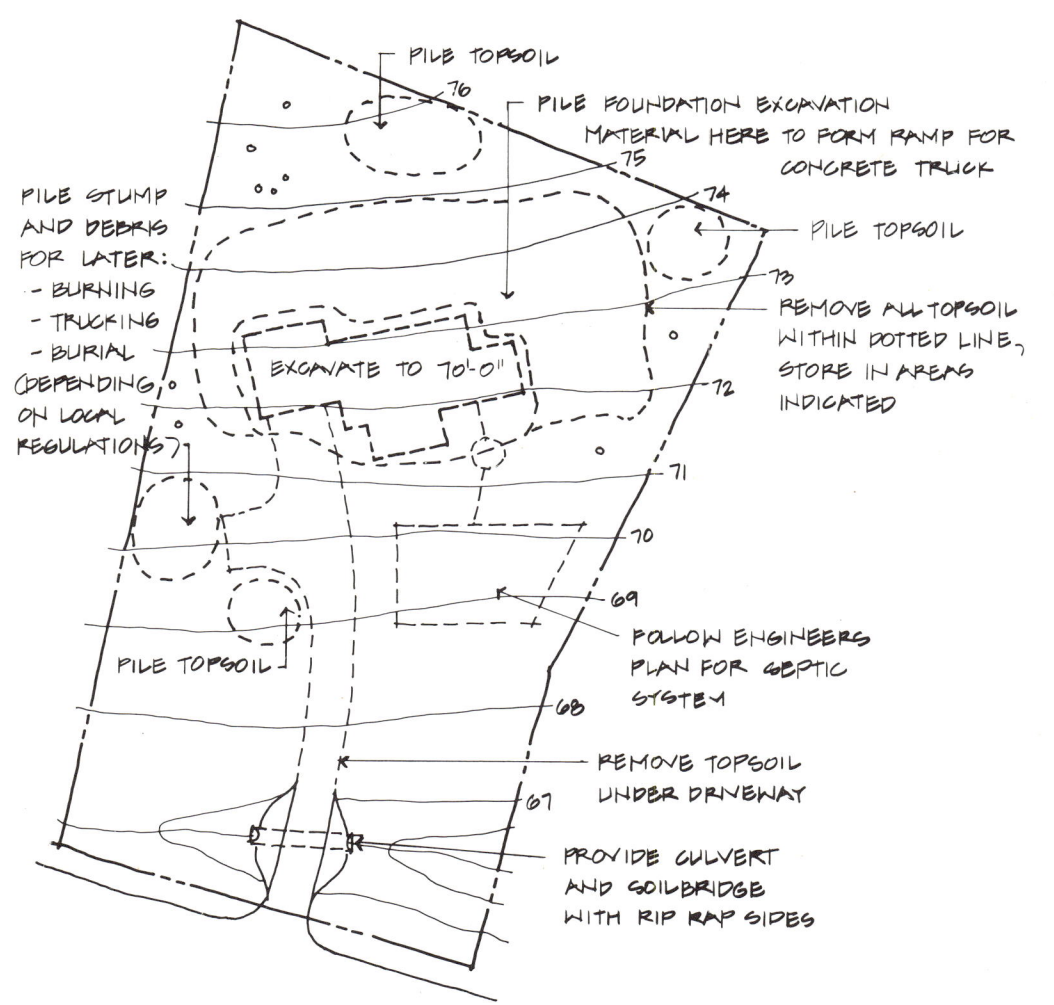

Fig. 8.13 An excavation plan for the sample site

In solar construction larger footings may be required for the increased loads transmitted from thermal mass walls, large glazed areas, or shared loads; Table 9.1 summarizes typical dead loads for these features. As always, footing depths should be below typical frost penetration levels. Perimeter drains are especially important in solar construction; when properly installed they effectively carry ground water away from the foundation. This lowers the risk of water leakage into the building and helps reduce the amount of heat loss from the building.

Builders should supervise carefully the installation of perimeter drains to ensure that pipes are properly joined and pitched to drain, though these may be standard practices.

The proper design and construction of retaining walls during the sitework and foundation phase gain importance in solar construction due to the growing use of earth berms. Major changes in site slope and finish grade require retaining walls to control erosion. These features also allow the earth berm to extend further around the building at a higher grade, which offers more protection from convective heat loss.

FOUNDATION

The type of foundation used to support the building often defines the extent of excavation required at a site. Selection of the foundation system is influenced by factors of site slope, soil characteristics, ground and surface water, building forms, construction budget, and the use of foundation spaces for thermal storage or below grade living areas. This section presents the types of foundations commonly found in residential construction and

SITEWORK AND FOUNDATIONS 125

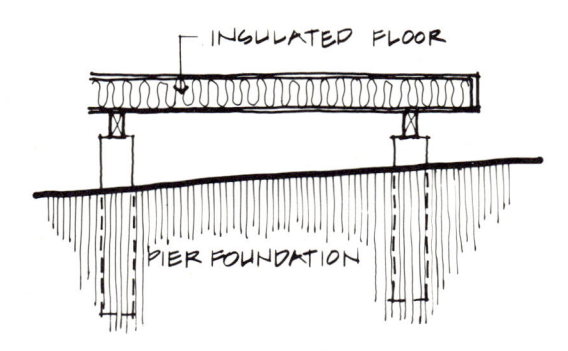

Fig. 8.14 Pier foundation

discusses the issues that are important when these various systems are used in solar construction.

Pier Foundations

Pier foundations may be concrete, masonry, or treated wood posts. When you use a pier foundation, the building structure is supported completely above the ground plane, providing minimum disturbance of the ground surface; thus, ground water and surface drainage conditions are not critical. This approach provides natural ventilation below the first floor deck, which must be insulated and utility penetrations must be protected against freezing. This type of foundation generally is best suited for warmer climates (Fig. 8.14).

Perimeter Foundations

Perimeter foundations consist of poured concrete or concrete block walls that extend to a depth below the deepest expected frost line and rest on a concrete footing. This type of foundation either can form a crawl space beneath the building, or it can serve as the foundation for slab on grade construction (Fig. 8.15). It is important to carefully specify and supervise the installation of utility sleeves and vent openings in the concrete forms prior to the pour. Typical penetrations through these foundation walls include waste line, water supply, underdrain and floor drain exits, and outside air feed for combustion makeup air. The proper installation of formed openings for vents at each opposing corner of the foundation is critical to moisture control in unheated crawl spaces, especially if the finish crawl space floor will consist of earth.

As in all types of construction, these foundations must be built to be square and level. Tops of walls that are uneven or not level will create gaps between the wall

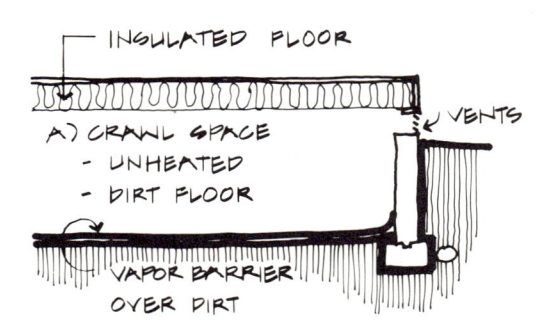

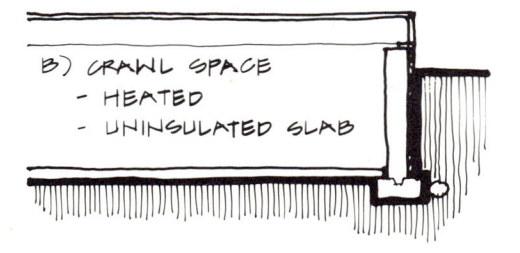

Fig. 8.15 Perimeter foundation showing unheated or heated full basement.

and sill where most air leakage in buildings occurs. Air leakage is not as serious a problem with unheated crawl spaces as with heated crawl spaces used as warm air plenums. Double shell buildings circulate tempered air from the crawl space through the double frame; other buildings locate auxiliary heaters in the crawl space and deliver warm air through floor registers in the main floor.

Concrete Slab on Grade

Slab on grade foundations and concrete slab floors in basements play an important role in solar construction, because they offer an economical means of increasing thermal storage inside a building (Fig. 8.16). Concrete slabs should be insulated below the slab in most cases. Selection of an insulation for use in this case is discussed later in this chapter. Concrete slabs used as thermal storage in sun tempered houses are often thicker than the 4-inch standard. Builders must account for the extra thickness when estimating the amount of material, time to cure, and finished floor heights. Slab thickness also may affect the height of frost walls.

As with any slab on grade construction, site preparation is the most critical factor in determining whether a slab will crack or leak. This is especially important when the slab floor is within finished living areas. The

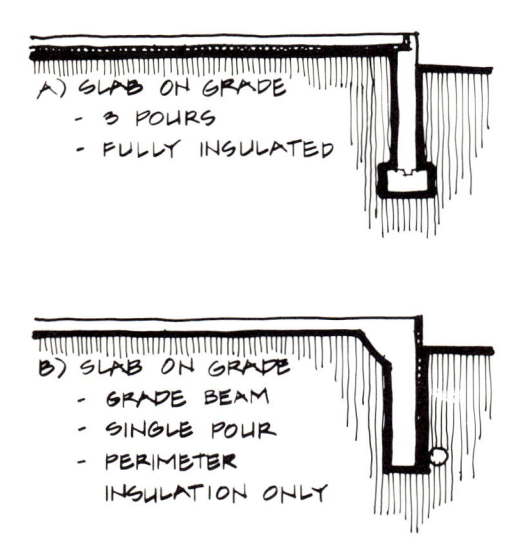

Fig. 8.16 Concrete slab on grade foundations

preparation of a gravel bed to support the slab includes the following steps:

- rough grading
- construction of additional footings
- installation of any cast-in-place utilities, drains, or outside air feeds
- spreading of 4 to 6 inches of gravel or crushed stone
- tamping and ponding
- installation of 6-mil vapor barrier with minimum joints
- installation of rigid board insulation onto gravel bed, and along foundation wall to insulate edges and serve as expansion joint
- placement of wire mesh and skreed boards

Rigid insulation placed on a level gravel bed will not damage easily if you walk on it during the pour; however, wheelbarrow tires will damage the materials. Builders also must be careful when installing skreed boards (or pipes). The layer or layers of rigid insulation hide the location of plumbing, electrical, and heating lines roughed-in beneath. Stakes to hold the skreed boards at the proper height are driven into the gravel bed, and could damage these lines if they strike them. Builders should map the location of pipes, wires, or ducts, and supervise the preparation of the site carefully, double-checking all work prior to the pour. Once the site is ready, the slab can be poured, skreeded, and floated like any other slab on grade.

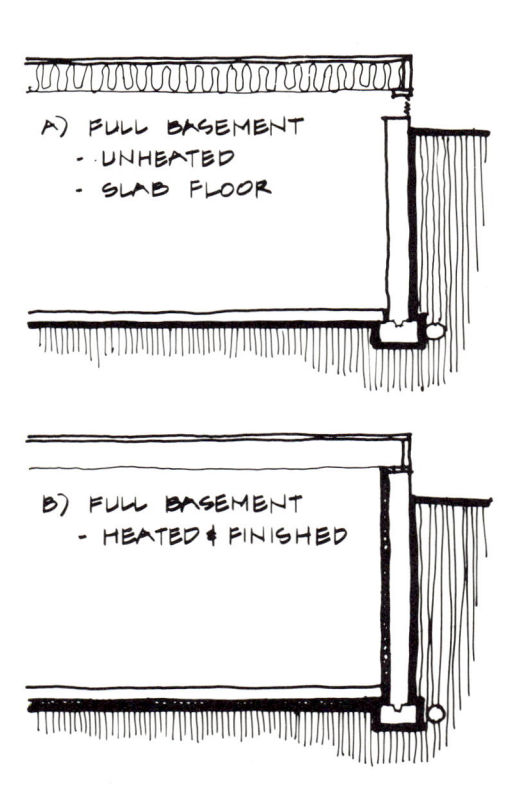

Fig. 8.17 Perimeter foundation showing unheated or heated full basement

The most common finish surfaces for concrete slab floors are various slate or ceramic tiles, but there are tools that can be used to cast a pattern into the new concrete after it has been floated. This offers a relatively inexpensive finish as an alternative to the more expensive tiles. Chapter 12 offers a more detailed presentation of finish floor surfaces.

Full Basement

Full basements typically have been left as unfinished areas used for recreation, mechanical equipment, and storage space (Fig. 8.17). Builders sometimes allow for future finishing by roughing-in a bathroom or heat distribution zone during initial construction. In solar construction full basements also are commonly used as finished living areas, where the south wall is opened to the sun and the other walls are covered with earth. Though most easily accomplished on south sloping sites, this is also possible on flat sites. In the case of earth sheltered houses, the earth berm extends along the east, north, and west walls and continues up onto the roof structure.

Fig. 8.18 This house has full foundation walls on east, north, and west, and a frost wall on the south side to allow for glazed areas.

The use of foundations as living space takes advantage of the sheltering effect of the earth, and can increase the thermal storage capacity of a building when the foundation walls are insulated on the outside. Foundations can be left open on the south, as shown in Figure 8.18, by building full or stepped walls on the east, north, and west, and by utilizing a frost wall on the south side. This open side then can be completely wood frame, allowing considerable flexibility in design of the south elevation. Another means of opening full foundations to the south requires casting forms with openings for windows and doors into the concrete walls, or building them into block foundations. Dimensions and locations of these openings must be accurate to avoid problems in subsequent phases. Builders should check all form work prior to the foundation pour, or block work during construction of block foundations.

Because of their proximity to finish grade, windows cast into the east, north, or west walls of full foundations used as living space should be placed high enough on the wall to avoid problems with snow build up and mud splash. Metal or concrete window areaways can be used to help reduce these problems. Windows and doors built into foundation walls require special details for fastening jamb extensions and casings to the concrete or block. These interior finishes are discussed more fully in Chapter 12.

The elevations of finish grades should be followed carefully during excavation to assure that the foundation and its doors and windows will be well integrated with finish grades. The same concerns for layout and installation of sleeves for various utility penetrations discussed earlier apply to full basements; the use of these areas for primary living space increases the importance of site and perimeter drainage, waterproofing, and foundation insulation.

MOISTUREPROOFING FOUNDATIONS

In order to protect a foundation from the effects of surface and ground water, builders should: (1) carefully select and apply foundation sealant on the outside surfaces; (2) install perimeter drains; (3) backfill with well drained soils; and (4) slope finish grade away from building.

In solar construction, keeping foundations relatively dry is important; it is not appropriate to cut corners here, or in applying the sealants to a foundation. A little extra time and money spent during this phase to assure the best possible waterproofing job will save an expensive call back for a leaky foundation—one of the most frequent home owner complaints in the building industry (Fig. 8.19).

Foundation Sealants

Careful selection of a foundation sealant is one of the most important steps to a waterproofed foundation, and compatibility of the sealant for use with rigid board insulation is crucial. Many different types of foundation

Fig. 8.19 Exterior foundation insulation must be protected from sunlight and physical damage where it is exposed above grade.

sealants are available; their costs, availability, and performance vary. The degree of waterproofing required, and the cost to attain it, depend on the use of the space inside the foundation. A full basement used as primary living space below grade requires more protection from ground moisture than a perimeter foundation enclosing a crawl space. Selection of a foundation sealant for concrete or block must also take into account the movement of ground water at the site, and the type of material used for backfill.

The most commonly used sealants are the asphalt based emulsions, which vary in both cost and quality. Besides their resistance to moisture, these sealants should be compared for compatibility with various foam sheathings that may be used to insulate the exterior of the foundation walls. Incompatible sealants will damage the insulations by melting holes in the material.

Foundation sealants also are available in cement or clay parges or reinforced plasters. These materials, when properly applied, can be very effective at reducing moisture movement into foundation walls. Because they are cement based, they adhere well to the concrete or block, and they are compatible with all of the appropriate below grade insulations. Their use as interior finishes is discussed in Chapter 12.

Another form of sealant utilizes clay filled, corrugated cardboard panels placed against the foundation and soaked with water. The wet clay expands and spreads to cover the adjacent surface. When it dries and sets, it offers excellent protection. The same clay is also available as a parge coating.

Many builders also include a layer of polyethylene in addition to one of the other waterproofings as an inexpensive extra measure to keep moisture away from the foundation. Rigid board insulation with low permeability used to insulate on the exterior of the foundation also helps reduce the amount of moisture reaching the walls, but it should not be used as the primary protection.

INSULATING FOUNDATIONS

Foundations and slabs should be insulated to reduce heat loss and to increase thermal storage in new and existing buildings. Foundations may be insulated on either the interior or the exterior surfaces, depending on the specific situation.

Foundation Insulation Materials

Insulation materials should be selected for their insulative value, moisture resistance, ease of installation, cost per square foot installed, and type and ease of finishing, where required. Insulation applied to the exterior surface of foundations and slabs must be suitable for below grade use as these surfaces are exposed to ground water, frost action, and insect or animal damage—all factors which contribute to the accelerated breakdown of the insulation materials over the life of the building. The most important factors to consider, though, are the movement of ground moisture through the insulation and the material's resistance to freeze-thaw conditions.

Table 8.1
Freeze-thaw cycles for various regions

Geographical region	Freeze-thaw cycles/year
(Miami, Fla.)	0
(San Francisco, Calif.)	0
(Macon, Ga.)	15
(Bowling Green, Ky.)	54
(Big Springs, Tex.)	26
(Amarillo, Tex.)	67
(El Paso, Tex.)	28
(Albuquerque, N.M.)	68
(San Bernadino, Calif.)	6
(Boston, Mass.)	42
(Elkins, W.Va.)	85
(Garden City, Kans.)	96
(Tonopah, Nev.)	103
(Pendleton, Ore.)	46
(Portland, Ore.)	15
(Yarmouth, N.S., Canada)	52
(Akron, Ohio)	63
(Ogallala, Neb.)	111
(Elko, Nev.)	137
(Juneau, Alaska)	52
(Millinocket, Me.)	71
(Grand Rapids, Mich.)	63
(Fort Peck, Mont.)	69
(Cranbook, B.C., Canada)	103
(Val d'Or, P.Q., Canada	49
(Winnipeg, Man., Canada)	46
(Mayo Landing, Y.T., Canada)	58
(Dawson, Y.T., Canada)	47
(Trout Lake, Ont., Canada)	36
(Baker Lake, N.W.T., Canada)	28

Chart 8.1
Water absorption of various rigid board insulations.

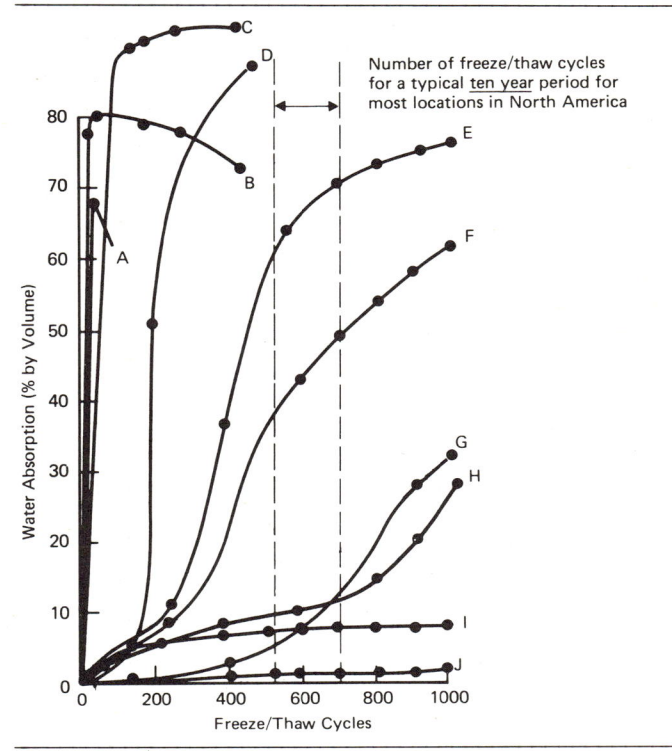

A. 3.81 cm thick cellular glass (144.2 kg/m^3)
B. 2.54 cm thick fiberglass roof insulation (221.4 kg/m^3)
C. 2.54 cm thick fiberboard (163.2 kg/m^3)
D. 2.54 cm thick polyisocyanurate, glass reinforced with aluminum facings (41.6 kg/m^3)
E. 2.54 cm thick molded bead polystyrene (16.0 kg/m^3)
F. 5.08 cm thick molded bead polystyrene (27.2 kg/m^3)
G. 5.08 cm thick German molded bead polystyrene (35.2 kg/m^3)
H. 3.56 cm thick polyurethane with asphalt felt facing, all sides sealed in asphalt (38.4 kg/m^3)
I. 2.54 cm thick polyurethane without skins
J. 2.54 cm and 5.08 cm thick extruded polystyrene skinboard (33.6 to 40.0 kg/m^3)

(The Dow Chemical Company, Midland, Mich. 1976)

Rigid board insulations most commonly used below grade may perform differently in this harsh environment. Materials that absorb ground water lose some of their insulative qualities (lower R-value) as heat is conducted more easily away from the foundation or slab through the saturated insulation. If the soil temperature drops to freezing, the moisture contained in the insulation will freeze and expand. Continuous freeze-thaw cycles will lead to the gradual disintegration of the insulation and an increase in the rate of heat loss through the foundation (Table 8.1). Chart 8.1 compares rigid board insulations currently used below grade throughout the country, including extruded polystyrene (blueboard or pinkboard), polyurethane, polyisocyanurate, and expanded polystyrene (beadboard) (Figure 8.20). Of these materials, extruded polystyrene absorbs the least amount of moisture per unit volume. This resistance to moisture allows the insulation to remain effective, and protects it from frost action due to the low level of moisture content. Polyurethane and polyisocyanurate are available with wax paper or foil facings that further reduce their moisture absorption. Expanded polystyrene is available in both molded and cut sheets. The molded sheets absorb less moisture than the cut sheets; however, neither form should be used below grade without special treatment in the form of waterproof mastic or parge applied to the outside surface of the insulation to further reduce moisture absorption. This approach does not prevent moisture from

Fig. 8.20 Various types of rigid board insulations are often used below grade; however, not all of them are suited for this application.

wicking-up into the insulation from the bottom edge at the footing.

Of the rigid board insulations commonly used for this purpose, extruded polystyrene is probably the most suitable, followed by polyurethane or polyisocyanurate with facings, and then expanded polystyrene with reinforced plaster finish. Expanded polystyrene (beadboard) should not be used below grade without protective coatings.

Insulation also is commonly used on the interior of frost wall foundations. These materials are also subjected to ground moisture and water vapor in crawl spaces; though they probably will not freeze, and will not be exposed to ultraviolet radiation, they must be selected carefully. Insulation beneath concrete slab floors and along their perimeters must be able to withstand conditions below grade, as well as resist compression from the weight of the concrete.

In the past block foundations have been insulated by filling the block cores with vermiculite. This method still allows free conduction of heat through the block webs, which are the major thermal bridge in this type of wall. Insulative sheathing wraps the entire wall, and it is much more effective in reducing heat loss.

Existing foundations are most easily insulated on inside surfaces that have been left exposed. A popular method of insulating these areas utilizes fiberglass batt insulation installed between wood or metal furring strips, attached to the foundation, and finished with sheet rock or paneling. Rigid board insulations including fiberglass can also be used here, by fastening them to the concrete with compatible adhesives or other devices. Be sure to select a material that meets local codes for flame spread and toxicity. Most foam sheathings used inside a building must be covered with a fire resistant material or finish. Due to the likelihood either of moisture condensing on the cool foundation wall, or the movement of ground water into the basement through the wall, the insulation should be selected for its absorption resistance. Installing a vapor barrier on the interior side of the insulation and, if fiberglass is used, leaving an air space between the insulation and the wall, can help.

Panel adhesives used to install insulative sheathings to either the inside or outside of the foundation must also be selected carefully. Not all adhesives are compatible with all of the various foam insulations. Those that are incompatible damage the insulations by melting holes into them, as shown in Figure 8.21.

All types of insulative sheathings used on the exterior of foundations need to be protected from ultraviolet degradation and physical damage where exposed above grade. Cement parges, reinforced plasters, metal flashings, and ¼-inch asbestos millboard all are used for this purpose. These materials should cover the insulation from 6 to 12 inches below grade to the bottom of the exterior siding, as detailed later in this chapter.

Insulating Outside the Foundation

Insulation can be applied on the *exterior* of foundations under the following conditions:

- full foundation/new construction
- perimeter foundation/crawl space
- perimeter foundation/slab on grade

Exterior insulation can be applied as soon as the foundation sealant is ready. By insulating the exterior of the walls, the thermal mass is left exposed to the inside where it can benefit the building's thermal performance.

SITEWORK AND FOUNDATIONS 131

Fig. 8.21 Panel adhesives used during installation of exterior foundation insulation must be compatible with the rigid board material. Read the labels.

Fig. 8.22 Extruded polystyrene insulation applied to the exteriors of full foundation walls and frost walls.

Sheets of insulation can be installed either vertically or horizontally against the wall. They should be fitted tightly together and temporarily held in place by either a small bead of compatible panel adhesive, or by propping pieces of lumber against them at random. The soil backfill eventually does the permanent job of holding the insulation in place.

Apply the insulation completely around the foundation that supports heated spaces. Depth of insulation will depend on soil type and climate; in cold climates the foundation should be insulated from the footing to the sill, whereas in warm climates this may not be necessary. The thickness of insulation will also vary with the climate and depend on whether the crawl space is heated or unheated (Fig. 8.22).

Some builders place a rigid insulation "shelf" almost perpendicular to the foundation. Theoretically, this reduces frost penetration into the soil, which in turn reduces the need for exterior insulation on the foundation below the level of the shelf.

The foundation insulation should be joined carefully at corners with lap joints, especially where it will be exposed above grade. On buildings that use the same insulative sheathing on the exterior of the wood frame, the foundation insulation can be allowed to run past the sill. As discussed later in Chapter 9, lapping the sill area will greatly reduce heat loss due to air leakage. On buildings that do not use insulative exterior sheathing on the frame, the sill or plate may be kicked-out the thickness of the insulation, so that the walls end up flush to the outside.

Insulating the exterior of a foundation does not take long, due to the wide coverage of the sheets, lightness of the materials, and the ease with which they can be cut and joined (Fig. 8.23). Usually one person cuts while another fits the pieces together and takes measurements for the next piece. This saves time climbing in and out of the hole, and it makes the job go smoothly. The cutter

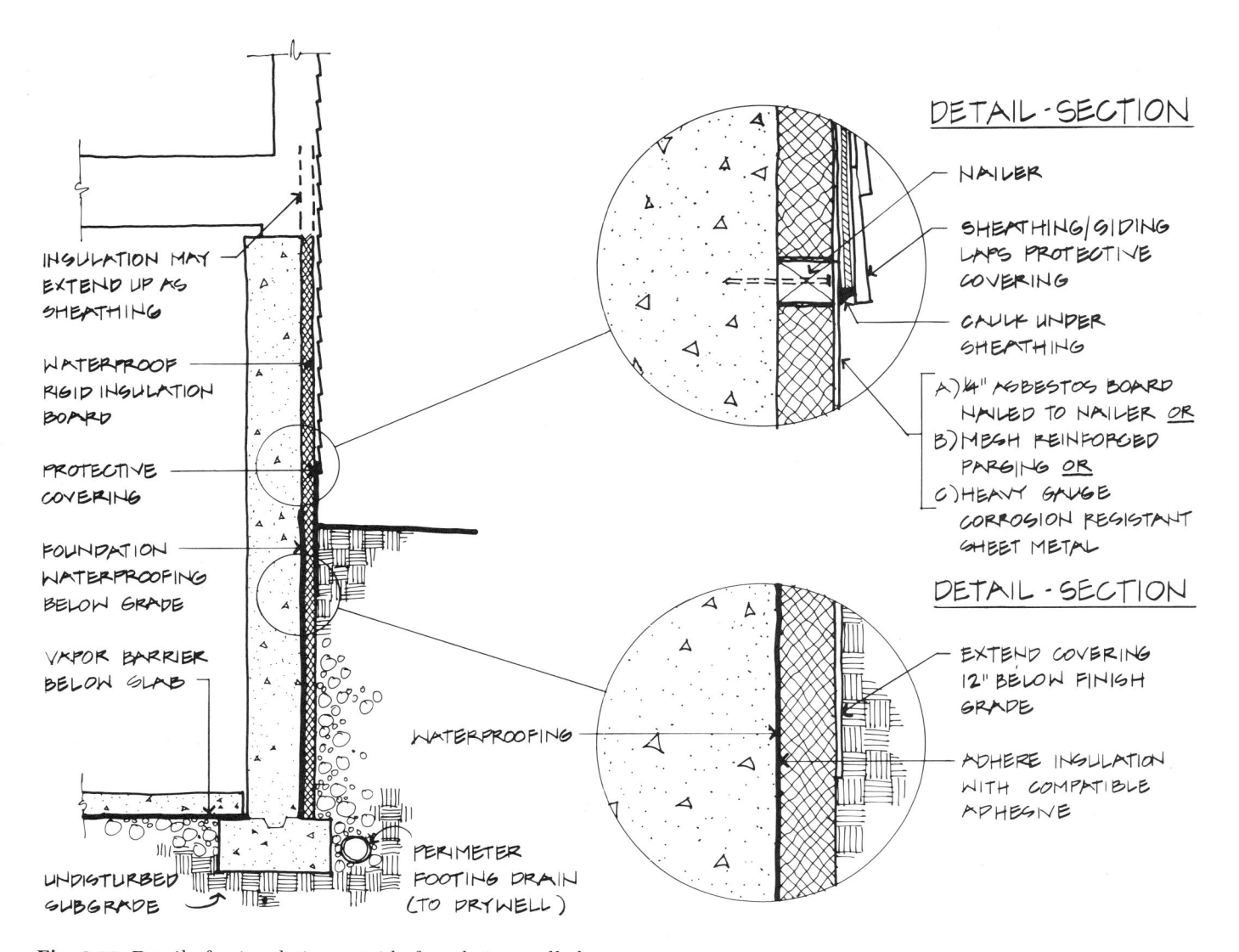

132 MATERIALS, DETAILS, AND TECHNIQUES OF SOLAR CONSTRUCTION

Fig. 8.23 Details for insulating outside foundation walls below grade.

needs a flat working surface, framing square, straight edge, and utility knife or small handsaw. When cutting polyurethane or polyisocyanurate, the worker should wear a mask for protection from dust.

Once the exterior of the foundation has been insulated, the areas of rigid foam that will be exposed above grade must be covered to protect them from ultraviolet radiation and physical damage (Fig. 8.25). Protective cover should extend from the bottom of exterior siding to a point 6 to 12 inches below finish grade (Fig. 8.26). This protection can be achieved by using any one of four techniques.

A cement or mortar parge mixed with water to the consistency of pancake batter can be applied to the rigid insulation with a wide mason's brush. To prepare the insulation for this treatment, brush any dust or degrading material from the surface with a stiff broom. The cement parge can then be "painted" on with smooth or stucco brush strokes. It is a good idea to apply more than one coat to fill holes, cover joints, and shape corners. The parge dries quickly and leaves the exposed areas looking like a concrete foundation.

Reinforced plaster finishes also are available as protective cover for rigid insulations. The application techniques vary, but they generally require layer by layer application of reinforcing fibers or mesh and plaster. These finishes are more labor intensive than the cement parge, as well as more expensive to purchase. However,

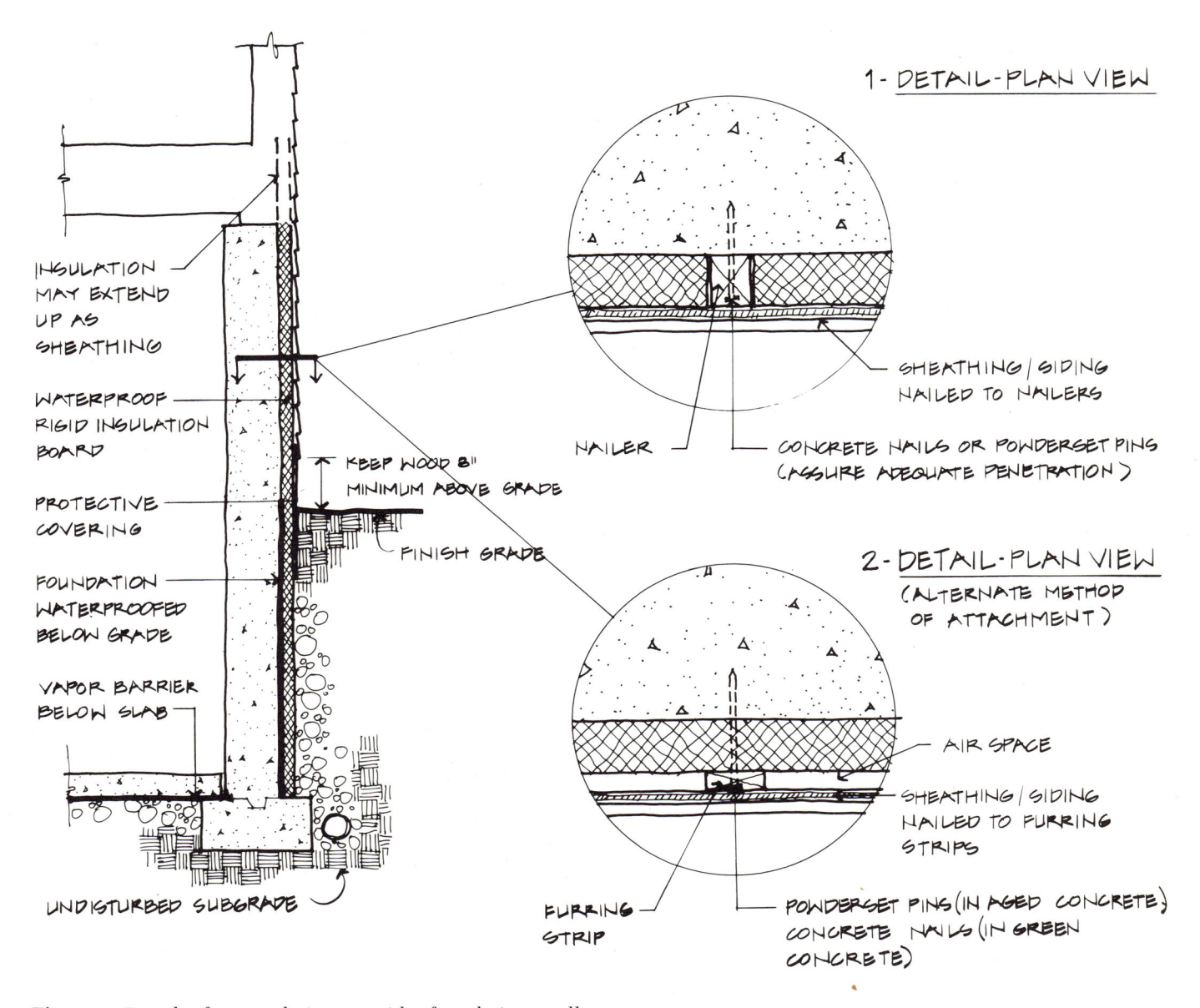

Fig. 8.24 Details for insulating outside foundation walls above grade.

they do offer a stronger finish which affords better protection from physical damage. These products leave a stucco finish on exposed areas of insulation.

Asbestos millboard, ¼-inch thick, commonly is used to protect this area. When installed, it extends into the soil 6 to 12 inches at the bottom, and is lapped by the lowest exterior siding at the top. Corners are made with lap joints. The material is strong and durable and gives the appearance of a concrete foundation. Asbestos boards can be nailed to the band joist, but nail holes should be predrilled since the material shatters easily. Workers cutting and installing this material should wear breathing masks to protect them from dust.

Metal flashing also can be used to cover rigid insulation above grade. The most commonly used material is 0.40 aluminum that is nailed up under the exterior siding and is extended into the ground 12 inches. Problems associated with metal covers are primarily aesthetic—the metallic appearance, waviness that results when the metal expands, and the potential for denting and corrosion.

134 MATERIALS, DETAILS, AND TECHNIQUES OF SOLAR CONSTRUCTION

Fig. 8.25 Properly installed reinforced stucco is a very durable finish for foundation insulation above grade.

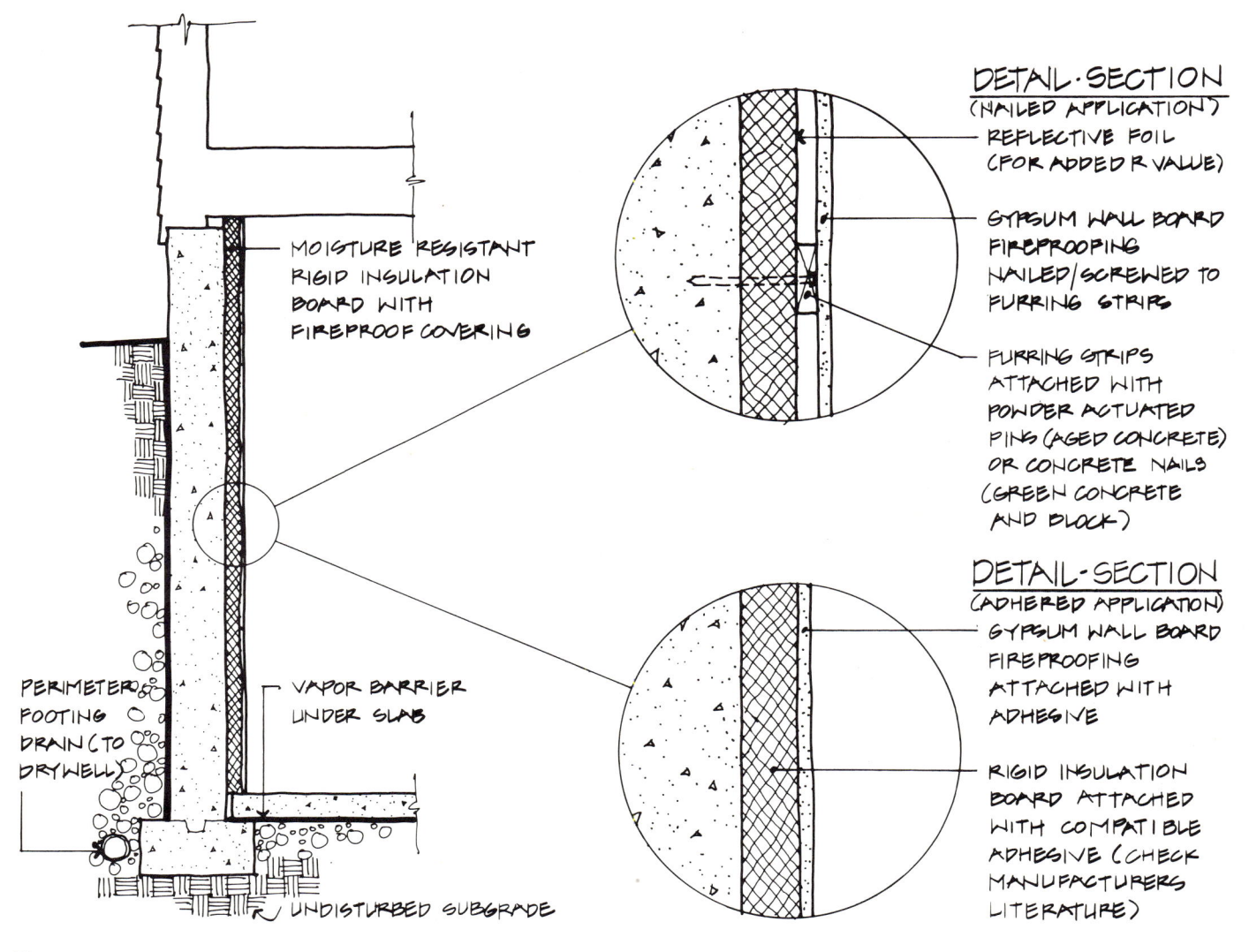

Fig. 8.26 Construction details for insulating inside foundation walls with rigid board insulation.

Fig. 8.27 Construction details for insulating inside foundation walls with fiberglass batt insulation.

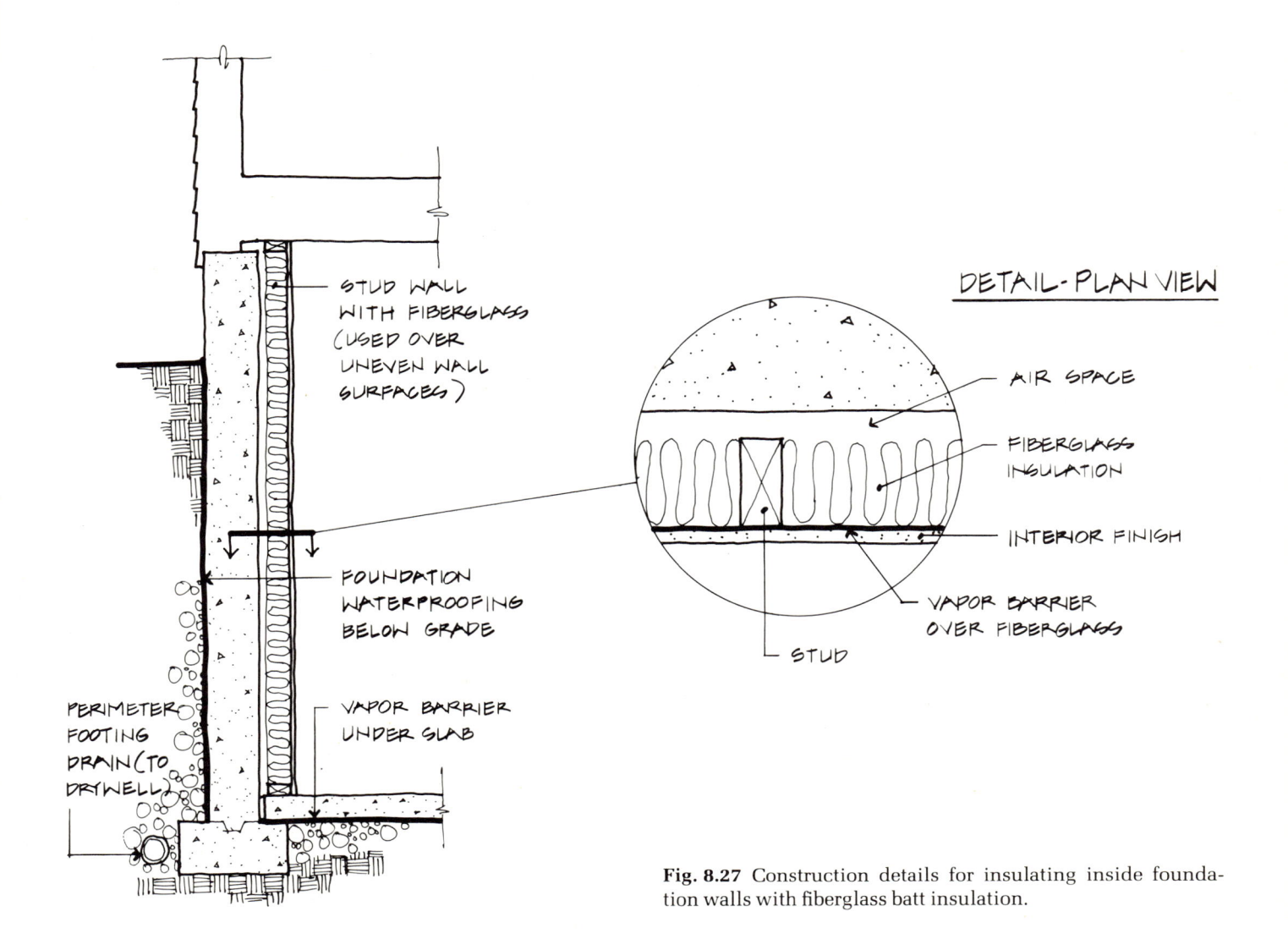

Insulating Inside the Foundations

Insulation usually is applied to the *interior* of foundations under the following conditions:

- full basement/existing building
- perimeter foundation/crawl space
- perimeter foundation/slab on grade

Although it is generally advantageous to insulate exterior surfaces of foundations and thereby keep the thermal storage in the building, it may not always be practical to do so, as in the case of existing buildings. Many designers and builders choose to insulate interior foundation surfaces, even in new construction. This is done most commonly on perimeter foundations/slab on grade, when the slab is well insulated on the exterior surface, thus offering the building more readily available mass.

Full foundation walls can be insulated on the inside with any rigid foam or fiberglass insulation, or fiberglass batts. All of these materials require a fire resistant surface finish between the insulation and building interior. The rigid sheet insulations can be fastened to foundation walls with a compatible panel adhesive; however, any moisture entering the building through the wall will damage the adhesive's holding power (Fig. 8.26).

Foundation walls also can be insulated on the inside by using furring strips attached to the wall to hold the insulation and interior finish. Walls can be studded in to provide an even deeper cavity for insulation. This latter approach would be suitable for fiberglass batts provided a 1-inch air space is left between the insulation

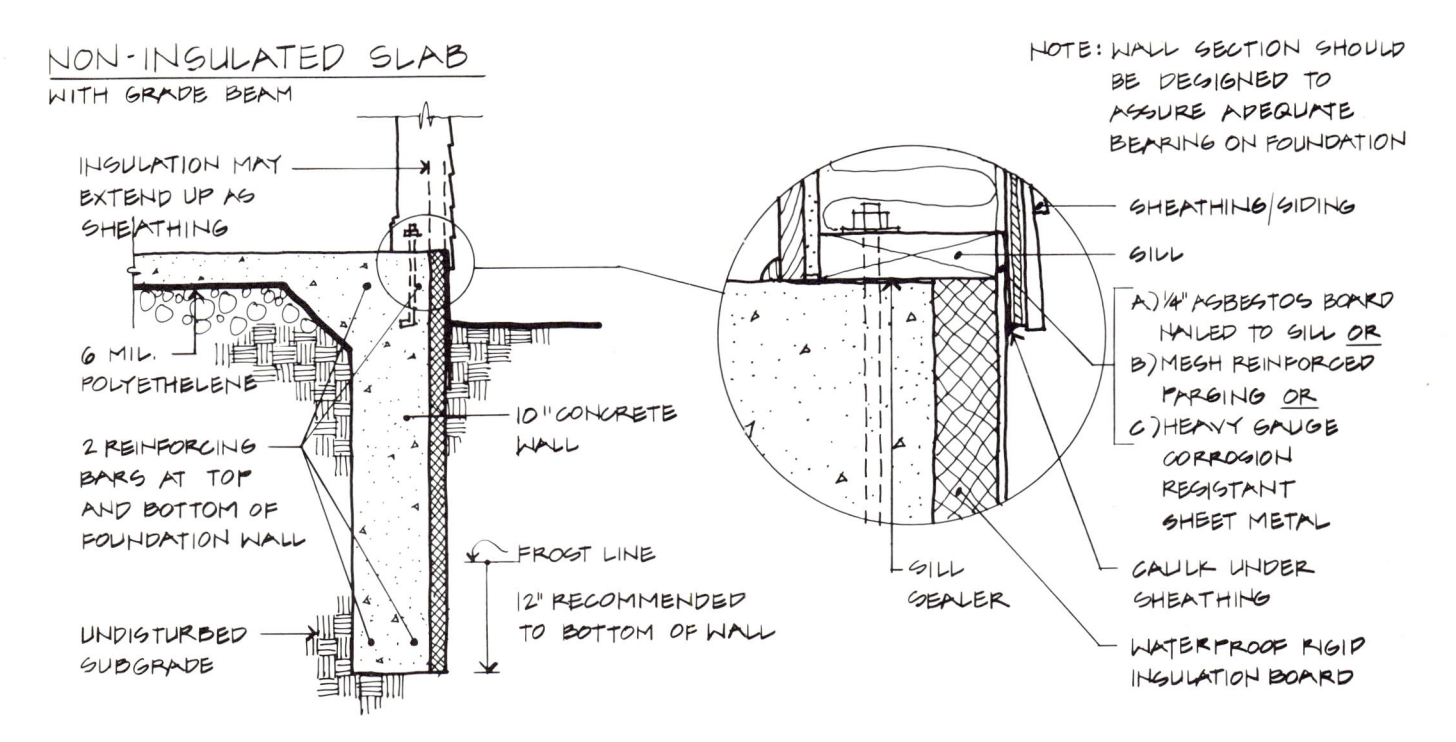

Fig. 8.28 Construction detail for concrete slab on grade foundation with grade beam.

and foundation. This air space will help keep the insulation dry. A 6-mil polyethylene vapor barrier also should be installed on the room side of the insulation (Fig. 8.27).

Insulation placed on the interior of perimeter foundations should be selected carefully due to the high levels of moisture that can be present both in the earth floor and the air. This application is also limited to those insulations suitable for below grade use. In this case, rigid insulation is installed vertically or horizontally along the walls, extending from the footing up to the sill. Since there is no exposure to ultraviolet radiation, the material need not be covered unless it is expanded polystyrene (beadboard), which requires moisture protection. The insulation can be fastened to the foundation by using a compatible panel adhesive or backfilling, or both.

Insulating Concrete Slabs

Concrete slab floors lose heat to the earth and foundation walls by conduction, and through the edges exposed to cold outside conditions by convection and radiation. The heat loss through uninsulated slab on grade foundations and floors is significant. Slab floors increasingly are used for solar heat storage; they should be well insulated with rigid board insulation beneath the slab, as well as completely around the perimeter, to seal the cold edges where most of the heat loss occurs (Fig. 8.28).

This work is scheduled as part of the preparation for pouring the slab, as discussed earlier in the chapter. Once the gravel bed has been raked, leveled, and tamped, and utility lines have been roughed-in, the 6-mil polyethylene vapor barrier can be installed. The rigid insulation is applied next. Once again, the insulation must be able to withstand conditions below grade. Sheets of rigid insulation should be laid out carefully and should fit tightly together. The pieces should be accurately notched around plumbing and electrical protrusions, or footings for posts, stairs, or chimney. If two layers are specified, the second layer should run perpendicular to the first (Fig. 8.29).

Details for edge insulation vary, depending on how the perimeter of the slab is supported (Fig. 8.30). If the slab stops at the foundation wall or footing, then strips of rigid insulation cut to a width equal to the slab's thickness should be placed on the wall with panel adhesive. This will reduce thermal bridging and serve as an expansion joint. If the slab runs out over the frost wall or

SITEWORK AND FOUNDATIONS **137**

Fig. 8.29 Once the slab bed has been properly prepared, and the insulation is in place—the slab is poured. Drying time may be increased due to the low permeance of extruded polystyrene.

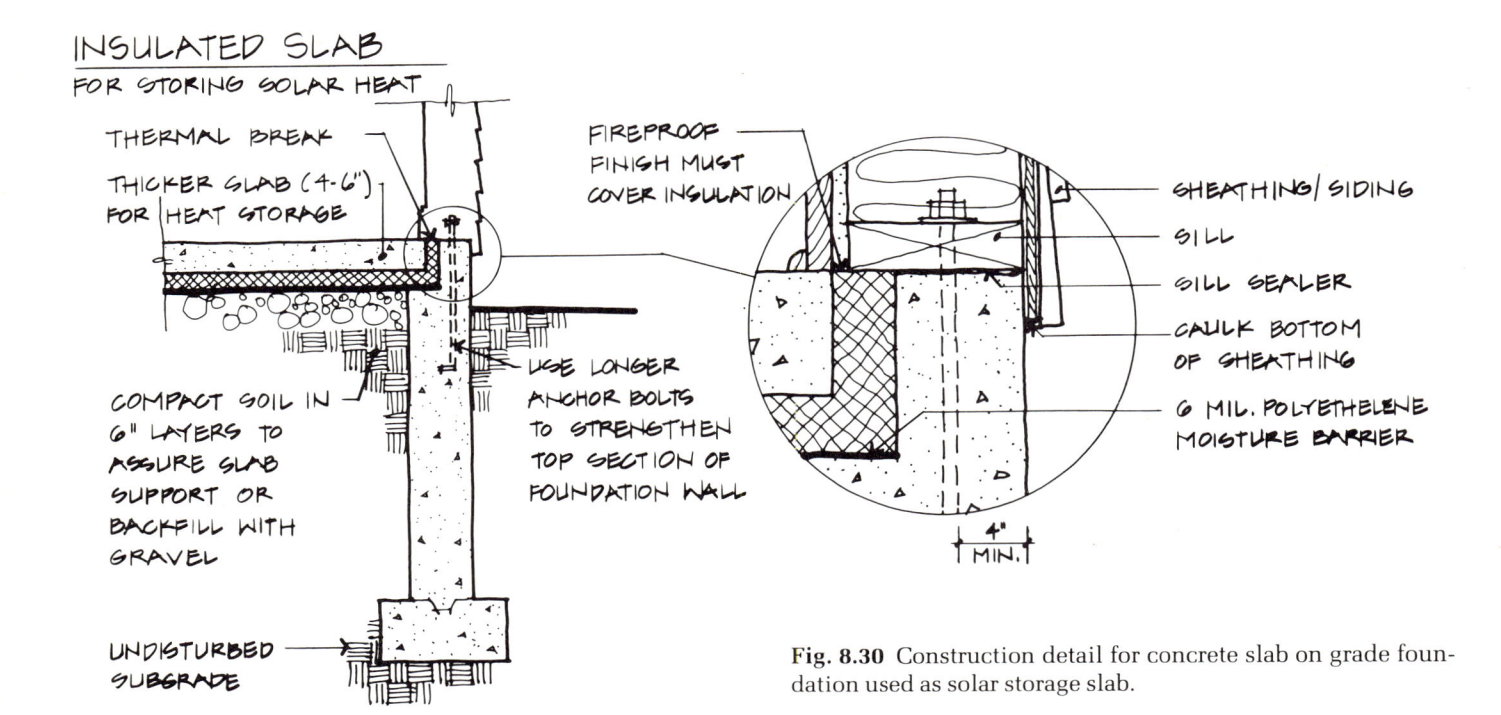

138 MATERIALS, DETAILS, AND TECHNIQUES OF SOLAR CONSTRUCTION

Fig. 8.30 Construction detail for concrete slab on grade foundation used as solar storage slab.

footing and ends flush to the outside, then the only effective means of insulating the edge is to insulate the exterior of the frost wall, and run the insulation from the footing to the sill (or beyond).

CHAPTER 9 THE INSULATED BUILDING SHELL

INTRODUCTION

The building shell controls the passage of sun, air, moisture, light, heat, and sound. Its shape, materials, and assembly will determine, to a large degree, the building's energy requirements for heating and cooling. Many priorities for solar construction must be considered when deciding on the details, materials, and level of workmanship required for this phase, which includes framing, sheathing, roofing, siding, insulating, and installing vapor barriers and vents. Although doors, windows, and glazings are usually considered part of the shell phase, their importance in solar construction is treated separately in Chapter 10.

The first priority of solar construction is to control heat loss and heat gain through the building shell, which can be accomplished by increasing the insulation and controlling air leakage through the shell with new materials and assembly techniques. Builders must adapt their current framing systems to accommodate insulation in areas usually left uninsulated; they also should select new framing details and components that allow for more insulation. The ultimate goal is to wrap the heated living spaces with a well insulated and "tight" exterior shell.

As the rate of air leakage is reduced through the building shell, the presence and movement of moisture within it requires greater attention. The measures taken to control the movement and accumulation of moisture in the shell combine the use of a carefully installed vapor barrier on the inside of the shell with vents properly sized and located to allow the moisture to escape from the shell. These controls help keep insulation, framing, and exterior sheathing dry, which increases their effectiveness over the life of the building.

The insulated building shell controls the relationship between the outdoor climate and the indoor environment, protecting the indoors from the harsh elements and admitting the favorable ones (Fig. 9.2). The shell is selectively opened and closed to control the passage of solar radiation and air movements as it works to warm the interior in winter and to cool it in summer. The location and size of windows and vents, the shape and dimension of overhangs, and the framing system and insulation used to form the building shell all must balance the requirements of local climate, building style, market, and building codes (Fig. 9.3).

Specifications and drawings must be backed up with careful supervision and inspection of workmanship throughout this phase. Even if there are very few changes in the shell, the quality of workmanship will have a tremendous impact on the rate of air leakage and moisture movement through it. The builder may have to explain new framing details to carpentry crews, to familiarize them with the sequence of assembly and acceptable tolerances. Once these new details have become standard, the amount of supervision necessary will decrease.

The work completed in all other job phases affects the exterior shell, so builders must carefully specify, supervise, and inspect the work done by subcontractors at all stages. The importance of a square and level foundation in reducing air leakage at the sill was explained in Chapter 8. Subsequent phases including the roughed-in plumbing, heating, and electrical components have an impact on the effectiveness of insulation and vapor barriers, as discussed later in this chapter and in Chapter 11.

The materials and techniques used to form the exterior shell of a building have undergone continuous

Fig. 9.1 The insulated building shell phase of construction includes framing, sheathing, roofing, installing rough mechanical and electrical runs, insulating and installing vapor barriers.

change and refinement throughout history. Framing, sheathing, insulation, siding, and roofing systems currently in use were all at one time new to builders. Now today's "standard practices" are undergoing further changes and refinement to improve the energy efficiency of exterior shells, and to form and support the special features used in solar construction. Changes in framing systems, exterior sheathing, insulation materials, vapor barriers, and venting all are included. This section presents issues that are critical in the selection of materials and techniques used in specific areas of typical buildings. All of these changes are interdependent, so we have organized the building shell phase into the following sequence: (1) floors; (2) walls; and (3) roofs and ceilings.

FLOORS

The construction of floors plays an important role in the energy performance of a home by controlling heat loss and reducing air leakage at three critical areas: (1) at the sill, where air leakage can account for up to 40 percent of the total building heat loss; (2) at the band joist, a typically uninsulated area that can create stripes of heat loss through an otherwise well insulated wall; and (3) in the floor cavities themselves, where insulation and vapor barriers may be required (depending on the conditions below the floor). Wood frame floors divide the living spaces within the building and separate them from crawl spaces and basements. Because the appropriate floor section varies with the conditions below, this discussion considers three residential wood frame floor situations: (1) on pier foundations; (2) over unheated crawl spaces; (3) over heated crawl spaces or full basements. Concrete slab on grade floors are discussed in Chapter 8. The components of the wood floor framing systems we will discuss in this chapter are identified in Fig. 9.4.

Solar construction may require structural changes in floor framing to support additional loads of internal

THE INSULATED BUILDING SHELL 141

Fig. 9.2 Completing the insulated shell requires careful coordination of many subtrades.

142 MATERIALS, DETAILS, AND TECHNIQUES OF SOLAR CONSTRUCTION

- CONTROL HEAT LOSS & HEAT GAIN THROUGH BUILDING SHELL
    - INCREASE INSULATION LEVELS IN WALLS, CEILINGS, ROOFS, FLOORS
    - USE FRAMING TECHNIQUES TO REDUCE HEAT LOSS
    - REDUCE AIR INFILTRATION

- INTERFACE WITH OTHER PHASES
    - FOUNDATION MUST BE LEVEL AND SQUARE
    - MECHANICAL & ELECTRICAL WORK MUST BE CAREFULLY COORDINATED WITH FRAMING, INSULATION AND VAPOR BARRIERS
    - RIGID INSULATION BOARD REQUIRES FIREPROOF FINISH

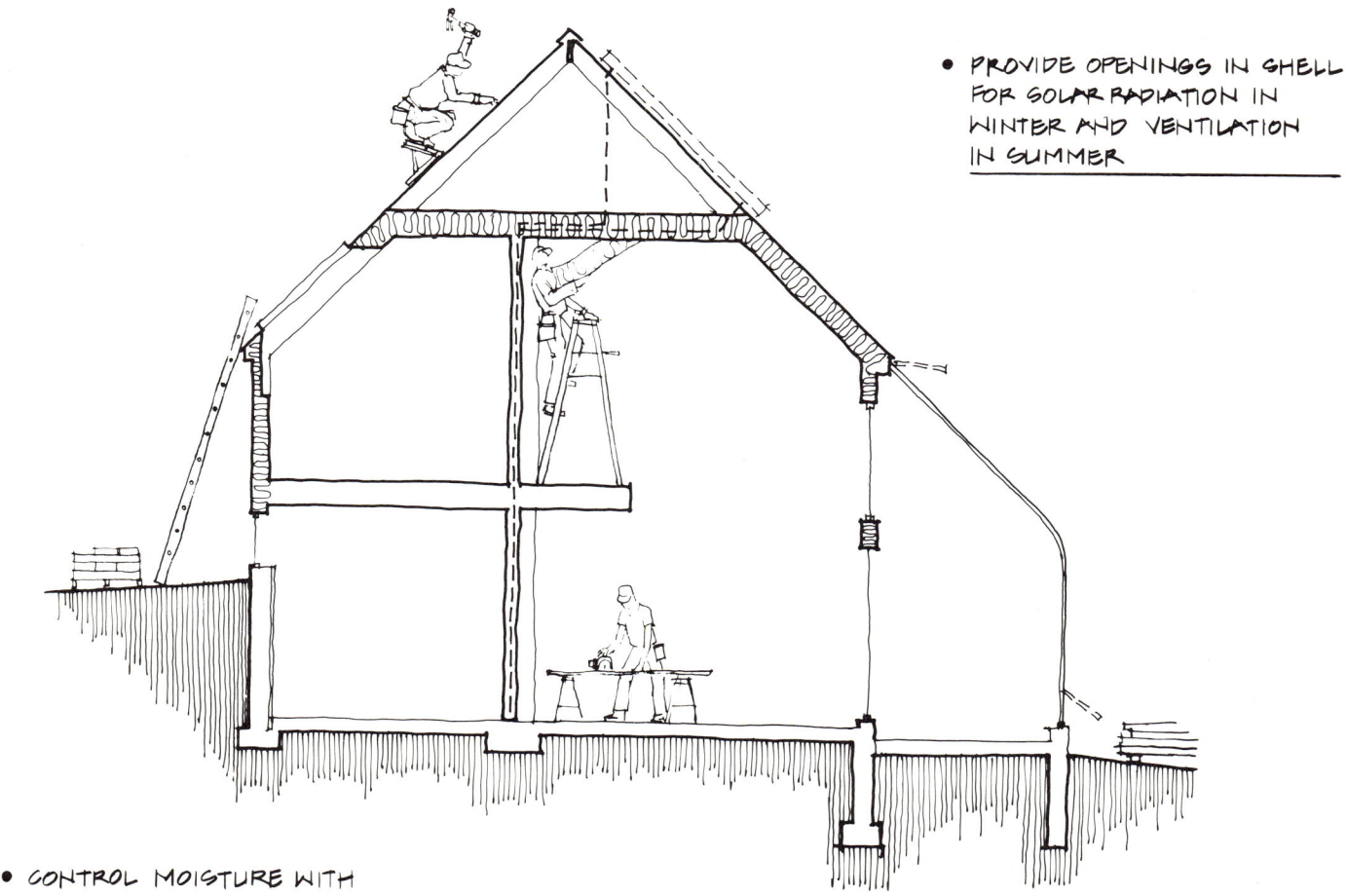

- PROVIDE OPENINGS IN SHELL FOR SOLAR RADIATION IN WINTER AND VENTILATION IN SUMMER

- CONTROL MOISTURE WITH VAPOR BARRIERS & VENTILATION
    - INSTALL CONTINUOUS VAPOR BARRIER ON WARM SIDE OF INSULATION
    - USE FOUNDATION VENTS OVER UNHEATED SPACES
    - VENTILATE ROOF CAVITIES

- PROVIDE FOR UNIQUE STRUCTURAL REQUIREMENTS
    - SUPPORT THERMAL MASS
    - SUPPORT SOLAR COLLECTORS
    - LONGER SPANS MORE COMMON IN OPEN FLOOR PLANS

Fig. 9.3 Solar priorities for the insulated shell phase of construction.

FLOOR DECK MEETS FOUNDATION

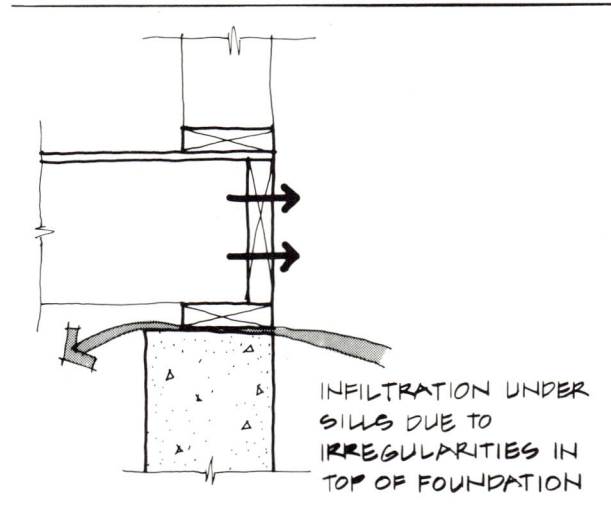

INFILTRATION UNDER SILLS DUE TO IRREGULARITIES IN TOP OF FOUNDATION

BETWEEN FLOORS

CONDUCTION THROUGH BAND JOIST

INFILTRATION BETWEEN COMPONENTS

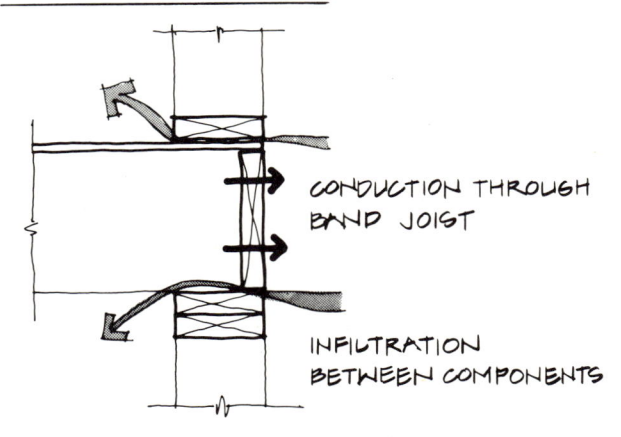

Fig. 9.4 How and where heat is lost through floors.

thermal mass in the form of masonry or water wall partitions, masonry veneers, thermal mass ceiling tiles, poured or precast concrete slabs, and ceramic tile or slate finish floors. These loads must be supported by the framing and transmitted to the foundation (Fig. 9.5). The design of open floor plans also can affect the structural design of wood frame floors, especially the upper floors. In order to create open areas, bearing partitions often are replaced with large beams. Floor trusses and changes in joist depth and spacing can be used to span greater distances without intermediate support. The following checklist gives guidelines for reducing heat loss through floors; it is followed by a more detailed discussion of the specific configurations.

Fig. 9.5 Masonry floors can be constructed on wood framing and used as thermal mass.

- Supervise to be sure foundation is level and square.
- Use fiberglass sill seal between foundation wall and sill.
- Consider rigid insulation lapping sill.
- Insulate band joist.
- Wood frame floors over vented crawl space—insulate floor cavity; vapor barrier on ground in crawl space; vents should be properly sized and operable.

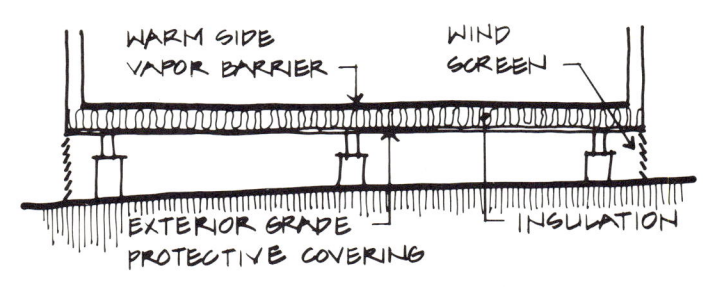

Fig. 9.6 Pier foundations are relatively inexpensive. However, the floor should always be insulated and the water lines must be protected from freezing in cold climates.

Fig. 9.7 Insulating wood frame floor on pier foundation.

- Wood frame floor over heated crawl space—insulate perimeter frost wall down to footing; insulate band joists.
- Wood frame floors over heated basements—do not insulate, allow heat flow from basement; insulate band joist; insulate foundation and slab floor.
- Wood floor over unheated basement—insulate floor; insulate band joist.

Floor on Pier Foundation

Wood frame floors built on pier foundations are subject to greater heat loss through the floor due to wind movement than are floors built on other types of foundations. This exposure to increased air movement also accelerates the rate of air leakage (Fig. 9.6).

Framing layout on piers and foundation walls always is affected both by the choice of exterior sheathing and siding, and by whether the exterior wall finish is flush with or extends beyond the foundation. For example, if the exterior wall sheathing is one-inch-thick rigid board insulation, and only the exterior finish siding is to lap the foundation, then the framing should be set in one inch from the outside line. The floor frame should be well insulated, including the perimeter beams or girders and the cavities between floor joists. The sequence for insulating between floor joists can follow two patterns. First, after the frame is complete, sheath the bottom of the joists with rigid board insulation or exterior wood sheathing. The insulation then can be installed from above, making the job somewhat easier. The sheathing helps protect the insulation from ground water and animal damage. If ground clearance is a problem, the floor can be framed and sheathed in sections, and assembled section by section. Second, construct the deck on top of the frame prior to insulating between floor joists. The insulation and sheathing must be installed from below, which can be difficult if the floor is close to the ground (Fig 9.7).

Insulation material commonly used to insulate floors on piers includes fiberglass blanket or batt, and rigid board insulation. Fiberglass insulation, equal in thickness to the floor joists, should be installed between framing members with paper or foil vapor barrier facings placed towards the living space above. Additionally, a continuous sheet vapor barrier is recommended to reduce the amount of moisture that comes through the floor from inside the building, especially in winter when vapor pressure is usually higher inside than outside. Insulation batts should fit snugly into the cavities and be installed carefully around any floor bridging. If exterior sheathing is not used on the bottom of joists, fiberglass batt insulation can be held in place with wire supports placed between floor joists, with chicken wire mesh nailed to the faces of the joists, or by creating a crisscross support system, stringing wire between nails in the framing.

Rigid board insulation also can be used to insulate between floor joists. Select a material that can withstand moisture and freezing conditions and also offers the desired level of insulation. The insulation must be cut to fit snugly between framing members. This can be a time consuming process, especially if the floor joists are at all out-of-square. Each bay must be measured separately. Solid blocking is easier to insulate with rigid board insulation than cross bracing. However, if cross bridging is used, carefully notch the insulation around it. The sheets can be either toenailed to the joists, or supported

THE INSULATED BUILDING SHELL

OVER UNHEATED BASEMENT

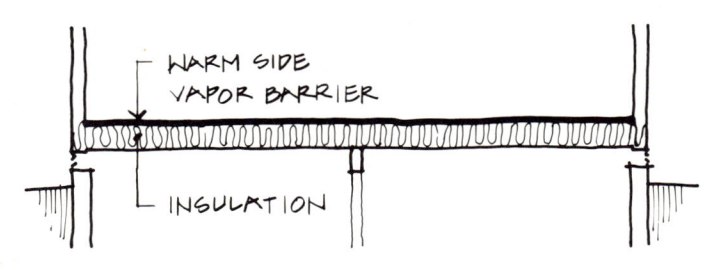

[Diagram labeled: WARM SIDE VAPOR BARRIER; INSULATION]

OVER UNHEATED CRAWL SPACE

[Diagram labeled: MAINTAIN 24" MIN. CLEARANCE; 6 MIL. VAPOR BARRIER ON GROUND IN CRAWL SPACE HELD IN PLACE WITH GRAVEL OR SAND]

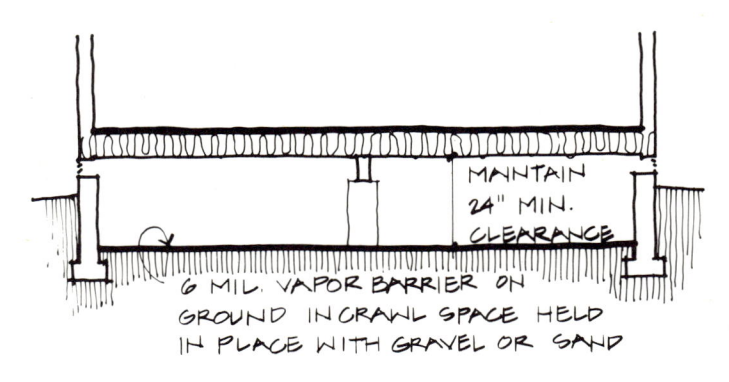

Fig. 9.8 Insulating a Floor over Unheated Basement or Crawl Space
- Perimeter foundation provides a more stable substructure
- Mechanical and electrical lines should be located within the heated envelope
- Crawl space must be ventilated.

by ledger strips, wire mesh, or plywood sheathing nailed to the joists.

Rigid board insulation also can be nailed to the bottom of the floor joists before the plywood sheathing to reduce thermal bridging through the joists. If this is done, sheathing from the exterior walls of the building should extend far enough past the floor framing to make a corner with the floor sheathing.

Pipe runs and ductwork installed in this floor configuration should be well insulated and located on the warm side of the floor. An important limitation of pier foundations is the need to adequately protect water pipes from freezing in cold climates. Supply lines from wells or mains, in addition to distribution and waste lines, require protection. Penetrations made in the underlayment must be stuffed with fibrous insulation or caulked to prevent air leakage. Another method for reducing air leakage through the floor is to cover the entire floor deck with a resin coated building paper, which allows the underlayment to breathe, but resists air movement. To further reduce the effects of air movement on the floor system, an apron can be constructed around the building; this helps divert wind, or at least slows the velocity of the wind before it passes under the building.

Floor Over Unheated Crawl Space

Wood floors over unheated crawl spaces are subjected to a more stable and less harsh climate than floors over piers. Temperature extremes and air movement are not as great (Fig. 9.8). A crawl space is tightly enclosed, so moisture rising out of the ground must be controlled with a vapor barrier ground cover. Moisture from the crawl space should be vented to the atmosphere through vent openings carefully sized and placed in the foundation walls. The air movement resulting from cross-ventilation will cool the floor in winter and increase the rate of conductive heat loss; therefore, these floors should also be well insulated (Fig. 9.9). All other sources of air leakage, including the sill/foundation joint and floor penetrations for plumbing, heating, and electrical lines, should be sealed. The foundation vents should open and close easily and should be sized to provide adequate ventilation of the crawl space.

Before framing the main floor deck, the crawl space floor should be prepared and a vapor barrier installed. Unheated crawl spaces usually enclose a gravel or crushed stone floor. On very wet sites, it may be necessary to place an interior perimeter drain in the gravel bed, to drain excess ground water from the crawl space. Guidelines for installation of interior perimeter drains are presented in Chapter 8. Once the crawl space floor is prepared, a 6-mil (.006) polyethylene vapor barrier ground cover should be installed. The crawl space floor should be covered with one layer of polyethylene installed with a minimum number of joints. Joints in the poly can simply overlap 6 inches, and need not be taped; it should also lap 6 inches up the perimeter walls. When the barrier is down, a small amount of gravel or sand will hold the edges in place. Another form of ground cover often used is 30-pound felt paper; but its limited widths result in more joints, which reduces its effectiveness. This work also can be done after the floor frame is in place; however, the sequence depends somewhat on the accessibility of the crawl space at various other stages of construction.

STANDARD CONSTRUCTION

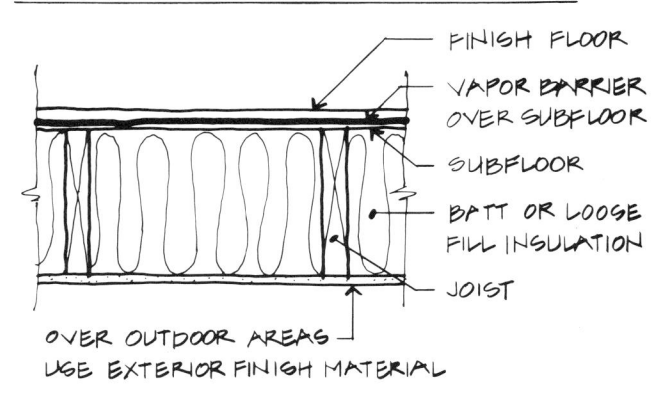

- FINISH FLOOR
- VAPOR BARRIER OVER SUBFLOOR
- SUBFLOOR
- BATT OR LOOSE FILL INSULATION
- JOIST

OVER OUTDOOR AREAS USE EXTERIOR FINISH MATERIAL

PLANK & BEAM
(BEAMS EXPOSED BELOW)

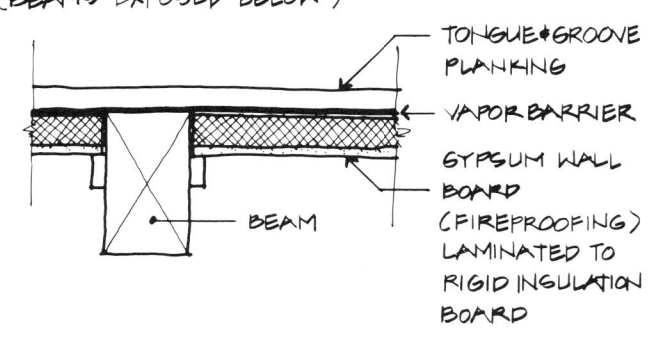

- TONGUE & GROOVE PLANKING
- VAPOR BARRIER
- GYPSUM WALL BOARD (FIREPROOFING) LAMINATED TO RIGID INSULATION BOARD
- BEAM

PLANK & BEAM
(PLANKS & BEAMS EXPOSED BELOW)

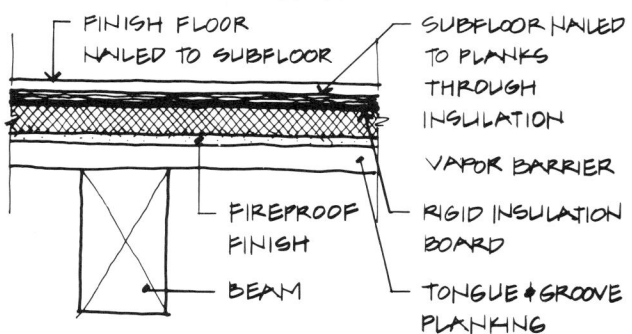

- FINISH FLOOR NAILED TO SUBFLOOR
- SUBFLOOR NAILED TO PLANKS THROUGH INSULATION
- VAPOR BARRIER
- RIGID INSULATION BOARD
- TONGUE & GROOVE PLANKING
- FIREPROOF FINISH
- BEAM

Fig. 9.9 Construction details of floor construction over unheated spaces.

Foundation vents also are critical in the effort to control moisture in unheated crawl spaces. The proper sizing and placement of these openings is discussed in Chapters 4 and 8. Vents should be installed before the floor framing for easier access to both sides of the wall. Depending on the type, vents can be installed by grouting with cement or framing them with wood. They are also available with integrated frames. Vents should be sealed around the bottom and sides when installed, and along the top after the sill sealer and sill have been installed. These edges can be sealed with a flexible caulk, mortar, or spray foam.

Layout of sill and band joist on all perimeter foundations is determined by the exterior sheathing, finish siding, and method of insulating the perimeter foundation. The priorities of solar construction are to prevent infiltration under the sill and to insulate the band joist. An effective detail for this intersection is to insulate on the outside with a rigid board foam. This foam sheathing can run up past the sill to lap the band joist, and intersect with the wall sheathing. Any joint between the foundation insulation and wall sheathing should not occur at the sill or shoe plate, or air will leak through the joint.

Sill sealer is another effective means of reducing air leakage at the sill (Fig. 9.10). It is a one-inch-thick fibrous material that helps fill gaps caused by irregularities in foundation and sill, and should be used if exterior sheathing does not overlap this critical intersection. If exterior sheathing does lap this area, sill sealer helps to level irregularities in the top of the foundation. It is most easily installed after the entire sill piece has been cut and drilled for anchor bolts. Select a width of material equal to the sill, and install it between the sill and top of foundation. The sill seal will press easily right over anchor bolts. After the sill sealer is in place, sill boards can be placed back onto the foundation, squared, bolted, and nailed. If the foundation is far out of level, and the sill must be shimmed, then gaps left unfilled by the sill sealer should be either stuffed with more material or caulked. This is especially important if the exterior surface of this area is not lapped by the sheathing.

The construction of the floor frame, including beams, band joists, and floor joists, follows standard procedures. The methods of insulating floors over unheated crawl spaces are similar to those used for floors built on pier foundations; there is no need to use exterior plywood or particle board sheathing on the underside of the floor frame. The most common support detail for fiberglass batts in this floor configuration is wire mesh stapled or nailed to the joists. Rigid board insulation can be installed in the same way as previously described.

THE INSULATED BUILDING SHELL 147

FLOORS OVER HEATED SPACES

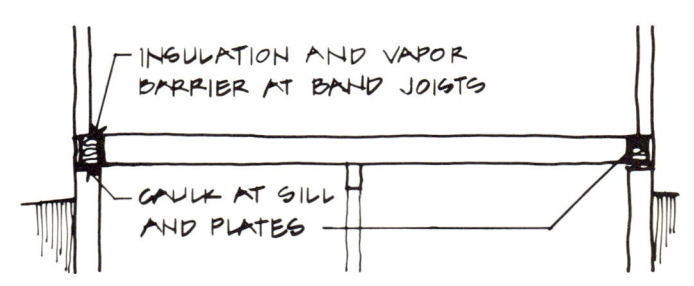

Fig. 9.11 In floors over heated spaces the heat loss at the band joist and sill is critical.

Floor Over Heated Crawl Space

Crawl spaces are considered heated if they enclose central heating equipment, serve as a plenum for warm air furnaces, or serve as an air plenum for double shell construction (Fig. 9.11). Wood frame floors built over crawl spaces that enclose or serve as air plenums for central heating systems generally are left uninsulated. Heat from the warm crawl space is allowed to conduct through the floor and into the living space, and sometimes it circulates to and from these areas through operable floor registers. Whether the crawl space floor is gravel or concrete, a vapor barrier ground cover is necessary, especially since these crawl spaces usually are unvented, to reduce heat loss. Air leakage control at the sill becomes more important, but sealing of floor penetrations is less critical, although local codes may require this as a fire-stop specification.

The rate of conductive heat loss through band joists is more significant because the crawl space is heated, so the joists should be well insulated either on the inside or outside (Fig. 9.12 & 9.13). As with unheated crawl spaces, the placement of the sill on the foundation depends on the choice of exterior sheathing or the use of rigid insulation inside or outside the foundation.

In many cases, heated crawl spaces and full basements are better insulated than other foundations, due to their higher temperatures and the use of the walls and floors for heat storage. The sill placement is affected by these considerations.

Double shell construction imposes a different set of conditions on floors built over crawl spaces used as air plenums. They may require structural changes in the framing as well as careful layout of special details. Wood frame floors in double shell construction gener-

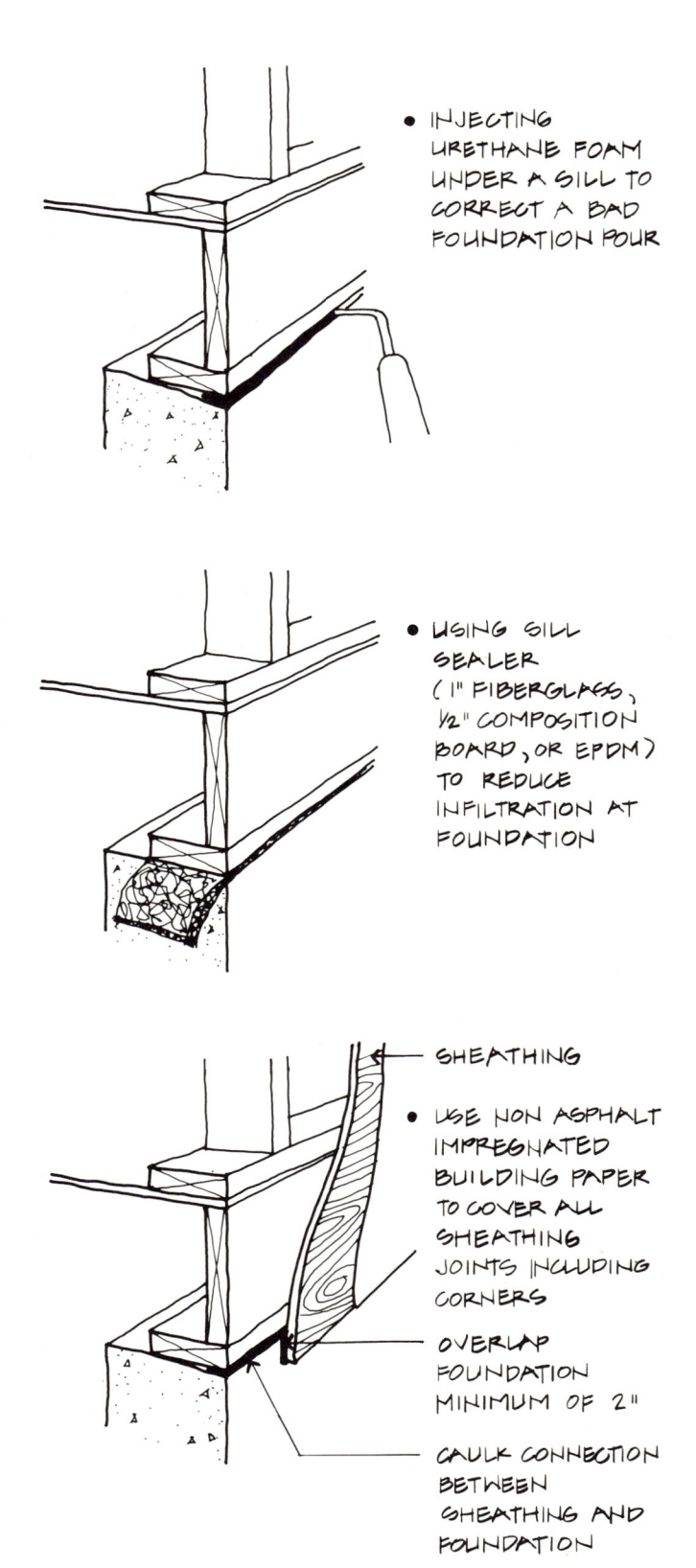

Fig. 9.10 Reducing infiltration at floor sill and foundation.

148 MATERIALS, DETAILS, AND TECHNIQUES OF SOLAR CONSTRUCTION

INSULATE INSIDE

- BATT INSULATION
- INTERIOR FOUNDATION INSULATION

Fig. 9.12 Insulating the band joist.

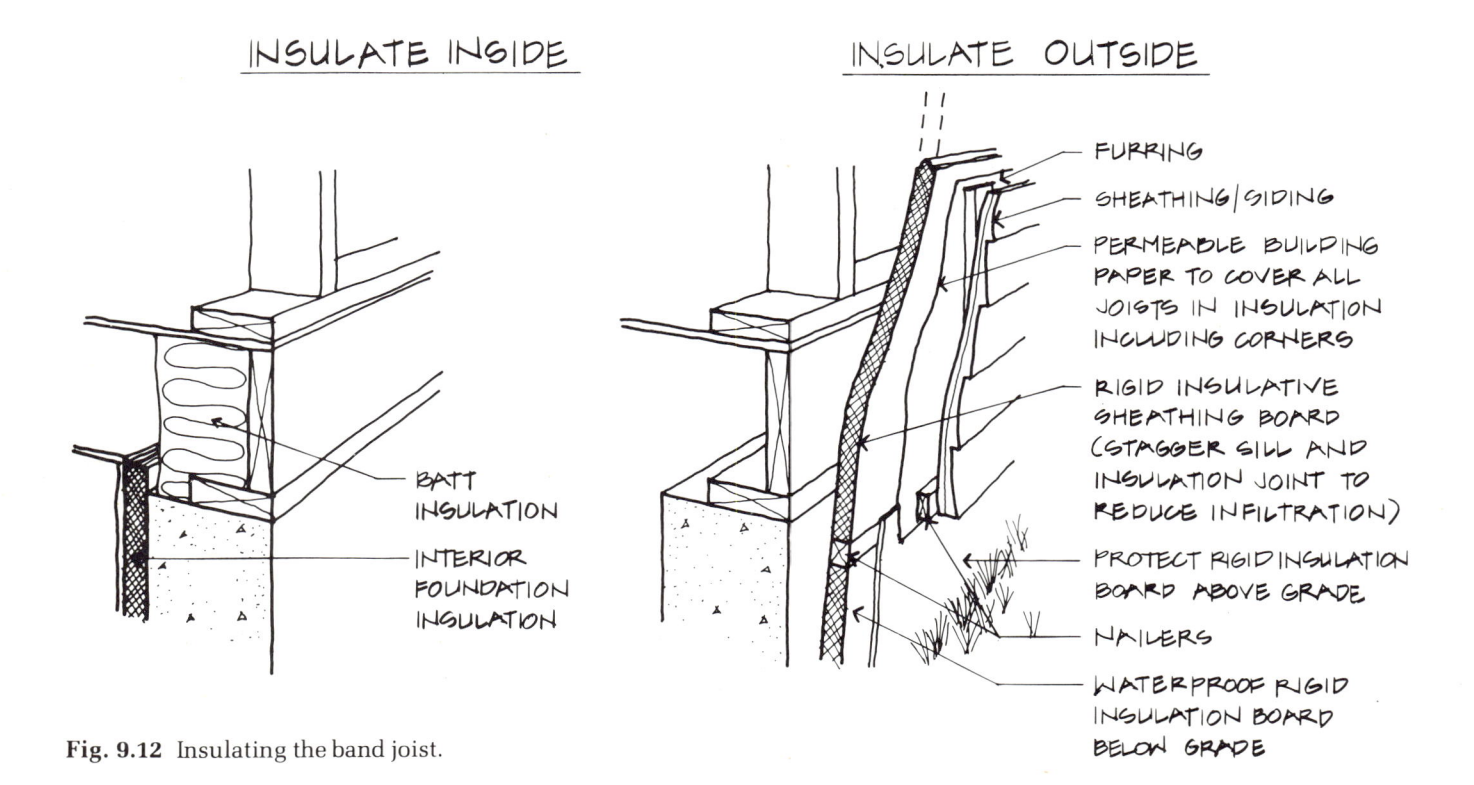

INSULATE OUTSIDE

- FURRING
- SHEATHING/SIDING
- PERMEABLE BUILDING PAPER TO COVER ALL JOISTS IN INSULATION INCLUDING CORNERS
- RIGID INSULATIVE SHEATHING BOARD (STAGGER SILL AND INSULATION JOINT TO REDUCE INFILTRATION)
- PROTECT RIGID INSULATION BOARD ABOVE GRADE
- NAILERS
- WATERPROOF RIGID INSULATION BOARD BELOW GRADE

Fig. 9.13 The band joist area should be insulated around the entire perimeter of the building.

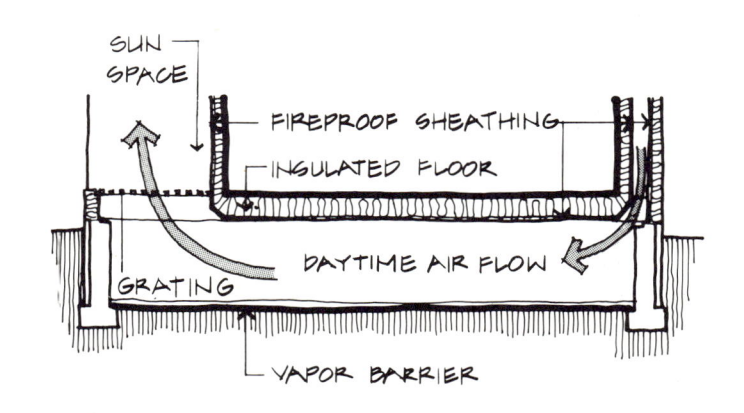

DOUBLE SHELL FLOOR

- SUN SPACE
- FIREPROOF SHEATHING
- INSULATED FLOOR
- DAYTIME AIR FLOW
- GRATING
- VAPOR BARRIER

Fig. 9.14 Insulating the floor in double shell construction.

ally are insulated in the same way as floors over unheated crawl spaces. Ground cover vapor barriers are very important in reducing the amount of moisture that enters the building and circulates within the double shell air space. The lack of a vapor barrier can cause serious rotting of structural lumber throughout the shell. The presence of moisture must be considered when selecting a sheathing material to cover the insulation in these floor systems. Sheathing may be necessary to satisfy local fire codes and reduce the circulation of dangerous fibers or dust. The most commonly used sheathing for this purpose is drywall, which also may be required as a sheathing for all other surfaces adjacent to the air space of the double shell's walls and ceilings (Fig. 9.14).

Floor layout and structural changes for double shell plenums may be necessary, depending on the specific building design. These include changes in the size of footings that share double wall loads and layout of framing to support loads of inner walls.

Floor Over Full Basement

Wood frame floors built over full basements usually are left uninsulated, especially when either central heating equipment is located in the basement, or the area is used as primary living space. In either case, controlling air leakage at the sill and moisture entering through the concrete slab floor is important, as discussed in previous sections of this chapter. As with the other types of perimeter foundations, the sill layout may depend on the approach taken in insulating the foundation walls. If the foundation walls are to be insulated on the inside, the use of sill sealer and band joist insulation becomes even more important.

Structural Changes in Floors for Solar Construction

In the preceding portions of this chapter, we have focused primarily on reduction of heat loss through the floor and foundation systems, and how different situations affect the placement of the frame on a variety of foundations. This section presents examples of structural changes that may be required in floor systems in solar construction, including:

- new internal loads from masonry or water wall partitions, masonry veneers, thermal mass ceiling tiles, poured or precast concrete slabs, and ceramic tile or slate finish floors
- framing details for slabs floated on wood framing

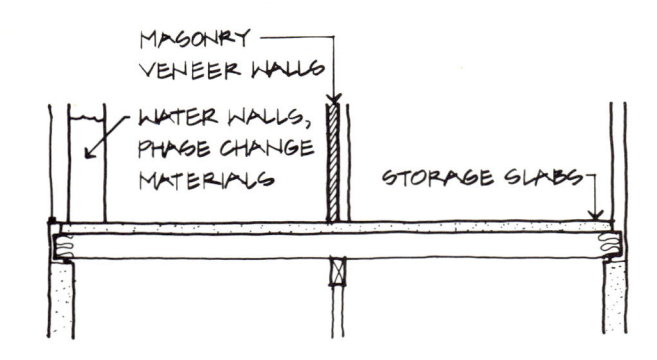

THERMAL MASS LOADS ON FLOORS

Fig. 9.15 Floor Supporting Thermal Mass Loads
- Larger joists and beams, closer spacing or shorter spans may be necessary to support distributed loads like slabs.
- Support of concentrated loads like water walls or masonry veneer may require lumber with higher compressive and shear strength as well as solid backing under mass.

- framing details for floor-wall intersection in double shell construction

Although construction materials used for thermal storage are most cost effective if they also serve structural functions, builders often do use nonstructural thermal mass (Fig. 9.15). These new dead loads must be supported by the floor and foundation systems and may necessitate changes in footing size and location, and in the size and spacing of framing members. Changes derived from calculating new loads must meet or surpass load guidelines established by local building codes. Table 9.1 gives examples of internal loads found in solar construction.

WALLS

Wall systems adapted for solar construction may undergo more changes in their materials and assembly than any other part of the building. The building walls form the openings for windows and doors, provide the structure that supports vertical loads and resists horizontal and racking forces, and create cavities for insulation. Changes in walls for solar construction include variations in the size and orientation of openings, new materials and techniques to increase insulation levels, increased vertical loads transmitted from large glazed

Table 9.1
Vertical loads for features commonly used in solar construction

Feature/material	Weights lbs/ft²
Glazings:	
1 layer glass	1.2–1.6
2 layers glass	3.5–4.5
1 layer FRP	0.25–0.29
2 layer FRP	0.7
2 layer Acrylic	0.25–1.0
Thermal storage floors:	
4″ concrete slab	50
6″ concrete slab	75
¾″ quarry tile	8.6
3″ brick (paver)	40
4″ brick	35
Thermal storage walls (without glazing system):	
8″ brick	78
12″ brick	117
8″ concrete	100
10″ concrete	125
12″ concrete	150
Masonry partitions:	
4″ concrete block	22
4″ metal lath and plaster	14–16
8″ concrete block	36
4″ brick veneer	37
Solar heat collectors:	
Aluminum frame, copper absorber, tempered glass (1 layer), insulation	5.5

areas or thermal mass components, and special attention to diagonal bracing due to changes in exterior sheathing materials. Masonry walls also may be adapted to serve the dual functions of structural support and heat storage distribution.

The wall system also supports exterior and interior sheathings and finish materials, as well as plumbing, heating, and electrical services. The details of construction and level of workmanship applied when installing exterior sheathing and siding, and interior vapor barriers and finishes, will affect greatly the rate of air leakage and moisture movement through the exterior shell. These factors are also critical when completing the shell by installing the doors, windows, and glazings, as discussed in Chapter 10.

Reduced wall heights can improve a building's energy efficiency by exposing less wall area to the wind, and by lowering ceiling heights, thus reducing the volume of air that requires heating or cooling. Typical 8-foot ceiling heights can be lowered to 7 feet 6 inches, resulting in greater comfort due to more even temperatures between the floor and ceiling.

The wall systems discussed in this section include: wood frame exterior shell, wood frame double shell, and masonry. The following general guidelines should be considered when comparing alternate wall systems:

- Avoid thermal bridging. Areas of special concern include headers, plates, corners, jack and stud assemblies.
- Never compromise structural integrity for energy performance.
- Consider insulative sheathing to replace structural plywood or composition board. Provide diagonal bracing with insulative sheathing.
- Increase insulation levels. Consider 2x6, 24″ on center framing to use less wood in wall cavities.
- Reduce infiltration. Assemble sheathing, siding, and trim accurately and tightly.
- Install continuous sheet vapor barrier on warm side of insulation. Patch all holes.
- Consider the vapor permeance of the whole built-up wall section. (See Chapter 3.)
- Minimize mechanical and electrical runs in insulated wall sections. Consider running all utility lines in interior walls and electrical wiring in raceway conduits.
- Any utility penetrations through walls should be sealed tightly by caulking or stuffing with insulation.

Wood Frame Exterior Shell

Wood frame exterior walls are most commonly constructed on site using platform (Western) framing techniques, or by erecting panelized sections that have been built off site. Both framing systems use similar materials and details and suffer from similar problems in terms of energy efficiency. Although our discussions of wall construction highlight on-site construction, they often apply to all types of wood frame wall systems (Fig. 9.16). The components of a typical light wood frame wall section, include top and bottom plates, studs, jacks, cripples, headers, corners, blocking, nailers, bracing, exterior sheathing and siding, insulation, vapor barriers, and interior finishes. Post and beam construction, an older and more labor intensive framing technique, is well suited to solar construction because of the long spans that can be achieved with minimal support. Use of this framing technique in buildings that utilize large

THE INSULATED BUILDING SHELL 151

Fig. 9.17 Post and beam construction allows builders to span large distances, creating more room for windows and glazings.

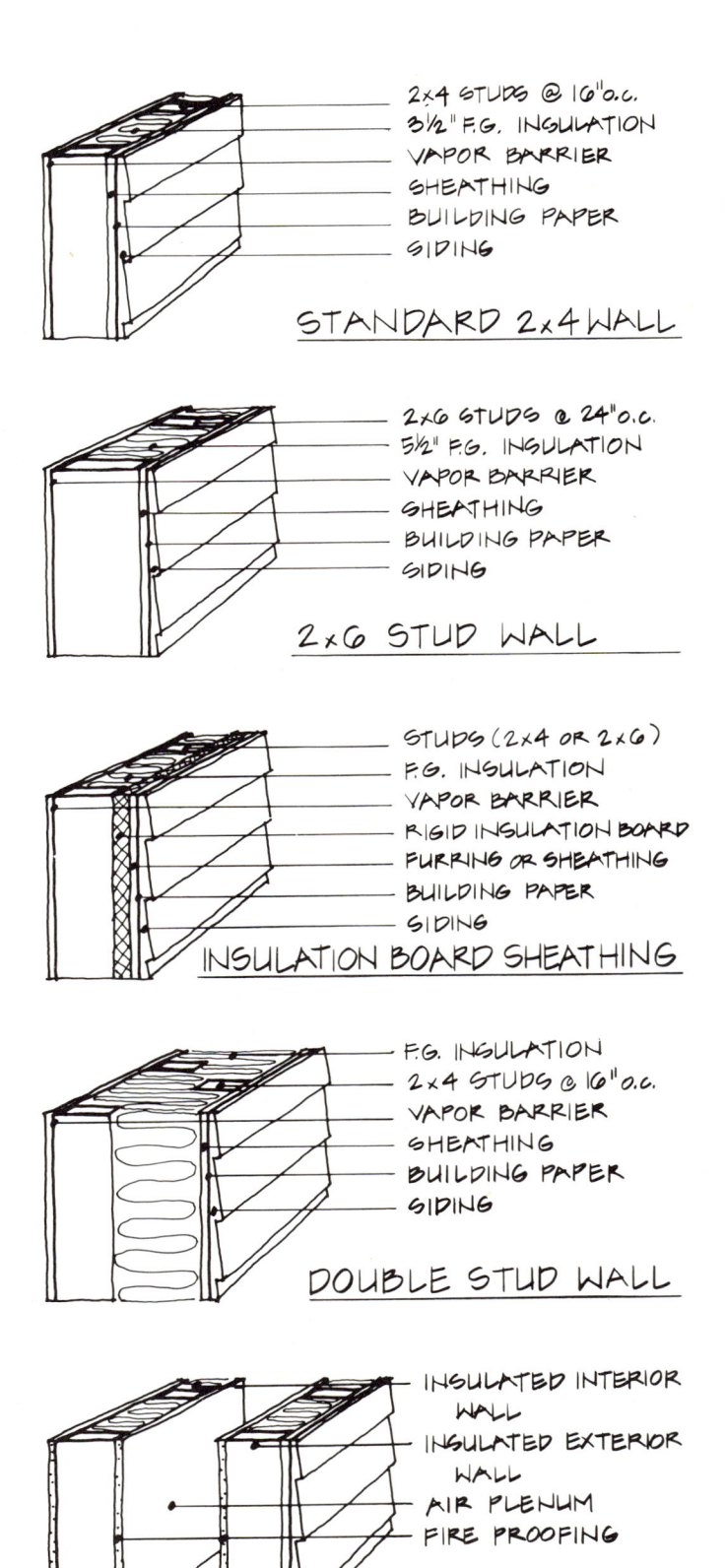

Fig. 9.16 Insulating wood frame walls.

glazed areas for solar heat collection allows flexibility in the structural design of window walls (Fig. 9.17). Depending on the building, builders may choose to combine wall systems, using stud framed walls on the north, east, and west sides, and post and beam framing on the south.

Standard stud wall construction typically has used nominal 2x4 studs spaced 16 or 24 inches on center, insulated with 3½-inch (R-11) fiberglass blankets or batts. This wall section provides an R-13, including ½-inch gypsum finish inside and ½-inch plywood sheathing and wood siding outside. At one time this amount of insulation was considered sufficient, but now it is generally recognized as inadequate in most climatic regions of the country. A simple modification that will greatly improve energy efficiency is to use insulative exterior sheathing in place of plywood or composite sheathing. By sheathing the R-13 wall with rigid board insulation, levels of R-18 or R-20 can be achieved (Fig. 9.18). In addition to increasing the R-value of the wall section, the insulative sheathing also covers the framing materials, reducing the amount of heat conduction or thermal bridging that occurs through them. With studs spaced 16 inches on center, as much as 20 percent of the gross wall area consists of framing lumber, through which one-third of the wall's total heat loss may be transmitted. By framing with studs spaced 24 inches on center, the amount of wall area in lumber may be reduced to 10 percent.

To increase the amount of insulation in walls beyond this level, the depth of the wall cavity may be en-

Fig. 9.18 The use of insulative sheathing to increase R-value of wall section.

larged by using 2x6 or even 2x8 studs, 24 inches on center. Stud walls framed with 2x6's provide a 5½-inch cavity that can be insulated with 5½-inch thick (R-19) fiberglass blankets or batts. These walls commonly are built using plywood or composite exterior sheathing rather than rigid board insulation, resulting in an R-21 insulation level. However, by sheathing 2x6 framed walls with insulative sheathing, the insulation level can reach R-26 to R-28. Walls framed with 2x8 studs can be used to achieve even higher R-values in the same manner.

Insulative Exterior Sheathing

Rigid board insulations used as exterior sheathings include extruded polystyrene, polyurethane, polyisocyanurate, foil boards, and expanded polystyrene. The considerations in selection of sheathing materials for this phase are different than those that apply to products used to insulate foundations, as discussed in Chapter 8. Exterior sheathing on above grade wood frame walls is not subjected to the harsh conditions that foundation insulations must withstand. Selection should take into account the following factors:

- Availabililty: type of material, available dimensions, "cost per R."
- Code approval: safety concerns of flame spread, toxicity, and structural implications.
- Strength: compressive materials may cause waviness in exterior walls by compressing against the

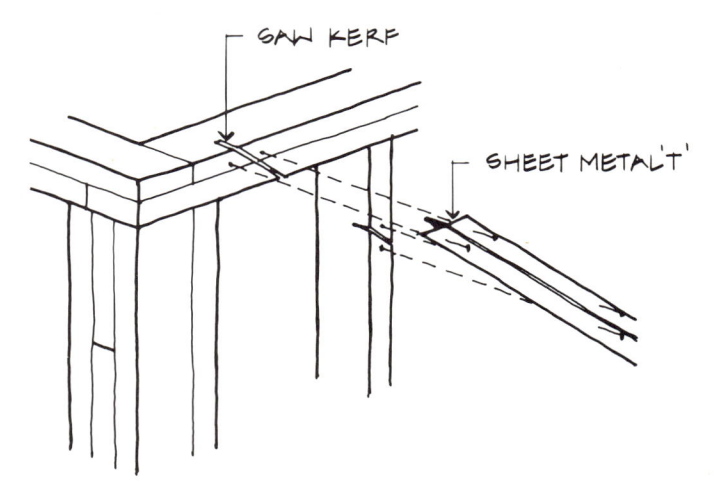

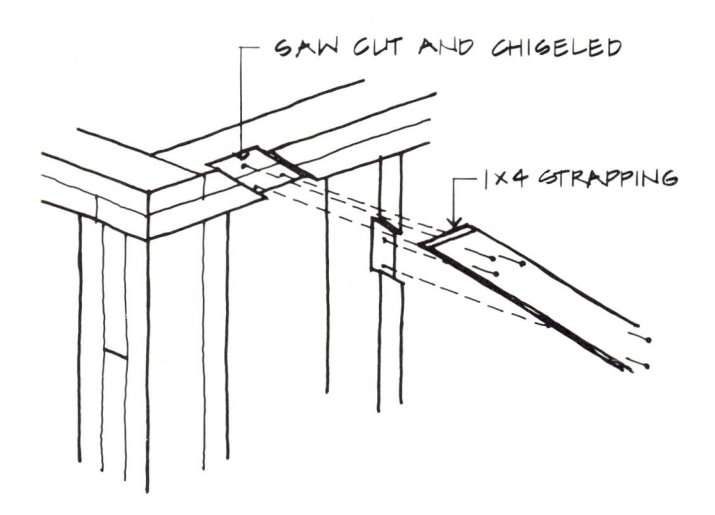

Fig. 9.19 Diagonal bracing techniques for use with insulative sheathing.

framing as siding is nailed. This is especially evident with horizontal sidings.
- Durability: resistance to animal and/or insect damage.

Insulative sheathing materials provide little diagonal reinforcing. A building shell's resistance to horizontal or racking forces caused by wind movement largely depends on the use of structural exterior sheathings like plywood or particle board. Replacement of these materials with nonstructural insulative sheathings requires the installation of diagonal bracing as part of the stud walls. Let-in braces consisting of 1x4 lumber, or metal banding as seen in Fig. 9.19, are effective in stiffening the frame, and have been approved for use in this manner by the International Conference of Building Officials, Southern Building Code Conference, Building Officials Code Association, and HUD/FHA.

A second method of stiffening the frame is to use at the corners both plywood and insulative sheathing that combine in thickness to equal (within one-sixteenth of an inch) the full thickness of insulative sheathing used elsewhere on the frame. A third way to assure torsional strength in the frame while using nonstructural insulative sheathing is to apply plywood finish siding over the sheathing. When properly nailed these sheets of paneling will serve to brace the frame.

Most insulative sheathings do not provide the continuous nailing surface for siding that plywood provides, although some laminated panels do include exterior plywood. This affects the layout of framing members and nailers or blocking, as well as the selection of finish exterior siding (Fig. 9.20). Basically, the use of vertical siding requires horizontal blocking for nailing; horizontal siding may be nailed through the sheathing directly into the studs. Special blocking may be necessary to provide nailing for the siding where it joins the corner boards, frieze, and bottom trim, and window and door casings.

The sheet of insulative sheathing can be cut with circular saw, table saw, or utility knife used with a straight edge. It is applied to the frame in a similar manner as other exterior sheathing materials. Nails used to fasten the sheathing to the frame vary with the thickness of the material and builders' preference. Galvanized roofing nails often are used because their large heads hold the relatively soft material without pulling through it. Common nails with metal discs, often used to hold roofing paper, can be used to fasten the sheathing without tearing into it. Table 9.2 presents some of the options available for fastening exterior insulative sheathing to the frame.

Fig. 9.20 The use of insulative exterior sheathing may require installing special nailers for exterior siding and trim.

Table 9.2
Recommended nailing of insulative sheathing to frame

Sheathing to framing

Sheathing thickness	Type of nails
¾ 1	2" galv. roofing nail or 6d galv. box nail with aluminum roofing paper disc
1¼ 1½	2½" galv. roofing nail or 8d galv box with disc

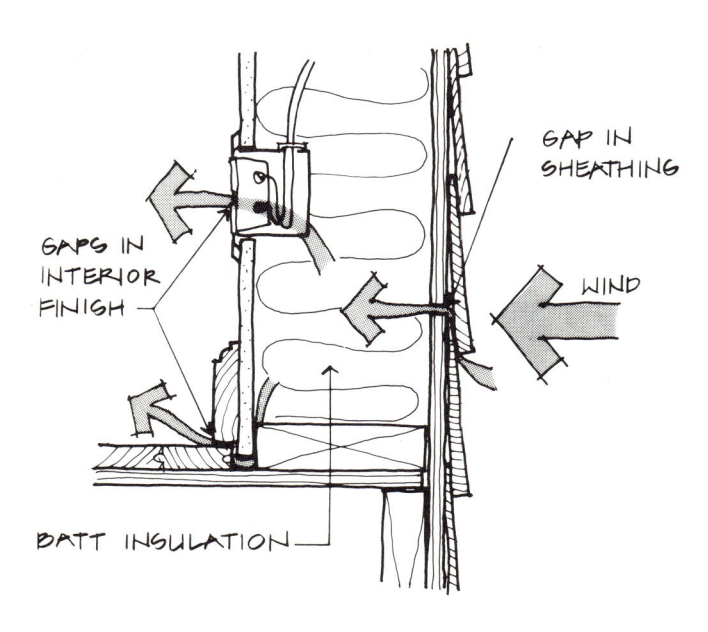

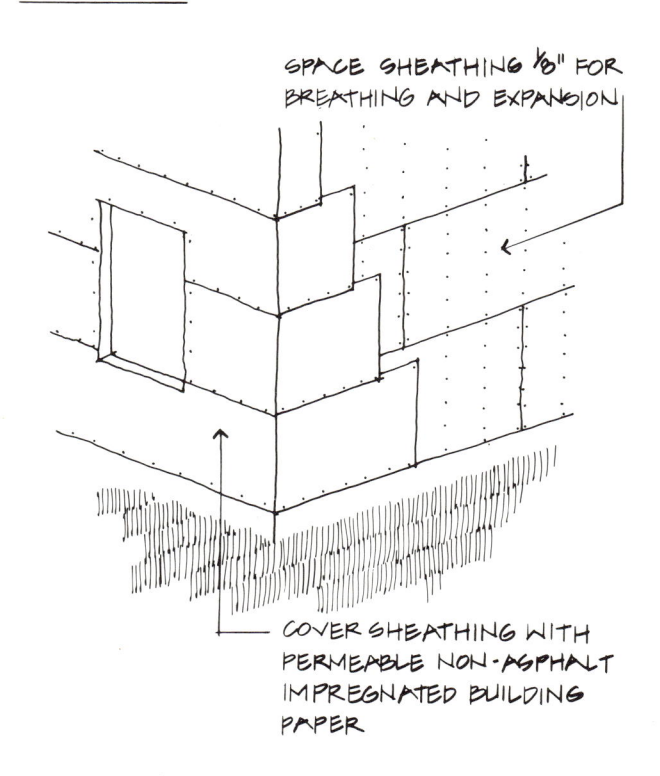

154 MATERIALS, DETAILS, AND TECHNIQUES OF SOLAR CONSTRUCTION

THE ISSUE:

INFILTRATION IN JOINTS IN SHEATHING

REMEDIES:

Fig. 9.21 Reducing infiltration at joints in sheathing.

Nailing patterns for these various sheathing products usually are specified by the manufacturer. Generally, the suggested pattern ranges from 8 to 12 inches on center along the studs, using the closer spacing along vertical joints between adjacent pieces. Sheathing should be nailed so that it is tight to the frame. Care must be taken to prevent either driving a fastener too far into the material, or damaging the sheathing with hammer marks that break through the material. To reduce air leakage, damaged sections should be replaced before siding is installed. Insulative sheathing can be placed over window and door openings, and later cut flush to the rough opening with a utility knife and straight edge, or with a hand saw (Fig. 9.21).

Siding

Exterior finish siding materials are installed over insulative sheathing in the same manner as over plywood. However, due to the fixed location of nailing, and the compressibility of insulative sheathing, more care must be taken to assure a flat and secure surface. Depending on the details and materials selected, siding may be installed before or after the windows, doors, and trim boards. Protect these intersections of siding with doors and window trim against air leakage by accurate cuts and caulking.

Wall Framing

Insulative exterior sheathing will reduce significantly the amount of heat conducted through the wall framing; however, other measures listed below control this source of heat loss: (Fig. 9.22)

- Built-up headers should be constructed with a one-inch-thick layer of rigid board insulation.
- Box headers should be filled with fiberglass or rigid board insulation as they are assembled.
- Box-type corner posts should be filled with insulation.
- Corner details and intersections between exterior wall and interior partitions may be adapted to allow more complete insulation.

Generally, the more wood in the frame, the less room is available for insulation; this applies to structural framing as well as nailing surfaces (Fig. 9.23). However, structural considerations and provisions for nailing of interior and exterior finishes are the first priorities in wall systems.

Framed wall sections built on site may be sheathed before or after they are erected. Before raising job built or factory built panelized sections into place, a bead of caulk should be applied to the deck where the bottom

THE INSULATED BUILDING SHELL   155

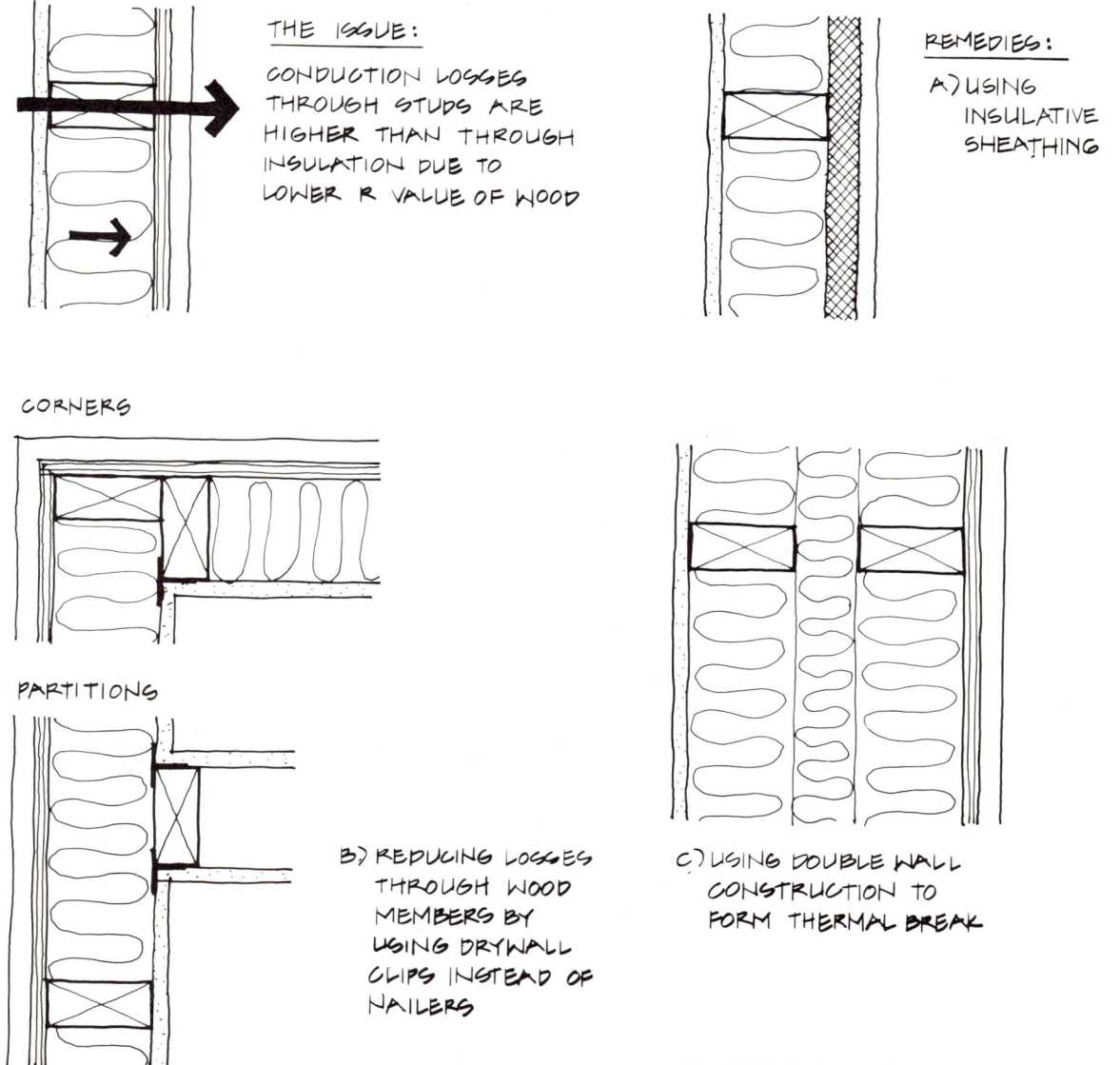

Fig. 9.22 Reducing heat loss through wood frame walls.

plate will rest. This will help reduce the amount of air leakage that occurs at this point. The position of the wall on the deck may be affected by the use of rigid board insulation on the exterior of the foundation.

Insulating Exterior Wall Cavities

The most common insulations used in wood frame walls in new construction are fiberglass blankets or batts (Fig. 9.24). These materials usually are installed after the plumbing, heating, and electrical services have been roughed-in, but this schedule often is changed. If these jobs are done after the insulation or vapor barriers are in place, builders should replace insulation and repair vapor barriers. By changing the layout of these utility systems, builders can avoid placement of pipes, ducts, and wiring in the exterior shell, as discussed in Chapter 11. This will help reduce the necessary number of penetrations of the wall surfaces, which helps control air leakage and the movement of moisture.

Fiberglass blanket or batt insulations are available in 2½-inch (R-8), 3½-inch (R-11), 5½-inch (R-19), and 9-inch (R-27) thicknesses, and in widths of 16 and 24 inches. They are also available with aluminum foil or

156 MATERIALS, DETAILS, AND TECHNIQUES OF SOLAR CONSTRUCTION

HEAVY LOAD
- 2×6 WALL

(TOP PLATE; 2" RIGID INSULATION BOARD)

MEDIUM LOAD
- PLYWOOD BOX BEAM —
PLYWOOD WEB GLUED
AND SCREWED TO
UPPER AND LOWER
LONGITUDINAL
MEMBERS

(BATT INSULATION, PLYWOOD WEB, LONGITUDINAL MEMBER)

MINIMAL LOAD
- JOISTS PARALLEL
WITH WALL
- BAND JOIST TAKES
WALL LOADS

(BATT INSULATION, CRIPPLE STUD @ 2'-0" O.C.)

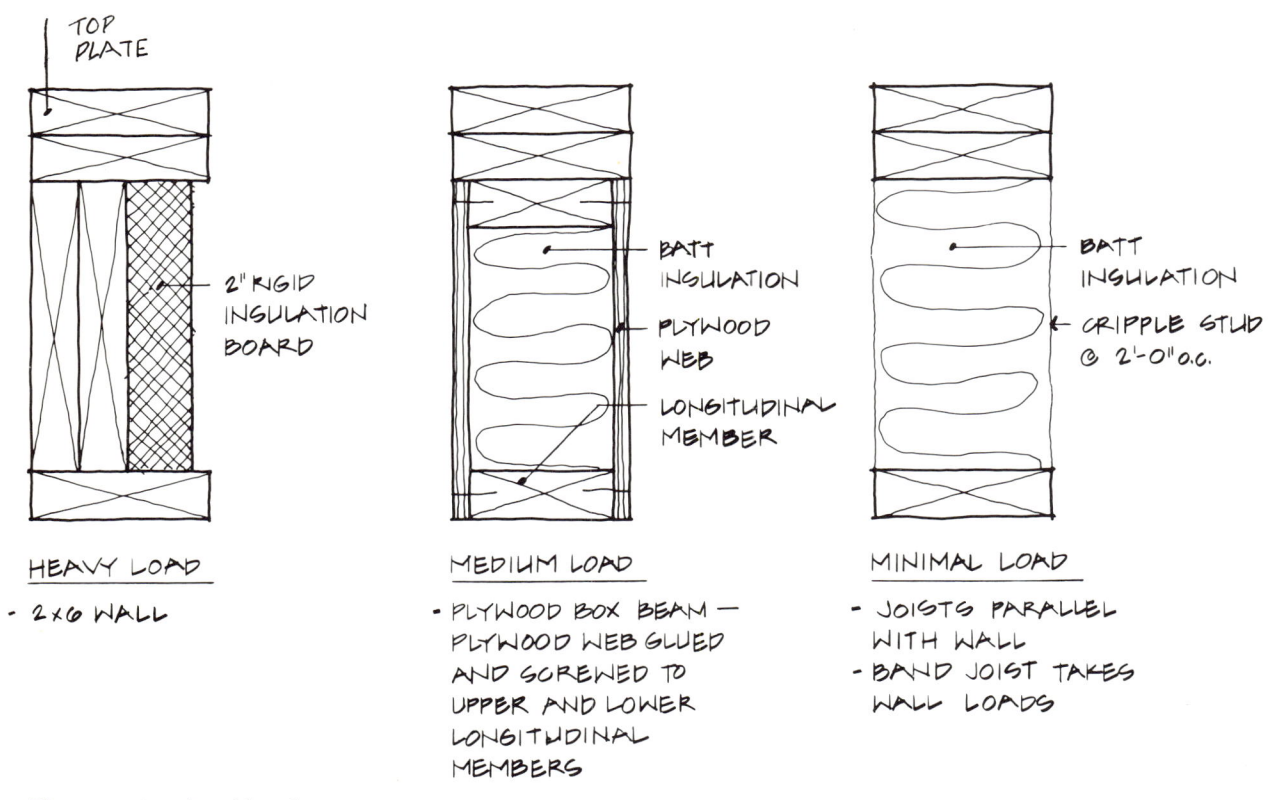

Fig. 9.23 Insulated headers.

kraft paper facings, or unfaced (friction fit). Although the facings can be used as vapor barriers, it is common practice to use a separate sheet vapor barrier over these materials. In order to achieve the specified R-values, these insulations must be properly installed. Supervision and inspection of this work will ensure the effectiveness of the insulation before the vapor barrier and interior finishes are installed. Builders should check the following:

- Blankets should be cut to fit accurately within the cavity, butt tightly together, and fill the entire cavity.
- Enough staples should be used to avoid gaps in the stapling flanges (not as critical when using separate sheet vapor barrier).
- Water piping and ductwork must be protected in exterior walls by wedging blanket insulation behind these components.
- Small areas between framing members at windows, doors, or partition corners should be stuffed with insulation or filled with spray foam.

- Exterior corners and intersections of interior partitions and exterior walls should be insulated between studs before exterior sheathing is applied.
- Electrical boxes can be insulated at the back with a separate small piece of insulation, while the rest of the blanket fits tightly around the sides.
- Insulate all walls between heated and unheated areas in multilevel houses.
- Exterior wall sections behind bath and shower units must be insulated before the units are installed.
- Band joists on upper floors should be insulated while accessible.

Loose fill insulation also may be used in wood frame wall cavities in both new and existing buildings. Cellulose insulation is rated at approximately R-4 per inch, and consists of shredded newspaper treated with a fire retardant chemical. It is applied by either dry-blowing it into the enclosed cavities or, when mixed with glue, spraying it onto the exterior sheathing from the inside (new construction or major renovation only). Fiberglass

Fig. 9.24 Fiberglass batt insulation in exterior wall cavity.

loose fill is rated at approximately R-2 per inch and is dry-blown into the wall section. Both types of loose fill materials can be expected to settle. For this reason, they are most often used in floors and ceilings where the material will have less tendency to compress under its own weight.

Vapor Barriers

In order to reduce the amount of moisture that enters a wood frame wall section from the building's interior in winter, a vapor barrier should be installed on the heated side of the wall after the utilities have been roughed-in and the cavities insulated. Materials commonly used as vapor barriers include:

- foil-backed wallboard
- foil or paper facings on fiberglass batt or blanket insulation
- rigid board insulation (when covered by drywall for fire protection)
- separate polyethylene or foil sheets stapled to framing

The effectiveness of any of these materials in controlling moisture and air movement depends upon its permeability and the quality of installation. Table 3.5 (Chapter 3) gives permeability ratings for typical vapor barriers. In selecting a vapor barrier, builders must consider many factors, the most important of which is the severity of the winter season as represented by the winter design temperature. The map in Fig. 3.6 (Chapter 3) presents various design temperatures for different parts of the country and uses these delineations to define the three condensation hazard zones as illustrated. Table 3.6 (Chapter 3) offers recommendations for the permeability and locations of vapor barriers in each zone. Zone A (severe) represents the region where condensation is a major consideration in construction, and identifies areas where the most effective moisture control measures should be incorporated. In Zone B (moderate) vapor barriers also should be used to control moisture movement into walls, although the conditions are less severe. Zone C (slight) identifies an area where there is little chance of condensation occuring in walls. In this region high temperature and vapor pressure differentials between inside and outside do not occur very often; therefore, vapor barriers on walls may be unnecessary.

Foil-backed wallboard products in 4 foot by 8 foot sheets may be used for moisture protection in Zones A and B when joints are made over framing members. This is accomplished most easily by installing the sheets vertically so that joints occur over studs; however, even this configuration will allow some vapor leakage.

Fiberglass roll and batt insulations are available with vapor barrier facings of asphalt impregnated foil or kraft paper. Most manufacturers recommend that barrier faced insulation be installed with the flanges stapled to the sides of the studs. This method makes it almost impossible to avoid forming gaps along the flange between fasteners. The gaps allow air and water vapor to move past the barrier; therefore, this means of moisture control should be limited to the areas of moderate or slight condensation hazards found in Zones B and C. In Zone A this method may be used when the flanges are stapled to the faces of studs. As a rule, however, a separate sheet-type vapor barrier is recommended for use with batt insulation.

Some **rigid board insulation** materials have a very low permeance and can be used as interior vapor barrier surfaces, while other rigid insulation products are manufactured with foil or waxed paper facings that resist moisture movement. When applied to the interior surface of a wall, they are most effective as vapor barriers if the joints occur over framing and are sealed with moisture resistant mastic or tape. Due to their flammability and toxicity, many of these materials must be covered with gypsum wallboard. Safe installation techniques for foam products usually are recommended by the manufacturers and must meet local codes.

The most effective vapor barrier is a **continuous layer of polyethylene or aluminum foil** stapled to the interior surface of stud walls. These materials are recommended for use in Zones A and B. The most common of these vapor barriers are 4-mil or 6-mil polyethylene. The 6-mil thickness is recommended because of its greater resistance to moisture and puncturing. The following installation guidelines apply to all separate sheet vapor barriers (Fig. 9.25 and 9.26).

- Vapor barrier should be applied to walls in large sections to minimize joints.
- Joints should lap 4 to 6 inches and occur over framing members.
- Sheets should be extended over window and door openings to be cut out at a later time.
- Vapor barrier should be carefully cut around and taped to electrical outlets and plumbing or heating penetrations.
- All tears should be repaired by taping with duct tape.
- Sheets should extend far enough in all directions to lap effectively with other sheets at corners, and intersections between walls and floors or ceilings.
- Vapor barrier (or a section) should be installed on exterior walls before interior partitions are framed, or before shower or bath units are installed.
- Vapor barrier should extend to cover inside of band joists on upper floors.

Insulation contractors usually are responsible for installing vapor barriers. It is very important for builders to supervise this phase of work to make sure that all critical areas are insulated and protected from water vapor. Subsequent work by drywall contractors and

Fig. 9.25 Continuous sheet vapor barriers should be installed in large sections to minimize joints.

finish carpenters must also be supervised, to make sure that the properly installed insulation and vapor barrier remain intact.

Wood Frame Double Shell

An increasingly common technique for wall framing in cold climates is the construction of double stud walls (Fig. 9.27). There are two basic approaches to double wall framing. One approach simply increasees the depth of the wall cavity to allow room for a thicker blanket of insulation than can be installed in single wall framing. These more heavily insulated buildings are sometimes called "superinsulated." The other approach, often called double shell or "envelope" construction, utilizes a double stud wall system to enclose an insulated air space. This air space usually is linked through openings in the floor to an insulated crawl space, where the earth temperature helps keep the air between the shells at a fairly stable temperature.

THE INSULATED BUILDING SHELL 159

THE ISSUE:

AIR INFILTRATION AND VAPOR MIGRATION AT ELECTRICAL OUTLETS

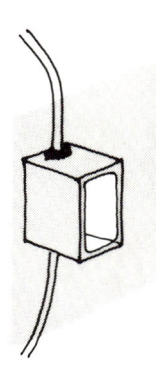

REMEDIES:
- USE BOXES WITHOUT SEAMS
- CAULK WIRE PENETRATION POINTS
- RUN VAPOR BARRIER OVER BOX AND CUT AWAY AFTER DRYWALLING

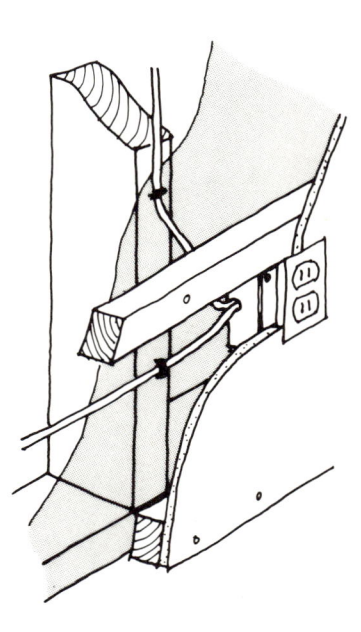

- FUR OUT WALLS TO CREATE ELECTRICAL CHASES ON THE INTERIOR SIDE OF THE VAPOR BARRIER
- UNPUNCTURED VAPOR BARRIER HELPS CONTROL VAPOR MIGRATION AND INFILTRATION
- DRILLING FOR WIRES IS ELIMINATED BUT WIRING MUST BE DONE AFTER INSULATING

Fig. 9.26 Reducing infiltration and vapor migration with the use of continuous sheet vapor barriers.

Fig. 9.27 The use of double stud wall framing.

Both systems offer advantages in energy conservation through the increase in R-value, reduction in heat loss by conduction through framing members, and reduction in air leakage. Buildings which use these techniques require a small fracton of the energy for heat that "conventional" houses do. Double framing adds to the initial cost of the building due to the additional material and labor used in framing, as well as in finish details at window and door jambs. These costs can be offset somewhat by the lower initial costs of supplemental heating and cooling equipment.

The two methods used for increasing the depth of the wall cavity are based on practices used to reduce sound transmission through walls; staggering the stud layout on common bottom and top plates; or splitting the plates and building two separate walls. The staggered stud wall creates an insulation cavity as deep as the width of the plates and reduces the number of thermal bridges in the frame. Staggered stud walls may be assembled at the site like single stud wall sections. The positioning of the wall on the deck in relation to foundation insulation or exterior insulative sheathing should follow the guidelines established in the preceding section. Considerations for the use of exterior sheathing, cavity insulation, and interior vapor barriers also are similar.

The other method used to increase the amount of insulation in wall sections is the use of double stud walls. This technique also uses 2x4 studs 16 or 24 inches on center, and it requires building two walls. The outermost wall must be placed according to foundation insulation and/or exterior sheathing details. The innermost stud wall can be placed to provide a deep cavity for various thicknesses of blanket, batt, or loose fill insulation materials. The two walls often are joined together by blocking or bridging, or by plywood gussets to reinforce their rigidity. Vapor barriers should be installed on the heated side of the inner frame using techniques recommended earlier in this chapter.

Double shell or envelope construction also makes use of double stud walls. Rather than filling the entire wall cavity with insulation, the stud cavities in each wall are insulated and the space between the two walls is left open to serve as an air passage. Both the depth of studs used to build each wall and the air space left between the walls vary with the building design. Double shell construction is another means of superinsulating a building. Heat loss through these wall systems is minimized because: (1) both exterior and interior stud walls are insulated; (2) the presence of earth tempered air between the stud walls acts as an effective buffer between interior and exterior temperatures; (3) the double stud wall system greatly reduces heat conduction through the framing; and (4) HVAC, plumbing, electrical and solar domestic hot water lines can be run through innermost wall cavity, reducing their impact on heat loss.

Lumber used to frame these walls includes 2x4, 2x6, and 2x8 studs. Some builders construct double 2x4 walls, while others use 2x6 or 2x8 studs for the exterior shell and 2x4 studs for the interior shell. The selection of stud size, especially for the exterior shell, will also vary due to climatic factors, with the larger dimensioned studs used in colder climates to create a deeper cavity for insulation.

The depth of the air space between the double walls is another variable in double shell construction that depends upon the approach selected, as discussed in Chapter 5. Some double shell buildings utilize a sunspace/greenhouse to heat air within the envelope. In this case the sunspace/greenhouse is used as part of the air buffer (Fig. 9.28). The air heated in the sunspace/greenhouse then circulates into an air space that may be from 4 to 12 inches wide, as it moves along the roof and down into the crawl space through the double north wall. This air movement is often assisted mechanically to avoid overheating in the sunspace. Other forms of double shell buildings use the 4-to 12-inch air space on the south rather than the large sunspace/greenhouse. Builders also vary the number of double walls used, with some double framing on the south and north walls only, and others double framing all of the walls and opening them to the earth tempered crawl space.

Construction sequence for double shell buildings follows the same sequence as for other forms of construction, where the exterior shell is framed and en-

Fig. 9.28 The use of a sunspace in double shell construction.

Table 9.3
Approximate U-values for uninsulated masonry walls

Wall type and nominal thickness	Plain wall no plaster	5/8" Lightweight interior plaster	Furred interior gypsum plaster
Solid wall			
6" Brick	0.68	0.54	0.35
8" Brick	0.48	0.41	0.29
Composite wall			
4" Brick + 4" structural clay tile	0.36	0.32	0.24
4" Brick + 4" concrete brick	0.49	0.41	0.29
Cavity wall			
4" Brick + 4" brick	0.33	0.29	0.23
4" Lightweight block + 4" lightweight block	0.21	0.18	0.16
Veneered wall			
4" Brick (clay or concrete) over wood frame	—	0.25	—
Hollow units			
8" Concrete block	0.35	0.31	0.24
8" Structural clay tile	0.36	0.32	0.25

closed first. The exterior walls that support the roof loads are placed on the foundation in relation to exterior foundation insulation and/or exterior sheathing (including rigid board insulation), as described earlier in this chapter. Once the exterior shell, including windows, has been enclosed, the outer walls can be insulated and a 6-mil polyethylene vapor barrier installed. Depending upon local codes, the inside surface of the wall then may have to be covered with gypsum wallboard to reduce the amount of dust circulating around the building and, most importantly, to protect the walls from fire in the air space. The inner walls also may require this same protection.

The inner stud walls can be framed after the exterior shell has been completed. If wallboard is required on the air space side of the wall, it can be applied to the framed wall sections before they are erected. Many designs utilize windows in the inner walls that line up with the windows in the outer shell. These inner windows also should be installed before the walls are set in place. Once the inner walls are in place, framing for window and door jambs can be completed, the services roughed-in, and the insulation installed. The use of an additional vapor barrier on the heated side of the innermost wall is also recommended; however, many builders omit this vapor barrier because the dew point temperature usually does not occur in this wall section, even in cold climates.

Masonry Walls

Exterior masonry wall systems used in residential construction include solid, hollow, and veneered walls constructed from brick, adobe, or cement blocks. Often these walls are used in conjunction with wood frame wall systems to form the exterior building shell. Masonry materials commonly are used in solar construction to collect, store, and reradiate heat which is collected from sunlight that strikes them directly or absorbed from other heat sources within the building. The selection of masonry material, specific wall thickness, and finish depends upon local availability and the building's design. Wall systems must be constructed from sound masonry and the correct mortar with careful workmanship to meet the specifications of local building codes.

Depending on their construction, masonry walls may contribute to conductive heat loss due to thermal bridging. Although solid walls conduct more heat than hollow ones, both types should be insulated on the exterior, especially if they are to be used as thermal mass. Rigid board insulation used in this manner can be finished with a stucco surface, or the outside of the wall

Fig. 9.29 This brick exterior wall has been constructed to absorb solar heat and transfer it to the interior of the building.

can be furred to provide nailing for exterior siding. Masonry wall sections should be insulated to a level comparable to wood frame wall sections for a given climatic region. Table 9.3 presents the approximate U-values of typical uninsulated masonry walls. In applications that prohibit use of exterior insulation, hollow walls may be filled with insulation, or solid walls may be insulated on the interior with rigid board insulation or insulated stud walls.

Thermal Storage Walls

Exterior masonry walls located on the south side of a building may be designed to collect, store, and deliver solar heat to the house (Fig. 9.29). Rather than insulate these mass walls, they are left exposed to the sun on one side and exposed to the living space on the other. A discussion of how these walls function is presented in Chapter 5.

Thermal storage walls may be made of concrete block (solid or filled), paving brick, adobe, and poured concrete. Typically the walls are double or triple glazed on the exterior with a window wall that may be hung on the wall surface, and supported by the foundation. The glazing system allows the sunlight to strike and heat the masonry surface, and reduces the amount of heat lost from the wall due to the multiple glazings and a 4-inch minimum air space. Greenhouse glazing systems are sometimes used to enclose mass walls. Both of these glazing approaches are examined in detail in Chapter 10.

Fig. 9.30 Interior view of a vented thermal storage wall.

Thermal masonry walls absorb heat and deliver it into the building by conduction through the wall and by subsequent radiation into the heated space. If vents are cast or built into the walls close to the floor and ceiling (with a minimum 6-foot vertical distance between them), air that is heated in the air space between the wall and glazing systems will rise and enter the room through the upper vents. This convective air movement draws cooler air into the air space through the lower vents, and continues to heat the air for 2 to 3 hours after the sun has stopped heating the wall. Operable vents can be used in these openings to control the rate of air flow. At night, upper vents should be left closed to prevent the reverse flow of warm air out of the living space and past the cool wall glazing. Construction details for manual and automatic dampers will be discussed in Chapter 12. Vent openings, as illustrated in Fig. 9.30, are formed either by eliminating single cement blocks at appropriate locations in the wall, or by casting 4-inch by 15-inch openings into poured concrete walls. Similar openings can be made in brick walls.

The amount of heat that the exterior surface of a thermal masonry wall can absorb depends on the color and type of material. Since dark colored materials absorb more solar heat than light colored ones, masonry materials like concrete, cement block, and adobe often are painted or dyed brown or black to enhance their performance. Paving bricks are naturally dark in color and often are used without paint.

Concrete and cement block walls must be prepared properly to receive either cement based paints, water thinned emulsions, or fill coats similar to the cement based applications. Holes in the wall surface should be filled with a block sealer to provide backing for the paint, and to help ensure an even colored surface. Because alkali in the concrete and cement materials will degrade oils and oil based materials, only alkali resistant coatings, or latex or resin based coatings, should be used. Before applying these coatings the contractor should clean concrete walls to remove oil residues from the forms, chalkiness from curing, and dust from construction. If a brick wall is to be painted, the selection of a coating depends on the age of the wall. If the mortar is well cured, almost any paint may be used due to the absence of alkali. However, new brick walls should be coated with paints recommended for concrete walls, because alkali is present in unseasoned mortar. Paints should be suitable for exterior use, because they will be exposed to temperature extremes, ultraviolet degradation, and a variety of moisture conditions. Follow manufacturer's instructions for surface preparation, coverage, suitable temperatures for application, and ventilation safety requirements while painting.

Two other important factors in the design and construction of a thermal masonry wall are the conductance of the chosen material and thickness of the wall using that material. Table 9.4 lists the various materials used, their conductance, and recommended thickness, all factors which determine the time required for solar heat to move through the wall before it starts to radiate to the living space. These factors also determine the length of time the heat will continue to radiate from the wall after the outside surface has stopped absorbing heat (at night or cloudy day), or after convective air flow is stopped by closing the dampers. As the conductance of the material increases, the optimum thickness increases. A wall built from highly conductive masonry must be thicker to avoid delivery of heat to the building before it is needed. Conversely, a wall built from materials which conduct heat poorly should be thin enough to permit the slow

Table 9.4
Effect of wall thickness on interior air temperature fluctuations

Material	Thermal conductivity (Btu/hr-ft-°F)	Recommended thickness (in)	Approximate indoor temperature (°F) fluctuation as a function of wall thickness[1]					
			4 in	8 in	12 in	16 in	20 in	24 in
Adobe	0.30	8–12	...	18°	7°	7°	8°	...
Brick (common)	0.42	10–14	...	24°	11°	7°	...	...
Concrete (dense)	1.00	12–18	...	28°	16°	10°	6°	5°
Brick (magnesium additive)[2]	2.20	16–24	...	35°	24°	17°	12°	9°

Notes: 1. Assumes a double-glazed thermal wall. If additional mass is located in the space, such as masonry walls and/or floors, then temperature fluctuations will be less than those listed. Values given are for winter-clear days.
2. Magnesium is commonly used as an additive to brick to darken its color. It also greatly increases the thermal conductivity of the material.

moving heat to reach the interior surface at the appropriate time of day.

Thermal masonry walls are constructed using standard trade practices for providing structural reinforcement. Very often these walls include vent, window, and door openings that allow air circulation, direct solar heat gain, view to the outside, and an entrance or exit. These openings must be constructed carefully.

Additional Details: Wall Systems

Sunspace and greenhouse areas often are built as additions to the main portions of buildings in new construction and retrofit applications. In many cases, the framing systems for these additions are attached to the exterior walls of adjacent buildings, either below the eaves or on the gable ends. Figure 9.31 and 9.32 show greenhouse framing details. Further details of sunspace/greenhouse glazing systems are discussed in Chapter 10.

ROOFS AND CEILINGS

All types of roof and ceiling systems are used in solar construction; the appropriate selection for a specific building must consider appearance, structural loads, control of heat loss and water vapor, fire resistance, and special requirements for various solar energy features such as overhangs, skylights, and solar heat collectors (Fig. 9.33). The selection of roof and ceiling systems also affects the cost of a building in terms of ease of insulation, type of roofing materials, the need for interior bearing walls, and the length of time to enclose it. Roof and ceiling systems discussed in this section include: truss roofs; rafter and joist systems; joist roofs; plank and beam; and panelized systems.

The extent to which heat loss through roofs and ceilings can be reduced depends on the building configuration, framing plan, and use of attic spaces. Heat from inside tends to collect at upper levels, causing a greater temperature differential than in other parts of the building (Fig. 9.34). Roofs and ceilings should be the most heavily insulated areas of the building. Attics are considered unheated if the insulation is located in attic floor joists (ceiling joists for room below), and heated if the insulation is between the rafters or on the roof deck. The following general considerations apply to most roof and ceiling installations:

- Framing members of roof or ceiling may restrict the depth of insulation. Using deeper framing provides more room for insulation but also provides larger spans, which enables floor plans to open up more for natural heat distribution.
- Attic hatchways and utility chases through ceiling should be insulated.
- Roof venting must be correctly sized and installed. Half of the vent area should be installed as inlet and half as outlet.
- Continuous sheet vapor barrier should be installed on the warm side of the insulation.

Truss Roofs

Truss roofs and ceiling systems are used throughout the country as an efficient way to enclose a building with a flat or sloped roof. Trusses spaced 24 or 48 inches on center may span the entire width of a building, allowing flexibility in the floor plan because interior bearing partitions are not needed. This can open up floor plans for natural circulation of heat and moisture throughout buildings.

Depending upon their design, trusses may either form usable second floor or attic spaces or simply enclose an unusable area. The selection of a truss design affects the amount and location of insulation installed in these roof systems. For example, trusses used to enclose

164 MATERIALS, DETAILS, AND TECHNIQUES OF SOLAR CONSTRUCTION

Fig. 9.32 Attached solar greenhouses must be securely fastened to wall or roof framing. (Sunplace Corp.)

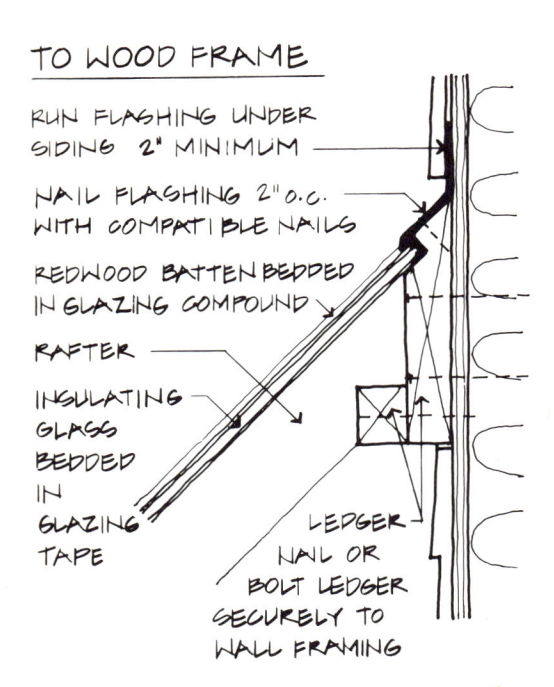

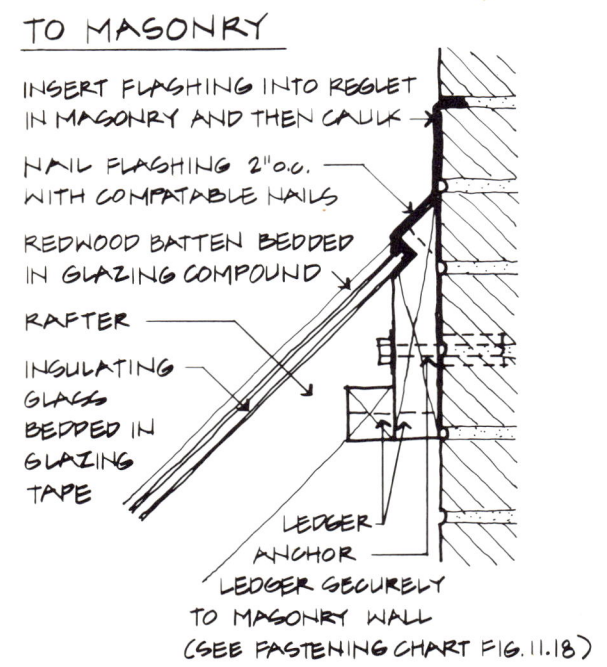

Fig. 9.31 Greenhouse framing into walls.

a second floor or attic may require insulation in the cavities formed by the top chords for a portion of the roof. Because truss roofs use smaller framing members in their construction than stick frames, the amount of insulation that can be installed properly in these cavities is limited. Typical truss designs that do not enclose usable space are not restricted in this way. These systems offer an easy means of increasing the insulation level in the roof/ceiling, using either loose fill or blanket materials installed between the lower chords to the desired depth (Fig. 9.35). Bottom chords generally serve as the ceiling framing to which the vapor barrier and interior finishes are attached; they also support the ceiling insulation, especially loose fill materials.

Double shell construction may require adaptation of standard truss designs to create an air passage above the ceiling. This can be accomplished by installing a special chord above the bottom chord at the job, or as specified in the truss design. Blanket insulation then can be installed in two layers; one between the bottom chords, and the other between the new upper chords, leaving the desired space between the layers.

Truss systems also may be designed to form fixed overhangs at the eaves to reduce solar heat gain in the summer by shading glazed areas. Design and construction details for fixed overhangs are presented later in this section.

Rafter and Joist Systems

Roofs and ceilings also commonly are framed using rafters and joists cut and assembled by carpenters at the job to form sloped roofs. Depending on the building design, these framing systems often require interior bearing walls to help carry the ceiling joists, which may

THE INSULATED BUILDING SHELL   165

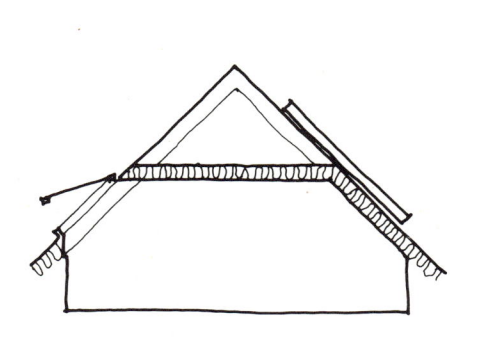

STEEPER ROOF PITCHES (DESIRABLE FOR MOUNTING SOLAR COLLECTORS) CREATE MORE ATTIC SPACE WHICH IN CONJUNCTION WITH ROOF WINDOWS MAY BECOME LIVING SPACE

ROOFS RECEIVING EXTENSIVE SUN SHOULD BE LIGHT IN COLOR AND WELL VENTILATED TO AVOID OVERHEATING ATTIC AND LIVING SPACE

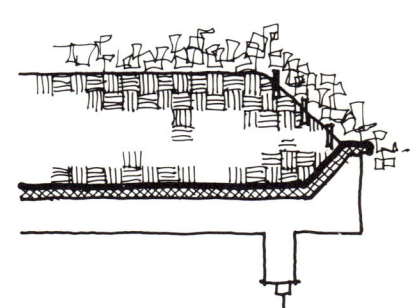

EARTH SHELTERED ROOF REQUIRES SPECIAL WATERPROOFING, VENTING AND STRUCTURAL DETAILING

Fig. 9.33 Selection of roof configuration should consider local climatic priorities.

ATTIC FLOOR
2×12 CEILING JOIST
80°
70°

HIGHER TEMPERATURES NEAR CEILING MAY REQUIRE THE USE OF MORE INSULATION HERE. DEEPER CEILING JOISTS ALLOW USE OF ATTIC SPACE FOR STORAGE

12" LOOSE FILL OR BLANKET INSULATION

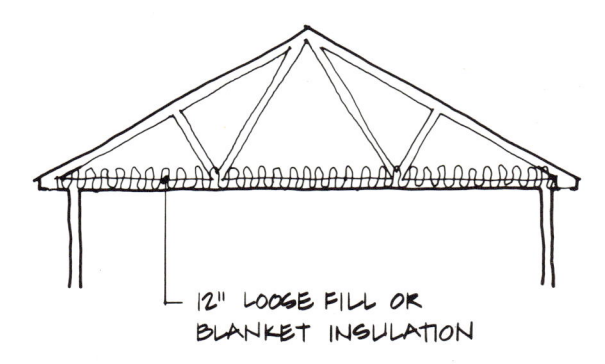

Fig. 9.35 Insulating Truss Roof Framing

- Insulation depth not limited to framing dimension
- Longer spans possible, inexpensive
- Attic unavailable for storage.

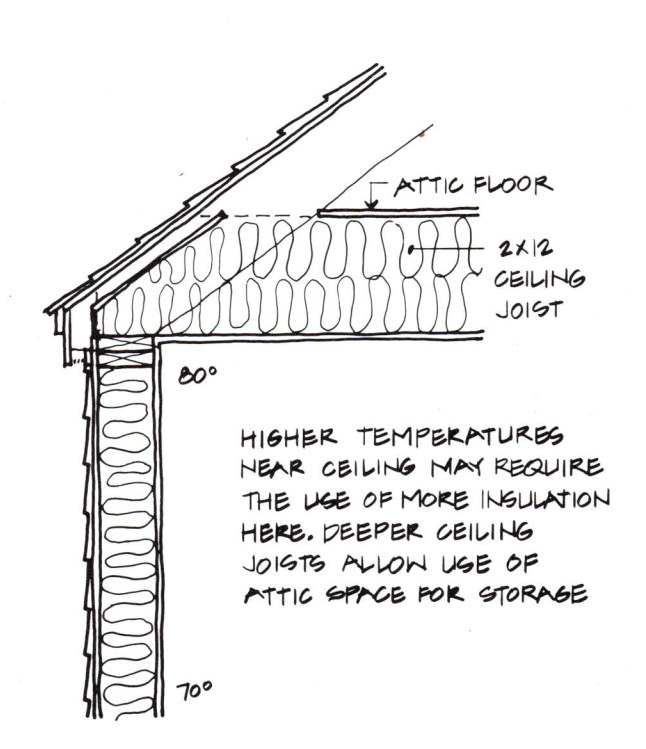

Fig. 9.34 Roofs and ceilings require higher levels of insulation due to greater temperature differential.

affect the layout of open floor plans. Typical layouts of rafters and joists include spacings of 16 or 24 inches on center depending on design loads and layout of wall framing. Open floor plans can be achieved by using deeper joists, built-up beams, or floor/ceiling trusses that span longer distances. Rafter and joist framing systems can be used to form heated second floor or attic

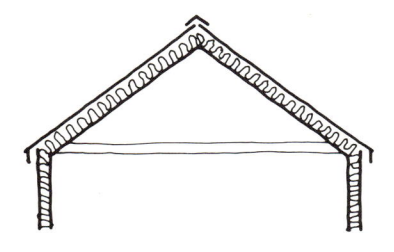

166 MATERIALS, DETAILS, AND TECHNIQUES OF SOLAR CONSTRUCTION

BATT INSULATION IS LIMITED TO RAFTER DEPTH MINUS 1" (FOR VENTILATION)

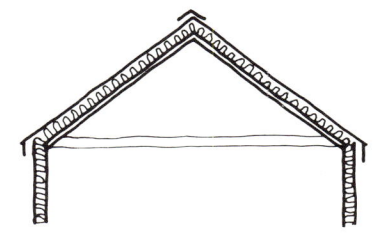

FIREPROOFED RIGID BOARD INSULATION INCREASES INSULATION VALUE WITHOUT INCREASING RAFTER DEPTH.

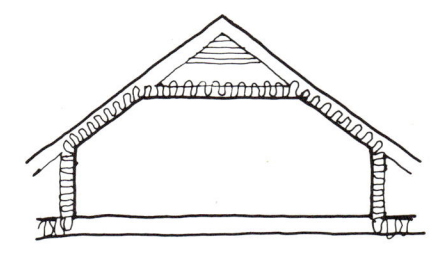

INSULATED CEILINGS AND KNEE WALLS PROVIDE PARTIAL "CATHEDRAL CEILINGS" WHILE SIMPLIFYING INSULATING AND VENTING DETAILS OF RAFTER CAVITIES

Fig. 9.36 Insulating rafter cavities.

spaces by insulating the rafter cavities, or may create unheated spaces by insulating the floor/ceiling joist cavities (Fig. 9.36) Other configurations often occur when knee-walls and collar ties become part of the insulated building shell.

In upper rooms used for heated storage space or intended for future expansion, insulation usually is installed between rafters or along collar ties. Typically rafter cavities are insulated with fibrous blanket or batt materials. The amount of insulation that can be applied in these areas is limited to the depth of the rafter, minus the one-inch air space that must be left between the insulation and roof sheathing for ventilation (Fig. 9.37). In order to increase the level of insulation achieved in this configuration, the depth of the cavity can be enlarged by using larger rafter material that will allow a thicker blanket of insulation. For example, 2x8 rafters normally insulated to R-19 can be replaced with 2x12's insulated to R-30. The fibrous insulation should be installed at its full thickness without obstructing the air space extending from low vents at the eaves to high vents (described in detail later). This increase in depth to accommodate thicker insulation also permits larger spans.

The use of rigid board insulation on the inside of the rafters, or in some cases on outside of the roof sheathing in addition to the fibrous materials, is another means of increasing the R-value of these roofs. This method is especially appropriate for use in vaulted ceilings or sloped portions of second floor ceilings (Fig. 9.38). Fire protection as defined by local building codes must be provided for many rigid board insulations used in this manner. Recommendations are similar to those found in the previous section on wall systems.

1" AIRSPACE ABOVE INSULATION FOR VENTILATION

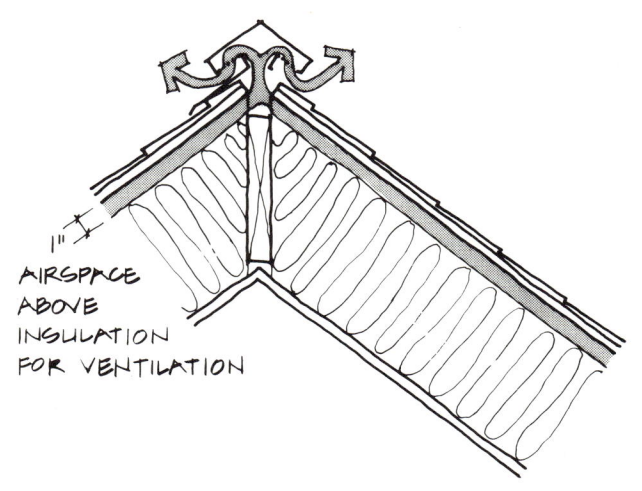

Fig. 9.37 Cathedral ceilings require special venting details to prevent overheating and condensation.

Insulation may be placed between floor/ceiling joists or collar ties when the attic space above them will remain unheated. It is easy to achieve high R-values in areas that will not be used for storage because blanket, batt, or loose fill insulation levels will not be limited by the size of framing members. However, if floor decking is installed on top of joists or collar ties to create usable cold storage areas, then the level of insulation that can be achieved is limited to the depth of the framing. In either case, rigid board insulation may be applied to the joists or collar ties to help increase the insulative value in the ceiling. Because many of these materials or their facings have relatively low permeabilities, they should be applied to the heated side of the ceiling.

THE INSULATED BUILDING SHELL 167

Fig. 9.38 The R-value of cathedral ceilings can be increased by applying rigid board insulation to them prior to the vapor barrier and interior finish. Builders should be sure to follow local building code requirements for fire protection.

Ceiling joists and collar ties may be insulated with faced or unfaced blankets or batts before the vapor barrier and finish surfaces have been applied below. If loose fill materials are used, they may be poured or blown into the attic from above after the vapor barrier and finishes are in place.

Joist Roofs

Joist roof systems make use of framing members that combine the functions of rafters and ceiling joists. These roofs may be flat or sloped and, depending upon the building design, may span the entire width or be supported by load bearing walls or beams. Framing is usually spaced 16 or 24 inches on center, depending upon roof loads and layout of wall framing.

- SMALL FLAT ROOFS
  - HOT ROOF
  - PRONE TO LEAKING IF DEAD FLAT

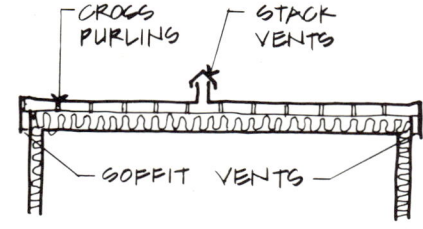

- LARGE FLAT ROOFS
  - HOT ROOF
  - PRONE TO LEAKING IF DEAD FLAT

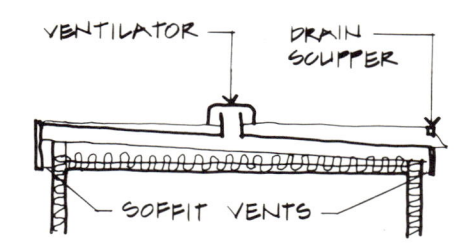

- SLOPED 'FLAT' ROOFS
  - BETTER VENTILATED AND COOLER THAN FLAT ROOF
  - NOT AS PRONE TO LEAKING BECAUSE WATER CANNOT POOL ON ROOF

Fig. 9.39 Alternate configurations of insulating and ventilating flat roofs.

Insulation levels in this roof and ceiling system are limited to the depth of the roof joists or trusses. Fibrous blankets or batts can be installed before the vapor barrier and ceiling finishes are applied, and must allow a minimum one-inch air space for ventilation of water vapor between the insulation and roof sheathing. To increase the R-value of those systems, roof joist size may be increased to allow a thicker blanket of fibrous insulation to be installed; rigid board insulation also may be applied to the interior surface of the joists before the vapor barrier and approved finish surfaces are applied (Fig. 9.39).

Plank and Beam Roof Systems

Plank and beam roof systems utilize framing members and roof decking that serve as both roof structure and finish ceilings. These roof systems may be used to form either flat or shallow sloped roofs, and most often are used on single story buildings. Because the framing is left open to the interior, insulation must be applied to the exterior surface of the roof decking (typically 2x6 or 2x8 tongue and groove or splined planks). Rigid board insulation may be fastened by nailing it to the decking or the framing, but avoid having nails protrude through the decking. This roof system is completed by framing above the deck and applying exterior sheathing over the insulation. Finish roofing is then nailed to the plywood sheathing. Construction details should allow a minimum one-inch air space between the rigid board insulation and the exterior roof sheathing.

Panelized Roof Systems

Panelized roof systems consist of premanufactured or job-built panels typically constructed with nominal two-inch framing members, interior finish ceiling material, rigid board insulation, and exterior sheathing to which finish roofing is nailed. These components are used to form either flat roofs or sloped roofs with vaulted ceilings. Panels may be applied over exposed post and beam framing, or supported by exterior walls and interior beams or partitions. The level of insulation that can be achieved in this roof system is limited to the thickness of the panels, which may be increased to accommodate more insulation. Both plank and beam and panelized roof systems limit the amount of insulation that can be applied to them, so they are best suited for use in the warmer climate regions.

Insulation

The two most commonly used insulations for ceilings are fiberglass batts and loose fill. The use of proper techniques for installing these insulations in floors, walls, roofs, and ceilings is critical to long-term energy efficiency in buildings. Although many of the insulation

Fig. 9.40 Insulating roof and ceiling cavities.

techniques discussed in other sections also apply to roof and ceiling systems, there are certain important differences that must be considered (Fig. 9.40).

When installing blanket and batt insulation, keep in mind:

- Insulation should cover the top wall plate without interfering with ventilation.
- Leave a minimum one-inch air space between top of insulation and underside of sheathing when soffit vents are included.
- When two layers of insulation are installed in ceiling joists or collar ties, run the second layer perpendicular to the first. This covers the framing, which reduces thermal bridging. The top layer should be unfaced to prevent condensation from occurring between the layers.
- Always butt the ends of adjoining pieces tightly together.
- Using insulation, fill gaps along top plates between the framing and insulation.
- Use separate pieces of insulation at framing offsets and intersections.
- Ceiling voids, such as areas around vent pipes and chimneys, should be filled with insulation.

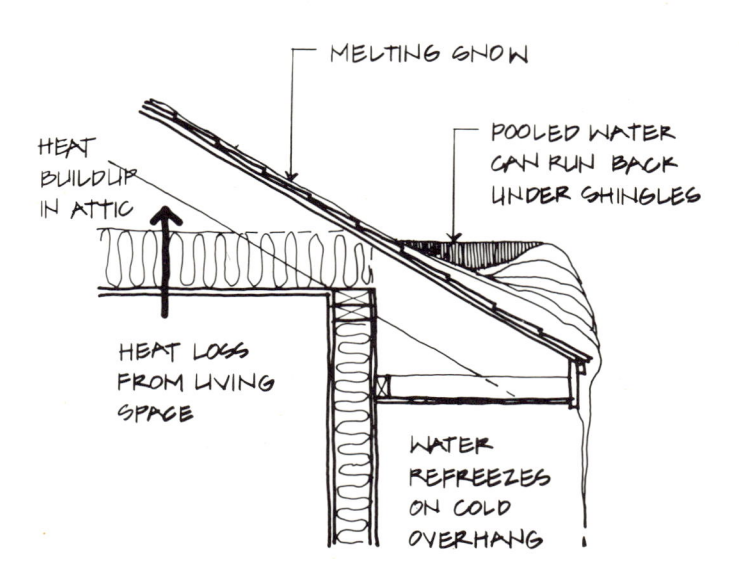

Fig. 9.41 Ventilating overhangs in cold climates to prevent ice damming.

- Recessed lighting fixtures should be avoided. If used they should not be covered with insulation, so that heat generated by them can dissipate.
- Dropped soffit areas such as bathroom or kitchen cabinets should be insulated.
- Attic access panels and doors should be insulated with rigid board insulation and their openings weatherstripped.

When installing loose fill insulation, remember:

- Maintain proper coverage, weight per square foot, and thickness as specified by the manufacturer to achieve desired R-value.
- To ensure ventilation when soffit vents are used, insulate areas along the eaves with blanket materials, or install corrugated vent components before loose fill is poured or blown in.
- Recessed light fixtures should not be covered.
- Dropped soffits should be covered with plywood or filled with insulation.
- Attic access panels and doors should be insulated with rigid board insulation and their openings weatherstripped.

Moisture Control

The control of moisture in roof and ceiling systems combines the use of a continuous vapor barrier installed on the heated side of the insulation, with properly designed and constructed vent openings, as introduced in Chapter 3. Table 3.3 presents the recommended qualities and locations of vapor barriers and sizes of vent openings for the three areas of the country defined by the map in Figure 3.6.

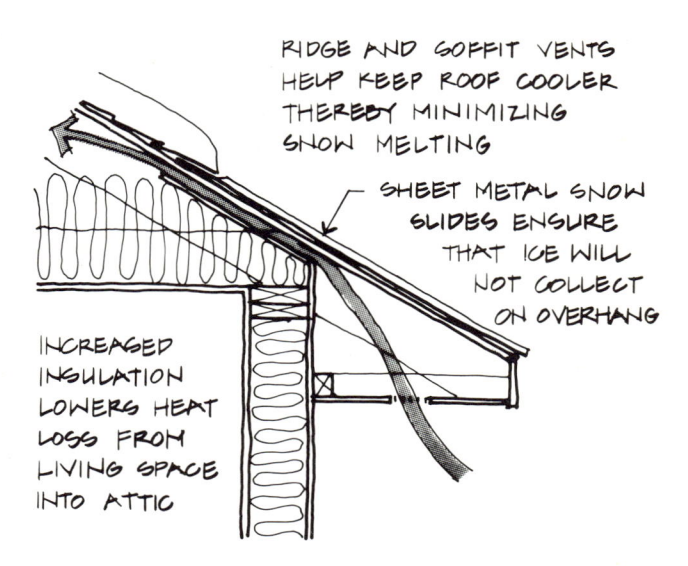

Vapor Barriers

Vapor barrier materials used in roof and ceiling systems are the same as those used in wall systems, and here again, the separate sheet type vapor barriers are most effective when properly installed. Although attic-type (truss or rafter) roof systems outside Zone A may not require vapor barriers, their use is recommended in all regions. Attic-less-type (joist roof) roof systems in all regions should be protected by vapor barriers due to the somewhat restricted opportunity to ventilate them. Plank and beam roof systems rely solely on edge ventilation for moisture protection to prevent the accumulation of moisture on wood decking; however, a vapor barrier is recommended for this type of roof in the colder portions of Zone A (design temperature -10°F), or in buildings where inside relative humidity is 40 percent in winter.

Once *all* of the framing is complete (including all nailers), the plumbing, heating, and electrical components have been roughed-in, and the insulation has been carefully installed, the vapor barrier can be applied directly to the framing with staples. If rigid board insulation is used inside, the vapor barrier can be held in place temporarily with nails driven through the insulation and into the frame. Interior ceiling finish materials eventually will hold the vapor barrier permanently in place. Recommended techniques for installing sheet-type vapor barriers are listed in the preceding section on wall systems.

Ventilation

The ventilation of roof and ceiling systems with outside air allows moisture to be vented from the building before it can condense and cause damage. This air movement, which is driven by wind movement or thermal convection, depending on the vents used, also cools the exterior roof surfaces; this is an advantage in both winter and summer. In winter cooler roof surfaces reduce the potential for ice dams to occur because less snow melts. Ice dams are created when melting snow runs down the roof, only to refreeze as it reaches the cold eaves. As the ice dam grows, it causes water to back up underneath roof shingles, increasing the possibility for leaks to develop. In summer, the air movement along the inside surfaces of the sheathing carries away heat that has been conducted through the roof (Fig. 9.41).

There are many different types of vents used for roof and ceiling ventilation, and they are most often used in combination to create the proper size openings for proper air flow. When sizing these openings, select vent components by their net free areas. Typical roof ventilations used in residential construction include roof louvers, soffit vents, gable end louvers, and continuous ridge vents.

These vents are available in plastic, wood, or aluminum, or may be job-built. They should be constructed to shed rain, and to keep insects and animals from entering the building through them. The design of these protective louvers and screens affects the net free area of the vents, which must be considered when vents are specified. Vent manufacturers specify the net free area of their products in square inches per vent or per linear foot of vent.

A widely used rule of thumb for sizing roof and ceiling vents holds that the minimum net free area is one three-hundredth of the attic floor area if a vapor barrier has been used; if a vapor barrier has not been used, the net free area should be doubled. The resulting net free area should be divided with half placed low on the roof, such as in the eaves, and half high on the roof, such as the ridge.

No venting system will operate as required if the air passages between the inlets and outlets are blocked with insulation or framing (Fig. 9.42). Insulation installed at

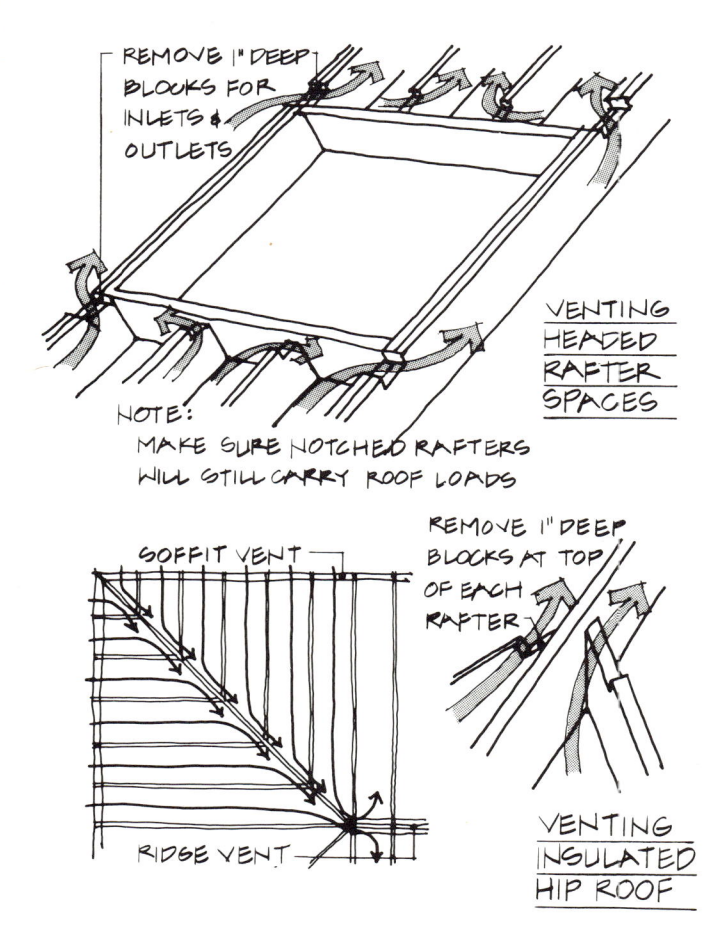

Fig. 9.42 Ventilating dead air spaces in cathedral ceiling roofs.

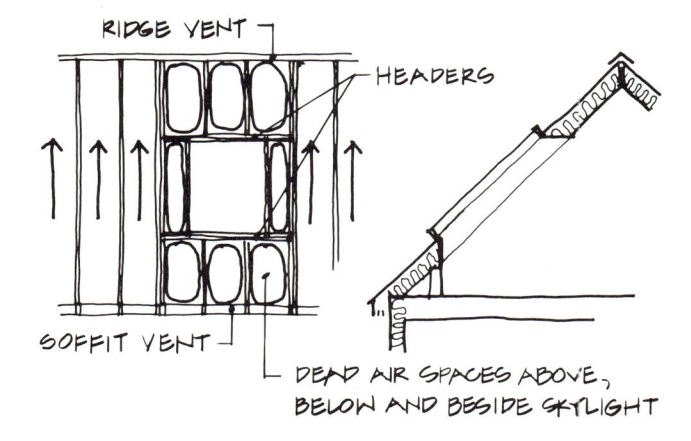

THE INSULATED BUILDING SHELL   171

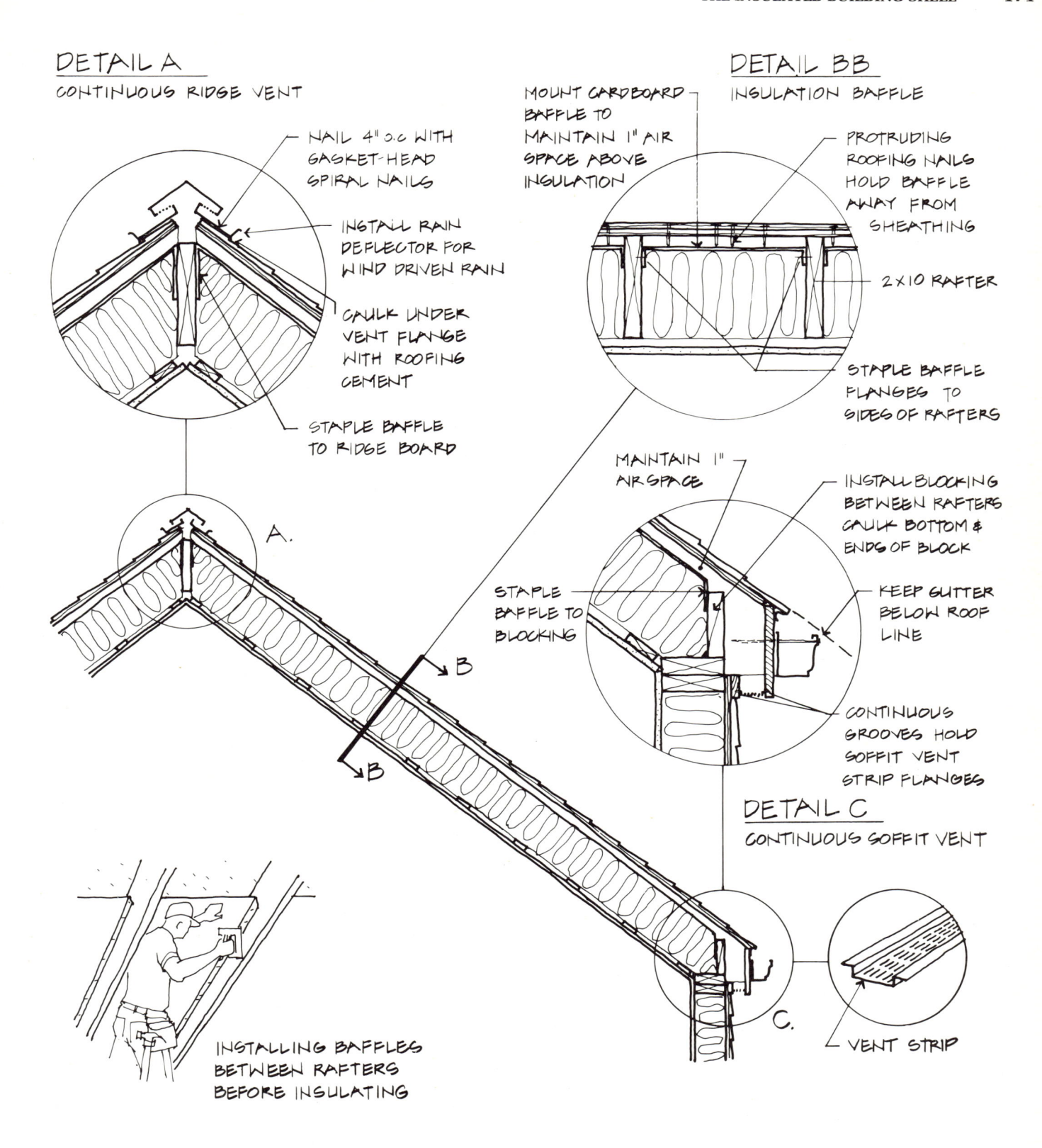

Fig. 9.43 Insulating and ventilating rafter cavity with soffit vent and continuous ridge vent.

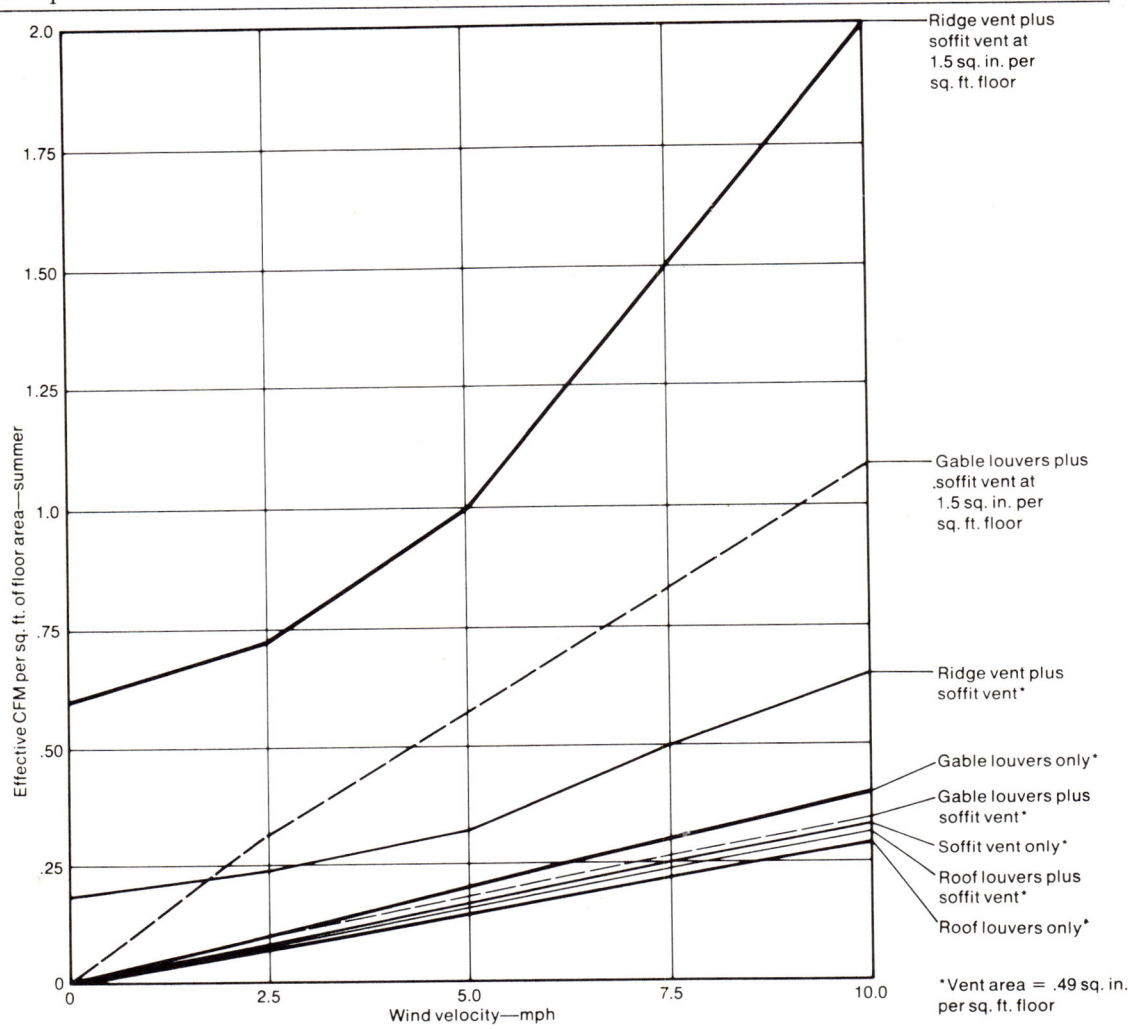

Chart 9.1
Comparison of air flow for various vent systems

[Chart: Effective CFM per sq. ft. of floor area—summer vs. Wind velocity—mph]

- Ridge vent plus soffit vent at 1.5 sq. in. per sq. ft. floor
- Gable louvers plus soffit vent at 1.5 sq. in. per sq. ft. floor
- Ridge vent plus soffit vent*
- Gable louvers only*
- Gable louvers plus soffit vent*
- Soffit vent only*
- Roof louvers plus soffit vent*
- Roof louvers only*

*Vent area = .49 sq. in. per sq. ft. floor

---

the eaves should be kept from extending too far beyond the top plates. Products are available which are installed between rafters and against the sheathing, and which allow the insulation to cover the top plates while the air flow remains open through preformed passageways.

Framing members such as headers for chimney openings, skylights, dormers, and site-built solar water heaters block the flow of air within the rafter cavities, increasing the importance of the vapor barriers in those areas. Although some builders drill holes in the rafters and headers in an attempt to move air past these blockages, the rate of flow is still decreased and may result in localized problems. Chart 9.1 compares the various systems used to ventilate attic-type sloped roofs. The table shows that continuous ridge and soffit vents offer the best combined performance. Typical construction details for vent openings are presented in Fig. 9.43. This vent system is especially appropriate for vaulted sloped ceilings framed with rafters.

Soffit vents are also often combined with roof louvers or gable end louvers to ventilate attic areas. Chart 9.2 can be used to determine the appropriate net free area for a range of attic floor areas, for each of the three combinations of vents most commonly used.

Roof systems that do not enclose an attic, such as flat or sloped joist roofs, must be ventilated at the ends of

THE INSULATED BUILDING SHELL 173

Chart 9.2

Ventilation calculator—Amount of ventilation required for various ventilating systems to obtain an air flow of 15 CFM per sq ft of attic floor at wind velocity of 75 mph.

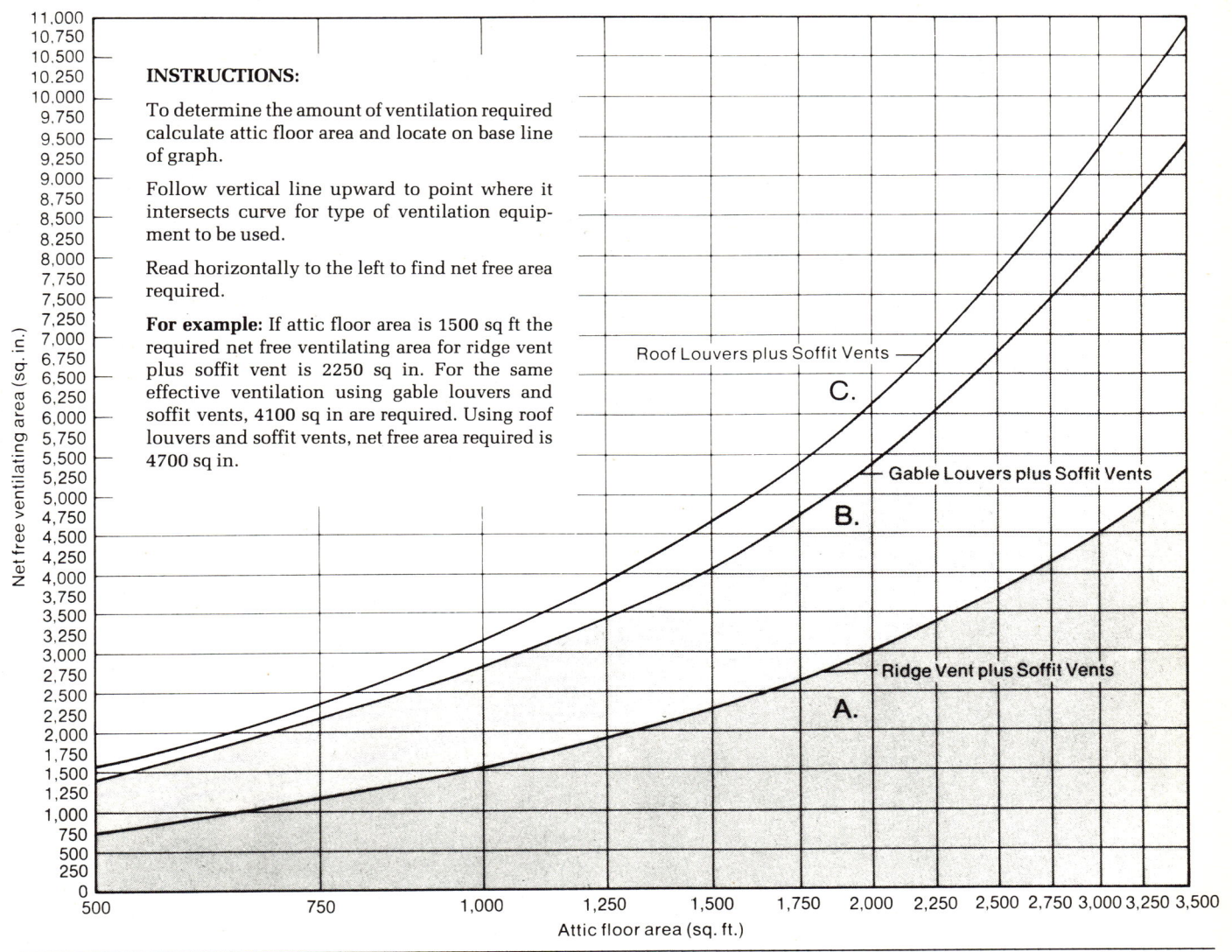

INSTRUCTIONS:

To determine the amount of ventilation required calculate attic floor area and locate on base line of graph.

Follow vertical line upward to point where it intersects curve for type of ventilation equipment to be used.

Read horizontally to the left to find net free area required.

For example: If attic floor area is 1500 sq ft the required net free ventilating area for ridge vent plus soffit vent is 2250 sq in. For the same effective ventilation using gable louvers and soffit vents, 4100 sq in are required. Using roof louvers and soffit vents, net free area required is 4700 sq in.

C. Roof Louvers plus Soffit Vents
B. Gable Louvers plus Soffit Vents
A. Ridge Vent plus Soffit Vents

Note: Direct multiples of data from chart may be used to determine ventilation requirements for attics of larger area than those shown.

each joist space. Individual vents or continuous soffit vents may be used to allow wind movement to draw air into the roof system. Continuous soffit vent openings ¾ inch wide are sufficient for most houses.

Plank and beam roof systems can be ventilated by using either edge or stack venting or, in buildings over 40 feet wide both techniques may be combined. Figure 9.44 shows a venting detail for a flat roof and Fig. 9.45 shows construction of an earth sheltered roof.

Wind direction has a major impact on the effectiveness of the various types and combinations of vents used in roof and ceiling systems.

Vents can be installed during various phases of construction, depending on the type selected. In general: soffit vents are installed as the roof trim and soffits are built; roof louvers with integral flashing are built into the finish roof surface as it is applied; ridge vents are assembled and installed after the finish roofing is

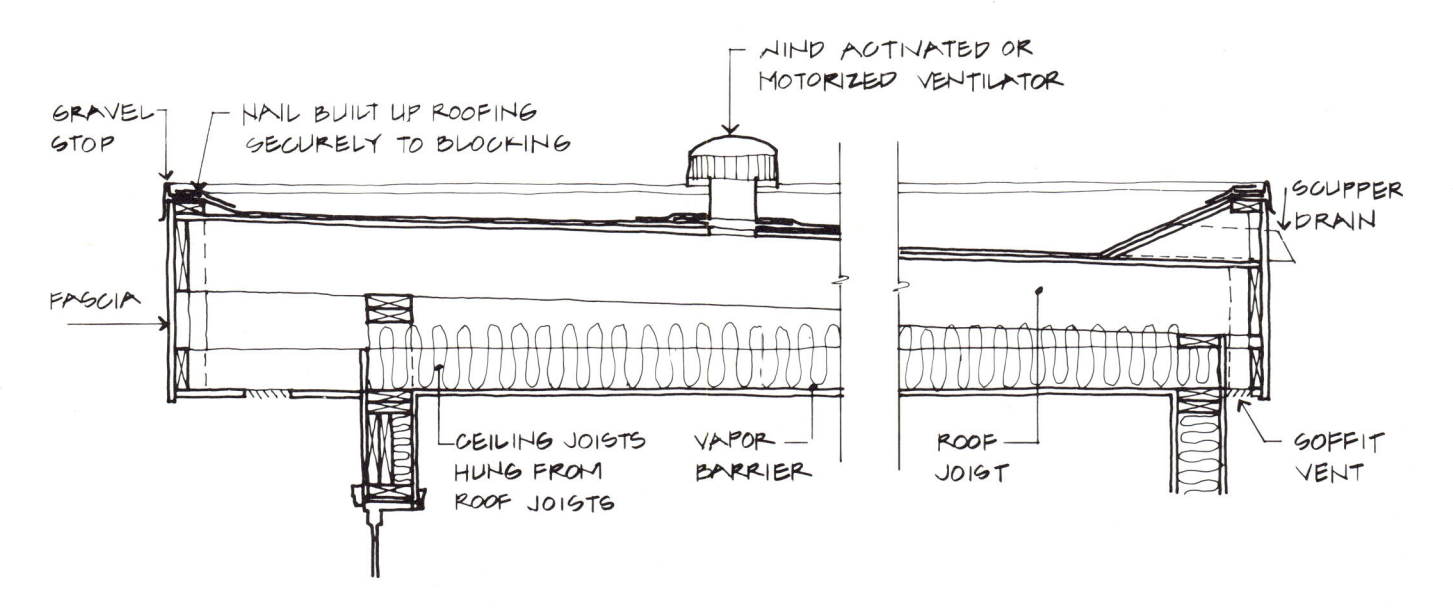

174 MATERIALS, DETAILS, AND TECHNIQUES OF SOLAR CONSTRUCTION

Fig. 9.44 Insulating and ventilating flat roof.

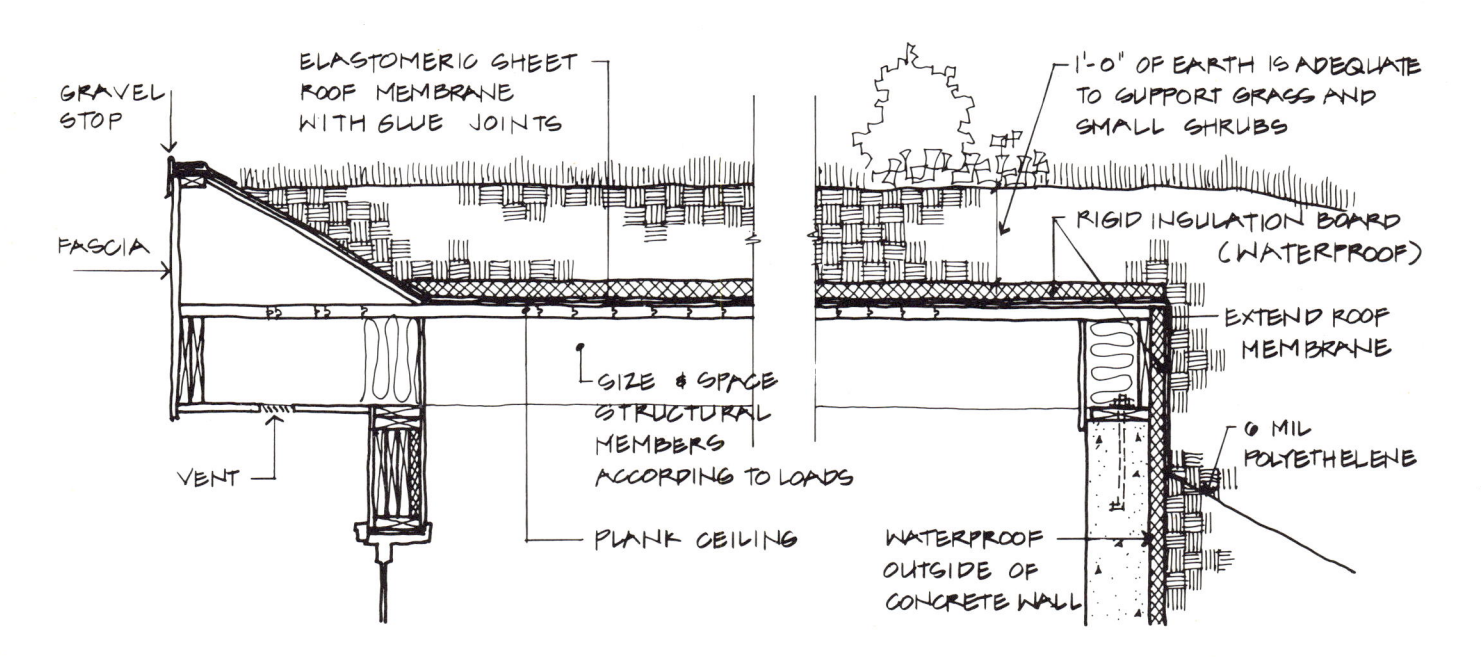

Fig. 9.45 Earth-supporting flat roof.

THE INSULATED BUILDING SHELL 175

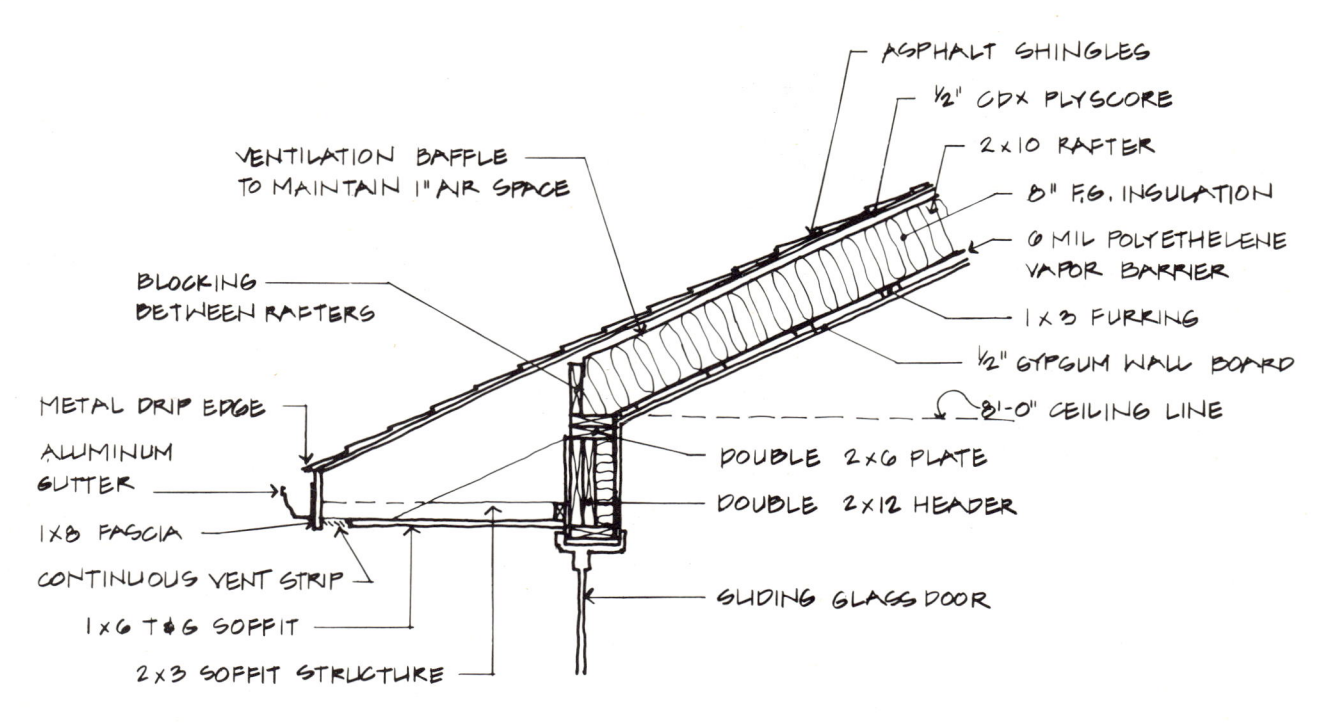

Fig. 9.46 Fixed overhang.

completed; and gable end louvers may be installed before or after exterior siding is applied, depending on type of siding and vent casing details.

ADDITIONAL DETAILS: ROOF AND CEILING SYSTEMS

Fixed Overhangs

Fixed overhangs can be creatd by extending the roof framing beyond the exterior walls, to form modified soffits or eaves. Details vary according to the site latitude, height of vertical glazings, and roof construction. Figure 9.46 presents typical construction details to form fixed overhangs. Other shading devices are presented in Chapter 12.

Sunspace/Greenhouse

Sunspace and greenhouse areas can be incorporated into the insulated building shell by glazing sloped roof areas and vertical walls. Sunspace/greenhouse areas added on to the main building can be integrated into the roof line, as shown in Fig. 9.47. This method may be used in new construction as well as retrofit applications.

Fig. 9.47 Sunspace or greenhouse roofs are sometimes integrated into the roof line of the main building.

Fig. 9.48 Framed opening in roof will later house site-built solar heat collectors.

Fig. 9.49 Site-built solar collector components that require the least changes in roof framing should be used. These components are designed for rafters or trusses spaced 24" o.c.

Depending on the components used, job-built solar collectors may also require framing modifications, including headers that enclose the collector area, nailers for roof sheathing, flashing and finishes, and metal or wood glazing components. The easiest method of integrating these modifications into the roof system is to select components that fit within standard rafter or truss spacings (Fig. 9.49). This approach requires the least change in framing layout and thereby saves time in getting the building enclosed. The same building and framing modifications can be made in building custom skylights into sloped roofs.

Solar Water Heaters and Skylights

Roof framing may need to be modified in order to provide fastening points for premanufactured solar heat collectors or to house job-built collectors (Fig. 9.48). Especially in the case of vaulted ceilings, fastening blocks should be installed as the roof is framed. Otherwise, builders may wait until the solar contractor identifies the exact location of the collectors during their installation before installing special framing. Many solar contractors will install this framing themselves, as needed. Mounting details and requirements for premanufactured units are presented in Chapter 11.

CHAPTER 10 DOORS, WINDOWS, AND GLAZINGS

INTRODUCTION

Exterior doors, windows, and glazings complete the insulated building shell. These components form the major openings in the shell, and provide for entry and exit, transmission of solar radiation, ventilation, daylighting, views, and protection from wind and precipitation.

Doors, windows, and other glazings account for a large percentage of a building's total heat loss. The materials used to construct them have far less resistance to heat conduction than the insulated wall and roof sections they replace. They are also the primary source of air leakage through the shell (Fig. 10.2). Reducing these heat losses requires careful selection and proper installation of energy efficient components. Heat loss through all doors and windows follows the same paths: conductive losses occur through the frame, sash, door, and glazing; infiltration losses occur between the rough opening and frame, and past casings, sills, and operable sash or door. The use of frame materials with low conduction rates, "thermal doors," and multiple glazings reduces conductive loss. Careful installation, caulking, and proper weatherstripping details to ensure tight closure for the life of the unit reduce infiltration losses (Fig. 10.3).

Sliding glass doors, windows, and skylights commonly are used to admit solar radiation directly into a building or into thermal storage walls and floors. Because glass is impermeable to moisture and is usually much cooler than moisture laden interior air (in winter), surface condensation first accumulates on windows, skylights, and glazed doors. Materials and details to avoid condensation should be selected and then finished with a surface that protects components from moisture damage.

Fixed glazings used in walls, sunspace/greenhouses, skylights, and solar collectors also must be selected and installed carefully. Although glass generally is recommended, some builders are using new products for these applications. The use of any glazing material in these configurations requires special consideration for support, flashing materials, details, and sequence of construction.

This chapter is organized into four sections. It begins with a comparison of materials used in the construction of doors, windows, and glazings. Wood, aluminum, polystyrene, glass, and acrylic all have important functions, and builders must know when and where to use each of these materials.

The next two sections discuss the many functions of doors and windows in solar construction, present the basis for choosing the right type for a specific application, and give guidelines for installation. Doors and windows perform many similar functions in a residence, and they are influenced by the objectives of solar construction in many of the same ways.

Fixed glazings are used much more in solar construction than in conventional construction. They make up many of the special applications of solar energy usage in residences, including window walls, greenhouses, thermal storage walls, and solar collector cover plates. This chapter concludes with a discussion of fixed glazings and their special application in solar construction.

NOTES ABOUT MATERIALS

A number of the same priorities consistently apply when selecting materials for use in solar construction. The resistance of the material to heat flow is always important; cost and availability are governed by local supply networks; materials, workability, expansion, and contrac-

178   MATERIALS, DETAILS, AND TECHNIQUES OF SOLAR CONSTRUCTION

Fig. 10.1 The installation of doors, windows, and glazings completes the insulated building shell.

Fig. 10.2 Careful selection and installation of door and window components are critical to a building's energy performance.

DOORS, WINDOWS, AND GLAZINGS 179

(Green Horizon)

(Downing and Leach)

(Downing and Leach)

Fig. 10.2 *(continued)*

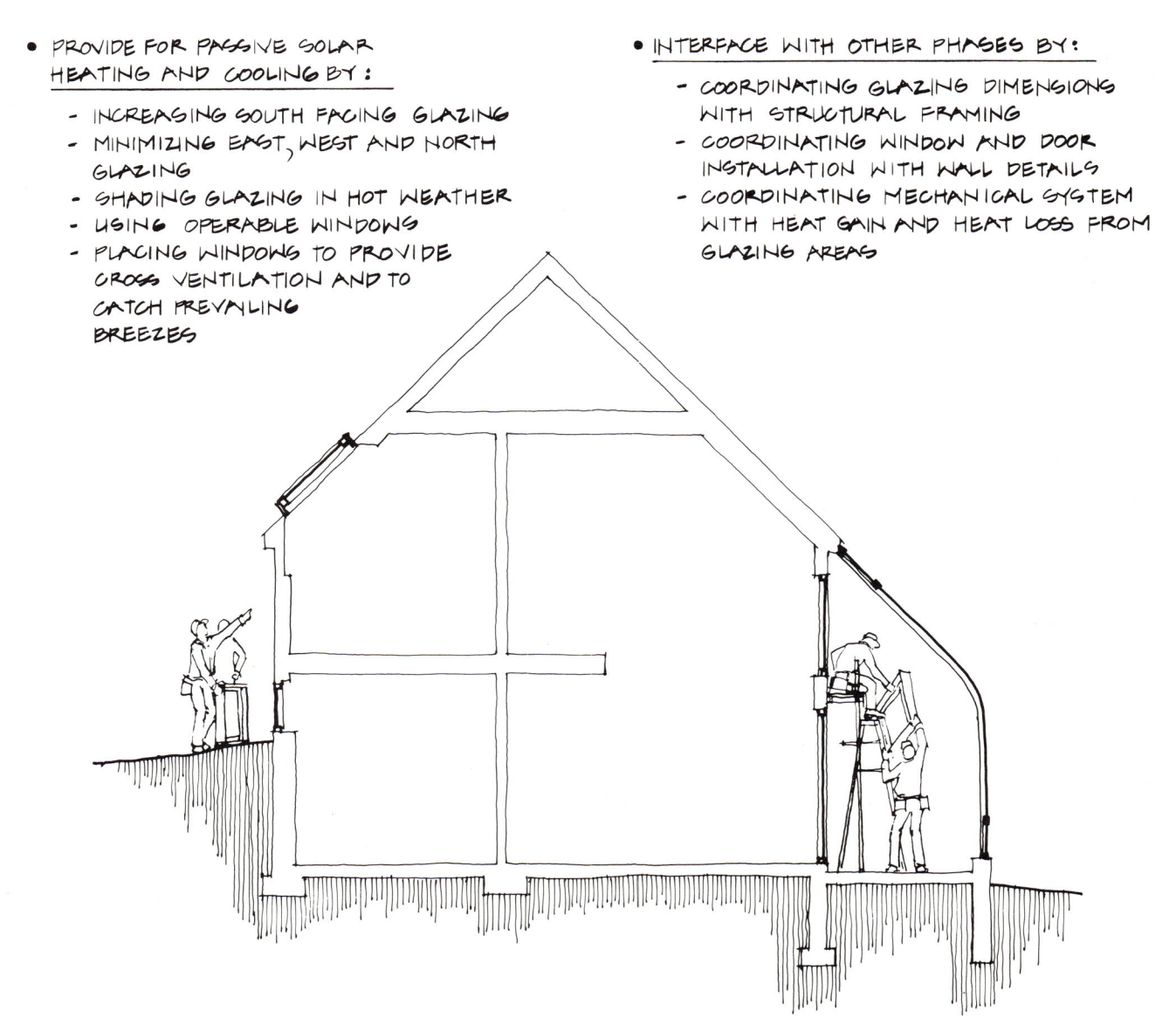

180 MATERIALS, DETAILS, AND TECHNIQUES OF SOLAR CONSTRUCTION

- PROVIDE FOR PASSIVE SOLAR HEATING AND COOLING BY:
    - INCREASING SOUTH FACING GLAZING
    - MINIMIZING EAST, WEST AND NORTH GLAZING
    - SHADING GLAZING IN HOT WEATHER
    - USING OPERABLE WINDOWS
    - PLACING WINDOWS TO PROVIDE CROSS VENTILATION AND TO CATCH PREVAILING BREEZES

- INTERFACE WITH OTHER PHASES BY:
    - COORDINATING GLAZING DIMENSIONS WITH STRUCTURAL FRAMING
    - COORDINATING WINDOW AND DOOR INSTALLATION WITH WALL DETAILS
    - COORDINATING MECHANICAL SYSTEM WITH HEAT GAIN AND HEAT LOSS FROM GLAZING AREAS

- REDUCE CONDUCTIVE HEAT LOSS THROUGH DOORS AND WINDOWS WITH:
    - MULTIPLE GLAZING
    - INSULATED DOORS
    - INSULATIVE FRAMES
    - MOVABLE WINDOW INSULATION

- REDUCE INFILTRATION THROUGH DOORS AND WINDOWS WITH:
    - GOOD WEATHERSTRIPPING
    - CAREFUL INSTALLATION
    - THOROUGH SEALING AND CAULKING OF FRAMES

- CONTROL CONDENSATION ON DOORS AND WINDOWS WITH:
    - MULTIPLE GLAZING
    - INSULATED DOORS
    - INSULATIVE FRAMES

Fig. 10.3 Solar priorities for the doors, windows and glazings phase of construction.

DOORS, WINDOWS, AND GLAZINGS   181

tion all must be compatible. Many material choices in this phase are made by the manufacturer. The builder's responsibility is to select particular components and then install them properly.

Wood and Metals

Wood and metals are used for frames in most windows and doors (Fig. 10.4). Though wood is more resistant to heat flow than aluminum or steel, the metal components usually are significantly less expensive. Thermal breaks of PVC, polystyrene, or other insulating materials are required with these metal units to prevent conductive loss through jambs, sills, and sash and to reduce condensation. The use of these metals in solar collector frames is discussed in the next chapter. Table 10.1 compares windows and doors made with different frame materials.

Glazings

While the choice of frame and sash materials is limited, the choice of glazings is far less limited; often it is the builder's responsibility to choose the glazing material (Fig. 10.5). Glazing materials are used throughout solar construction, in windows, doors, skylights, solar collectors, thermal storage walls, and greenhouses. (In window and door selection, the builder's choice usually is limited to comparing alternate configurations of multiple glazing.) Later in this chapter we will examine in detail the applications and availability of various glazing options. The following characteristics define which glazings may be used in certain situations (Table 10.2 summarizes some of these.):

- Transmission of solar radiation
- Resistance to heat conduction
- Strength and durability under extreme conditions of temperature, moisture, wind, and ultraviolet radiation
- Optical clarity
- Thermal expansion and contraction
- Weight—impact on structural requirements
- Ease of installation and maintenance
- Aesthetics, cost, and availability
- Approval by local building codes

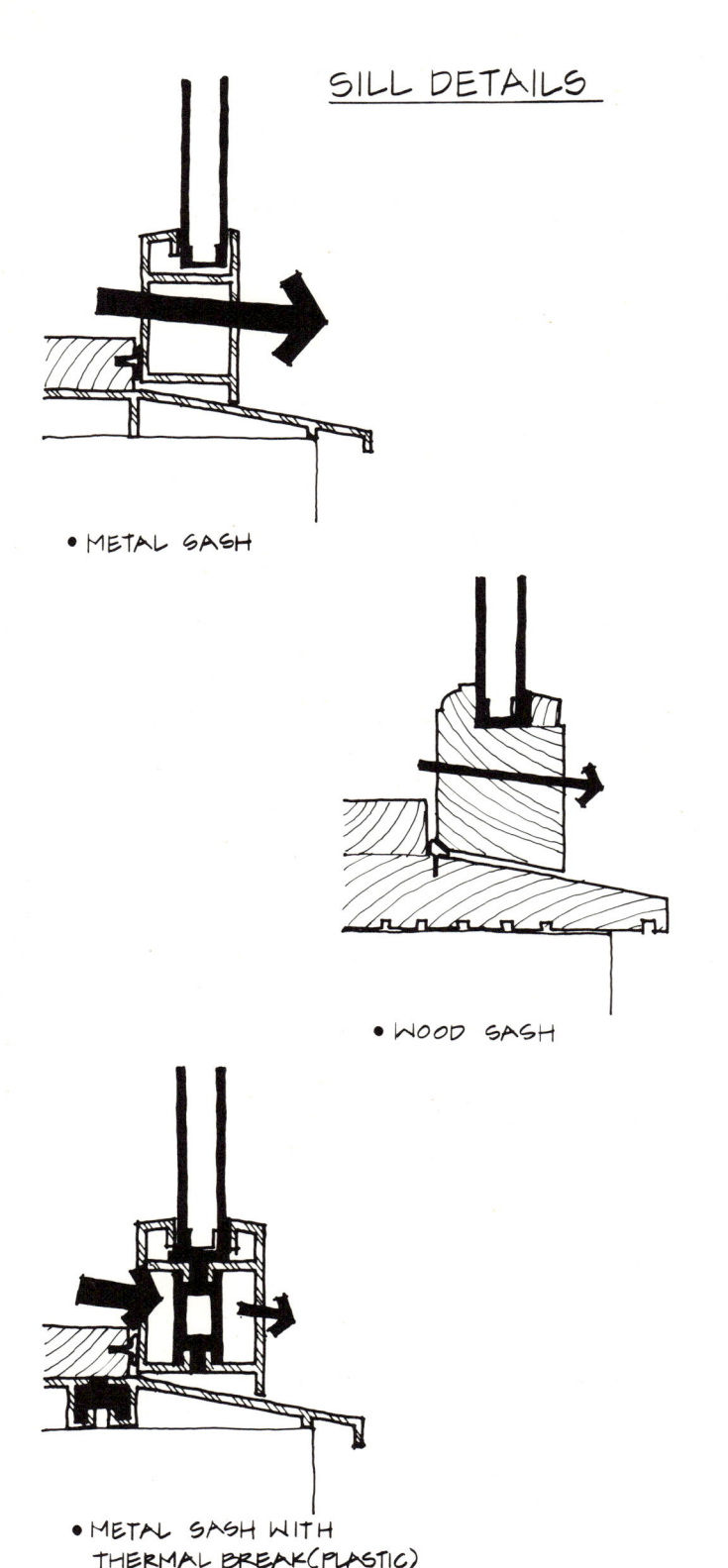

Fig. 10.4 Comparing the use of wood and metal in door and window components.

Table 10.1
Comparison of windows and sliding patio doors with different frame and sash materials

| | Insulating glass with separate storm panel ||| Single glass and storm windows ||| Sliding patio doors ||||
| | Metal sash, no thermal break | Metal sash with thermal break | Wood sash | Metal storm over metal prime | Metal storm over wood prime | Wood storm over wood prime | Single glass || Insulating glass ||
Window description							Metal sash	Wood sash	Metal sash	Wood sash
Single-hung windows, patio doors, and fixed (picture) windows	0.716	0.650	0.617	0.820	0.782	0.745	1.420	1.310	1.002	0.940
	0.595	0.529	0.496	0.699	0.661	0.624	1.299	1.189	0.881	0.819
	0.534	0.468	0.435	0.638	0.601	0.563	1.238	1.128	0.820	0.758
	0.463	0.397	0.364	0.567	0.529	0.492	1.167	1.057	0.749	0.687
Patio doors and fixed (picture) windows with adjacent operable windows	0.836	0.770	0.737	0.940	0.902	0.865	1.540	1.430	1.122	1.060
	0.669	0.603	0.570	0.773	0.736	0.698	1.373	1.263	0.955	0.893
	0.586	0.520	0.487	0.690	0.653	0.615	1.290	1.180	0.872	0.810
	0.487	0.421	0.388	0.591	0.554	0.516	1.191	1.081	0.773	0.711
Double-hung windows	0.955	0.889	0.856	1.059	1.022	0.984				
	0.744	0.678	0.645	0.848	0.810	0.773				
	0.638	0.572	0.539	0.742	0.704	0.667				
	0.512	0.446	0.413	0.616	0.579	0.541				
Awning, hopper, and casement windows	1.075	1.009	0.976	1.179	1.142	1.104				
	0.818	0.752	0.719	0.922	0.885	0.847				
	0.690	0.624	0.591	0.794	0.756	0.719				
	0.537	0.471	0.438	0.641	0.604	0.566				
Amount of glass assumed	80%	80%	70%	80%	80/70%	70%	85%	80%	85%	80%
U_t transmission heat loss only	0.396	0.330	0.297	0.500	0.463	0.425	1.100	0.990	0.682	0.620

Table 10.2
A summary of glazing materials characteristics

Material	Thickness (in.)	Solar transmittance	Sheet size (ft)	Weight (lbs/ft²)	Thermal expansion	Max. temp. (F)
Tempered glass	0.125	0.90	2, 3, 4 × 8 3, 4 × 7	1.6	0.47	—
Fiberglass reinforced polyesters (FRP)	0.40	0.86–0.88	4, 5 wide × variable length	0.25–0.29	2.0–2.3	300°
Acrylics and polycarbonates	0.125	0.89–0.93	4, 6 × 8	0.25–1.0	4	200°–230°
Plastic films	0.001–0.004 (1 mil)–(4 mil)	0.93–0.96	58, 64 inch wide × variable length	0.02–0.77	2.80–5.85	200°–300°

DOORS, WINDOWS, AND GLAZINGS 183

Fig. 10.5 Materials used for glazings in solar construction include glass, fiberglass reinforced polyesters, acrylics and polycarbonates.

Glass

Glass is the best material for use in most glazing applications. It is strong and durable, and allows for clear views and relatively free transmission of solar radiation. Glass is unaffected by heat, ultraviolet radiation, and moisture, and it is generally available and aesthetically pleasing. Builders may be limited to sash units as supplied by a manufacturer, or they may choose glass types purchased without sash for use in job-built applications. Single, double, and triple layered glass units are available with either fully tempered or nontempered glass. Builders may form multi-layered windows using single layers of job-placed glass or, as is more commonly done, they may install multi-layered, factory sealed units. The most economical way to buy glass is in the standard sizes used by window and door manufacturers. These materials are available from glass and window suppliers as replacement units for the standard products.

The types of glass used for residential glazings are sheet (window), float, and plate glass, available in a wide range of sizes and thicknesses. Glass types also vary in the amount of solar radiation that passes through them and how much is either reflected by the outside surface or absorbed by the glass. The amount of solar heat absorbed depends on the iron content and thickness of a particular type. Ideally, glass that allows most of the solar radiation (85 to 95 percent) through it into the building should be selected. This usually requires special ordering of low iron glass from a distributor. Generally builders are limited to the glass types used by window manufacturers; if the glass is purchased without sash, however, builders can select types that have high solar transmission ratings, as well as meet their other requirements.

Insulated Glass

Heat conduction through window glazings can be reduced by using multiple layers or movable insulation (See Chapter 12). Glass, a poor insulator, conducts heat freely. The R-value of a $1/8$-inch sheet of glass is only .01; however, air films close to both surfaces of the glass will increase the effective R-value to approximately R-1, depending on outside wind speeds. Additional layers of glass create dead air spaces which further increase the R-value of the window, depending on the size of the air space and rate of wind movement. Table 10.2 compares available insulated glass units and R-values, which also apply to job-built fixed glazings used in multiple layers. Remember that the dimensions used to describe insulated glass thickness refer to outside dimensions of the two or three layers, and not to the air space between them. For example, $5/8$-inch insulated glass actually has only a $1/4$-inch air space. Air spaces of one-half inch up to three-quarter inch are generally thought to be optimum. Air spaces larger than three-quarter inch allow convective air movement between the glazings, which reduces their efficiency. A number of approaches to provide multiple glazing in windows are discussed later in this chapter (Fig. 10.6).

Fiberglass-reinforced Polyesters

One alternative to glass in fixed glazings is a fiberglass-reinforced polyester (FRP) material. When new, these products allow almost as much solar radiation to pass through them as the best glass. However, their exposure to ultraviolet radiation, air, and rain pollutants, as well as high temperatures, may cause a measurable decrease in the transmission of solar radiation due to discoloring of the glazing. Some products are treated with ultraviolet protective coatings to reduce some of these effects. These materials are already clouded when new, and should only be used in areas where view out is not important, such as skylights, solar heat collectors, some solar greenhouses, and thermal storage walls.

FRP materials are available in a variety of thicknesses, widths, and lengths and can be purchased in rolls, single sheets, or multi-glazed panels. Other characteristics of these glazings are presented in Table 10.2. At present these materials are not as readily available as other glazing options, and builders may need to allow for some delay in delivery.

One noteworthy characteristic about FRP glazings is the significant amount of expansion and contraction that occurs in them as they change temperature. This thermal movement must be considered when determining clearances from glazing supports, types and locations of fasteners, sealants, and flashing details. Thermal movement also affects the aesthetic appearance of the glazing, causing it to buckle or form a wavy surface when warm and returning to a flatter appearance when cool. This is especially true in applications that place FRP glazings in close proximity to a warm surface, when used as the covers for solar collectors or thermal storage walls. It is not as critical when they are used to glaze skylights and solar greenhouses.

Construction details have been developed that allow FRP materials to expand and contract while maintaining a consistent concave shape. Double glazed panels consisting of two layers of FRP mounted on aluminum frames also can be used to maintain a relatively flat surface, since most FRP materials expand and contract at a rate close to that of aluminum. These components are used to glaze both solar heat collectors and thermal masonry walls. In the case of thermal masonry walls,

DOORS, WINDOWS, AND GLAZINGS   185

INSIDE
AIR FILM
(STILL)
R=.60

OUTSIDE
AIR FILM
(MOVING)
R=.17

A) AIR FILMS DETERMINE
R VALUE FOR GLASS

B) MULTIPLE GLAZING
INCREASES EFFECTIVENESS
OF AIR FILMS

1"

C) OPTIMUM AIR SPACE
APPROXIMATELY 1"

Fig. 10.6 The use of multiple layers of glass reduces heat loss through glass. A) A single pane of glass by itself has virtually no R-value. Its effective R-value comes from the air films which cling to its surfaces. B) Multiple layers of glass increase the number and effectiveness of the air spaces. C) The optimum air space is about 1". A smaller dimension decreases the size and effectiveness of the interior air films. If the air space is greater than 1", convection currents begin to occur which disturbs the air films.

provision must be made for summer venting of the air space between the glazing and the wall. Exposure to high temperatures will accelerate the degradation of these materials.

Acrylics and Polycarbonates

Plastic glazing materials such as acrylics and polycarbonates also may be used in certain applications. Acrylics and polycarbonates transmit high levels of solar radiation when new; however, they also are damaged by ultraviolet radiation, and can suffer surface damage from dust and pollutants. Clouding resulting from this damage both reduces the ability of the glazing to transmit solar radiation and mars the appearance. These factors should be addressed when considering plastic glazings for various applications.

Thermal expansion and contraction are also important considerations with acrylic and polycarbonate glazings. Plastic glazings are best suited for window walls, solar greenhouses, and skylights. Their use as covers for solar heat collectors or thermal masonry walls is not recommended, due to a low melting temperature and high degree of thermal movement.

Acrylic and polycarbonate glazings are available in various thicknesses, widths, and lengths (Table 10.2). They are available as single layers, or double glazed units which are used in sunspace/solar greenhouse construction. Normally transparent, the materials lose this characteristic when applied in two layers, and should be used in locations where view out is not important. Double glazed plastic does diffuse sunlight, thus these products are useful in reducing glare.

DOORS

Exterior doors used in residential construction operate either by swinging on hinges or by sliding in tracks, and are constructed from wood or metal and glass. The best exterior doors are strong, present an attractive appearance, reduce heat conduction, and seal tightly against air leakage when closed (Fig. 10.7). Primary exterior doors should be located on protected sides of a building and should open into vestibules or mud rooms. Every time an exterior door is opened in winter, warm inside air rushes out through the opening and is replaced with cold outside air. In summer the opposite occurs. Double door entries help reduce this air leakage; even when a hinged door is closed, however, it may allow considerable air leakage around edges, beneath the sill, past the jambs, and through the lock set. Exterior doors must close tightly, even after years of use. The quality of the doors and the way they are hung affect their tightness when closed (Fig. 10.8).

Insulated hinged doors with weatherstripping offer the best options for energy efficiency in exterior doors. The use of a storm door with primary door will reduce heat loss further. In summer, these exterior doors with a screened sash, rather than storm sash, can allow natural ventilation of the building. Most storm doors are constructed from aluminum because of its strength and durability under constant use; however, these doors will conduct more heat than wood storm doors.

Sliding glass doors often are used in residential construction. These components provide large glazed areas that can be installed and finished quickly, so many builders use them to increase the solar collection area on

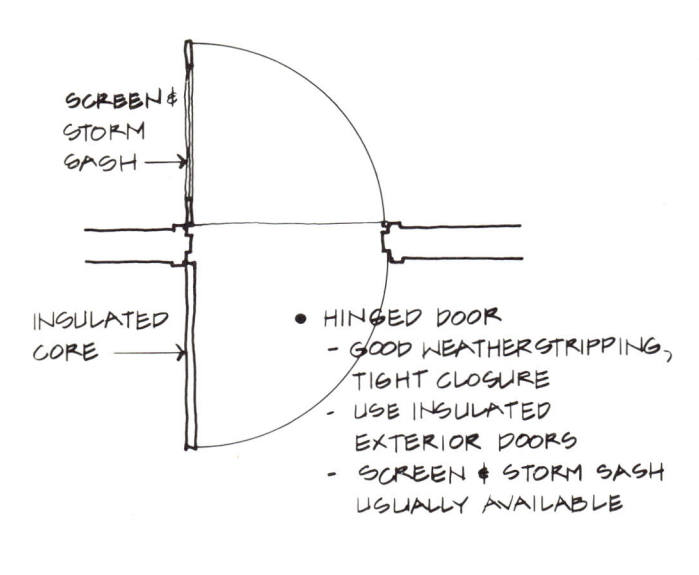

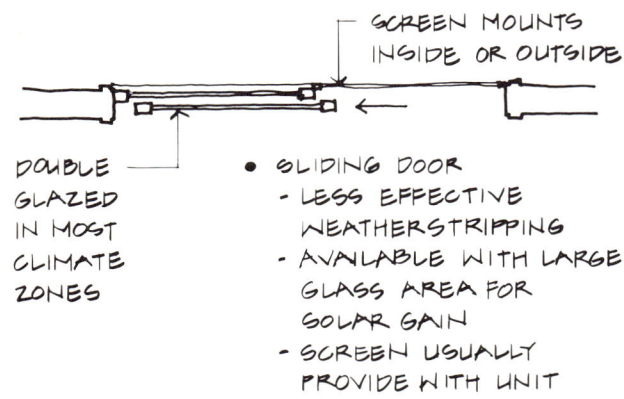

186 MATERIALS, DETAILS, AND TECHNIQUES OF SOLAR CONSTRUCTION

Fig. 10.7 Energy considerations in selecting door types

south facing exterior walls. However, these door systems allow considerable air leakage past the sliding sections and thus should be used only in protected areas where entry and exit are necessary. They should not be used as primary doors. For example, sliding glass doors used to divide interior living areas from attached sunspace/greenhouse areas will transmit solar radiation directly into the building, and effectively control air movement between the areas; yet, they are not subjected directly to air leakage because of the buffering effect provided by the sunspace/greenhouse.

Choosing Doors

Exterior doors lose or gain heat by conduction through wood or metal frame members and finish facings or panels (Fig. 10.9). Wood doors conduct heat at a slower

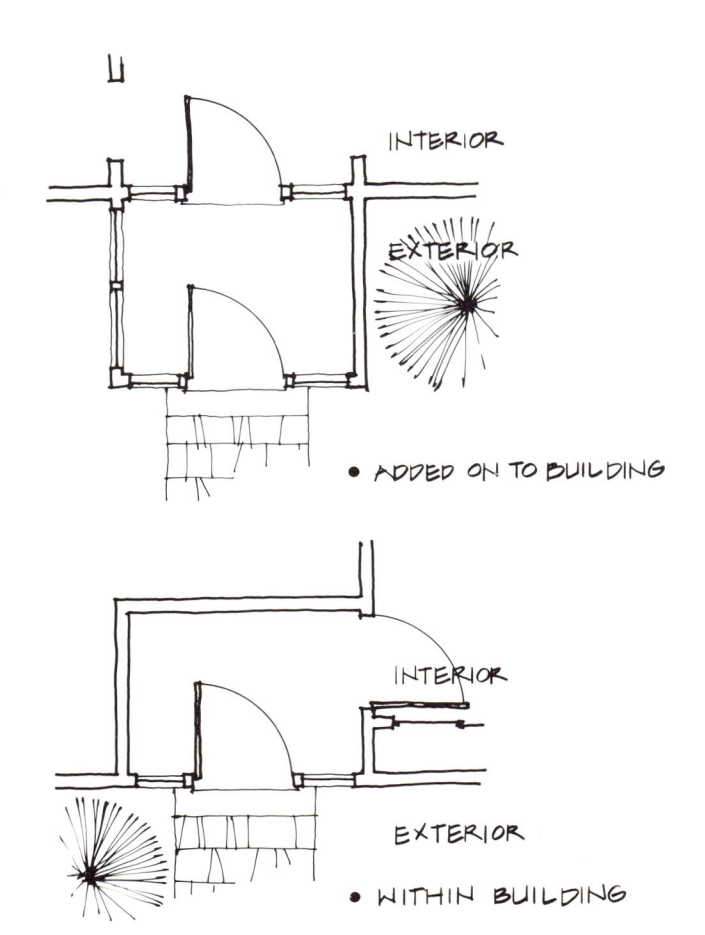

Fig. 10.8 Double door entries or vestibules are very important features in solar construction.

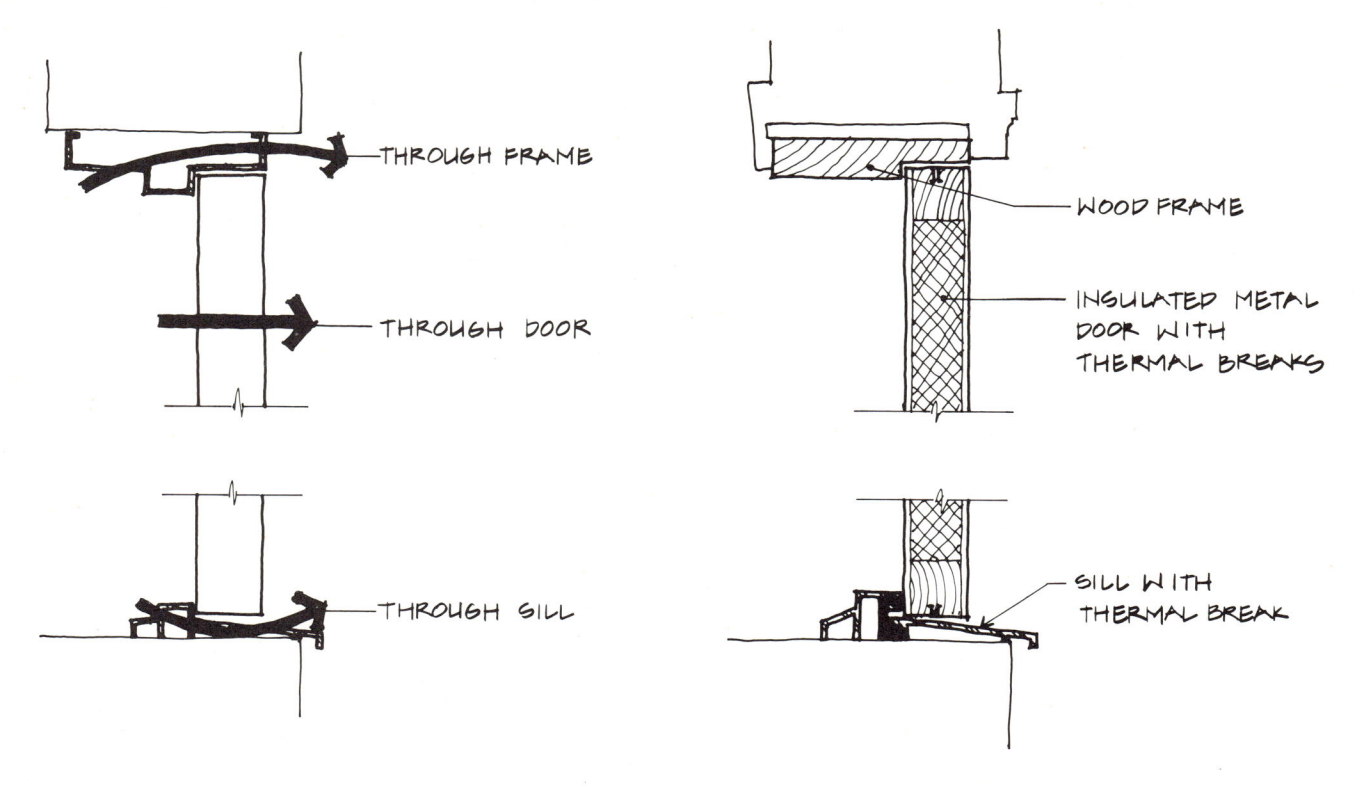

Fig. 10.9 Paths of conductive heat loss through doors and frames

Fig. 10.10 Provide doors that resist heat flow through them.

rate than metal doors; however, both types of doors should be constructed with insulated cores. Insulated metal doors should be equipped with wood or plastic thermal breaks between the interior and exterior surfaces (Fig. 10.10). Thermal breaks in metal door components not only reduce heat conduction but also reduce condensation of moisture on cold interior metal surfaces in winter. Prehung units also should include thermal breaks in metal sills and jambs. The use of insulated doors must be approved by local building codes, as many of the foam insulations used in these doors are flammable.

Insulated wood doors should be built to resist warpage and also to remain square when hung. A sagging door operates poorly due to binding action between the sill and weatherstrip sweep. This problem will also increase the amount of air leakage occurring at the top of the sagging door. Wood doors have a tendency to swell in humid summer air and shrink in dry winter air. This movement must be accommodated by the weatherstripping components to provide a good seal all year.

Metal doors are less likely to warp than wood doors. Their dimensional stability assures good sealing properties when they are used with carefully installed weatherstrip components. One advantage of using metal doors is the ability to utilize magnetic weatherstripping. Metal sills also may be adjusted in these systems, which can help ensure a good seal at the bottom.

Hinged doors should be sealed when closed by compressive, magnetic, or interlocking weatherstrip components, which can be installed by manufacturer or builder. Exterior doors on existing buildings can be retrofitted with these materials to reduce air leakage through door assemblies. Figure 10.11 compares various options available for weatherstripping doors.

Sliding glass doors generally conduct more heat than insulated hinged doors, due to their large glazed panels. The following measures to reduce conductive heat movement should be considered. Door jambs and sills should be made of wood (clad or unclad); if metal, a thermal break should be provided. Door panels should have wood frames or metal frames with thermal breaks. Glazings should be at least 5/8-inch double insulating tempered glass in most regions, with a third layer recommended for severely cold climates.

In selecting sliding glass doors, consider the details and materials used to reduce air leakage. Weatherstrip features are very important for sliding glass doors and must provide a positive seal, even after years of use. Typical weatherstrip materials include vinyl flanges, compressible vinyl covered urethane foam, or wool pile strips. Weatherstripping is critical along sills and jambs,

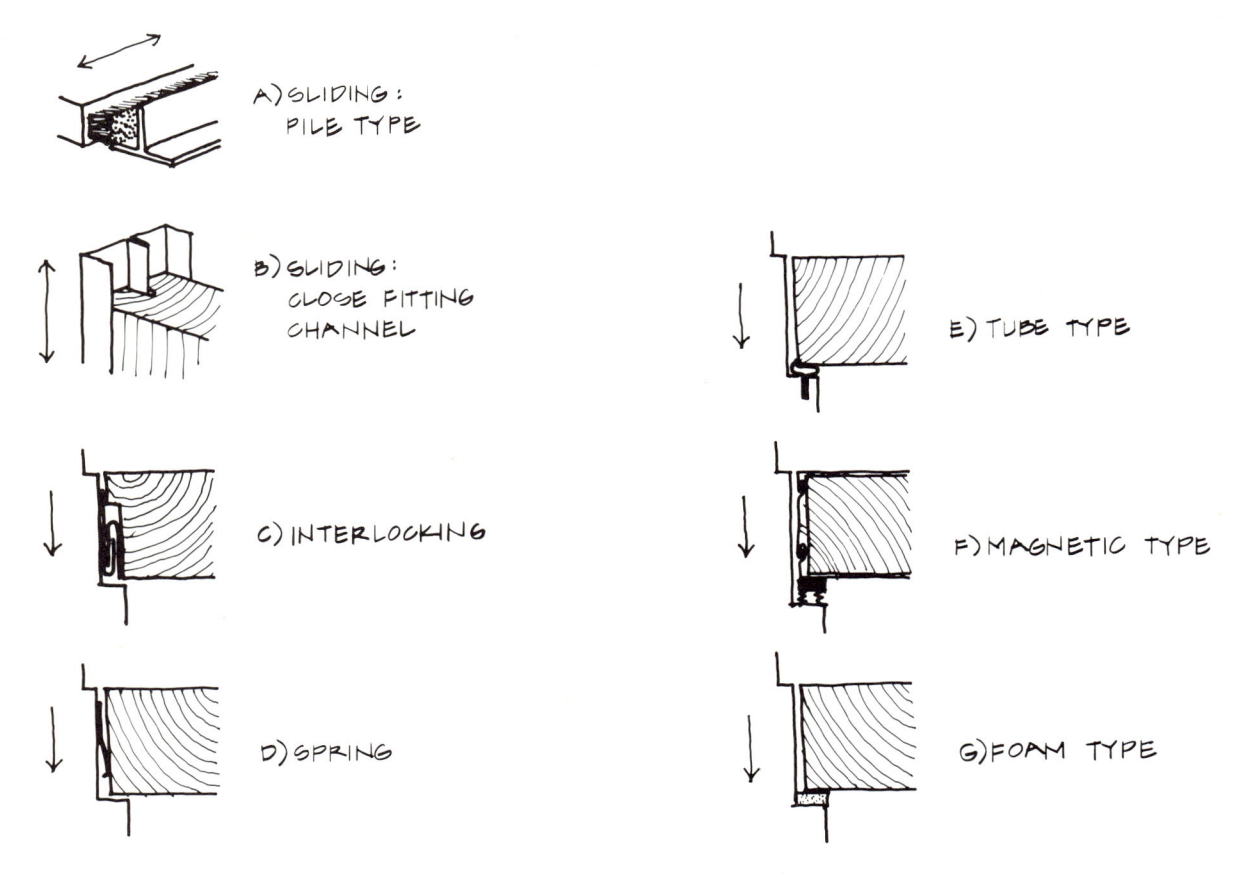

Fig. 10.11 Weatherstripping Options for Doors and Windows
A) Pile type—Best for sliding applications if installed properly. B) Close fitting channel (metal or plastic)—The required close fit for weathertightness may hinder sliding operation of unit. C) Interlocking (metal or plastic)—Best metal type for tightness but can create closing problems if deformed. D) Spring (metal or plastic)—Good, all around weatherstripping. E) Tube type (plastic)—Effective, especially for installations with large gaps such as garage doors. F) Magnetic type—Very effective but limited to steel doors and tends to be less durable than most types. G) Foam type—Low cost and initially very effective but wears out quickly.

Notes on materials and installation: The most durable materials are non-rusting metals such as bronze or stainless steel. These are usually applied on the job and must be carefully installed to achieve proper weathertightness. Plastic forms the best seal initially because of its inherent resiliency. However, over time it will break down and require replacement. Brush type weatherstripping can wear out quickly if the unit bears heavily against it due to poor installation or if the unit becomes roughened by weathering or corrosion.

and at the meeting stile where sliding and fixed sections interlock. For specific details, compare manufacturers' literature or display units at local lumber yards.

Installing Doors

Proper installation of all exterior doors is critical to their energy performance. Techniques discussed here focus on reducing air leakage and ensuring tight closure for the life of the unit (Fig. 10.12).

Swinging doors must be mounted accurately and snugly; hinges should be fastened securely to ensure tight fit. At installation check for proper functioning of weatherstripping and accurate adjustment of thresholds to guarantee snug fits. Many types of weatherstripping are available for installation on exterior doors, should this detail not be present in the purchased component. Air leakage past door jambs, casings, and sills can be reduced greatly by the following installation techniques:

- Fill the shim space between the jambs and the framing with spray foam or fibrous insulation.

DOORS, WINDOWS, AND GLAZINGS   189

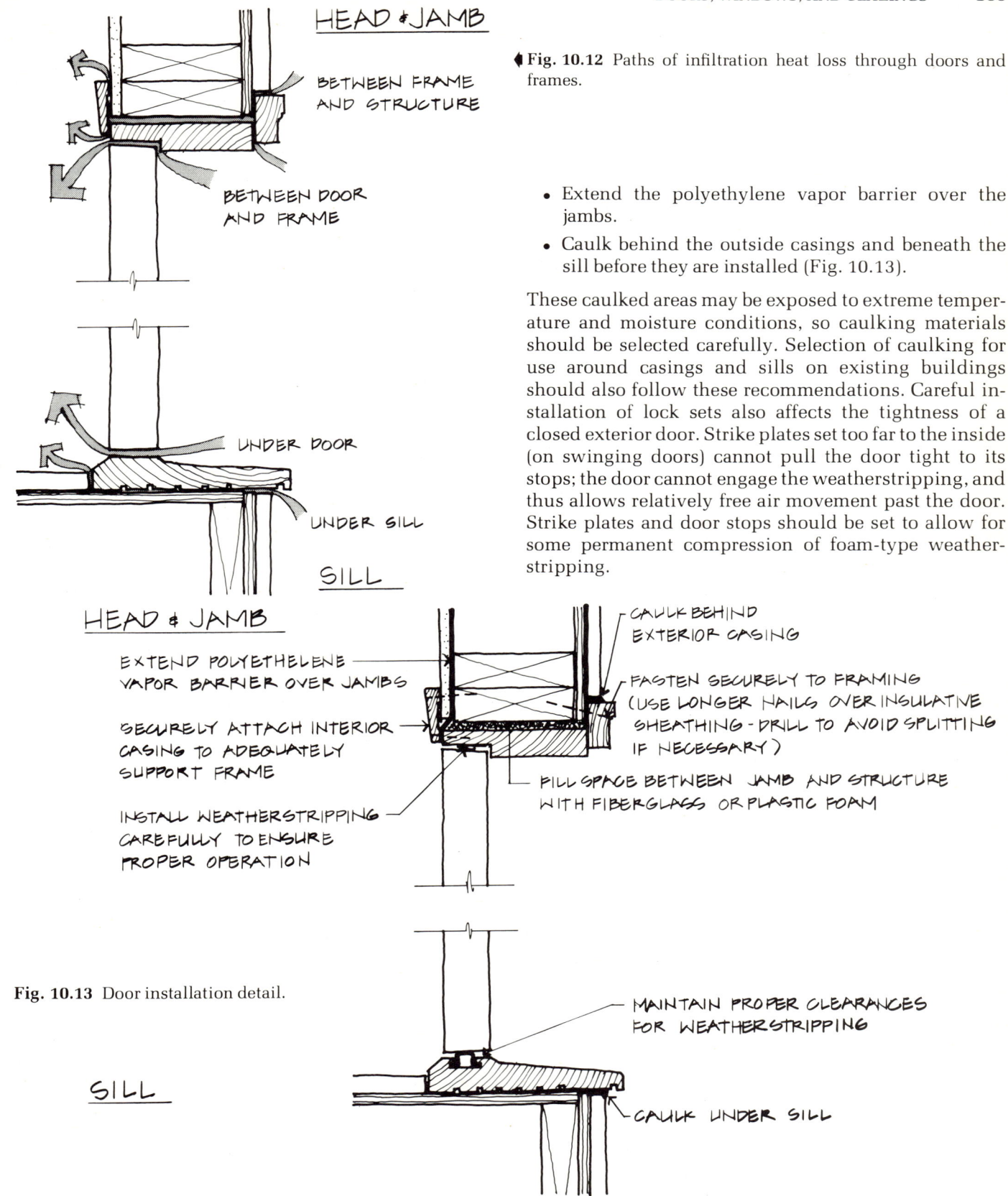

Fig. 10.12 Paths of infiltration heat loss through doors and frames.

- Extend the polyethylene vapor barrier over the jambs.
- Caulk behind the outside casings and beneath the sill before they are installed (Fig. 10.13).

These caulked areas may be exposed to extreme temperature and moisture conditions, so caulking materials should be selected carefully. Selection of caulking for use around casings and sills on existing buildings should also follow these recommendations. Careful installation of lock sets also affects the tightness of a closed exterior door. Strike plates set too far to the inside (on swinging doors) cannot pull the door tight to its stops; the door cannot engage the weatherstripping, and thus allows relatively free air movement past the door. Strike plates and door stops should be set to allow for some permanent compression of foam-type weatherstripping.

Fig. 10.13 Door installation detail.

190 MATERIALS, DETAILS, AND TECHNIQUES OF SOLAR CONSTRUCTION

Insulative sheathing used on the exterior of a wall requires the use of larger nails in fastening outside casings of wood or metal doors to the framing. Jamb extensions to bring jambs flush with the interior wall finishes may be either provided with the door or job-built.

When assembling sliding glass door frames, be sure to caulk and fasten the jambs and sill as specified by the manufacturer. Before the frame is placed into the rough opening, a bead of caulk should be placed along the sill where it sits on the floor decking. Caulking also should be placed on the exterior sheathing or siding where the outside casings will be fastened, to reduce air movement. The frame then can be installed. Make sure the sill is level, so the heavy glass doors will operate smoothly. If shimming is required, this area should be recaulked. Side jambs should be plumbed and held straight with shims at fastening points, so closure and weatherstrip details will function properly. Once the frame has been leveled, squared, and fastened, the door panels can be installed. Fixed units typically are screwed to the frame against factory installed weatherstripping. Additional caulking around the fixed unit will improve its resistance to air leakage. This panel should be fastened securely so the sliding panel will not disrupt it as it is opened and closed. The sliding unit should be adjusted to operate smoothly and engage properly with weather seal and security components. Outside casings are secured to the sheathing or framing in the same manner as described for hinged doors, depending on the use of exterior insulative sheathing.

OPERABLE WINDOWS

Operable windows provide daylight, ventilation, emergency egress, and views. In solar construction they also transmit solar radiation directly into the building, often in combination with fixed glazings. Operable windows open and close by either swinging on hinges or sliding within a track. These types of windows are available in wood (clad or unclad) or aluminum, and consist of the following components:

- Window frame—including side and head jambs and sill
- Window sash—consisting of horizontal rails, vertical stiles, and the single, double, or triple glazing
- Weatherstripping
- Exterior casings

Swinging and sliding windows lose or gain heat in the same way as swinging and sliding exterior doors.

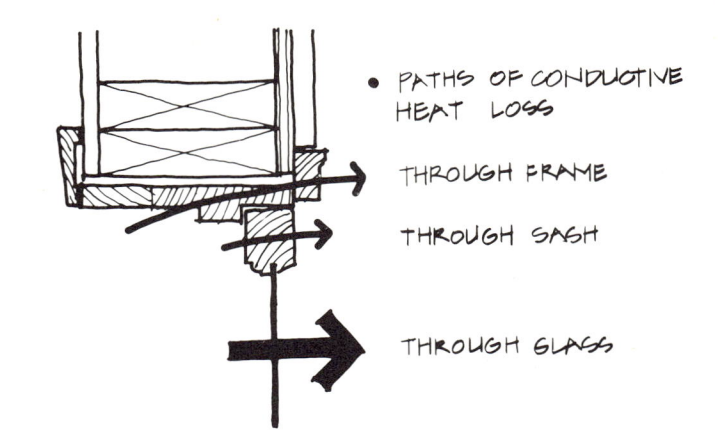

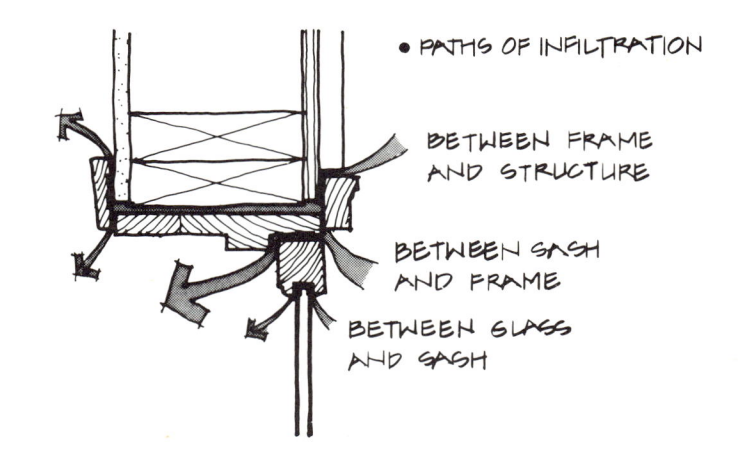

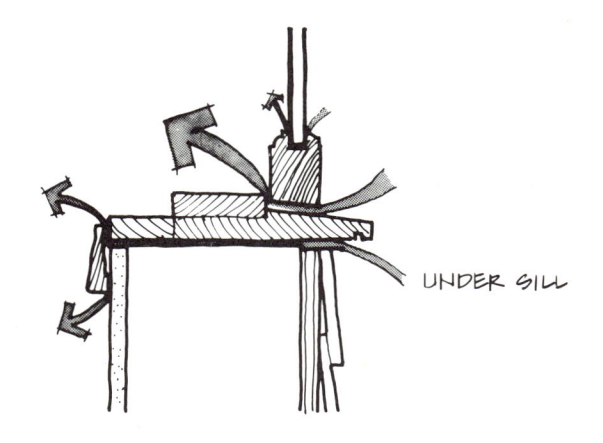

Fig. 10.14 Heat loss through windows

DOORS, WINDOWS, AND GLAZINGS   191

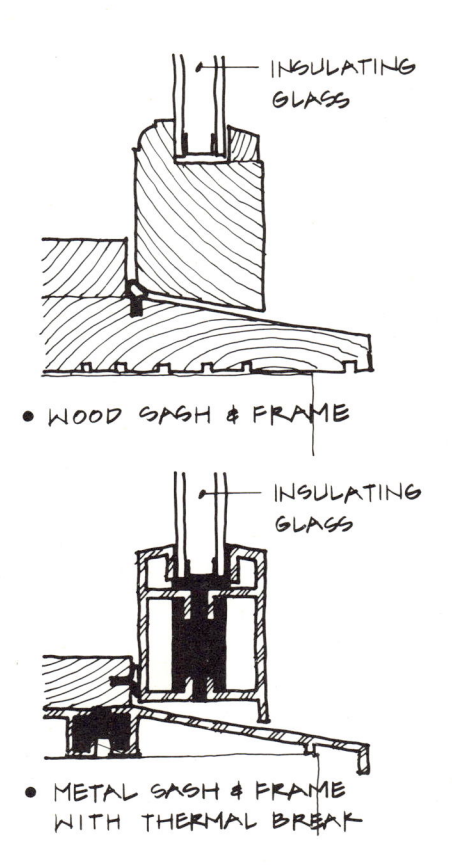

Fig. 10.15 Provide windows that minimize conductive heat loss.

Heat is conducted through the frame, sash, and glazing, while air leaks past the sash, behind the casings, and past the jambs and sills (Fig. 10.14). Windows that reduce heat conduction (Fig. 10.15), close tightly against durable weatherstripping, and reduce condensation should be selected. They must be installed properly so that they operate smoothly, close tightly, and resist air leakage (Fig. 10.16).

Another consideration in window selection is the potential for ventilation offered by different types of windows (Fig. 10.17). This is important for cooling and natural dehumidifying in the summer and in warm climates. Ventilation is especially important in sunspace/greenhouses and thermal masonry wall systems (Fig. 10.18).

Choosing Windows

Depending on their quality, **hinged windows** such as casements, awnings, and hoppers, offer greater potential energy efficiency than do sliding windows, primarily due to the tighter closure that swinging windows can

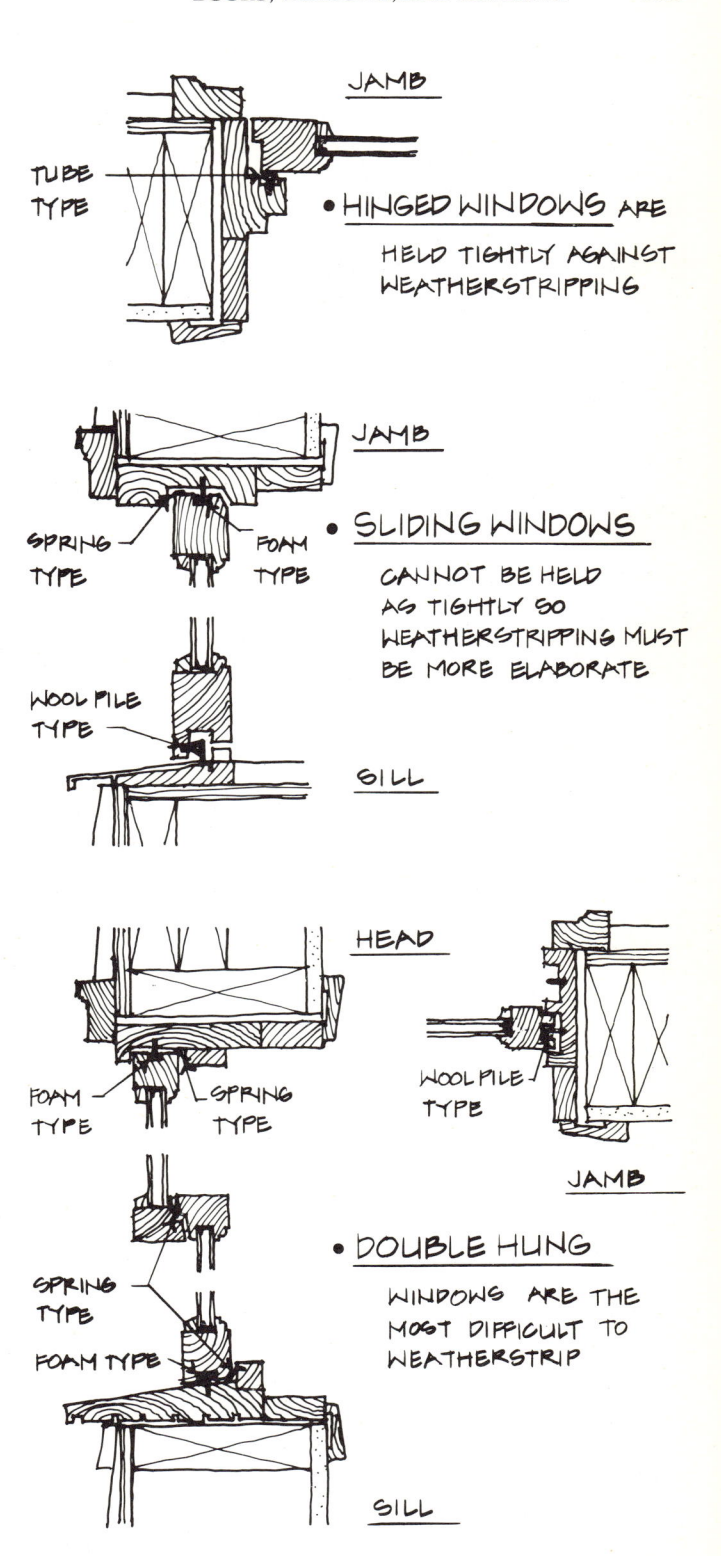

Fig. 10.16 Select and Install Windows Carefully. Proper window detailing includes the use of the suitable weatherstripping for the action involved (compression or sliding), durable materials, and tight fits at corners.

Fig. 10.17 Casement windows are more effective for natural ventilation than double hung.

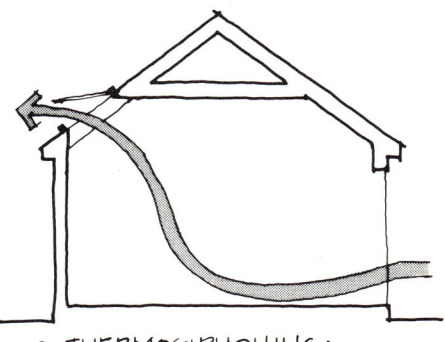

Fig. 10.18 Careful window placement is important for effective ventilation.

achieve (Fig. 10.19). Both types, however, lose considerable heat by conduction. Units constructed with wood frame and sash conduct less heat than metal framed windows, unless the metal units have thermal breaks. Metal windows with thermal breaks perform comparably to wood windows.

Casement, awning, and hopper windows can open fully and encourage ventilation by diverting the air moving along the exterior wall surfaces into the building. The direction of opening should consider prevailing wind directions of the site. These windows often are used to vent sunspace/greenhouses.

Double hung and horizontal **sliding windows** are usually less energy efficient than hinged windows due to the higher rate of air leakage that occurs around the sash (Fig. 10.20). Weatherstripping allows the window to operate while providing a tight seal. Window manufacturers supply a variety of weatherstripping with their units, including rigid vinyl ribs, vinyl covered foam, and rigid vinyl leaf.

Sliding windows are less effective than hinged windows for ventilation, limiting the actual openings to approximately 50 to 60 percent of the total window area. These windows cannot open to divert outside air movement through them.

Multiple Glazing

The importance of using double and triple glazing to reduce heat conduction through glass was discussed earlier. There are many ways to provide multiple layers of glass in windows. When selecting components, consider the insulating properties of the unit and the likelihood of condensation forming on the inner surface or between layers. Double and triple glazed windows are available in the following configurations (Fig. 10.21):

DOORS, WINDOWS, AND GLAZINGS 193

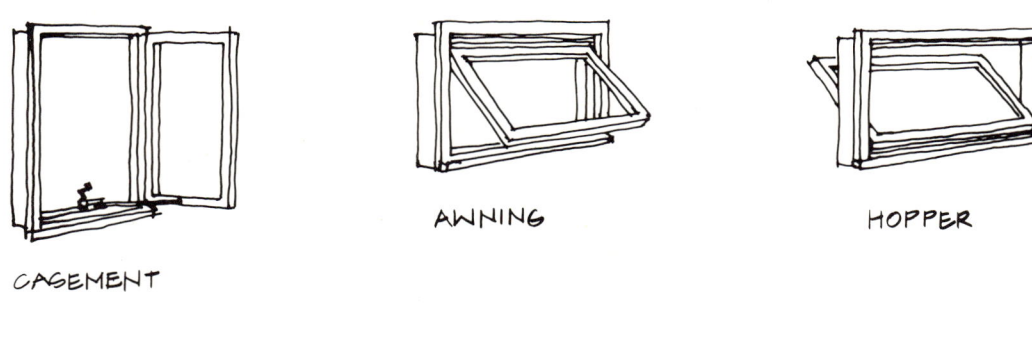

Fig. 10.19 Comparing hinged windows

Fig. 10.20 Comparing sliding windows

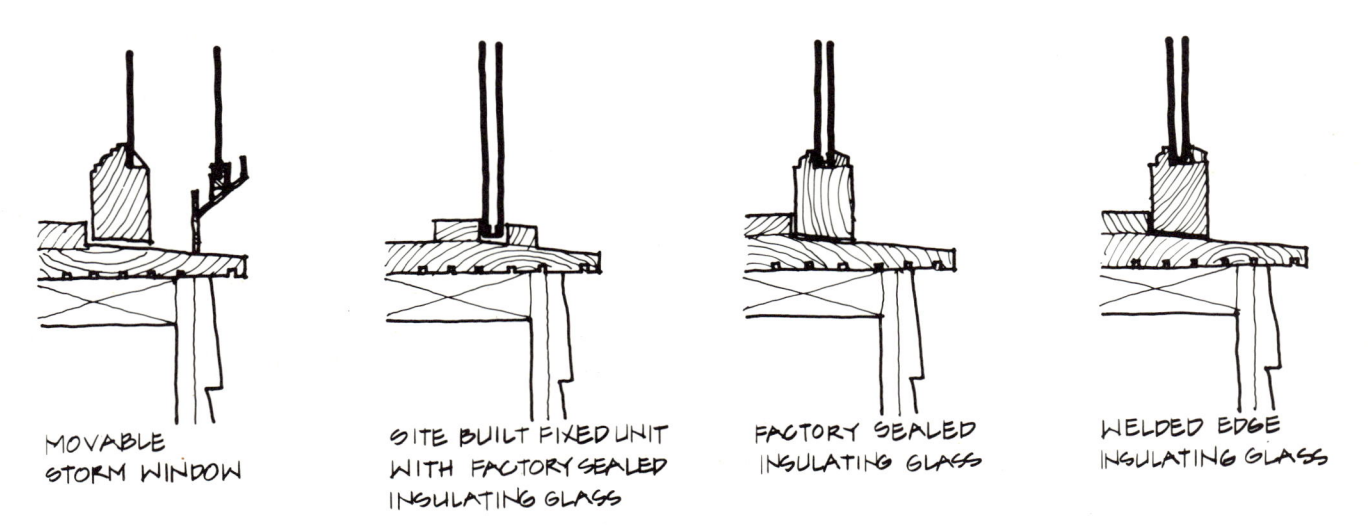

Fig. 10.21 The use of multiple glazings in doors and windows

- Sash with factory sealed double or triple glazings
- Single glazed sash with single or double glazed storm insert applied to inside or outside
- Single or double glazed sash with storm sash applied to the outside
- Double glazed sash with single glazed insert panel applied to inside or outside

Condensation can cause problems in any window configuration. Ice build-up fogs the windows, impairing view out and the transmission of solar radiation into the building. The ice then melts and forms puddles on muntins, sash, and sills. Continued moisture build-up eventually causes wood and metal window components to deteriorate. Single glazed windows usually have the greatest problem with condensation. These windows are often below interior dew point temperature due to their direct contact with cold outside air. By adding another layer of glass with an air space between them, the interior surface of the inner layer remains relatively warm, thus reducing condensation (Fig. 10.22). However, if the additional glazing is applied on the inside of the window, moisture may move past the warm inner glazing and condense on the cooler outer glazing. This may occur even with storm sashes that have vinyl weatherstripping along their perimeters. If windows with interior storm sash are to be used, condensation may be reduced by selecting windows that are double glazed with a single glazed insert.

Factory sealed insulated glass units are joined together at the edges with either aluminum channel and sealant or a separate piece of glass welded to them. Usually air space is dehumidified with a dessicant. Condensation may occur between the layers if the edge seal breaks, allowing moist air to enter and condense on the cool outer layer. Problems also may arise after a number of years when the dessicant has become saturated with absorbed moisture.

If storm sashes are used with either single or double glazed windows, condensation can be avoided by placing the additional layer on the outside. This configuration keeps the tight, factory installed glazing on the inside and puts the looser, site installed glazings on the outside. The putty and paint used to seal the connection between the primary sash and glass will reduce the amount of moisture moving to the outer secondary glazing. This, coupled with small air movement between the layers, lowers the potential for condensation to form there. Remember that the inside glazing should fit tightly and be weatherstripped, and outer glazing should be allowed to breathe (Fig. 10.23).

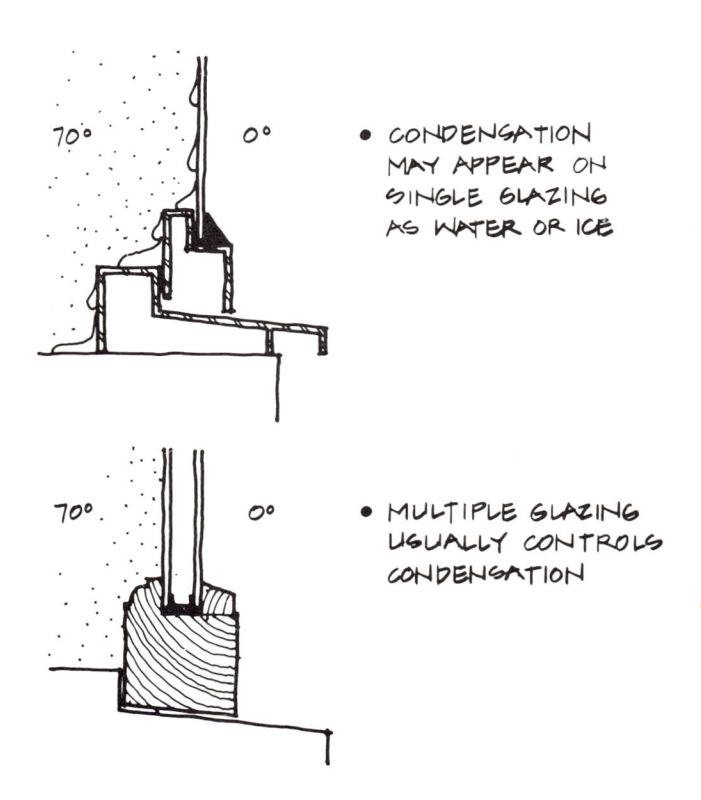

Fig. 10.22 Controlling condensation on doors and windows

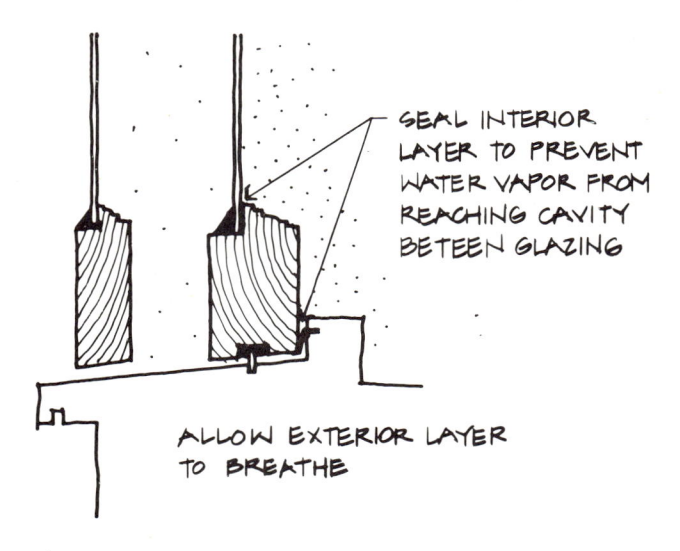

Fig. 10.23 Installing non-factory sealed double glazing or storm sash

Installation of Windows

Installation affects the amount of air leakage that occurs with windows. Prior to placing the window into the rough opening, a bead of butyl or other suitable caulk should be placed on the sheathing or siding around the opening, where the casing will meet the exterior sheathing. The window then can be set in place, leveled, shimmed, and nailed. If insulative sheathing has been used on the outside, longer nails will be required for nailing the casings to the frame. Caulking between the casing and sheathing and below the sill reduces air leakage. Some manufacturers provide an anchoring flange and windbreak on vinyl clad windows which is integral with the exterior casings and sill. Others provide a flexible foam bead on the back side of the casing. Finally, the window operation should be checked to make sure that the sash operates smoothly and closes tightly against the weatherstripping along its total perimeter.

FIXED GLAZINGS

Fixed glazings in solar construction form window walls, thermal storage wall glazings, sunspace/greenhouses, skylights, and sidelights (Fig. 10.24). In some cases fixed glazings are single layered, while in other applications they may be double or triple glazed. These window components can be supplied by a manufacturer in a sash ready to install or can be job-built from separate components assembled at the site. These units, or the components used to build them, are available in a full range of sizes and materials, allowing flexibility in the design of glazing details.

Fixed glazings are generally more energy efficient than operable windows of the same size and number of layers, because they resist air leakage more effectively. Greater efficiency can be achieved only if these units are installed and sealed properly. Fixed glazings cannot be used for ventilation; therefore, they are often used in combination with operable windows.

Fig. 10.24 Fixed glazings are commonly used in various solar construction applications.

This section presents various applications of fixed glazings in solar construction, the materials appropriate for specific uses, and construction details and techniques for proper installation. Fixed glazings form an important part of the exterior shell of a building, and they must provide weathertight, waterproof seals as their primary function. This requires proper selection and installation of sealants, fasteners, and flashings. Further attention to detail when installing fixed glazings reduces air leakage around the perimeter of the window and condensation of moisture on inner surfaces or between multiple layers.

Mounting systems for fixed glazings range from factory applied sash, exterior casings, and sill to job-built window stops, jambs, casings, and sills. In some instances the glazing manufacturer also offers factory made, site-assembled glazing support systems designed specifically for their products. In other cases the builder designs (or has designed) his or her own details using locally available components. In many applications, fixed glazings are used in combination with operable windows to provide ventilation and emergency egress.

Window Walls

South facing window walls allow solar radiation to enter directly into a building, and usually combine fixed glazings with operable windows or sliding glass doors. Insulating glass is most commonly used in this application because it provides a clear view out from the living areas. If large expanses of glass are used, the units should be built with fully tempered glass to take advantage of its greater strength and safety characteristics. As discussed in Chapter 5, these glazings can be relatively small or large, depending on the building's size, floor plan, capacity for heat storage, and resistance to heat loss or gain (Fig. 10.25).

Fixed glazings may be installed after the building has been framed and sheathed. In this application they are placed into openings in the exterior supporting walls of the building. If they are factory or shop built and supplied with exterior casings, they may be installed prior to the exterior siding when horizontal siding is used, or after the siding when vertical siding is selected. The sequence of installation is similar to the placement of operable windows described in the preceding section. Emphasis should be placed on sealing between the exterior casings and the sheathing or siding to reduce air leakage. This may be accomplished by caulking or using components that have either compressible foam on the back side of the casings or an integral plastic anchoring flange and windbreak.

Fig. 10.25 South facing window areas should be carefully sized to avoid overheating during the day and overcooling at night.

Fixed glazings built at the job using window or patio door replacement glass require careful workmanship during framing of the rough opening, and in preparing the opening to receive the glass. The openings should be square, free of twists, and built from materials strong enough to bear the weight of the glass units. The actual window frames may be built-up from finish interior and exterior jambs applied to the framing, or solid structural members may be rabbetted to receive the glass. Design of jambs and rabbet cuts should include the thickness of glazing compounds or tapes used to seal the opening. In sizing the finished openings, allow for clearance around the entire perimeter of the unit to permit expansion of the glass, or racking and settling of the building without damage to the window wall. Table 10.3 presents recommended clearances and rabbet depths for various insulating glass sizes.

Table 10.3
Recommended clearances and rabbet depths for various glass sizes

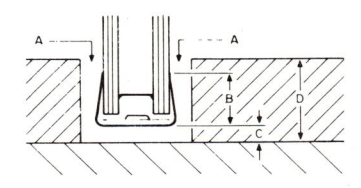

Factory-fabricated, Thermopane dimensions cannot be changed at point of use. Adequate clearances and rabbet depths must be provided for all units so that metal seal is not visible.

		½" and ¾" units ⅛" glass	⅝" and ⅞" units ³⁄₁₆" glass	¾" and 1" units ¼" glass
A	Face clearance	⅛"	⅛"	⅛"
C	Metal edge depth	⅜"	⅜"	⅜"
C	Edge clearance	⅛"	¼"	¼"
D	Minimum rabbet depth	⅝"	¾"	¾"

Although job-built glazings may be installed from either the inside or outside of the building, builders may choose to install fixed window wall glazings from the inside so that the exterior shell may be completed without interruption. In this case, after the sill or job-built frame has been set into the rough opening, the finish exterior stops or jambs can be fastened securely to the framing, flush to the outside of the exterior sheathing or siding, depending on the specific application. Glazing putty or tape then is applied to the jamb along the surfaces against which the glass will rest. Next, neoprene setting blocks should be placed at the bottom corners of the opening to act as spacers. The glass unit is placed on these blocks and tilted up into the opening. Final positioning of the unit to center it in the opening should be done before the glass is pressed firmly against the jamb and sealant to produce a good seal all the way around. The glazing then can be held in place with temporary inside stops until the interior finish work begins.

Thermal Storage Walls

Fixed glazings used in thermal storage walls include single or multiple layers of fully tempered glass or fiberglass-reinforced polyester. Because the masonry wall often serves as structural support for roof loads and upper floors, the glazing systems need only support their own dead loads and withstand wind loads. The framework for these fixed glazings may be constructed with factory, shop, or job-built wooden millwork including mullions, muntins, and sills, or they may be assembled from metal prefabricated components designed for use with specific types and sizes of glazing materials. Glazing frames may be hung from the thermal wall with lag screws or supported on part of the foundation and steadied with fasteners tied into the wall. The design of a glazing system and selection of its components should consider:

- Type and number of glazing layers
- Design of job-built glazing supports
- Availability of prefabricated glazing bars
- Means of assembly and support
- Heat loss through framing
- Details and materials for weatherproofing
- Durability and maintenance
- Cleaning and/or replacement of glazing sections
- Provisions for summer venting
- Allowances for thermal expansion and contraction

Glazing components used in these applications are installed from the outside. The glazing, applied after the wall has been painted, should be scheduled so that installation coincides with the application of other exterior surfaces, trim, and flashings. All materials used in the construction of glazing systems for thermal storage walls must be able to withstand extreme conditions of wind, precipitation, interior moisture, temperature, and ultraviolet radiation. These components must be installed carefully to reduce air leakage, using sealants that are suitable for use under the above mentioned conditions. Figure 10.26 show typical construction details for glazing systems used to enclose thermal storage walls.

Sunspace/Greenhouses

Sunspace/greenhouse applications utilize large areas of fixed glazings, often combined with some form of operable windows for venting excess heat and moisture. The primary solar collection area consists of multiple layers of fixed glass, FRPs, or plastic glazings. Depending on the design, these fixed glazings may be installed either vertically or in a sloped position. These details are determined by the shape, size, appearance, and intended use as discussed in Chapter 5 (Fig. 10.27).

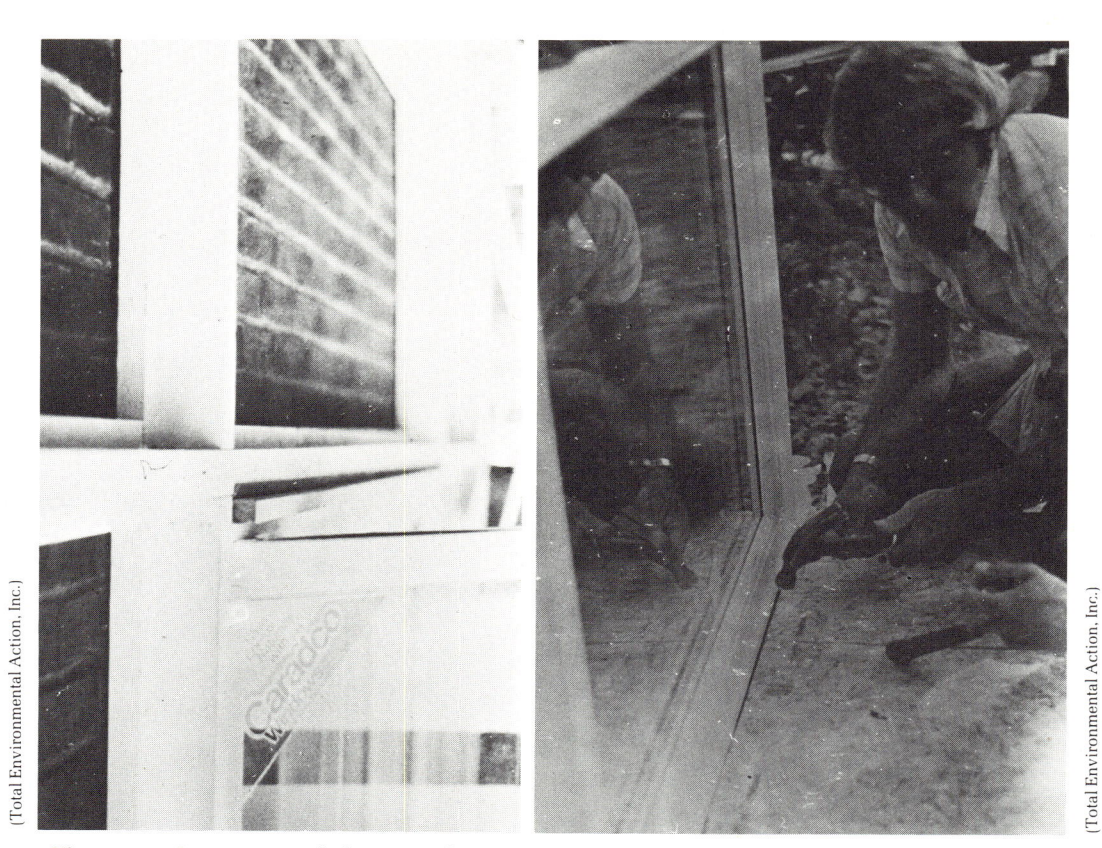

Fig. 10.26 One means of glazing a thermal storage wall

The frames used to support fixed glazings in these applications may be job-built with treated or durable lumber, such as redwood or cedar, or they may be prefabricated from aluminum extrusions. Job-built wood frames can either be built-up or rabbetted to receive glazing materials usually applied from the outside and held down with wood or aluminum battens. The clearance requirements for expansion and contraction of materials discussed in regard to window walls apply here. Prefabricated aluminum glazing systems are available in kit form; they provide either an extruded channel that houses the glazing materials or simply a surface upon which to support and fasten them. Builders may choose to purchase an entire greenhouse kit including frame, glazings, vents, sealants, and flashings from a supplier and assemble it at the site (Fig. 10.28). Builders also may elect to subcontract this work to a solar greenhouse specialist.

The most important features of any glazing system used in a sunspace/greenhouse are structural integrity, weather resistance, solar radiation transmission, and

DOORS, WINDOWS, AND GLAZINGS 199

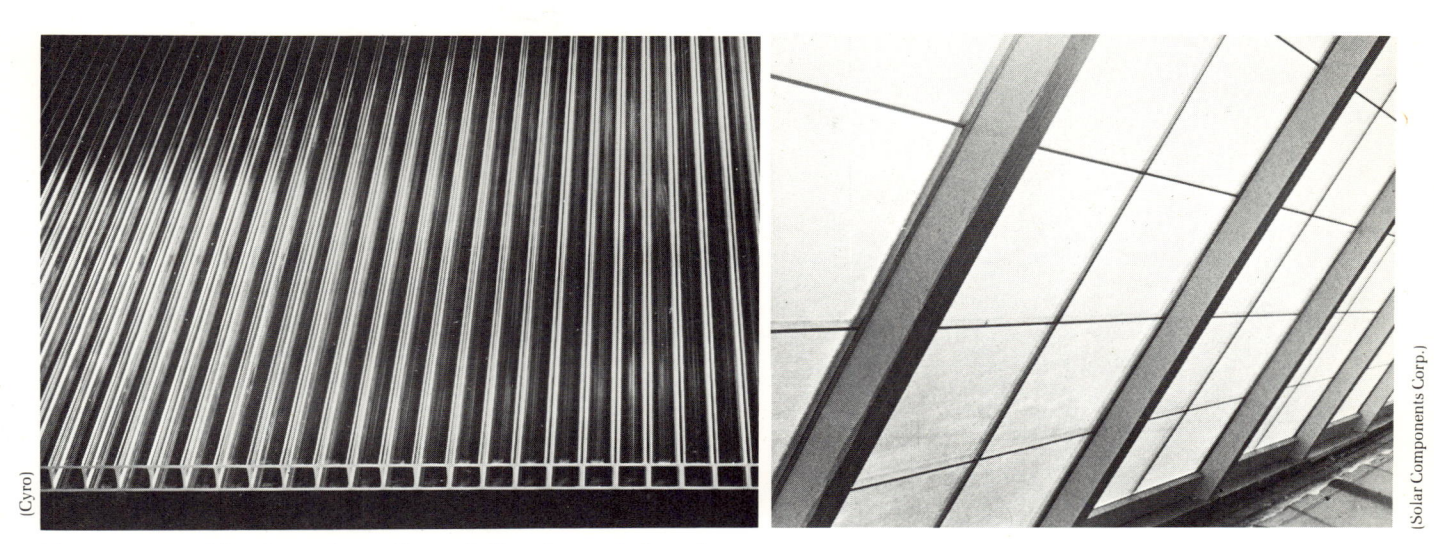

Fig. 10.27 Double skinned acrylic and fiberglass reinforced polyester glazing panels are widely used in solar construction.

Fig. 10.28 The erection of a factory-built solar greenhouse kit

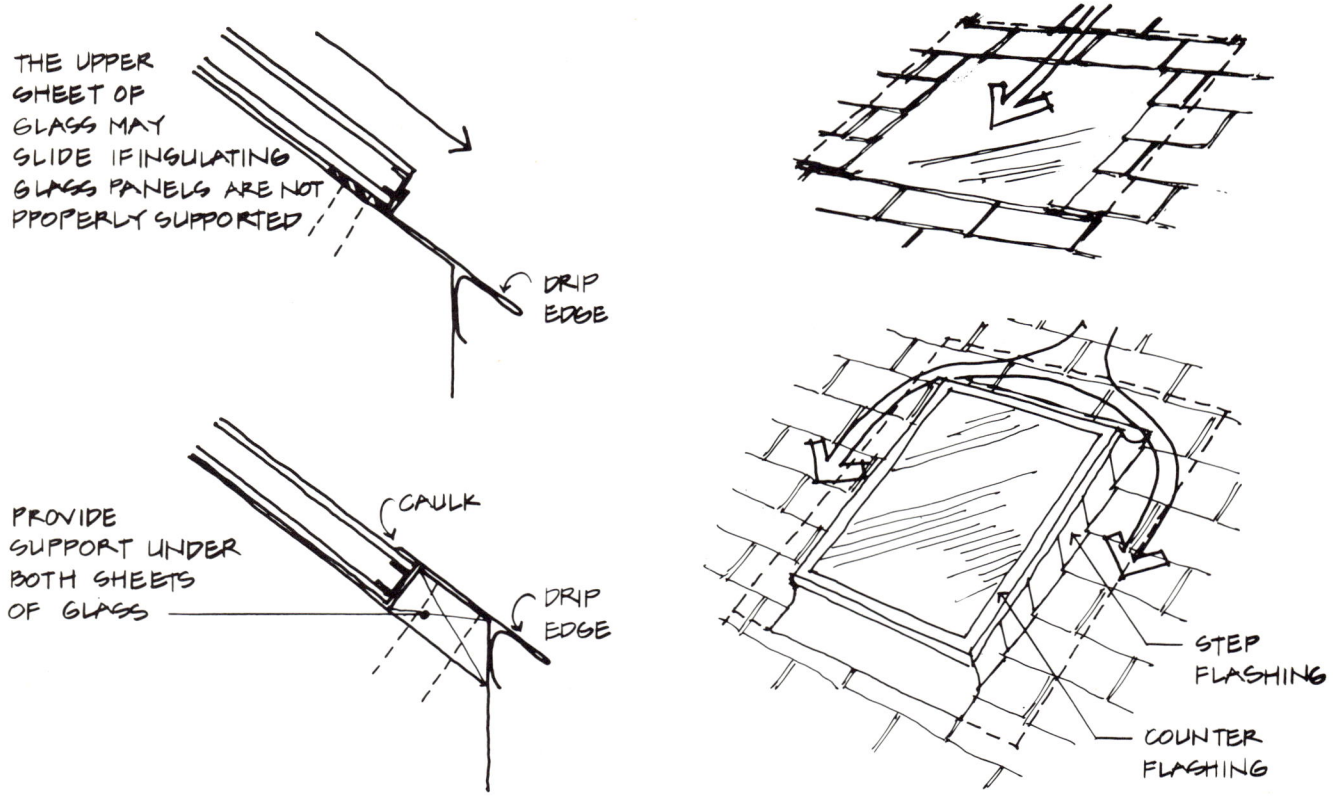

200   MATERIALS, DETAILS, AND TECHNIQUES OF SOLAR CONSTRUCTION

Fig. 10.29 Insulating glass units must be fully supported when installed in sloped position.

Fig. 10.30 Fixed skylights should be raised above the plane of the roof to ensure waterproofing.

energy conservation. Materials must be able to withstand extreme environmental conditions both inside and outside the structure. Details used to prevent water from entering the building, especially when sloped glazings are used, must be properly designed and built. This also applies to details used to prevent damage from moisture generated within the space that condenses on the inner glazing surfaces, runs down them, and eventually accumulates on muntins or sills.

Materials used to glaze vertical and sloped sunspace/greenhouses must meet local building code requirements, especially where overhead sloped glazings are used. Builders also should be sure that glazing manufacturers approve the installation of their products for specific applications. For example, some producers of fully tempered insulating glass units will not warrantee their products for sloped applications. When applied in this manner, the upper layer of glass may not be fully supported and may shift, breaking the edge seal and resulting in condensation between the glazings (Fig. 10.29).

Construction sequence for fixed greenhouse/sunspace glazings depends on the specific design. Sloped glazings integrated with shingled or metal roofing must be installed and flashed as the finish roofing is applied to adjacent areas. Vertical glazings may be scheduled in the same way as for window walls.

Skylights and Collectors

Glazing materials and details used to construct fixed skylights are the same as those used in sloped sunspace/greenhouses. They may be installed using job-built or prefabricated support and fastening components, and must be carefully sealed and flashed to provide weathertight, waterproof protection. This is very important when using glazing materials that are constantly expanding and contracting due to temperature changes. Figure 10.30 illustrates construction details for job-built fixed skylight glazings and collector glazings. Once again, local building codes will define acceptable practices and applications.

CHAPTER 11
HVAC, PLUMBING, ELECTRICAL, AND SOLAR DHW

INTRODUCTION

This chapter discusses the selection, installation, and operation of HVAC, plumbing, electrical, and solar domestic hot water (DHW) components used in residential solar construction. In many cases new components and installation techniques may be employed as further means of reducing energy consumption in buildings. These services, which deliver supplemental heating or cooling, hot and cold water, and light and power, are designed to meet the comfort requirements of the building occupants, whose use of these conveniences and necessities ultimately determines the level of energy consumed in operation. The actual energy efficiency of HVAC, plumbing, and electrical systems, including solar water heaters, is beyond the control of the builder; however, he or she should provide components, controls, and appliances designed for energy efficient operation and carefully sized to meet specific loads, rather than randomly selected as has been the usual practice (Fig. 11.2).

Even the best components will not function efficiently if improperly installed and maintained. Heating and cooling equipment, plumbing fixtures, solar water heaters, and electrical controls especially are affected by poor installation, and problems with these components may continue undetected for a time if the malfunction only impairs their operation instead of preventing it. Selection of experienced subcontractors who will warrantee and service their equipment and workmanship will minimize the number of problems that arise, and solve those few that do with the least amount of inconvenience to the owners.

HVAC, plumbing and electrical services are installed in two phases: (1) roughed-in ductwork, piping, and wiring installed during the shell phase; and (2) mechanical equipment, components, and finish fixtures installed as the construction proceeds to completion.

It is important for builders to schedule the installation of these components into the sequence of construction, and consider the impact they will have on work already completed, especially as ductwork, piping, and wiring are roughed-in after the shell has been completed, but before insulation and finishes are applied. Double-check the layout and workmanship of this work using guidelines to be discussed later in this chapter. Equipment and components should be tested and balanced by the subcontractor after installation, to assure proper operation and functioning (Fig. 11.3).

HVAC

Heating and Cooling

As we improve the energy efficiency of buildings, conventional heating and cooling systems play an increasingly supplemental role. Improved construction techniques, from increased insulation levels and proper siting to some of the more elaborate solar features which reduce heating and cooling loads, allow builders to install less costly, sized-down HVAC equipment. The use of open floor plans and other techniques to encourage natural energy movement within buildings saves time and materials used to install heating and cooling distribution systems. In many instances these direct savings will offset the added costs of new framing technique, increased insulation, mechanical equipment, and increased glazed areas.

Centralized or decentralized heating and cooling systems fueled by any source should be designed to meet the specific loads of energy efficient buildings. Once the building has been designed, heat loss/gain

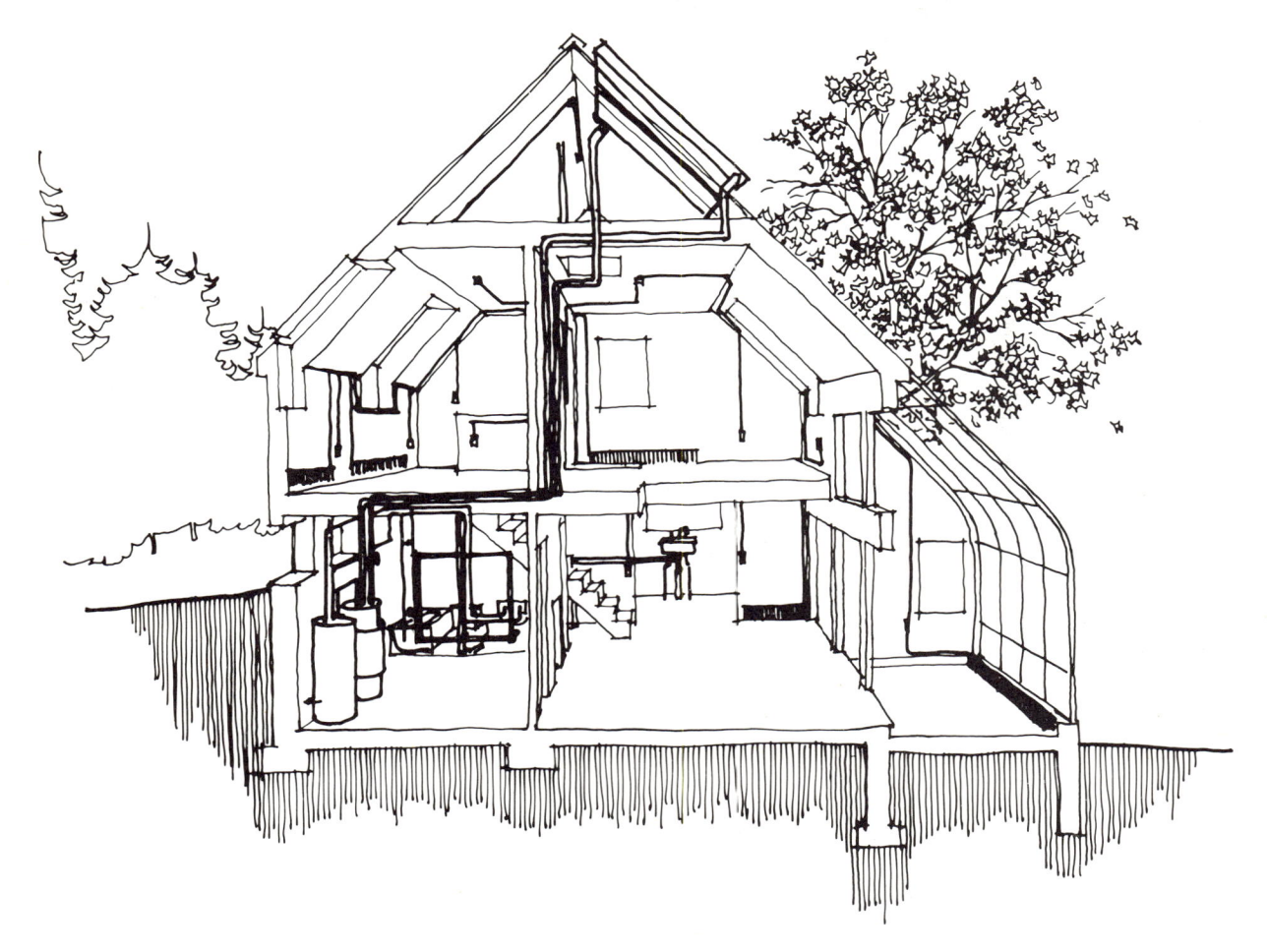

Fig. 11.1 The mechanical and electrical phase of construction includes the installation of heating, ventilating, air conditioning, plumbing, electrical, and solar hot water equipment.

calculations can be computed and the most efficient equipment selected. In some areas, builders are required by lenders or building officials to install conventional heating systems sized to meet 100 percent of the load, even in buildings which are 30 to 50 percent solar heated. In these cases, builders often select systems that have low initial costs though they may be more expensive to operate (such as electric resistance baseboard), and assume that the system will not be required to operate very frequently. Builders also may find lenders and building officials receptive to their sizing the conventional systems to the reduced loads, rather than installing 100 percent backup.

Manufacturers of heating and cooling equipment are improving the efficiency of their products and introducing new components, including: more efficient heat pumps; wood, oil, gas, and electric fired boilers and furnaces; automatic stack dampers that close the flue when the boiler or furnace is off; radiant heat panels; and air conditioners. New components should be evaluated on the basis of energy performance (EER rating), installed cost, reliability, expected maintenance, and warrantee conditions. The selection of equipment also must consider the type and size of house and amount of space devoted to mechanicals, and the costs and availability of various fuel sources projected over the life of the building. These components should be coupled with control systems that offer energy saving features, which are described later in this section.

Ventilation and Air Quality

Source Ventilation

As buildings become "tighter" builders must plan for venting odors, moisture, and harmful dust to the atmosphere through one or a combination of approaches. In

Fig. 11.2 Proper selection and installation of equipment is always critical in solar construction.

MATERIALS, DETAILS, AND TECHNIQUES OF SOLAR CONSTRUCTION

Fig. 11.3 Energy priorities for mechanical and electrical phases

- INCREASE THE ENERGY EFFICIENCY OF MECHANICAL AND ELECTRICAL SYSTEMS BY:
  - CAREFULLY SELECTING AND ACCURATELY SIZING THE HEATING AND COOLING SYSTEMS
  - LAYING OUT HVAC AND PLUMBING SYSTEMS TO MINIMIZE LENGTH OF PIPING AND DUCT RUNS
  - USING ENERGY EFFICIENT APPLIANCES
  - USING ENERGY EFFICIENT LIGHTING FIXTURES
  - KEEPING HEATING DUCTS AND PIPING OUT OF EXTERIOR WALLS
  - INSULATING HOT WATER LINES

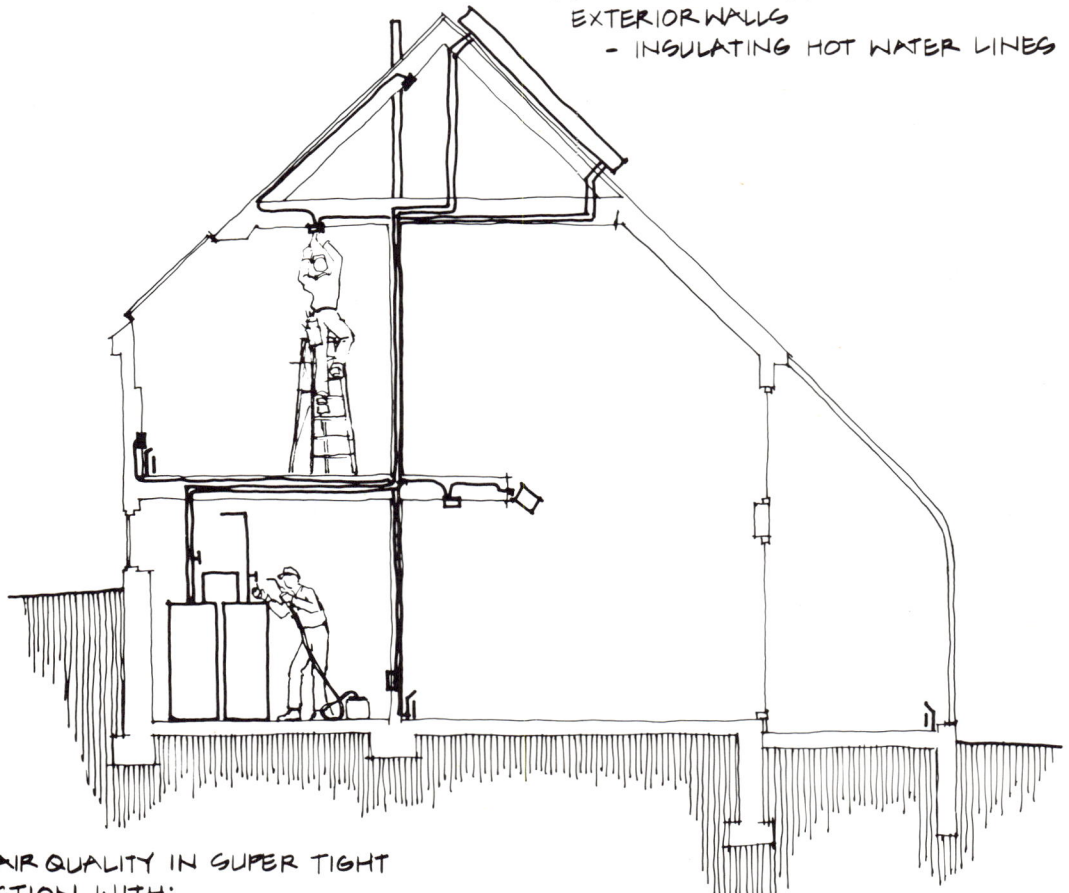

- ASSURE AIR QUALITY IN SUPER TIGHT CONSTRUCTION WITH:
  - SOURCE VENTILATION
  - AIR TO AIR HEAT EXCHANGERS

- CONSIDER PROVIDING A SOLAR DOMESTIC HOT WATER SYSTEM USING ONE OF THESE PRIMARY SYSTEMS:
  - ANTIFREEZE
  - DRAINBACK
  - THERMO SIPHON
  - RECIRCULATING
  - BATCH HEATER

- INTERFACE WITH OTHER PHASES BY:
  - COORDINATING INSTALLATION OF MECHANICAL AND ELECTRICAL COMPONENTS TO MINIMIZE PENETRATIONS OF THE HEATED SHELL (ESPECIALLY VAPOR BARRIERS)
  - ACCURATELY PLANNING AND INSTALLING ROUGH PLUMBING, HVAC, ELECTRICAL LINES IN FOUNDATION AND FRAMING PHASES

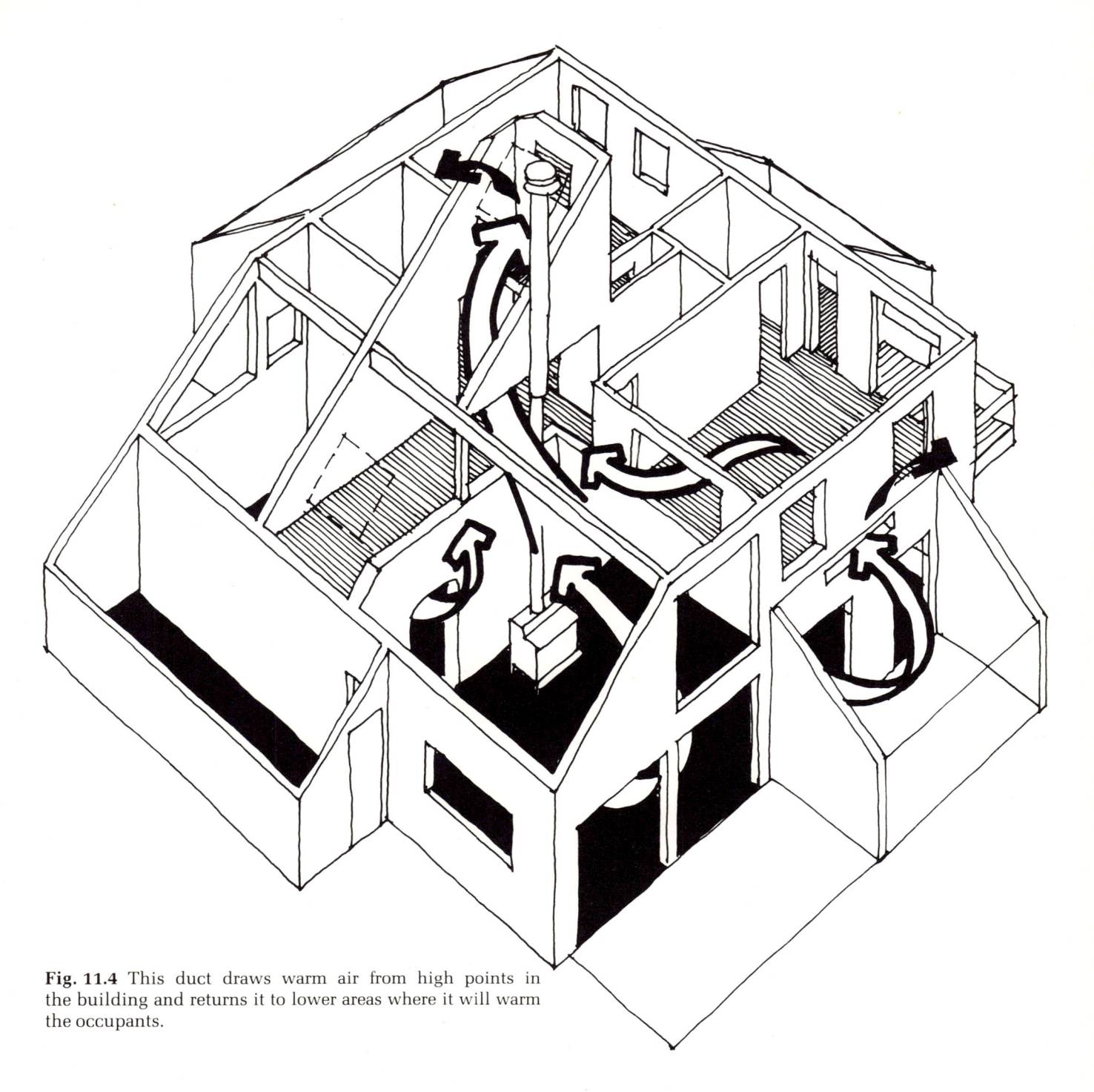

Fig. 11.4 This duct draws warm air from high points in the building and returns it to lower areas where it will warm the occupants.

older buildings, these elements are diffused by the considerable amount of air leakage occurring through the building shell. In new buildings, strategically located and properly sized mechanical ventilators must be used to remove these gases and particles from the building interior. New components also may be used to introduce a controlled source of fresh air into "tight" buildings for health and comfort, and as a combustion makeup source.

Venting moisture and odors at their source effectively reduces both the amount of moisture that accumulates in the building, thus reducing the formation of surface condensation, and the build-up of unpleasant odors. Vent fans ducted to the outside from kitchen range hoods, and laundry, bathroom, and greenhouse vents, can be used, and the outlets from these vents can be located on exterior walls, soffits, or roof openings. These components should be equipped with automatic or manual dampers that prevent air leakage through them when the fans are not in use.

Attic Fans

Attic fans also may be used to ventilate and cool buildings. These may be located either in an upper ceiling, central to the building, or in a gable end of an attic; usually they are used in the summer, or in warm climates, to remove large volumes of moist air at night. Because of the general ventilation they provide, their operation in winter, or in cold climates, results in significant heat loss, making them impractical for use.

Heat Recovery

Ventilation equipment and components also may be used to move heated air from warm areas to cooler areas, or to remote storage. Systems may be as simple as thermostatically controlled ceiling fans that recirculate warm air stratified near the ceiling, or as elaborate as vents, ducts, and fans built into walls, floors, and ceilings, and used to transport warm air from ceiling to floor, or room to room (Fig. 11.4). These *heat recovery* systems often are used to help even temperatures in existing buildings. In solar construction they may be used to move heated air from areas of high solar gain (greenhouses and other direct gain areas) to areas of low solar gain, or even into contact with masonry walls or floors used as heat storage. Builders should avoid the need for mechanical heat recovery by planning properly for natural convective air and heat movement within their buildings. Fans and blowers should be employed only when other approaches will not perform the whole job efficiently.

Air Quality

The air quality within a structure determines, to a large degree, the health and comfort of a building's occupants. The accumulation of odors, harmful dust particles, and gases resulting from combustion can be controlled to some extent through the use of source ventilators, as previously described, or more thoroughly through the use of air-to-air heat exchangers (Fig. 11.5). These components serve as central ventilators, expelling interior air (and odors, moisture, particles) at a controlled rate. In doing so they transfer heat from the

Fig. 11.5 Air to air heat exchanger (Mitsubishi)

warm outgoing air to preheat the cooler, incoming fresh air. This results in effective ventilation without excessive heat loss. Again, these components must be properly sized and located to perform as desired.

Another element of air quality affecting health and comfort is the relative humidity maintained within a building. This is an important factor in all climates during all seasons, as discussed in more detail in Chapter 3. Depending on climate, season, tightness of the shell, and lifestyle, the relative humidity inside the building may need to be controlled through the use of a humidifier or a dehumidifier.

PLUMBING

Plumbing systems for hot and cold water supplies should be designed to include water conserving fixtures and appliances. The resulting reduction in water usage helps save valuable water as well as energy used to produce hot water.

Water Conservation

Water conservation can be achieved through the use of special fixtures installed on faucet, bath, and shower heads, and new toilet tank components, and by using dishwashers and washing machines supplied with special water level settings. These components and appliances have been designed to provide full service while using a fraction of the water typically consumed. They are available generally through plumbing wholesalers and contractors, and are installed in the same manner as their conventional counterparts.

Energy Conservation

By reducing the total water consumption in their buildings, builders reduce directly the amount of hot water consumed and, thus, the energy required. Further measures should be taken to reduce energy used to provide domestic hot water. Water heaters are available in many forms: integrated into central heating and cooling equipment; separate large volume storage tanks; or small volume/high capacity instantaneous source heaters. They may be fueled by wood, oil, gas, electricity, coal, or solar energy. The following recommendations apply to selection, installation, and operation:

- Equipment should be sized to meet expected requirements of the building's occupants.
- Location close to water fixtures and appliances helps reduce length of pipe runs and distribution heat loss.
- Thermostat settings should be at minimum possible, as defined by manufacturer, occupants, and appliances (dishwashers, washing machines).
- Tank-type water heaters should be insulated to R-11 by manufacturer or plumbing contractor. (See discussion of solar water heater tank insulation later in this chapter.)
- Hot water distribution piping should be properly laid out and insulated. (See roughing-in section later in this chapter.)
- Dishwashers with booster heaters and washing machines with special low temperature cycles should be provided.
- Burners, resistance coils, and water tanks should be maintained properly for continued efficient operation.
- Tank-type electric water heaters should be metered separately to take advantage of off-peak electricity rates (where locally available), especially when used in conjunction with solar preheating.

Water heater manufacturers also are improving the energy performance of their products. Some are increasing the levels of insulation provided to reduce standby heat loss; others are developing new components for water heating, like the air-to-liquid heat pump pictured in Fig. 11.6. This water heater may be installed as an add-on to existing equipment, or with original equipment, and concentrates heat from indoor air which is transferred to the domestic water circulating through it from the tank.

ELECTRICAL

Electrical components and systems in residential construction provide lighting and power for heating and cooling equipment, electrical controls, and various appliances. Builders should equip their buildings with energy efficient electrical products to offer reduced operating expenses to buyers.

Fig. 11.6 One type of air to water heat pump designed to heat domestic water

Lighting

Depending on the specific building design, solar construction can increase the level of natural daylighting provided to interior spaces. Clerestories, dormers, skylights, and large windows admit solar radiation as light which, when it strikes interior surfaces, is converted to heat. Natural lighting eliminates the need for electrical lighting during daylight hours, even on cloudy days. Electrical lighting fixtures provided for use when natural lighting is insufficient should provide appropriate levels of illumination for various tasks throughout the house, and should utilize low energy incandescent or fluorescent bulbs with reflectors or diffusers. Avoid using recessed lighting fixtures, especially in upper ceilings where they protrude into the attic; these fixtures are limited in their range of illumination, and are sources of heat loss, and air and moisture leakage.

Heating Equipment and Electrical Controls

Electricity also powers various components of wood, oil, gas, and coal fired heating systems (i.e., burners, blowers, pumps, valves, and dampers), as well as electric resistance baseboard, radiant panels, and storage electric equipment. Strategically placed thermostatic controls activate or deactivate the generation and delivery of heat to the portions of the house in which they are located when the temperature there is either below or above the desired setting. Thermostatic controls can be either unit mounted on electric baseboard components, or wall mounted. If wall mounted thermostats are used, avoid placing them on exterior walls or in locations where cold air drafts will affect them, such as near exterior doors.

Thermostatic controls that automatically lower nighttime settings should be used to reduce heating costs; these components operate on a 24-hour clock and can be set by the occupants. Automatic setback thermostats are recommended for use with all types of heating systems except heat pumps. Thermostatic controls also are used to control solar water heating equipment and are discussed later in this chapter.

Appliances

Energy efficient models of all major appliances currently are available from a variety of manufacturers. Builders can choose from a selection of colors and capacities, while providing equipment that requires far less energy to operate than has been the standard. Among the energy efficient features included with these appliances are:

- Automatic washers: cold wash settings, cold rinse settings
- Clothes dryers: variable temperature settings
- Refrigerators and freezers: increased insulation levels, magnetic door gaskets for positive seal, natural draft condensers (eliminates electric fan)
- Dishwashers: short wash cycles which reduce hot water usage; cool dry cycle which uses fan for speed drying, rather than electric heater; booster heaters that allow lower tank temperature settings.

ROUGHED-IN DUCTWORK, PIPING, AND WIRING

Ductwork, piping, and wiring are roughed-in at various stages of construction; depending on the specific building design, this work may be scheduled to occur during preparation for concrete slab floors, and after the exterior shell has been enclosed (before insulation, vapor barrier, and interior finishes are applied). Installation of these components affects the resistance of the exterior walls to air leakage and heat conduction, the movement of moisture through the shell, and the efficiency of heat and hot water distribution. They should be laid out and installed both to minimize their impact on the building's structural and thermal performance and to improve their efficiency.

While their impact on the performance of the shell is not as critical as elsewhere, components installed in or beneath concrete slab floors must be laid out carefully to assure proper placement, especially where they protrude from the slab at designated locations. Double-check the layout and heights of components coming up through the slab, and ensure their stability prior to pouring the concrete. This phase of construction must be built right the first time. Components typically roughed-in at this stage include:

- exterior makeup air feeds for combustion
- plumbing, heating, and electrical distribution lines
- radiant heat distribution components.

Wherever possible, avoid cast-in-place plumbing, heating, and electrical components which are difficult to maintain. When this approach is selected, be sure to provide utility sleeves or conduit for plumbing and electrical lines that allow future replacements. Distribution piping or ductwork used to transport solar heat, domestic hot water, or warm air to specific delivery points should be insulated from the slab and the gravel bed with pipe or duct insulation suitable for use below grade. The high cost of these materials may influence the builder to seek other alternatives for these components.

Plumbing, heating, and electrical lines that run through the wood frame walls, floors, and ceilings of the exterior shell may impair the effectiveness of the insulation and vapor barrier by taking up space within the cavities and by penetrating through the interior finish at various locations. When the insulation and vapor barriers are installed after lines are run, more time and care will be required to insulate properly behind the roughed-in components, and to seal their penetration through the vapor barrier (Fig. 11.7).

Piping and ductwork placed within exterior framing also will be subject to heat loss or freezing, which reduces their efficiency and may even cause damage to the building. Builders should review the layout and installation of those components located in the exterior shell with subcontractors, to help minimize the impact on previous work, reduce the difficulty of subsequent

HVAC, PLUMBING, ELECTRICAL, AND SOLAR DHW   209

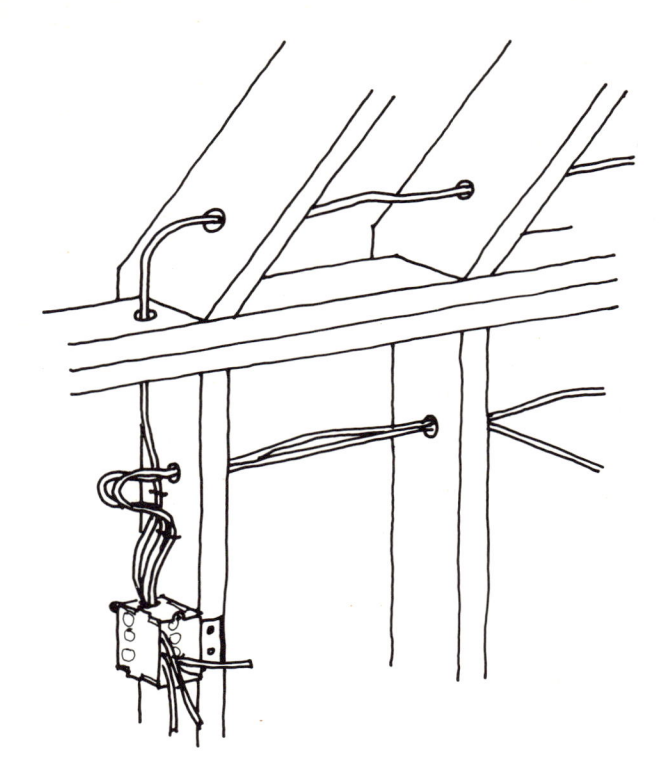

THE ISSUE:

CUTTING ACROSS INSULATION CAVITIES MAKES INSULATING MORE DIFFICULT AND COMPROMISES R-VALUE

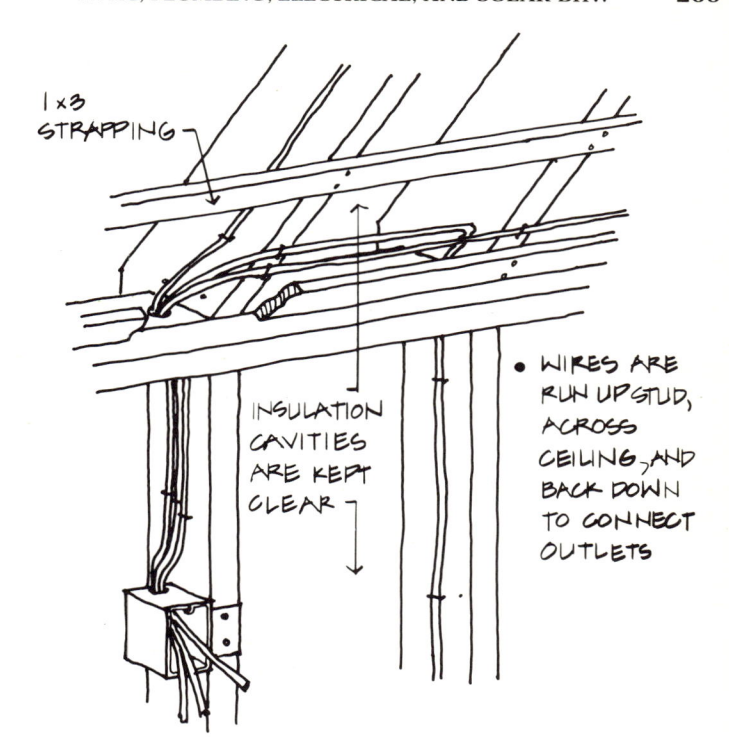

REMEDY:

USE OF CEILING STRAPPING ENABLES WIRES TO RUN ACROSS UNDERSIDE OF RAFTERS OR CEILING JOISTS. MAKE ALL CROSS FRAMING RUNS HERE RATHER THAN THROUGH THE MIDDLE OF MEMBERS. ALTHOUGH SLIGHTLY MORE WIRE IS USED, DRILLING IS MINIMIZED AND CEILINGS CAN BE SMOOTHER.

- 1×3 STRAPPING
- INSULATION CAVITIES ARE KEPT CLEAR
- WIRES ARE RUN UP STUD, ACROSS CEILING, AND BACK DOWN TO CONNECT OUTLETS

Fig. 11.7 Running electric lines to improve effectiveness of a building's insulation

work, and prevent problems from occurring after the building is occupied. Changes in the layout of roughed-in distribution systems, to remove as many of these components from the exterior shell as possible, should be considered. In some cases, new components that reduce the need to penetrate the shell may be used.

The following recommendations apply to the installation of HVAC, plumbing, electrical, and solar DHW distribution lines installed in the exterior shell:

- Heating and cooling ducts should be joined together tightly, and joints lapped with duct tape to reduce leakage.
- All heating and cooling air ducts, hot water piping, and solar heat transfer piping should be well insulated, as illustrated in Fig. 11.8. Table 11.1 compares insulation materials used for these purposes.

Fig. 11.8 Insulate all heating and cooling air ducts, hot water piping, and solar heat transfer piping.

Table 11.1
Comparison of pipe insulation materials and application techniques

		Application			
Material	Type of adhesive	Underground	Exterior	Interior	Workability
Closed cell foams usually 6' lengths pre-slit or unslit wall thicknesses from ¼" (R-1 to R-4)	Contact cement, tape secure cut joints	If in *waterproof* jacket	If in weatherproof jacket, or protective paint	Suitable	Very workable Easily formed around fittings and components
Glass fiber usually 3' lengths pre-slit in a variety of wall thicknesses	Seal sealing tape, staples secure paper jacket	Same as above	Same as above	Suitable	Relatively workable Easy to cut around components large outside diameter may cause space restriction.
Rigid foams (Urethane) usually 3' lengths pre-slit with a 1" wall thickness (R-6)	Vinyl tape, PVC cement, and staples secure thin PVC jacket	Available in PVC pipe for use below grade	If protected from ultraviolet radiation and moisture	Suitable Fire protection required	Less workable Cuts made with hack saw Dust creates adhesive problem Pre-formed fittings make for very good appearance
Glass fiber duct insulation	Duct tape and contact cement or self-sealing tape, secure vinyl jacket	Not advised		Suitable Especially good for DHW tanks	Very workable Duct tape may not hold in long term

- Avoid running lines through unheated crawl spaces. When this is necesssary, components must be well insulated.
- Utility penetrations through walls, floors, and roofs must be sealed properly against air and moisture movement.
- Penetrations of ductwork, piping, and wiring through the vapor barrier should be sealed carefully with duct tape (Fig. 11.9).
- If components are roughed-in or changed after insulation and vapor barrier have been installed, the plumber or electrician must replace or repair any materials damaged as a result of his or her work.

Problems associated with plumbing, heating, and electrical distribution components placed within the framing of the exterior shell can be avoided by changing the layout of these systems, or by using products that do not require penetrating the vapor barrier in their installation. Following are recommendations for making these changes:

- Locate plumbing, heating, and electrical distribution lines within interior utility chases and partitions (Fig. 11.10).
- Insulate domestic hot water and solar heat transfer piping as discussed in the preceding section.

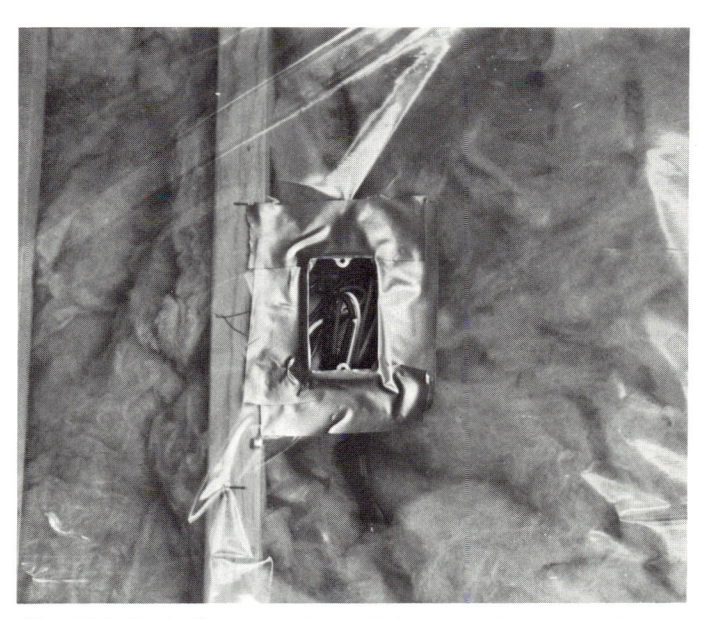

Fig. 11.9 Seal all penetrations of the vapor barrier with duct tape.

- Utilize flour mounted electrical outlets or surface mounted electrical strips for service along exterior walls (Fig. 11.11).

HVAC, PLUMBING, ELECTRICAL, AND SOLAR DHW

SOLAR DHW

The selection and installation of solar water heating equipment follows the same general guidelines for selecting and installing conventional HVAC, plumbing, and electrical components. Solar DHW systems chosen must be suitable for use under specific climatic conditions, and sized to meet a predetermined portion of the total expected hot water requirement of the building's occupants. Information on system design is best obtained from local suppliers, who also should be able to provide an estimated cost and performance analysis for their equipment when used in specific applications. Chapter 6 discusses various generic types of systems used in residential solar construction.

Selecting Components

Solar DHW system components are generally available in two forms, commercially available and site-built systems.

Commercially Available Kits

Solar water heater kits consist of components produced by several companies but assembled by one company (a solar collector or water heater tank manufacturer, for example), and sold as integrated packages (Fig. 11.12). Many of the components supplied with these kits are standard off-the-shelf products, while others (such as differential thermostatic controls and flat plate collectors) have been produced specifically for solar applications. These systems are especially suitable for retrofit installations. Among the factors that should be considered in selecting commercially manufactured components are:

- strength, durability, and warranty of all components
- efficiency of heat transfer
- appearance of collectors
- ease of assembly and stability of collector mounting details and hardware
- ease of assembly and practicality of collector plumbing connections
- simplicity of system operation
- expected maintenance of equipment
- installed cost
- compliance with local building, plumbing, and electrical codes.

Commercially available kits generally include solar heat collectors, storage tank, heat transfer fluid, and heat

Fig. 11.10 Whenever possible locate plumbing and electrical lines within interior partitions.

Fig. 11.11 Surface mounted electrical strip

212 MATERIALS, DETAILS, AND TECHNIQUES OF SOLAR CONSTRUCTION

Fig. 11.12 Solar water heater kit delivered to a job site

exchanger (depends on type of system), differential thermostatic "controls" and sensors, circulating pumps, and various air elimination and fluid expansion components. The materials supplied by the installer in this case include copper tubing, fittings, valves, gauges, pipe insulation, additional tank insulation, hangers, and supports. If the collectors are to be installed on a roof, wall, or ground mounted rack, materials with which to build the rack may be supplied by either the manufacturer or the installing contractor.

Components supplied as a package purchased from one source usually include product warranties written by each manufacturer. Builders should become familiar with the specific warranty provisions set forth by the manufacturers in order to understand fully the protection (or lack of protection) offered for systems under consideration.

Site-built Systems

Site-built solar water heaters are similar to commercially available kits, except that they are built at the site rather than in a factory. One of the best applications for site-built solar heat collectors is on new buildings. Properly constructed site-built solar collectors can perform as efficiently as premanufactured collectors; if purchased and installed carefully, they also can be less expensive and more attractive because they avoid the added-on appearance of collectors built in the factory (Fig. 11.13).

All of the other components used in these systems are the same as those used in the solar DHW kits. In this case the installing contractor is the collector manufacturer, who supplies all of the components used in building the collectors into the roof, including insulation, absorber plates, glazing materials, sealants, and fasteners. The installer is also responsible for providing all other components and materials necessary to assemble the particular type of system selected. Some components may be purchased from specialized distributors, including the insulation, absorber plates, glazings, differential thermostatic controls and sensors, and solar storage tanks. Other components and materials, such as pumps, copper tubing, fittings, valves, gauges, pipe insulation, tank insulation, hangers, and supports, may be obtained through conventional plumbing and heating wholesalers.

Among the factors that should be considered in selecting materials and details from which to assemble site-built collectors are:

- spacing between rafters or trusses

Fig. 11.13 Site-built solar water heater

- absorber plate materials and coatings, dimensions, and plumbing connections
- glazing materials, sealants, and fasteners
- flashing materials and details
- ease of installation and maintenance
- efficiency of heat transfer
- strength and durability of all materials
- appearance of collectors
- installed costs
- compliance with local building and plumbing codes.

Components supplied by subcontractors for site-built installations should be protected by individual warranties. The collectors may be limited to the coverage for workmanship provided by the installer, although they also may include a warranty from the absorber manufacturer.

Selecting a Subcontractor

Builders must select not only properly sized and long-lasting equipment, but also an experienced subcontractor to install it. Subcontractors who install solar water heaters may be specialized solar contractors or plumbing and heating contractors, but they should have proven experience with solar DHW systems, and offer good quality workmanship and reliable service. Even the best equipment will perform poorly if installed improperly.

Good installers must be qualified in a variety of trade skills. In addition to knowledge of solar energy theory, they also must have experience in general construction, including plumbing, heating, electrical, roofing, and carpentry. Subcontractors also must be licensed to secure the building, plumbing, and electrical permits required by local regulations. Depending on these restrictions, solar DHW installations may be completed by a single subcontractor, or may require several people to complete specialized portions of the work. The latter situation will make careful scheduling of the installation more important. Besides appropriate licensing, builders should also require:

- certificates of insurance
- description of work
- statement of estimated costs
- scheduled time period of work
- payment schedule
- warranty statement
- service contract proposal

Solar DHW installations can be subcontracted either as part of the total plumbing and heating job, or separately, depending on the availability and scope of qualified contractors. Many of the problems encountered are with contractors installing their first system. Builders should visit at least one system installed by a potential subcontractor, and check references for other installations. Do not assume that any subcontractor can install a solar water heater successfully the first time he or she tries. If you would like to continue working with reliable plumbing and heating subcontractors who have not yet installed their first solar DHW systems, you may decide to let them gain experience on upcoming projects. It should be noted that the first solar installations for which these subcontractors are responsible will, and should, take longer than subsequent installations, or than if the work was done by experienced solar contractors.

Most of the work required during the actual installation of solar DHW systems will be familiar to experienced plumbing and heating subcontractors; areas that may be unfamiliar to them include: determining site feasibility (See Chapter 6), system layout, roof work, insulating supply and return piping, and system startup and operation.

System Layout

The decisions regarding system layout must balance input from three main areas of concern: location of collectors, pipe runs from the collectors to the mechanical room, and arrangement of components in the mechanical room. The exact location of the solar heat collectors will help determine the layout of the rest of the system. The length and location of pipe runs connecting the collectors with the domestic water storage can influence the efficiency and operation of the system, and should be planned carefully.

Collectors

Collectors may be located on the roof, on a wall mounted rack, or on a ground mounted rack (Fig. 11.14). Collectors mounted on the roof should receive adequate direct solar radiation and avoid interference with other roof penetrations or flashings (Fig. 11.15). Also they should be placed in a position that will allow secure fastening to roof framing, access for pipe penetrations, minimal build-up of water, snow and ice, protection from wind loads, and an aesthetically pleasing appearance.

Additional considerations for awning and ground mounted collectors include:

- Awning mounted arrays should not obstruct window view or operation, or cause unwanted shade.

Fig. 11.14 Typical locations for solar collectors

- Location should present minimum safety hazard.
- Location should minimize the potential for damage to the collectors from ice and snow falling from the roof.

Pipe Runs
Insulated pipes run from collectors installed on roofs, walls, or ground mounted racks should enter the building shell as soon as possible through properly sealed penetrations, in order to reduce the length of runs outside. Even well insulated pipes lose a considerable amount of heat between the collectors and storage, especially if they are exposed to ambient temperatures.

Pipe runs for solar water heaters, along with other plumbing, should be located in interior partitions and chases in new construction, or in closets and utility rooms in retrofits. This reduces the rate of heat loss from these lines by avoiding the cooler temperatures of exterior walls, and leaves the wall cavities open for more complete insulation.

Mechanical components
Although manufacturers and designers will specify the exact schematic plan, actual layout of components in the mechanical area is defined by the installing subcontractor, and by the space available for insulated pipes and components. Storage tanks should be located for ease of connection to collector piping, cold water inlet,

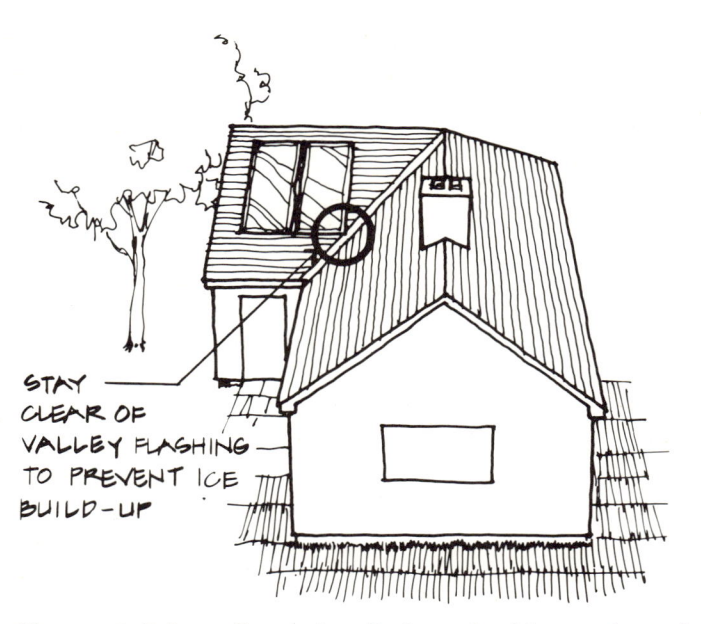

Fig. 11.15 Solar collector installations should stay clear of roof flashings.

Fig. 11.16 Prepackaged solar components save time during the installation but cost more than components purchased separately.

hot water outlet, and auxiliary energy sources (electricity, gas, oil). The layout of all components in this area should be compact, yet allowing sufficient space for ease of maintenance, and inspection of components. Several component packages are available, as pictured in Fig. 11.16, that save time in installation and space in the mechanical areas. Builders should become familiar with installation details so they prepare their buildings for the system, schedule the phases of installation, and supervise the work knowledgeably.

Scheduling

In new construction, the solar DHW system installation must interface with the progress of other work. Installation sequence depends on the status and type of roof construction, walls, interior partitions and chases, electrical work, and domestic plumbing. As the building shell is completed the collector supply and return lines may be roughed-in, pressure tested, and insulated at the same time that other plumbing components are installed. Sensor wires running between the collectors and the controller are also roughed-in at this stage.

The installation of the mechanical components and storage tank can start whenever the mechanical area is ready. Completion of this phase must await the installation of the collectors, electrical service, cold water supply, and hot water distribution to the fixtures and appliances. Roof mounted solar heat collectors must be built or installed either while the finish roofing is applied or after it has been completed, depending on specific construction details and whether they are site-built or premanufactured. For wall or ground mounted applications, builders generally use premanufactured collectors which can be installed as soon as the racks have been constructed and fastened to the wall framing or concrete footings.

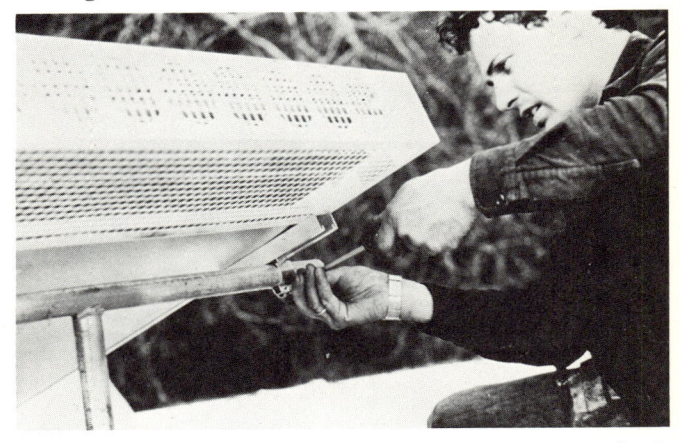

Fig. 11.17 Collector mounting configurations vary with the manufacturer.

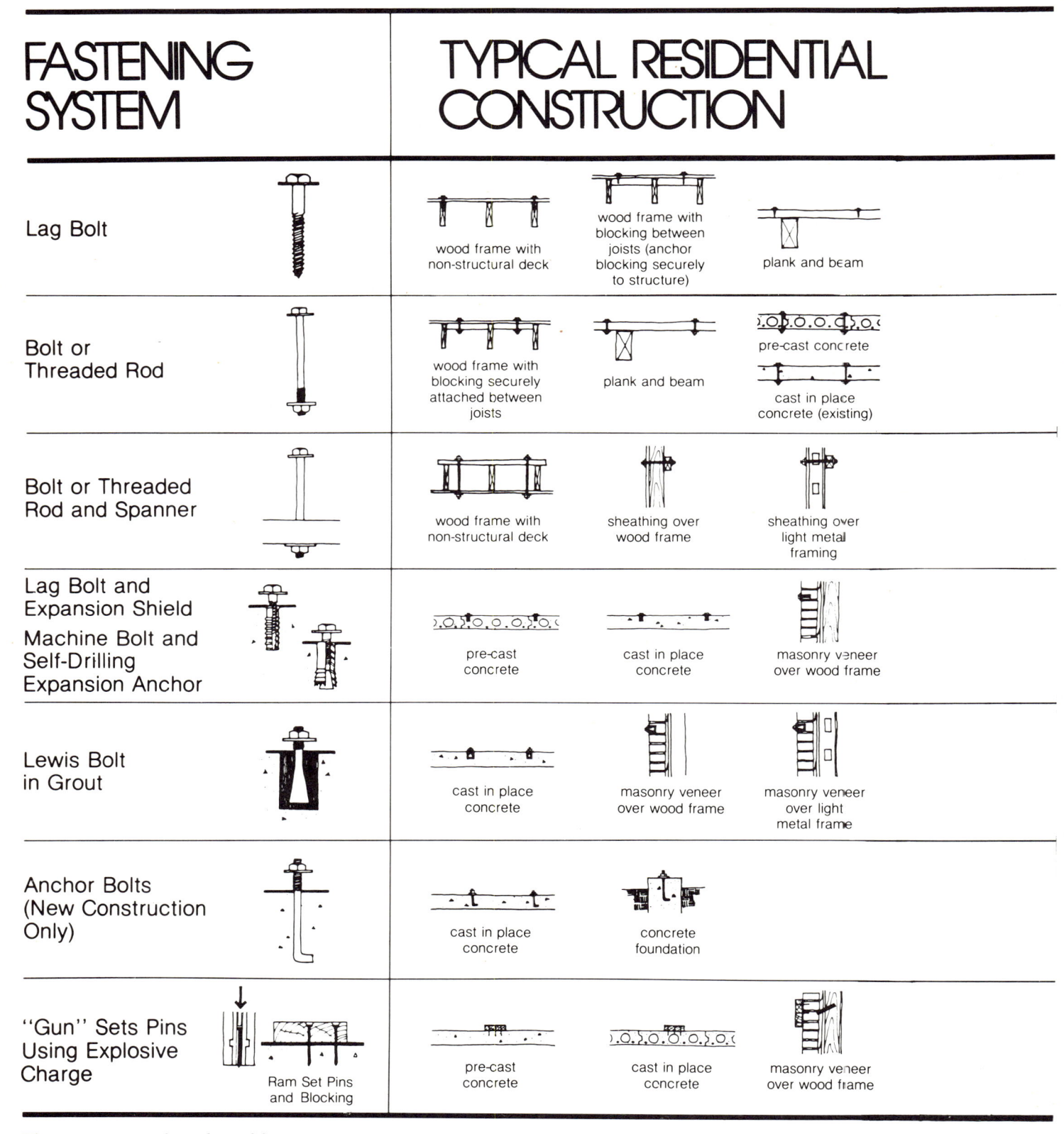

216　MATERIALS, DETAILS, AND TECHNIQUES OF SOLAR CONSTRUCTION

FASTENING SYSTEM		TYPICAL RESIDENTIAL CONSTRUCTION		
Lag Bolt		wood frame with non-structural deck	wood frame with blocking between joists (anchor blocking securely to structure)	plank and beam
Bolt or Threaded Rod		wood frame with blocking securely attached between joists	plank and beam	pre-cast concrete / cast in place concrete (existing)
Bolt or Threaded Rod and Spanner		wood frame with non-structural deck	sheathing over wood frame	sheathing over light metal framing
Lag Bolt and Expansion Shield / Machine Bolt and Self-Drilling Expansion Anchor		pre-cast concrete	cast in place concrete	masonry veneer over wood frame
Lewis Bolt in Grout		cast in place concrete	masonry veneer over wood frame	masonry veneer over light metal frame
Anchor Bolts (New Construction Only)		cast in place concrete	concrete foundation	
"Gun" Sets Pins Using Explosive Charge	Ram Set Pins and Blocking	pre-cast concrete	cast in place concrete	masonry veneer over wood frame

Fig. 11.18 Typical residential fastening systems.

SITUATIONS	CHARACTERISTICS OF FASTENING SYSTEM	
sheathing over wood frame / masonry veneer over wood frame	• good holding power • must be attached to structural member—sheathing attachment not reliable in long term • if underside of structure is accessible, blocking can be installed giving greater freedom in locating mounts	
sheathing over wood frame / masonry veneer over wood frame / solid masonry or block wall	• excellent holding power—limited only by strength of member to which it is attached • both ends of bolt must remain accessible to permit loosening of nut and removal of collectors	• when tightening nuts, care is necessary so as not to deform construction (such as compressing a masonry veneer wall)
masonry veneer over wood frame / masonry veneer over light metal frame	• excellent holding power • spanner serves two functions: makes location of mounting points more flexible reinforces individual structural members	• since spanner will be visible on the inside, its application is limited to surfaces that will remain unfinished • when tightening nuts, care is necessary so as not to deform construction (such as pulling sheathing or masonry veneer out of line)
masonry veneer over light metal framing / solid masonry or block wall	• good holding power if installed correctly • quality of workmanship is critical to strength of connection • self-drilling type simplifies installation	note: masonry veneer is not designed to resist heavy pulling loads
solid masonry (not hollow core block)	• good holding power if installed correctly • quality of workmanship very important to strength of connection • not feasible in hollow core block or plank	note: masonry veneer is not designed to resist heavy pulling loads
	• excellent holding power • new construction only	note: masonry veneer is not designed to resist heavy pulling loads
masonry veneer over light metal frame / solid masonry or block wall	• pins set with special gun • although individual pins have variable holding power, numerous pins used to attach blocking, pad, or other broad shape form unit with good holding power • attached block forms base to which	another fastening system can be attached • ram set threaded studs are also available, however, their individual holding power is variable; they should not be relied upon to resist concentrated loads

218 MATERIALS, DETAILS, AND TECHNIQUES OF SOLAR CONSTRUCTION

System Installation

The variety in available types of solar DHW equipment, and the differences in building materials and techniques throughout the country, make it difficult to present all system installation details. This section, therefore, focuses on typical materials, details, and techniques used to complete the portions of the solar installation that may be least familiar to builders and subcontractors. Specific installation procedures provided by equipment manufacturers should be followed closely to assure proper system performance and to stay within the protection of warrantees. This discussion deals primarily with mechanical solar DHW systems that utilize roof mounted, flat plate collectors, and covers:

- premanufactured collector installation
- site built collector construction
- insulated pipe runs
- system controls
- maintenance and troubleshooting

Additional details at the end of this section present options for construction of wall and ground mounted racks, as well as for installation of passive solar water heaters.

Premanufactured Collector Installation

Premanufactured collectors typically are installed on a finished roof surface in both new construction and retrofit applications. They may be installed parallel to the roof pitch, or on a rack used to adjust their tilt on shallow or flat roofs. With either method, the collectors or racks must be securely fastened to the roof framing, and penetrations made through the finish surface must be sealed properly.

Collector mounting details and hardware vary with the manufacturer; some of the approaches used are presented in Fig. 11.17. Bolts, lag screws, or threaded rod used to connect the collectors to the roof framing should be resistant to corrosion and, along with the collector components, must hold the collectors solidly in place under extreme conditions of temperature and moisture, as well as wind and snow loading.

Although most residential framing techniques used in roof construction are strong enough to carry the additional collector loads, builders should have roof framing plans approved by building officials prior to construction. Any changes or additions required relate more to the collector fastening systems than to the structural support of dead and live loads, and may include the installation of solid blocking between rafters or trusses, or spanners nailed to the inside of the roof framing. The

Fig. 11.19 Parallel mounted collectors must be raised off of the roofing to allow moisture movement and ventilation of the roof materials.

selection of a specific fastening system depends on the finished ceiling treatment directly behind the collectors, future access to connections, and local building code requirements. Figure 11.18 compares appropriate applications and characteristics of fastening components and details. Framing requirements should be verified by the installing subcontractor to ensure proper location of blocking or spanners. In many cases he or she may install this special framing during the course of the system installation. Collectors or racks should never be fastened solely to the roof sheathing.

Solar heat collectors mounted parallel to sloped roof surfaces should be spaced off the roofing at least one-half inch to allow water to course under the collectors and, most importantly, to allow air to circulate behind them. This air movement allows the roof to breathe and helps prevent the rotting of wood or asphalt shingles and sheathing materials. Figure 11.19 illustrates the means of achieving this air space through the use of racks, or mounting legs. The optimum collector height off the roof may be influenced by the height of roof flashings through which supply and return pipes are run, as discussed later in this section.

Roof surface penetrations made for collector or rack mounting fasteners must be either sealed carefully with a durable caulk or mastic, or made above the plane of the roof. The use of a flashed mounting shim allows the collectors or racks to remain in place during reroofing, whereas other methods of mounting require removal of the array. If sealants are used here or in any other exterior locations, they must be able to withstand extreme conditions of temperature, moisture, expansion and contraction of system components, and ultraviolet radiation without losing their ability to seal.

Racks used to hold collectors at the proper tilt or orientation should be constructed from strong and durable materials, such as galvanized or aluminum channel. Metals selected for this use should also be compatible

HVAC, PLUMBING, ELECTRICAL, AND SOLAR DHW

Fig. 11.20 Collector racks may either be supplied by the manufacturer or built by the contractor.

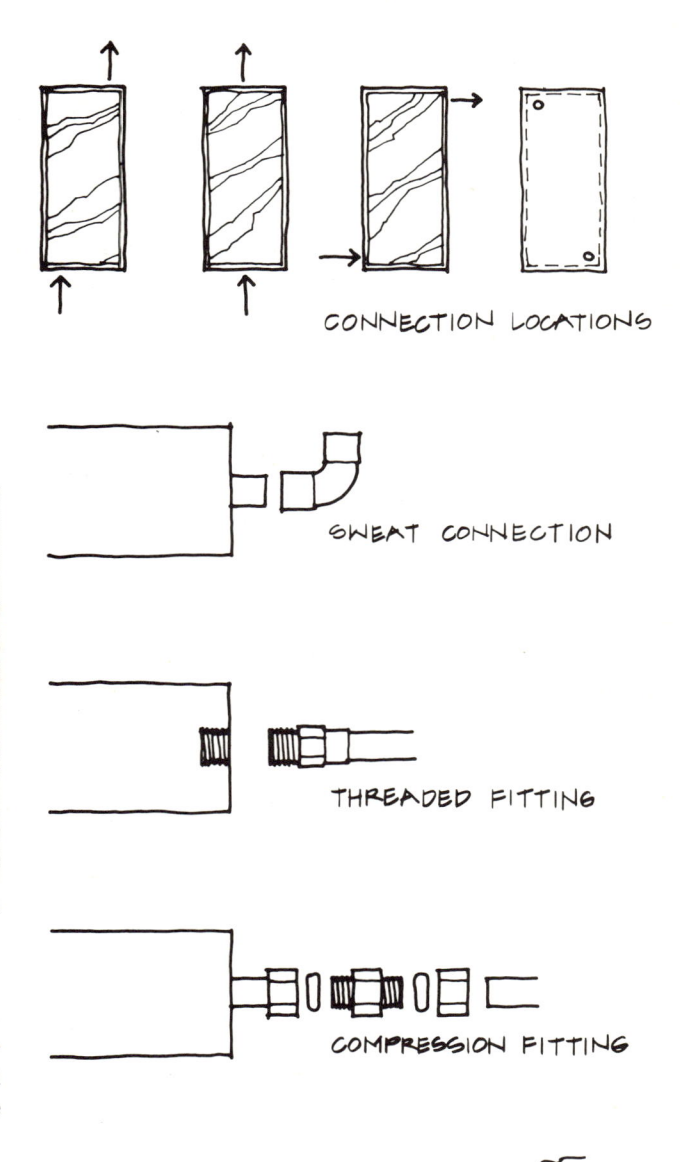

Fig. 11.21 Many types of plumbing connections are required for different solar collectors.

with, or isolated from, metal collector frames and fastening components to avoid galvanic corrosion. Racks can be either built by the installer or purchased with the solar DHW kit (Fig. 11.20).

The location and types of plumbing connections provided with commercially available collectors also depend on the manufacturer. The most common locations for these connections are at the ends of the collectors. Collectors with end connections require more external piping than for side-to-side connections; they should be used only for systems that rely on draining for freeze protection, or with freon-circulating systems where piping must be carefully pitched. The use of side-to-side connections will reduce not only the amount of external piping (and heat loss), but also the amount of copper tubing, fittings, pipe insulation, and time required to install the collectors. Side-to-side connections also may be used in draining systems by tilting the array towards the supply pipe.

Figure 11.21 illustrates typical plumbing connections and fittings used to join collectors to one another and to their supply and return lines. The type of connection used during the initial installation may affect the sequence of installation and the ease or difficulty of collector maintenance or repair, and should be considered during equipment selection and system layout. The collectors should be connected to supply and return lines as suggested by the manufacturer to ensure proper

Fig. 11.22 Standard stack flashing used for solar supply and return piping.

flow of heat transfer fluid through the entire array. If improperly installed, the fluid may be distributed unevenly through the collectors, resulting in inefficient performance.

In order to minimize external pipe runs, collector supply and return lines should emerge from and re-enter the building as close as possible to the collectors. Penetrations through the roof must be flashed properly to provide a long-lasting waterproof seal. Standard roof flashings typically used with vent stacks also can be used to flash insulated solar system piping. When ¾-inch copper tubing insulated with 1-inch thick pipe insulation is run through a common 3-inch roof flashing, the neoprene boot fits snugly around the 3-inch outside diameter pipe insulation to create a tight seal (Fig. 11.22).

The vertical distance between the roof surface and the top of the flashings may determine the optimum height off the roof at which to set the solar collectors on their mounting legs or racks. If set properly, the insulated supply pipe can pass through the flashing, make a 90 degree turn towards the first collector and, at the same height as the collector fitting, run directly into it. The same technique can be used to run the insulated return line out of the last collector and down through the other roof flashing. This approach saves time and materials and creates a neat, compact appearance which adds to the quality of the installation.

Site-built Collector Construction

Site-built solar collectors typically are integrated into the framing and finish surface of a building's southerly roof. Since they form an important part of the exterior shell, details must be designed accurately and glazing and flashing materials carefully selected and installed to prevent leaks from occurring.

When collectors are built into the roof in this manner, the rafters are used as the enclosures; the glazing system may be flush with, or slightly raised above, the finish roofing, and the back of the absorber can be insulated separately or in conjunction with the roof insulation. Pipe runs that connect site-built collectors with the components in the mechanical area should be installed according to the standards for all solar heat transfer piping.

The sequence of collector construction depends on the specific design of the collectors, and their integration into the finish roofing. In most cases the glazing and flashing systems must be installed as the roofing materials are applied. Also sequence is influenced by the techniques used to install and connect the absorbers. If the absorbers are installed from outside the building, they should be in place, connected, and pressure tested before the glazing is installed and, therefore, prior to finishing the roof. Some contractors install the absorbers from inside the building. If this approach is used, the glazing and flashing system and finish roofing can be completed independently. An important factor in the selection of one of these methods is future accessibility to the absorbers for maintenance and repair. If the collectors are built into an unfinished attic roof, and access from inside is assured, builders may decide to install the absorbers from the inside. If, however, the collectors are built into a finished vaulted ceiling, or inaccessible from the inside location, then the absorbers should be installed from the outside, and provisions for future main-

Fig. 11.23 Framed opening for site built collectors.

tenance should be included in the glazing and flashing system.

Most site-built collectors are integrated into the roof framing, so the roof pitch determines the collector tilt. Roofs (or sections) designed to include site-built collectors should be built within 5 degrees plus or minus of the site latitude.

Rafters that will be within the arrray should be relatively dry, straight, and accurately spaced. Absorber plate or glazing dimensions can be accommodated by framing an opening that creates the necessary enclosure and glazing supports (Fig. 11.23). However, the availability of 22½-inch-wide absorbers and 23-inch glass or 24- and 48-inch-wide plastics allows the collector to be assembled without disrupting normal rafter or truss layout of 24 inches on center. If rafters or trusses are spaced on 24-inch centers, the only extra framing necessary is boxing-in the length of each absorber space at the top and bottom of the array. These framing members create glazing support and nailing surfaces for roofing and flashings, and isolate the collectors from convective air movement within the roof section.

The actual construction of the absorber plates is best left to specialized manufacturing companies. There are a variety of absorber designs built with different materials and coatings, at a range of prices. These components may be obtained from specialized suppliers, or directly from companies that use them in premanufactured solar collectors. The size of the absorber may influence the roof framing layout; the most cost effective sizes are those that require little or no framing change.

Absorbers used for site-built collectors may either be expanded or extruded tube-in-fin components. Materials used include copper, aluminum, and EPDM (a rubberlike material). While EPDM absorbers are increasing in popularity, copper absorbers still are most commonly used. Absorbers with aluminum fluid passages should be avoided.

The use of absorbers that have side-to-side plumbing connections will save time and materials during installation. These components can be installed either from inside or outside the building, depending on the specific scheduling considerations as described earlier. Absorbers can be connected to one another prior to installation if the rafters have been notched to receive them. Absorbers placed into the notched openings from inside the building remain at the back of the enclosures and may receive undesirable shading from the adjacent rafters. Notches made in these rafters must be reinforced with plywood or metal strapping.

Absorbers installed from outside the building are placed in notches cut into the upper edges of the framing. This leaves the absorber surfaces closer to the glazing, thereby reducing shading from the sides of the collector enclosures. If glazing materials are transparent, this technique will create a better visual appearance.

The glazing system, including the glazing materials, glazing bars or extruded battens, fasteners, flashings, and sealants must be carefully selected and installed. Because they replace a section of finish roofing, these materials must serve as both light transmitting covers and waterproof roof surfaces. Materials selected for this application must be able to withstand ultraviolet radiation, precipitation, and thermal expansion and contraction. In many localities they also must meet guidelines established by building codes for finish roof surfaces.

The glazing materials commonly used for site-built collectors include fully tempered, low iron glass, and fiberglass reinforced polyesters. The characteristics of these materials are described in Chapter 10. Because the collector enclosure can reach relatively high temperatures (350° to 400°F), acrylic and polycarbonate materials usually are avoided in these applications.

Although fully tempered, low iron glass is recommended, any glazing material used depends on the fastening and flashing materials and details to create a weathertight seal. Figure 11.24 presents glazing and flashing details typically used with both glass and fiberglass reinforced polyesters. Glazing systems may utilize commercially available components or site-fabricated components. Flashing details must follow accepted roofing practices, and should be installed in a manner that will not prevent future maintenance or replacement of either absorbers or glazing materials. Metal components used in the glazing and flashing systems must either be compatible with, or insulated from, each other to avoid galvanic corrosion.

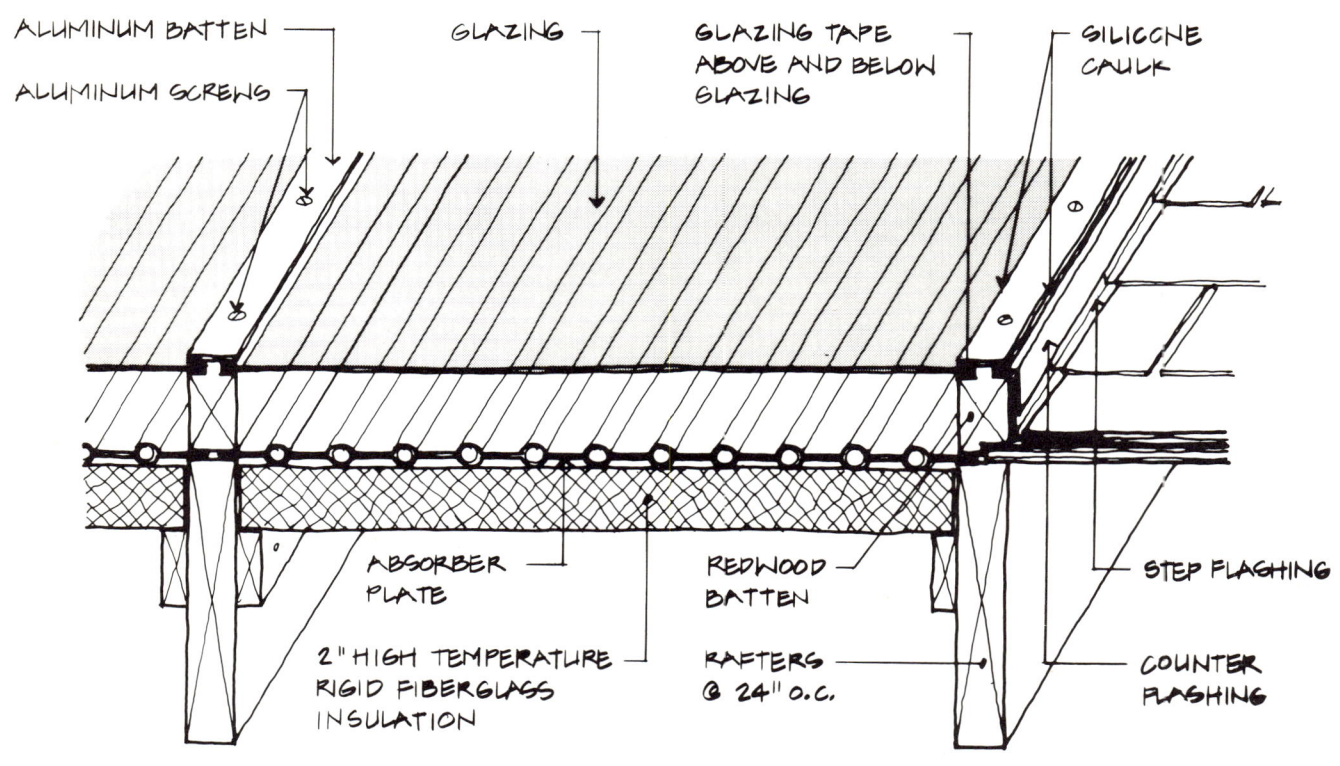

Fig. 11.24 Construction detail for site-built water heater

Rigid board insulations typically used to insulate the backs of collector absorbers include fiberglass, polyurethane, and polyisocyanurate. Depending on the location of the absorber within the rafter cavity, these materials may be either cut to fit snugly between the rafters or applied to the back of the rafters in full sheets. Because the absorbers often reach high temperatures, foam insulations should be isolated from them with a layer of fiberglass insulation. High temperature fiberglass insulation available in 4-foot by 8-foot sheets of 1- and 2-inch thickness can be used directly behind the absorbers without further protection. Collector insulation can be backed by additional roof insulation to increase the R-value in that area. Foams used for this purpose should be covered with a fire resistant interior surface.

Insulated Pipe Runs

The successful transfer of solar heat absorbed at the collectors and carried by the fluid to the storage tank or heat exchanger depends largely on the amount of heat lost through the piping along the way. The effect of this heat loss on overall system efficiency can be significant; therefore, all interior and exterior supply and return pipe runs must be well insulated. These same techniques also apply to hot water pipes used to distribute heat and domestic hot water.

Insulation is applied to piping after all connections in the system have been made, and a pressure test has revealed no leaks. Table 11.1 compares various insulation materials and application techniques. Selection should consider insulative value, availability, durability, workability, and compliance with local building codes. Insulation exposed to weather must be resistant to moisture and ultraviolet radiation, and all joints must be sealed tightly (Fig. 11.25).

System Controls

Proper installation of the differential thermostatic controls used to operate solar water heaters is critical to the correct functioning of the system and its components. Controls must be installed as specified by the system supplier or control unit manufacturer, and installation procedures also must comply with local electrical codes.

Some system packagers install the temperature sensors on the absorber and storage tanks, and prewire the control unit to accept the sensor leads at the job. Others provide controllers and sensors as separate components that must be installed by the subcontractor. When con-

HVAC, PLUMBING, ELECTRICAL, AND SOLAR DHW 223

Fig. 11.25 Insulated supply and return pipes

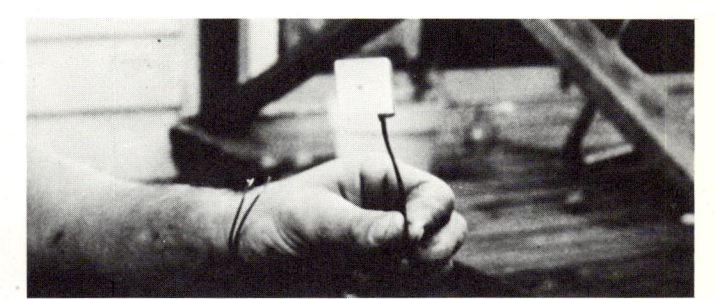

Fig. 11.26 Collector sensor

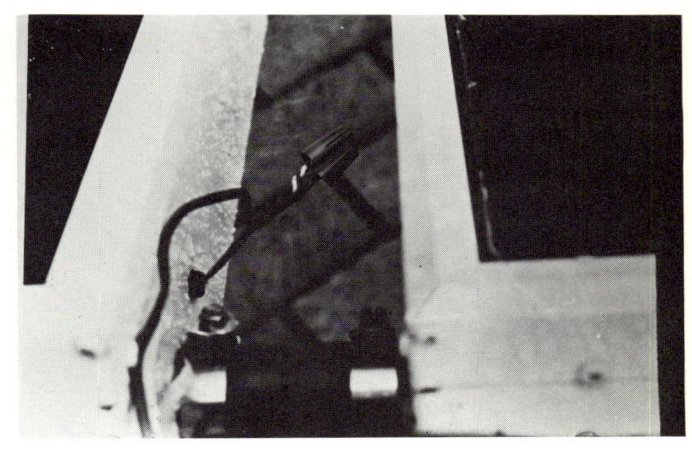

Fig. 11.27 Sensor wiring run with return piping

trollers and sensors are provided as separate components, the following points should be considered.

Collector Sensors
- Follow manufacturer's suggestions for locating and mounting sensors.
- Install sensor as close to the absorber as possible, typically at the return pipe from collector to storage (Fig. 11.26).
- Provide good thermal contact, securely fasten, and insulate the sensor when the pipe is insulated.

Storage sensors
- Locate as specified by the manufacturer, usually on lower third of tank.
- Fasten securely to the side of the tank with epoxy or clip provided behind access panel.

Wire runs
- Use twisted double-lead thermostat wire to minimize induction interference.
- Assure good connection using wire nuts or crimped couplings. Seal wire connections with silicone caulk.
- Indoor wiring can be stapled to interior surfaces, run through electrical conduit, or strapped to pipe insulation.
- Outdoor wiring should be protected from ultraviolet radiation by either running it through conduit or fastening it to the outside of the pipe insulation. Wire can be run with return pipe through roof flashings (Fig. 11.27).

Controller
- Mount close to circulator pump and electrical supply.
- Connect leads from sensor to appropriate terminals and double-check.
- Wire or plug components pump into control unit as specified by manufacturer or local codes.

Maintenance

System maintenance for solar hot water systems consists of regular operational checks and scheduled maintenance. Operational checks usually are performed by the owner/operator. Scheduled maintenance may be performed by either the owner/operator or the installing

Table 11.2
Troubleshooting chart

The following guidelines illustrate troubleshooting procedures in general. Contact component manufacturers for specific information concerning their products. These steps are described by symptom, component, problem, and corrective action, and can save some of the guesswork involved in troubleshooting faulty operation.

Symptom	Component	Problem	Correction
Not enough hot water	Collectors	Improperly faced	Check direction. Face collectors due south.
		Improperly sloped	Check slope, dorm, water, make lat. − or + 5°.
		Partially shaded	Remove shadowing material or move collectors.
		Insufficient area	Increase collector area.
		Unequal flow	If collectors are unequally warm, repurge system to equalize flow, assure reverse return piping layout.
	Differential Thermostatic Controller	Loose or incorrect electrical connections	Check wiring schematic for correct connections, tighten loose wiring.
		Sensors not insulated from surrounding air	Check and insulate.
		Faulty sensors	Dip alternately in hot and cold water to test whether switches start and stop pump.
		Faulty thermostat	Check to see if thermostat contacts close. CAUTION: DO NOT JUMP COMMON AND LOAD TERMINALS TO TEST.
	Tank	Too small	Install second tank.
		Improper electrical connection	Check power source wiring.
		High storage losses	Check insulation and location of tank.
	Piping	Night convection losses	Check piping. Install check-valve if necessary.
		Excessive heat loss	Check insulation.
	Mixing valve	Improperly adjusted	Check adjustment temperature indicator and set higher if necessary.
		Faulty	Replace
Water leak	Collectors	Leak at connections	Check and tighten fittings
		Internal leak	Repair leak or contact manufacturer.
	Relief valves	Set too low	Adjust pressure setting or replace.
		Do not re-seat (close)	Clean seat or replace unit.
		High system pressures	Install pressure reducing valve in water supply line.
Drop in system pressure	Collectors	Slow leak	Inspect and repair or replace.
	Relief valve	Spitting fluid	Inspect and repair or replace adjustable relief valve.
	Air vents	Spitting fluid	Inspect and repair or replace
	Expansion tank	Loss of pressure	Recharge to 12 psi.
	Piping	Leak in heat exchanger	Replace tank
		Leaky joints	Locate and repair.
Noisy system	Piping	Entrapped air	Purge system and install vents as needed at high points.
		Air purge installed backwards	Reverse. Face arrow in direction of flow.
		Pipe vibration	Prevent vibration. Isolate tube from hard surface.
		Air hammer	Install shock suppressor.

Table 11.2 (Continued)

Symptom	Component	Problem	Correction
Noisy system	Air vents	Not working	Check for tight cap. Operate plunger manually. Replace if necessary.
		Insufficient number	Install additional vents at intermediate high points.
	Pump	Air locked	Loosen venting screw in body. Vent air and tighten.
No flow	Collectors	Air locked	Purge system and install vents as necessary.
No flow	Pump	Too small	Check system pumping head and change pump if pump is not adequately large.
		Air locked	Loosen venting screw in body. Vent air and tighten.
		Impeller bound	Loosen impeller screw.
		Installed backwards	Reverse. Check flow direction arrow and reverse if necessary.
		Closed off	Open throttling lever on pump head.
		Installed incorrectly	If installed horizontally, place motor to side. Check pump installation book.
		Low speed on pump	Increase speed to high and check pump size.
	Piping	Air locked	Force purge; install air vents if necessary.
		Too small	Increase piping size or add second pump.
	Vents	Insufficient number	Install additional vents.
		Faulty	At high points not already vented operate vent plunger manually. Replace vent if necessary.
	Shut-off valves	Shut off	Open
	Flow regulator	Clogged	Open and clean out venturi.
		Installed backwards	Check arrow for flow. Reverse if necessary.
Decreasing performance	Collectors	Increased shading	Remove shade or move collectors.
		Dirty	Clean periodically.
		Deterioration of absorber coating	Contact reverse.
Decreasing performance	Piping	Night convection losses.	Install solenoid shut-off valve or thermal loop.
	Tank	Sludge in bottom	Drain water from tank periodically.
System stays on	Differential thermostat controller	Sensors improperly placed	Inspect, fasten securely to surface, cover with insulation.
		Sensors faulty	Inspect, replace.
		Faulty on-off-auto switch setting	Inspect, replace. Check and reset if necessary.
		Wired incorrectly	Check wiring diagram for correct connections.

contractor, as defined in the installation or service contract. Operational checks may include the following:

- Check for leaks at penetrations, pumps, tanks, joints, fittings, valves, etc.
- Check color of intermediate fluid and pressure in intermediate loop.
- Check the valve positions for proper operating position.
- Check operation of solenoid valves.
- Check thermostat settings on differential controller, mixing valve, and backup equipment.
- Check that pressure gauges, thermometers, and flow meters (if installed) are reading in acceptable range.
- Check for proper controller functioning. Is the pump running all night?)
- Check insulation for possible deterioration.
- Check all materials for any unusual degradation, especially at the collector absorber plate.
- Check for continued strength and proper support of all components.
- Check collector sensor contact.

Scheduled maintenance should include all of the above, plus the following:

- Monitor heat transfer fluid quality, and replace if required.
- Remove sediment from strainers and valve filters.
- Lubricate mechanical equipment and motors, according to schedule.
- Drain and flush storage tanks once a year.
- Wash collector cover, if necessary.
- Repressurize system if pressure has dropped below acceptable level.
- Eliminate air by manually venting at vent locations.
- Check and clean heat exchangers.
- Open and reset all temperature/pressure relief valves.

Troubleshooting

Table 11.2 shows a troubleshooting matrix covering symptoms, possible sources of the problem, causes, and recommended corrective action. This matrix will diagnose most problems associated with small residential hot water systems. For further information, contact the manufacturer or system supplier.

CHAPTER 12 INTERIOR FINISHES AND SPECIAL CONSTRUCTION

INTRODUCTION

The installation of interior finishes and specially constructed features represents the last major phase of construction, important because the materials selected as finishes, and the ways in which they are installed, define the aesthetic conditions within the building. Special functional features installed during this phase also must be well built and aesthetically pleasing.

In solar construction, interior finishes and special features may serve energy related functions, so their selection and proper application affect the overall energy efficiency of the building. Finishes applied to concrete slab floors, concrete and masonry walls, and ceilings must be selected for their color and ability to reflect, absorb, conduct, store, and reradiate heat, as well as for their appearance. The selection process may bring builders into contact with previously unfamiliar materials. The evaluation of new materials, details, and techniques should follow the same criteria at this phase as elsewhere in solar construction (Fig. 12.2).

Woodwork details also may be affected by techniques used in solar construction. For example, the use of insulative sheathing either on the inside or outside of walls requires special jamb extensions for doors and windows. Woodwork attached to concrete or masonry requires special fastening techniques, and may also affect the installation sequence.

Scheduling this phase of solar construction is the same as in conventional construction, except where new materials which require special or advance ordering are involved. The finish work moves from one component or area of the building to the next and requires careful scheduling and supervision of subcontractors. Builders must make sure that work done in this phase does not damage work done in preceding stages, especially regarding the vapor barrier and insulation.

For the purposes of our discussion we have organized this phase of construction into the following sequence:

- Interior finishes—colors, floors, walls, ceilings, woodwork
- Special construction—movable insulation, shading devices.

INTERIOR FINISHES

Colors

Solar radiation transmitted through glazed areas of south facing walls, skylights, and clerestories is reflected or absorbed by the interior finish surfaces. The degree of reflection or absorption depends on the color and texture of the finish; lighter colors and glossy surfaces reflect more than darker, matte finishes. In addition to affecting the rate of heat absorption, color and texture of interior surfaces near glazed areas also can reduce glare. As discussed throughout this chapter, a variety of standard finish materials and coatings can be used to achieve pleasant finishes and the balanced distribution of sunlight and heat.

Masonry floors used to store solar heat should be medium-dark in color to allow the surface to absorb some of the energy striking it, and reflect the rest deeper into the building where other masonry surfaces are located. The use of very dark colors on floor areas exposed to solar radiation for long periods may cause too much heat absorption in that area, resulting in local-

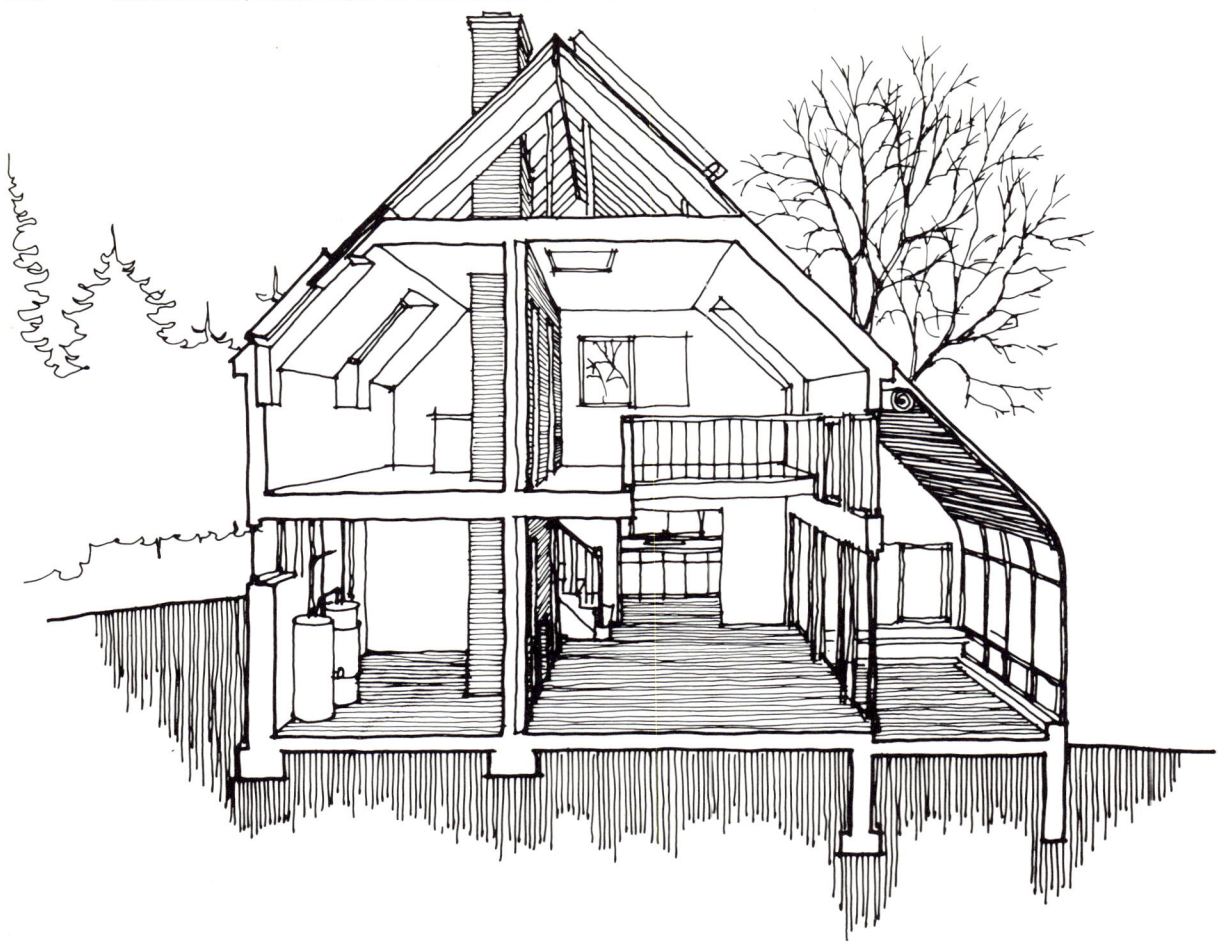

Fig. 12.1 Interior finishes and special construction complete the building.

ized overheating and discomfort. This also applies to wall surfaces.

Masonry walls can be finished with any color. Even light-colored surfaces will absorb 20 to 30 percent of the solar radiation striking them, and will reflect the rest onto other masonry surfaces. This reflection also aids natural daylighting of interior spaces.

Lightweight construction (wood frame partitions) exposed to solar radiation should be light in color to reflect sunlight onto masonry floor or wall surfaces. Dark colored materials that have low heat storage capacities will quickly heat up and begin reradiating heat into the living space during the daytime rather than storing it for use later. This also results in localized overheating and discomfort.

Floor Finishes

Concrete slab floors often are used for thermal storage in solar construction. The type of finish surface and its installation can either aid or impair the absorption, conduction, and reradiation of heat in the slab. Ceramic tiles of varying thicknesses can be bonded to the slab in a portland cement, mortar setting bed, or thin-set bond coat. Sealers and waxes used to protect and preserve tile and brick surfaces should leave nongloss finishes.

Masonry floors typically used in this application include slate, quarry tiles, and paver tiles. All of these materials have some heat storage capacity, determined by color, thickness, surface area, and density, and they will add to the total thermal mass of a building no matter where they are located within the heated space. However, their use in areas exposed to direct solar radiation for long periods should be in conjunction with the added thermal mass of a concrete slab subfloor. If used over wood subflooring alone, these thin materials quickly will reach their limited storage capacity and contribute to overheating.

Since it is important for these products to absorb and conduct heat into the slab subfloor, the contact between the finish surface and the slab is critical. A poor bond between these materials impedes heat conduction-

INTERIOR FINISHES AND SPECIAL CONSTRUCTION   229

- ENHANCE THE PASSIVE SOLAR FUNCTION OF THE BUILDING BY:
  - USING FINISH MATERIALS THAT HAVE THERMAL MASS WHERE POSSIBLE
  - USING DARK COLORS FOR MASSIVE MATERIALS AND LIGHT COLORS FOR NON MASSIVE MATERIALS
  - USING LIGHT COLORS TO ENHANCE NATURAL LIGHTING

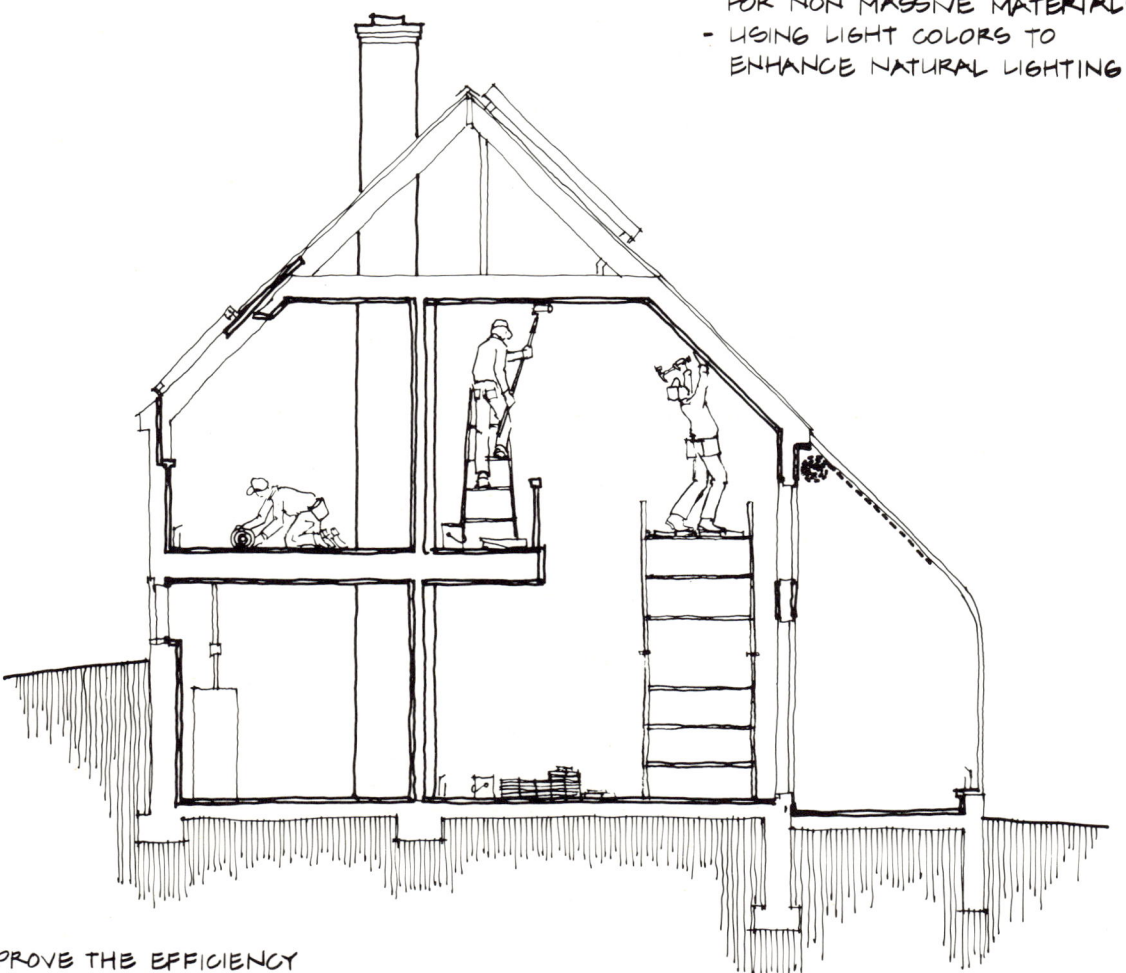

- IMPROVE THE EFFICIENCY OF FIREPLACES BY:
  - PLACING THE CHIMNEY ON THE INTERIOR
  - PROVIDING GLASS DOORS AND EXTERIOR AIR FEEDS
  - PROVIDING AIR OR WATER HEAT EXCHANGER GRATES
  - SUBSTITUTING AN AIRTIGHT WOOD STOVE

- CONTROL SOLAR RADIATION WITH:
  - ADJUSTABLE AWNINGS
  - WINDOW BLINDS OR SHADING
  - MOVABLE WINDOW INSULATION

Fig. 12.2 Energy priorities for interior finishes and special construction

by isolating the finish surface from the slab. Careful selection of the material used to bond the masonry finish to the concrete slab is crucial to the functioning of this floor, both in how the surface wears over time and how well it serves as a means of heat storage and distribution. Because of their ability to conduct heat, mortar and portland cement setting beds, rather than chemical glues and adhesives, should be used. Glues and adhesives insulate the finish surface from the subfloor, thus interrupting the flow of heat in both directions.

The surface of the slab subfloor may determine the best approach to bonding the finish masonry to the concrete. Concrete slabs should be cured before applying the tiles or bricks, and they should be constructed properly using an adequate thickness of concrete and proper reinforcement and drainage techniques. Slabs used for this purpose must also be well insulated following the recommendations presented in Chapter 8.

Mortar setting beds level and adhere the finish surface to the subfloor. If the top of the slab floor is out of level by one-half inch in 10 feet, then a thicker mortar bed will be required to bring the tiles or bricks to a level position. Conventional mortar bed thicknesses of ¾-inch to 1¼-inch may be required in this situation to slow the rate of heat conduction into and out of the slab and reduce its effectiveness. Therefore, it is important for slabs to be relatively level, within one-quarter inch in 10 feet, so that a layer of mortar 1/16-inch to 1/4-inch thick can be used which will improve the conduction of heat between the finish and subfloor. Manufacturers' recommendations concerning the proper temperatures to maintain during application and subsequent curing should be followed carefully.

Tiles or bricks should be set into the mortar and tamped into position to achieve a good bond. After the floor has cured properly, standard materials and techniques may be used in applying the grout. This material may be selected for its visual impact; however, builders should follow the recommendations for color selection as described previously. After the recommended curing time has lapsed, sealers and waxes then can be applied to the floor. Select a finish or technique that provides good protection without a glossy surface.

Masonry floors used for (solar) heat storage should be left exposed to the living space as much as possible. This is especially true in areas close to southerly glazings where direct radiation strikes the floor. Furniture and rugs or carpeting will block the solar radiation and prevent it from being stored for later use. In other areas where sunlight does not fall directly onto the floor, small rugs may be used to soften the impact of the masonry, without having a great effect on its heat flow characteristics. Large carpeted areas over concrete slab floors should be avoided, since they will block the use of the slab for heat storage and reradiation.

Wall Finishes

Concrete and masonry walls are used in solar construction to increase the thermal storage capacity of a building (See Chapters 5 and 9). However, these materials (except brick, perhaps) are not acceptable as interior finish surfaces, and they should be treated with finishing stain, paint, or dyed plaster to improve their appearance and allow heat to be absorbed and reradiated by the wall.

Plaster materials offer the best choice of finish surface for this application. They are available in standard gray or white, and may be dyed to achieve pastels or earth tones or painted to achieve almost any color desired. Plaster can be built-up to cover irregularities in the wall surface, and to fill gaps that will inevitably exist between the concrete or masonry and woodwork (such as window and door casings, chair rails, and baseboards). In addition, the finish top coat can be applied with a trowel, and then tooled or floated to form a variety of textures. Stains and paints can be used alone, but they only color the wall, leaving irregularities, joints, and imperfections visible from the living space. These products should be used to darken the exterior surfaces of thermal storage walls, as described in Chapter 9.

Concrete and masonry walls must be prepared properly to receive the finishes. Some of these preparations should occur shortly after the walls have been constructed, while the concrete and mortar are still uncured. All tie wires should be broken back three-quarters of an inch from the surface, and the resulting holes should be patched with mortar. Ridges and irregularities in concrete and uneven mortar in block walls should be smoothed before the material cures completely. With the plaster finishes, this can be done later.

Prior to finishing, the wall surfaces should be cleaned with muriatic acid and water (one part acid to two parts water), rinsed with water, and allowed to dry. The acid wash dissolves oils left from concrete forms and the rinse washes away the acid and construction dust. When applying any finish, follow the manufacturer's recommendations, especially concerning optimum temperature for application. Wall surfaces to be finished with plaster should be prepared further by applying a liquid bonding agent before the first coat of mortar.

Plaster finish surfaces usually require a preliminary scratch coat of mortar applied with a notched trowel,

INTERIOR FINISHES AND SPECIAL CONSTRUCTION   231

Fig. 12.3 Interior plaster finish on concrete wall

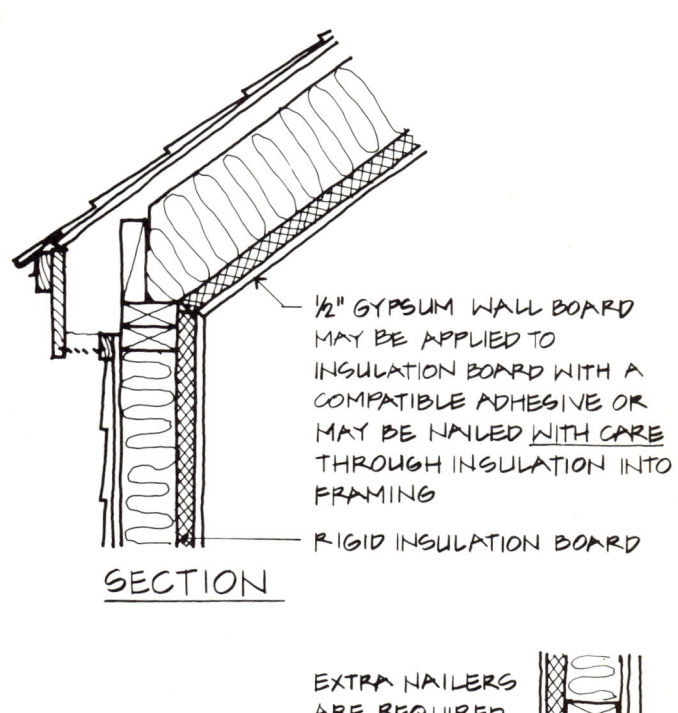

Fig. 12.4 The use of gypsum wall board as fire protection for rigid board insulation applied on the interior

followed by the finish (float) coat (Fig. 12.3). The treatment of the float coat determines the finish color and texture of the wall. Dye may be added to the plaster mix while still dry and the finish surface may be tooled or floated to achieve either a flat sand finish or a stucco appearance. The float coat should be brought up to woodwork already in place or to a predetermined line where woodwork will be installed. If there are large gaps to fill, it is best to build the wall out first in thin coats so that it will not crack, and then apply the float coat.

Some plasters require gradual mist spray curing, while others do not. The temperature and relative humidity inside the building at the time of application influences the need for this, as specified by most manufacturers. After the plaster has dried and cured, cracks may be touched up with more plaster. If the walls are to be painted, allow sufficient time for drying and curing. Latex paints are recommended for use over plaster finish surfaces.

Interior finishes of wood framed walls may not require modification for use in solar construction. However, certain applications of standard finishes increase thermal storage within low mass buildings, and provide fire protection for combustible insulation materials used in the wall cavity.

Multiple layers of gypsum wallboard, an economical way to increase the amount of thermal mass within wood framed buildings, are applied to exterior walls and interior partitions using the same techniques as for single layer applications. However, only the last layer receives corner and edge beads, tape, and joint compound. As each additional layer of gypsum is added, be sure to select properly sized nails or drywall screws. Multiple layers of gypsum will increase the thickness of the wall section and require adjustments in the dimensions of window and door jambs and sills, as discussed later in this chapter. Interior dimensions also will be affected by the added thickness and must be considered in using this technique.

The use of insulative sheathing on interior surfaces may require fire protection in the form of gypsum wallboard, as defined by the insulation manufacturer and local building codes (Fig. 12.4). The fasteners used to attach the gypsum will need to be sized properly according to the combined thickness of the insulation and wallboard. Because the insulation actually brings the gypsum away from the framing, builders must assure proper nailing surfaces for corner and edge beads. Window and door jambs and sills require adjustment to the thicker wall section.

Wood framed walls also may be finished by using new laminates that combine rigid board insulation and gypsum wallboard. Some of these products include an additional bonded layer of composite exterior sheathing. These products are installed during the construction of the shell, and their use saves time when the building enters the finish phase. Special care must be taken to protect these and any other finishes installed while rough carpentry and interior work still is being done.

Ceiling Finishes

Materials used to finish ceilings also play an important role in solar construction. They can reflect sunlight onto other surfaces including masonry walls and floors, or absorb, store, and radiate heat. Air registers installed in ceilings during this phase encourage natural convective air, heat, and moisture circulation to achieve more even comfort levels.

Sunlight entering a building through any of its glazed openings is reflected from surface to surface, bringing sunlight to areas distant from the point at which it entered. Ceilings finished in light colors can aid greatly the distribution of natural daylight throughout a building. The reflection of sunlight to other surfaces, especially masonry materials, increases the collection of solar energy for direct and delayed heating.

Phase-change Tiles

Ceilings also may be finished with special tiles designed specifically for heat absorption, storage, and distribution. These tiles contain phase-change materials which have a high capacity for heat storage (as discussed in Chapter 5). In some applications, sunlight is reflected directly onto the dark-colored tile surfaces and the heat is absorbed and stored. In other applications, the sun-

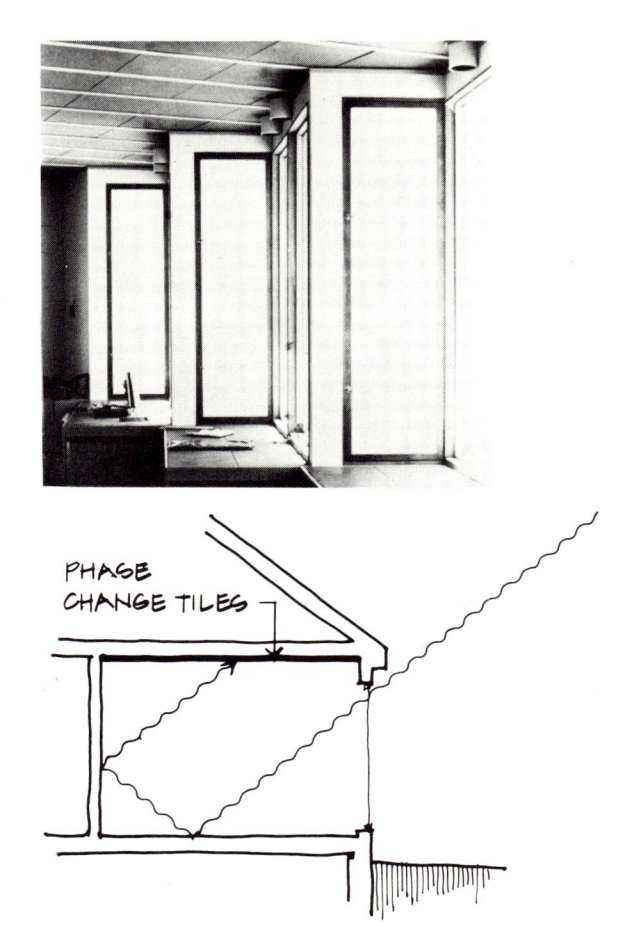

Fig. 12.5 Phase change ceiling tiles used for thermal storage

light simply is reflected off other interior surfaces until it strikes and is absorbed by the ceiling tiles (Fig. 12.5).

The use of these tiles and other new products brings builders into contact with unfamiliar materials, installation details, and techniques. As new products are developed and sold, manufacturers also will develop practical approaches for their installation. These and other new finish products increase the options available to builders who decide to utilize interior finishes for thermal storage; however, the builder must take into account the impact on structural requirements due to added dead loads, and any other concern as dictated by local building codes.

Ceiling/Floor Registers

Air registers placed into framed openings in ceiling/floor sections are installed during the finish phase of construction. They should be situated to allow warm air to rise into upper floors through centrally located registers and cool air to settle to the lower floor through registers located along exterior walls. Air registers used in this manner should be operable to allow control of air movement, privacy, and noise. Local building codes may place other restrictions on their use.

Woodwork

Interior woodwork installed during this phase may undergo modifications in construction details and techniques. The use of double wall framing, rigid board insulation (either interior or exterior), masonry construction, and multi-layered interior finishes increase the thickness of the wall, requiring wider jambs, sills, and thresholds on windows and doors. Inside casings installed onto masonry walls or wood framed walls with interior insulative sheathing require changes in fastening details. Further modification of window jambs or casings also may be necessary to accommodate the integration of movable insulation, as discussed in the next section.

Windows and doors are available with factory installed (or separately supplied) extension jambs that run flush to the inside of interior wall finishes. Due to the limited widths of jambs, even with standard extensions, custom extension jambs may need to be built in a shop or at the job site. The need for custom built jambs depends on the thickness of the wall section. Figure 12.6 pictures custom window jamb extensions used in a masonry opening. Window sills and door thresholds also may need to be extended or custom built to make up for added thickness in walls.

Window and door jamb extensions must be shimmed properly and fastened securely to the materials forming the rough opening. In concrete and masonry construction, jambs may be either nailed to wooden nailers cast into the rough opening, or screwed into expansion shields placed in the concrete or masonry. Screw heads should be countersunk, so that holes can be plugged and finished. Inside window and door casings may require new fastening details, depending on the materials to which they are applied. When installed onto masonry walls, they can be fastened using screws and expansion shields driven into properly sized holes drilled into the wall. If casings are installed onto wood frame walls, or cast-in nailers which are covered with interior insulative sheathing, longer nails will be required to fasten them to the framing. Other interior trim, such as baseboards, used in these configurations are fastened in the same way.

Interior window and door casings and baseboards installed onto masonry walls with plaster finishes should be installed before the plaster surfaces are applied. This

Fig. 12.6 Depending on the thickness of the wall section, window and door jambs, sills and thresholds may require custom-built extensions.

will allow the plaster to be brought up to the woodwork, and built-up to fill the unavoidable gaps between the woodwork and the rough concrete or masonry surface. The woodwork should be protected from the plaster and tools with masking tape during this work.

SPECIAL CONSTRUCTION

Movable Insulation

In an effort to further reduce winter heat loss through glazed areas in walls and ceilings, builders may utilize movable insulation products, along with multiple glazings. These products also are known as night time insulations (Fig. 12.7).

Movable insulations installed during this phase are designed to cover windows, glass doors, skylights, and greenhouse glazings. They can be applied either on the inside wall surface or exterior to the building, and are intended for use at night or during heavily overcast days when considerable heat is lost through these areas. They require daily management by the homeowner; the builder cannot control this, yet it is vital to the cost effectiveness of these special features. Some products are available with automatic motorized operation, a feature that adds considerably to cost and complexity.

Many of the movable insulation products currently available are similar to traditional drapes, roller shades,

234 MATERIALS, DETAILS, AND TECHNIQUES OF SOLAR CONSTRUCTION

Fig. 12.7 Many builders design and assemble custom movable insulation.

Fig. 12.8 Shading devices include fixed overhangs, venetian blinds, and adjustable awnings.

INTERIOR FINISHES AND SPECIAL CONSTRUCTION 235

TRIPLE OR QUADRUPLE GLAZING

INSULATING DRAPES - INTERIOR

SLIDING SHUTTERS - INTERIOR/EXTERIOR

SWINGING SHUTTER - INTERIOR/EXTERIOR

ROLL UP SHADES - INTERIOR

'ROMAN' SHADES - INTERIOR.

ROLL UP STACKING BLINDS - INTERIOR/EXTERIOR

ADJUSTABLE LOUVERS - INTERIOR/EXTERIOR

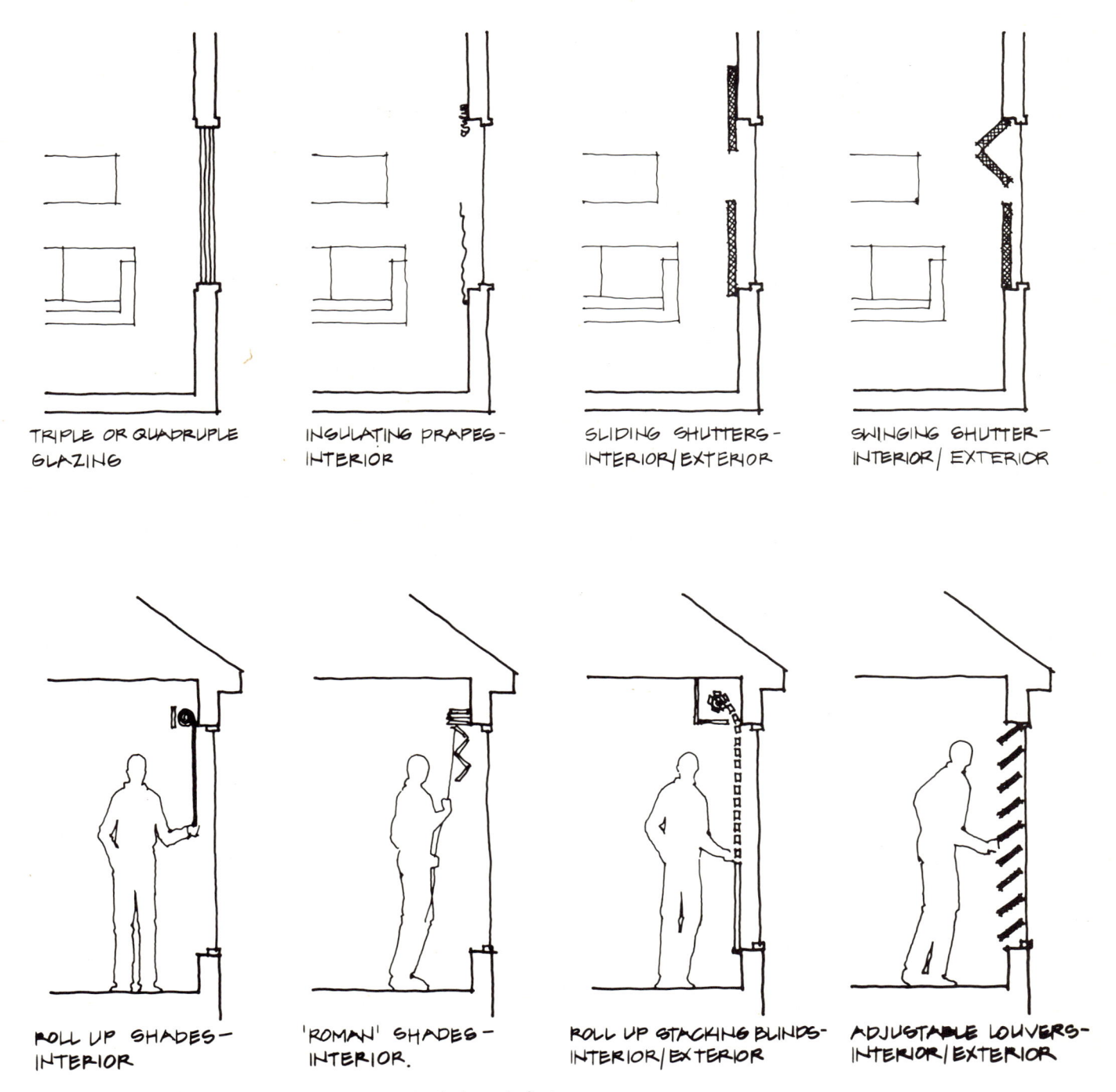

Fig. 12.9 Techniques for shading east or west windows in hot weather

and shutters; however, they generally are constructed from insulative materials. Due to the limited availability of premanufactured products, builders often customize these components themselves. The selection of materials from which to build movable insulation, or the selection of a particular product, must consider the effects of ultraviolet radiation, moisture, heat, and years of operation. These materials and products must be acceptable by fire safety local codes due to the common use of plastic foams, films, and synthetic fibers.

As is true with so many details in solar construction, the quality of workmanship in installing movable insulations affects performance over their designed effective lives. Those products that cover the inside surfaces of glazings usually are installed onto the jambs or inside casings. It is important for the components to seal effectively along the edges when closed to reduce the occurrence of condensation on the inner glazing surface. The presence of the movable insulation there lowers the glass temperatures, which increases the likelihood of condensation. Tight edge seals also help reduce air leakage at windows and doors. Builders should design or purchase components that will provide reliable operation through years of daily use. Figure 5.9 presents the generic types of movable insulations most commonly used, including insulative drapery liners, roll down shades, folding insulated shutters, and sliding pocket shutters.

Shading Devices

Shading devices are important features in solar construction; they control the amount of solar radiation that strikes and enters a building, which controls heat gain and reduces glare. These features can be integrated into the structure, as with fixed overhangs, or added onto the finished interior or exterior surfaces, as with venetian blinds or adjustable awnings (Fig. 12.8). The best approach to shading takes into account the size and orientation of glazings, and the availability of natural shade from vegetation. Another factor in the selection of shading devices is the likelihood of homeowner maintenance of seasonal components.

Chapter 9 presents considerations for designing and building fixed overhangs at the eaves of the roof. Although properly sized modified soffits oriented toward the south are effective in shading vertical glazings in the summer, their fixed positions also cause shading during periods of the heating season when direct sunlight is desired. Alternatives to fixed overhangs include adjustable awnings and trellis overhangs with vegetative cover.

Providing shade for glazed areas on the east and west ends of a building is as important as shading windows oriented toward the south. Unshaded glazings on the east and west ends are major contributors to overheating in summer; because of the low sun angles in morning and afternoon, they are particularly hard to protect. Fixed overhangs do not offer effective shade in this configuration, and builders must either rely on careful siting to utilize vegetation, or install adjustable awnings over each window (Fig. 12.9).

Sloped glazings are also hard to protect with fixed overhangs, and are best shaded by vegetation and interior or exterior shades (which also may serve as movable insulation). This is especially important where glazings are integrated into the ceilings above living areas (Fig. 12.10).

Fig. 12.10 Shading of sloped glazings is especially important to prevent overheating.

CHAPTER 13 CASE STUDIES

INTRODUCTION

Parts I and II present the technical issues of solar construction; equally important are the considerations of how solar construction affects a builder's business. In this chapter we look at the business of solar construction in five profiles of businesses working successfully within several solar markets. We identify issues common to all builders, and also describe each individual's approach to solar construction.

We have mentioned already several aspects of business management—purchasing, scheduling, selecting subcontractors, meeting local codes, and marketing—all of which vary greatly throughout the country, and often within the same state. Builders must apply new techniques within the context of their own local climate, code restrictions, availability of materials, and marketplace.

Another variable that affects how management concerns can be influenced by solar construction is the builder's type of business and approach to construction. We all have our own approaches to management, just as we approach construction from different perspectives. We each build a different number of houses per year and pursue varied markets. Therefore, the costs of any of the features presented in this book will differ, depending on the same factors that affect the cost of any building component; these factors include the level of detail, cost of materials, and quality of workmanship.

Builders can not change their markets suddenly; rather, they should make a gradual transition into solar construction on all levels, from sales meetings to job sites. This is not to say that a transition starts and ends at some given point. Builders can start the process at any time, using any of the techniques presented in this book.

Buildings are products. Builders buy the pieces and assemble them at a site. They must be careful when working with new ideas, materials, and people, and should be practical and keep things simple when considering change. And they must always work to provide the best possible product. If builders can do this, and at the same time continue to apply what they learn in new areas, then buildings will improve and the adjustments made to enter new markets will not disrupt ongoing operations.

The businesses presented in the following profiles serve as examples, rather than as models. They vary in geographic location, scale of operation, and approach to solar construction. Each one has gained experience within the bounds of local conditions, and has adapted his or her business according to their own particular plans. They have learned that there are no hard-and-fast rules that apply to solar construction, just as there are none to guide builders in any market. But they have also learned some valuable lessons that help their businesses continue to grow along with the demands for energy efficient housing. These profiles offer an opportunity to learn from others' experiences which, as with any of the information in this book, must be interpreted by the reader and made relevant to his or her own local constraints.

The first profile presents Peterson Construction Company of Nebraska. Founded in 1932, this company builds approximately one hundred homes per year. Their involvement in solar construction is an extension of energy improvements they have been making in their buildings since 1954. Early experience with a federally funded demonstration solar home has given this builder a new direction in a growing market.

The second business profile on Mayhill Homes Corporation of Georgia focuses on the changes this innovative manufactured home company has gone through in their transition to solar construction. Manufactured homes account for 30 percent of the average annual building starts nationwide. By developing passive solar models, this company has applied the efficiencies and controls of factory built housing to solar construction. This is an important step in ensuring that affordable solar homes are available to all markets.

The third presentation is the profile of Green Horizon, located in New Mexico. This company has specialized in the design and construction of custom sunspace/greenhouse additions, as well as standardized prefabricated kits. Solar retrofits like these can play an important role in a builder's attempts to diversify his or her business by entering new energy related markets. This profile illustrates that these options can be applied profitably.

The fourth profile, Sunrise Solar Services of Connecticut, features a master plumber who has established his family business as one of the leading solar contractors in the country. By reading this profile, builders can learn more about the characteristics of reliable subcontractors, and how they approach solar domestic hot water installations.

Finally, the fifth business profile presents Dennis Davey, Inc., a Connecticut builder of passive solar homes. This builder has applied many of the concepts presented in Parts I and II, to produce buildings that cost less than $100 per year to heat in a 6500-degree-day climate. He also has worked closely with his banker and realtor who, as a result of their experience with him, are now encouraging other builders to enter the solar market.

The people introduced in each of these profiles have certain traits in common. They are innovative business men and women who have combined their concern for energy with their business plans. They look to the future of their construction businesses and see that energy is one of the most important issues facing them, and they have taken the first steps to assure a place in the ever-changing future of the building industry. The most notable trait shared by these people also is shared by thousands of other builders, plumbers, solar contractors, architects, and engineers across the country—the fact that all of these people are working in solar construction *today*.

Fig. 13.1 Bob Peterson, solar home builder, Peterson Construction Company, Lincoln, Nebraska.

PETERSON CONSTRUCTION COMPANY
Lincoln, Nebraska
Bob Peterson, President

Bob Peterson, president of Peterson Construction Company is a builder making the transition to solar construction. Founded by his father the company has been in business since 1932, and has always had a reputation for innovative work. At present the company employs fifty people who work in the company's residential and commercial divisions. Peterson's first major residential tract, started in 1953, consisted of 800 detached single family units on 250 acres. In 1960 they started a 1000-unit development on 300 acres, and are just completing a 900-unit project, including multifamily residences, on 290 acres. Plans for a solar subdivision are also underway (Fig. 13.2). They first became involved in solar construction as a participant in the federal solar demonstration program, and this early experience helped them shape an approach to solar heating that is practical, low cost, and marketable.

Peterson's growing commitment to solar construction is helping mold his business to the shape of a new market. Improving the energy performance of buildings has been an important area of concern for him and has stimulated his company's movement toward energy conservation. Their promotional brochures and advertising clearly call out the energy conserving features which, along with the other construction details, make up the Peterson "Preferred Homes" (Fig. 13.3).

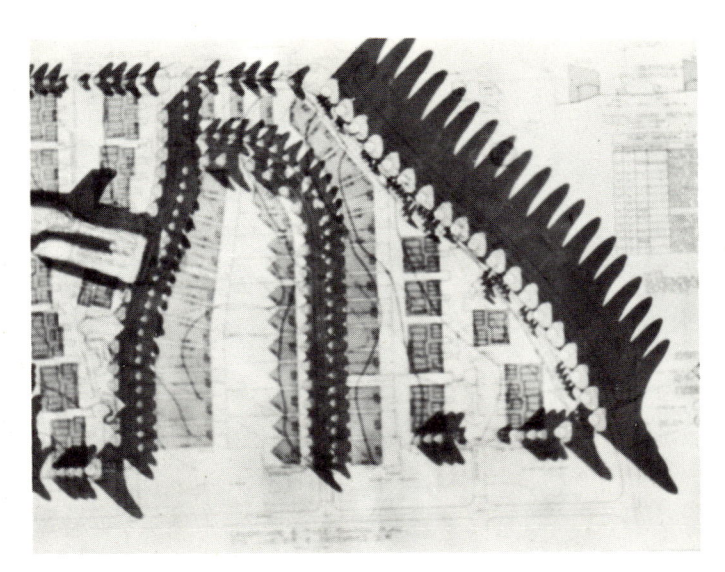

Fig. 13.2 Plot layout for planned solar subdivision.

Peterson began improving his buildings' energy performance in 1957, by minimizing the window areas on the east and west sides in an attempt to reduce cooling loads. He already had been insulating these homes with 1½ inches of rock wool in the side walls and 4 inches of blown fill in the attic since 1954. During the late 1950s when Owens Corning first promoted heavier insulation, FHA recognized 6 inches of attic insulation in their initial valuation. Peterson then incorporated this R-value level into his homes.

By 1971 Peterson Construction Company was using R-11 in the side walls and R-19 in the roof. In 1977, the city of Lincoln adopted a "local thermal ordinance" setting these same levels of insulation as the standard. The only thing Peterson had to change in order to comply was to insulate more basement walls. Most of his competitors, however, had not been insulating buildings to this level, and for them the thermal ordinance posed more of a change in a short period of time. Another Farm Home upgrade in 1977 brought Peterson's level of insulation to where it currently stands, with R-13 blanket plus R-5 styrofoam exterior sheathing Peterson had already been testing in the side walls, and R-33 blown rock wool in the ceiling.

For an innovative builder there is always more risk involved than usual, but the builder who recognizes a new idea as part of a long-term transition rather than a short-lived trend can emerge as an early leader. In 1948, Peterson Construction Company was one of the first builders in their area to use roof trusses in residential construction, and built them for their own buildings until they became available from specialized suppliers. They also built prefabricated wall sections from 1958 to 1978. Both of these concepts are widely used today.

Builders who succeed at becoming innovative leaders in their markets are careful business men and women who plan their changes after study and review. A decision to include energy conserving features was Peterson's first step in his transition to solar construction. This decision was made only after he became familiar with how his buildings performed, reviewed new energy conserving materials and techniques, found where energy improvements could be made, and determined the cost. He built dozens of energy efficient homes before he even considered his first solar home.

The transition to solar construction has not been completely smooth for Peterson; he quickly learned from early experiences, and uses them to avoid repeated problems. At the job site he maintains close supervision of his subcontractors, as well as his own crews. He feels that less supervision will be required as soon as they get used to the "new" materials, details, and techniques, and the delays that these changes may cause initially will decrease steadily.

The plans that Peterson Construction Company develops for their buildings have always been extremely detailed. They feel it is important to plan carefully (especially detailing new areas of concern), provide drawings as a reference for carpenters and subcontractors, and have everyone work from these plans. Standard details often are left out of their building plans because of repeated use. Eventually, the new energy-related details also become routine; until that time, builders need to help each trade understand changes that may be required. Peterson is developing a loose-leaf notebook that catalogues all current construction details, for use as an additional reference at the job site.

The transition to solar construction also requires some adjustment from the standpoint of business management. In the design phase of their early solar homes, Peterson Construction Company designers needed more time to develop new details, from foundation insulation to finished valances for movable insulation on the windows. If a new product or material is selected, delays often occur while waiting for specifications and details, and often for the product.

Similar scheduling problems occur when special subcontractors, such as solar DHW installers, are hired. There are frequently delays and scheduling problems—and attempts to avoid them "next time." These are not problems associated solely with solar construction, but they can be exaggerated in early solar projects if the builder does not try to foresee and divert them.

Fig. 13.3 Suntempered 1½ story home built for a "sweat equity" buyer. First floor kitchen/family room has brick floor over concrete and brick alcove for woodstove.

Fig. 13.4 Solar home by Peterson Construction built for HUD Cycle V solar demonstration program.

Fig. 13.5 Passive solar home by Peterson Construction featuring direct gain with "Sniffer" duct and fan to direct warm air to bedroom.

Marketing was another area of Peterson's business management that required some initial adjustment. Although the energy conserving features of their standard designs had always been promoted in advertising and publications, they were always presented as part of the total list of features offered in a Peterson Home. This total package promotes their homes as being well-built, comfortable, and economical. When their first solar home was marketed, they tried a different approach, and emphasized more strongly the solar heating system and energy features. When the home was opened to the public, the large crowd that was anticipated was actually only slightly larger than normal. Peterson has since learned that the home buyer must like the house for all of its features, and not simply because it is energy efficient. His sales staff promotes all the benefits of their homes, such as the quality of materials, floor plan, open bright spaces, and low operating cost. Peterson's approach is to first interest a person in buying the house, then try to close the sale by promoting the energy features—without overdoing it (Fig. 13.4).

Fortunately, Peterson has not encountered any resistance from lenders on these projects. He feels that though the first solar homes did cost more, they soon became more in line with his regular operations. Working with new details and materials can slow construction and complicate management initially; however, with experience, these problems can be avoided. Careful attention to cost estimating is critical to ensure a reasonable profit margin, especially when estimating the costs for unfamiliar materials and techniques. This skill also must be acquired over time. The best guarantee of a profitable venture into solar construction, though, is the fact that these homes sell faster than standard models. The solar home that is sold quickly—often prior to completion—improves cash flow and reduces the amount of interest paid on financing.

Peterson Construction Company's early involvement in solar construction has given them an edge over their competition. They have had the chance to try different approaches, evaluate new materials and techniques, and educate their designers, work crews, and sales staff. They have continued to live up to the reputation for quality homes, innovative construction, and leadership that has kept their business alive and growing since 1932. Not only are they prepared to respond to the growing solar market—but they also are helping to shape it (Fig. 13.5).

Fig. 13.6 John Odegaard, solar designer and manufactured home builder, Mayhill Homes, Gainesville, Georgia.

MAYHILL HOMES CORPORATION
Gainesville, Georgia
John Odegaard, Vice President Product Development

Mayhill Homes Corporation is an innovative manufacturer of factory built panelized homes. Since forming in 1972, they have delivered more than five thousand units; they are among the first manufactured home companies to offer energy conserving/sun tempered models that are simple and affordable. John Odegaard has played an important role in Mayhill Homes' decision to develop passive solar designs. As vice president of product development, he is responsible for their ambitious "Model-A-Month" program, through which Mayhill Homes offers builders a new model home every month. All new models include energy conserving features. More recent models include the Stovehaus, designed to be heated by a single airtight woodstove; a sun tempered home that utilizes a solarium to collect solar heat; and other passive solar designs.

Mayhill Homes offers a full line of homes, more than 100 models which are 884 square feet and larger. They sell their homes to builders who erect the panelized building at the site. The typical Mayhill Homes package includes framing from bottom plates to roof decking, factory applied exterior siding, installed double glazed sliding windows and doors, and interior and exterior trim. The builder must provide the site, foundation, labor, plumbing, all mechanical equipment and installation, roofing, and finishes. In 1980, 1300 units were delivered to their 250 builder-customers in the Southeast and Midwest.

Fig. 13.7 Mayhill's solar homes are built in one of their factories and erected at the site by their many builder-customers.

©1980—E. Alan McGee—Atlanta

CASE STUDIES 245

Fig. 13.8 The Stovehaus was designed to be heated by a single centrally located wood stove.

A lot of thought goes into the design of a manufactured home. Companies like Mayhill Homes are trying to develop a large volume market by offering a wide variety of sizes and styles that appeal to a broad group of home buyers. This volume is necessary to make the manufactured approach efficient, and to cover the relatively high cost of overhead for shop facilities, tools, and equipment. These buildings also are designed to make the most efficient use of materials and quick, accurate assembly by the builder at the site (Fig. 13.7). Because home manufacturers plan so thoroughly and cautiously, many home builders look to them to set the trends they will follow.

Mayhill Homes decided to introduce another priority into their design process—energy efficiency. Through their "Positive Energy Performance" program, their homes are designed to include such energy conserving features as high capacity, soffit and ridge venting, insulated and weatherstripped exterior doors, double glazed windows, foam caulking at jamb openings, R-19 walls, and a continuous polyethylene vapor barrier. Ceiling insulation, supplied by the builder, can be any thickness up to 10 inches.

Having taken the first step by improving the thermal performance of all of his designs, Odegaard began to develop more advanced models. Soon Mayhill Homes introduced the "Stovehaus," an energy efficient model designed to be heated by a single airtight wood stove

246 MATERIALS, DETAILS, AND TECHNIQUES OF SOLAR CONSTRUCTION

Fig. 13.9 The Mayhill Sunburst

Fig. 13.10 The Mayhill Apollo

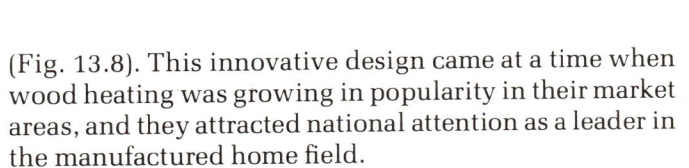

(Fig. 13.8). This innovative design came at a time when wood heating was growing in popularity in their market areas, and they attracted national attention as a leader in the manufactured home field.

Continuing the development of new energy efficient models, Odegaard designed Mayhill Homes' first passive solar model. This 1050-square-foot single story home (Fig. 13.9) combines the direct gain of a solarium with a thermal storage wall exposed to direct and diffuse solar radiation. The house is only 50 feet wide (including a carport) so it can be turned on average sized lots to face south. The lot for this model is designed to have the south generally at the rear.

Another Mayhill passive solar model is a 1786-square-foot single story house (with solarium) that utilizes a 248-square-foot greenhouse on the back for indirect solar gain (Fig. 13.10). The latest additions to the Mayhill Homes passive solar line are two split foyer models. They have approximately the same amount of solar contribution as the one story models, but they are larger in floor area (Fig. 13.11).

As Odegaard designs the Mayhill series of passive solar homes, he tries to develop models that will work in

Fig. 13.11 The Mayhill Sunburst

terms of slope and orientation on various sites. He also tries to keep the solar designs within the range of marketable styles that has been defined for their other models. The solar models are designed to eliminate changes in the factory production, by using coded components and materials also used in other models. Some of the differences in the solar designs do require stocking special components, such as tempered glass used in the greenhouses, special windows with built-in shading devices, and vents. By utilizing Mayhill's standard format for production, the passive solar models have not required special retooling for the factory operation or training of workers.

Odegaard has found that the successful marketing of these solar homes also fits within their standard sales approach and procedures. Mayhill salespeople "soft pedal" the solar features, focusing on the quality of materials used and the durability of the building; this same sales technique is used for all their models. The solar greenhouse is promoted as a "nice, bright, attractive, and warm new room that can be used year round." Their first passive solar model was sold by one of Mayhill's builder-customers before it was completed. On a walk-through of the house, the builder did not even tell the prospective buyers about the solar features. The buyers liked the design of the house so much that the solar heat contribution was just an added benefit. What sold them was the open floor plan, split bedrooms, natural lighting, sunspace, and the sense of comfort they felt while they were there.

This early market acceptance of Mayhill Homes' passive solar models is very encouraging to Odegaard. He plans to continue introducing energy conserving passive solar homes through his "Model-A-Month" program because he believes that this is the direction the entire building industry soon will follow. Manufactured home companies are seen as trendsetters because their designs anticipate future markets rather than respond to current ones. By carefully leading the market without being too far ahead of it, these companies can continue to get builders to buy and construct their products. Mayhill Homes, by attempting to anticipate the market changes, offers builders a product that can give them a jump on their competition—a product builders would find difficult to develop soon enough to stay ahead. Mayhill Homes assists their builders in marketing their homes by providing sales literature, radio and television ads, and periodic educational conferences held at their plant facilities. These builders now have a full line of energy conserving sun tempered homes to offer at very competitive prices. The leadership and innovation displayed by John Odegaard and Mayhill Homes over the past years has proven that they truly are trendsetters.

Fig. 13.12 Valerie Walsh, solar greenhouse designer/builder, Green Horizon, Santa Fe, New Mexico.

GREEN HORIZON
Santa Fe, New Mexico
Valerie Walsh, President

Valerie Walsh, president of Green Horizon, is a designer and builder who specializes in custom solar greenhouse additions. Her company, founded in 1976, has gained a reputation for creative design and quality construction, and is growing as a result. Green Horizon's greenhouses are designed and built to provide supplemental heat for the home while adding valuable living and planting areas. Walsh has focused on a specialized but growing market within the building industry, and her company is expanding and diversifying to meet the demand. As the demand for solar greenhouses increases, the number of contractors who build them also increases. Through careful planning and management, innovative design and construction, and targeted marketing and public relations, she and her company try to set themselves apart from their competitors.

Walsh has been a licensed contractor since 1977, and has organized her business to respond to current markets while still planning for the future. Her work crews change in size depending on the season; winter is her busiest time of the year. She generally runs one job at a time during the other seasons, when heating bills are farther from homeowners' minds.

After Green Horizon has been contracted by a homeowner, and greenhouse plans have been finalized, the construction begins. Much of the work takes place in Walsh's shop, where the greenhouses are built in modules. After the foundation has been completed, the entire greenhouse is transported to the job site and erected. Depending on interior finish details, completion may take three weeks (Fig. 13.13).

Walsh utilizes functional elements of the greenhouse as thermal storage, especially when an adobe exterior wall is not enclosed by the addition. These may take the form of masonry and stucco planting beds, sitting surfaces, and concrete slab floors finished with decorative clay tile. In some cases she supplements the masonry thermal storage by including hot tubs that contain several hundred gallons of water. She also uses electric radiant heat panels in the ceiling as a backup system.

In marketing her custom greenhouses, Walsh has primarily focused on upper middle class buyers; many potential customers have retired to Santa Fe, attracted by both the unique style of Pueblo and Spanish architecture and the climate. These adobe buildings, some 100 to 200 years old, commonly have exposed vigas for roof beams, corner handmade kiva (beehive) fireplaces, ceramic tile work, and brick or flagstone floors. As a solar retrofit designer, Walsh must plan carefully how the solar greenhouse addition will blend with the existing home, especially when the home has historical significance. Adobe homes usually have irregular contours, with many curves and round edges; her greenhouses, with their curved lines of wood and glass, blend into this overall aesthetic appearance and feeling (Fig. 13.14).

Green Horizon pursues the custom greenhouse market in various ways. In each approach they present their philosophy that solar greenhouse additions should be attractive and enhance the house and owner's lifestyle (Fig. 13.15). Walsh often finds that her efforts to promote her business require a simultaneous effort to educate the public about solar greenhouses, through newspaper and magazine advertisements, exhibits at trade and home shows, bank window displays, and slide show presentations. She has also added a solar greenhouse showroom onto an existing commercial nursery (Fig. 13.16). This showroom is open to the public seven days a week and houses flowering plants and indoor trees, as well as Green Horizon brochures, solar energy fact sheets, and a descriptive diagram of the solar greenhouse and its applications. All of this effort to reach and educate the public is another factor in Walsh's success. Although these activities require a lot of time and expense, they have helped identify Green Horizon as

Fig. 13.13 Walsh greenhouse, interior view

Fig. 13.14 Walsh greenhouse, exterior view

CASE STUDIES   251

Fig. 13.15 Green Horizon promotes solar greenhouse construction through various means including newspaper advertisements.

Fig. 13.16 The Green Horizon showroom is open to the public seven days a week.

252 MATERIALS, DETAILS, AND TECHNIQUES OF SOLAR CONSTRUCTION

produced in large numbers at lower costs, may increase the builder's profit margin.

Diversification is an important consideration for all builders. Companies that serve a variety of markets are less vulnerable to the fluctuations of the building industry than those that specialize in only one market. For example, builders who offer both new construction and retrofit services can operate even when the number of new housing starts drops by focusing on renovations and additions in the interim.

By specializing (in a diversified manner) within the markets that solar retrofits offer, Valerie Walsh and Green Horizon filled a void that existed in their area. Their early entry into this market has helped them gain valuable experience and exposure. Walsh is trying to meet the needs of the public by developing standard solar greenhouse products; however, her reputation is based on creative custom designs, which is the work she most enjoys (Fig. 13.17).

Fig. 13.17 Green Horizon greenhouse

knowledgeable builders who can communicate what they offer to potential customers. The increased exposure and credibility is important to the growth of their business.

Although the custom greenhouse business is growing, Walsh has plans to diversify in order to reach contractors, developers, and architects. Green Horizon has begun to prefabricate their curved laminated mahogany greenhouses for wider distribution, and has developed several models (in various sizes) for contractor installation. Many builders prefer to purchase a predesigned, modular greenhouse, rather than design and experiment with building one on-site. The use of greenhouse kits can aid builders in estimating and, because they are

Fig. 13.18 Ed and Ellie Butler, solar contractors, Sunrise Solar Services, Suffield, Connecticut.

SUNRISE SOLAR SERVICES
Suffield, Connecticut
Ed Butler, President

Ed Butler, President of Sunrise Solar Services, Inc., is a licensed master plumber who, since installing his first solar water heater in 1976, has become one of the most experienced solar contractors in the United States. He has installed hundreds of systems throughout the Northeast and, in the spring of 1979, was subcontracted

Fig. 13.19 Ed. Butler was the master plumber for the solar water heater installed on the White House, Washington, D.C.

to help install the solar water heater on the White House in Washington, D.C. (Fig. 13.19). His reputation for innovation, craftsmanship, and reliability has been important to Sunrise Solar Services' continued growth and leadership within the solar DHW field.

Butler is typical of many plumbing and heating contractors operating small family businesses. Unlike most, however, he started installing solar DHW systems early in their development, and he supplemented the occasional solar heating jobs with conventional work. As his interest grew he began contracting jobs away from home and gained experience with a wide range of solar DHW equipment and generic system types. He also became an experienced troubleshooter. By 1977 Butler was installing conventional plumbing only on jobs where both solar and conventional work were included in the same bid.

As mentioned in Chapter 11, solar contractors should have experience in a wide range of building trade skills and be able to secure the building, plumbing, or electrical permits required by local codes. Butler's background in construction work includes two years as a commercial roofer; he also has his master plumber's license. In most localities in which Butler works, his license is required to obtain plumbing permits for solar DHW installations, primarily because they tie in to the potable water service.

At times throughout his plumbing career, Butler has been exposed to challenging and innovative projects. While still an apprentice, he gained experience working with strict specifications and complex layout, installing the plumbing and waste systems in college chemistry laboratories. While a journeyman, Butler worked for a while as a shipyard steamfitter and, as a leading solar contractor, he has often installed one-of-a-kind, prototypical solar heating systems for equipment manufacturers and researchers.

Although innovative jobs still come along, the routine work for Sunrise Solar Services consists of solar water heater sales and installation (Fig. 13.20). Due to the large number of existing buildings in the Northeast, the primary market for their systems is in commercial and residential retrofitting. Butler markets their services to homeowners by representing the company at home shows, educational workshops, and local club meetings, and through direct mail and advertisements in several publications. He has found, however, that a large percentage of jobs are obtained through word-of-mouth. This is also the experience of other solar contractors, and it demonstrates the importance of a good reputation, both for quality of workmanship during the installation, and for reliable follow-up service whenever a problem arises.

Butler also consults with builders, architects, and engineers on their plans to include solar DHW systems in new buildings. Early input from an experienced subcontractor during the planning and design phase can help to pinpoint possible problems, and ensure logical layout and realistic scheduling of the solar installation. After a Sunrise Solar Services' bid has been accepted, Butler meets with the builder to finalize the system layout, identify special structural or mounting requirements in the framing, and define the job schedule.

One of the problems often encountered in scheduling a solar installation is availability of the specialized components. Through the years, Butler has installed equipment manufactured by both large and small companies, and has had to delay jobs due to shipment problems. This has occurred regardless of the manufacturing company's size, and has led him to rent extra storage

Fig. 13.20 Typical Sunrise Solar Services solar DHW installation

areas adjacent to his office where he stocks solar heat collectors, storage tanks, mechanical components, and materials for collector racks. He also keeps an inventory of copper tubing, fittings, assorted hardware, and pipe insulation—more for convenience and savings from quantity purchasing than availability. These components are usually readily available from plumbing wholesalers and insulation suppliers.

As the installation begins, Butler reviews with the two installers that make up each of his two crews the plans for placement of collectors, layout of pipe runs, and location of mechanical equipment (Fig. 13.21). These workers are already familiar with the procedures he has standardized, and with his requirements for quality of installation at every step. Together they determine whether any last-minute adjustments are required before proceeding with the installation. Although Butler usually works on each installation, he also must obtain permits, oversee other jobs in progress, order materials, and contact sales leads for future work. The key to his ability to fulfill these other responsibilities is his confidence that the installation crews will follow his instructions, and use their own considerable experience to avoid problems and complete the job on time.

The length of time required for installation of solar water heaters varies and this directly affects scheduling. The period of work is influenced by the experience of the installer, quality of workmanship, generic type of system, number of collectors, collector mounting details, collector plumbing connections, height of roof, roof type and flashing details, and the weather.

Butler feels that most problems with solar DHW systems can be avoided through careful planning and supervision of the installation. Still, problems do arise and must be solved quickly to minimize their impact on the building and its occupants. Again, experience is the key to understanding the symptoms of operational problems, and in determining the best approach to correcting them. Sunrise Solar Services warranties their installations and offers service contracts that extend beyond the warranty period, as do most reputable solar contractors.

Fig. 13.21 Ed Butler reviews installation procedures with work crew.

Sunrise Solar Services was one of the first plumbing and heating firms in the Northeast to specialize in solar DHW installation. Although they are a small family business, they have managed to gain a widespread reputation for their work; by 1978 they had solar systems operating in all of the New England states. Though the number of qualified installers throughout the region is growing, Butler has focused on a smaller, more serviceable territory, supported by the increase in local demand for solar water heaters.

Ed Butler has watched the interest in solar energy grow within the plumbing trade, and is no longer surprised to find the plumber next to him at the supply house ordering components for a solar job. Butler has seen plumbing wholesalers change, too, from the days when he would debate the merits of the solar equipment with them to the present, as he orders that same equipment from them. These changes have brought growth to his business, and have allowed him to continue planning for improved organization and marketing and the development of innovative projects. And people still go out of their way to meet the "sunshine plumber" (Fig. 13.22).

256 MATERIALS, DETAILS, AND TECHNIQUES OF SOLAR CONSTRUCTION

Fig. 13.22 Sunrise Solar Services' installation

Fig. 13.23 Dennis Davey, solar builder, Dennis Davey Inc., Tolland, Connecticut.

DENNIS DAVEY, INC.
Tolland, Connecticut
Dennis Davey, President

Dennis Davey, President of Dennis Davey, Inc., is an architect and builder of passive solar homes. Since 1976, when he built his first "low energy" house, he has gained experience with a variety of sun tempering approaches as well as designs that are based on double shell construction. Davey currently builds five to six custom solar homes per year. He has successfully teamed with his local banker and realtor to offer, without government funding, innovative homes that are cost-competitive in his markets. Most of these solar homes have sold well before completion.

Davey's first energy efficient house combined the basic passive solar concepts of careful siting, increased insulation (2x6 stud walls), an open floor plan with daytime living spaces located on the south, and a central mass fireplace (Fig. 13.24). This 1300-square-foot, three bedroom, slab on grade house was designed to be 30 percent passive solar heated. It was sold long before construction was complete.

Davey's home building techniques evolved from simple energy conservation measures to the use of attached solar greenhouses, earth bermed walls, thermal mass walls and floors, insulated draperies and shutters, and wood stoves (Fig. 13.25). Davey also has built a number of houses using double shell construction; however, he redesigned these buildings after evaluating the original concept and details. His redesign reduces the building's reliance on solar heat gain, and emphasizes the more constant earth tempering effect of the air circulated from the crawl space. Davey feels that it is this earth tempered air, and not the solar heat gain, which makes these designs work.

He has also gone through a transition in his approach to these houses. He started by designing and building a home similar to the original envelope configuration, utilizing large areas of south glazing in the form of a sunspace. He now uses smaller glazed areas on the south, to provide direct gain and daylighting more than to provide a driving force for the convective loop (Fig. 13.26).

All of Davey's solar homes have solar domestic water preheaters which further reduce operating costs.

Fig. 13.24 Early energy efficient home built by Davey

His first houses were equipped with active solar systems; more recent designs incorporate passive batch-type water preheaters, usually located in a solar greenhouse or sunspace, as seen in Fig. 13.27.

When he started building solar homes, Davey was concerned about marketing his designs and worked hard at making them fit in with local types. He also tried to make each house somewhat different, to demonstrate that energy conservation and sun tempering could be effective with any type of house design, and on many different lot orientations.

Davey has tried to control the costs of his buildings by using panelized siding materials, less concrete, less interior trim, inexpensive flooring, and truss framing in the floors and roofs. All phases of construction are subcontracted. Through the years Davey has developed a good relationship with reliable subcontractors, and now uses the same ones almost exclusively. He finds that they enjoy the challenge of the innovative work, and that they feel it is good for their own reputations to be involved with solar construction.

At first, Davey's realtor and banker were uncertain that his designs would work—and sell—but by taking the time to help educate them about energy conservation and solar construction, Davey opened the door to

Fig. 13.25 Davey earth bermed, suntempered home

Fig. 13.26 Davey has built a number of double shell homes such as the one pictured here.

Fig. 13.27 Batch-type solar water heaters are standard in Davey's homes.

Fig. 13.28 Davey solar home.

what has become a successful and cooperative business relationship. His realtor is especially enthusiastic about the ease of selling the solar homes, and has encouraged other builders in his area to enter the market. Advertisements placed in the real estate sections of local newspapers and in real estate magazines have brought immediate response and early sales.

Davey's banker developed a new approach to financing solar construction that allows more flexibility in the schedule of progress payments. The normal sequence of phase-related payments can cause cash flow problems in solar construction due to added steps that may be required at certain phases. For example, payment made for the foundation phase normally does not cover the costs of insulating the foundation and slab. Money for insulation usually is released at a later stage. Davey avoided this problem by using a system of payments that releases money in time intervals rather than at the completion of a phase.

Many concepts work well in theory. In practice, Davey's buildings have resulted in documented heating costs consistently below $100 a year, in the 6500-degree-day climate of northeastern Connecticut. He feels that he has reached the point where he can repeat details learned from each of his buildings, and knows how new materials will perform under various conditions. He has tried several approaches to solar construction, and continues to apply what he learns in an effort to refine his skills as a solar home builder (Fig. 13.28).

GLOSSARY

Absolute Humidity: A measure of the water vapor content of air.

Absorber: A solid surface (commonly black or dark) which transforms radiant solar energy to heat energy.

Active Solar System: A system which uses solar heat collectors and mechanical devices to collect, store, and distribute solar energy.

Air Changes: Expression of ventilation rate in terms of room or building volume in air changes per hour.

Altitude, Solar: The angle of the sun above the horizon (winter, low; summer, high).

Ambient Temperature: Surrounding temperature.

ASHRAE: Abbreviation for the American Society of Heating, Refrigeration and Air-conditioning Engineers.

Azimuth, Solar: The angular position of the sun in a horizontal plane measured from true south. At solar noon, the sun is due south; the Azimuth angle = 0°.

Berm: A natural or man-made mound of earth often utilized on the north side of a building for wind protection.

BTU (British Thermal Unit): A heat measurement; the amount of heat needed to raise 1 pound of water 1°F. The burning of one match is approximately one BTU.

BTU/DD/Ft^2 (Heated Area): A unit commonly used to express the rate of heat loss in buildings.

Chimney Effect: Air movement caused by warm air rising and cooler air sinking to replace it. *See* **Convection**.

Clerestory: A vertical window placed high in a wall at the eaves, or between a lower roof and a higher roof, used for light, heat gain, and ventilation.

Climate: The effects of temperature, precipitation, humidity, wind, and other meteorological conditions characteristic of a region.

Collector Angle: The angle between the surface of a solar collector and the horizon.

Collector, Flat Plate: A building component containing a panel of metal (usually flat black on its sun side) that absorbs sunlight and converts it into heat. This panel is usually in an insulated box, covered with glass or plastic on the sun side to retard heat loss. The heat in the collector transfers to a circulating liquid or gas (e.g. air, water, oil, or antifreeze) to be transferred for immediate use or stored for later use.

Collector, Solar: Any device which collects solar radiation and converts it to heat energy.

Condensation: The production of liquid which results when warm, moist air comes in contact with a colder surface and deposits moisture onto that surface. In colder climates, the condensate may appear as frost.

Conductance (C): A measure (in BTU's) of the thermal conducting properties of a single material through one square foot in one hour when there is a 1°F temperature difference between them. To determine the conductance (C) for a particular thickness, divide the conductivity (k) of the material by its thickness (X).

Conduction: The transfer of heat through materials by passage of kinetic energy from molecule to molecule.

Conductivity (k): The quantity of heat (in BTU's) that will flow through one square foot of a material one inch thick in one hour, when there is a temperature difference of 1°F between both surfaces.

Convection: The transfer of heat by movement of a fluid (liquid or gas).

Convection, Forced: Heat transfer resulting from forced circulation of a fluid, as by a fan or pump.

Courtesy of Sunrise Builders School, Grafton, Vermont

Convection, Natural: Heat transfer of a fluid resulting from density differences, i.e.; the natural rising of the lighter, warm fluid and the sinking of the heavier, cool fluid.

Convective Loop: The flow of air in a closed path induced by rising hot air and falling cold air.

Cooling Load: The rate (calculated on a daily, monthly, or yearly basis) at which heat must be removed from a space to maintain room air temperature at the constant value which was assumed when calculating heat gain.

Dead Air Space (Still Air Space): A confined space of air which reduces heat loss through both conduction and convection, as is utilized in virtually all insulating materials and systems (e.g.; double glazing, fiberglass batts, rigid foam panels, vermiculite, rock wool).

Declination: The angular distance of the sun north or south of the celestial equator. The declination varies between ±23° (summer, winter).

Degree Day (DD), Cooling: See degree day for heating, except that the base temperature is established at 65°F, and cooling degree days are measured above the base.

Degree Day (DD), Heating: A unit of heat measurement equal to one degree variation from a standard temperature (usually 65°) in the average temperature of one day. If the standard is 65°F and the average outside temperature for one day is 50°F, then the number of degree days recorded for that day would be 15.

Delta T (ΔT): A difference in temperature.

Density: The mass of a substance which is expressed in pounds per cubic foot.

Dehumidification: The condensation of water vapor from air by cooling it below the dewpoint or removal of water vapor from air by chemical or physical methods.

Design Temperature: A designated temperature close to the most severe winter or summer temperature extremes of an area, used in estimating heating and cooling demand.

Diffuse Radiation: The total solar energy reaching the earth's surface after being reflected or scattered by the atmosphere.

Direct Gain: A passive solar heating system whereby solar radiation is admitted directly into the conditioned space.

Direct Radiation: Solar energy that reaches the earth's surface and has not been reflected or scattered by the atmosphere.

Equinox: The two times of the year when the sun crosses the equator, thereby making day and night of equal length. The spring equinox occurs about March 21; the fall equinox about September 21.

Eutectic Salts: Salts that melt at low temperatures, absorbing large quantities of heat and then, as they re-crystalize, release that heat. (One method used for storing solar energy as heat.)

Evaporation: Change of state from liquid to vapor.

Exfiltration: Indoor air leakage to the exterior through the building envelope caused by a pressure differential.

Glazing: A covering of transparent or translucent material (glass or plastic) used for admitting light.

Glazing, Double: A sandwich construction of two separated layers of glass or plastic enclosing air to create an insulating barrier.

Greenhouse Effect: The heat build-up that occurs when a glazing material transmits solar radiation (short wave) into an enclosure and traps the long wave radiation.

Heat Capacity: The ability of a material to store thermal energy (heat) over a given change in temperature.

Heat Exchanger: A device specifically designed to transfer heat between two fluids.

Heat Gain: The amount of heat gained by a space from all its sources, including occupants, lights, equipment, solar radiation. The total heat gain represents the amount of heat that must be removed from a space to maintain desired indoor conditions during cooling.

Heat Lag: The resulting time delay of heat transfer through a material due to its heat capacity and thermal resistance. This principle is utilized in passive solar design, through thermal mass, to sustain daytime warmth throughout the night.

Heat Loss: A decrease in the amount of heat contained in a space, resulting from heat flow through floors, walls, doors, windows, roofs, and other building envelope components.

Heat Loss Coefficient (UA): The rate of energy transfer through the walls, roof, and floor of a house, calculated in BTU/Hr/°F.

Heat Pump: A refrigeration system designed so that the heat extracted at a low temperature and the heat rejected at a higher temperature may be used alternately for heating and cooling functions respectively.

Heat Recovery: Reuse of heat which would otherwise be wasted.

Heat Sink: A heat reservoir large enough that significant quantities of heat may be added or taken from it without appreciably changing its temperature.

Heat Transfer: The methods by which heat may be conveyed from one place to another; e.g.: conduction, convection, radiation.

Heat Transfer Medium: A medium (e.g.: liquid, air, or solid) through which thermal energy is transported.

Humidify: To increase the moisture content of air.

Humidity: Water vapor and air mixture.

HVAC System: Mechanical systems fueled by conventional sources of energy to provided controlled heating, ventilating, and air conditioning.

Hybrid System: A solar heating system that combines active and passive solar features.

Indirect Gain system: A solar heating system in which sunlight first strikes a thermal storage wall located between the sun and a living space. The sunlight absorbed by the mass is converted to heat and then transferred into the living space through convection and radiation.

Infiltration: The uncontrolled leakage of cold air into buildings through cracks and joints in any building section, and around windows and doors of a building, caused by the pressure effects of wind.

Insolation: The total amount of solar radiation incident upon an exposed surface measured in Btu/hr/ft^2 or in Langleys.

Insulation: A material which is used to retard the flow of heat. Good insulators have low k values (thermal conductivity) and high R values (thermal resistance). Four major classifications of building insulating materials are: batt, loose fill, reflective, and rigid.

Internal Heat Gain: The heat generated by equipment, appliances, lights, and people.

Isolated Gain System: A system where solar collection and heat storage are isolated from the living spaces.

Latitude: Angular distance north (+) or south (−) of the earth's equator, measured in degrees of arc.

Magnetic South: South as indicated by a compass; changes markedly with the geographic location.

Mean Radiant Temperature: That single temperature of all enclosing surfaces which would result in the same heat emission as the same surfaces with various different temperatures.

Microclimate: Climate at a specific site as defined by local variations in the regional climate caused by topography, vegetation, soils, water conditions, as well as man-made construction.

Movable Insulation: Insulation placed over windows when needed to prevent heat loss or gain, and removed for light, view, venting, or solar heat gain.

Natural Circulation: Circulation of a gas or liquid due to density differences resulting from temperature variations; hot air rises, cold sinks.

Natural Convection: Transfer of heat by natural circulation.

Orientation: The position of a building relative to the influences of the natural environment, mainly the sun and wind. In general, a passive solar building should be oriented so that its long side faces south.

Passive Solar System: An integral energy system or assembly of natural and architectural components (including collectors, thermal storage devices, and transfer fluid) in which no appreciable off-site energy is used to accomplish the transfer of thermal energy.

Payback: An economic decision criterion that divides the additional cost of a solar system over a conventional system by the annual expected dollar savings resulting from the system.

Radiation: The direct transport of energy through a space by means of electromagnetic waves.

Radiation, Solar: Radiant energy emitted from the sun in the wavelength range between 0.3 and 3.0 microns. Of the total solar radiation reaching the earth, approximately 3 percent is in ultraviolet region, 43 percent in the visible region, 54 percent in the infrared region.

Reflected Radiation: Solar radiation reflected by light colored or polished surfaces. Can be used to increase solar gain.

Reflectivity: The capacity of a material to reflect radiant energy.

Relative Humidity: A measure of the degree of saturation of the air at a given dry-bulb temperature.

Resistance (R): The tendency of a material to retard the flow of heat. The R-value is the unit of thermal resistance used for comparing insulating values of different materials. the higher the R-value of a material, the greater its insulating capabilities.

Retrofitting: Installing solar water heating and/or solar heating or cooling systems in existing buildings.

Selective Surface: A coating with high solar radiation absorptance and low thermal emittance, used on the surface of an absorber to increase system efficiency.

Skylight: A clear or translucent panel set into a roof to admit sunlight into a building.

Solar Altitude: The angle of the sun above the horizon.

Solar Energy: Energy received from the sun in the form of electromagnetic radiation.

Solar Noon: The time of day when the sun is due south (i.e. when the solar azimuth is zero and the solar altitude is maximum).

Solstice: The time of year when the sun is highest in the sky (summer solstice, near June 21) or lowest in the sky (winter solstice, near December 21).

Specific Heat: The number of BTUs required to raise the temperature of one pound of a material 1°F.

Stratification: The formation of thermal layers in a room or heat storage tank where the top layer is warmer than the bottom due to the natural tendency of heated fluids to rise and cooler fluids to sink.

Sun Tempered Building: A structure which is designed or oriented to take into account climatic conditions but which does not necessarily possess strict passive features such as thermal mass or overhangs.

Thermal Break (Thermal Barrier): A material of low thermal conductivity placed in such a way as to reduce the flow of heat between two materials of high thermal conductivity.

Thermal Energy: Heat energy.

Thermal Lag: The time delay in the transmission of heat from a hot area to a cool area.

Thermal Mass: A thermally absorptive building component used to store heat energy. In a passive solar system, the thermal mass absorbs the sun's heat during the day and radiates it at night as the temperatures drop. Thermal mass can also refer to the amount of potential heat storage capacity available in a given system or assembly.

Thermal Storage Wall: A passive system in which the heat storage mass is a wall located between a window wall and living space(s) to be heated. The mass can be a variety of materials including water or masonry.

Transmissivity: The capacity of a material to transmit radiant energy.

Trombe Wall: A passive heating concept consisting of a south-facing masonry wall with glazing in front. Solar radiation is absorbed by the wall, converted into heat and conducted and radiated into the building. Vents may be used to circulate the warm air from the space between the glass and wall to the building.

U-Value (Coefficient of Heat Transfer): The number of BTUs that flow through one square foot of roof, wall or floor, in one hour, when there is a 1°F difference in temperature between the inside and outside air, under steady-state conditions. $U = \dfrac{1}{R}$

Vapor Barrier: A layer of material with low permeance to moisture used to prevent hidden condensation of water within building sections.

Ventilation, Forced: Mechanically assisted movement of fresh air through a building using fans or blowers.

Ventilation, Induced: The thermally assisted movement of fresh air through a building.

Ventilation, Natural: The unassisted movement of fresh air through a building.

Water Wall: A passive solar heating system, implementing water-filled containers, for collecting and storing solar energy.

Weatherstripping: Narrow or jamb-width sections of thin metal, fabric, or other materials used to prevent infiltration of air and moisture around windows and doors.

INDEX

absorber plates, for solar
    collector, 221
acrylics, 185
air change per hour (ACH), 43
air envelope construction, 160
air films, 29, 184
air lock entry, 29
air quality, indoor, 32, 43-44,
    202-206
air temperature, 12
    outdoor, 51
air to air heat exchanger, 44, 206
air velocity, 13
appliances, energy conserving, 208
attic fans, 206
automatic setback thermostats, 208
automatic washers, 208
awning, adjustable, 71, 236

band joist
    heat loss at, 140
    insulating, 148
basement, full, 126
batch heaters, 96
british thermal units (BTU'S), 11
building
    interior finishes, 104, 232
    layout, 115-120
    materials, selection of, 103
    orientation, 115-120
    shape, 60-65
    shell, 139-176
    shell, solar priorities, 142
    symbols in drawings, 112
Butler, Ed, 252

cathedral ceilings, insulating and
    venting, 167
caulking

doors, 189
    sliding glass doors, 190
ceiling finishes, 232-233
ceiling/floor registers, 232
ceilings, 163-176
    comparing alternate systems, 163
    rafter and joist, 164
chimney mass, 75
circulator, 94
clear sky conditions, 47
clearances from glazing
    supports, 184
climate zones of the United States, 45
climate
    effect on comfort, 12
    elements of, 46
closed loop system, 93
clothes dryers, 208
collector
    arrays, 99
    glazings, 98
    installation, premanufactured, 218
    installation, site-built, 220-222
    job-built, 99
    mounting details, 218
    mounting, roof penetration, 218
    sensor, 93
    shading, 99
    supply and return lines, 220
color, effect on reflection and
    absorption, 227
combustion makeup air, 205
comfort range, 72
compass south, 65
concrete slabs
    finishes, 228
    insulating, 136-138
    storage, 73
condensation

hazard zones, 37
    controlling, 36, 194
    hidden, 36
    surface, 35
conductance (C), 9
conduction, 9
    through doors and windows, 177
construction sequence, 103
controller, differential
    thermostatic, 94
controls, for solar hot water
    system, 222
convection, 9
conventional water heater, 97
cost estimating, 104, 243
cross ventilation, 54

Davey, Dennis, 256
daylighting, 71
degree-day, 51
delivery delays, 103
Dennis Davey, Inc., 256
design temperature, 51
dessicant, 194
deviation, 120
dew point, definition of, 13, 33
diagonal bracing for insulative
    sheathing, 152
differential thermostat, 93, 222
direct gain buildings, 73
dishwashers, 207, 208
domestic hot water, 91
doors, 185-190
    comparing types, 186-188
    hinged, 185
    in solar construction, 28, 30
    installing, 188-190
    priorities for solar construction, 180
    reducing heat loss, 28-30

reducing infiltration, 188
storm, 185
weatherstripping, 187
double shell houses, 86
drain back systems, 95
drainage, 58, 123
duct work, rough in, 208-211

earth berm, 82
earth sheltered construction, 82
earth temperature, 89
EER rating, 202
electric water heaters, 92
electrical
controls, 208
phase, solar priorities of, 202
systems, 207-208
emergency egress, 104
emergency regulations, 106
equinox, 49
estimating, 103
evaporation, 11
evaporative cooling, 11
excavation, 58, 123
extension jamb, 190, 227, 233
exterior air feeds, 27
exterior doors, 185

factory built panelized homes, 243
fiberglass reinforced polyester, 184
as collector cover, 221
finish grades, 127
fire prevention, 104
fire-resistant finishes, 104
fixed glazings,
framing for, 196
installing, 195
mounting systems for, 196
flag lots, 65
flat plate solar collectors, 93, 218
flat roofs, insulating and venting, 167
floor finishes, 228-230
floor plans, 65
floors, 140-149
in double shell construction, 148
on pier foundation, 144, 145
over full basement, 149
over heated crawl space, 147-149
over unheated crawl space, 145-146
reducing heat loss, 143
structural changes for solar construction, 149
footing drains, 119
footings, 123
foundation
protection of insulation, 132
sealants, 127
vents, 145
walls as thermal mass, 76
foundations, 124-138
as living spaces, 127
concrete slab on grade, 125
insulating, 128-138

insulating inside the, 135-136
insulating outside the, 130-134
insulation materials, 128
moistureproofing, 127-128
perimeter, 125
pier, 125
solar priorities, 116
framing
double shell, 158
superinsulated, 158
freeze-thaw cycles, 129
freezers, 208
fresh air supply, 13

galvanic corrosion, 221
glare, 69, 71
glass, 184
insulated, 184, 194
low iron, 184
tempered and non-tempered, 184
glazed areas, sizing, 68
glazing
compounds, 196
frames, 197
installation, codes, 200
multiple, 29, 68, 192
vertical, 71
choosing, 181
fixed, 195, 200
shading sloped, 236
sloped, 71, 84
types, 181-185
grading and drainage plan, 119
Green Horizon, 249-252
greenhouse effect, 14
greenhouses, 83-86, 197-200
attached, 85
kits, 198
framing, 175
integrated with floor plan, 84
ventilation, 86
ground water, 114

heat distribution, mechanical, 15
heat energy
measurement of, 11
principles of, 7-11
sources of in buildings, 14-16
heat exchange coil, 93
heat flow, 7
heat gain in buildings, 31
heat load, 68
heat loss
conductive, 16
controlling, 20-30
convective, 16
in buildings, 16-20
infiltration, 17
radiative, 20
through doors and windows, 177
heat pump, air-to-liquid, 207
heat recovery, 206

heat storage, 85
heat transfer fluid, 93, 95, 211
hot water
consumption, 91
distribution piping, 207
heaters, selecting, 207
tanks, 91
thermostat settings, 207
humidity, 52
HVAC, 201-207

ice damming, preventing, 169
indoor pollution,
reducing, 43
sources of, 32, 43
infiltration, 10, 17
controlling at doors, 188
reducing at floor framing, 147
through doors and windows, 177
insolation, 47
insulated headers, 156
insulated pipe runs, 222
insulating
ceiling, roofs and attic spaces, 27, 163-169
concrete slab, 25, 136
exterior wall cavities, 155-161
floors, 25, 141-149
foundations, 128-138
masonry and concrete walls, 24
roofs, 163-169
walls, 26, 151
insulation
definition of, 7
exterior, 76
for use in solar collectors, 222
principles of, 22
types of, 22
used below grade, 129
use of, 20-28
insulative sheathing, diagonal bracing for, 152
interior finishes, 227-233
effect on vapor barrier and insulation, 227
solar priorities for, 229
interior trim, effect of solar construction on, 233
internal heat gains, 86
inversion, 55
isogonic map, 120

jamb extensions, 190, 227, 233
job estimates, 104
job supervision, 104

k-value, 9

landscape planning, 58
layout, 103
light fixture
recessed, 207
task, 207

INDEX

lighting, 207
low iron glass, as collector cover, 221

macroclimate, 45
maintenance, solar hot water system, 223
marketing solar construction, 243, 248, 249, 253, 257
masonry partitions, 73
masonry walls, 161
mass configurations, 73
mass walls, 77, 79
materials take-offs, 104
Mayhill Homes Corporation, 243-248
mean radiant temperature, 13
mechanical heating and cooling, 201
mechanical phase, solar priorities of, 202
mechanical systems
   comparing, 202
   role in maintaining thermal comfort, 14
   rough in, 208-211
mechanical ventilators, 205
microclimate, 45, 47-54
moisture control, 37-43
movable insulation, 233-246
mud rooms, 185

natural
   convection, 10
   daylighting, 207
   ventilation, 31

Odegaard, John, 243
off-peak electricity, 92, 207
optical clarity of glazings, 181
orientation of building, 60-65, 97
overhang, fixed, 71, 175, 236

panel adhesives used with foundation insulation, 131
panelized roof, 168
passive cooling, 60
passive solar heating, 60
permeance, 34
   of building materials, table of, 34
   of wall section, 41
Peterson Construction Company, 238-243
Peterson, Bob, 238
phase-change tiles, 232
phases of construction, 106
pipe insulation materials, 92, 210
piping, rough in, 208-211
plank and beam roof, 168
plumbing systems, 206-207
polycarbonates, 185
precipitation, 52
prehung doors, 186
production schedule, 103
purchasing, 103

R-value, 9
   table of, 18
rabbet depths, 197
radiant heat, 11
radiation
   diffuse, 47
   direct, 47
   thermal, 11
rafter and joist framing, 164
recirculating systems, 95
reducing infiltration with vapor barrier, 159
refrigerators, 208
relative humidity, 13, 32
residential fastening systems, 216
resistance (R), 9
retaining walls, 123
roof and ceiling vents, types, 170
roof venting, 41
roofs, 163-176
   comparing alternate systems, 163
   panelized, 168
   plank and beam, 168
   rafter and joist, 164
   truss, 163
room layout, 65
Russian fireplace, 75

scheduling
   problems, 239
   solar hot water installation, 253
sensor
   ambient, 95
   collector, 223
   storage, 223
   tank, 94
shading
   devices, 236
   obstructions, 118
sheathing, insulative, 152-154
siding, 154
sill
   heat loss at, 140
   sealer, 146
site
   analysis, 113-115
   clearing, 120-123
   feasibility, 65
   orientation, 55, 114
   planning, 65
   planting, 120-123
   slope, 55, 114
site-built collector
   components, 212
   construction, 220
sitework, 113-124
   solar priorities, 116
siting
   solar collectors, 97-99
   the building, 58
sizing and selecting water heaters, 97
skylights
   framing, 176

   glazing, 200
sliding glass doors, 185
   selecting, 187
soil types, 115
solar
   access, 106
   altitude, 49
   angles, 48
   azimuth, 49
   business profiles, 237-257
   collectors
      mounting, 213
      plumbing connections, 219
   constant, 47
   construction, what's different, 3-6
   contractors, 100, 253
      selecting a, 213
   domestic hot water, 211-226
      components, selection of, 211-226
   energy transmission, 71
   gain, 67
   greenhouse, 249
   heat collector
      glazing, 97, 200, 211
      tilt, 97
   heated building, 60-90
   hot water system
      installation, 218-223
      layout, 213-214
      maintenance, 223-226
      installation scheduling, 215
      mechanical room layout, 214
      site-built, 212
      warranties, 254
   radiation, 14, 47-51
      effect of microclimate on, 49
   water heater, 91
      framing, 176
      kits, warranties, 212
      pipe runs, 214
   water heating, 93-100
solstice, 49
special construction, 233-236
   solar priorities for, 229
stack dampers, 202
subdivision layout, 58, 65
sun-tempered building, 58
Sunrise Solar Services, 252-255
sunshine, percent of possible, 49
sunspace, 83-86, 197-200
   attached, 85
   framing, 175
suntempering, 65-73
superinsulated houses, 27, 86
supervision at job site, 239
surface drainage patterns, 115
system layout, 99

temperature differential, 7, 16
temperature swings, 72
thermal break, 9, 187
   in doors and windows, 28

thermal comfort, 11-14
thermal conductivity (k), 9
thermal expansion, 185
   glazing materials, 182
thermal mass, 15, 73-82
thermal ordinance, 239
thermal storage, 73
   slabs and walls, finishes for, 230
   walls, 77-82, 161
      glazing, 197
      venting, 197
thermosiphoning collectors, 94
thermostat settings, 92
thermostatic controls, 208
thresholds, adjustment of, 188
time lag, 73
topography, 54-58
transmission of solar radiation, 181
trees
   coniferous, 120
   deciduous, 120
   protection of, 121
troubleshooting chart for solar hot water systems, 224
true south, 65
truss roofs, 163

U-value, 9
   for multiple glazings, 29
ultraviolet degradation, 69
utility sleeves, 125

vapor barriers, 20
   in crawl space, 145
   installing, 157-158
   roofs and ceilings, 169
   selecting type, 157
   use of, 39
   walls, 157
vapor pressure, 33
vegetation, 114
vent types, 41
ventilation, 71
   mechanical, 202-206
   source, 202
   windows for, 192
venting area, net free, 40
venting
   foundation, 145
   roofs and ceilings, 27, 169-175
   source, 40
   structure, 40-43
vestibules, 185

wall finishes, 230-232
wall framing, 154
walls, 149-163
   changes for solar construction, 149
   comparing alternate systems, 150
   insulating exterior, 155-161
   insulating wood frame, 151
   masonry, 161
   thermal storage, 161-163, 197
Walsh, Valerie, 249
water
   conservation, 206
   conserving appliances, 92
   lines, insulated, 92
   saving fixtures, 92
vapor
   movement, 32
   effect on materials, 34
   sources of, 32
water walls, 73, 82
wind
   control, 53-54
   directions, 53
   speed, 53
windbreaks, 53
window
   orientation, 67
   placement, 67-69
   shading, 69-73
   walls, 196
windows
   choosing, 191-192
   hinged, 191
   in solar construction, 28-30, 180
   installation of, 195
   operable, 190-191
   reducing heat loss, 28-30
   sliding, 192
winter overheating, 71
wire runs, for solar hot water controls, 223
wiring, rough in, 208-211
woodwork, 233
workmanship, 103